Public Enterprise

Special Publications Series
Institute of Latin American Studies
The University of Texas at Austin

PUBLIC ENTERPRISE
An International Bibliography

Compiled by Alfred H. Saulniers

Office for Public Sector Studies
Institute of Latin American Studies
University of Texas at Austin

INSTITUTE OF LATIN AMERICAN STUDIES
THE UNIVERSITY OF TEXAS AT AUSTIN

William P. Glade, *Director* Robert M. Malina, *Associate Director*

Library of Congress Cataloging in Publication Data

Saulniers, Alfred H., 1945-
Public enterprise.

(Special publications series/ Institute of Latin American Studies, the University of Texas at Austin)
Includes index.
1. Government ownership—Latin America—Bibliography. 2. Government ownership—Bibliography. 3. Government business enterprises—Latin America—Bibliography. 4. Government business enterprises—Bibliography. I. University of Texas at Austin. Institute of Latin American Studies. Office for Public Sector Studies. II. Title. III. Series: Special publication (University of Texas at Austin. Institute of Latin American Studies)
Z7164.S84S28 1985 016.351009'2 85-14601
[HD4010.5]
ISBN 0-86728-014-x
ISBN 0-86728-013-1 (pbk).

The paper used in this publication meets the minimum requirements of American National Standard for Information Sciences—Permanence of Paper for Printed Library Materials, ANSI 239.48-1984.

First Edition, 1985

Contents

INTRODUCTION

The Office for Public Sector Studies (OPSS) of the Institute of Latin American Studies (ILAS) was established in 1976 to study the increasingly important role of the public sector in Latin America, to develop specialized graduate-level courses about the public sector, and to disseminate information on public sector activities. It was viewed as an appropriate academic response to a neglected and understudied aspect of Latin American development.

Since then, the OPSS has concentrated on several important areas of public sector activity, including regional development, public health, high-technology policies, and cultural policies. By far, however, its major focus has been on public enterprise studies. Our integrated approach to examining this aspect of the public sector has combined case studies; conferences; seminars; lectures; articles; technical papers; in-depth country study; graduate-level courses on the entrepreneurial state; consultancies for public enterprises, national governments, and international organizations; and visiting professors and researchers.

Public enterprises produce or sell goods or services. Definitional controversies exist over the degree of separate legal personality from the general government and over the degree of government ownership of company equity necessary for an entity to be considered a public enterprise.[1] This bibliography does not propose a specific definition to resolve those controversies; instead, it includes many and varied uses of the term by other authors to provide broad coverage. Some entities in the definitional gray area are included, for example, worker self-managed firms, which, typically, although the capital is not government owned, rely heavily on other government inputs in lieu of ownership. The Latin American approach to public enterprise definition has evolved almost exclusively along legal lines, concentrating on juridical status and formal, often direct, ownership. Unfortunately, legal definitions are too country- and period-specific to support any but the most cursory international comparative analytical efforts. Less commonly employed are public administration approaches that stress effectiveness of government control over company management, the structure of objectives for company creation, and, to a lesser extent, motives for company existence. The definition presented above, more economic in scope, conforms to more current approaches, which seek to define a public enterprise on the basis of ownership characteristics, engagement in business activities, and market orientation for production.

Many public enterprises are large and economically important. Sixty-nine companies in the *Fortune* magazine listing of the top 500 industrial corporations outside the United States in 1983 were government owned, with 31 of those in the top 150.[2] Indeed, public enterprises are the largest industrial enterprises in many countries, heading the country list in twenty of the forty-two countries represented. Even in the United States, one of the best-kept secrets of economic organization has been the more than 7,000 local, regional, state, and interstate public authorities whose combined investment expenditures in 1981 exceeded $26 billion.[3]

Although public enterprises are stereotyped as losers and "parasitic parastatals," most of the government-owned corporations represented on the 1983 list showed a profit. On what basis, then, is their popular image sustained? Part of the stereotype comes from really spectacular cases, such as Argentina's petroleum producer, YPF, a company whose management has, except for a short period in the 1920s, been extremely politicized, stripped of autonomy, subject to bureaucratic bottlenecks, and forced to funnel funds to the government at the expense of company financial health. YPF's serious defects have important negative repercussions on the entire concept of public enterprise.[4] Likewise, the British case has attracted attention as a paradigm of public enterprise inefficiency without arriving at the obvious conclusion, based on a wider frame of reference, that the British performance reflects more on the absence of adequate conditions in Britain than it does on the nature of equity holdings. Of the eighty-seven British firms on the list, five were government owned. All showed losses, with British Steel trailing YPF as the big money losers. Of the eighty-two private British firms, ten showed losses, but their combined losses did not exceed British Steel's. Attention has also focused on Italy. Its spectacular loser, ENI, ranked third in losses, must also be placed in perspective: although both Italian public enterprises for which information is recorded lost money, so did three of the seven private companies.

To conclude, the image of public enterprises as losers has less basis in reality than is commonly believed. My recent comparison of financial indicators for both public and private enterprises in Latin America demonstrated that, in most cases, the source of equity ownership does not account for statistically significant differences in company behavior.[5] Focus, particularly by the business media, on the spectacular losses of a few companies in an even smaller number of countries, without placing such losses in global perspective, has regularly obscured the profits earned by the majority of government-owned companies. Broader studies have demonstrated that public enterprises do earn an operating surplus, even though thc environment in which they are forced to operate is so hostile that their rates of return on capital are low, usually because government-imposed pricing systems distort company performance.[6]

Public enterprises became public for a variety of reasons. Ideological predilection, fear of foreign ownership, and national security are often-stated government objectives. To these, however, must be added natural and economic disasters, retribution for past grievances, the rescue of failing private firms, and sheer accident. For Latin America, the traditional historical view that public enterprises entered the public portfolio according to some unidirectional, additive, inevitable historical logic has been debunked by a set of recent in-depth studies of the nineteenth and early twentieth century state.[7] Many exceptions and counterexamples to the expected growth of the public portfolio from a nineteenth-century position of subservient support to private, foreign, extractive-based capital, to provision in the post-Depression and Second World War period of public services and transport to support the purported phase of easy import substitution demonstrate that the governments were clearly important owners of the means of production at a much earlier date than expected, and that such growth did not conform to the evolving motivational patterns predicted by previous scholarship.[8] The commonly accepted notion that the advent of the public enterprises marks the second quarter of this century as the start of a radical departure from earlier government practices has been clarified. A revisionist view of public enterprise evolution, based on a newer, more careful, and detailed examination of government actions, reveals the effects of a set of government policies that were often changed, modified, countermanded, reversed, and then reinstated under different guises. Consequently, public enterprises were created, dissolved, merged, or allowed to atrophy during their long history. Present portfolio composition is but a glimpse of the convoluted evolutionary process that has marked the Latin American public sector, an evolution that will only be revealed through a more thorough analysis of the entrepreneurial role of several national governments throughout their histories.

Although public enterprises became public for a variety of reasons, the taxonomic approach, which classifies such firms according to known motives for incorporation into the public portfolio, suffers from serious defects. One of the most noteworthy is its failure to acknowledge, in the rush to explain government actions rationally, that many public enterprises became public by accident. Thus, although many motives cover company creation, they do not adequately explain specific portfolio composition, particularly for Latin America. Although preliminary examination of data from a limited number of non-Latin American countries indicates that some countries at similar levels of development have similar public enterprise portfolios, recent Latin American data indicate rapid growth of the portfolio and "accidental" shifts in its composition in several countries via massive nationalizations of banks, financial holding companies, or the family holdings of deposed dictators.[9] One of the largest European public enterprises, now held up as a model for Latin American governments, rose to a position of prominence via accidental nationalization. IRI, the Italian industrial development holding company, was originally founded in 1933 to temporarily take over banks that were threatened with collapse, but, as it acquired a number of miscellaneous, subsidiary, and not very related enterprises, it became a de facto industrial development agency.[10] The rush of bank nationalizations in Latin America after 1970 provides ample examples of accidental nationalization. In Peru, a variety of unintended public enterprises entered the portfolio following the preemptive takeover of the Banco Popular in 1970. These included textile mills, a chain of movie theaters showing soft-core pornography, and, it was widely rumored, a bordello. Similarly, the September 1982 bank nationalizations in Mexico swept private banks' portfolio holdings into the public sector without any decision having been taken on the rationale of government ownership of individual firms. Although exact estimates vary, it is commonly accepted that the nationalization increased the number of government holdings between 30 and 50 percent—without any underlying rationale. Current efforts to sanitize the portfolio by hiving off activities deemed nonessential have led to the disposal of shares in many such accidentally nationalized firms.[11] Post-1980 nationalizations in Peru and Chile have produced similar results.

Results of accidental nationalization are predominantly found in agriculture, industry, and services. Consequently, broad sectoral similarities may be found in other sectors of the economy. Basic infrastructure, including electricity, gas, water, and wastewater, is overwhelmingly public, whereas communications, air and rail transportation are less heavily dominated by public enterprises.[12] Although the public enterprise share of manufacturing typically reaches a lower level than in those sectors mentioned above, Mitra examines the case for extending heavy state intervention to one segment of manufacturing, the capital goods sector.[13] Thus, externalities, infant industry, and commanding-heights arguments often induce the government to take the leading position in steel, mining, and petroleum. Of the sixty-nine government corporations appearing on the *Fortune* list, more than a third, twenty-four, are petroleum enterprises; eleven produce steel; and seven are mining enterprises.

Because definitional aspects of national accounting data emanating from international financial organizations systematically exclude public financial institutions from consideration with other entities in the public portfolio, the exact portfolio size and the haphazard nature of its formation have been systematically neglected.[14] Rational nationalization, based on derivation of motives that have guided government intervention, has long been the subject of academic inquiry. Similar attention should be placed on accidental nationalization to provide a broader picture of the nature and scope of government action.

Prior to 1970, public enterprises remained a neglected topic of analysis for Latin Americanists. Since then, however, with the advent of *Fortune*-like, annual country-specific and continentwide industrial listings, the importance of public enterprises in explaining the magnitude and direction of Latin American development has become more apparent. During the 1970s, two major and opposing trends in public enterprise growth became apparent. First, natural resource-based industries were nationalized wholesale during the decade, often with associated marketing operations. Chile, Jamaica, and Peru followed the natural resource nationalization pattern, which was also echoed in Africa's major mining countries, Zambia and Zaire. The second major trend, privatization, occurred later and was particularly exemplified in Pinochet's Chile, where privatization became a watchword for reversing the massive growth in the public portfolio that had occurred during the presidency of Salvador Allende. The evolution of the direct and indirect holdings of CORFO, the development finance corporation, is instructive. In 1970, it controlled 44 companies. During the next three years under Allende, its holdings increased to 178 controlled firms, minority ownership in a further 70, and 259 companies that had been intervened, but in which the government had no equity participation. Under the Chicago-style policies of General Pinochet, all intervened firms were returned to their former owners, 122 companies were sold directly, bank shares were disposed of, other firms were closed and their assets liquidated, so that by 1979, CORFO had been shrunk to only 2 banks and 31 other companies.[15] However, notwithstanding the decade-long emphasis placed on privatization, Chile by 1984 had one of the highest concentrations of public enterprises among its top firms, where 7 of the top 10, when ranked by sales, were government owned. One other, although having no government equity, was under government administration as a result of private sector failures. The privatization trend became more visible in Thatcherian England, resulting in large, well-publicized equity sales.[16] Elsewhere, the fires of privatization smolder, but the roaring blaze that was expected to engulf and destroy the rampant public portfolio never occurred.

Far more significant, however, than privatization of equity is the movement toward privatization of public enterprise management through the introduction and nurturing of a climate for company action that stresses clear and attainable objectives, with minimal government interference in management decisions, makes managers responsible for results, gives them appropriate incentives for action, and upgrades their management skills.[17] Privatization of the management environment for public enterprises must be carefully balanced against national needs to control macro variables. In Brazil, where the post-1964 growth had been based on creating a corporate environment similar to that of the private sector, government inability to control the sources and uses of funds led to the creation in 1979 of the Secretariat for Control of State Enterprises (SEST) to monitor and approve the budgets of the largest companies at the national level.[18]

Indeed, the conspicuous failure of privatization efforts to achieve the expectations of their promoters suggests that the well-known Peacock and Wiseman hypothesis about the nature of public sector growth in general may be modified to account for the growth of the public enterprise portfolio.[19] In its general form, the hypothesis states that temporary changes in the acceptable sphere of government activity lead to more permanent changes. The portfolio analogue is that, once a temporary disturbance has increased the actual portfolio size, the tolerable portfolio size also increases, making it more difficult to decrease the number of government holdings.

An ongoing OPSS project has been to compile bibliographies on various facets of public sector action. Within this project, naturally, the area of public enterprises came in for an important concentration. This bibliography was prepared specifically to help diffuse information on the increasingly studied problem of public enterprise management. Although it is strong on materials dating from the 1950s to the 1970s, the newer, more analytically oriented materials of the early 1980s are heavily represented as unpublished conference papers, many of which are located in our own collections, or as chapters in edited volumes. The standard bibliographies on public enterprises have been consulted for inclusion in this work, notably those of Smith; the Latin American Center for Economic and Social Documentation (CLADES); Marsden; Maurice and Miller; and several versions and updates of the important work compiled under the sponsorship of the Interamerican Development Bank (BID) and the Brazilian government at the Interamerican School of Public Administration (EIAP) of the Getúlio Vargas Foundation in Brazil (FGV).[20] So, too, have the materials on public enterprises generated by the programs and projects of the International Center for Public Enterprises in Developing Countries (ICPE) in Ljubljana, Yugoslavia, and reported in its first bibliography been consulted.[21] A year's stay in East Africa, while on leave of absence from the University of Texas, provided me with access to public enterprise-related materials from a part of the world not usually well studied by Latin Americanists.

Certain materials have been deliberately omitted from the bibliography. The small library attached to the Office for Public Sector Studies and the much larger Nettie Lee Benson Latin American Collection (BLAC) have made special efforts to collect the raw material of public enterprise studies, namely, the economic and financial information published by the companies themselves. These efforts have met with considerable success. Likewise, official publications of controlling agencies, including, but not limited to, comptrollers' reports, are also well represented in BLAC for the Latin American nations. These are present on the Austin campus, but are not included in this bibliography for reasons of space. Their inclusion would have expanded this already-unwieldy volume far beyond manageable limits. A complete listing of these materials must await a possible companion volume. Similarly, the large collection of U.S. government documents that deal with public enterprises has also been omitted with the expectation that a later supplement will cover them in detail.

The form of the bibliography merits explanation. Many bibliographies opt for a limited classification of entries by topical or country descriptors, with additional references listed at the end of each classification. The flexible, on-line computer program designed for the OPSS permits a wider classification so that each entry can be referenced by up to ten separate descriptors, with no explicit ordering. The program permits the retrieval of specialized bibliographies based on a descriptor profile. Consequently, in this hard-copy version of the on-line data base, the entries are presented in alphabetical order, with the index serving as the principal reference source. Alphabetization also avoids the need for a long introductory section specifying the peculiarities of author-specific classifications. Index and analytical classification categories are based on a subset of USPSD (United States Political Science Documents) descriptors augmented by country names and by specific terms especially relevant for public enterprise studies. Basing the descriptors on a widely employed and accepted set makes for wider acceptance of then classificatory scheme. When possible, call numbers and library location are provided for entries available on the UT campus.

A list of abbreviations employed in the bibliography has been provided. To make the information more widely accessible, the use of abbreviations within citations has been kept to a minimum, with University of Texas and United Nations divisions accounting for the vast majority of the entries in the list of acronyms.

Inspiration for the international public enterprise bibliography project came from William P. Glade, ILAS director, who has advocated, fostered, and undertaken studies of public enterprises for years. A similar tribute to his interest in disseminating public enterprise information is found in the acknowledgments of the Maurice and Miller bibliography, which mentions an intellectual indebtedness to William P. Glade, "who was instrumental in initiating the work on the bibliography." I recognize a greater debt level, because he went much further than initiating this work. He was a constant source of encouragement, always available for consultation, and frequently called new works to my attention.

A series of research assistants gathered and verified much of the raw material that makes up the bibliography. Their contributions deservedly merit recognition. Among those who participated in various phases during the past years are Marta Ardila, David Bowie, Marcella Case Lesher, Paul Charney, Lewis DiFelice, Greg Estep, Floriano Gomes da Silva, Timothy Hlavinka, Donald Hebard, José Hernández, Jorge Hidrobo, Greg Koury, Luis Leriche-Guzmán, Elizabeth Mahan, Mao Guo Ping, Daniel Mattes, Katherine Murray, Patricia Quintero, Linda Seaman, Douglas Washburn, and Michael Whitehead. Their diverse backgrounds and the diversity of tasks they accomplished are only matched by their current geographical dispersal. Wherever they are, they merit our thanks.

The raw material was entered into a flexible input-output bibliography especially designed for the Office for Public Sector Studies as a project under the direction of Dr. Eleanor Jordan of the UT School of Business. Randall Bryan, in particular, provided many of the key insights, designed essential program elements, and brought the project to fruition long after it had emerged from Eleanor's control. Various consultants at the UT Computation Center have aided in clearing up successive generations of bugs. L. Stuart Vance deserves particular mention for his recent attention to the project.

Kathryn Bork and Mary E. Moran of ILAS's publications office regularly provided pertinent answers to pesky problems, maintaining unfailing good humor about an impertinent professor who kept uncovering or perhaps inventing those problems. Mao Guo Ping, Jorge Hidrobo, and Peter Conaty provided much of the final proof editing and consistency checking. The rest of the Institute staff provided unfailing moral and unceasing nutritive support. My wife, Suzanne, showing her customary good sense, was continents away during the months that the bibliography neared completion, a separation that purged both ritual guilt and pleasant distractions from the inevitable long hours devoted to final checking.

OPSS will continue to provide catalytic stimulation for the study of public enterprises in Latin America with the objectives of raising the technical level of such studies, increasing their coverage, and contributing to the use of new research findings in solving management problems in and about the public enterprises. Detailed analysis of one geographical area has repercussions on the development of our knowledge base for the study of public enterprises in other parts of the world. Broader diffusion of information leading to cross-cultural comparative studies may shed more light on the public enterprise phenomenon removed from a strictly national context and may lead to more skillful and efficient reliance on public enterprise as a policy tool and a more careful delineation of the areas of possible public enterprise action and those that may be placed beyond the pale of the public sector.

The objective of this bibliography is to serve as a useful reference tool for scholars, researchers, government officials, and international advisers who have an interest in public enterprises. Although aimed principally at economists and public administrators, I hope that others, too, will find it useful.

Alfred H. Saulniers
Coordinator, Office for Public Sector Studies

NOTES

1. Although there is still no single "correct" definition of "public enterprise" on which scholars and practitioners agree, Andreja Böhm summarized the recent debate on definitional issues at a conference sponsored by the International Center for Public Enterprises in Developing Countries, and proposed general and operational definitions in his 1981 article, "The Concept, Definition and Classification of Public Enterprises," *Public Enterprise* 1, 4:72-78. Leroy Jones proposed a more formal economic approach in a set-theoretical formulation encompassing different definitional criteria in *Public Enterprise and Economic Development: The Korean Case* (Seoul: Korea Development Institute, 1975).

2. *Fortune* (Aug. 20, 1984), "The International 500: The Fortune Directory of the Largest Industrial Corporations Outside the U.S.," pp. 200-215.

3. Peter Saunders and Friedrich Klan, "The Role of the Public Sector: Cause and Consequences of the Growth of Government," *OECD Economic Studies*, No. 4 (1985), p. 77.

4. Solberg stresses possibilities of discrediting the concept of government-owned oil companies when detailing the mismanagement, financial shortages and inefficiencies during YPF's early years: *Oil and Nationalism in Argentina: A History* (Stanford, Cal.: Stanford University Press, 1979), p. 64.

5. Alfred H. Saulniers, *Public Enterprises in Latin America: The New Look?* Technical Papers series, no. 44 (Austin: University of Texas at Austin, Institute of Latin American Studies, Office for Public Sector Studies, 1985). The work is also available in Spanish: "Empresas públicas en América Latina: Una nueva visión?" in *Seminario sobre planeamiento y control del sector de empresas públicas - Documentos* (Brasília: IPEA/CEPAL, 1983); and Portuguese: "Empresas públicas na América Latina: Novas Funções?" in *Seminário sobre planejamento e controle do setor de empresas estatais - Documentos* (Brasília: IPEA/CEPAL, 1983).

6. R. P. Short, "The Role of Public Enterprises: An International Statistical Comparison" (Washington: International Monetary Fund, DM/83/34, 1983); and Mary Shirley, *Managing State-Owned Enterprises, World Bank Staff Working Papers,* Number 577 (Washington, 1983), pp. 10-17.

7. Gene E. Bigler, *La política y el capitalismo de Estado en Venezuela* (Madrid: Editorial Técnos, 1981); Steven Topik, *The Evolution of the Economic Role of the Brazilian State, 1889-1930,* Technical Papers series, no. 15 (Austin: University of Texas at Austin, Institute of Latin American Studies, Office for Public Sector Studies, 1981); Alfred H. Saulniers and Julio E. Revilla, "The Economic Role of the Peruvian State: 1821-1919," paper presented at the XI International Congress of the Latin American Studies Association, Mexico City, 29 Sept. - 1 Oct. 1983.

8. For traditional views of the temporal evolution of the nature of Latin American public enterprises, see E. V. K FitzGerald, *The Public Sector in Latin America*, Cambridge University Centre of Latinamerican Studies Working Paper, no. 18 (Cambridge, 1974); idem, "Some Aspects of the Political Economy of the Latin American State," *Development and Change* 7 (1976):119-133; and Economic Commission for Latin America, "Public Enterprises: Their Present Significance and Their Potential in Development," *Economic Bulletin for Latin America* 16 (1971):1-70.

9. The massive nationalization of Trujillo's property to the Dominican Republic's public enterprise portfolio led to the formation of a holding company, CORDE. In Nicaragua, however, the extensive Somoza holdings were split among the sectoral ministries. See Maritza Amalia Guerrero, "Las empresas públicas en la República Dominicana," paper presented at the Seminar on Public Enterprises and Planning in Central America and the Caribbean, San José, Costa Rica, 1-3 July 1981; Bernhard Wittich, "La situación operativa y productiva de las empresas de CORDE" (Santo Domingo: Corporación Dominicana de Empresas Estatales, 1983); and Instituto Nicaragüense de Administración Pública, Centro de Instrucción para la Dirección Estatal, "Los problemas de las empresas públicas en un proceso revolucionario" (Managua, 1981). For the non-Latin American analysis of portfolio similarities, see Leroy P. Jones and Edward S. Mason, "Role of Economic Factors in Determining the Size and Structure of the Public Enterprise Sector in Less-developed Countries in Mixed Economies," in Leroy P. Jones et al., *Public Enterprise in Less-developed Countries* (New York: Cambridge University Press, 1982), pp. 17-47.

10. The number of references in the published literature to accidental public enterprises is extremely limited. On IRI, see N. S. Carey Jones, S. M. Patankar, and M. J. Boodhoo, *Politics, Public Enterprise and the Industrial Development Agency: Industrialization Policies and Practices* (London: Croom Helm, 1974), p. 23; and Stuart Holland, "The National Context," in Stuart Holland, ed., *The State as Entrepreneur: New Dimensions for Public Enterprise: The IRI State Shareholding Formula* (London: Weidenfeld and Nicolson, 1972), pp. 57-59.

11. See Héctor Fernández Moreno, "Experiencias y planteamientos para la planeación y control de las empresas del sector público," paper presented

at the seminar "State Control and Planning of Public Enterprises," Brasília, 15-17 June 1983; Ewell E. Murphy, Jr., "The Mexican Bank Expropriation in Retrospect," *The Mexican Forum* 5, no. 3 (1985):15-19; "Reestructuración de la industria paraestatal," *El Mercado de Valores* 45, no. 14 (8 Apr. 1985):33-37; and idem, "Venta de acciones de empresas no prioritarias con participación estatal," *El Mercado de Valores* 45, no. 16 (22 Apri. 1985):376-377.

12. Shirley, *Managing State-Owned Enterprises*, p. 8; and International Bank for Reconstruction and Development, *World Development Report 1983* (Washington, 1983), pp. 48-50.

13. Jayati Datta Mitra, *The Capital Goods Sector in LDCs: A Case for State Intervention?* World Bank Staff Working Paper, no. 343 (Washington, 1979).

14. For a background to international positions on definitional discrepancies, see United Nations Statistical Commission, "Reconciliation of the United Nations Draft Manual in Public Sector Statistics"; and the International Monetary Fund draft, "Manual on Government Finance Statistics, Report of the Secretary General," prepared for the Nineteenth Session of the Statistical Commission, New Delhi, 6-19 Nov. 1976.

15. The data are taken from CORFO internal reports. Chile, Corporación de Fomento de la Producción, *Privatización de empresas y activos 1973-1978* (Santiago, n.d.), Anexo No. 2; and idem, *Actividades realizadas por CORFO en 1980 y perspectivas para 1981: Información real al 30 de junio de 1981* (Santiago, 1981), Anexo no. 1.

16. David Steel and David Heald, "Privatizing Public Enterprise in the Record of the UK Conservative Government, 1979-83," paper presented at the conference "State Shrinking: A Comparative Inquiry into Privatization," Austin, Tex., 1-3 Mar. 1984; "Privatization in Britain: Making the Modern Dinosaur Extinct," *The Economist* 294, no. 7382 (23 Feb.-1 Mar. 1985):76-78.

17. For additional stress on the proper environment for public enterprise improvement, see *World Development Report 1983*, pp. 74-87. A provocative and insightful analysis of privatization issues is found in William P. Glade, "The Privatization and Denationalization of Public Enterprises," in G. Ram Reddy, *Public Enterprise: Essays in Honor of Professor V. V. Ramanadham* (London: Frank Cass and Co., 1983), pp. 67-97.

18. Brazil, Presidency of the Republic, Planning Secretariat, Secretariat for Control of State Enterprises, *State Enterprises in Brazil and the Control of the SEST: Background and 1980 Results* (Brasília, 1981).

19. Alan Peacock and Jack Wiseman, *The Growth of Public Expenditure in the United Kingdom* (Princeton, N.J.: Princeton University Press, 1961).

20. Hadley F. Smith, *Public Enterprise and Economic Development: An International Bibliography*, International Public Administration Series, no. 3 (Los Angeles, Cal.: University of Southern California, International Public Administration Center, 1964); Centro Latinoamericano de Documentación

Económica y Social, *Bibliografía sobre empresas públicas* (Santiago, 1972); R. P. Marsden, *Bibliography of Public Enterprise with Special Reference to the Developing Countries Based on the Collections of Professor A. H. Hansen* (Leeds: University of Leeds, 1973); Nelson R. Maurice and Richard U. Miller, *The Management of Public Enterprise: A Bibliography* (Madison: University of Wisconsin-Madison, Center for International Business Research, 1975); Escola Brasileira de Administração Pública - Fundação Getúlio Vargas, and Centro Brasileiro de Apoio à Pequena e Média Empresa, *Empresas estatais, indicador bibliográfico* (São Paulo, 1977); and Escuela Interamericana de Administración Pública, Fundación Getúlio Vargas, *Empresas públicas: indicador bibliográfico* (Mexico City: Editorial Limusa, 1979).

21. Manca Umek and Matjaž Musek, *Bibliography of ICPE, 1974-1981* (Ljubljana: International Center for Public Enterprises in Developing Countries, 1982).

LIST OF ABBREVIATIONS

AICC - All India Congress Committee
ALIDE - Latin American Association of Development Finance Institutions
BAPEG - Boston Area Public Enterprise Group
BBC - British Broadcasting Corporation
BID - Inter-American Development Bank
CAFRAD - African Center for Administrative Training and Research for Development
CARICAD - Caribbean Centre for Development Administration
CEDES - Center for the Study of State and Society
CEE - European Economic Community
CEEP - European Center for Public Enterprise
CEMLA - Center for Latin American Monetary Studies
CEPAL - Economic Commission for Latin America
CETAI - Centre for International Business Studies
CIDE - Center for Economic Teaching and Research
CIRIEC - International Committee for the Study of the Financing of Public Undertakings in European Countries
CLACSO - Latin American Social Science Council
CLAD - Latin American Center of Development Administration
CLADES - Latin American Center for Economic and Social Documentation
COFIDE - Development Finance Corporation
CONASUPO - National Company for Basic Foodstuffs
DESA - Department of Economic and Social Affairs
ECA - United Nations Economic Commission for Africa
ECAFE - United Nations Economic Commission for Asia and the Far East
ECE - United Nations Economic Commission for Europe
ECLA - Economic Commission for Latin America
ECOSOC - Economic and Social Council

EEC -	European Economic Community
EIAP -	Inter-American School of Public Administration
ENI -	National Hydrocarbon Authority
ESCAP -	Economic and Social Council for Asia and the Pacific
FAO -	Food and Agricultural Organization
FGV -	Getúlio Vargas Foundation
FIEL -	Foundation for Latin American Economic Research
FINEP -	Financier for Studies and Projects
FIPAD -	International Foundation for Development Alternatives
FUNDAP -	Foundation for Administrative Development
HIID -	Harvard Institute for International Development
HRC -	Humanities Research Center
IBRD -	International Bank for Reconstruction and Development
ICAP -	Central American Institute of Public Administration
ICPE -	International Centre for Public Enterprises in Developing Countries
IDB -	Inter-American Development Bank
IIAS -	International Institute of Administrative Sciences
ILAS -	Institute of Latin American Studies
ILET -	Latin American Institute of Transnational Studies
ILO -	International Labour Organisation
ILPES -	Latin American Institute for Economic and Social Planning
IMF -	International Monetary Fund
INAP -	National Institute of Public Administration
INI -	National Industrial Institute
INTAL -	Institute for Latin American Integration
IPEA -	Institute for Applied Economic and Social Research
IRI -	Institute for Industrial Reconstruction
LAC -	Nettie Lee Benson Latin American Collection
NIPA -	National Institute of Public Administration
OCDE -	Organization for Economic Cooperation and Development
OECD -	Organization for Economic Cooperation and Development
OPSS -	Office for Public Sector Studies
OPTIMA -	Optimal Performance through Integral Management Action
PCL -	Perry-Castañeda Library
SBP -	Strengthening the Bargaining Position
SIAP -	Inter-American Planning Society
TOT -	Transfer of Technology
TVA -	Tennessee Valley Authority
UAR -	United Arab Republic
UGL -	Undergraduate Library

UNCTAD - United Nations Conference on Trade and Development
UNDESA - United Nations Department of Economic and Social Affairs
UNDP - United Nations Development Programme
UNECA - United Nations Economic Commission for Africa
UNECAFE - United Nations Economic Commission for Asia and the Far East
UNECE - United Nations Economic Commission for Europe
UNECLA - United Nations Economic Commission for Latin America
UNESCO - United Nations Educational, Scientific, and Cultural Organization
UNIDO - United Nations Industrial Development Organization
UNILPES - Latin American Institute for Economic and Social Planning
UNTAA - United Nations Technical Assistance Administration
UT - University of Texas

Public Enterprise

1. Abani, A. S. 1973 "Cost Audit in Public Enterprises." Lok Udyog (New Delhi), V. 7, No. 2, pp. 35-40. /India /Costs /Control process /354.54 L836 PCL

2. Abani, A. S. 1974 "Budgeting in Public Enterprises." Lok Udyog (New Delhi), V. 7, No. 12, pp. 49-58. /India /Budgetary process /354.54 L836 PCL

3. Abani, A. S. 1978 "Professional Management in State Level Public Enterprises." Lok Udyog (New Delhi), V. 11, No. 12, pp. 29-36. /India /Management /State government /354.54 L836

4. Abaya, Bonifacio A., ed. 1975 Laws Affecting Government Owned or Controlled Corporations. Quezon City, Philippines: University of the Philippines, Law Center, Institute on Government Owned or Controlled Corporations. /Philippines /Law

5. Abbott, C. C. 1937 "The Government Corporation as an Economic Institution." Harvard Business Review V. 15, pp. 295-312. /United States of America /Economic analysis /HF 5001 H3

6. Abbott, John C. 1967 "Agricultural Marketing Boards in the Developing Countries." Journal of Farm Economics V. 49, No. 3, pp. 705-722. /Developing nations /Marketing boards /Agricultural sector /338.105 J826 PCL

7. Abbott, John C., and H. C. Creupelandt. 1966 Agricultural Marketing Boards: Their Establishment and Operation. Rome: UNFAO. /Agricultural sector /Marketing boards /Developing nations / HP 9000.6 A2 PCL

8. Abdalla, Ismail-Sabri. 1979 "Secteur publique et stratégies du développement." Dossier FIPAD No. 7. /Economic development /OPSS

9. Abdallah, I. S. 1969 Organization of Public Sector. Cairo: Dar El-Maaref. /Egypt /Organization formation

10. Abdel Monein, Abdel Salam. 1974 Empresas industriales públicas en el Sudán, corporación para la producción industrial. Ljubljana: ICPE. /Sudan /Industrial sector /Development corporation

11. Abdul Rahman, Wan Zahir Bin Heikh. 1980 "Management of Transfer of Technology by Public Enterprises in Malaysia." Paper presented at the Regional Workshop on Management of Transfer of Technology by Public Enterprises in the ESCAP Region, 10-15 Nov., Bangalore, India. Ljubljana: ICPE /Malaysia /Technology transfer

12. Abdul Wahab, Subkey bin, and Abdul Jalil bin Mohamed Ali. 1979 "Training in Public Enterprises: Ministry of Public Enterprises Malaysia; Country Report." Paper presented at the International Seminar on Management and Training in Public Enterprises in Developing Countries, 1-13 Oct., Ljubljana, Yugoslavia. Ljubljana: ICPE. /Malaysia /Training /Management

13. Abdulla, A. 1954 "Pakistan, Industrial Development Corporation." Pakistan Quarterly (Karachi, Pakistan), pp. 48-54. /Pakistan /Industrial sector /Development corporation

14. Abegaz, Haile Yesus. 1982 The Organization of State Farms in Ethiopia after the Land Reform of 1975. Fort Lauderdale/Plantation, Fla.: Breitenbach Publishers. /Ethiopia /Agrarian reform /Collective farming /Economic development / Socialist economy

15. Abel, Albert S., and Gabriel Wilner. 1970 "The Public Corporation in the United States." In W. G. Friedmann and J. F. Gardner, ed(s). Government Enterprise, A Comparative Study. New York: Colombia University Press. pp. 181-200. /United States of America /Bibliography / 350.0092 G746 PCL

16. Abel, Deryck. 1957 "British Conservatives and State Ownership." Journal of Politics V. 19, pp. 237-239. /United Kingdom /Mixed enterprises /320.5 J825

17. Abel, Martin E. 1975 "Irrigation Systems in Taiwan: Management of a Decentralized Public Enterprise." Minneapolis: University of Minnesota, Department of Agricultural and Applied Economics. /China, Rep. of /Irrigation systems /Water resources development / OPSS

18. Abente, Diego. 1982 "Las corporaciones regionales en la Venezuela contemporánea." Paper presented at the Tenth National Meeting of the Latin American Studies Association, Washington, D C., 4-6 March. /Venezuela /Regional development / OPSS

19. Aberle, G. 1972 "Die Abgabenpolitik bei offentlich angebotenen gutern: das Beispiel der verkeh verkehrsinfrastruktur." (Duty Policy in the Case of Public Goods: The Traffics Infrastructure Example. With English summary). Zeitschrift fur Wirtschafts- und Sozial wissen schaften. V. 92, No. 1. /Germany, Federal Rep. of /Highways and roads / H 5 J2 PCL

20. Abeywickrama, Don Sepala Herat. 1980 "Preparations and Negotiations for the Technology Transfer Agreement for the Sri Lanka Tyre Corporation." Paper presented at the International Workshop on Preparations and Negotiations of Technology Transfer Agreements for Public Enterprises in Developing Countries, 27-31 Oct., Ljubljana, Yugoslavia. Ljubljana: ICPE. /Sri Lanka /Technology transfer /Tire industry / Industrial sector /Case studies /

21. Abib, Abdelkrim. 1976 "L'accès à la technologie: le cas Algérien; l'avance dans la maîtrise des technologies à travers les investissements des entreprises publiques dans le secteur productif." Lausanne, Switzerland: Université de Lausanne. /Algeria /Technology transfer / Investment

22. Abraham, Henry J. 1956 Government as Entrepreneur and Social Servant. Washington, D. C.: Public Affairs Press. /Entrepreneurial activity /Social welfare policy /338.973 Ab82g

23. Abrams, M. 1963 "State Industry and the Public." In M. Shanks, ed(s). Lessons of Public Enterprise. London: Jonathan Cape. pp. 207-218. /United Kingdom /Industrial sector

24. Abramson, R. 1975 "Behavioral Science Application in the Management of Public Enterprises - An East African Case Study." Improving Performance in Public Enterprise, Report of an International Conference, Arusha, Tanzania, 2-5 Dec. Arusha, Tanzania: East African Community Management Institute. pp. 92-109. /Management /Organization development /East Africa /Case studies

25. Abramson, R. 1979 "Planning for Improved Performance and Organization Development in East African Public Corporations." Paper presented at the Regional Workshop on Planning in Public Enterprises of the African Region, 10-15 Dec., Accra, Ghana. Ljubljana: ICPE. /East Africa /Africa /Planning process /Productivity /Management

26. Abramson, R., and W. Halset. 1979 "Planning for Improved Enterprise Performance: A Guide for Managers and Consultants." International Productivité Gestion des entreprises publiques. Geneva: ILO. No. 15. /Planning process /Management /Productivity

27. Abranches, Sérgio Henrique. 1980 "A empresa pública como agente de polítocas do estado: Fundamentos teóricos do seu papel, inclusive em face de nossas relações com o exterior." A empresa pública no Brasil: Uma abordagem multidisciplinar. Brasília: IPEA. pp. 5-32. /Brazil /Economic policy /Political economy /Control process

28. Abranches, Sérgio Henrique. 1981 "Economía política e democracia: Notas sobre a lógica da ação estatal." Dados, Revista de Ciencias Sociais V. 24, No. 1, pp. 3-23. /Brazil /Political economy / G305 D127 LAC

29. Abranches, Sérgio Henrique. 1984 "State Enterprise and Modes of Privatization. A Critical View Based on Brazilian Examples," Paper presented at the conference: "State Shrinking: A Comparative Inquiry into Privatization," Austin, Tex., 1-3 Mar. /Brazil /Privatization /OPSS

30. Abranches, Sérgio Henrique. n.d. "Empresa estatal e capitalismo: Uma análise comparada." Unpublished. /Brazil /Capitalism /Comparative analysis / OPSS

31. Abtan, Aziz Jaffar Hussan. 1979 "Development of Control Concept and the Control over the Public Enterprises in Iraq." Paper presented at the Interregional Workshop on Control Systems for Public Enterprises in Developing Countries, 9-13 July, Ljubljana, Yugoslavia. Ljubljana: ICPE. /Iraq /Control process

32. Abu Bakar, B. Taib. 1968 A Study into the Social and Economic Aspects of FLDA Scheme at Sg. Buava Eawang. Kuala Lumpur: University of Malaya, Faculty of Agriculture, 4th Year Agricultural Economic Project Paper. /Malaysia

/Agricultural sector /Agricultural development /Case studies /Economic development /Social development

33. Abyan, Ibrahim M. 1980 "Survey of Rural Development: (Togdheer and Nugal Regions)." Paper presented at the Expert Group Meeting on the Role of Public Enterprises in Regional Development in Developing Countries, 7-11 Dec., Ljubljana, Yugoslavia. Ljubljana: ICPE. /Rural development

34. Acharya, S. N. 1972 "Public Enterprise Pricing and Social Benefit-Cost Analysis." Oxford Economic Papers V. 24, No. 1, pp. 36-53. /India /Gas utility industry /Price policy /Social welfare policy /Cost benefit analysis /330.6 OX2 PCL

35. Acharya, S. N. 1978 "Pricing and Profit Policy of the Assam Gas Company Limited." In K. R. Gupta, ed(s). Pricing in Public Enterprises. India: Atlantic Publishers & Distributors. pp. 161-163. /India /Assam, India (State) /Gas utility industry /Price policy / HB 236 I4 P75 PCL

36. Acosta Gómez, Germán. 1955 "Los trabajadores contratados indirectamente en la industria venezolana del petróleo." Revista del Trabajo (Caracas), V. 5, No. 19, pp. 111-166. /Venezuela /Oil industry /Labor relations /Employment policy /G331.80987 R327

37. Acosta Suárez, Ricardo. 1984 "A Conceptual Approach to Interlinkages." Public Enterprise V. 4, No. 3, pp. 33-48. /Economic analysis /Political role / OPSS

38. Adak, R. 1963 "Une forme d'entreprise publique turque: L'organisme économique d'Etat." Synthèses (Brussels), V. 18, No. 205, pp. 269-279. /Turkey /Law

39. Adar, Zvi, and Yair Aharoni. 1980 "Risk Sharing Managers of State Owned Enterprises." Paper presented at the Second BAPEG Conference: Public Enterprises in Mixed Economy LDCs, Boston, April. /Management /OPSS

40. Adedeji, A. 1969 Problems and Techniques of Administrative Training in Africa. Ibadan, Nigeria: University of Ife Press. /Africa /Administrative management /Training

41. Adizes, I. 1971 "The Role of Management in Democratic (Communal) Organization Structures. A Study of the Yugoslav Self-Management, the Israeli Kibutz and the Peruvian Comunidad Industrial." Annals of Public and Cooperative Economy /Yugoslavia /Israel /Peru /Worker self management /330.5 An73

42. Adizes, I., and Elisabeth Mann Borgese, eds. 1975 Self-Management: New Dimensions to Democracy. Santa Barbara, Cal.; Oxford, England: American Bibliographical Center; Clio Press. /Management /Worker self management /Yugoslavia /Israel /Norway / OPSS

43. Adjei, Kwame E. 1975 "The Staffing and Training of Public Enterprise Management in Africa." Improving Performance in Public Enterprise, Report of an International Conference,

Arusha, Tanzania, 2-5 Dec. Arusha, Tanzania: East African Community Management Institute. pp. 150-163. /Training /Africa /Nigeria

44. Adler, R. W., and R. F. Mikesell. 1966 Public External Financing of Development Banks in Developing Countries. Eugene, Or.: Bureau of Business and Economic Research, University of Oregon. /Financial institutions /Development banks / 332.15 Ad59p PCL

45. Affonso, Sebastião Baptista. 1980 "Relações entre as empresas públicas e o governo: Análises, recomendações e alternativas de institucionalização dessas relações." A empresa pública no Brasil: Uma abordagem multidisciplinar. Brasília: IPEA. pp. 325-382. /Brazil /Control process /Law

46. Agarin, L. 1960 "Contronto fra l'efficienzia della siderurgia statale in Italia." Rivista del Instituto di Science Economique e Comericali pp. 26-36. /Italy /Steel industry /Efficacy

47. Agarwal, B. K. 1973 "Marketing Information Systems." Lok Udyog (New Delhi), V. 7, No. 4, pp. 43-46. /India /Information system /Marketing /354.54 L836 PCL

48. Agarwal, N. P. 1981 "Measuring Financial Strength Through Common-Size Balance Sheets of Aluminium Industry in India." Lok Udyog (New Delhi), V. 15, No. 2, pp. 43-58. /India /Financial performance /Metal manufacturing industry /354.54 L836 PCL

49. Agarwal, O. P. 1963 "Developments in Training Programmes for Public Sector Employees." Indian Journal of Public Administration (New Delhi), V. 9, pp. 114-124. /India /Employment policy /Training / JA 26 I55 Pub Aff

50. Agarwal, R. C. 1961 State Enterprise in India. Allahabad, India: Chaitanya Publishing House. /India /Evaluation /338.954 Ag148s

51. Agarwal, R. D. 1965 "Industrial Development Bank: A Model for Underdeveloped Countries." Indian Economic Journal V. 11. /Development banks / 330.5 In16

52. Agarwal, R. D. 1973 "Setting Objectives for Success." Lok Udyog (New Delhi), V. 7, No. 8, pp. 5-10. /India /Goal setting /354.54 L836 PCL

53. Agarwal, S. C. 1973 "Productivity Concept and Measurement - Meaning, Techniques and Methods." Lok Udyog (New Delhi), V. 7, No. 1, pp. 13-20. /India /Productivity /Methodology /354.54 L836 PCL

54. Agarwala, Umesh N. 1978 "Is Promotion Contingent on Performance in Public Sector Enterprises." Lok Udyog (New Delhi), V. 12, No. 2, pp. 35-38. /India /Personnel management /Evaluation /354.54 L836 PCL

55. Agpalo, R. E. 1961 The Political Process and the Nationalization of the Retail Trade in the Philippines. Quezon City: University of Philippines, Office of Coordinator of Research. /Philippines /Retail trade /Nationalization /Marketing / 658.87 Ag78p

56. Agpalo, R. E. 1961 "Nationalization of Retail Trade in the Philippines." Philippine Journal of Public Administration (Manila), V. 5, No. 2, pp. 129-143. /Philippines /Retail trade /Nationalization /Marketing

57. Agrawal, Govind R. 1981 "Education and Training in Public Enterprise in Nepal." Paper presented at the Regional Workshop on Management Training and Development in Public Enterprises of Developing Countries, 5-15 Jan., Karachi, Pakistan. Ljubljana: ICPE. /Nepal /Training /Management /Also published in Public Enterprise, Vol. 2, No. 1(1981), pp. 53-56. /OPSS

58. Agrawal, N. C. 1958 "Management of Public Enterprise in India." Indian Journal of Commerce (Allahabad, India). V. 11, No. 4. /India /Management

59. Agudelo Montoya, Oscar, and Néstor López G. 1975 "Empresas públicas de Medellín (Colombia): Aspectos principales." Rio de Janeiro: FGV-EIAP. /Colombia /Medellin, Colombia / OPSS

60. Agudelo Montoya, Oscar, et al. 1976 "El sector público descentralizado de Colombia." Rio de Janeiro: FGV-EIAP. /Colombia /Control process /Economic history / OPSS

61. Aguilar Chávez, A., H. F. Corrales C., and Miguel Angel Martínez B. 1975 "La empresa pública en Paraguay." Rio de Janeiro: FGV-EIAP. /Paraguay /Directory / OPSS

62. Aharoni, Yair. 1977 Markets, Planning, and Development: The Private and Public Sectors in Economic Development. Cambridge, Ma.: Ballinger Publishers. /Management /Comparative analysis

63. Aharoni, Yair. 1981 "Managerial Discretion." In Raymond Vernon and Yair Aharoni, ed(s). State-Owned Enterprises in the Western Economy. New York: St. Martin's Press. pp. 184-193. /Management

64. Aharoni, Yair. 1982 "State-owned enterprise: an agent without a principal." In Leroy P. Jones et al., ed(s). Public enterprise in less-developed countries. New York: Cambridge University Press. pp. 67-76. /Control process /Goal setting /Accountability / /HD 3850 P83 PCL /Paper originally presented at the Second BAPEG Conference in Boston, April 1980.

65. Ahluwalia, P. S. 1977 "HMT's Roll Forging Machine for Rural Upliftment." Lok Udyog (New Delhi), V. 11, No. 9, pp. 59-60. /India /Metal manufacturing industry /Rural development /Case studies /354.54 L836 PCL

66. Ahmad, Abdullah Sanusi. 1981 "Financial Profitability and Losses in Public Enterprises." Paper presented at the International Workshop on Financial Profitability and Losses in Public Enterprises, 1-5 June, Ljubljana, Yugoslavia. Ljubljana: ICPE. /Profits

67. Ahmad, Aftabuddin. 1979 "Management and Training in Public Enterprises: Country Report of Bangladesh." Paper presented at the International Seminar on Management and Training in Public Enterprises in Developing Countries, 1-13 Oct., Ljubljana, Yugoslavia. Ljubljana: ICPE. /Bangladesh /Training /Management

68. Ahmad, Ashraf Uddin. 1980 "Management and Training of Public Enterprises of Bangladesh." Paper presented at the Interregional Seminar on Training Management in Public Enterprises in Developing Countries, 29 Sept. - 10 Oct., Ljubljana, Yugoslavia. Ljubljana: ICPE. /Bangladesh /Management /Training

69. Ahmad, M. 1974 "Planning and Public Sector Enterprises in Bangladesh: National Paper of Bangladesh." Paper presented at the International Seminar ´74: Planning in Public Enterprises in Developing Countries, 23 Sept. - 9 Oct., Ljubljana, Yugoslavia. Ljubljana: ICPE. /Bangladesh /Planning process

70. Ahmad, M. 1980 <u>Public Sector Industrial Enterprises in Bangladesh.</u> Ljubljana: ICPE. /Bangladesh /Industrial sector

71. Ahmad, M. 1980 <u>Public Enterprise in South Asia: A Study in Comparison.</u> Ljubljana: ICPE. /Asia /South Asia /Comparative analysis

72. Ahmad, M. 1980 <u>Public Sector in a Developing Economy: A Politico-Economic Study of Bangladesh.</u> Ljubljana: ICPE. /Bangladesh /Economic analysis /Political analysis /

73. Ahmad, M. 1982 <u>Public Enterprises in South Asia.</u> Ljubljana: ICPE. /Asia /South Asia

74. Ahmad, M. 1982 "Political economy of public enterprise." In Leroy P. Jones et al., ed(s). <u>Public enterprise in less-developed countries.</u> New York: Cambridge University Press. pp. 49-64. /Political economy /HD 3850 P83 PCL /Paper originally presented at the second BAPEG seminar, Boston, April 1980. /OPSS

75. Ahmad, M., and Pavle Sicherl. 1977 "Guidelines for Preparation of the National Report: The Role of the Public Sector in Developing Countries." Paper presented at the Meeting of the International Research Project on "The Role of the Public Sector in Developing Countries," 7-11 Dec., Ljubljana, Yugoslavia. Ljubljana: ICPE. /Developing nations

76. Ahmad, N., and E. Becher. 1965 "Development Banks and Corporations in Africa." <u>Nigerian Journal of Economic and Social Studies</u> (Ibadan), V. 7. /Africa /Development banks /Development corporation

77. Ahmed, Allauddin, and Viqar Ahmed. 1965 "Coordinator of Public Enterprises: Country Study for Pakistan." In A. S. H. K. Sadique, ed(s). *Public Enterprise in Asia: Studies on Coordination and Control.* Kuala Lumpur: Asian Centre for Development Administration. pp. 449-488. /Pakistan /Control process / HD 4276 P8 PCL

78. Ahmed, Jalaluddin. 1981 "Pre Course Assignment." Prepared for the Interregional Seminar on Training Management in Public Enterprises in Developing Countries, 19-28 Oct., Ljubljana, Yugoslavia. Ljubljana: ICPE. /Training /Management

79. Ahmed, Mohamed Said. 1965 "The Autonomy of Public Enterprises in Developing Nations: A Critique, with Special Reference to the United Arab Republic." Los Angeles, Calif.: University of Southern California. /Egypt /Control process

80. Ahmed, Viqar. 1980 "Education and Training in Public Enterprises in Developing Countries: Country Paper of Pakistan." Paper presented at the Expert Group Meeting on the Research Project on Education and Training in Public Enterprises in Developing Countries, 17-22 Mar., Ljubljana, Yugoslavia. Ljubljana: ICPE. /Pakistan /Training /Management

81. Ahmed, Z. U. 1980 "Investment Criteria and Investment Decision-Making Processes: Some Issues concerning Policy and Practice in Pakistan." Paper presented at the International Workshop on Investment Criteria and Investment Decision-Making Processes, 20-24 Oct., Ljubljana, Yugoslavia. Ljubljana: ICPE. /Investment /Pakistan /Decision making process

82. Ahmed, Z. U. 1981 "Financial Profitability and Losses in Public Enterprises." *Public Enterprise* V. 2, No. 1, pp. 8-21. /Profits /OPSS

83. Ahmed, Z. U. 1981 "Public Enterprises and Engineering Goods Sector in Developing Countries: Some Policy Considerations." Paper presented at the International Workshop on Financial Profitability and Losses in Public Enterprises, 1-5 June, Ljubljana, Yugoslavia. Ljubljana: ICPE. /Manufacturing industry /Profits

84. Ahmed, Z. U. 1981 "Management Perspectives and Problem Areas in the Foundry and Mechanical Workshop (Warshadda Birta Yxamar)." Paper presented at the National Workshop of Public Enterprises, 9-13 Aug., Mogadishu, Somalia. Ljubljana: ICPE. /Management /Industrial sector /Case studies

85. Ahmed, Z. U. 1982 "A Review of the Expert Group Meeting on Wage and Renumeration Policies in Public Enterprises." *Public Enterprise* V. 3, pp. 34-84. /Brazil /India /Wages /Personnel management /Productivity / Statistics / OPSS

86. Ahmed, Z. U., ed. 1982 *Pricing Policy and Investment Criteria in Public Enterprises.* Ljubljana: ICPE. /Price policy /Investment

87. Ahsan, A. K. M. 1967 Top Level Management and Personnel Problems of Public Enterprises. Lahore, Pakistan: NIPA Seminar on Problems of Public Enterprises. /Administrative management /Personnel management

88. Ahuja, S. K. 1976 "Public Relations and Public Enterprises." Lok Udyog (New Delhi), V. 10, No. 2, pp. 45-48. /Public relations /354.54 L836 PCL

89. Aingh, Ajit. 1972 "Holding Company and the Public Sector." Lok Udyog (New Delhi), V. 6, No. 4, pp. 5-14. /Holding company /354.54 L836 PCL

90. Aitken, Hugh G. J., ed. 1959 The State and Economic Growth. New York: Social Science Research Council. /Economic growth policy / HC 51 C58

91. Akabane, Takeo. 1976 "Some Problems Faced by Japanese Public Enterprises." Approaches to the Public Enterprise Policy in Asia on Investment, Prices and Returns Criteria. Kuala Lumpur: UN Asian Centre for Development Administration. pp. 153-161. /Japan / HD 4276 A8 1976 PCL

92. Akinsanya, Adeoye. 1978 "Reforming a Public Enterprise Through a Management Audit: Any Lessons From the Former Western Nigeria Development Corporation?" Indian Journal of Public Administration V. 24, No. 4, pp. 1016-1031. /Nigeria /Control process /Public financing /Administrative reform /Budget auditing /JA 26 I55 Pub Aff

93. Akinsanya, Adeoye. 1980 The Expropriation of Multinational Property in the Third World. New York: Praeger Publishers. /Nationalization / HD 2755.5 A49 LAC

94. Al-Fadel, Youssif. 1968 "Problems of the National Oil Companies." Paper presented at the Seminar on Petroleum Economics and Development, Kuwait. Kuwait: Kuwait Institute for Economic and Social Planning in the Middle East. /Oil industry

95. Al-Jammal, Z. 1967 Public Enterprises. Cairo: Yousef Press. /Egypt

96. Alain, Jean-Marc. 1978 "Les entreprises publiques: Une recherche bibliographique /Public Enterprises A Bibliography." In André Gélinas, ed(s). Public Enterprise and the Public Interest. Ontario: The Institute of Public Administration of Canada. pp. 215-266. /Bibliography

97. Alaoui Mdaghri, D. 1981 "The Limits of State Control over Public Enterprises in Morocco." Public Enterprise V. 2, No. 1, pp. 41-52. /Morocco /Administrative reform /Control process / OPSS

98. Alaraji, Asim. 1983 "Public Enterprises as Instruments of State Policies in Management Development." Paper presented at the 19th International Congress of Administrative Sciences, West Berlin, 19-23 Sept. /Middle East /Iraq /Goal setting /OPSS

99. Alario Méndez, Mario, and Carlos Espinosa Facío Lince. 1978 Las entidades descentralizadas en Colombia. Cartagena, Colombia: Gráficas El Faro. /Colombia

100. Albanese, G. 1958 "L´Impresa pubblica." Tempi Moderni pp. 458-460. /Italy

101. Albano, Osvaldo. 1975 "El presupuesto integrado de las empresas del Estado." Revista de la Asociación Interamericana de Presupuesto Público V. 2, No. 6, pp. 57-122. /Latin America /Budgetary process / OPSS

102. Albergaria Filho, Jason Soares. 1972 "A natureza jurídica das fundações públicas." Revista de Direito Administrativo (Rio de Janeiro), No. 109, pp. 34-40. /Brazil /Law

103. Albergo, Salvatore d´. 1969 Positive System of Public Corporations in Italian Organization. Milan, Italy: A. Giuffre. /Italy /Structural characteristics

104. Albergo, Salvatore d´. 1970 Le participazioni statali. Milan, Italy: Ed. Giuffre. /Italy /Planning process

105. Alberts, Tom, et al. 1978 "The Bargaining Gap in Technology: A Major Obstacle in the Implementation of Development Strategies for Satisfying Basic Human Needs." Paper presented at the International Workshop on Management of Transfer and Development of Technology in Public Enterprises in Developing Countries, 19-25 June, Ljubljana, Yugoslavia. Ljubljana: ICPE. /Technology transfer

106. Albi, F. 1960 Tratado de los modos de gestión de las corporaciones locales. Madrid. /Spain /Management /Local government

107. Albian, Daniel, and François Souflage. 1979 "Le rôle de l´entreprise publique dans la planification." Revue Française de Gestion No. 20, pp. 64-66. /France /Planning process

108. Albino de Oliveira, Fernando A. 1973 "Concessão dos serviços públicos de energia eléctrica: Sua evolução na dereito brasileiro." Revista de Direito Público (São Paulo), V. 6, No. 23, pp. 40-60. /Brazil /Electrical utility industry /Law /Economic history

109. Albu, A. 1955 "Renault Miracle." New Statesman V. 50, pp. 502-503. /France /Automobile manufacturing industry

110. Albu, A. 1963 "Ministerial and Parliamentary Control." In M. Shanks, ed(s). Lessons of Public Enterprise. London: Jonathan Cape. pp. 90-113. /United Kingdom /Management /Evaluation / Control process /Parliament

111. Alby, P. 1969 "Mission de l´entreprise publique." Association des Cadres Dirigeants de l´Industrie pour le Progrès Social et Economique; Bulletin No. 246, pp. 370-383. /Goal setting

112. Alegría, Rosa Luz. 1978 "Criterios para la evaluación de la acción de las empresas públicas." In Rosa Luz Alegría et al., Empresas públicas. Mexico City: Presidencia de la República. pp. 77-84. /Mexico /Evaluation /HD 4013 E479 1978 LAC

113. Alejo, Francisco Javier. 1979 "La verdad de las paraestatales." Económica (Mexico City), No. 5, pp. 10-16. /Mexico /Profits

114. Alessi, Lewis de. 1982 "On the Nature and Consequence of Private and Public Enterprises." Minnesota Law Review V. 67, pp. 197-203. /Private enterprises /Mixed enterprises

115. Alexander, K. C. 1972 "Participative Management in India: Two Case Studies." Lok Udyog (New Delhi), V. 5, No. 12, pp. 1215-1224. /India /Worker management participation /Case studies /354.54 L836 PCL

116. Alexander, R. H. 1978 "The Financing of Public Utilities in Jamaica." Paper presented at the Interregional Workshop on Financing of Public Enterprises in Developing Countries, 22-26 May, Ljubljana, Yugoslavia. Ljubljana: ICPE. /Jamaica /Public financing /Public utility industry

117. Alfaro, Juan. 1959 "La organización administrativa de la programación económica." Documentación Administrativa (Madrid), No. 16, pp. 5-14. /Spain /Planning process /Administrative management /Organization formation

118. Alfaro, Juan. 1962 "La organización administrativa española y el desarrollo económico." Documentación Administrativa (Madrid), No. 58, pp. 37-46. /Spain /Economic development /Administrative management /Organization formation

119. Alfred, Helen L., ed. 1961 Public Ownership in the U.S.A.--Goals and Priorities. New York: Peace Publications. /United States of America /Planning process / 338.973 Ae29p PCL

120. Algeria. Bureau des Statistiques Industrielles. 1972 "Les sociétés nationales à caractère industriel." Algiers. /Algeria /Statistics /Industrial sector

121. Alhadeff, David A. 1968 Competition and Controls in Banking: A Study of the Regulation of Bank Competition in Italy, France and England. Berkeley: University of California Press. /Italy /France /United Kingdom /Financial institutions / 331.2 Al39c PCL

122. Ali, Abduljawad N. 1974 "Public Sector and Planning in Public Enterprises in Iraq: National Paper of Iraq." Paper presented at the International Seminar ´74: Planning on Public Enterprises in Developing Countries, 23 Sept.-9 Oct., Ljubljana, Yugoslavia. Ljubljana: ICPE. /Iraq /Planning process

123. Ali, Kebede. 1980 "The Adams Special Printing Plant: A Case from Ethiopia." Paper presented at the Regional Workshop on

Development of Training in Methologies for Internal Consultants in African Public Enterprises, 1-6 Dec., Addis Ababa, Ethiopia. Ljubljana: ICPE. /Ethiopia /Training /Methodology /Consultant services / Case studies

124. Ali-Toudert, A. 1980 "Les structures financières de l'Algérie." Intégrations: Revue du CMERA No. 12, pp. 66-88. /Algeria /Public financing /Credit policy /Public administration / Banking system / OPSS

125. Allen, G. C. 1968 "The Public and Co-operative Sectors in Japan." Annals of Public and Cooperative Economy V. 39, pp. 133-156. /Japan /Cooperatives / 330.5 An73 PCL

126. Allen, Kevin. 1972 "Regional Intervention." In Stuart Holland, ed(s). The State as Entrepreneur. London: Wiedenfeld and Nicolson. pp. 165-183. /Italy /Regional development /Holding company /HD 487 H6 1973 Pub Aff /HD 3616 I83 H65 PCL

127. Alleyne, D. H. N. 1980 "The State Petroleum Enterprise and the Transfer of Technology." State Petroleum Enterprises in Developing Countries. New York: Pergamon Press. pp. 109-122. /Oil industry /Technology transfer

128. Alleyne, D. H. N. 1980 "Financial Provisions of State Petroleum Enterprises in Developing Countries." State Petroleum Enterprises in Developing Countries. New York: Pergamon Press. pp. 151-173. /Oil industry /Financing

129. Alleyne, D. H. N. 1980 "Energy Utilization for Economic Development in Developing Countries and the Role of the State Petroleum Enterprises." State Petroleum Enterprises in Developing Countries. New York: Pergamon Press. pp. 174-192. /Oil industry /Developing nations

130. Almenara, María Rosario. 1981 "Tax links between Public Enterprises and the Central Government: Case of Peru." Austin, Tx.: unpublished master's thesis. /Peru /Taxation policy

131. Almiro, A. 1966 "As empresas estatais e a unidade de comando financeiro." Revista de Finanças Públicas (Rio de Janeiro), No. 246, pp. 6-10. /Brazil /Financing

132. Alonso-Villalobos, E. Gorostiaga. 1973 "Notas sobre el régimen legal de telecomunicaciones en la República de Perú." Revista de Administración Pública (Madrid), No. 72, pp. 431-440. /Peru /Communication industry

133. Alphandery, C., Y. Bernard, and F. Boloch-Laine. 1968 Pour nationaliser l'Etat. Paris: Editions du Seuil. /France /Nationalization

134. Alvarez Gendín, A. 1967 "La empresa pública como un instrumento de industrialización administrativa." Documentación Administrativa (Madrid), No. 107, pp. 95-112. /Industrialization /Economic development /Planning process

135. Alvarez Gendín, A. 1969 "A industrialização estatal." Estudios Administrativos /Brazil /Industrialization

136. Alvarez Gendín, A., and Arvids Kalnins K. 1974 "La prestación de los servicios públicos en Colombia." Revista Latinoamericana de Administración Pública (Bogotá), No. 2, pp. 36-41. /Colombia /Public services /Financing

137. Alvarez Gendín, Sabino. 1970 Servicios públicos. La empresa municipal como procedimiento de gestión del servicio local. Medellín, Colombia: Congreso Interamericano de Municipios. No. 13. /Colombia /Public services

138. Alvarez Rico, M. 1975 "Las tarifas de abastecimiento de agua." Revista de Estudios de la Vida Local No. 185, pp. 81-93. /Price policy /Public utility industry

139. Alvarez del Castillo, Enrique. 1979 "Regulación de la empresa pública--aplicación del régimen constitucional y legal del trabajo a las personas jurídicas del derecho público." Paper presented at the International Seminar on Regulation of the Public Enterprise, Mexico City. /Mexico /Control process /Law / OPSS

140. Alves, Sérgio Francisco, and Ecila Mutzenbecher Ford. 1975 "O comportamento tecnológico das empresas statais: A seleção das empresas de engineering, a escolha de processos industriales, e a compra de bens de capital." Finep, Grupo de Pesquisas (preliminary version) /Brazil /Technology /OPSS

141. Alvi, Shahiruddin. 1981 "A Survey of Management Training Needs of Public Enterprises in Pakistan." Paper presented at the Regional Workshop on Management Training and Development in Public Enterprises of Developing Countries, 5-15 Jan., Karachi, Pakistan. Ljubljana: ICPE. /Pakistan /Management /Training /Evaluation

142. Amado, Antônio Augusto Oliveira. 1980 "O planejamento nas empresas públicas: Programação, acompanhamento, controle e avaliação aos planos e programas de governo." A empresa pública no Brasil: Uma abordagem multidisciplinar. Brasília: IPEA. pp. 385-449. /Planning process /Brazil

143. Amerasinghe, A. R. B. 1976 "Public Corporations in Sri Lanka." Law and Public Enterprise in Asia. New York: Praeger for the International Legal Center. pp. 313-373. /Sri Lanka /Law /Private enterprises /Comparative analysis /HD 4283 L32

144. American Society of Planning Officials. 1952 Authorities for the Financing and Administration of Public Improvements. Chicago: American Society of Planning Officials. /United States of America /Public authority /Public financing /Public works policy

145. Ammar, Zeineb ben. 1982 "Responsabilités des entreprises publiques dans le développement de l´emploi feminin et dans l´amélioration de la condition de la femme: Le cas de la Tunisie." Ljubljana: ICPE. /Tunisia /Women´s studies

/Employment policy

146. Amonoo, E. 1975 "Internal Marketing Systems for Basic Foodstuffs and Government Involvements in the Central Region of Ghana (1970-1973)." I.S.S. Occasional Papers, No.50. The Hague, Netherlands: Institute of Social Studies. /Ghana /Food industry /Price policy /Marketing /Retail trade /Statistics /Marketing boards /Africa /OPSS

147. Amoroso, G. 1962 "Aspetti giuridici delle impresa pubblica." *Impresa Pubblica* (Rome), V. 6, No. 2, pp. 77-83. /Law

148. Anakioski, Dusan. 1977 "Planning in Public Enterprises in Developing Countries: Objectives and Contents of Planning in Public Enterprises." Ljubljana: ICPE. /Developing nations /Planning process

149. Anandarao, C. R. 1980 "Financial Management vis-à-vis Committee on Public Undertakings." *Institute of Public Enterprises Journal* V. 3, pp. 19-47. /India /Financial performance / Financial management /Control process

150. Anantaram, K. 1964 "State Trading: Catalyst of Economic Development." *Asian Economic Review* (Hyderabad), pp. 168-182. /Economic development /State trading organizations

151. Anastassopoulos, Jean-Pierre. 1973 "The Strategic Autonomy of Government-Controlled Enterprises in a Competitive Economy." Unpublished Ph.D. dissertation, Columbia University. /France /Electrical utility industry /Automobile manufacturing industry / Communication industry

152. Anastassopoulos, Jean-Pierre. 1979 "Les voies de l´autonomie." *Revue Française de Gestion* No. 20, pp. 52-57. /Autonomy /France

153. Anastassopoulos, Jean-Pierre. 1979 "Les bonnes à tout faire de la politique conjoncturelle." *Revue Française de Gestion* No. 20, pp. 67-71. /France /Price policy /Wages

154. Anastassopoulos, Jean-Pierre. 1981 "The French Experience: Conflicts with Government." In Raymond Vernon and Yair Aharoni, ed(s). *State-Owned Enterprises in the Western Economies.* New York: St. Martin´s Press. pp. 99-116. /France /Control process / HD 3850 S79 PCL

155. Andean Development Corporation. 1975 *Operational Criteria and Regulations of the Andean Development Corporation.* Caracas, Venezuela. /Andean Pact Countries /Development banks /Law / OPSS

156. Anderson, Paul S. 1959 "State Development Credit Corporations." *Development Corporations and Authorities.* Washington, D. C.: Government Printing Office. pp. 82-96. /United States of America /Development banks /Credit policy

157. Andrade, G. 1971 *Empresa Portuaria de Chile. Análisis de su organización y funcionamiento.* Santiago, Chile: Oficina de Planificación. /Chile /Postal service /Organization behavior

158. Andrade, Sudá de. 1959 Teoria da empresa pública. Rio de Janeiro: Konfino. /Economic theory / G380.1622 An24t

159. Andreieu, P. E. 1965 La contribución de la actividad empresarial del Estado al desarrollo económico. Rome: I.S.V.E. /Economic development

160. Andres Alvarez, V. 1950 "Introducción al estudio de la empresa pública." Revista de Administración Pública (Madrid), No. 3, pp. 41-52. /Spain

161. Andrews, Charles H., Jr. 1967 "An Evaluation of the Economic Performance on the Compañía Pacífico, S. A." Unpublished Ph.D. dissertation Vanderbilt University. /Chile /Steel industry /Economic efficiency /Economic analysis / FILM 4146 LAC Abridged version published in Studies in Latin American Business No. 9, Bureau of Business Research, Austin: UT, 1970.

162. Andric, S., and M. Sever-Zebec. 1969 Bibliography on Workers´ Participation in Management in Yugoslavia. Zagrab, Yugoslavia: Ekonomiski Institut. /Yugoslavia /Worker management participation /Bibliography

163. Andrieu, Pedro Enrique. 1975 Empresas públicas: El rol del Estado en el crecimiento económico y el cambio social. Buenos Aires: Editorial El Coloquio. /Argentina /Italy /France /United Kingdom /Latin America / HD 3850 A53 LAC

164. Angel, A. D. 1947 "British Use of Public Corporations." Social Research V. 14, pp. 321-331. /United Kingdom 305 Sc123 PCL

165. Angel, A. D. 1950 "The Great Lakes-St. Lawrence Project." Land Economics V. 26, pp. 222-231. /United States of America /Public works policy / 305 J824 PCL

166. Annable, James E. Jr. 1974 "A Theory of Wage Determination in Public Enterprises." Quarterly Review of Economics and Business V. 14, No. 4, pp. 43-58. /Wages / 330.5 Q23 PCL

167. Ansari, Javed A. 1981 "Comparative Study of Impact of Public and Private Manufacturing Sectors in Selected Developing Countries." Paper presented at the Expert Group Meeting on the Changing Role and Function of the Public Industrial Sector in Development, Vienna, Austria, 5-9 Oct. (Vienna: UNIDO). ID/WG.343/10. /India /Pakistan /Private sector /Comparative analysis /OPSS

168. Anselme-Rabinovitch, L. 1966 "Les nationalizations d´Algérie devant les tribunaux français." Banque (Paris), V. 41, No. 239, pp. 331-336. /Algeria /Nationalization /Law

169. Ansorena, Claudio, Salvador Amato, and Juan Carlos del Bello. 1981 "Contrato llave en mano: El caso de una destilería en Costa Rica." Paper presented at the Reunión regional de expertos "Estrategias e instrumentos para reforzar la negociación (SBP) de las empresas públicas en los países en desarrollo en las transacciones tecnológicas,"

23-27 Nov., San José Costa Rica. Ljubljana: ICPE. /Costa Rica /Technology transfer /Alcohol industry / Contractual relations

170. Antonov, N. 1953 Nationalization of Private and Industrial and Mining Property. Washington, D. C.: Mid-European Studies Center. /Europe /Private sector /Industrial sector /Mining industry /Nationalization

171. Antonov, N. 1963 "Aperçu sur le secteur public et semipublic mixte en France." Annales d'Economie Collective pp. 623-642. /France /Mixed enterprises

172. Anumudu, Theodore A. 1974 "Planning in Public Enterprises, the Nigerian Experience: National Paper of Nigeria." Paper presented at the International Seminar '74: Planning in Public Enterprises in Developing Countries, 23 Sept.-9 Oct., Ljubljana, Yugoslavia. Ljubljana: ICPE. /Nigeria /Planning process

173. Anyemedu, Kwasi. 1979 "National Planning and Public Enterprises in Ghana." Paper presented at the Regional Workshop on Planning in Public Enterprises of the African Region, 10-15 Dec., Accra, Ghana. Ljubljana: ICPE. /Ghana /Planning process

174. Aopi, Gerea. 1980 "Statutory Authorities in Papua New Guinea." Paper presented at the Reginal Workshop on Corporate Planning in Public Enterprises in the Asian and Pacific Region, Kuala Lumpur, 17-21 Nov. Ljubljana: ICPE. /Papua New Guinea /Law /Control process /Planning process

175. Apati-Bassah Dogbedi, K. A. 1982 Les entreprises d'Etat au Togo. Paris: Institut International d'Administration Publique. /Togo

176. Apicella, Vincenzo. 1964 "The Development of the Public Sector." Annals of Public and Cooperative Economy V. 35, pp. 5-42. /Italy

177. Appleby, Paul. 1956 Re-Examination of India's Administrative System. New Delhi, India: Government of India, Cabinet Secretariat. /India /Public administration

178. Appy, Robert. 1976 "Enfim um exemplo vigoroso a favor da privatização." Industria e Desenvolvimento V. 9, No. 5, pp. 20-21. /Brazil /Privatization / G333.0981 In2 LAC

179. Appy, Robert. 1976 "Resoluções do BNDE, novas amerças do estatização." Industria e Desenvolvimento V. 9, No. 8, pp. 20-21. /Brazil /Development banks /Holding company /G333.0981 In2 LAC

180. Aquina, Herman J. 1983 "A Bridge Too Many: The Prins Willem Alexander Toll-Bridge as an Instrument of a State Policy." Paper presented at the 19th International Congress of Administrative Sciences, West Berlin, 19-23 Sept. /Goal setting /Transportation industry /Case studies /OPSS

181. Arakelian, A. 1950 Industrial Management in the U.S.S.R. Washington, D. C.: Foreign Affairs Press. /Union of Soviet Socialist Reps.

182. Arana Sagnier, A. 1969 Algunas perspectivas sobre la evolución del sistema financiero yugoslavo. Barcelona: Centro de Estudios de Planificación. /Yugoslavia /Economic history /Public financing

183. Arapé Morales, Alberto, and Bernardo Kliksberg. 1981 Diagnóstico de la situación del adiestramiento en la administración pública venezolana. Caracas: Presidencia de la República, Oficina Central de Personal. /Venezuela /Personnel management /Public administration /Training /Management /OPSS

184. Araujo, J. T. 1974 "Escolha de técnicas e rentabilidade das empresas governamentais." Pesquisa e Planejamento Econômico (Rio de Janeiro), V. 4, No. 2, pp. 447-462. /Brazil /Profits /Technology / HC 186 P47 LAC

185. Araujo, J. T., and Vera Maria Dick. 1974 "Governo, empresas multinacionais e empresas nacionais: O cara de indústria petroquímica." Pesquisa e Planejamento Econômico (Rio de Janeiro), V. 4, No. 3, pp. 629-654. /Brazil /Oil industry /Multinational corporations /HC 186 P47 LAC

186. Arcenegui, Isidro E., and Luis M. Cosculluela. 1969 "La Empresa Nacional Iberia y la nacionalización del transporte aéreo." Revista de Administración Pública (Madrid), No. 1, pp. 349-385. /Spain /Air transportation industry /Nationalization

187. Archibugi, F. and S. Lombardini. 1963 Piano economico e impresa publica. Centro di Studi e Piani Economici, Turín. Studi Di Politica Economica. No. 1. Turin, Italy: Pablo Boringhieri. /Italy /Planning process

188. Ardant, Gabriel. 1952 "La mesure du rendement des entreprises et des services publics." Revue Economique (Paris), No. 4, pp. 449-491. /France /Evaluation /Financial performance /Public services / Profits / 330.5 R3282 PCL

189. Ardant, Gabriel. 1952 "Signification théoretique et portée pratique d'une méthode nouvelle; la mesure du rendement des entreprises et des services publics." Revue Economique (Paris), No. 4, pp. 449-491. /France /Public services /Financial performance /Evaluation /Profits /Economic theory /330.5 R3282 PCL

190. Ardant, Gabriel. 1953 "La medida de la productividad en las empresas nacionales y los servicios públicos." Revista de Trabajo No. 6, pp. 711-722. /France /Evaluation /Financial performance /Public services / 330.5 An73

191. Ardant, Gabriel. 1957 "The Measurement of Productivity in State Undertakings and Public Services." Annals of Collective Economy V. 24, pp. 79-96. /France /Evaluation /Financial performance /Public services /Profits /330.5 An73

192. Ardhanari, T R. 1979 "Project Implementation and Contracting for Fertilizer Factories in India." Lok Udyog (New Delhi), V. 13, No. 5, pp. 5-8. /India /Project management /Fertilizer industry /Contractual relations /354.54 L836 PCL

193. Ardouin, P. 1949 "Les chemins de fer marocains." Société Belge d'Etudes et d'Expansion (Liège, Belgium), No. 136. /Morocco /Railway industry

194. Arévalo, Alberto. 1971 "Sociedades anônimas mixtas con predominio estatal." Ciencias Administrativas (La Plata), V. 35, pp. 65-72. /Brazil /Mixed enterprises

195. Arellano, Vladimiro. 1975 "La evaluación de las acciones del sector público." Revista de la Asociación de Presupuesto Público V. 2, No. 7, pp. 15-90. /Evaluation / OPSS

196. Argentina. 1976 Las empresas públicas en la economía argentina, relevamiento de los principales indicadores de las empresas públicas y su importancia en la economía argentina. /Argentina /Statistics /Economic system / OPSS

197. Argentina. Banco Central. 1972 La creación del Banco Central y la experiencia monetaria argentina. Buenos Aires. /Argentina /Central banks /Monetary policy /Economic history

198. Argentina. Dirección Nacional de Programación e Investigación. 1972 Inversión del sector público argentino por regiones: Años 1968-1971. Buenos Aires: Dirección de Programación e Investigación. /Argentina / Q HJ 905 A74 197

199. Arief, S. 1967 The Political Process and the Management Process of State-Owned Enterprise: The Indonesian Case. Kuala Lumpur: Kajian Ekonomi Malaysia. /Indonesia /Political influence /Management

200. Arino Ortiz, Gaspar. 1972 Administración institucional: Mito y realidad de las personas jurídicas en el Estado. Madrid: Ed. Instituto de Estudios Administrativos. /Spain /Public administration /Law

201. Arino Ortiz, Gaspar. 1973 "Sobre el concepto y significado institucional de la expresión `establecimiento público´." Documentación Administrativa (Madrid), No. 155, pp. 7-27. /Taxonomy /Law

202. Arino Ortiz, Gaspar. 1980 "El control del gobierno sobre las empresas públicas en España: Autonomía versus dependencia." Revue Internationale des Sciences Administratives V. 46, No. 1, pp. 69-88. /Spain /Control process /Public administration /Decentralized authority / Accountability

203. Armand, Louis. 1957 "The French National Railways: A National Service." Annals of Collective Economy V. 28, pp. 301-310. /France /Railway industry / 330.5 An73 PCL

204. Armengaud, André. 1951 Vingt ans de capitalisme d'Etat. (Paris). /France

205. Armitage, S. 1969 _The Politics and Decontrol of Industry: Britain and United States._ London: Weidenfeld and Nicolson. /United Kingdom /United States of America /Political influence /Privatization /Decentralization /Industrial sector /322.3 Ar55p

206. Armstrong, Aubrey B. 1976 "The Development of Public Enterprises in Guyana: An Overview." _Bulletin of ICPE_ V. 2, No. 3, pp. 12-16. /Guyana

207. Armstrong, Aubrey B. 1978 "Personnel and Manpower Planning in Public Enterprises in Developing Countries: Outline of Lecture." Paper presented at the International workshop on Planning in Public Enterprises in Developing Countries, 20-25 Nov., Ljubljana, Yugoslavia. Ljubljana: ICPE. /Planning process /Employment policy /Personnel management / Manpower planning

208. Armstrong, Aubrey B. 1979 "Management Development and Training in Public Enterprises in Developing Countries: A Look at Policy and Strategy." Paper presented at the International Seminar on Management and Training in Public Enterprises in Developing Countries, Ljubljana, Yugoslavia, 1-13 Oct. Ljubljana: ICPE. /Training /Management /Developing nations

209. Armstrong, Aubrey B. 1979 "Report of the International Seminar on Management and Training in Public Enterprises in Developing Countries, Ljubljana, October 1-13, 1979." Ljubljana: ICPE. /Training /Management /Developing nations

210. Armstrong, Aubrey B., and Stane Mozina, eds. 1980 _Managing Training and Training Managers in Public Enterprises in Developing Countries._ Ljubljana: ICPE. /Developing nations /Management /Training /India /Egypt /Bangladesh / Malaysia /Philippines / OPSS

211. Armstrong, Aubrey B. 1980 "Les stratégies du dévelpppement de la gestion et de la formation dans les entreprises publiques dans les pays en voie de développement." Paper presented at the Séminaire international sur la gestion et la formation dans les entreprises publiques dans les pays en voie de développement, Ljubljana, Yugoslavia, 3-15 March. Ljubljana: ICPE. /Developing nations /Planning process /Training /Management

212. Arnfred, Niels. 1983 "Autonomy and Control in the Process of Transformation of Public Enterprise - the Case of the Danish State Railways." Paper presented at the 19th International Congress of Administrtive Sciences, West Berlin, 19-23 Sept. /Autonomy /Control process /Denmark /Railway industry /Case studies /OPSS

213. Arora, R. S. 1961 "Rise of the Public Corporation in India: Some Constitutional Aspects." _Public Law_ (London), pp. 362-385. /India /Economic history /Economic growth policy /Constitutional law / Law / 350.5 P962

214. Arora, R. S. 1966 "State Liability and the Public Corporation in India." Public Law (London), pp. 239-247. /India /Law / 350.5 P962

215. Arora, R. S. 1968 "Public Relations of British Nationalized Industries: Safeguards for Consumer Interests." Lok Udyog (New Delhi), pp. 875-883. /United Kingdom /Industrial sector /Public interest / Public relations /Consumer relations /354.54 L836

216. Arora, R. S. 1969 "Administration of Government Industries: Three Essays on the Public Corporation." New Delhi: Indian Institute of Public Administration. /India /Management

217. Arora, R. S. 1969 "Nationalization of Banks and Fundamental Rights in India." (Part 1) Lok Udyog (New Delhi), V. 3, No. 9, pp. 1037-1043. /India /Banking agency /Nationalization /354.54 L836

218. Arora, R. S. 1970 "Nationalisation of the Banks and the Fundamental Rights in India." (Part 2) Lok Udyog (New Delhi), V. 3, No. 10, pp. 1173-1178. /India /Banking agency /Nationalization /354.54 L836 PCL

219. Arora, R. S. 1973 "Audit and Accountability of Public Enterprises in India and Britain." Lok Udyog (New Delhi), V. 7, No. 7, pp. 29-42. /India /United Kingdom /Accountability /Control process /354.54 L836 PCL

220. Arrate, J., H. Assael et al. n.d. "Las fronteras del area de propiedad social." Panorama Económico (Santiago, Chile), No. 263, pp. 16-26. /Chile /Worker self management /G330.983 P194 LAC

221. Arrieche, Victor José, and Gustavo Chuecos Pérez. 1975 "La empresa pública en Venezuela." Rio de Janeiro: FGV-EIAP. /Venezuela /Control process /Public financing /Public administration /Law / Planning process / OPSS

222. Arrow, Kenneth J. 1981 "On Finance and Decision Making." In Raymond Vernon and Yair Aharoni, ed(s). State-Owned Enterprise in the Western Economies. New York: St. Martin's Press. pp. 63-69. /Management /Financing /HD 3850 S79 PCL

223. Arroyo Gómez, M. A. 1980 "La empresa pública en España: Consideraciones generales sobre su experiencia histórica y su papel en el futuro." Revista Latinoamericana de Administración Pública No. 10-1, pp. 437-451. /Spain /Economic history / JL 1974 R485 LAC

224. Artamonoff, G. L. 1965 State Owned Enterprises of Thailand. Bangkok: USAID. /Thailand /Evaluation

225. Asare, Jacob Kwame. 1978 "Transfer and Development of Technology: Ghanaian Experience." Paper presented at the International Workshop on Management of Transfer and Development of Technology in Public Enterprises in Developing Countries, Ljubljana, Yugoslavia, 19-25 June. Ljubljana: ICPE. /Ghana /Technology transfer

226. Ashley, Charles A., and R. G. H. Smails. 1965 Canadian Crown Corporations: Some Aspects of Their Administration and Control. Toronto: MacMillan Company of Canada Ltd. /Canada /Control Process / Management

227. Ashwell, J. 1965 Four Steps for Progress. The Operation of a Municipal Transport System with Workers Control. Hull: Humberside Voice. /Transportation industry /Worker self management / Public services

228. Asian Centre for Development Administration. Asian Think Tank Meeting. 1976 Approaches to the Public Enterprise Policy in Asia on Investment, Prices, and Returns Criteria. Kuala Lumpur: U.N. Asian Centre for Development Administration. /Asia /Investment /Price policy /HD 4276 A8 1976 PCL

229. Asian Development Bank. 1969 Development Banks of Asia, 4th Regional Conference: Summary of Proceedings. Manila: Asian Development Bank. /Asia /Development banks

230. Assael, H. 1966 "Planning the Public Sector." Economía pp. 23-46. /Chile /Planning process

231. Assmann, G., and W. Furbase. 1968 "L'Evolution de la gestion économique dans les entreprises nationalisées." Deutsche Finanzwirtschaft No. 14. /Management

232. Asthana, B. N. 1981 "Creativity and Innovation in Management." Lok Udyog (New Delhi), V. 15, No. 6, pp. 35-38. /India /Management /354.54 L836 PCL

233. "Atividade empresarial dos governos federal e estaduais." 1973 Conjuntura Económica (Rio de Janeiro), V. 27, No. 6, pp. 66-96. /Brazil /G330.981 F962c

234. Atti del V Congresso del Centre Européen de l'Entreprise Publique. 1966 Il finanziamento delle impresa pubbliche e el problema delle tariffe. Rome: Tavola Rotonda. /Italy /Financing /Price policy

235. Atti del V Congresso del Centre Européen de l'Entreprise Publique. 1971 L'évolution des entreprises publiques dans la Comunauté Européenne au cours des dernières années. Brussels: Ed. CEEP. /Europe

236. Aubert, J. B. 1937 Les sociétés d'économie mixte. /France /Mixed enterprises

237. Auby, Jean-Marie. 1969 Grands services publics et entreprises nationales. Paris: Presses Universitaires de France. /France /Public services

238. Audat, P. L. 1968 "Décentralisation et développement - L'exemple de l'Afrique de l'Ouest." Cahiers Africains d'Administration Publique (Tangier, Morocco), pp. 1-57. /Africa /Decentralization /Economic development

239. Augarde, M. 1966 "Worker Participation and Similar Schemes." *Annals of Public and Cooperative Economy* V. 37, No. 4, pp. 369-387. /Worker management participation

240. Aujac, H., J. Normand, and F. Tiquet. 1960 *La coopération entre les entreprises - Expériences et problèmes.* Liège, Belgium: Institut de Sociologie, Sciences Sociales, et Administration des Affaires. No. 11. /Belgium /Entrepreneurial activity

241. Austria. Congrès International des Cours des Comptes. 1962 *Contrôle des entreprises de droit privé nationalisées.* Vienna. /International law /Control process

242. Austria. Federal Ministry of Transport and Nationalized Undertakings. 1952 "The Nationalization of Austria's Basic Industries." *Annals of Collective Economy* V. 23, No. 1, pp. 1-39. /Austria /Nationalization / 330.5 An73 PCL

243. Austria. Institute of Economic Research. 1964 *Development Banks and Corporations in Africa.* Munich: Institute of Economic Research. /Africa /Development banks /Development corporation

244. Avendano, Jorge, et al. 1980 *Workers' Self-Management and Participation in Decision-Making in as a Factor of Social Change and Economic Progress in Developing Countries: National Reports.* Ljubljana: ICPE. V. 1. /Bangladesh /Malta /Peru /Yugoslavia /Worker management participation

245. Avendano, Jorge, et al. 1981 *Workers' Self-Management and Participation in Decision-Making as a Factor of Social Change and Economic Progress in Developing Countries: National Reports.* Ljubljana: ICPE. V. 2. /Algeria /Guyana /India /Tanzania /Worker self management / Worker management participation

246. Avery, R. S. 1954 "The TVA and Labor Relations: A Review." *Journal of Politics* V. 16, No. 3, pp. 413-440. /United States of America /River valley development projects / Labor relations / 320.5 J825

247. Avery, R. S. 1954 *Experiment in Management: Personnel Decentralization in the Tennessee Valley Authority.* Knoxville, Tenn.: University of Tennessee Press. /United States of America /Personnel management /Decentralization /River valley development projects / 309.973 T256Ya

248. Avilés, Mauro. 1974 *República del Ecuador. Seminario Latinoamericano: Las empresas públicas y sus relaciones con el gobierno central.* CLAD/SEM 1/D 13/74. Caracas: CLAD. /Ecuador /Control process

249. Avione, M. L. 1964 "Applicazione dell'analise dei costi e dei benefici alle imprese pubbliche." *Impresa Púbblica* (Rome), V. 8, No. 12. pp. 486-492. /Italy /Cost benefit analysis

250. Ayatallah, B. 1980 L'Office National de l'Electricité. Rabat, Morocco: Ecole Nationale d'Administration Publique. /Morocco /Electrical utility industry /Control process /Structural characteristics /OPSS

251. Ayo, Edward Olajide. 1980 "Policies and Practices in Nigeria on Investment Decisions Affecting Public Enterprises." Paper presented at the International Workshop on Investment Criteria and Investment Decision-Making Processes, Lubljana, Yugoslavia, 20-24 Oct. Ljubljana: ICPE. /Nigeria /Investment /Decision making process

252. Ayoubi, Sadiq al-, and Ahmed A. F. Mourad. 1983 "Public Projects and Development in the Syrian Arab Republic." Public Enterprise V. 3, pp. 49-66. /Syria /Economic history /Control process /Law /Evaluation /Financing / Public administration /Management / OPSS

253. Ayub, M. 1957 "Pakistan Industrial Development Corporation." Pakistan Quarterly (Karachi), V. 7, No. 2. /Pakistan /Industrialization /Development corporation

254. Ayub, Tan Sri Datuk Abdullah bin. 1976 "Public Enterprises in Malaysia." Approaches to the Public Enterprise Policy in Asia on Investment, Prices, and Returns Criteria. Kuala Lumpur: U.N. Asian Centre for Development Administration. pp. 86-106. /Malaysia /Investment /Price policy /Profits /HD 4276 A8 1976 PCL

255. Ayyar, J. M. 1976 "Public Sector Profits in True Perspective." Lok Udyog (New Delhi), V. 10, No. 6, pp. 45-48. /India /Profits /354.54 L836 PCL

256. Ayyar, J. M. 1979 "Evaluation of Financial and Physical Performance of the Public Sector Enterprises." Lok Udyog (New Delhi), V. 13, No. 9, pp. 23-24. /India /Evaluation /Financial performance /Economic efficiency /354.54 L836 PCL

257. Ayyar, J. M. 1980 "Role and Objectives of Public Enterprises in Developing Economy." Lok Udyog (New Delhi), V. 14, No. 1, pp. 13-16. /Economic development /Goal setting /354.54 L836

258. Azrael, J. R. 1966 Managerial Power and Soviet Politics. Cambridge, Mass.: Harvard University Press. /Union of Soviet Socialist Reps. /Management / 658.0947 Az73m UGL

259. Baade, H. W. 1960 "Indonesian Nationalization Measures before Foreign Courts--A Reply." American Journal of International Law V. 54, pp. 801-835. /Indonesia /Nationalization /International law /Law / 341.05 Am35

260. Babeau, A. 1968 Los consejos obreros en Polonia. Colección Trabajo y Sociedad. Barcelona: Ed. Nova Terra. No. 4. /Poland /Worker management participation

261. Bachelet, Vittorio. 1970 "Estructuras y garantías de la actividad empresarial del Estado." La Empresa Pública. Zaragoza, Spain: Publicaciones del Real Colegio de España en Bolonia. pp. 135-154. /Spain /Control process

262. Bachri, A. 1962 Le rôle de l'administration industrielle dans les établissements du secteur publique. Cairo: NIMD. /Egypt

263. Bacigalupo, V., M. Pumarino, and J. Dekovic. 1969 Proyecto de automatización del Banco del Estado de Chile. Santiago, Chile: Ediciones del Banco del Estado. /Chile /Central banks

264. Backman, J., and E. Kurnow. 1954 "Pricing of Government Services." National Tax Journal V. 7, pp. 121-140. /Price policy

265. Backskai, T. 1970 "New Developments in the Taxes on Enterprises in Some Socialist Countries: The Hungarian Experience." Public Finance (The Hague), V. 25, No. 2, pp. 212-232. /Hungary /Taxation policy / 336.05 Op2

266. Backskai, T. 1971 "New Developments in State Enterprise Taxation in Hungary." Acta Oeconomica V. 6, No. 1-2, pp. 107-122. /Hungary /Taxation policy / 330.5 Ac81

267. Badaqui, A. 1964 Contrôle des institutions publiques. Paris: Librairie Anglo-Egyptien. /France /Control process

268. Badawi, Abd-Assalam. 1969 Control of Public Enterprise. Cairo: Anglo-Egyptian Bookshop. /Egypt /Control process

269. Badouin, R. 1965 Les banques africaines du développement. Paris: Editions A. Pedone. /Africa /Development banks

270. Baena del Alcazar, Mariano. 1964 "La supresión de intervenciones como medida preliminar al desarrollo económico." Documentación Administrativa (Madrid), No. 74, pp. 47-58. /Spain /Economic development /Decentralization

271. Baena del Alcazar, Mariano. 1965 "El papel del derecho administrativo en la economía." Documentación Administrativa (Madrid), No. 94, pp. 43-54. /Public administration /Law

272. Baena del Alcazar, Mariano. 1966 Régimen jurídico de la intervención administrativa de la economía. Madrid: Editorial Tecnos. /Spain /Law /Planning process

273. Baer, W. 1969 The Development of the Brazilian Steel Industry. Nashville, Tenn.: Vanderbilt University Press. /Brazil /Steel industry /G338.47672 B145d LAC

274. Baer, W. 1971 "O papel das empresas governamentais na industrialização da América Revista Econômica (Fortaleza, Brazil), V. 2, No. 8, pp. 40-59. /Latin America /Industrialization

275. Baer, W. 1973 "A recente experiência brasileira do desenvolvimento: Uma interpretação." Pesquisa e Planejamento Econômico (Rio de Janeiro), V. 3, No. 2, pp. 265-302. /Brazil /Economic development

276. Baer, W. 1974 "The Role of Government Enterprises in Latin America's Industrialization." In David T. Geithman, ed(s).

Fiscal Policy for Industrialization and Development in Latin America. Gainesville, Fla.: University Presses of Florida. pp. 263-281. /Industrial sector /HJ 799.52 L38 1971 LAC

277. Baer, W. 1979 The Brazilian Economy: Its Growth and Development. Columbus, Ohio: Grid Inc. /Brazil /Economic development /Second edition published in New York by Praeger. /HC 187 B147 1983 LAC.

278. Baer, W., I. Kerstenetzky, and A. Villela. 1973 "The Changing Role of the State in the Brazilian Economy." World Development V. 1, No. 11, pp. 23-35. /Brazil /Economic development / Economic history

279. Baer, W., and A. Figueroa. 1981 "State Enterprises and the Distribution of Income: Brazil and Peru." In Thomas Bruneau and Phillipe Faucher, ed(s). Authoritarian Capitalism: Brazil´s Contemporary Economic and Political Development. Boulder, Co.: Westview Press. pp. 59-84. /Brazil /Peru /Income distribution /Paper earlier presented at the second BAPEG conference, April 1980. /HC 187 A798 LAC

280. Baer, W., and A. Figueroa. n.d. "Equity and State Enterprises: Reflections Based on the Cases of Brazil and Peru." (unpublished). /Brazil /Peru /Income distribution /OPSS

281. Baer, W., and Anibal Villela. 1980 "The Changing Nature of Development Banking in Brazil." Journal of Interamerican Studies and World Affairs V. 22, No. 4, pp. 423-440. /Financial institutions /Brazil /G 980.605 J826 LAC

282. Baer, W., et al. 1965 "Transportation and Inflation: A Study of Irrational Policy Making in Brazil." Economic Development and Cultural Change V. 13, No. 2, pp. 188-202. /Brazil /Transportation industry /Inflation /Policy analysis /330.5 Ec66

283. Baer, W., et al. 1976 "On State Capitalism in Brazil: Some New Issues and Questions." Inter-American Economic Affairs V. 30, No. 6, pp. 68-92. /Brazil / HC 161 I585 LAC

284. Baeza V., Sergio. 1976 Programación de la oferta de viviendas del sector público. Documento de Trabajo. Santiago, Chile: Instituto de Economía-Universidad Católica de Chile. No. 42. /Planning process /Investment /Housing industry / OPSS

285. Baginski, Raúl. 1982 "La acción descentralizada de fomento: La experiencia brasileña." San Juan, P.R.: ALIDE. /Brazil /Planning process /Decentralized authority / OPSS

286. Bagota, B., and T. Halai. 1967 Dirección y estimulos materiales en la industria húngara. Moscow: Izdvo Ekonomika. /Hungary /Industrial sector /Incentive systems /Management

287. Bahadur, S. R. 1980 "Development & Growth of Ancillary Industries in Central Public Enterprises." Lok Udyog (New Delhi), V. 13, No. 12, pp. 31-34. /India /Private

enterprises /Subsidiaries /354.54 L836 PCL

288. Bahadur, S. R., and R. Sampat. 1980 "Maintenance Managemnt Scheme in Central Public Sector Enterprises." Lok Udyog (New Delhi), V. 13, No. 10-1, pp. 47-54. /India /Management /354.54 L836 PCL

289. Bahrampour, Keyoumars. 1976 "Public Enterprises in Iran." Approaches to the Public Enterprise Policy in Asia on Investment, Prices, and Returns Criteria. Kuala Lumpur: U.N. Asian Centre for Development Administration. pp. 143-152. /Iran /Statistics / HD 4276 A8 1976 PCL

290. Baidoo, Philip Kwesi. 1980 "Ghana Industrial Holding Corporation: Problems of Production and Distribution in GIHOC." Paper presented at the Interregional Seminar on Training Management in Public Enterprises in Developing Countries, Ljubljana, Yugoslavia, 29 Sept. - 10 Oct. Ljubljana: ICPE. /Ghana /Industrial sector /Productivity /Holding company

291. Baier, Michel M. 1978 "Transfer and Development of Technology: Romanian Experience." Paper presented at the International Workshop on Management of Transfer and Development of Technology in Public Enterprises in Developing Countries, Ljubljana, Yugoslavia, 19-25 June. Ljubljana: ICPE. /Romania /Technology transfer

292. Bails, A. 1949 "The Payment of Workers under the National Dock Labour Board." Journal of the Institute of Transport pp. 181-185. /United Kingdom /Trade unions /Wages

293. Bain, J. S. 1961 "The Political Control of Nationalized Industries in Britain." Studies in Political Science. New York: Asia Publishing House. pp. 291-317. /United Kingdom /Public administration /Industrial sector /Political analysis /Control process

294. Bain, J. S., R. E. Caves, and J. Margolis. 1966 Northern California´s Water Industry: The Comparative Efficiency of Public Enterprise in Developing a Scarce Natural Resource. Baltimore, Md.: Johns Hopkins Press. /United States of America /California (State) /Water resources development /Comparative analysis /Private sector

295. Baker, R. J. S. 1962 The Management of Capital Projects: Studies in the Coal, Transport and Electrical Supply Industries. London: Bell. /United Kingdom /Coal mining industry /Electrical utility industry /Transportation industry /Investment /Management /Project management /338.942 B176m

296. Bakhru, Mira, and Vatsala Nagarajan. 1982 "Perception of Public Sector Managements: An Exploratory Survey." Lok Udyog (New Delhi), V. 15, No. 11, pp. 23-38. /Management /354.54 L836 PCL

297. Bakhshi, Viqar Rustam. 1980 "Management Development and Training in State Enterprises in Pakistan." Paper presented

at the Interregional Seminar on Training Management in Public Enterprises in Developing Countries, Ljubljana, Yugoslavia, 29 Sept. - 10 Oct. Ljubljana: ICPE. /Pakistan /Management /Training

298. Baki, Adel Abdel. 1983 "Public Enterprises as Instrument of State Policy." Paper presented at the 19th International Congress of Administrative Sciences, West Berlin, 19-23 Sept. /Egypt /Law /OPSS

299. Baklanoff, Eric N. 1975 Expropriation of U.S. Properties in Cuba, Mexico, and Chile. New York: Praeger Publishers. /Cuba /Mexico /Chile /Nationalization /HG 5160.5 A3 B34 LAC

300. Baklanoff, Eric N. 1983 Copper in Chile: The Expropriation of a Partially Nationalized Industry. Austin, Tex.: OPSS Technical Papers Series, No. 38. /Nationalization /Chile /Mining industry / OPSS

301. Baklanoff, Eric N. 1984 "The State and Economy in Portugal: Perspectives on Corporatism, Revolution, and Reform." Paper presented at the conference "State Shrinking: A Comparative Inquiry into Privatization," Austin, Tex., 1-3 Mar. /Portugal /Privatization /OPSS

302. Balakrishna, R. 1941 "Rate Structure of Public Utilities in a Socialist State." Indian Journal of Economics V. 21, pp. 383-394. /Public utility industry /Price policy /Socialist economy / 330.5 In2

303. Balakrishna, R. 1949 "Public Enterprise in a Mixed Economy." Indian Journal of Economics V. 30, pp. 3-21. /India /Mixed enterprises / 330.5 In2

304. Balakrishnan, K. 1984 "Internationalizing LDC Firms: A Strategic Search Model." Public Enterprise V. 4, No. 3, pp. 23-32. /Developing nations /International economic relations /Mixed enterprises / OPSS

305. Balassa, B. 1970 "Growth Strategies in Semi-Industrial Countries." Quarterly Journal of Economics V. 84, No. 1, pp. 24-47. /Developing nations /Economic growth policy /330.5 Q2

306. Baldwin, G. B. 1957 "Public Enterprise in Indian Industry." Pacific Affairs pp. 3-21. /India /Industrial sector /Evaluation

307. Baldwin, George. 1955 Beyond Nationalization: The Labor Problems of British Coal. Cambridge, Mass.: Harvard University Press. /United Kingdom /Labor relations /Coal mining industry /338.0954 B193i

308. Baldwin, George. 1959 Industrial Growth in South India. Glencoe, Ill.: Free Press. /India /Industrialization /331.182233 B193i

309. Baldwin, John R. 1975 The Regulatory Agency and the Public Corporation: The Canadian Air Transport Industry. Cambridge, Mass.: Ballinger. /Canada /Air transportation industry /HE

9815 1334 1975 PCL

310. Balestrini Contreras, G. 1971 La industria petrolera en América Latina. Caracas: Universidad Central de Venezuela, Ediciones de la Biblioteca. /Latin America /Oil industry /Nationalization /HD 9574 L3 B35 LAC

311. Balgir, A. S. 1983 "A Study of Managerial Perceptions of Indian Public and Private Sector Organizations." Lok Udyog (New Delhi), V. 16, No. 10, pp. 19-24. /India /Private enterprises /Comparative analysis /354.54 L836 PCL

312. Ball, A. G. 1975 "Implications of Government Land Banks and Residency Requirements for Agricultural Land Use in Canada." Canadian Journal of Agricultural Economics V. 23, pp. 143-146. /Canada /Land use policy /Agricultural sector /Development banks / 338.1971 C16 PCL

313. Ball, R. E. 1958 "Government Corporations and Bigness." American Journal of Economics and Sociology V. 17, pp. 249-260. /United States of America /Control process /330.5 Am311 PCL /H 1 A48 Pub Aff

314. Balla, J. S. 1960 "What Form of Organization - Public Industrial Enterprises." Economic Weekly V. 12, pp. 1649-1652. /India / 330.954 Ec74 PCL

315. Ballarin Marcial, Alberto. 1970 "La cuestión de la empresa pública agraria." La Empresa Pública. Zaragoza, Spain: Publicaciones del Real Colegio de España en Bolonia. pp. 735-750. /Spain /Agricultural sector

316. Balls, H. R. 1960 "Canadian Crown Corporations: Accountability and Control." Indian Economic Journal (Bombay), pp. 223-234. /Canada /Accountability /Control process / 330.5 In16

317. Balls, H. R. 1970 "Improving Performance of Public Enterprises through Financial Management and Control." Canadian Public Administration (Ontario), V. 13, No. 1, pp. 100-123. /Canada /Control process /Financing /Financial performance / Financial management / 350.5 C16

318. Balog, Nikola. 1959 "Les associations des organisations économiques en Yougoslavie." Annales de l'Economie Collective V. 547-5, pp. 125-143. /Yugoslavia /Economic organization

319. Balog, Nikola. 1966 Administrative Management of Public Enterprises. Brussels: IIAS, General Report, XIIIth International Congress of Administrative Sciences, Paris, 20-23 July 1965. /Management /Public administration /Control process /JA 35.5 I6 1965 Pub Aff

320. Balog, Nikola. 1967 "A organização administrativa das empresas públicas." Revista de Direito Administrativo (Rio de Janeiro), No. 88-9. /Brazil /Organization behavior

321. Balogh, András, ed. 1979 Studies on Contemporary Problems of the Indian Subcontinent. Budapest: Hungarian Academy of Sciences, Institute for World Economy. /India /Development process

322. Balogh, T. 1943 "Compensation and Public Boards." Oxford University Institute of Statistics Bulletin V. 5, pp. 277-280. /Public financing /Wages

323. Bandara, Wijayananda Jayaweera. 1978 "Report of the International Workshop Planning in Public Enterprises in Developing Countries, Ljubljana, November 20-25, 1978." Ljubljana: ICPE. /Developing nations /Planning process

324. Bandeira de Mello, Celso Antonio. 1968 Natureza e regime jurídico das autarquias. São Paulo: Ed. Revista dos Tribunais. /Brazil /Law

325. Bandeira de Mello, Celso Antonio. 1973 Prestação de serviços públicos e administração indireta. São Paulo: Ed. Revista dos Tribunais. /Brazil /Public administration /Public financing

326. Banerjee, A. M. 1964 "Managerial Personnel for Public Enterprises." Indian Journal of Public Administration (New Delhi), pp. 513-523. /India /Management / JA 26 I55 Pub Aff

327. Banerjee, A. M., and M. L. Laroia. 1980 "Role of Maintenance in Optimising Production and Profitability in the Steel Industry." Lok Udyog (New Delhi), V. 14, No. 7, pp. 21-28. /India /Economic efficiency /Profits /Steel industry /Case studies /354.54 L836 PCL

328. Banerjee, S. 1977 "Public Accountability and Responsibility of Public Sector Managements." Lok Udyog (New Delhi), V. 11, No. 5, pp. 41-46. /India /Accountability /354.54 L836 PCL

329. Banerjee, S. 1980 "Personnel Management in Public Enterprises - Some Issues." Lok Udyog (New Delhi), V. 13, No. 10-1, pp. 41-46. /India /Personnel management /354.54 L836 PCL

330. Banerjee, Shyamal. 1983 "Value Orientation in Management in Government." Lok Udyog (New Delhi), V. 16, No. 11, pp. 5-12. /India /Management /354.54 L836 PCL

331. Bansal, B. L. 1968 Pricing Policies in Public Sector. Bombay: Vora and Co. /India /Price policy

332. Bansal, B. L. 1970 Financing Planning and Public Enterprises. Bombay: Vora and Co. /Financing /Planning process

333. Baptist, Osmond. 1979 "Systems of Control: Guyana State Corporation GUYSTAC." Paper presented at the Interregional Workshop on Control Systems for Public Enterprises in Developing Countries, Ljubljana, Yugoslavia, 9-13 July. Ljubljana: ICPE. /Guyana /Control process

334. Bar, Ludwik. 1970 "Las empresas del Estado en la R.P.P." La Empresa Pública. Zaragoza, Spain: Publicaciones del Real Colegio de España en Bolonia. pp. 1707-1762. /Evaluation /Poland

335. Bar, Ludwik. 1983 "Autonomy, Control, and Interference of the State in Public Enterprises." Paper presented at the 19th International Congress of Administrative Sciences, West Berlin, 19-23 Sept. /Autonomy /Control process /Poland /OPSS

336. Barañano, Diego. 1979 "Los recursos humanos en la empresa pública." In EIAP-FGV, ed(s). Administración de empresas públicas. Mexico: Editorial Limusa. pp. 15-54. /Personnel management /HD 3850 A333 LAC

337. Baratz, M. S. 1964 "Public Investment in Private Enterprise: A West Africa Case Study." Nigerian Journal of Economic and Social Studies (Ibadan, Nigeria), V. 6, pp. 60-71. /Nigeria /Private enterprises /Investment /Case studies / Africa

338. Barbadero, L. Metano. 1960 "Industria di stato e sviluppo economico." Civilitá delle Machine pp. 453-462. /Italy /Economic development

339. Barbe, Raoul P. 1967 "Régime fiscal des entreprises publiques au Canada." Canadian Public Administration (Ontario), V. 10, No. 2, pp. 147-160. /Canada /Public financing / 350.5 C16

340. Barbe, Raoul P. 1969 "Le contrôle parlementaire des entreprises au Canada." Administration Publique du Canada V. 12, No. 4, pp. 463-480. /Canada /Parliament /Control process

341. Barbedo, Alceu Otacílio. 1960 "Concessão de serviços públicos: Encampação desapropriação." Revista de Direito Administrativo (Rio de Janeiro), No. 59, pp. 490-497. /Brazil /Law

342. Barbet, H. 1958 "Empresas públicas en Francia y problemas de derecho público." A. Pravn. Fak. (Belgrade), pp. 44-57. /France /Law

343. Bard, Erwin Wilkie. 1939 The Port of New York Authority. New York: Columbia University Press. /United States of America /New York (State) /Port authority /330 C723 no.468

344. Barea Tejeiro, José. 1969 "Las cuentas de las empresas públicas." Economia Financiera Española (Madrid), No. 31-3, pp. 81-92. /Spain /Accounting

345. Barenstein, Jorge. 1981 "Naturaleza y estrategia de las empresas del Estado en paises en vias de desarrollo." Paper presented at the seminar on public enterprises in development planning for Central America and the Caribbean, San José, In ed(s). Costa Rica, 1-3 July. /Goal setting /Private enterprises /Comparative analysis /OPSS

346. Barenstein, Jorge. 1982 La gestión de empresas públicas en México. Mexico City: CIDE, Centro de Investigación y

Docencia Económica. /Mexico /Management

347. Barenstein, Jorge. 1982 "Nature and Strategy of Public Enterprises in Developing Countries." Lok Udyog (New Delhi), V. 16, No. 9, pp. 29-36. /Developing nations /354.54 L836

348. Barenstein, Jorge. 1983 Algunas cuestiones relevantes para la gestión de empresas públicas en México. Mexico City: CIDE, Centro de Investigación y Docencia Económica. /Mexico

349. Barettoni Aieri, Alberto. 1967 L'ordinamento ed il controllo della spesa púbblica in Francia. Milan: Ed. Giuffré. /France /Control process /Administrative management

350. Bari, R. R. 1981 "Hidden Cash in Public Sector Undertakings." Lok Udyog (New Delhi), V. 15, No. 1, pp. 11-18. /India /Financing /354.54 L836 PCL

351. Barletti, Bruno, and Luis Fernández Zavala. 1976 "Empresas públicas y burocracia empresarial del Estado." Lima: Instituto Nacional de Administración Pública (INAP) and Pontifícia Universidad Católica del Perú. /Peru /Control process /Statistics /Government bureaucracy / OPSS

352. Barmin, V. 1955 "Análisis de la realización del programa de producción por las empresas comunales." Firancy Kredit pp. 76-82. /Evaluation

353. Barnouti, Souad N. 1981 Thoughts about the Probable Employment Conditions of Women in Public Enterprises. Ljubljana: ICPE. /Women's studies /Employment policy

354. Barquín Alvarez, Manuel. 1979 El control del ejecutivo y la administración publica federal sobre el sector paraestatal. Paper presented at the international seminar on regulation of the public enterprise, Mexico City. /Mexico /Control Process /Public administration / OPSS

355. Barré, Albert. 1957 "The Organization of the Cereal Market in France." Annals of Collective Economy V. 28, pp. 212-227. /France /Marketing boards / 330.5 An73 PCL

356. Barreda, José E. 1980 "Case History of Acquisition of Technology by a Public Enterprise in Peru." Paper presented at the International Workshop on Preparations and Negotiations of Technology Agreements for Public Enterprises in Developing Countries, Ljubljana, Yugoslavia, 27-31 Oct. Ljubljana: ICPE. /Peru /Technology transfer /Case studies

357. Barrett, J. T., and I. B. Lobel. 1974 "Public Sector Strikes - Legislative and Court Treatment." Monthly Labor Review V. 97, No. 9, pp. 19 22. /United States of America /Labor relations /Legislature / Film 7161 UGL HD 8051 A78

358. Barria, L. 1972 "La participación de los trabajadores." Principios (Santiago, Chile), No. 144, pp. 82-91. /Chile /Worker management participation / G335.405 P935 LAC

359. Barrie, D. S. M. 1950 "Railway Public Relations." Journal of the Institute of Transport (London), pp. 14-18. /Railway industry /Public relations

360. Barrington, T. J. 1975 "Roles and Relationships of Government, Board and Chief Executive in Irish Public Enterprises." Improving Performance in Public Enterprise, Report of the International Conference, Arusha, Tanzania, 2-5 Dec. Arusha, Tanzania: East African Community Management Institute. pp. 38-53. /Control process /Ireland

361. Barros, F. 1969 Información contable para un sistema de costos: La experiencia de ferrocarriles del Estado. Santiago, Chile. /Chile /Accounting /Costs /Railway industry

362. Barroso, Geonício C. 1972 "Perfil nacional e internacional da Petrobrás." Petróleo e Petroquímica No. 7, pp. 22-23. /Brazil /Oil industry

363. Barry, E. E. 1965 Nationalization in British Politics: The Historical Background. Stanford, Cal.: Stanford University Press. /United Kingdom /Nationalization /338.942 B279n 1965L

364. Barta, Jan. 1983 "Autonomy, Control, and Interference of the State in Public Enterprise." Paper presented at the 19th International Congress of Administrative Sciences, West Berlin, 19-23 Sept. /Socialist economy /Control process /OPSS

365. Bartsch, William H. 1971 "The Impact of the Oil Industry on the Economy of Iran." Foreign Investment in the Petroleum and Mineral Industries. Baltimore, Md.: Johns Hopkins University Press. pp. 237-263. /Iran /Oil Industry /338.23 M589f PCL,Pub Aff

366. Basak, Aroon K. 1975 "Management and Performance of Public Enterprises in Developing Countries - The Need for Further Research." Lok Udyog (New Delhi), V. 9, No. 3, pp. 9-16. /Developing nations /Economic efficiency /Financial performance /354.54 L836 PCL

367. Basic, A., and M. Konopnicki. 1969 "L´économie publique et coopérative en Italie." Annales de l´Economie Collective pp. 291-331. /Italy

368. Baskaran, P. S. 1976 "Operational Efficiency of a Public Sector Industry - A Case Study." Lok Udyog (New Delhi), V. 10, No. 8, pp. 31-36. /India /Economic efficiency /Case studies /354.54 L836 PCL

369. Bassi, Franco. 1967 "Azionariato púbblico e procedure concusnuali." Revista Trimestrale di Diritto Púbblico (Rome), pp. 896-913. /Italy /Management /Law

370. Bassino Galli, C. 1964 Los presupuestos por programa en las actividades públicas; su aplicación a una institución estatal. Santiago, Chile. /Chile /Public financing /Budgetary process

371. Bastos de Avila, F. 1959 "Es lícito nacionalizar?" Sintese Política Econômica Social (São Paulo), pp. 30-37. /Nationalization

372. Basu, Prahlad Kumar. 1976 "Issues and Problems of Public Enterprise Policy on Prices, Investment and Prices and Returns Criteria." Approaches to the Public Enterprise Policy in Asia on Investment Prices and Returns Criteria. Kuala Lumpur: U.N. Asian Centre for Development Administration. pp. 64-75. /Asia /Price policy /Investment /Profits / HD 4276 A8 1976 PCL

373. Basu, Prahlad Kumar. 1976 Managerial Civil Service in Asia. /Asia /Management /Civil service /Public administration

374. Basu, Prahlad Kumar. 1977 "The Context of Public Enterprise Experience in Asia. Problems of Management Development-Civil Services, Public Enterprises Cadres and Transplanted Private Managers; The Future of Cadernization and Training." Paper presented at the International Seminar on Management and Training in Public Enterprises in Developing Countries, Ljubljana, Yugoslavia, 10-28 Oct. Ljubljana: ICPE. /Asia /Management /Training

375. Basu, Prahlad Kumar. 1978 "Education and Training for Public Enterprise Administrators in Asia and Pacific Region: Issues for In-Depth Analysis." Paper presented at the International Seminar on Management and Training in Public Enterprises in Developing Countries, Ljubljana, Yugoslavia, 18 Sept.-6 Oct. Ljubljana: ICPE. /Asia /Training /Management

376. Basu, Prahlad Kumar. 1979 "A Note on Management and Training in Public Enterprises in India." Paper presented at the International Seminar on Management and Training in Public Enterprises in Developing Countries, Ljubljana, Yugoslavia, 1-13 Oct. Ljubljana: ICPE. /India /Training /Management

377. Basu, Prahlad Kumar. 1980 "Linkage Between Policy and Performance: Empirical and Theoretical Considerations on Public Enterprises in Mixed Economy L.D.Cs." Paper presented at the second BAPEG conference, Boston, April. /India /Economic Policy /OPSS

378. Basu, Prahlad Kumar. 1981 "Training Public Enterprise Managers: Issues and Achievements." Paper presented at the Regional Workshop on the Evaluation of Training Packages for Public Enterprise Managers, Bangkok, Thailand, 10-14 Aug. Ljubljana: ICPE. /Training /Management

379. Basu, Prahlad Kumar. 1982 Public Enterprises--Policy, Performance and Professionalization. Bombay: Allied Publishers Private Limited. /India /Evaluation /Training /Management /Policy development / Developing nations /Mixed enterprises

380. Basu, S. K. 1965 Theory and Practice of Development Banking: A Study in the Asian Context. Bombay: Asia Publishing. /Asia /Development banks

381. Basu, S. K., et al. 1971 Report on the Monetary and Non-Monetary Work Incentives in Public Enterprises of West Bengal. New Delhi: Planning Commission, Research Programmes Committee. /India /Wages /Employee benefits /West Bengal, India

382. Basurto, J. 1978 El conflicto internacional en torno al petróleo de México. Mexico City: Siglo Veintiuno Editores. /Mexico /Oil industry /Nationalization /International relations / International economic relations

383. Bates, R., and M. Webb. 1968 "Government Control Over Investment Planning in the Nationalized Electricity Supply Industry." Bulletin of the Institute of Economics and Statistics V. 30, No. 1, pp. 37-53. /United Kingdom /Electrical utility industry /Investment /Control process /310.5 Ox2 PCL

384. Bates, R., and Neil Fraser. 1974 Investment Decisions in the Nationalized Fuel Industries. New York: Cambridge University Press. /United Kingdom /Public utility industry /Investment /HG 4028 C4 B35 Pub Aff,PCL

385. Batley, Richard. 1979 "The Brazilian National Housing Bank: Establishment and Adaptation." DAG Occasional Paper 6. Birmingham, England: University of Birmingham, Institute of Local Government Studies, Development Administration Group (DAG). /Brazil /Housing industry /Financial institutions /Credit policy / OPSS

386. Battacharya, D., and S. P. Pal. 1981 "Economic Evaluation of Cement Industry in India- The Question of Optimal Cement Pricing." Lok Udyog (New Delhi), V. 15, No. 7+8, pp. 3-12. /India /Price policy /Cement manufacturing industry /354.54 L836 PCL

387. Bauchet, P. 1962 Propriété publique et planification: Entreprises publiques non-financières. Paris: Cujas. /Public administration /Planning process /338.74 B323p

388. Bauchet, P. 1966 "Las empresas públicas francesas y el Mercado Común." Documentación Administrativa (Madrid), No. 106, pp. 11-32. /France /European Economic Community /Evaluation

389. Bauer, Ludwig. 1980 "Cooperation among State Petroleum Enterprises in Developed and Developing Countries." State Petroleum Enterprises in Developing Countries. New York: Pergamon Press. pp. 77-81. /Oil industry

390. Bauer, P. T. 1961 Indian Economic Policy and Development. New York: Frederick A. Praeger. /India /Planning process /Economic development / 338.954 B362u 1961

391. Bauermeister, G., and R. Bauer. 1966 "Zu einegen Problemen des Praenienwesens." Arbeits Oekonomik (Berlin), V. 10, No. 3, pp. 228-238. /Germany, Federal Rep. of /Wages

392. Baum, Warren C. 1958 *French Economy and the State.* Princeton, N. J.: Princeton University Press. /France

393. Baumol, William J., ed. 1980 *Public and Private Enterprise in a Mixed Economy: Proceedings of a Conference Held by the International Economic Association in Mexico City.* New York: St. Martin's Press. /Mixed enterprises /Private enterprises /HD 3842 P87 PCL

394. Bavu, Immanuel K. 1981 "A Description of the Structure of State Control and Management of Public Enterprises in Tanzania." Ljubljana: ICPE. /Tanzania /Control process /Management

395. Bayali, Abdelovahal. 1980 "Quelques réflexions sur la gestion et la formation dans les entreprises publiques dans les pays en voie de développement: le cas du Maroc." Paper presented at the Séminaire international sur la gestion et la formation dans les entreprises publiques dans les pays en voie de développement, Ljubljana, Yugoslavia, 3-15 Mar. Ljubljana: ICPE. /Morocco /Management /Training

396. Bayer, R. J. F. 1955 "The Statutory Corporation in the Cultural Field, the Australian Broadcasting Commission." In A. H. Hanson, ed(s). *Public Enterprise.* Brussels: IIAS. pp. 501-502. /Australia /Broadcasting industry / HD 3850 H28 Law

397. Beach, Philip E. 1963 "Industrial Development Banks: Operating Practices." In Warren H. Hausman, ed(s). *Managing Economic Development in Africa.* Cambridge, Mass.: MIT Press. pp. 112-120. /Africa /Economic policy /Financial institutions / 338.96 Mlm PCL

398. Beacham, A. 1950 "Nationalization in Theory and Practice." *Quarterly Journal of Economics* V. 64, pp. 550-558. /Nationalization /330.5 Q2

399. Beacham, A. 1951 "Planned Investment in the Coal Industry." *Oxford Economic Papers* pp. 125-154. /United Kingdom /Coal mining industry /Investment /330.6 Ox2 PCL

400. Beaglehole, J. H. n.d. "Malay Participation in Commerce and Industry: The Role of R.I.D.A. and M.A.R.A." *Journal of Commonwealth Political Studies* V. 7, No. 3, pp. 216-245. /Malaysia /Investment /Industrial sector /Commercial sector

401. Beatrix, L. 1948 *L'industrie électrique en France avant et après la nationalisation.* Paris. /France /Electrical utility industry /Nationalization

402. Becker, David. 1983 *The New Bourgeoisie and the Limits of Dependency: Mining, Class, and Power in "Revolutionary" Peru.* Princeton, N.J.: Princeton University Press. /Mining industry /Nationalization /Peru /Comparative analysis /HC 227 B357 1983 LAC

403. Becker, R. 1968 *Les entreprises publiques en Afrique du Nord: L'expérience de l'autogestion en Algérie.* Tangier, Morocco: CAFRAD. /Algeria /Africa /Evaluation

404. Becker, R. 1968 The Experiment of Self Management in Algeria. Tunis: UNECA. Seminar, Dec. 9-20. /Algeria /Worker self management

405. Becker, R., and M. Nour. 1968 Public Enterprises in Algeria, Libya and Morocco. Tunis: UNECA. Seminar, Dec. 9-20. /Algeria /Libya /Morocco /Evaluation

406. Beckman, Björn. 1977 "Public Enterprise and State Capitalism." In Yash Ghai, ed(s). Law in the Political Economy of Public Enterprise: African Perspectives. Uppsala: Scandinavian Institute of African Studies. New York: International Legal Centre. pp. 127-136. /Political economy /Ideology / Africa 76 L41 Law

407. Bederman, S. H. 1968 The Cameroons Development Corporation. Partner in National Growth. Bota, Cameroon: Development Corp. /Cameroon /Agricultural development /Development corporation

408. Bedoya, J. M. de. 1971 "Los fallos de la empresa pública." Informaciones (Madrid), V. 14.58, No. 2. /Evaluation /Spain

409. Beesley, M. E., and C. D. Foster. 1965 "The Victoria Line: Social Benefit and Finances." Journal of Royal Statistical Society pp. 67-88. /United Kingdom /Railway industry

410. Beesley, M. E., and G. M. White. 1973 "The Industrial Reorganization Corporation: A Study in Choice of Public Management." Public Administration V. 51, pp. 61-89. /United Kingdom /Management / JA 8 P8 Pub Aff

411. Beesley, M. E., and Tom Evans. 1981 "The British Experience: The Case of British Rail." In Raymond Vernon and Yair Aharoni, ed(s). State-Owned Enterprise in the Western Economies. New York: St. Martin's Press. pp. 117-132. /United Kingdom /Railway industry /HD 3850 S79 PCL

412. Beever, Miles. 1950 "The Accountability of the British Transport." British Transport Review (London), pp. 146-152. /United Kingdom /Transportation industry /Accountability

413. Begaum-Francotte, Colette. 1970 "La empresa pública en la Union Soviética." La Empresa Pública. Zaragoza, Spain: Publicaciones del Real Colegio de España en Bolonia. pp. 1763-1892. /Union of Soviet Socialist Reps. /Evaluation

414. Belanger, Gérard. 1972 "Le secteur publique: Un budget croissant pour des services constants." Revue Economique (Paris), V. 23, No. 1, pp. 70-85. /France /Budgetary process /330.5 R3282 PCL

415. Belgium. Telegraph and Telephone Corporation. 1958 "The Telegraph and Telephone Corporation." Annals of Collective Economy V. 29, pp. 509-514. /Belgium /Communication industry /Telephone industry /Telegraph industry /330.5 An73 PCL

416. Bell, Reginald W. 1951 "Selection and Training for Management in British Nationalized Industries." Law and

Contemporary Problems V. 16, No. 4, pp. 633-651. /United Kingdom /Management /Personnel recruitment / 340.5 L44 PCL

417. Bell, Reginald W. 1951 "The Relation of Promotion and Training to Higher Management in British Nationalized Industries." *Public Administration* (London), pp. 201-216. /United Kingdom /Industrial sector /Training /Employment policy / JA 8 P8 Pub Aff

418. Bell, Vernon W. 1979 "Systems of Information and Control of Public Enterprises in Developing Countries: Jamaica." Paper presented at the Interregional Workshop on Control Systems for Public Enterprises in Developing Countries, Ljubljana, Yugoslavia, 13-18 Nov. Ljubljana: ICPE. /Jamaica /Control process / Information management

419. Belloula, Tayeb. 1977 *De l´organisation socialiste des enterprises.* Algiers: Edition du Parti. /Algeria

420. Ben Aissa, Mohamed Salah. 1974 "Le principe de spécialité et les établissements publiques économiques en droit tunisien et en droit français." Unpublished thesis, University of Tunis: Centre d´Etudes, de Recherches et de Publications. V. 3. /Tunisia /France /Law

421. Benachenhou, M. 1969 *Problèmes sociologiques de l´autogestion agricole en mitidja.* Bordeaux: Université de Bordeaux, Faculté de Lettres et Sciences Humaines. /Agricultural sector /Worker self management

422. Benadusi, L. 1968 "Programmazione economica e riforma dell´impresa publica." *Questitalia* (Venice), V. 2, No. 120, pp. 29-54. /Administrative reform /Management

423. Bendekovic, Jadranko. 1979 "Evaluation of Corporate Plans." Paper presented at the Regional Workshop on Planning in Public Enterprises of the African Region, Accra, Ghana, 10-15 Dec. Ljubljana: ICPE. /Planning process /Evaluation

424. Bendekovic, Jadranko. 1980 "Additional Criteria in the Planning of the Public Enterprise Development." Paper presented at the Regional Workshop on Planning of Public Enterprises in the Latin American and Caribbean Region, Kingston, Jamaica, 11-15 Feb. Ljubljana: ICPE. /Planning process

425. Bendekovic, Jadranko. 1980 "Evaluation of Corporate Plans." Paper presented at the Regional Workshop on Planning of Public Enterprises in the Latin American and Caribbean Region, Kingston, Jamaica, 11-15 Feb. Ljubljana: ICPE /Planning process /Evaluation

426. Bendekovic, Jadranko. 1980 "Shadow Rate of Foreign Exchange in Investment Project Planning." Paper presented at the Regional Workshop on Corporate Planning in Public Enterprises in the Asian and Pacific Region, Kuala Lumpur, Malaysia, 17-21 Nov. Ljubljana: ICPE. /Planning process /Foreign exchange /Investment

427. Benedict, D. 1971 Intervención de los trabajadores en la dirección de las empresas. Geveva: Foro Sindical. /Worker management participation

428. "Benefits to State Economies arising from Central Public Enterprises." 1976 Lok Udyog (New Delhi), V. 10, No. 3, pp. 53-56. /India /Regional development /354.54 L836 PCL

429. Benítez de Castro, C. 1969 Política de participación: Participación en los beneficios, accionario obrero, capitalismo popular, y cogestión. Buenos Aires: Eudeba. /Worker management participation /Labor relations /Participatory democracy

430. Benítez, Jesús. 1973 "Análisis legal de la economia mixta." Espejo (Mexico City), V. 13, No. 99, pp. 28-33. /Law /Mixed enterprises / 330.5 Es64 LAC

431. Benmatti, Nadir Abdullah. 1982 "Rapport national sur le thème `L´Entreprise publique comme instrument des politiques de l´Etat´." Paper presented at the Tokyo Round Table preparatory to the 19th International Congress of Administrative Sciences, 13-17 Sept. /Algeria /Management /Law /Control process /Economic history /OPSS

432. Bennett, Douglas, and Kenneth Sharpe. 1979 "El Estado como banquero y empresario: El cáracter de última instancia de la intervención económica del Estado mexicano, 1917-1970." Foro Internacional (Mexico City), V. 20, pp. 29-72. /Mexico /Banking system /Economic history / G056.8 F71 LAC

433. Bennett, Peter D. 1968 Government´s Role in Retail Marketing of Food Products in Chile. Studies in Latin-American Business No. 6. Austin, Tex.: UT Bureau of Business Research and ILAS. /Chile /Food industry /Marketing /Price policy /Economic policy /Entrepreneurial activity /Taxation policy /HD 9014 C52 B4 Pub Aff

434. Benzo Mestre, F. 1973 Equilibrio entre empresa pública y privada, la empresa pública industrial en España. Madrid: Instituto de Estudios Fiscales. /Spain /Industrial sector /Evaluation /Private sector

435. Berckholtz, Pablo. 1980 "A Case on Restrictive Practices in Transfer of Technology in an Andean Country." Paper presented at the International Workshop on Preparations and Negotiations for Technology Transfer Agreements for Public Enterprises in Developing Countries, Ljubljana, Yugoslavia, 27-31 Oct. Ljubljana: ICPE. /Andean Pact Countries /Technology transfer

436. Berczi, Andrew. 1977 "A Proposal for Improving Public Sector Management through Systematic Measurement of Operational Performance." Annals of Public and Cooperative Economy V. 49, pp. 279-298. /Management /Economic efficiency /330.5 An73

437. Berend, Pierre. 1952 "Les prix de reivient et le contrôle de la gestion dans les manufactures de tabacs du service

d'exploitat ou industrielle des Tabacs et des Allumettes." Revue Economique (Paris), No. 4, pp. 499-516. /France /Industrial sector /Control process /Price policy /Tobacco industry /Match manufacturing industry /330.5 R3282 PCL

438. Berend, Pierre. 1954 "Le monopôle français des tabacs." Revue Administrative (Paris), pp. 356-370. /France /Monopoly /Tobacco industry

439. Bergamini de Abreu, Armando. 1979 "La divisionalización como instrumento de descentralización." In EIAP-FGV, ed(s). Administración de empresas públicas. Mexico City: Editorial Limusa. pp. 123-218. /Management /Brazil / HD 3850 A333 LAC

440. Bergendohl, Goran. 1971 "Aspects of Pricing Policy for Private and Public Transportation." The Swedish Journal of Economics V. 73, No. 2, pp. 204-224. /Sweden /Mixed enterprises /Price policy /Land transportation industry /HB 9 E6 PCL

441. Bergsman, Joel. 1970 Brazil: Industrialization and Trade Policies. London: Oxford University Press. /Brazil /Industrialization /Economic policy /G338.0981 B454b

442. Bergson, A. 1964 The Economics of Soviet Planning. Studies in Comparative Economics, No.5. New Haven: Yale University Press. /Union of Soviet Socialist Reps. /Planning process /338.947 B454e

443. Bergson, A. 1972 "Optimal Pricing for Public Enterprises." Quarterly Journal of Economics V. 86, No. 4, pp. 519-544. /Price Policy / 330.5 Q2 PCL

444. Bergson, A. 1978 "Managerial Risks and Rewards in Public Enterprises." Journal of Comparative Economics V. 2, pp. 211-225. /Management / HB 1 J568

445. Bergson, A., et al. 1953 Soviet Economic Growth: Conditions and Perspectives. Evanston, Ill.: Row, Peterson and Co. /Union of Soviet Socialist Reps. /Economic growth policy /Economic analysis /330.947 B454s

446. Berkovitch, Israel. 1977 Coal on the Switchback. London: Allen & Unwin. /United Kingdom /Coal mining industry /HD 9551.5 B43 UGL

447. Berlanga Laurent, Luis. 1978 Control por parte del gobierno federal de las instituciones nacionales de credito, organizaciones auxiliares nacionales de credito y las instituciones nacionales de seguros y finanzas. Mexico City: Comisión Nacional de Salarios Mínimos. /Mexico /Credit policy /Financial institutions / OPSS

448. Berliner, Joseph S. 1952 "The Informal Organization of the Soviet Firm." Quarterly Journal of Economics V. 66 I, No. 3, pp. 342-365. /Union of Soviet Socialist Reps. /Management /330.5 Q2 PCL,Law /HB1 Q3 Pub Aff

449. Berliner, Joseph S. 1957 Factory and Manager in the U.S.S.R. Cambridge, Mass.: Harvard University Press. /Union of Soviet Socialist Reps. Industrial sector /Management / 658.5 B455f

450. Berlinski, Julio, and Héctor C. Dieguez. 1977 "Análisis de la evolución de precios de empresas públicas en la Argentina, un comentario." Desarrollo Económico (Buenos Aires), V. 17, pp. 159-168. /Argentina /Price policy /Economic analysis /Evaluation / HD 85 S7 D48 LAC

451. Bermúdez, A. J. 1963 The Mexican National Petroleum Industry: A Case Study in Nationalization. Stanford, Cal.: Stanford University Press. /Mexico /Oil industry /Nationalization /G338.2 B456dT

452. Bermúdez, A. J. 1976 La política petrolera mexicana. Mexico City: Editorial J. Mortiz. /Mexico /Oil industry /Political analysis /HD 9574 M6 B475 LAC

453. Bernard, F. 1954 "La centralisation administrative dans les houillières britanniques." Revue française de science politique (Paris), pp. 564-579. /United Kingdom /Administrative management /Centralization /Coal mining industry /320.5 R3273

454. Bernard, M. 1968 Les entreprises publiques en Côte d'Ivoire. Abidjan, Ivory Coast: Ecole National d'Administration. /Ivory Coast /Evaluation

455. Bernheim, P., et al. 1977 Séminaires du secteur publique productif: Place du secteur publique productif, filiales et participations des entreprises publiques. Paris: Ecole Nationale d'Administration. /France /Public financing / OPSS

456. Bernier, Ivan. 1981 "State Trading and the GATT." In M. M. Kostecki, ed(s). State Trading in International Markets. New York: St. Martin's Press. pp. 245-260. /State trading organizations /Economic integration /HF 1410.5 S7 1981 M. Also found in Les Cahiers du Cetai, no 79-14, June, 1979 /OPSS

457. Berrada el Azizi, Abdelmoula. 1980 "Le transfert de maîtrise industrielle: Exemple de l'Office pour Développement Industriel (I'O.D.I.)." Paper presented at the Séminaire international sur la gestion et la formation dans les entreprises publiques dans les pays en voie de développement, Ljubljana, Yugoslavia, 3-15 March. Ljubljana: ICPE. /Training /Management /Industrial sector

458. Berrie, T. W. 1967 "The Economics of System Planning in Bulk Electricity Supply." Electrical Review, 15th, 22nd, and 29th September. V. 181. /Electrical utility industry /Economic analysis /621.305 EL26 /Reproduced in R. Turvey, Public Enterprise, /338.001 R869e PCL /HD 3850 T89 Pub Aff

459. Berthomieu, Claude. 1970 La gestion des entreprises nationalisées: Critique de l'analyse marginaliste. Paris: Presses Universitaires de France. /India /Price Policy /330.5 In16 PCL

460. Besson, L. 1947 Nationalisation et organisations des assurances. Paris: Droit Social. /France /Financial institutions /Nationalization /Organization formation / Law /Insurance industry

461. Betancourt, R. 1967 Venezuela, política y petróleo. Caracas, Venezuela: Editorial Senderos. /Venezuela /Oil industry /Political analysis /Nationalization / G987.063 B456ven

462. Betancourt, R. 1978 Venezuela's Oil. London: George Allen & Unwin. /Venezuela /Oil industry /Nationalization /Political analysis / HD9574 V42 B4

463. Bevis, H. L. 1936 "The AAA and TVA Decisions." Harvard Business Review V. 14, No. 3, pp. 272-278. /United States of America /River valley development projects / Decision making process /Control process / HF 5001 H3

464. Bewlay, S. 1964 Towards an Assessment of the Economic Cost of Nationalization. London: Aims of Industry Study. /United Kingdom /Nationalization /Economic analysis /Costs

465. Bezdanov, Stevan. 1977 "Alternation of Work and Education in Yugoslavia: A Study Based on the Examples of Two Enterprises." Paper presented at the Séminaire international sur la gestion et la formation dans les entreprises publiques dans les pays en voie de développement, Ljubljana, Yugoslavia, 3-15 March. Ljubljana: ICPE. /Yugoslavia /Training /Management

466. Bezdanov, Stevan. 1977 "Facilities and Training Activities in Enterprises." Paper presented at the International Seminar on Management and Training in Public Enterprises in Developing Countries, Ljubljana, Yugoslavia, 10-28 Oct. Ljubljana: ICPE. /Yugoslavia /Training /Management

467. Bhalla, D. N., and M. F. Anabtawi. 1959 Devolution of Powers to Autonomous Institutions, with Special Reference to Autonomous Public Corporations. The Hague, Netherlands: Institute of Social Studies. V. 3 I, No. 68. /Netherlands /Management / Control process /Accountability

468. Bhalla, G. S. 1965 "Problems of Compensation in Nationalized Industries in India." Annals of Public and Cooperative Economy V. 34, No. 2-3, pp. 391-399. /India /Industrial sector /Nationalization / Wages

469. Bhalla, G. S. 1968 Financial Administration of Nationalized Industries in the U. K. and India. Meerut: Meenakshi. /United Kingdom /India /Industrial sector /Financing /HD 4293 B43 1968

470. Bhalla, G. S. 1971 "Financing Public Enterprises in India." Lok Udyog (New Delhi), V. 5, No. 4, pp. 353-364. /India /Financing /354.54 L836 PCL

471. Bhalla, G. S., and S. S. Mehta. 1970 "Rates of Return in Public and Private Sector Industries in India." Lok Ugyog (New Delhi), V. 4, No. 2, pp. 147-157. /India /Private

sector /Industrial sector / Profits / /354.54 L836

472. Bhalla, P. N. 1971 "Reporting System in State Trading Corporation." Lok Udyog (New Delhi), V. 5, No. 2, pp. 145-158. /India /Information system /State trading organizations /354.54 L836 PCL

473. Bhalla, P. N. 1975 "Role of Finance in Accountability." In R. C. Dutt and Raj K. Nigam, ed(s). Towards Commanding Heights. New Delhi: Vivek Joshi. pp. 220-231. /India /Accountability /HD 4293 T68 PCL

474. Bhambhri, Chandra Prakash. 1960 Parliamentary Control over State Enterprises in India: A Study in Public Administration. New Delhi, India: Metropolitan Book Company. /India /Control process /Parliament / 338.954 B469p

475. Bhandari, A. S. 1979 "Joint Venture and Public Enterprise in India." Paper presented at the International Seminar on Joint Ventures and Public Enterprises in Developing Countries, Ljubljana, Yugoslavia, 4-12 Dec. Ljubljana: ICPE. /India /Mixed enterprises

476. Bhandari, Basant Raj. 1978 "Cooperation among State Trading Orgnizations of Asian Developing Countries." (Geneva: UNCTAD). TD/B/C.7/17 /State trading organizations /Bangladesh /Burma /India /Indonesia /Malaysia / Pakistan /Sri Lanka /OPSS

477. Bhandari, K. 1962 Nationalization of Industries in India: Doctrinaire Adherence Redundant. Calcutta, India: Academic Publishers. /India /Industrial sector /Nationalization /338.954 B469h

478. Bhandari, M. C. 1967 "The Role of Chartered Accountants in Public Sector Undertakings." Lok Udyog (New Delhi), /India /Accounting

479. Bhandari, R. M. 1969 "Investment in Public Enterprises." (Part 1) Lok Udyog (New Delhi), V. 3, No. 9, pp. 1023-1029. /India /Investment /354.54 L836

480. Bhandari, R. M. 1970 "Investment in Public Enterprises." (Part 2) Lok Udyog (New Delhi), V. 3, No. 10, pp. 1147-1152. /India /Investment /354.54 L836 PCL

481. Bhandari, R. M. 1970 "Investment in Public Enterprises." (Part 3). Lok Udyog (New Delhi), V. 3, No. 11, pp. 1267-1272. /India /Investment /354.54 L836 PCL

482. Bhandari, R. M. 1971 "Management Information System in Industrial Projects." Lok Udyog (New Delhi), V. 5, No. 2, pp. 139-144. /India /Information system /Project management /354.54 L836 PCL

483. Bhandari, R. M. 1978 "Public Enterprises in India." Paper presented at the Interregional Workshop on Financing of Public Enterprises in Developing Countries, Ljubljana, Yugoslavia, 22-26 May. Ljubljana: ICPE. /India /Financing

484. Bhandari, S. K. R., and A. S. Abani. 1975 "Management Audit with Reference to Indian Public Enterprises." Lok Udyog (New Delhi), V. 9. No. 3, pp. 27-32. /India /Accountability /Control process /354.54 L836 PCL

485. Bhandari, S. K. R., and A. S. Abani. 1975 "Management Audit in Public Enterprises." Lok Udyog (New Delhi), V. 9, No. 4, pp. 27-30. /Accountability /Control process /354.54 L836 PCL

486. Bharathan, V. 1977 "Organising R & D for Heavy Machine Tool Industry." Lok Udyog (New Delhi), V. 10, No. 11, pp. 45-54. /India /Research and development /Metal manufacturing industry /354.54 L836 PCL

487. Bhargava, P. K. 1972 "Indian Tax Structure--A Brief Review." The Indian Journal of Public Administration (New Delhi), V. 18, No. 3, pp. 436-442. /India /Taxation policy /JA 26 I55 Pub Aff

488. Bhargava, R. N. 1962 Indian Public Finances. London: George Allen & Unwin. /India /Public financing /336.54 B469i

489. Bhatia, B. M. 1969 "A Landmark in Evolution of Public Sector." Lok Udyog (New Delhi), pp. 495-601. /India /Investment /354.54 L836

490. Bhatla, A. C. 1967 "Public Sector Enterprise for Greater Profits." Lok Udyog (New Delhi), pp. 37-41. /India /Profits

491. Bhatt, V. V. 1970 "Financial Institutions in Economic Development." Lok Udyog (New Delhi), V. 4, No. 7, pp. 793-797. /Financial institutions /354.54 L836 PCL

492. Bhatt, V. V. 1978 "Decision Making in the Public Sector: Case Study of Swaraj Tractor." Washington, D. C.: IBRD. /India /Tractor manufacturing industry

493. Bhatt, V. V. 1982 "Decision structure, technological self-reliance, and public-enterprise performance." In Leroy P. Jones et al., ed(s). Public enterprise in less-developed countries. New York: Cambridge University Press. pp. 129-140. /Decision making process /Tractor manufacturing industry /India /HD 3850 P83 PCL /Earlier version presented at Second BAPEG seminar, Boston, April 1980. /OPSS

494. Bhatt, V. V. 1982 "Development Banking: Top Management Tasks and Structure." In William Diamond and V. S. Raghavan, ed(s). Aspects of Development Bank Management. Baltimore, Md.: The Johns Hopkins University Press. pp. 18-32. /Management /HG 3550 A8 PCL

495. Bhatt, V. V. 1982 "Financial Institutions and Technology Policy." In William Diamond and V. S. Raghavan, ed(s). Aspects of Development Bank Management. Baltimore, Md.: The Johns Hopkins University Press. pp. 144-158. /Development banks /Technology transfer /HG 3550 A8 PCL

496. Bhattacharyya, N. K. 1968 "Audit of Public Undertakings." Lok Udyog (New Delhi), pp. 25-31. /India /Accounting /354.54

L836

497. Bhattacharyya, S. C. 1972 "Management Development by Environmental Influence in the Public Sector Industries." Lok Udyog (New Delhi), V. 6, No. 4, pp. 53-56. /India /Control process /Training /354.54 L836 PCL

498. Bhattacharyya, S. K. 1969 "Management Reporting System in Public Undertaking." Economic and Political Weekly (Bombay), pp. 43-54. /Management /Information system /330.954 Ec75

499. Bhattacharyya, S. K. 1971 "Management Reporting in Public Undertakings." Lok Udyog (New Delhi), V. 5, No. 2, pp. 125-139. /India /Information system /354.54 L836 PCL

500. Bhattacharyya, S. K. 1975 "The Nature and Mechanics of the Accountability of Public Undertakings." In R. C. Dutt and Raj K. Nigam, ed(s). Towards Commanding Heights. New Delhi: Vivek Joshi. pp. 92-119. /India /Accountability /HD 4293 T68 PCL

501. Bhaya, Hiten. 1978 "Management of Transfer and Development of Technology in Public Enterprises in Zambia." Paper presented at the International Workshop on Management of Transfer and Development of Technology in Public Enterprises in Developing Countries, Ljubljana, Yugoslavia, 19-25 June. Ljubljana: ICPE. /Developing nations /Technology transfer /Management / Zambia /Africa

502. Bhaya, Hiten. 1983 Methods and Techniques of Training Public Enterprise Managers. Ljubljana: ICPE. /Training /Management

503. Bhoothalingam, S. 1972 "Plan for Holding Company - Division of Powers and Responsibilities." Lok Udyog (New Delhi), V. 6, No. 7, pp. 21-24. /India /Subsidiaries /Holding company /354.54 L836 PCL

504. Bianchi, R. 1960 "Aspetti e prolemi dell´impresa pubblica in Gran Bretagna." L´Impresa Pubblica (Rome), V. 4, pp. 433-438. /Italy /Evaluation

505. Bianchi, R. 1961 "Aspetti giuridici della proprieta pubblica in Francia." L´Impresa Pubblica (Rome), V. 5, No. 4, pp. 251-255. /France /Law

506. Bianchi, T. 1963 La nacionalizzazione delle impresa eletriche. Riflessi sul mercato del credito. Milan, Italy: A. Giuffre. No. 7. /Italy /Electrical utility industry /Nationalization

507. Bienstock, G., S. M. Swartz, and A. Yugow. 1944 Management in Russian Industry and Agriculture. Oxford: Oxford University Press. /Union of Soviet Socialist Reps. /Industrial sector /Management /Agricultural sector /HC 335 B5 1944 HRC

508. Bigler, Gene E., II. 1979 "State Economic Control vs. Market Expansion: The Third Sector in Venezuelan Politics, 1928-1978." Unpublished Ph.D. dissertation, The Johns

Hopkins University. /Venezuela /Political analysis /Policy analysis /Economic development /FILM 13,986 LAC

509. Bigler, Gene E., II. 1979 "Styles of Management in the Third Sector: Some Implications of Public Economic Expansion in Venezuela." Paper presented at the 40th National Conference of the American Society of Public Administration, 1-4 Apr. /Venezuela /Management /OPSS

510. Bigler, Gene E., II. 1981 _La política y el capitalismo de Estado en Venezuela._ Madrid: Editorial Tecnos. /Venezuela /Economic history /Public administration /Political analysis /HC 237 B52 1981

511. Bilandzic, D. 1967 _Management of Yugoslav Economy, 1945-1966._ Belgrade: Yugoslavia Trade Union. /Yugoslavia /Public administration /Planning process /Economic history /658.3152 B49uTh

512. Bilandzic, D. 1971 "Social Self Management in Yugoslavia." _Indian Left Review_ (New Delhi), V. 1, No. 2, pp. 78-88. /Yugoslavia /Worker self management

513. Bilandzic, D., et al. 1980 _The Role of the Public Sector in Developing Countries: Yugoslav National Report._ Ljubljana: ICPE. /Yugoslavia

514. Bilkey, Warren J. 1971 "Public Enterprise Models and a Caribbean Experience." _Inter-American Economic Affairs_ No. 25, pp. 39-55. /Caribbean Region /Evaluation /HC161 I585 LAC

515. Billimoria, R. P. 1967 "Joint Consultations in Tata Steel." _Indian Journal of Labour Economics_ (Bombay), pp. 104-115. /India /Worker management participation /Steel industry /331 0954 In2

516. Billimoria, R. P. 1975 "Human Resources Management." In R. C. Dutt and Raj K. Nigam, ed(s). _Towards Commanding Heights._ New Delhi: Vivek Joshi. pp. 176-189. /India /Personnel management /HD 4293 T68 PCL

517. Billimoria, R. P. 1978 "Steel Works in Developing Countries: Outside Participation (Non-Technical Aspects) - The Indian Experience." _Lok Udyog_ (New Delhi), V. 11, No. 10, pp. 9-18. /India /Steel industry /Multinational corporations /354.54 L836 PCL

518. Billimoria, R. P. 1980 "Management of Industrial Relations." _Lok Udyog_ (New Delhi), V. 14, No. 5, pp. 3-13. /Labor relations /Industrial relations /Personnel management /354.54 L836

519. Bird, Frederick L. 1949 _A Study of the Port of New York Authority._ New York: Dunn and Bradstreet. /United States of America /New York (State) /Port authority

520. Bird, Frederick L. 1949 "The Contribution of Authorities to Efficient Municipal Management." _The Authority_ pp. 2-5. /Local government /Public administration /Management /Public

authority

521. Bird, Richard. 1950 "Public Bodies and Public Accountability." Lloyd´s Bank Review V. 15, pp. 12-22. /Public authority /Public administration /Accountability /330.5 L779 PCL

522. Bird, Richard. 1980 "Central-Local Fiscal Relations and the Provision of Urban Public Services." Research Monograph No. 30. Canberra: Australian National University, Centre for Federal Financial Relations. /Australia /Public financing /Local government /Public services

523. Bird, T. A. 1953 "British Electricity 1952-53." Local Government Finance (London), pp. 278-280. /United Kingdom /Electrical utility industry

524. Bitar, S. 1974 "Efecto de las áreas de propiedad social y mixta en la industria chilena." El Trimestre Económico (Mexico City), V. 41, No. 163, pp. 543-567. /Chile /Industrial sector /Mixed enterprises /Worker self management /G330.972 T735

525. Bitar, S., and H. Trivelli. n.d. Cálculo de rentabilidades financieras y económicas de empresas industriales chilenas. Santiago, Chile: Centro de Planejamento. /Chile /Industrial sector /Financial performance /Profits

526. Bizaguet, A. 1967 Les entreprises publiques dans la Communauté Européenne. Paris: Dunod. No. 20. /European Economic Community /Evaluation

527. Bizaguet, A. 1973 "French Public Enterprises." The Evolution of the Public Enterprises in the Community of the Nine. Brussels: CEEP Editions. pp. 117-165. /France /Statistics /OPSS

528. Bizaguet, A., et al. 1964 Les banques de développement dans le monde. Paris: Dumond. /Development banks

529. Blagojevic, Borislov. 1970 "Algunas características de las empresas públicas en Yugoeslavia." La Empresa Pública. Zaragoza, Spain: Publicaciones del Real Colegio de España en Bolonia. pp. 1789-1806. /Yugoslavia /Evaluation

530. Blair, Calvin Pat. 1964 "Nacional Financiera: Entrepreneurship in a Mixed Economy." In Raymond Vernon, ed(s). Public Policy and Private Enterprise in Mexico. Cambridge, Mass.: Harvard University Press. pp. 191-240. /Mexico /Mixed enterprises /Credit policy /Entrepreneurial activity /G330.972 V598p

531. Blair, J. P. 1976 "The Politics of Government Pricing: Political Influences on Rate Structures of Publicly-Owned Electric Utilities." American Journal of Economics and Sociology V. 35, No. 1, pp. 31-36. /United States of America /Electrical utility industry /Price policy /330.5 Am311 PCL /H 1 A48 Pub Aff

532. Blair, T. L. 1969 The Land to Those Who Work it. Algeria's Experiment in Workers' Management. New York: Doubleday. /Algeria /Agricultural sector /Worker self management /HD 5660 A4 B55 1976

533. Blakenney, A. E. 1953 Saskatchewan's Crown Corporation, a Case Study. Ontario, Canada: Institute of Public Administration of Canada, Proceedings of 5th Annual Conference. /Canada /Evaluation / Case studies

534. Blanc, Georges. 1982 "Les entreprises multinationales publiques." Paper presented to the International colloquium "Les Multinationales en Mutation," Paris, 15-16 Nov. /Multinational corporations /OPSS

535. Blanco y Perez del Camino, Manuel. 1947 "El primer caso en la administración local de una empresa mixta immobiliaria." Revista de Estudios de la Vida Social (Madrid), No. 35, pp. 701-708. /Spain /Local government /Mixed enterprises

536. Bland, F. A. 1929 "The Administration of Government Enterprises." Economic Review V. 5, pp. 1-21. /Control process /Management

537. Blase, M. G., W. Gottman, and C. G.Mcnabb. 1972 "Public Water Supply Districts: Evaluation of a New Institution." Land Economics V. 48, No. 3, pp. 273-276. /United States of America /Water resources development / 305 J824 PCL

538. Bloch, Roger. 1964 L'entreprise remise en question. Entreprise publique. L'exemple des entreprises de transport en Europe Occidentale. Socialisation des économies européennes. Paris: Librairie générale de droit et de jurisprudence. /Europe /Socialization /Transportation industry /Evaluation /338.74 B62e

539. Bloch-Laine, F. 1964 "L'entreprise, ses téchniques et son Gouvernement. 1, L'entreprise et son environnement." Economie Appliquée (Paris), V. 17, No. 2-3, pp. 158-446. /Evaluation

540. Blonk, W. A. G., and M. E. Van der Linden. 1973 "Public Enterprises in the Netherlands." The Evolution of the Public Enterprises in the Community of the Nine. Brussels: CEEP Editions. pp. 265-287. /Netherlands /Statistics /OPSS

541. Blunt, M. E. 1964 "Place of Ideology in Nigerian Public Enterprise." Nigerian Journal of Economic and Social Studies (Ibadan, Nigeria), V. 6, pp. 333-350. /Nigeria /Evaluation /Political influence

542. Blunt, M. E. 1970 "State enterprise in Nigeria and Ghana. The end of an era?" African Affairs (London), V. 69, No. 274, pp. 27-43. /Nigeria /Ghana /Evaluation /Comparative analysis / Africa 960.5 Af82

543. Boada, C. 1973 El INI, sus realidades y su problemática. La empresa pública industrial en España: el INI. Madrid: Instituto de Estudios Fiscales. /Spain /Industrial sector

/Holding company

544. Boekmeyer, M. J. 1970 Yugoslav Workers' Self Management-Proceedings. Dordrecht, Holland: D. Reidel Publishing Co. /Yugoslavia /Worker self management

545. Boeninger, Edgardo, and Eduardo Palma. 1978 "Empresas estatales: El caso chileno y un análisis general." Paper presented at the Seminar on Planning Process in Latin America and Public Enterprises, Lima, Aug. /Chile /Economic history / OPSS

546. Boeren, J. A. 1961 "Energy Administration in the Netherlands." International Review of Administrative Sciences V. 2, No. 27. /Netherlands /Energy utility industry /Administrative management /JA 1 A1 I6 PCL

547. Bohm, Andreja. 1981 "The Concept, Definition and Classification of Public Enterprises." Public Enterprise V. 1, No. 4, pp. 72-78. /Taxonomy / OPSS

548. Boire, G. 1957 "The Paris Public Transport System." Annals of Collective Economy V. 28, pp. 322-333. /France /Mass transportation industry / 330.5 An73

549. Boiteux, M. 1956 "Sur la gestion des monopoles publiques astrients à l'équilibre budgetaire." Econometrica V. 24, No. 1, pp. 22-40. /Management /Economic theory /Economic policy /330.5 Ec74e

550. Boiteux, M. 1971 "On the Management of Public Monopolies Subject to Budgetary Constraints." Journal of Economic Theory V. 3, No. 3, pp. 219-240. /Management / Economic theory /Economic policy / 330.5 J8265

551. Boiteux, M. 1980 "Public Enterprise and Advanced Planning Techniques: The Experience of Electricité de France." In William J. Baumol, ed(s). Public and Private Enterprise in a Mixed Economy. New York: St. Martin's Press. pp. 97-111. /Management /Electrical utility industry /France /HD 3842 P87 PCL

552. Boiteux, M., et al. 1965 Le fonctionement des entreprises nationalisées en France. Paris: Ed. Dalloz. /France /Management

553. Boix Raspall, José María. 1965 "Incautación de empresas." Nueva Enciclopedia Jurídica. No. 12, pp. 131-133. /Law /Nationalization

554. Bokhari, Riyaz H. 1982 Subvention Policy and Practices for Public Enterprises. Ljubljana: ICPE. /Subsidization policy /Price policy

555. Boldrini, M. 1965 "State Intervention in the Economy." Indian Journal of Public Administration (New Delhi), V. 11, pp. 1-10. /India / JA 26 I55 Pub Aff

556. Boldyrev, B. G. 1970 "New Tendencies in the Development of the Soviet System of Payments of Industrial Enterprises into the Budget." Public Finance (The Hague), V. 25, No. 2, pp. 233-243. /Union of Soviet Socialist Reps. /Industrial sector /Budget record /336.05 Op2

557. Bolivia. Comisión Investigadora Nacional. 1965 "Daños y costos del sindicalismo al Comibol." Informe No. 4. /Mining industry /Bolivia /

558. Bolona Behr, Carlos. 1977 Las importaciones del sector público en el Perú: 1971-74. Lima, Peru: Universidad del Pacífico, Centro de Investigación. /Peru /Imports / OPSS

559. Bonavia, M. R. 1971 The Organization of British Railways. London: Ian Allan. /United Kingdom /Railway industry /Organization behavior /HE 3016 B63 PCL

560. Bonbright, J. C. 1961 Principles of Public Utility Rates. New York: Columbia University Press. /Public utility industry /Price policy /

561. Boneo, H. 1965 "El control de las empresas públicas." Revista de Administración Pública (Buenos Aires), /Control process /JA 5 R483 LAC

562. Boneo, H. 1968 La regulación de las empresas públicas. Buenos Aires: Centro de Investigaciones en Administración Pública, Instituto Torcuato Di Tella. /Law /Control process

563. Boneo, H. 1969 Las relaciones entre las empresas públicas y el gobierno central: Su efecto sobre la eficiencia. New York: UNDP. /Public administration /Control process /Economic efficiency

564. Boneo, H. 1973 La ampliación de la planta siderúrgica de Santa Ana: Un caso de decisión en empresa pública. Lima: Escuela Superior de Administración Pública. /Peru /Steel industry /Case studies /

565. Boneo, H. 1973 Las empresas públicas industriales en el Uruguay: Partes seleccionadas, selección no revisada. Montevideo: Presidencia de la República, Oficina Nacional del Servicio civil. /Uruguay /Industrial sector /HD 4123 B663 LAC

566. Boneo, H. 1974 Algunos aspectos esenciales a considerar en la estructuración de una compañía. Caracas: Comisión para la Reforma Integral de la Administración Pública. /Venezuela /Structural characteristics /Organization change

567. Boneo, H. 1974 Una propuesta para la reestructuración del sistema de empresas públicas venezolanas. Caracas: Comisión para la Reorganización de la Administración Pública. /Venezuela /Organization change

568. Boneo, H. 1974 Metodología de trabajo para la reorganización de la Corporación Venezolana de Fomento. Caracas: Comisión de Administración Pública. /Venezuela /Development

corporation /Structural characteristics /Organization change

569. Boneo, H. 1975 La regulación de las empresas públicas: Proyecto de investigación regional, sugerencias metodológicas. Caracas: CLAD. /Latin America /Regional development /Law /Methodology / HD 3850 B654 LAC

570. Boneo, H. 1976 "Políticas estatales y el sistema regulatorio: El problema de congruencia." Austin, Tex.: Paper presented at the Conference on Implementation in Latin America´s Public Sector, "Translating Policy into Reality," April. /Control process /Public administration /Law / OPSS

571. Boneo, H. 1978 "Las relaciones entre gobierno central y empresas públicas: Planteamiento del problema." In Horacio Boneo et al., ed(s). Gobierno y empresas públicas en América Latina. Buenos Aires: Ediciones SIAP. /Control process /Public administration / Latin America / OPSS

572. Boneo, H. 1978 "La regulación de las empresas públicas en América Latina." In Horacio Boneo et al., ed(s). Gobierno y empresas públicas en América Latina. Buenos Aires: Ediciones SIAP. /Law /Control process /Latin America / OPSS

573. Boneo, H. 1979 "Planificación, presupuesto y empresas públicas en América Latina." Paper presented at the First Latin American Conference on Public Policy, São Paulo. Buenos Aires: Centro Estudios de Estado y Sociedad. V. 2, No. 4. /Latin America /OPSS

574. Boneo, H. 1979 "Las empresas estatales en América Latina." Lima: Paper presented at the Seminar on The Planning Process in Latin America and Public Enterprises, August. /Latin America / OPSS

575. Boneo, H. 1979 Las empresas estatales en América Latina. Caracas: CLAD. /Latin America

576. Boneo, H. 1979 "Planificación, presupuesto y empresas públicas en América Latina." Estudios CEDES No. 2. /Latin America /Planning process /Budgetary process / HD 4010.5 B66 LAC

577. Boneo, H. 1979 "Regimenes Politicos Y Empresas Publicas." paper presented at the First Latin American Conference on Public Policy, São Paulo, December, 1979. /OPSS

578. Boneo, H. 1980 Saber ver las empresas públicas. San José, Costa Rica: Editorial Universitaria Centroamericana. /Planning process /Control process /Government authority /Law / OPSS

579. Boneo, H. 1980 "Political Regimes and Public Enterprises." paper presented at the Second BAPEG Conference: "Public Enterprise in Mixed Economy LDCs," Boston, April 1980. /Argentina /Management /Political role /OPSS

580. Boneo, H. 1980 "Regímenes políticos y empresas públicas: Algunas cuestiones vinculadas al ambito y dimemsión del

sector productivo estatal." Estudios CEDES V. 3, No. 7. /Argentina /Management /Political role /HD 4084 B65 LAC

581. Boneo, H. 1980 "Empresas estatales: Tres preconceptos y sus consecuencias." Revista Argentina de Administración Pública No. 3. /Argentina /Evaluation

582. Boneo, H. 1980 "Some Notes on the Definition and Taxonomy of Public Enterprises." Paper presented at the Expert Group Meeting on Concept, Definition and Classification of Public Enterprises, Tangier, Morocco. Ljubljana: ICPE. /Taxonomy

583. Boneo, H. 1980 Political Regimes and Public Enterprises. Austin, Tex.: OPSS Technical Papers Series No. 31. /Argentina /Management / Political Role / OPSS

584. Boneo, H. 1981 "Government Control over Public Enterprises in Latin America." Ljubljana: ICPE. /Latin America /Control process

585. Boneo, H. 1981 "On Goals, Planning, Controls and Evaluation: A Conceptual Overview." Paper presented at the Expert Group Meeting on Performance Criteria and the Implementation of Performance Evaluation Systems in Public Enterprises in Developing Countries, Ljubljana, Yugoslavia, 23-27 Nov. Ljubljana: ICPE. /Control process /Planning process /Evaluation

586. Boneo, H. 1981 "Las Empresas públicas en el proceso de desarrollo." Paper presented at the seminar on public enterprises in development planning for Central America and the Caribbean, San José, Costa Rica, 1-3 July. /Latin America /Economic development /Goal setting /State trading organizations /OPSS

587. Boneo, H. 1983 Government Control over Public Enterprises in Latin America. Ljubljana: ICPE. /Latin America /Control process

588. Boneo, H. 1983 "Government and Public Enterprise in Latin America." In G. Ram Reddy, ed(s). Government and Public Enterprise: Essays in honour of Professor V. V. Ramanadham. Bombay, India: N. M. Tripathi Private Limited. pp. 157-180. /Latin America /Government authority

589. Boneo, H. 1984 "Some Preliminary Thoughts on Privatization." Paper presented at the March 1-3 Conference "State Shrinking: A Comparative Inquiry into Privatization," Austin, Tex. /Argentina /Privatization /OPSS

590. Boneo, H., and Víctor García González. 1973 Las empresas públicas y la capacitación de su personal. Lima: ESAP, primer seminario sobre políticas de capacitación en empresas públicas. /Training

591. Boneo, H., et al. 1978 Gobierno y empresas públicas en América Latina: Seminario del Centro Latinoamericano de Administración para el Desarrollo. Buenos Aires: Ediciones SIAP. /Latin America

592. Boneschi, Luca. 1964 "Aspetti giuridici dell'intervento economico dello stato: Gli enti di coordinamento." Revista de Diritto Industriale (Milan, Italy), No. 3, pp. 213-270. /Italy /Law /Control process

593. Bonie, J. A. 1947 "Are Public Boards Efficient; Who Should Be on Them?" Industry (London), pp. 22-24. /United Kingdom /Business regulation policy /Control process

594. Bonilla, F. (Comp.) 1973 Sistema nacional de control de las empresas públicas. Lima: Editorial Mercurio. /Peru /Law /Control process /Peru 37 G746 Law

595. Bonnefous, E. 1977 Rapport d'information fait au nom de la Commission des Finances, du contrôle budgetaire et des comptes économimiques de la nation sur le contrôle des entreprises publiques en 1977 (filiales et prises de participation ....). Paris: Sénat. /France /Control process /Air transportation industry /Parliament / Automobile manufacturing industry / OPSS

596. Bonsignore, J. 1979 "El Estado y las empresas públicas en Uruguay." Revista Latinoamericana de Administración Pública (Mexico City), No. 8-9, pp. 81-94. /Uruguay /Control process /Productivity /Economic history / JL 974 R485 LAC

597. Boodhoo, Martin J. 1980 "An Action-Oriented Approach to the Concept and Classification of Public Enterprises." Paper presented at the Regional Workshop on Corporate Planning in Public Enterprises in the Asian and Pacific Region, Kuala Lumpur, Malaysia, 17-21 Nov. Ljubljana: ICPE. /Asia /Taxonomy / Also presented at the Expert Group Meeting on Concept, Definition, and Classification of Public Enterprises, Tangier, Morocco, Dec. 15-19, 1980.

598. Boodhoo, Martin J. 1980 "The Relevance of Management Information Systems to Corporate Planning in Public Enterprises." Paper presented at the Regional Workshop on Corporate Planning in Public Enterprises in Asian and Pacific Region, Kuala Lumpur, Malaysia, 17-21 Nov. Ljubljana: ICPE. /Planning process /Management /Information system

599. Boodhoo, Martin J. 1983 "Management Information Systems in Public Enterprise." In G. Ram Reddy, ed(s). Government and Public Enterprise: Essays in honour of Professor V. V. Ramanadham. Bombay, India: N. M. Tripathy Private Limited. pp. 113-126. /Information system

600. Boodhoo, Martin J., and J.-C. Kapur. 1979 "Public Enterprise Management: A Select Bibliography." London: Commonwealth Secretariat, Commonwealth Programme of Applied Studies in Government. /United Kingdom /British Commonwealth /Management /Control process / Bibliography

601. Boon, J., F. Mortiaux, and F. Hoosemans. 1958 "The Belgium National Broadcasting Corporations." Annals of Collective Economy V. 29, pp. 515-522. /Belgium /Broadcasting industry /330.5 An73

602. Booyer, R. 1957 "The Statutory Corporation as a Democratic Device." Public Administration (Sydney, Australia), pp. 29-36. /Australia /Law /Participatory democracy

603. Bopp, Karl R. 1946 "Nationalization of the Bank of England and the Bank of France." Journal of Politics V. 8, No. 3. pp. 308-318. /United Kingdom /France /Central banks /Nationalization / Comparative analysis / 320.5 J825

604. Bora, P. M. 1983 "Public Distribution System: An Instrument of State Policy in India." Paper presented at the 19th International Congress of Administrative Sciences, West Berlin, 19-23 Sept. /India /Food industry /OPSS

605. Bordier, L. 1952 Le champ d´application du statut du personnel des industries électriques et gazières. Paris: Droit Social. /France /Electrical utility industry /Gas utility industry / Personnel management /Law

606. Borella, F. 1966 "Le droit publique économique de l´Algérie." Revue Algerienne des Sciences Juridiques Politiques et Economiques (Algiers), No. 3, pp. 499-562. /Algeria /Law

607. Borella, François. 1969 "Les entreprises publiques en Algérie depuis l´independence." Perspectivas del Derecho Público en La Segunda Mitad del Siglo XX. (Madrid), /Algeria

608. Bornstein, M. 1962 "The Soviet Price System." American Economic Review V. 52, No. 1, pp. 64-103. /Union of Soviet Socialist Reps. /Price policy / 330.5 Am312

609. Bornstein, M. 1969 "The Soviet Debate on Agricultural Price and Procurement Reforms." Soviet Studies V. 21, No. 1, pp. 1-20. /Union of Soviet Socialist Reps. /Agricultural sector /Price policy / 947.005 So89

610. Borrani Williams, Jorge. 1982 Empresas públicas en el Perú. Austin, Tex.: OPSS Technical Papers Series, No. 37. /Peru /OPSS

611. Borrel y Macia, José. 1946 El intervencionalismo del Estado en las actividades económicas. Barcelona, Spain: Ed. Bosh. /Spain

612. Bortolani, Sergio. 1975 Central Banking in Africa. Milan, Italy: Cassa di Resparnio delle Provincie Lombarde. /Africa /Central Banks /Financial institutions

613. Bos, Dieter. 1981 Economic Theory of Public Enterprise. New York: Springer-Verlag. /Economic theory /HD 3850 B68 PCL

614. Bosa, G. 1966 Uganda Credit and Savings Bank. Makerere, Uganda: Institute of Social Research. /Uganda /Credit policy /Financial institutions / East Africa

615. Boskey, Shirley. 1959 Problems and Practices of Development Banks. Baltimore, Md.: Johns Hopkins University Press, for the International Bank for Reconstruction and Development.

/Development banks / HG 4517 B6 Pub Aff 332.66 B 652p

616. Botchwey, Kwesi. 1979 "The Political Economy of Public Enterprise in Ghana." Council for the Development of Economic and Social Research in Africa, Project on the Public Sector and Development. /Ghana /Political economy

617. Botswana. Central Statistics Office. 1974 "An Economic Analysis of Government Industries, 1972-1973." (Gaborone). /Botswana /Economic analysis

618. Boulin, R. 1977 _La politique du gouvernement à l'égard des entreprises publiques._ Paris: Ministère de l'Economie et des Finances. /France /Control process

619. Boulois, Jean. 1952 "A propos de la responsabilité des administrateurs délégués de l'Etat dans les sociétés d'économie mixte." _Revue de Science et Legislation Financière_ (Paris), /Accountability /Mixed enterprises

620. Boulois, Jean. 1953 "Régime des biens et statut financier des entreprises nationalisées." _Jurisclasseur Administratif_ (Paris), No. 158. /France /Public financing /Law

621. Boulois, Jean. 1953 _Le personnel des entreprises nationalisées._ _Jurisclasseur Administratif_ (Paris), pp. 2-30. /France /Personnel management

622. Boulois, Jean. 1953 "Les opérations de nationalisation." _Jurisclasseur Administratif_ (Paris), No. 155. /France /Nationalization

623. Boulois, Jean. n.d. "L'Activité des entreprises nationalisées." _Jurisclasseur Administratif_ (Paris), /France

624. Boulois, Jean. n.d. "Régime et organisation générale des entreprises nationalisées." _Jurisclasseur Administratif_ (Paris), /France /Public administration /Structural characteristics

625. Bourgault, Jacques. 1983 "Le processus de nomination des dirigeants d'entreprises publiques comme instrument du contrôle gouvernemental: le cas du Québec." Paper presented at the 19th International Congress of Administrative Sciences, West Berlin, 19-23 Sept. /Control process /Quebec, Canada (Province) /Economic history /Autonomy /Law /OPSS

626. Bourne, Compton. 1981 "Issues of Public Financial Enterprise in Jamaica: The Case of the Jamaica Development Bank." _Economic and Social Studies_ (Mona, Kingston, Jamaica), V. 30, No. 1, pp. 197-208. /Caribbean Region /Jamaica /Case studies /Development banks /G330.97292 So13 LAC

627. Bousoumah, M. 1980 "L'Entreprise industrielle socialiste en Algérie." Ph.D. dissertation, Université de Nancy II. /Algeria /Control process / Personnel management / OPSS

628. Bradbury, Katharine L., Phillip I. Moss, and Joseph S. Slavet. 1976 "Shifting Local Services to the State:

Boston." National Tax Journal V. 29, No. 1, pp. 95-107. /United States of America /Public services /Tax reform /HJ101 N3 Pub Aff /336.205 N213 PCL

629. Bradley, A. W., and J. P. W. B. McAuslan. 1970 "Public Corporations in East Africa." In W. G. Friedmann and J. F. Garner, ed(s). Government Enterprise: A Comparative Perspective. New York: Colombia University Press. /Tanzania /Kenya /Uganda / East Africa / 350.0092 G746

630. Bradshaw, K. A. 1950 Parliament and the Public Corporation. Cambridge: Cambridge Journal. /United Kingdom /Parliament

631. Braga, Carlos Alberto Primo. 1980 "Siderugia no Brasil: História e análise da competividade internacional do setor nos anos 70." Master´s thesis, Universidade de São Paulo. /Brazil /Steel industry

632. Braga, L. 1964 "Sociedade de economia mista, natureza, personalidade jurídica e regime tributário." Revista de Direito da Procuradoria Geral (Rio de Janeiro), V. 12, No. 12, pp. 81-488. /Brazil /Law /Public financing /Mixed enterprises

633. Braibant, G. 1979 "Las relaciones entre el Estado y las empresas públicas." Revista Latinoamericana de Administración Pública No. 8-9, pp. 95-100. /France /Control process / JL 974 R485 LAC

634. Branch, Brian. 1981 "Change and Continuity in the Peruvian Public Sector." Austin, Tex.: unpublished M.A. thesis, ILAS. /Peru /Privatization

635. Branch, Brian. 1982 Public Enterprises in Peru: The Perspectives for Reform. Austin, Tex.: OPSS Technical Papers Series, No. 37. /Peru /Privatization / OPSS

636. Branchon, Jacques. 1970 "La réforme des entreprises publiques." Entreprise (Paris), No. 755, pp. 88-97. /France

637. Brand, R. H. 1949 "Nationalization." Lloyd´s Bank Review V. 12, pp. 1-11. /Nationalization

638. Brandão Cavalcanti, T. 1973 "Empresas públicas e sociedades da economia mista." Revista de Ciencias Políticas (Rio de Janeiro), V. 7, No. 4, pp. 35-52. /Brazil /Mixed enterprises

639. Brandenbusch, W. 1966 Funktion und Rechtliche Ausgestaltung der Arbeitnehmermitwirkung in Arbeitsgesetzbuch Mitteldentschlands-Mainz. Mainz: Universitat, Rechts-Wirtschaftswissenschaftliche Fakultaet. /Germany, Federal Rep. of /Law /Labor relations

640. Brandt, H. 1959 Die Finanzierung der Staatlichen Sozialistischen Industriebetriebe. Berlin: Volk und Vissem. /Germany, Democratic Rep. of /Public financing /Socialist economy / Industrial sector

641. Brandt, H. 1959 _Financing the State Socialist Industrial Enterprise._ Berlin: Volk und Wissen. /Germany, Democratic Rep. of /Industrial sector /Financing

642. Branger, Jacques. 1959 _Etude sur les participations financières de l´Etat: Rapport du Conseil Economique._ Paris: Conseil Economique. /France /Public financing /Investment

643. Brasdefer, Gloria, et al. 1976 _Las empresas públicas en México: Su importancia en el sector industrial y comercial; bases jurídicas de su acción._ Mexico City: Instituto Nacional de Administración Pública. /Mexico /Industrial sector /Commercial sector / Law / HD 4013 E475 LAC

644. Bratus, S. N. 1953 "El contrato económico como forma legal de la distribución de la producción entre las empresas estatales." _Bravo_ pp. 74-88. /Productivity /Planning process /Law

645. Bravo, Víctor. 1981 "La política petrolera." _Realidad Económica_ V. 44, pp. 93-109. /Oil industry /Argentina /HC 171 R424 LAC

646. Brazil. Conferencia Nacional de Administração Pública. 1963 "Categorias de empresas públicas no direito brasileiro." _Atualidades Administrativas_ (Rio de Janeiro), V. 5, No. 17, pp. 5-74. /Brazil /Law /Taxonomy

647. Brazil. Departamento de Imprensa Nacional. 1952 _Os fundamentos da Petrobrás._ Rio de Janeiro. /Brazil /Oil industry

648. Brazil. FGV. Instituto Brasileiro de Economia. 1972 _Atividade empresarial dos governos estaduais._ Rio de Janeiro. V. 1. /Brazil /State government

649. Brazil. Instituto de Planejamento Econômico e Social. 1976 _Aspectos da participação do governo na economia._ Rio de Janeiro. /Brazil /Mixed enterprises /Planning process /HC 187 A788 LAC

650. Brazil. Ministerio da Minas e Energia. 1983 "Estrutura tarifária de referência para energia elétrica." Paper presented at the ECLA seminar: "State Control and Planning of Public Enterprises," Brasília, 15-17 June. Brasília: UNECLA. /Brazil /Electrical utility industry /Price policy /OPSS

651. Brazil. Secretaria de Obras Públicas (Guanabara). 1967 _Uma nova política salarial. Modernos métodos gerenciais aplicados a empresas públicas._ Rio de Janeiro. /Brazil /Wages /Incentive systems

652. Brazil. Secretariat for Control of State Enterprises. (SEST) 1981 _State Enterprises in Brazil and the Control of SEST: Backgroud and 1980 Results._ Brasília. /Brazil /Control process /Economic history /Decision making process /Budgetary process / OPSS

653. Bredi, Jean-Denis. 1957 L'Entreprise semi-publique et publique et le droit privé. Paris: Librairie générale de droit et de jurisprudence. /France /Mixed enterprises /Law

654. Brekic, Jovo. 1977 "System of the Development of Cadres in Public Enterprises." Paper presented at the International Seminar on Management and Training in Public Enterprises in Developing Countries, Ljubljana, Yugoslavia, 10-18 Oct. Ljubljana: ICPE. /Training /Management /Also presented at similar conference at Ljubljana, Yugoslavia from Sep. 18 to Oct. 6, 1978.

655. Brenna, A. 1968 "Impresa pubblica e programmazione economica in Italia." Relazioni Social V. 8, No. 2, pp. 172-192. /Italy /Planning process

656. Bresser Pereira, Luiz C. 1982 "State Expenditures, Distribution, and Value." Paper presented at the 10th National Meeting of the Latin American Studies Association, Washington, D.C., 4-6 March. /Brazil /Political analysis /OPSS

657. Brewer-Carías, Allan-Randolph. 1967 Las empresas públicas en el derecho comparado: Estudio sobre el régimen de las actividades industriales y comerciales del Estado. Caracas: Universidad Central de Venezuela, Facultad de Derecho. /Venezuela /Industrial sector /Public administration /Law /Comparative analysis

658. Brewer-Carías, Allan-Randolph. 1978 "Algunos aspectos jurídicos de las relaciones entre el gobierno central y las empresas del Estado." Gobierno y empresas públicas en América Latina. Buenos Aires: SIAP. pp. 151-184. /Law /Control process /OPSS

659. Brewer-Carías, Allan-Randolph. 1978 "Las empresas públicas y las empresas privadas en el sistema económico venezolano." Paper presented at the Latin American Conference of Public Administration, Mexico City, Nov. /Venezuela /Law /OPSS

660. Brewer-Carías, Allan-Randolph. 1980 "Las empresas públicas y las empresas privadas en el sistema económico venezolano." Revista Latinoamericana de Administración Pública No. 10-1, pp. 609-632. /Venezuela / Private enterprises /Comparative analysis /JL 974 R485 LAC

661. Brewer-Carías, Allan-Randolph. 1980 "Régimen jurídico de las empresas públicas en Venezuela." (Caracas: Ed. Art). /Venezuela /Law / HD 4133 B73 1980 LAC

662. Brewer-Carías, Allan-Randolph. 1981 "Aspectos organizativos de la industria petrolera nacionalizada en Venezuela." Archivo de Derecho Público y Ciencias de la Administración. V. 3, pp. 407-491. /Venezuela /Oil industry /Control process /Law

663. Briceno, R. 1981 "El control de gestión." Revista de Control Fiscal (Mexico City), No. 100, pp. 39-43. /Control process /Management G336.87 C7685 LAC

664. Bricola, Franco. 1970 "El derecho penal de la empresa pública." La empresa pública. Zaragoza, Spain: Publicaciones del Real Colegio de España en Bolonia. pp. 551-686. /Law

665. Briere, J. 1969 "Les nationalisations et la gestion démocratique comme base de la democracie réelle sur la voie du socialisme." Economie et Politique (Paris), No. 182, pp. 3-87. /Nationalization /Political analysis

666. Briere, J. 1969 "Les nationalisations, pour une démocracie avancée." Economie et Politique (Paris), No. 179, pp. 19-34. /Nationalization

667. Briseno Sierra, Humberto. 1970 "La empresa estatal en México." La Empresa Pública. Zaragoza, Spain: Publicaciones del Real Colegio de España en Bolonia. pp. 1839-1858. /Mexico /Evaluation

668. Bristow, J. A. 1966 "State Enterprises in the Republic of Ireland." Annals of Public and Cooperative Economy V. 37, No. 1, pp. 25-41. /Ireland /Cooperatives / 330.5 An73

669. Bristow, J. A. 1969 "The Public and Cooperative Sectors in Ireland." Annals of Public and Cooperative Economy pp. 347-371. /Ireland /Cooperatives / 330.5 An73

670. Bristow, J. A., and C. F. Fell. 1971 "Bord Na Mona: A Cost-Benefit Study." /Ireland /Cost benefit analysis /Evaluation

671. British Institute of Management. 1950 Management Efficiency in Nationalized Undertakings. London: British Institute of Management. /United Kingdom /Management /Economic efficiency /Evaluation

672. Brochard, P. 1952 "Nationalisation et cogestion." Revue de l'Action Populaire (Paris), pp. 525-553. /Nationalization /Worker management participation /

673. Broderick, John P. 1972 "Banco de Fomento, the First Thirty Years: A Case History/The Government Development Bank for Puerto Rico." San Juan, P. R.: Government Development Bank for Puerto Rico. /Puerto Rico /Development banks /Economic history /Case studies

674. Bronde, Henry W. 1959 "The Role of the State in American Economic Development, 1820-1890." In Hugh G. J. Aitken, ed(s). The State and Economic Growth. New York: Social Science Research Council. pp. 4-25. /United States of America /Economic development /Economic history /338.91 C763

675. Bronstein, Arturo (ed.) 1981 Las relaciones laborales en las empresas estatales de América Latina. Geneva: ILO. /Mexico /Peru /Venezuela /Trade unions /Labor relations /Oil industry / HD 8013 L29 B76

676. Bronstein, Arturo. 1981 "Las relaciones laborales en las empresas estatales de América Latina:" Estudio comparativo." In Arturo Bronstein, ed(s). Las relaciones laborales en las

empresas estatales de América Latina. Geneva: ILO. pp. 1-103. /Labor relations /Latin America / HD 8013 L29 B76

677. Brook, W. F. 1944 "The German TVA." Land Economics V. 20, pp. 217-222. /Germany, Federal Rep. of /Regional planning /305 J824 PCL

678. Broseta Pont, Manuel. 1966 "Las empresas públicas en forma de sociedades anónimas." Revista de Derecho Mercantil No. 100, pp. 267-290. /Evaluation / 347.7 R327 LAC

679. Brown, Adlith. 1981 "Issues of Public Enterprise." Social and Economic Studies (Mona, Kingston, Jamaica), V. 30, No. 1, pp. 1-16. /Caribbean Region /Financial performance /G330.97292 So13 LAC

680. Brown, E. C. 1966 Soviet Trade Unions and Labor Relations. Cambridge, Mass.: Harvard University Press. /Union of Soviet Socialist Reps. /Trade unions /Labor relations /HD 6732 B7

681. Brown, Gardner, Jr., and M. Bruce Johnson. 1969 "Public Utility Pricing and Output under Risk." American Economic Review V. 59, pp. 119-128. /United States of America /Price policy / 330.5 Am312 PCL

682. Brown, J. C. 1969 The Role of Public Enterprises in Mauritius. Mauritius: UNECA Seminar on Role of Public Enterprises in Planning and Plan Implementation, Sep. 16-26. /Mauritius /Evaluation

683. Bruce, M. 1981 "Evaluation of the British Airways Airline Management Workshop." Paper presented at the Regional Workshop on the Evaluation of Training Packages for Public Enterprise Managers, Bangkok, Thailand, 10-14 Aug. Ljubljana: ICPE. /United Kingdom /Air transportation industry /Training / Management /Efficacy

684. Bruckmeyer, M. J. 1970 "Proceedings of Amsterdam Symposium." Yugoslav Workers´ Self Management. Dordrecht, Netherlands: D. Riedel. /Yugoslavia /Worker self management

685. Brugarola, M. 1961 "Nacionalización de las empresas o capitalismo popular?" Mundo Social (Madrid), pp. 163-170. /Nationalization

686. Brulle, D. 1965 "La democracie économique dans les entreprises nationatisées britanniques et françaises." Annales d´Economie Collective pp. 513-548. /United Kingdom /France /Participatory democracy

687. Brunella, D. 1969 "La administración de las empresas públicas: La experiencia de YPF." Paper presented at the meeting of experts on Administration in Latin America and the Caribbean, Santiago, Chile, 17-22 Nov. ST/ECLA/Conf.35/L.4 /Argentina /Oil industry /Case studies

688. Brzezinski, W. 1966 Le système de l´économie planifiée et la place de l´entreprise nationale dans ce système. Paris: International Political Science Association. Documentation

of the Jablonna Round Table Meetings, 19-24 Sep. 1966. /Planning process

689. Buck, J. de. 1965 "Les nationalisations en Syrie." Correspondence d'Orient; Etudes (Brussels), No. 7, pp. 61-67. /Syria /Nationalization

690. Buckingham, W. S., Jr. 1953 "Compensation and Profits in British Nationalized Industries." Journal of Finance V. 8, pp. 422-435. /United Kingdom /Profits /Wages /332.05 J827 PCL

691. Buczkowski, S. 1966 "La position de l'entreprise d'état dans l'appareil de l'état et dans la circulation économique." Paris: International Political Science Association. Documentation of the Jablonna Round Table Meetings. 19-24 Sep. 1966. pp. 19-24. /Evaluation /Control process

692. Budhiraja, S. B. 1977 "Multi-Purpose Distribution Centres of Indian Oil - A New Concept in Rural Marketing." Lok Udyog (New Delhi), V. 11, No. 6, pp. 7-10. /India /Oil industry /Rural development /Marketing /Retail trade /Case studies /354.54 L836 PCL

693. Bueno, Gerardo M. n.d. El financiamiento de la creación y la operación de empresas públicas industriales en México. Santiago, Chile: UNECLA. /Mexico /Industrial sector /Public financing

694. Bukhari, Bukhari Mahmoud. 1980 "Development of Training Methodologies for Internal Consultants in African Public Enterprises: Sudanese Case." Paper presented at the Regional Workshop on Development of Training Methodologies for Internal Consultants in African Public Enterprises, Addis Ababa, Ethiopia, 1-6 Dec. Ljubljana: ICPE. /Sudan /Training /Methodology /Consultant services / Case studies

695. Bukovic, Janez, et al. 1978 "Programmes for Training of Managers and Specialists in Public Enterprises." Paper presented at the International Seminar on Management and Training in Public Enterprises in Developing Countries, Ljubljana, Yugoslavia, Sept. 18 - Oct. 6. Ljubljana: ICPE. /Training /Management /Also presented at a similar seminar in Ljubljana, Yugoslavia, Oct. 10-28, 1977.

696. Bukow, W. 1965 "Les entreprises publiques dans la République Fédérale d'Allemagne." Annales de l'Economie Collective V. 53, No. 1, pp. 7-15. /Germany, Federal Rep. of /Evaluation

697. Bulhoes, O. G. de. 1969 "O Estado como empresário." Visão (Rio de Janeiro), V. 34, No. 12. /Brazil / G056.81 V82

698. Bullard, F. J. 1968 Mexico's Natural Gas. Austin, Tex.: UT Press. /Mexico /Gas utility industry /G338.09806 T312s

699. Bulme, H. 1971 Organizational Aspects of Agro-Industrial Development Agencies. Munich: Weltform Verlag. /Germany, Federal Rep. of /Agricultural sector /Industrial sector

700. Bunbury, Henry. 1944 "The Public Corporations." Public Administration (London), No. 3, pp. 137-142. /United Kingdom /320.5 J826 PCL /JA 8 P8 Pub Aff

701. Bunge, A. 1933 La guerra del petróleo en la Argentina. Buenos Aires. /Argentina /Nationalization /Oil industry /Economic history / G338.2 B883g

702. Buonocuore, Vincenzo. 1970 "Las sociedades con participación del Estado: Reseña de la doctrina italiana." La empresa pública. Zaragoza, Spain: Real Colegio de España en Bolonia. pp. 1667-1706. /Italy /Law /Mixed enterprises

703. Buract, I. K. 1969 Problems of Control on Public Sector. Cairo Al-Ahram. /Egypt /Control process

704. Burdett, E. W. 1906 "Municipal Ownership in Great Britain." Journal of Political Economy V. 14, pp. 257-314. /United Kingdom /Local government / 330.5 J82

705. Burgierman, Nelson. 1976 "Modelo de simulação económica-financiera da Companhia Paulista de Fôrça e Luz." Rio de Janeiro: FGV-EIAP. /Brazil /Electrical utility industry /Simulation / OPSS

706. Burgierman, Nelson. 1979 "Modelo de simulación económico-financiera de la Compañía Paulista de Fuerza y Luz." In EIAP-FGV, ed(s). Administración de empresas públicas. Mexico City: Editorial Limusa. pp. 523-546. /Electrical utility industry /Simulation /Brazil /HD 3850 A333 LAC

707. Burkhead, J. 1954 "Le contrôle des entreprises publiques dans les pays économiquement avancés et dans les pays sous développés." Cahiers Economiques /Developed nations /Developing nations /Control process

708. Burkhead, Jesse. 1971 "A elaboração orçamentária e o contrôle da empresa pública." Orçamento Público (Rio de Janeiro), pp. 521-556. /Brazil /Control process

709. Buru, Duncan. 1951 "The National Coal Board." Lloyd's Bank Review (London), No. 19, pp. 33-45. /United Kingdom /Coal mining industry /Management

710. Bustamante, Alberto, et al. 1977 "Propiedad social: Modelo y realidad; Manual para trabajadores de base." Lima: Centro de Estudios y Promoción del Desarrollo. /Peru /Worker self management /HD 5660 P4 P757 LAC

711. Bustamante, E. 1962 "Control de las empresas del Estado." Revista de Economía (Mexico City), V. 25, No. 9, pp. 346-350. /Mexico /Control process

712. Bustamante, Luis. 1981 "El sistema de relaciones laborales en las empresas del sector público en el Perú." In Arturo Bronstein, ed(s). Las relaciones laborales en las empresas públicas de América Latina. Geneva: ILO. pp. 107-133. /Peru /Labor relations / HD 8013 L29 B76

713. Busto, Armando. 1978 "Asignación de recursos en las empresas públicas y privadas." Paper presented at the 4th General Assembly of the Latin American Association of Public Administration, Mexico City, 6-11 Nov. /Financing /Private enterprises /Comparative analysis /OPSS

714. Butlin, N. G. 1950 "Public Enterprise in Australian Economic Development, 1860-1880." *Explorations in Entrepreneurial History* V. 2, pp. 141-158. /Australia /Economic history /Economic development

715. Buttgenbach, A. 1964 *La nozione di impresa pubblica secondo l'Art. 90 del Tratado Istituto del Mercato Commune Europeo: Il colloquio di Bruxelles sulla concorrenza tra settore pubblico e privato nella C.E.E.* Milan, Italy. /European Economic Community /Law

716. Butts, John D. de. 1971 "The Management of Complexity." *Public Utility Fortnightly* V. 88, No. 9. /United States of America /Management

717. Bye, R. T. 1929 "Composite Demand and Joint Supply in Relation to Public Utility Rates." *Quarterly Journal of Economics* V. 44, pp. 40-62. /Price policy /Public utility industry / 330.5 Q2 PCL

718. Bye, Vegard. 1979 "Nationalization of Oil in Venezuela: Re-defined Dependence and Legitimization of Imperialism." Lund, Sweden: Prepared for the Nordic Symposium on Development Strategies in Latin America and the New International Economic Order. /Venezuela /Oil industry /Nationalization / OPSS

719. Byrnes, T. J. 1983 "Profitability vis-à-vis the Public Interest: A New Approach." Paper presented at the 19th International Congress of Administrative Sciences, West Berlin, 19-23 Sept. /Profits /Ireland /Law /Financial performance /Public interest /OPSS

720. CAFRAD. 1969 *Memorandum on the Organisation and Management of Public Enterprises in Africa.* Tangier, Morocco: CAFRAD. /Africa /Management

721. CDES. Centro de Documentación Económica-Social. 1965 *Las empresas estatales en el Perú.* Lima: CDES. /Peru /Economic history / G380.1622 C333e

722. CEEP. 1971 *L'entreprise publique, élément dynamique de la politique industrielle.* Proceedings of the Fifth Congress of CEEP, Rome, 27-28 May. Ghent, Belgium: Imprimeris Erasmus Ledeberg. /European Economic Community

723. CIRIEC. 1964 "Le imprese pubbliche a la cooperazione in Italia." *Edizioni di Communita* (Milan, Italy), /Italy

724. CLAD. 1974 "Corporación Dominicana de Empresas Estatales (CORDE)." Paper presented at the Latin American seminar "Las empresas públicas y sus relaciones con el gobierno central." CLAD/SEM 1/D 14/74. Caracas: CLAD. /Dominican Republic

/Holding company

725. CLAD. 1976 Las Empresas Públicas en América Latina (Versión Preliminar). Caracas: CLAD. /Latin America /OPSS /Final version published in 1979

726. CLAD. 1978 "Informe final del seminario sobre la gestión de las empresas públicas de América Latina e Italia." Rome. /Latin America /OPSS

727. CLAD. 1979 "Primer coloquio sobre experiencias en reforma administrativa: Estrategias y metodologías." Mexico City: INAP. /Latin America /Administrative reform

728. Caballero Ortíz, J. 1980 "El control ejercido por la Contraloría General sobre las empresas públicas." Revista de Control Fiscal (Caracas), No. 99, pp. 121-138. /Control process /Venezuela

729. Cabral, L. F. R. 1974 "Productivity in Indian Airlines - A Preliminary Comparative Study." Lok Udyog (New Delhi), V. 7, No. 11, pp. 47-60. /India /Air transportation industry /Productivity /354.54 L836 PCL

730. Cabral, Nuno. 1981 "Criteria for the Control of Public Enterprises." Annals of Public and Cooperative Economy V. 51, No. 1-2, pp. 27-48. /Control process /330.5 An73

731. Cabrera, J. G. 1966 The Role of Public Enterprise in Bolivia´s Agricultural Development. Leeds, England: Seminar Essay, Social Studies Department, University of Leeds. /Bolivia /Agricultural development /Agricultural sector

732. Cadbury, G. W. 1955 "Public Enterprises in the Province of Saskatchewan." In A. H. Hanson, ed(s). Public Enterprise. Brussels: IIAS. pp. 110-118. /Canada /Saskatchewan, Canada (Province) / HD 3850 H28 Law

733. Cadic, Jean-Yves. 1979 "Le contrat de programme: Essai de rationalisation de la gestion des entreprises publiques." L´Actualité Juridique - Droit Administratif (20 Dec.) No. 12, pp. 12-27. /France /Management /Control process /Financing / Contractual relations

734. Caetano, Marcello. 1970 "Empresas públicas." Manual de Direito Administrativo. Rio de Janeiro: Forense. pp. 345-348. /Brazil /Evaluation /Law

735. Cagno, V. A. 1965 "La nazionalizzazione dell´industria elettrica in Italia." Revue Française de l´Energie (Paris), V. 16, No. 167, pp. 192-204. /Italy /Electrical utility industry /Nationalization

736. Cahen Salvador, Jean. 1945 "La régie nationale des usines Renault." Droit Social (Paris), /France /Management

737. Callanan, Brian. 1983 "The Work of Shannon Free Airport Development Company." Paper presented at the 19th International Congress of Administrative Sciences, West

Berlin, 19-23 Sept. /Ireland /Air transportation industry /OPSS

738. Callendar, Guy S. 1902 "The Early Transportation and Banking Enterprises of the States in Relation to the Growth of Corporations." Quarterly Journal of Economics V. 17, pp. 111-162. /United States of America /Transportation industry /Banking system / Economic history / 330.5 Q2 PCL

739. Calvo, E. 1971 Estadísticas generales de un grupo de empresas públicas chilenas. Santiago, Chile: CEPAL/ILPES. /Chile /Statistics

740. Camargo Pinuelas, S. 1964 "Nationalization of Resources." Revista de Economía (Mexico City), V. 27, No. 9, pp. 265-272. /Mexico /Nationalization

741. Camejo, Enrique. 1980 "La empresa pública en Cuba." Ljubljana: ICPE. /Cuba

742. Campbell, W. J. 1952 "The Statutory Corporation in New South Wales." Public Administration (Sydney, Australia), pp. 108-118. /Australia /Development corporation / New South Wales, Australia(State)

743. Campbell, W. J. 1955 "New South Wales." In A. H. Hanson, ed(s). Public Enterprise. Brussels: IIAS. pp. 492-500. /Australia /New South Wales, Australia(State) / HD 3850 H28 Law

744. Campo Pamliega, J. 1962 "The Public Sector and Spanish Economy, 1954-1957." Revista de Economía Política (Madrid), No. 30, pp. 95-112. /Spain /Economic development

745. Campo, Walter E., and José Estevez Paulos. 1976 Problemas jurídicos tributarios suscitados por las empresas binacionales. Montevideo: COMCORDE. /Law /Multinational corporations /HD 69 I7 C347 LAC

746. Campos Rivera, Jorge. 1977 Las exportaciones del sector público en el Perú: 1972-1975. Lima: Centro de Investigación de la Universidad del Pacífico. /Peru /Exports / OPSS

747. Campos, Roberto de Oliveira. 1966 "O diálogo entre a empresa pública e a empresa privada." Digesto Económico (São Paulo), V. 22, No. 190, pp. 11-19. /Brazil /Private sector /G330.981 D569 LAC

748. Canada. Dominion Bur. of Stat. Pub. Fin. & Trans. Div. Pub. Fin. Section. 1962 Financial Statistics of Federal Government Enterprises, 1958, 1959, and 1960. Ottawa, Canada: Queens Printer. /Canada /Public financing /Statistics

749. Candiani, M. 1959 "Le imprese pubbliche nello sviluppo economico." L'Impresa Pubblica (Rome), pp. 294-298. /Italy /Economic development

750. Canessa, J. V. 1957 La verdad sobre el petróleo argentino. (Buenos Aires). /Argentina /Oil industry

751. Cannan, E. 1899 "Ought Municipal Enterprises to be Allowed to Yield a Profit." Economic Journal V. 9, pp. 1-9. /Price policy /Profits /Local government / 330.5 Ec7

752. Cannegieter, C. A. 1957 The Capital Structure of the Electricity Corporation of Nigeria. Sessional Paper. Lagos: Government Printer. No. 3. /Nigeria /Electrical utility industry /Investment /Africa

753. Cannegieter, C. A. 1968 Los aspectos humanos de la lucha entre la empresa privada y la empresa pública. Monterrey, Mexico. No. 9, pp. 549-564. /Mexico /Private sector

754. Cannon, C. M. 1966 "The Limited Application of Minimum Profitability Requirement to Capital Expenditure Proposals." Journal of Industrial Economics (London), pp. 54-65. /Profits /Investment / 330.5 J81

755. Capek, Darel. 1970 "La empresa del Estado en Checoslovaquia." La Empresa Pública. Zaragoza, Spain: Publicaciones del Real Colegio de España en Bolonia. pp. 1289-1304. /Czechoslovakia

756. Capo, G. 1952 "Legislative Control of Works and Public Service Contracts." Economia (Rome), V. 9, No. 2, pp. 5-50. /Control process /Public services /Legislature /Contractual relations

757. Caraballo, G., Jr. 1965 "La empresa del Estado en la República Argentina." Revista de Administración Pública (Buenos Aires), V. 5, No. 19, pp. 9-95. /Argentina /Law /JA 5 R483 LAC

758. Carballo Millan, Rogelio. 1981 "Basic Concepts of Government Control for Public Enterprises." Paper presented at the International Workshop on Financial Profitability and Losses in Public Enterprises, Ljubljana, Yugoslavia, 1-5 June. Ljubljana: ICPE. /Control process

759. Cardenas, K. G. 1979 La gestion administrative et le financement de las SNIAS (Société Nationale Industrielle Aérospatiale. Paris: Université de Paris. /France /Air transportation industry /Control process /Investment /Economic history /OPSS

760. Cardon, Ruben C. A. 1981 "New Dimensions in Modern Government Auditing." International Journal of Government Auditing V. 8, No. 2, pp. 7-10; 15. /Latin America /Budget auditing

761. Carey Jones, N. S. 1971 "The Impact of Planning and Public Enterprise on Public Administration and Measures for Administrative Reform." Paper presented at the Interregional Seminar on Major Administrative Reforms in Developing Countries, 25 Oct. - 2 Nov. /Public administration /Administrative reform /Planning process

762. Carey Jones, N. S., S. M.Patankar, and M. J. Boodhoo. 1974 Politics, Public Enterprise and the Industrial Development Agency: Industrialization Policies and Practices. London: Croom Helm. /Industrialization

763. Caria, E. 1969 La tutela della libertá di concorrenza nella C.E.E. con particolare riguardo alle imprese pubbliche. Milan, Italy: CIRIEC. /European Economic Community /Law

764. Carlson, Sune. 1960 "Management of State-Owned Industries: Some Scandinavian Experiences." Skandinaviska Banken Quarterly Review pp. 81-90. /Scandinavia /Management

765. Carlston, Kenneth S. 1958 "Concession Agreements and Nationalization." American Journal of International Law V. 52, pp. 260-279. /Nationalization /Law / 341.05 Am35

766. Carlston, Kenneth S. 1959 "Nationalization: An Analytical Approach." Northwestern University Law Review V. 54, No. 4, pp. 405-433. /Nationalization /Law

767. Carmoy, G. de. 1971 Le dossier européen de l´énergie: les marchés, les industries, les politiques. Paris: Editions d´Organisation. /Europe /Energy utility industry

768. Carney, David Edward. 1961 Government and Economy in British West Africa: A Study of the Role of Public Agencies in the Economic Development of British West Africa in the Period 1947-1955. New York: Bookman Associates. /Africa /Economic development /Economic history / 338.966 C217q

769. Carnot, R. 1920 L´étatisme industriel. Paris: Ed. Payot. /France /Capitalism /Industrialization

770. Carr, T. H. 1951 "Les conseils des consummateurs dans les industries britanniques nationalisés." Problèmes Economiques (Paris), No. 157, pp. 21-23. /United Kingdom /Consumer relations

771. Carr, T. H. 1953 "Local Advisory Committees--A Chairman´s Point of View." British Electricity pp. 402-404. /United Kingdom /Electrical utility industry /Consumer relations

772. Carranza, Roque. 1981 "La subsidariedad del Estado." Realidad Económica (Buenos Aires), V. 43, pp. 37-43. /Argentina /Subsidization policy /Economic history /HC 171 R424 LAC

773. Carrazedo, R. O. 1966 "Do conceito da sociedade de economia mista." Revista de Direito Público e Ciencia Política (Rio de Janeiro), V. 9, No. 4, pp. 5-15. /Mixed enterprises /Law /Brazil

774. Carrillo Castro, A. 1976 Las empresas públicas en México: Su importancia en el sector industrial y comercial. Mexico City: Ediciones INAP. /Mexico /Economic history /Law /Economic analysis /Control process /HD 4013 E475 LAC

775. Carrillo Castro, A. 1978 "La empresa pública y la reforma administrativa." In Rosa Luz Alegría et al. Empresas públicas. Mexico City: Presidencia de la República. pp. 9-50. /Mexico /Administrative reform /HD 4013 E479 1978 LAC

776. Carrillo Castro, A. 1979 "La regulación jurídico administrativa de la empresa pública en México." Paper presented at the First Latin American Seminar on Public Policies, São Paulo. /Mexico /Law /Control process /OPSS

777. Carrillo Castro, A., and F. Solana. 1980 La reforma administrativa en México (1971-1979). Mexico City: Editorial Porrúa. /Mexico /Administrative reform / OPSS

778. Carrillo Castro, A., and Sergio García Ramírez. 1981 Las empresas públicas en México. Mexico City: Editorial Porrúa. /Mexico /Control process /Administrative reform /Economic development /Law / Planning process /Evaluation /Economic history

779. Carrión Hernández, Joaquín. 1978 "Metodología de evaluación en una empresa eléctrica de servicio público." /Electrical utility industry /Evaluation / OPSS

780. Carron, A. 1969 La notion d'établissement public industriel et commercial. Paris: CIEG. /Law /France

781. Carvalho, Getúlio Pereira. 1973 "Empresa pública: Uma análise administrativa." Revista de Administração Municipal (Rio de Janeiro), V. 20, No. 116, pp. 5-27. /Brazil /Public administration / JS 41 R484 LAC

782. Carvalho, Getúlio Pereira. 1974 A empresa pública: Uma análise administrativa. Rio de Janeiro: FGV. /Public administration / HD 4093 C379 LAC

783. Carvalho, Getúlio Pereira. 1975 "Petrobrás: Duas décadas e um dilema." Revista de Administração Pública (Rio de Janeiro), V. 9, No. 1, pp. 14-39. /Brazil /Oil industry /Management / G350.5 R3261 LAC

784. Carvalho, Getúlio Pereira. 1975 "Empresa pública e modernização administrativa." Tendencia (Rio de Janeiro), V. 3, No. 27. /Brazil /Administrative reform

785. Carvalho, Getúlio Pereira. 1976 Petrobrás: Do monópolio aos contratos de risco. Rio de Janeiro: Forese-Universitária. /Brazil /Oil industry /Economic history /Nationalism /Nationalization / Contractual relations / HD 9574 B82 C33 LAC

786. Carvalho, Getúlio Pereira. 1976 "Petrobrás: A Case Study of Nationalism and Institution Building in Brazil." Storrs, Conn.: University of Connecticut unpublished Ph.D. dissertation. /Brazil /Evaluation /Oil industry /FILM 14,695 LAC

787. Carvalho, Getúlio Pereira. 1979 "La empresa pública: un análisis administrativo." In EIAP-FGV, ed(s). Administración

de empresas públicas. Mexico City: Editorial Limusa. pp. 54-77. /Law /Management /Autonomy /HD 3850 A333 LAC

788. Carvalho, Getúlio Pereira. 1980 "Report of the Regional Meeting of Latin America and Caribbean Countries on the Role of the Public Sector in Developing Countries, January 14-19, 1980, Mexico City." Ljubljana: ICPE. /Developing nations

789. Carvalho, Getúlio Pereira. 1980 "The Role of the Public Sector in Brazil." Paper presented at the Regional Meeting of Latin American and Caribbean Countries on the Role of the Public Sector in Developing Countries, Mexico City, 14-19 Jan. Ljubljana: ICPE. /Brazil

790. Carvalho, Getúlio Pereira. 1981 "The Role of the Public Sector in Brazil." Public Enterprise V. 2, No. 1, pp. 31-40. /Brazil / OPSS

791. Carvalho, L. N. de. 1971 "As instituções de crédito do sector público em Portugal." Juridica (Rio de Janeiro), V. 16, No. 113, pp. 72-113. /Portugal /Financial institutions

792. Carvalho, L. N. de. 1971 Subsidios para un estudo das empresas públicas em Portugal. Lisbon: Centro de Estudos de Planeamento. /Portugal

793. Casanova, Mario. 1970 "Evolución de la disciplina de las empresas públicas en Italia. Empresa pública y empresa privada en el Constitución." La Empresa Pública. Zaragoza, Spain: Publicaciones del Real Colegio de España en Bolonia. pp. 1399-1426. /Italy /Private sector /Law

794. Casas Gonzalez, Antonio. 1975 Empresas multinacionales regionales en América Latina. Buenos Aires: BID-INTAL. /Latin America /Multinational corporations /HD 2810.5 C37218 LAC

795. Case, H. L. 1955 Personnel Policy in a Public Agency: The TVA Experience. New York: Harper. /United States of America /River valley development projects Personnel management / /351.1 C266p

796. Caselli, L. 1970 L'Impresa pubblica nella economia di mercato. Milan, Italy: Ed. A. Giuffre. /Italy

797. Caso, F. de. 1972 "La informática en la empresa pública." Innovación Empresa No. 148. /Information system

798. Cassandro, P. E. 1961 "On Administrative Account-Taking in Public Enterprises." Rivista dei Dottori Commercialisti (Milan, Italy), V. 12, No. 5, pp. 593-600. /Accounting

799. Cassandro, P. E. 1966 Le gestioni erogatrici pubbliche UTET. Turin, Italy. /Italy /Management

800. Cassell, F. 1956 "The Pricing Policies of the Nationalized Industries." Lloyd's Bank Review (London), V. 42, pp. 1-18. /United Kingdom /Price policy /Nationalization

801. Cassese, Sabino. 1962 Elementi per una bibliografia sulle imprese pubbliche in Italia. Milan, Italy: Ed. CIRIEC. /Italy /Bibliography

802. Cassese, Sabino. 1970 "Los aspectos financieros del sistema de las participaciones estatales." La Empresa Pública. Zaragoza, Spain: Publicaciones del Real Colegio de España en Bolonia. pp. 1455-1482. /Spain /Financing

803. Cassese, Sabino. 1980 "Il controllo delle partecipazioni stratali." Rivista Trimestrale di Diritto Pubblico (Rome), No. 4, pp. 1215-1234. /Italy /Control process /Public administration

804. Cassese, Sabino. 1981 "Public Control and Corporate Efficiency." In Raymond Vernon and Yair Aharoni, ed(s). State-Owned Enterprise in the Western Economies. New York: St. Martin's Press. pp. 145-156. /Control process /Economic efficiency /HD 3850 S79 PCL

805. Castagnede, B. 1971 L'équilibre financier des entreprises publiques. Paris: Armand Colin. /France /Financial performance

806. Cathelineau, J. 1965 Le personnel d'Electricité de France et de Gaz de France. Paris. /France /Electrical utility industry /Gas utility industry / Personnel management

807. Cavalcanti, T. B. 1971 "Sociedade de economia mista." Revista de Direito Administrativo (Rio de Janeiro), No. 103, pp. 1-15. /Brazil /Mixed economy / G350.981 R327

808. Cavalcanti, T. B., et al. 1964 "A empresa pública e a sociedade de economia mista." Paper presented at the round table organized by FGV, Rio de Janeiro, 1-9 Dec. 1963. Revista de Direito Público e Ciencia Política (Rio de Janeiro), V. 7, No. 2, pp. 5-72. /Brazil /Mixed economy /340.05 R325 LAC

809. Cavalcanti, T. B., et al. 1973 "Empresas públicas e sociedades de economia mista." Revista de Ciencia Política (Rio de Janeiro), V. 7, No. 4, pp. 35-52. /Brazil /Mixed economy

810. Cavalieri, Duccio. 1968 Gli apporti al fondo de dotazione o al capitale sociale e le anticipazioni del tesoro, in studi sul finanziamiento delle imprese pubbliche. Milan: Ed. CIRIEC. /Italy /Public financing / Subsidization policy

811. Cavalieri, Duccio. 1977 "The Crisis in the System of State Shareholdings in Italy." Annals of Public and Cooperative Economy V. 49, No. 4, pp. 435-450. /Italy /Mixed enterprises /330.5 An73

812. Cazenave, O. 1978 "Les sociétés d'économie mixte." Ph.D. dissertation, Université de Poiters. /France /Construction industry /Law /Decentralized authority / Mixed economy /Control process / OPSS

813. Ceballos Merino, Heliodoro. 1970 "Coloquios sobre protección y prevención industrial en las empresas del I.N.I." *I.N.I. Revista de Información* No. 56, pp. 53-69. /Holding company /Industrial sector /Spain

814. Celier, C. 1945 *Quelques données historiques du problème des nationalisations.* Paris: Droit Social. /France /Nationalization

815. Celler, Emanuel. 1961 "Congress, Compacts, and Interstate Authorities." *Law and Contemporary Problems* V. 26, No. 4, pp. 682-702. /United States of America /Public authority /Law

816. Centellas, G. J. M. 1961 "Nationalization of Mines in Bolivia." *Combate* V. 3, No. 17, pp. 26-33. /Bolivia /Mining industry /Nationalization

817. "Central Government Public Enterprises: Performance during 1975-76." 1977 *Lok Udyog* (New Delhi), V. 11, No. 3, pp. 49-60. /India /Financial performance /Economic history /Statistics /354.54 L836 PCL

818. Centre de Développement de l´OCDE. 1974 *Public Enterprises with Particular Reference to Developing Countries.* Paris: Centre de Développement de l´OCDE. /Bibliography /Developing nations

819. Centre de Développement de l´OCDE. n.d. *Bibliography (1973-1976) of Articles and Essays Dealing with the Government-owned Enterprises in Latin America and Elsewhere.* Paris: Centre de Développement de l´OCDE. /Bibliography /Latin America

820. Cernovsek, Branko J. 1979 "The Consultant´s Approach." Paper presented at the Interregional Workshop "Developing Problem Solving Skills in Public Enterprises," Ljubljana, Yugoslavia, 2-17 Apr. Ljubljana: ICPE. /Consultant services

821. Cervantes Delgado, A. 1963 "El control de los organismos y empresas del Estado." *Const. Ext.* V. 13, No. 5, pp. 329-333. /Control process

822. Cesarini, F. n.d. *Il ricorso al mercato obbligazionario in studi sul finanziamento delle imprese pubbliche.* Milan: Ed. CIRIEC. /Italy /Public financing

823. Chaban-Delmas, M. 1971 "Faire sortir les entreprises publiques de leur ghetto." *Agence Economique et Financière* (Paris), No. 205. /Public administration /Management

824. Chabanol, Daniel. 1974 "Entreprises publiques et rentabilité. Quelques reflexions." *Analyse et Prévision* (Paris), V. 17, No. 2. /Evaluation /Profits

825. Chabas, J. 1965 "Le domaine national du Senegal." *Annales Africaines* pp. 33-70. /Senegal

826. Chakaravarti, A. 1972 "The Social Profitability of Training Unskilled Workers in the Public Sector in India." *Oxford Economic Papers* V. 24, No. 1, pp. 11-123. /India /Training /330.6 Ox2 PCL

827. Chakraborty, S. K. 1979 "Restructuring the Debt/Equity Ratio of Public Enterprises - A Methodological Note." *Lok Udyog* (New Delhi), V. 13, No. 4, pp. 43-48. /India /Financial performance /Methodology /354.54 L836 PCL

828. Chakravorty, D. K. 1980 "Construction Technology and Management Techniques followed by NFL in Execution of Giant Sized Fuel Oil Plants at Nangal, Bhatinda and Panipat." *Lok Udyog* (New Delhi), V. 14, No. 2, pp. 43-50. /India /Construction industry /Project management /Case studies /354.54 L836 PCL

829. Chambers, David. 1983 "Target-Setting and Performance Assessment in Public Enterprises." In G. Ram Reddy, ed(s). *Government and Public Enterprise: Essays in honour of Professor V. V. Ramanadham.* Bombay, India: N. M. Tripathi Private Limited. pp. 48-66. /Evaluation /Accountability

830. Chanda, A. K. 1956 "Public Accountability of State Undertakings: Company Form of Management is Well within Parliamentary Control." *Commerce* (Bombay, India), V. 92, No. 2345. /India /Accountability /Parliament /Control process

831. Chandra Suri, Prakash. 1957 "Some Problems of Organization of Public Enterprises in India." *Annals of Collective Economy* V. 28, pp. 81-87. /India /Control Process /330.5 An73

832. Chandra, Gyan. 1975 "Performance Evaluation of Public Sector Enterprises: Selection of Criterion." *Annals of Public and Cooperative Economy* V. 46, pp. 13-22. /India /Evaluation /330.5 An73

833. Chandra, Prasanna. 1979 "Financial Appraisal of Investment by State Electricity Boards - A Critique." *Lok Udyog* (New Delhi), V. 12, No. 9, pp. 19-24. /India /Electrical utility industry /Investment /Financing /354.54 L836 PCL

834. Chandra, Shushil. 1979 "Technical Education and Training: Indian Experience." Paper presented at the International Workshop on Education and Training in Public Enterprises in Developing Countries, Ljubljana, Yugoslavia, 12-17 Feb. Ljubljana: ICPE. /Training /India

835. Chandra, Shushil. 1980 "Training of Public Enterprise Managers: Some Perspectives." Paper presented at the Interregional Seminar on Training Management in Public Enterprises in Developing Countries, Ljubljana, Yugoslavia, 29 Sept. - 10. Oct. Ljubljana: ICPE. /Training /Management

836. Chandra, Shushil. 1981 "Human Resource Development." Paper presented at the Interregional Seminar on Training Management in Public Enterprises in Developing Countries, Ljubljana, Yugoslavia, 19-28 Oct. Ljubljana: ICPE. /Training

837. Chandy, K. T. 1964 "Managerial Personnel for Public Enterprises." Indian Journal of Public Administration (New Delhi), V. 10, No. 4, pp. 601-607. /India /Personnel management /Training / JA 26 I55 Pub Aff

838. Chanes Nieto, José. 1978 "Insuficiencia del marco jurídico de la denominada administración pública paraestatal en México." Paper presented at the Round Table on Public Enterprise of the 10th General Assembly of the Latin American Association of public Administration. Mexico City. /Mexico /Public administration /Law / OPSS

839. Chaney, Armadeo. 1976 La actividad empresarial del Estado. Lima: Instituto Nacional de Administración Pública. /Peru

840. Chang, Yu-nan. 1956 "Industrial Administration in Communist China." Western Political Quarterly V. 9, No. 4, pp. 850-872. /China, People's Rep. of /320.5 W525

841. Chao, Kang. 1970 Agricultural Production in Communist China. Madison: University of Wisconsin Press. /China, People's Rep. of /Agricultural Production / 338.10951 C3635a

842. Chapel, Yves. 1956 "Aperçu sur les services parastataux en Allemagne Fédérale." International Review of Administrative Sciences V. 12, No. 3, pp. 119-145. /Germany, Federal Rep. of /Public services / JA 1 A1 I6 PCL

843. Chapman, R. A. 1971 "The Bank of England: Not a Nationalised Industry or a Public Corporation, but a Nationalized Institution." Parliamentary Affairs (London), V. 24, No. 3, pp. 208-221. /United Kingdom /Central banks

844. Chappez, J. 1972 Le contrat de programme entre l'Etat et l'O.R.T.F. France: L'Actualité Juridique (Droit Administratif) /France /Planning process /Accountability /Communication industry /Contractual relations

845. Charles, Roger. 1951 "Port Development in the United Kingdom: Review of a Century of Enterprise and Development." Port and Harbour Authority (London), /United Kingdom /Port authority

846. Chase, S. M., Jr. 1968 Applying Benefit Cost Analysis to Public Programmes. Washington, D. C.: Brookings Institution. /Cost benefit analysis /Evaluation

847. Chatelus, M., et al. 1969 L'entreprise publique et la tarification. Paris: Edition Cujas. /Price policy

848. Chatterjee, Pareshnath. 1975 "Productivity Audit: Some Basic Considerations." Lok Udyog (New Delhi), V. 9, No. 3, pp. 17-26. /Accountability /Control process /354.54 L836 PCL

849. Chatterjee, S. K. 1955 "New Patterns of Public Enterprise in India." Calcutta Revue (Calcutta), pp. 119-133. /India /Evaluation

850. Chattopadhyay, P. 1982 "Relevance of Management Techniques in Underdeveloped Countries with Special Reference to India." Lok Udyog (New Delhi), V. 16, No. 7, pp. 33-42. /India /Management /354.54 L836 PCL

851. Chaudhary, A. S. 1981 "Professionalism among Managers in Industrial Organization in Public Sector." Lok Udyog (New Delhi), V. 14, No. 12, pp. 35-40. /India /Management /354.54 L836 PCL

852. Chauhan, A. B., and S. G. Deobhankar. 1981 "Restructuring of Commercial Banks in India - Some Thoughts." Lok Udyog (New Delhi), V. 15, No. 6, pp. 21-26. /India /Banking system /354.54 L836 PCL

853. Chauvey, D. 1970 Autogestion. Paris: Editions du Seuil. /Worker self management

854. Chavanon. 1939 Essai sur la notion et le régime juridique du service publique industriel et commercial. Paris. /France /Law

855. Chavez, Fermín. 1980 "IME (Industrias Mecánicas del Estado): Industria y tecnología nacional también es soberanía." Realidad Económica (Buenos Aires), pp. 28-34. /Argentina /Air transportation industry / HC 171 R424 LAC

856. Cheema, G. Shabbir. 1981 "The Organization and Management of Public Enterprises for Regional Development in Asia: Some Issues." Paper presented at the Expert Group Meeting on the Role of Public Enterprises in Regional Development in Developing Countries, Ljubljana, Yugoslavia, 7-11 Dec. Ljubljana: ICPE. /Asia /Regional development /Management /Organization development / Control process

857. Cheema, G. Shabbir. 1982 "The Organization and Management of Public Enterprises for Regional Development in Asia." Public Enterprise V. 2, No. 4, pp. 21-36. /Asia /Regional development /Management /Control process / OPSS

858. Chenot, Bernard. 1949 Premiers résultats de la nationalisation des mines. Paris: Droit Social. /France /Nationalization /Mining industry

859. Chenot, Bernard. 1955 "Les paradoxes de l'entreprise publique." Revue Français de Science Politique (Paris), V. 5, No. 4, pp. 725-734. /France /Evaluation

860. Chenot, Bernard. 1956 Les entreprises nationalisées. Paris: Presses Universitaires de France. /France

861. Chenot, Bernard. 1965 Organization économique de l'Etat. Paris: Dalloz. /France

862. Chesshire, John. 1980 "The Public Enterprise and Consumers." Paper presented at the 13th International Congress of Public and Cooperative Economy, Lisbon, 2-4 June. /Consumer relations /OPSS /Published in Annals of Public and Cooperative Economy, Vol. 52, Nos. 1-2, (1981): pp. 157-170.

863. Chessi, Vincent. 1963 "Development Banks." Organization, Planning, and Programming for Economic Development. Washington, D. C.: Government Printing Office. V. 8, pp. 137-144. /Development banks

864. Chester, D. N. 1948 British Public Utility Services. London: Longmans. /United Kingdom /Public utility industry /914.206 B777 no.27

865. Chester, D. N. 1950 "Note on the Price Policy Indicated by the Nationalization Acts." Oxford Economic Papers V. 2, pp. 69-74. /Price policy /Nationalization /United Kingdom /330.6 Ox2 PCL

866. Chester, D. N. 1950 "Organization of Nationalized Industries." Political Quarterly (London), V. 21, pp. 122-134. /United Kingdom / 320.5 P76p

867. Chester, D. N. 1951 The Nationalized Industries: A Statutory Analysis. London: Institute of Public Administration. /United Kingdom /Law / HD 4147 C44 HRC

868. Chester, D. N. 1952 "Management and Accountability in the Nationalized Industries." Public Administration (London), V. 30, pp. 27-47. /Australia /Management /Accountability /Evaluation / JA 8 P8 Pub Aff

869. Chester, D. N. 1953 "The Nationalized Industries." Three Banks Review (London), V. 16, pp. 23-46. /United Kingdom

870. Chester, D. N. 1953 Public Corporations and the Classification of Administrative Bodies. London. pp. 34-52. /United Kingdom /Public administration

871. Chester, T. E. 1955 "Private Pensions on State Benefits?" National Westminster Bank Quarterly Review V. 26, pp. 43-55. /United Kingdom /Retirement Systems / HC 251 A1 N36 PCL

872. Chester, T. E. 1955 "Public Enterprise in South-East Asia." Political Quarterly V. 26, pp. 43-55. /Asia /Southeast Asia /320.5 P76p

873. Chester, T. E. 1956 The Nationalized Industries of Great Britain. Transactions of the Third World Congress of Sociology. London: International Sociological Association. V. 2, pp. 49-55. /United Kingdom

874. Chester, T. E., and H. A. Clegg. 1954 "Nationalization and the Problem of Communication." British Management Review (London), V. 12, No. 6, pp. 307-316. /Nationalization /

875. Chester, T. E., and H. Smith. 1959 Management under Nationalization. London: Acton Society Trust. /United Kingdom /Nationalization /Management

876. Chester, T. E., and G. Forsyth. 1961 "Nationalisation et bureaucratie." Sociologie du Travail (Paris), V. 3, No. 3, pp. 209-220. /France /Nationalization /Management /331.05 So14 PCL

877. Chevrier, J. 1957 "The French Electricity Supply Company: The First Ten Years" Annals of Collective Economy V. 28, pp. 284-300. /France /Electrical utility industry / 330.5 An73

878. Chevrier, J. 1965 "Public Enterprise in a Free Society: Practical Experience of `Electricité de France´." Annals of Public and Cooperative Economy V. 36, No. 2-3, pp. 213-234. /France /Electrical utility industry

879. Chiancone, A. 1970 "Les entreprises publiques comme instrument de politique anticonjuncturelle." Revue de la Société Belge d´Etudes et d´Expansion (Liège, Belgium), No. 243, pp. 932-944. /Evaluation

880. Chilcote, Ronald H. 1968 Spain´s Iron and Steel Industry. Austin, Tex.: UT Bureau of Business Research. /Spain /Steel industry /Trade unions /Economic history /Price policy /Economic policy /Private enterprises /338.476691 C435s PCL /HD 9525 S8 C4 LAW

881. Chile. Banco Central. 1967 El Banco Central de Chile. Santiago, Chile: Editoria del Pacífico. /Chile /Central banks / G332.10983 B222ban LAC

882. Chile. Banco Central. 1970 Realizaciones del Banco Central, 1964-1970. Santiago, Chile. /Chile /Central banks

883. Chile. Conserjería Nacional de Promoción Popular. 1966 La administración del Estado y sus servicios públicos. Santiago, Chile. /Chile /Government bureaucracy /Administrative management /Public services

884. Chile. ODEPLAN. 1971 Planes operativos de las empresas del area social y mixta. Santiago, Chile. /Chile /Mixed enterprises /Planning process

885. Chile. ODEPLAN. n.d. "Participación de los trabajadores en las empresas del area de propiedad social y mixta." In G. Martner, ed(s). El pensamiento económico del gobierno de Allende. pp. 284-288. /Chile /Mixed enterprises /Worker management participation

886. Chileshe, Leo Marsan. 1978 "Management of Transfer and Development of Technology in Public Enterprises in Zambia." Paper presented at the International Workshop on Management of Transfer and Development of Technology in Public Enterprises in Developing Countries, Ljubljana, Yugoslavia, 19-25 Jun. Ljubljana:ICPE. /Zambia /Technology transfer /Management

887. Chirico, Giulio. 1970 "Programazione economico e funcioni dell´imprenditorialita pubblica." Foro Administrativo No. 11, pp. 856-869. /Italy /Planning process

888. Chitale, M. P. 1975 "Some Basic Issues in the Joint Sector." In R. C. Dutt and Raj K. Nigam, ed(s). Towards Commanding Heights. New Delhi: Vivek Joshi. pp. 374-385. /India /Mixed enterprises /HD 4293 T68 PCL

889. Chlepner, B. S. 1949 "Reflexions sur le probléme des nationalisations." *Revue de l´Institut de Sociologie Solvay* (Brussels), No. 2, pp. 207-232. /Nationalization

890. Choksi, Armeane. 1979 *State Intervention in the Industrialization of Developing Countries: Selected Issues. World Bank Staff Working Paper No. 341.* Washington, D. C. /Industrialization /Economic analysis

891. Cholvis, Francisco. 1973 "Princípios generales del papel del estado en la economía nacional." *Función del Estado en la economía.* Buenos Aires: Cuenca Ediciones. /Argentina /Economic analysis /Management /HD 85 S7 F85 LAC

892. Chopfel, J. 1965 "Les entreprises publiques envahissent largement le secteur privé." *L´Usine* /France /Private sector /Economic analysis

893. Chopra, O. P. 1982 "Identification of Mission and Objectives among Public Sector Undertakings in India." *Lok Udyog* (New Delhi), V. 15, No. 10, pp. 7-13. /India /Goal setting /354.54 L836 PCL

894. Chotani, Abdul Hamid. 1980 *Report of the Regional Workshop on Management of Transfer of Technology by Public Enterprises in the ESCAP Region, Bangalore, India, November 10-15, 1980.* Ljubljana: ICPE. /Technology transfer /Management

895. Choudhury, S. 1978 "Project Performance Measurement and Control." *Lok Udyog* (New Delhi), V. 12, No. 5, pp. 17-24. /Project management /354.54 L836 PCL

896. Choudhury, S. 1979 "Project Planning, Scheduling & Monitoring System Concepts." *Lok Udyog* (New Delhi), V. 13, No. 7, pp. 21-26. /Project management /354.54 L836 PCL

897. Choudhury, S., and P. K. Rudra. 1981 "Performance Costing A New Technique for Project Cost Control." *Lok Udyog* (New Delhi), V. 15, No. 1, pp. 19-32. /Economic efficiency /Control process /Cost benefit analysis /Financial performance /Project management /354.54 L836 PCL

898. Chowdhary, R. K. 1973 "Improving Productivity of the Indian Railways." *Lok Udyog* (New Delhi), V. 7, No. 8, pp. 11-20. /India /Railway industry /Productivity /354.54 L836 PCL

899. Chowdhury, R. C. 1947 "Nationalization." *Indian Journal of Economics* V. 27, pp. 373-387. /Nationalization / 330.5 In2

900. Chuayffet Chemor, Emílio. 1979 "Formas legales de control administrativo de las empresas públicas en México." Paper presented at the International Seminar on Regulation of the Public Enterprise, Mexico City. /Mexico /Public administration /Control process /Law / OPSS

901. Chubb, B. 1954 "Public Control of Public Enterprises." *Administration* (Dublin), V. 2, No. 1, pp. 21-32. /Ireland /Control process

902. Chung, J. S. 1966 "Trends in the North Korean Industrial Enterprise: Control, Concentration and Managerial Functions." In J. S. Chung, ed(s). Patterns of Economic Development: Korea. Kalamazoo, Mich.: Korea Research and Publications. pp. 80-103. /Korea, People´s Democratic Rep. of /Industrial sector /Control process /Management

903. Cibotti, R., and E. Weffort. 1967 "La planificación del sector público. Una perspectiva sociológica." Desarrollo Económico (Buenos Aires), V. 7, No. 26, pp. 37-57. /Argentina /Planning process / HD 85 S7 D48 LAC

904. Cibotti, R., and E. Sierra. 1970 El sector público en la planificación del desarrollo. Mexico City: Siglo XXI Editores. /Planning process / G330.9806 C482s

905. Ciller, Tansu U. 1980 "Classification and Taxonomy of Public Enterprise: (An Explanatory Perspective)." Paper presented at the Expert Group Meeting on Concept, Definition and Classification of Public Enterprises, Tangier, Morocco, 15-19 Dec. Ljubljana: ICPE. /Taxonomy

906. Cincunegui, Jorge Eduardo. 1979 Objetivos da firma pública: Um caso. São Paulo: FUNDAP/CLASCO. /Brazil /Goal setting /Management / OPSS

907. Cingi, Selçuk, and Güllay Coskun. 1983 "Control of the Public Economic Enterprises in Turkey." Paper presented at the 19th International Congress of Administrative Sciences, West Berlin, 19-23 Sept. /Turkey /Control process /OPSS

908. Citrine, Lord. 1951 "Problems of Nationalized Industries." Public Administration (London), No. 4, pp. 317-332. /United Kingdom /Industrial sector / 320.5 J826 PCL

909. Citrine, Lord. 1952 "Electricity." In Sir Herbert Houldsworth, ed(s) Efficiency in the Nationalized Industries. London: Allen & Unwin. /United Kingdom /Electrical utility industry

910. Citti, L. 1979 "Pour un réseau national d´essais." Annales des Mines pp. 97-106. /France /Industrialization /Planning process /Control process

911. Clapp, Gordon R. 1936 Supervisory Training in the Tennessee Valley Authority. Chicago: Civil Service Assembly. /United States of America /River valley development projects /Training

912. Clapp, Gordon R. 1943 "Problems of Union Relations in Public Agencies." American Economic Review V. 33, pp. 184-196. /United States of America /River valley development projects /Labor relations /330.5 Am312

913. Clapp, Gordon R. 1955 "TVA´s Working Philosophy of Industrial Relations." In A. H. Hanson, ed(s). Public Enterprises. Brussels: IIAS. pp. 71-78. /United States of America /River valley development projects /Industrial relations / HD 3850 H28 Law

914. Clapp, Gordon R. 1955 The TVA: An Approach to the Development of a Region. Chicago: University of Chicago Press. /United States of America /River valley development projects / Regional development / 309.973 T256Yc

915. Clapp, Martin C. 1955 "Public Enterprise in the Industrial Field in Puerto Rico." In A. H. Hanson, ed(s). Public Enterprise. Brussels: IIAS. pp. 167-177. /Puerto Rico /Industrial sector / HD 3850 H28 Law

916. Clark, R. 1964 The Management of the Public Sector of the National Economy. London: Athlone Press. /United Kingdom /Management

917. Clark, R. 1966 "The Public Sector." Public Administration (London), pp. 61-72. /United Kingdom / 320.5 J826

918. Clavero Arevalo, Manuel Francisco. 1952 Municipalización y provincialización de servicios en la ley de régimen local. Madrid. /Spain /Decentralization /Decentralized authority

919. Clawson, Marion. 1967 "The Federal Lands as Big Business." Natural Resources Journal V. 7, No. 2, pp. 183-193. /United States of America /Land use policy /Management /HC 10 N3 Pub Aff Law

920. Clegg, H. A. 1950 Industrial Democracy and Nationalization. Oxford: Oxford University Press. /United Kingdom /Nationalization / 331.15 C587i

921. Clegg, H. A. 1950 Labour in Nationalized Industry. Oxford: Oxford University Press. /United Kingdom /Labor relations /335 F112re no.141

922. Clegg, H. A. 1950 Labour Relations in London Transport. Oxford: Oxford University Press. /United Kingdom /Land transportation industry / Labor relations / 331.1856 C5871

923. Clegg, H. A., and T. E. Chester. 1953 "The North of Scotland Hydroelectric Board." Political Studies (London), No. 3, pp. 213-234. /United Kingdom /Scotland /Hydroelectric power /320.5 P77 PCL

924. Clegg, H. A., and T. E. Chester. 1953 The Future of Nationalization. Oxford: Basil Blackwell. /United Kingdom /Nationalization

925. Clegg, I. 1971 Workers' Self-Management in Algeria. London: Penguin Press. /Algeria /Worker self management

926. Clemens, E. W. 1950 Economics and Public Utilities. New York: Appleton-Century-Crofts. /Public utility industry /Public utility regulation policy

927. Climbes, B. L. 1951 "A Miner Considers the Effects of Nationalisation." Fortnightly Review pp. 148-152. /United Kingdom /Nationalization /Mining industry /Working conditions

928. Cloete, J. J. N. 1982 "Problems of Public Enterprise." Paper presented at the Tokyo Round Table preparatory to the 19th International Congress of Administrative Sciences, 13-17 Sept. /Control process /Accountability /OPSS

929. Cloete, J. J. N. 1983 "The Public Enterprise as an Instruemnt of Economic Policy." Paper presented at the 19th International Congress of Administrative Sciences, West Berlin, 19-23 Sept. /Economic policy /OPSS

930. Cluseau. 1946 "Réflexions sur la nouvelle organisation du crédit et la nationalisation des banques." Revue de Science et Législation Financière (Paris), No. 61. /France /Nationalization /Credit policy /Banking agency

931. Coase, R. H. 1945 "Price and Output Policy of State Enterprise--a Comment." Economic Journal V. 55, pp. 112-113. /Price policy / Film 9093 Micro 330.5 Ec7

932. Coase, R. H. 1947 "The Origin of the Monopoly of Broadcasting in Great Britain." Economics (London), /United Kingdom /Broadcasting industry

933. Coase, R. H. 1950 British Broadcasting: A Study in Monopoly. Cambridge, Mass.: Harvard University Press. /United Kingdom /Broadcasting industry / 380.162 C631b

934. Coatman, John. 1951 "Constitutional Position of the BBC." Public Administration (London), pp. 160-172. /United Kingdom /Constitutional law /Broadcasting industry / 320.5 J826 PCL

935. Coburn, John F., and Lawrence H. Wortzel. 1984 "The Problem of Public Enterprise: Is Privatization the Solution?" Paper presented at the conference, "State Shrinking: A Comparative Inquiry into Privatization," Austin, Tex., 1-3 March. /Privatization /OPSS

936. Cockerill, Anthony. 1980 "Steel and the State in Great Britain." Annals of Public and Cooperative Economy V. 51, No. 4, pp. 439-458. /United Kingdom /Steel industry /330.5 An73

937. Cohn, G. 1910 "Municipal Socialism." Economic Journal V. 20, pp. 561-568. /Local government / 330.5 Ec7

938. Cohn, Gabriel. 1968 Petróleo e nacionalismo. São Paulo: Difusão Européia do Livro. /Brazil /Oil industry /Nationalism

939. Colanovic, Braiuslav. 1974 Planificación al servicio del desarrollo y bases del sistema de planificación en Yugoslavia. Ljubljana: ICPE. /Yugoslavia /Planning process

940. Colanovic, Branislav, Radomir Jovanovic, and Joze Zakonjsek. 1974 "Planning to Serve Development and the Foundations of Planning in Yugoslavia." Paper presented at the International Seminar '74: Planning in Public Enterprises in Developing Countries, Ljubljana, Yugoslavia, 23 Sept. - 9 Oct. Ljubljana: ICPE. /Yugoslavia /Planning process

941. Cole, G. D. H. 1948 The National Coal Board. London: Fabian Research Series. /United Kingdom /Coal mining industry /335 F112re no.129

942. Cole, G. D. H. 1948 Why Nationalize Steel? London: Fabian Research Series. /United Kingdom /Steel industry /Nationalization

943. Cole, G. D. H. 1950 "Labour and Staff Problems under Nationalization." Political Quarterly (London), V. 21, pp. 160-170. /United Kingdom /Labor relations /Personnel management / 320.5 P76p

944. Cole, Margaret. 1949 Miners and the Board. London: Fabian Research Series. /United Kingdom /Labor relations /Mining industry / 335 F112re No.134

945. Cole, Redcliff Cecil Ayodele. 1979 "An Overview of the Philosophies, Strategies of Education and Training for Public Enterprises in the Republic of Sierra Leone." Paper presented at the International Seminar on Management and Training in Public Enterprises in Developing Countries, Ljubljana, Yugoslavia, 1-13 Oct. Ljubljana: ICPE. /Sierra Leone /Training

946. Colin, J. P. 1966 "La nature juridique des marchés de travaux passés par les sociétés d'économie mixte." Actualité Juridique - Droit Administratif (Paris), V. 1. /France /Law /Labor relations

947. Colliard, C. A. 1959 "Il controllo dell'impresa pubblica in Francia." Revue de l'Institut de Sociologie (Paris), pp. 199-218. /France /Control process

948. Colliard, C. A. 1965 "L'Entreprise publique et l'évolution du marché comun." Revue Trimestrelle de Droit Européen (Paris), /Europe /European Economic Community

949. Collins, B. A. N. 1975 "The Role of a Management Development Institute in Improving Performance in Public Enterprises." Improving Preformance in Public Enterprise, Report of an International Conference, Arusha, Tanzania, 2-5 Dec. Arusha, Tanzania: East African Community Management Institute. pp. 138-149. /Training /East Africa /Case studies

950. Collins, Paul. 1971 The Working of Tanzania's Rural Development Fund: A Problem in Decentralization. University of Sussex: Institute of Development Studies. No. 62. /Tanzania /Rural development /Development corporation /Decentralized authority /Evaluation /OPSS

951. Colloque de Grenoble. 1956 Le fonctionnement des entreprises nationalisées. Paris: Ed. Dalloz. /France /Economic efficiency /Financial performance

952. Colman Sercovich, Francisco. 1980 "State-Owned Enterprises and Dynamic Comparative Advantages in the World Petrochemical Industry." Development Discussion Paper. Cambridge, Mass.: HIID. No. 96. /Oil industry / OPSS

953. Colombia. Comité de Regalías. 1981 "Orígenes del registro en Colombia." Paper presented at the Reunión regional de expertos "Estrategias e instrumentos para reforzar la negociación (SBP) de las empresas públicas en los países en desarrollo en la transferencia internacional de transacciones tecnológicas," San José, Costa Rica, 23-27 Nov. Ljubljana: ICPE. /Colombia /Technology transfer

954. Colombia. Federación de Loterías de Colombia. 1976 "Información sobre entidades oficiales y instituciones privadas." _Directorio de despachos públicos._ Bogotá: Federación de Loterías de Colombia (FEDELCO). /Colombia /Directory /Mixed enterprises /Private sector /JL 2821 D564 LAC

955. Colombia. Ministerio de Agricultura. 1970 _La Corporación Nacional para el Desarrollo del Chocó._ Bogotá: Ministerio de Agricultura. /Colombia /Regional development /Agricultural development / HD 4105 C45 A5 LAC

956. Colombia. Secretaría Técnica del Comité de Superintendencia de Industria y Comercio. 1981 "Recuentes de las labores del Comité de Regalías de Colombia, 1967-1977." Paper presented at the Reunión regional de expertos "Estrategias e instrumentos para reforzar la negociación (SBP) de las empresas públicas en los países en desarrollo en la transferencia internacional de transacciones tecnológicas." San José, Costa Rica, 23-27 Nov. Ljubljana: ICPE. /Colombia /Technology /Technology transfer /Economic history

957. Colombia. Secretaría Técnica del Comité de Superintendencia de Industria y Comercio. 1981 "Manual para el trámite de contratos de transferencia de tecnología ante el Comité de Regalías." Paper presented at the Reunión regional de expertos "Estrategías e instrumentos para reforzar la negociación (SBP) de las empresas públicas en los países en desarrollo en la transferencia internacional de transacciones tecnológicas." San José, Costa Rica, 23-27 Nov. Ljubljana: ICPE. /Colombia /Technology transfer /Law

958. Colombo, L. 1961 _Nationalization of the Electricity and Gas Industry in Great Britain and France._ Milan: A. Giuffre. /United Kingdom /France /Electrical utility industry /Gas utility industry / Nationalization

959. Comiseti, L. 1952 "Théorie du quatriéme pouvoir (pouvoir économique) la nationalisation des entreprises." _Annales de l'Economie Collective_ pp. 281-294. /Nationalization

960. Commonwealth Secretariat. 1976 "Training Systems and Curriculum Development for Public Enterprise Management: Recommendations." Paper resulting from the Expert Group on Training Systems and Curriculum Development for Public Enterprise Management. /British Commonwealth /Training /Management

961. Commonwealth Secretariat. 1977 _Seminar on the Role and Management of Public Enterprises._ Kingston, Jamaica: Commonwealth Secretariat. /British Commonwealth /Management

962. Commonwealth Secretariat and Institute of Development Management. 1978 Seminar on Performance Evaluation of Public Enterprises. Gaborone, Botswana: Commonwealth Secretariat; Institute of Development Management. /British Commonwealth /Africa /Evaluation

963. Commonwealth Secretariat. 1978 Seminar on Issues in Public Enterprises Development. New Delhi: Commonwealth Secretariat. /British Commonwealth

964. Comyns Carr, A. 1962 "Our Economy and our Nationalized Industries." Calcutta Review (Calcutta), pp. 132-134. /India /Economic analysis /Industrial sector

965. Concha, V. H. 1969 La Empresa Nacional de Electricidad S. A. (Endesa) como organismo del sector público. Santiago, Chile: UNECLA Meeting of Experts on Administration of Publicc Enterprises in Latin America and Caribbean. pp. 17-22. /Chile /Electrical utility industry /Public administration

966. Confalonieri, Antonio. 1958 Note sul finanziamento delle azienca pubbliche a carrattere industriale. Milan: Ed. CIRIEC. /Italy /Industrial sector /Financing /Taxation policy

967. Confalonieri, Antonio. 1963 Il finanziamento delle imprese pubbliche. Milan: Ed. Comunista. /Italy /Public financing

968. "Conference on Public Relations in Public Enterprises." 1964 Lok Udyog (New Delhi), pp. 423-441. /India /Public relations

969. Connoch, M. 1917 Constitution d'une nouvelle société financière d'Etat, en vue de financement des entreprises en difficulté: Italia. Paris: Agence Economique et Financière. V. 116, No. 1. /Italy /Financial institutions /Financial performance

970. Connoch, M. 1950 "Los consejos obreros y los consejos de gestión en Yugoslavia." Ekonomsk Politika (Belgrade), V. 4, No. 8, pp. 355-360. /Yugoslavia /Worker management participation

971. Connoch, M. 1962 "El control de empresas del Estado." Revista de Administración Pública (Buenos Aires), V. 2, No. 5. /Argentina /Control process / JA 5 R483 LAC

972. Connoch, M. 1972 "Modelo soviético: Las empresas soviéticas ante la difícil encrucijada." Dirección y Progreso (Madrid), /Union of Soviet Socialist Reps.

973. Connois, R. 1959 La notion d'établissement publique en droit administratif français. Paris: Librairie générale de droit et de jurisprudence. /France /Administrative law

974. Coombers, David. 1965 "The Scrutiny of Ministers' Powers by the Select Committee on Nationalized Industries." Public Law (London), pp. 9-29. /United Kingdom /Law /Control process 350.5 P962

975. Coombes, David. 1966 The Member of Parliament and the Administrations: The Case of the Select Committees in Nationalized Industries. London: Allen & Unwin. /United Kingdom /Parliament / 328.42 C781m

976. Coombes, David. 1971 State Enterprise: Business or Politics? London: Allen & Unwin. /United Kingdom / HD4145 C6 Pub Aff

977. Coombes, David. 1972 "The Conservative Party and Public Ownership: Some Recent Developments in British Public Enterprise." Rivista Trimestrale di Diritto Pubblico (Rome), No. 2, pp. 819-832. /United Kingdom /Evaluation

978. Coons, Arthur. 1939 "The Development of Public Corporations in Economic Enterprise." Annals of the American Academy of Political and Social Science pp. 161-170. /Economic history

979. Corbin, C. 1957 Financement, auto-financement et administration des grandes entreprises: Application au secteur nationalisé. Paris: Dalloz. /France /Financing

980. Cordero, Salvador H., and Sylvia Gómez Tagle. 1979 "Estado y trabajadores de las empresas estatales en México." Paper presented at the Round Table on Public Enterprise of the Tenth General Assembly of the Latin American Association of Public Administration. Mexico City. /Mexico /Labor relations /OPSS

981. Cordoba, J. n.d. "La capacidad inversionista del sector publico en Costa Rica." Economía y Finanzas (San José, Costa Rica), No. 421. /Costa Rica /Investment / OPSS

982. Cordoba, J., Santiago Ruiz, and Víctor Valle. 1978 La capacitación y el desarrollo del personal de dirección en las entidades públicas autónomas del Istmo Centroamericano. San José, Costa Rica: ICAP. /Central America /Personnel management /OPSS

983. Corna-Pellegrini, G. 1961 "Public and Private Enterprises as Instruments of Social and Economic Progress." Vita e Pensiero (Milan), V. 44, No. 3-4, pp. 257-275. /Evaluation /Comparative analysis

984. Corporación Andina de Fomento. 1975 Corporación Andina de Fomento, S. A. Caracas. /Andean Pact Countries /Development corporation / OPSS

985. Correa Álvarez, Alberto Miguel. 1983 The Role of Public Enterprises in the Advancement of Women in Mexico. Ljubljana, ICPE. /Mexico /Women's studies /Law

986. Correa, Carlos María. 1979 "Possible Scope, Content and Structure of Instruments to be Elaborated within the Framework of ICPE's TOT Project." Paper presented at the Expert Group Meeting on Structuring of Contractual Relations in Transfer of Technology Transactions of Public Enterprises in Developing Countries (Model Contracts/ Provisions for Licensing), Ljubljana, Yugoslavia, 22-26 Oct. Ljubljana: ICPE. /Technology transfer /Planning process / Training

/Contractual relations

987. Correa, Carlos María. 1979 "Possible Ways for Improving Available Information on TOT to PEs in DCs." Paper presented at the Expert Group Meeting on Structuring of Contractual Relations in Transfer of Technology Transactions of Public Enterprises in Developing Countries (Model Contracts/Provisions for Licensing), Ljubljana, Yugoslavia, 22-26 Oct. Ljubljana: ICPE. /Developing nations /Technology transfer /Information system / Training /Contractual relations

988. Correa, Carlos María. 1980 Legal Nature and Contractual Conditions of Know-How Transactions. Ljubljana: ICPE. /Technology transfer /Law / Contractual relations

989. Correa, Carlos María. 1981 "Empresas públicas y transferencia de tecnología en América Latina." Paper presented at the Reunión regional de expertos "Estrategias e instrumentos para reforzar la negociación (SBP) de las empresas públicas en los países en desarrollo en la transferencia internacional de transacciones tecnológicas San José, Costa Rica, 23-27 Nov. Ljubljana: ICPE. /Latin America /Technology transfer

990. Correa, Carlos María. 1981 "National Legal Policies on the Transfer and Development of Technology: The Experience of Developing Countries." Paper presented at the Reunión regional de expertos "Estrategias e instrumentos para reforzar la negociación (SBP) de las empresas públicas en los países en desarrollo en la transferencia internacional de transacciones tecnologícas," San José, Costa Rica, 23-27 Nov. Ljubljana: ICPE. /Developing nations /Technology transfer /Law

991. Correia, M. M. 1973 Nuevos rumbos para algunos sectores de administración pública. Lisbon: Imprensa Nacional. /Public administration

992. Corry, J. A. 1936 "The Fusion of Government and Business." Canadian Journal of Economics and Political Science (Toronto), V. 2, pp. 301-316. /Mixed enterprises /305 C16

993. Cortés, F. F. 1968 "Formas del sector parastatal en México." Economía Política (Mexico City), V. 5, No. 2, pp. 195-200. /Mexico

994. Corti, G. 1976 "Perspectives on Public Corporations and Public Enterprises in Five Nations." Annals of Public and Cooperative Economy V. 47, No. 1, pp. 47-86. /France /Germany, Federal Rep. of /Italy /Sweden /Japan /330.5 An73

995. Coskun, Gülay, and Selçuk Cingi. 1983 "Measuring the Effectiveness of a Public Enterprise in the Implementation of an Economic Policy - A Case from Turkey." Paper presented at the 19th International Congress of Administrative Sciences, West Berlin, 19-23 Sept. /Turkey /Economic efficiency /Agricultural development /Development banks /Case studies /OPSS

996. Cosmo, G. 1951 "State Participation in Business Concerns in Italy." Banca Nazionale del Lavoro Review V. 4, pp. 202-212. /Italy /Mixed economy /Mixed enterprises

997. Costa Rica. Escuela Superior de Administración Pública. 1966 Las empresas públicas del Istmo Centroamericano. San José, Costa Rica. /Central America

998. Costa Rica. Escuela Superior de Administración Pública. 1968 "Les entreprises publiques en Amérique Central." Bulletin de l'Institut International d'Administration Publique (Paris), No. 8. /Central America

999. Costa Rica. Oficina de Planificación. 1970 Previsiones del desarrollo económico y social 1969-1972, y planes del sector público. San José, Costa Rica. V. 1. /Costa Rica /Planning process

1000. Costa Rica. Oficina de Planificación Nacional y Política Económica. 1980 "Objetivos de la Unidad Técnica de Empresas Asociativas (UTEA) y del subsistema de empresas asociativas." San José, Costa Rica. /Costa Rica /Planning process

1001. Costa, Célia Maria Leite. 1980 "Política intervencionista nos anos 30: o IAA." Dados, Revista de Ciencias Sociais V. 24, No. 1, pp. 37-60. /Brazil /Alcohol industry /G305 D127 LAC

1002. Costa, D. E. P. W. 1952 "State Enterprise in Asia's Industries." Industrial Review (Athens), pp. 62-63. /Asia

1003. Costa, M. L. da. 1968 "Sociedades de economia mista e participação do Estado na capital de sociedade anonima." Revista de Ciencia Política (Rio de Janeiro), No. 5, pp. 135-142. /Brazil /Mixed enterprises /Investment

1004. Costa, Rubens Vaz da. 1969 "O equilíbrio entre iniciativa governamental e o setor privado." Economia e Desenvolvimiento (Rio de Janeiro), pp. 21-26. /Brazil /Management /Incentive systems /Private sector

1005. Cotrim Neto, Alberto Bittencourt. 1966 "Empresas do Estado na França." Direito administrativa da autarquia: Um Estado sobre expedientes de administração indireta no Estado contemporaneo. Rio de Janeiro: Freitas Bastos. pp. 107-122. /France /Public administration /Administrative law

1006. Cotrim Neto, Alberto Bittencourt. 1966 "Empresas do Estado na Itália." Direito administrativo da autarquia: Um Estado sobre expedientes de administração indireta no Estado contemporaneo. Rio de Janeiro: Freitas Bastos. pp. 103-107. /Italy /Public administration /Administrative law /Law

1007. Cotrim Neto, Alberto Bittencourt. 1966 "Empresas do Estado na Rússia Soviética e na área socialista." Direito administrativo da autarquia: Um Estado sobre expedientes de administração indireta no Estado contemparaneo. Rio de Janeiro: Freitas Bastos. pp. 122-131. /Union of Soviet

Socialist Reps. /Eastern Europe /Administrative law /Public administration /Law

1008. Cotrim Neto, Alberto Bittencourt. 1966 "Conceito jurídico de entidade `paraestatal´." Revista de Direito Administrativo (Rio de Janeiro), No. 83, pp. 32-43. /Brazil /Law

1009. Cotrim Neto, Alberto Bittencourt. 1966 "Empresas do Estado na área de Common Law.´" Direito administrativo da autarquia: um estudo sobre expedientes de administração indireta no Estado Contemporaneo. Rio de Janeiro: Freitas Bastos. pp. 143-152. /Law

1010. Cotrim Neto, Alberto Bittencourt. 1972 "Autarquias e empresas públicas." Revista de Direito Público (Rio de Janeiro), V. 5, No. 20, pp. 48-63. /Brazil /Decentralized authority / Law

1011. Cotrim Neto, Alberto Bittencourt. 1975 "Teoria da empresa pública de sentido estrito." Revista de Direito Administrativo (Rio de Janeiro), No. 122, pp. 21-56. /Law

1012. Cotta, P. 1975 O petróleo é nosso? Rio de Janeiro: Guavira Editores. /Brazil /Oil industry / HD 9574 B82 C64 LAC

1013. Cottino, Gastone. 1970 "Participación pública en la empresa privada e interés social." La Empresa Pública. Zaragoza, Spain: Publicaciones del Real Colegio de España en Bolonia. /Spain /Mixed enterprises

1014. Coulson, H. C. H. 1951 Control of Public Corporation: Functions of the Auditor. London: Ed. Accountant. /United Kingdom /Control process / Accountability

1015. Coutinho, Luciano Galvão. 1979 "Evolucão da administracão descentralizada em São Paulo: Questiones relevantes para as políticas públicas." Revista de Administracão de Empresas (Rio de Janeiro), V. 19, No. 2, pp. 43-61. /Brazil /Sao Paulo, Brazil (State) /Public administration / Decentralized authority / OPSS

1016. Coutinho, Luciano Galvão. 1980 "Evolução da administração descentralizada em São Paulo: Questões relevantes para as políticas públicas." A empresa pública no Brasil: Uma abordagem multidisciplinar. Brasília: IPEA. pp. 453-494. /Economic policy /Decentralization /Sao Paulo, Brazil (State)

1017. Coutinho, N. A. 1966 "COPERBO, sua origem, dificuldades e perspectivas. Sociedades de economia mista-PE." Brasil Açucareiro (Rio de Janeiro), V. 68, No. 4, pp. 15-25. /Brazil /Mixed enterprises

1018. Cox, R. W., K. F. Walker, and Greyfie de Bellecombe. 1967 "Workers Participation in Management." Bulletin of the International Institute for Labor Studies (Geneva), No. 2, pp. 64-125. /Worker management participation

1019. Coyle, Peter D. 1973 "Public Enterprises in Ireland." The Evolution of the Public Enterprises in the Community of the Nine. Brussels: CEEP Editions. pp. 167-184. /Ireland /Statistics /OPSS

1020. Crabbe, V. 1959 "Le contrôle de l'entreprise publique en Belgique. Pages de documentation d'histoire." Res Publica (Louvain, Belgium), pp. 38-57. /Belgium /Control process

1021. Crabbe, V. 1964 "La empresa pública en Bélgica." Información Comercial Española (Madrid), /Belgium

1022. Crappe, C. 1958 "The National Housing Institute." Annals of Collective Economy V. 29, pp. 697-699. /Belgium /Housing industry / 330.5 An73

1023. Crazut, Rafael J. 1970 El Banco Central de Venezuela: Notas sobre la historia y evolución del instituto, 1940-1970. Caracas: El Banco Central de Venezuela. /Venezuela /Central banks /Economic history / HG 2976 C728 LAC

1024. Creacic, Vladimir, and Phyllis Green. 1982 "Public Enterprise Study: Jamaica Railway Corporation." Public Enterprise V. 3, pp. 97-118. /Jamaica /Railway industry /Economic history /Personnel management /Case studies /Evaluation /OPSS

1025. Cremoux, R. 1969 Le problème des entreprises publiques en Afrique. Mauritius: UNECA Seminar on Role of Public Enterprises in Planning and Plan Implementation. /Africa

1026. Crespi Reghizzi, Gabriele. 1970 "La sociedad como forma empresarial en la experiencia soviética." La Empresa Pública. Zaragoza, Spain: Publicaciones del Real Colegio de España en Bolonia. /Union of Soviet Socialist Reps.

1027. Crespigny, A. R. C. 1958 "Labour Party Policy and the Nationalized Industries in Great Britain." South African Journal of Economics (Pretoria), V. 26, pp. 280-293. /United Kingdom /Labor party /Nationalization

1028. Cretella, José, Junior. 1971 "Regime jurídico das emprêsas públicas." Revista de Direito Administrativo (Rio de Janeiro), No. 106, pp. 62-80. /Brazil /Law / G350.981 R327

1029. Cretella, José, Junior. 1973 Empresa pública. São Paulo: Editora da Universidade do São Paulo. /Brazil /Decentralized authority /Law /Public administration / HD 4092 C747 LAC

1030. Crew, M. 1966 Pennine electricity board: A study in tariff pricing. London: Thomas Nelson. /United Kingdom /Price policy /Electrical utility industry / Abridged version reprinted in R. Turvey, Public Enterprise. /338.001 T869e PCL /HD 3850 T89 Pub Aff

1031. Crosland, C. A. R. 1950 "Prices and Costs in Nationalized Undertakings." Oxford Economic Papers V. 2, No. 1, pp. 51-68. /Price policy / 330.6 Ox2 N.S. PCL

1032. Crosland, C. A. R. 1961 "The Future of Public Ownership." Encounter pp. 60-65. /United Kingdom

1033. Crosser, Paul K. 1960 State Capitalism in the Economy of the United States. New York: Brokman Associates. /United States of America / 338.973 C884s

1034. Crowther, E. 1951 "Administration in the Gas Industry." Public Administration (London), No. 4, pp. 333-334. /United Kingdom /Gas utility industry / 320.5 J826 PCL

1035. Crowther, Warren. 1981 "Latin American Public Enterprises and the Negotiation of Technological Transfer: A Model and Recommendations." Paper presented at the Reunión regional de expertos "Estrategias e instrumentos para reforzar la negociación (SBP) de las empresas públicas en los países en desarrollo en la transferencia internacional de transacciones tecnológicas," San José, Costa Rica, 23-27 Nov. Ljubljana: ICPE. /Latin America /Technology transfer

1036. Crowther, Warren. 1981 "Los estudios de costo-beneficio como instrumento de dependencia o como ejercicio pedagógico: La experencia de la Empresa Pública Chilena de Ferrocarriles." Paper presented at the seminar on public enterprises in development planning for Central America and the Caribbean, San José, Costa Rica, 1-3 July. /Chile /Case Studies /Cost Benefit Analysis /Railway Industry /OPSS

1037. Crozier, M. 1968 "Le rapprochement actuel entre administrations publiques et grands entreprises privés et ses conséquences." Revue Internationale des Sciences Sociales (Paris), /France /Comparative analysis

1038. Cruz de Arrillaga, Juan. 1965 "Eficacia y dinamismo de los organismos autónomos." Documentación Administrativa (Madrid), No. 80, pp. 27-40. /Spain /Economic efficiency /Evaluation

1039. Csikos, B. 1967 "Quelques problemes de la planification des prix dans l'économie hongroise." Economie Appliquée (Paris), No. 1-2, pp. 59-72. /Hungary /Price policy

1040. Csikos-Nagy, L. 1966 "Les experiences hongroises de la planification des prix." Economie Appliquée (Paris), No. 1, pp. 53-67. /Hungary /Price policy /Planning process

1041. Cue de Duarte, I. 1979 "La empresa pública: Referencias constitucionales y su inclusión en la Ley Orgánica de la Administración Pública Federal." Revista Latinoamericana de Administración Pública (Mexico City), No. 8-9, pp. 151-158. /Mexico /Law /Constitutional law / Mixed enterprises

1042. Cugis, C. de. 1956 Le imprese pubbliche in Italia dal 1861 alla prima guerra mondiale. Milan: Ed. CIRIEC. /Italy /Economic history

1043. Culbert, Samuel A., and Jerome Reisel. 1970 Organization Development: A Tool for Managers on Public Enterprise in Development Stores. Washington. /Organization development

/Organization theory

1044. Culbert, Samuel A., and Jerome Reisel. 1971 "Organization Development: An Applied Philosophy for Managers of Public Enterprises." Public Administration Review V. 31, No. 2, pp. 159-169. /Organization development /Organization theory

1045. Cummings, Ian G. 1980 "Corporate Planning in the Public Sector." The Sri Lanka Journal of Management Studies V. 1, No. 1, pp. 1 5. /Sri Lanka /Planning process

1046. Cunningham N. J. 1966 "Public Funds for Public Enterprise: The International Finance Corporation." Journal of Development Studies V. 2, No. 3, pp. 268-296. /Investment /Development corporation / 338.9105 J826

1047. Cuomo, G. 1963 "Observations on the Limits of Control of the Audit Office over Bodies Subsidised by the State." Rassegna di Diritto Pubblico (Naples, Italy), V. 18, No. 1, pp. 26-41. /Italy /Control process

1048. Curran, C. J. 1967 The Selection of Top Management in B.B.C. Lahore, Pakistan: NIPA Seminar. /United Kingdom /Broadcasting industry /Management / Case studies

1049. Curtis, H. A. 1952 "The TVA and the Tennessee Valley: What of the Future?" Land Economics V. 28, pp. 333-340. /United States of America /River valley development projects /305 J824 PCL

1050. Cvetanovic, Milivoje. 1978 "Internal and External Audits: Their Roles and Procedures in Assisting Management and Owners to Assess the Financial Results of Public Enterprises." Paper presented at the Workshop on Information System for the Evaluation of Business Efficiency in Public Enterprises in Developing Countries, Ljubljana, Yugoslavia, 13-18 Nov. Ljubljana: ICPE. /Management /Budget auditing

1051. Cvetanovic, Milivoje. 1979 "Control Systems for Yugoslav Public Enterprises." Paper presented at the Interregional Workshop on Control Systems for Public Enterprises in Developing Countries, Ljubljana, Yugoslavia, 9-13 July. Ljubljana: ICPE. /Yugoslavia /Control process

1052. Cvetanovic, Milivoje. 1981 "Performance Evaluation System in the Yugoslav Organization of Associated Labour." Paper presented at the Expert Group Meeting on Performance Criteria and the Implementation of Performance Evaluation Systems in Public Enterprises in Developing Countries, Lijubljana, Yugoslavia, 23-27 Nov. Ljubljana: ICPE. /Yugoslavia /Trade unions /Evaluation

1053. Czachorski, Witold. 1970 "Responsabilidad del director de la empresa pública frente al Estado socialista." La Empresa Pública. Zaragoza, Spain: Publicaciones del Real Colegio de España en Bolonia. /Spain /Management

1054. Czechoslovakia. Prague Institute of Management. 1971 The State and the Enterprise. Prague: Prague Institute of

Management. /Czechoslovakia /Management

1055. Dagli, Vadilal, ed. 1969 The Public Sector in India: A Survey. Bombay: UBS Publishers' Distributors. /India /354.54092 D133p

1056. Dain, Sulamis. 1977 "Empresa estatal e política econômica no Brasil." Rio de Janeiro: FINEP. /Brazil /Political economy /OPSS

1057. Dain, Sulamis. 1979 "Empresa estatal e capitalismo maduro." Paper presented at the First Latin American Seminar on Public Policies, São Paulo, Brazil, 3-5 Dec. /Brazil /Economic theory / OPSS

1058. Daintith, J. C. 1970 "The Mixed Enterprise in the United Kingdom." In Wolfgang G. Friedmann and J. F. Garner, ed(s). Government Enterprise, A Comparative Study. New York: Columbia University Press. pp. 53-78. /United Kingdom /Mixed enterprises / 350.0092 G746

1059. Dakshinamurthy, D., and G. Prasad. 1981 "Changing Structure of Finance in Government Corporate Sector in India, 1961-78." Lok Udyog (New Delhi), V. 15, No. 6, pp. 7-20. /India /Financing /Economic history /354.54 L836 PCL

1060. Dalal, B. C., and S. C. Mehta. 1963 State Trading Corporation of India, Ltd. Boston: Graduate School of Business Administration, Harvard University. /India /State trading organizations / 016.65807 H261c

1061. Dallari, Adilson Abreu. 1980 "O controle politico das empresas públicas." A empresa pública no Brasil: Uma abordagem multidisciplinar. Brasília: IPEA. pp. 171-201. /Control process

1062. Dallmayr, Winfried R. 1961 "Public and Semi-Public Corporations in France." Law and Contemporary Problems V. 26, No. 4, pp. 755-793. /France /Mixed enterprises /Administrative law / KF 5698 L353 Arch KF1 L3 Pub Aff

1063. Dangeard, Frank-Emmanuel. 1983 "Nationalisations et dénationalisations en Grande Bretagne." Notes et Etudes Documentaires, Nos: 4739-4740. (14 Nov). /United Kingdom /Nationalization /Privatization

1064. Daniel, G. H. 1960 "Public Accountability of the Nationalized Industries." Public Administration (London), V. 38, No. 1, pp. 27-34. /Accountability /JA 8 P8 Pub Aff

1065. Dans, Albina M. 1981 "The Junior Managers Training." Paper presented at the Regional Workshop on the Evaluation of Training Packages for Public Enterprise Managers, Bangkok, Thailand, 10-14 Aug. Ljubljana: ICPE. /Training /Management

1066. Dargent, J. R. 1963 "Nationalized Industries and Economic Policy." In M. Shanks, ed(s). Lessons of Public Enterprise. London: Jonathan Cape. pp. 248-269. /United Kingdom /Economic policy / 335.5 Sh181

1067. Das, A. K. 1980 "Performance Budgeting with Special Reference to the Indian Railways." _Lok Udyog_ (New Delhi), V. 14, No. 3, pp. 15-24. /India /Railway industry /Budgetary process /Case studies /354.54 L836 PCL

1068. Das, N. 1971 "Unrest in Public Enterprises." _Lok Udyog_ (New Delhi), V. 4, No. 12, pp. 1371-1374. /India /Labor relations /354.54 L836 PCL

1069. Das, Nabagopal. 1955 "Management of State Industries--Problems and Policies." _Major Industries of India_ V. 6, pp. 241-248. /India /Management

1070. Das, Nabagopal. 1955 _The Public Sector._ New Delhi, India: Eastern Economist. /India

1071. Das, Nabagopal. 1966 _The Public Sector in India._ New York, Bombay: Asia Publishing House. /India / 338.954 D26p 1966

1072. Das, S. K. 1958 "Management of State Enterprises in India." _Indian Journal of Commerce_ (Allahabad, India), V. 11, No. 4. /India /Management

1073. Das, S. K. 1969 "Workers Participation in Management of Public Enterprises in the U. K." _Lok Udyog_ (New Delhi), pp. 1007-1011. /United Kingdom /Worker management participation /354.54 L836

1074. Das, Tushar K. 1974 "Organisational Change in Commercial Banks." _Lok Udyog_ (New Delhi), V. 7, No. 12, pp. 5-12. /India /Organization development /Banking system /354.54 L836 PCL

1075. Dasappa, H. C. 1961 "Parliamentary Control and Accountability of Public Undertakings." _Indian Journal of Public Administration_ (New Delhi), V. 7, pp. 136-144. /India /Accountability /Control process /Parliament /JA 26 I55 Pub Aff

1076. Dasgupta, B. 1971 _The Oil Industry in India: Some Economic Aspects._ London: Cass. /India /Oil industry

1077. Daskalakis, George D. 1955 "Public Enterprise in Greece." In A. H. Hanson, ed(s). _Public Enterprise._ Brussels: IIAS. pp. 231-240. /Greece / HD 3850 H28 Law

1078. Datta, Uma. 1961 "Growth of Government Companies (1950-51 to 1958-59)." _Economic Weekly_ (London), pp. 1405-1408. /India /Economic history

1079. Davico, Jasa. 1958 "Publicly-Owned Enterprises in Yugoslavia and Control of Their Operation." Paper presented at the Congress of the International Political Science Association, Rome. /Yugoslavia /Control process

1080. Davies, David G. 1971 "The Efficiency of Public versus Private Firms, The Case of Australia's Two Airlines." _Journal of Law and Economics_ V. 14, No. 1, pp. 149-165. /Australia /Air transportation industry /Economic efficiency

/Comparative analysis /KF 1 J58 Pub Aff

1081. Davies, David G. 1977 "Property rights and economic efficiency - the Australian Airlines revisted" Journal of Law and Economics V. 20, No. 1, pp. 223-226. /Australia /Law /Air Transportation Industry /Private Sector /Economic Efficiency /KF 1 J58 Pub Aff

1082. Davies, Ernest. 1940 The State and the Railways. London: Victor Gollancz. /United Kingdom /Railway industry

1083. Davies, Ernest. 1946 National Enterprise: The Development of the Public Corporation. London: Victor Gollancz. /United Kingdom /Economic history

1084. Davies, Ernest. 1950 "Ministerial Control and Parliamentary Responsability of Nationalized Industries." Political Quarterly (London), V. 21, pp. 150-159. /United Kingdom /Control process /Parliament / 320.5 P76p

1085. Davies, Ernest. 1952 Problems of Public Ownership. London: Labour Party. /United Kingdom

1086. Davies, Ernest. 1955 "Government Policy and the Public Corporation." Political Quarterly (London), V. 26, pp. 104-116. /United Kingdom /Economic policy / 320.5 P76p

1087. Davies, Ernest. 1961 "Reorganization of Nationalised Transport." Political Quarterly (London), V. 32, No. 2, pp. 182-192. /United Kingdom /Mass transportation industry /Administrative reform / 320.5 P76p

1088. Davignon, Etienne. 1980 "Future for the European Iron and Steel Industry." Annals of Public and Cooperative Economy V. 51, No. 4, pp. 507-520. /European Economic Community /Steel industry /330.5 An73

1089. Davis, Grant M. 1973 "In Defence of Public Utility Advertising." Public Utilities Fortnightly V. 92, No. 2. /Public utility industry / 388.9 P97

1090. Davis, M. T. de Carvalho Britto. 1969 Tratado das sociedades de economia mista: A empresa estatal brasileira perante o cenário jurídico e econômico. Rio de Janeiro: J. Konfino. /Brazil /Law /Mixed enterprises

1091. Davletshin, T. 1969 "La situación legal de la empresa industrial de propiedad del Estado en la URSS." Estudios sobre la Unión Soviética (Munich), V. 7, No. 21, pp. 48-57. /Union of Soviet Socialist Reps. /Law /Industrial sector

1092. Dayal, Ishwar. 1975 "The Manager of State Enterprises." In R. C. Dutt and Raj K. Nigam, ed(s). Towards Commanding Heights. New Delhi: Vivek Joshi. pp. 208-219. /India /Management /Control process /HD 4293 T68 PCL

1093. Dayal, M. 1964 "Atomic Power Planning and Programme in India." Indian Journal of Public Administration (New Delhi), V. 10, No. 3. /India /Nuclear power /Planning process /JA 26

I55 Pub Aff

1094. Dayal, V. 1975 "The Common Managerial Cadre for the Public Sector." Rivista Trimestrale di Scienza della Administrazione (Milan, Italy), No. 1, pp. 51-60. /Public administration /Management

1095. Daykin, David S. 1979 "The Venezuelan Guyana Corporation and Urban Development in Ciudad Guyana: A A Case Study of the Impact of State Enterprises on Urban Housing Policy." Paper presented at the Latin American Studies Association Meetings on Case Studies of Decision- Making, Operational Styles and Performance of State Enterprises and Development Banks. /Venezuela /Ciudad Guayana, Venezuela /Housing industry /OPSS

1096. Daykin, David S. 1980 The Venezuelan Guayana Corporation ad Urban Development in Ciudad Guayana: A Case Study of the Impact of State Enterprises on Urban Housing Policies. Austin, Tex.: OPSS Technical Papers Series, No. 27. /Venezuela /Ciudad Guayana, Venezuela /Housing industry /OPSS

1097. De Brulle, Daniel. 1964 "A Short Account of the Principal Public Enterprises in Great Britain." Annals of Public and Cooperative Economy V. 35, No. 4, pp. 338-341. /United Kingdom /Evaluation / 330.5 An73

1098. De Brulle, Daniel. 1965 "Economic Democracy in Nationalized Undertakings in France and Great Britain." Annals of Public and Cooperative Economy V. 36, pp. 461-491. /France /United Kingdom / 330.5 An73

1099. De Brulle, Daniel. 1966 "An Assessment of State and Public Enterprise." Annals of Public and Cooperative Economy V. 37, pp. 434-441. /Evaluation / 330.5 An73

1100. De Brulle, Daniel. 1966 "The Labour Plan for Renationalization of the British Iron and Steel Industry." Annals of Public and Cooperative Economy No. 3, pp. 188-215. /United Kingdom /Metal manufacturing industry /Nationalization / 330.5 An73

1101. De Brulle, Daniel. 1966 "Public Enterprise as a Motivation." Annals of Public and Cooperative Economy V. 37, No. 4, pp. 427-433. /Evaluation / Motivation / 330.5 An73

1102. De Brulle, Daniel. 1966 "Le projet travailliste de renationalisation de la sidérurgie britannique." Annales de l'Economie Collective V. 54, No. 2, pp. 137-200. /United Kingdom /Steel industry /Nationalization /

1103. De Flores, Louis Joseph. 1968 "The Evolution of the Role of the Government in the Economic Development of Mexico." Ph.D. dissertation: University of Southern California. /Mexico /Economic development /Planning process /Economic history /Political history /FILM 4297 LAC

1104. De Hejia, V. T. 1968 "Financing the Public Sector." State Bank of India Monthly Review (New Delhi), /India /Financing

1105. De Kerchove, Anne-Marie. 1979 "Demand Patterns and Risk-Sharing in a Labor-Managed Industry." Annals of Public and Cooperative Economy V. 50, No. 2, pp. 63-74. /Worker self management /Theoretical framework /330.5 An73

1106. De Michel Garcia, Pedro. 1974 El intervencionismo y la empresa pública. Madrid. /Spain

1107. De Ru, H. J. 1983 "The Public Enterprise as an Instrument of State Policies." Paper presented at the 19th International Congress of Administrative Sciences, West Berlin, 19-23 Sept. /Netherlands /Economic analysis /Law /Policy analysis /Mixed enterprises / Multinational corporations /OPSS

1108. De Vos, M. 1958 "The Belgium National Railways (S.N.C.B.)". Annals of Collective Economy V. 29, pp. 523-529. /Belgium /Railway industry /330.5 An73

1109. De la Madrid Hurtado, Miguel. 1978 "Algunas cuestiones actuales del financiamiento de la empresa pública." In Rosa Luz Alegría et al., Empresas públicas. Mexico City: Presidencia de la República. pp. 85-94. /Mexico /Financing /HD 4013 E474 1978 LAC

1110. De la Peña, Francisco and Emilio Alanis Patiño. 1955 "Public Enterprise in Mexico." In A. H. Hanson, ed(s). Public Enterprise. Brussels: IIAS. pp. 157-166. /Mexico / HD 3850 H28 Law

1111. De, Nitish R. 1975 "Organization Development as a Technique for Improving Performance in Public Enterprises." Improving Performance in Public Enterprise, Report of an International Conference, Arusha, Tanzania, 2-5 Dec. Arusha, Tanzania: East African Community Management Institute. pp. 164-188. /Organization development

1112. De, Nitish R. 1976 "Coordination of Public Enterprises: Country Study for India." In A. S. H. K. Sadique, ed(s). Public Enterprise in Asia: Studies on Coordination and Control. Kuala Lumpur: Asian Centre for Development Administration. pp. 219-276. /India /Control process /HD 4276 P8

1113. De, Nitish R. 1979 "An Exercise in Curriculum Development for Personnel Mangement in Public Enterprises." Lok Udyog (New Delhi), V. 13, No. 3, pp. 5-16. /Training /Personnel management /354.54 L836 PCL

1114. De, Nitish R. 1980 "Specific Input Needs for Training of Public Enterprise Managers: A Framework." Paper presented at the Interregional Seminar on Training Management of Public Enterprises in Developing Countries, Ljubljana, Yugoslavia, Sept.29-Oct.10. Ljubljana: ICPE. /Training /Management /Shorter version presented at the Interregional Seminar on Training Management in Public Enterprises in Developing Countries, Ljubljana, Yugoslavia, Sept. 29 - Oct. 10, 1980.

1115. Deaglio, M. 1966 Private Enterprise and Public Emulation: A Study of Italian Experience with IRI and the Lessons of Britain's IRC. London: Institute of Economic Affairs. /Italy /United Kingdom /Comparative analysis / Holding company

1116. Dean, A. J. H. 1975 "Earnings in the Public and Private Sectors 1950-1975." National Institute Economic Review V. 7, No. 74, pp. 60-70. /United Kingdom /Profits /Comparative analysis /330.6 N214n

1117. Decelis Contreras, R. 1978 "La empresa, la alianza para la producción y el entorno social." Paper presented at the Round Table on Public Enterprise of the Tenth General Assembly of the Latin American Association of Public Administration. /Mexico / OPSS

1118. Dechert, Charles R. 1962 "Ente Nazionale Idrocarburi: A State Corporation in a Mixed Economy." Administrative Science Quarterly V. 7, pp. 322-348. /Italy /Oil industry /Mixed enterprises

1119. Dechert, Charles R. 1963 Ente Nazionale Idrocarburi, Profile of a State Corporation. Leiden: E. J. Brill. /Italy /Oil industry / 338.27282 En82Yd Geol

1120. Degani, A. H. 1964 "The Land Development Authority--An Economic Necessity." Malayan Economic Review (Singapore), /Malaysia /Land use policy

1121. Delbouille, M., and A. Moureau. 1950 "The Liège Electricity Company: An Intercommunal Cooperative Society Comprising Only Public Authorities." Annals of Collective Economy V. 29, pp. 589-599. /Belgium /Cooperatives /Electrical utility industry / 330.5 An73

1122. Deleon, Aser. 1959 "Workers' Management." Annals of Collective Economy V. 30, pp. 143-169. /Worker self management / 330.5 An73

1123. Delion, André G. 1958 L'Etat et les entreprises publiques. Paris: Sirey. /France /Government authority

1124. Delion, André G. 1959 "Le contrôle des entreprises publiques. La Commission de Verification." Droit Social (Paris), No. 1, pp. 1-9. /France /Control process

1125. Delion, André G. 1959 "Le contrôle des entreprises publiques. Le contrôle parliamentaire." Droit Social (Paris), No. 2, pp. 265-274. /France /Parliament /Control process

1126. Delion, André G. 1960 "Les filiales des entreprises publiques." Droit Social (Paris), V. 23, No. 7-8, pp. 381-394. /France /Subsidiaries

1127. Delion, André G. 1961 "Le plan d'adaptation des charbonnages français." Droit Social (Paris), /France /Coal mining industry /Planning process

1128. Delion, André G. 1963 Le statut des entreprises publiques. Paris: Berger-Levrault. /France /Law

1129. Delion, André G. 1963 "Les participations financières des collectivités locales." Gestion (Paris), /France /Financing /Subsidiaries

1130. Delion, André G. 1965 "Les participations financières des entreprises publiques." Gestion (Paris), /France /Financing /Subsidiaries

1131. Delion, André G. 1966 "Entreprises publiques et Communauté Economique Européene." Revue du Marché Commun (Paris), /European Economic Community

1132. Delion, André G. 1968 Financial Aspects of Manufacturing Enterprises in the Public Sector. Paris. /Manufacturing industry /Public financing /Economic analysis

1133. Delion, André G. 1970 "L´Institut national d´industrie et les entreprises publiques." L´Actualité Juridique (Droit Administratif) No. 1, pp. 4-17. /Industrial sector

1134. Delion, André G. 1971 "Les impératifs de gestion des entreprises publiques." Les Cahiers Français (La Documentation Française) (Paris), No. 150, pp. 21-31. /France /Management

1135. Delion, André G. 1972 "La politique contractuelle entre l´Etat et les entreprises publiques en France." Annales de l´Economie Collective No. 2. /France /Control process /Contractual relations

1136. Delion, André G. 1978 "Les entreprises publiques en France." In André Gélinas, ed(s). Public Enterprise and the Public Interest. Ontario: The Institute of Public Administration of Canada. pp. 119-147. /France /Law /Control process

1137. Delion, André G. 1981 "Les entreprises publiques et le concept d´efficacité." Revue Française d´Administration Publique (Paris), No. 20, pp. 13-30. /Control process /Economic efficiency

1138. Delion, André G., and Michel Durupty. 1982 Les Nationalisations 1982. Paris: Economica. /France /Nationalization /Law

1139. Dell, Sidney. 1971 The Inter-American Development Bank: A Study in Development Financing. New York: Praeger Publishers. /Financial institutions /Development financing /Latin America / HG D384 Pub Aff

1140. Delville, A. 1969 L´information dans l´entreprise. Paris: Dunod. /France /Information system

1141. Demichel, André. 1974 Grands services publiques et entreprises nationales. Paris: Dalloz. /France

1142. Dempsey, J. 1962 "Labour Relations in the State-Sponsored Organizations." Administration (Ibadan, Nigeria), pp. 29-35. /Nigeria /Labor relations

1143. Denduyver, J. 1975 "De overheidstussenkomst ten voordlle von de nationale moatschopiij der belgische spoorwegen" ("Government Intervention in Favor of the Belgian Railways Company"). Economisch en Sociaal Tijdschrift (Antwerp), V. 29, No. 2, pp. 61-83. /Belgium /Railway industry / 305 Ec74

1144. Denis, Jean-Emile. 1981 "Export Performance of the Marketing Boards in LDCs - the Case of Cocoa and Coffee in West Africa." In M. M Kostecki, ed(s). State Trading in International Markets. New York: St. Martin's Press. pp. 221-244. /State trading organizations /Africa /Agricultural services / HF 1410.5 S7 1981 M.

1145. Denis, Maurice. 1958 "The Liège City Electricity Board." Annals of Collective Economy V. 29, pp. 638-640. /Belgium /Electrical utility industry / 330.5 An73

1146. Derber, M. 1970 "Crosscurrents in Workers Participation." Industrial Relations V. 9, No. 2, pp. 123-136. /Worker management participation

1147. Derwish, Ghazi Abdul Wahab. 1978 "Aspects of Technology Transfer in Iraq." Paper presented at the International Workshop on Management of Transfer and Development of Technology in Public Enterprises in Developing Countries, Ljubljana, Yugoslavia, June 19-25. Ljubljana: ICPE. /Iraq /Technology transfer

1148. Deryck, A. 1957 "British Conservatives and State Ownership." Journal of Politics /United Kingdom /Political analysis /320.5 J826

1149. Desai, S. R. 1980 "Transactional Analysis - A New Way to Managerial Effectiveness." Lok Udyog (New Delhi), V. 14, No. 7, pp. 5-10. /India /Management /Organization behavior /354.54 L836 PCL

1150. Desazars de Montgaillard, L. 1949 "Les caractères de l'entreprise publique." Droit Social (France), /France /Evaluation / Law

1151. Deshpanda, R. A. 1962 "Pricing Policy of Public Enterprises." Indian Journal of Public Administration (New Delhi), /India /Price policy / JA 26 I55 Pub Aff

1152. "Design of an Effective Reporting System". 1971 Lok Udyog (New Delhi), V. 5, No. 2, pp. 180-196. /Information system /354.54 L836 PCL

1153. Despicht, Nigel. 1972 "Diversification and Expansion: The Creation of Modern Services." In Stuart Holland, ed(s). The State as Entrepreneur. London: Wiedenfeld and Nicolson. pp. 127-164. /Transportation industry /Communication industry /Italy /Holding company HD 3616 I83 H65 PCL /HD 487 H6 1973 Pub Aff

1154. Destanne de Bernis, G. 1962 "Le rôle du secteur public dans l´industrialisation: Cas des pays sous-développés." Economie Appliquée (Paris), V. 15, No. 1-2, pp. 135-174. /Industrialization /Developing nations

1155. Devaraj, A. Francis. 1978 "Price Policy of Public Enterprises in a Developing Economy." In K. R. Gupta, ed(s). Pricing in Public Enterprises. New Delhi, India: Atlantic Publishers and Distributors. pp. 133-144. /Developing Nations /Price Policy / HB 236 I4 P75

1156. Devarajan, P. N. 1980 "Transfer of Technology by Public Enterprises." Paper presented at the Regional Workshop on Management and Transfer of Technology in Public Enterprises in the ESCAP Region, Bangalore, India, 10-15 Nov. Ljubljana: ICPE. /Technology transfer /Developing nations

1157. Devarajan, P. N. 1980 "Research and Development Activities at HOC." Lok Udyog (New Delhi), V. 14, No. 9, pp. 3-6. /India /Research and development /Case studies /354.54 L836

1158. Devolve, P. 1970 "Les marchés des enteprises publiques." Revue du Droit Public et de la Science Politique en France et à l´Etranger (Paris), No. 6, pp. 287-352. /France /Marketing

1159. Deyrup, F. J. 1957 "Limits of Government Activity in Underdeveloped Countries." Social Research V. 24, pp. 191-201. /Developing nations / 305 So123 PCL

1160. Dhar, R., and Arun Elhance. 1982 "Relative Growth of Private and Public Sectors." Lok Udyog (New Delhi), V. 16, No. 1, pp. 15-28. /India /Private enterprises /Comparative analysis /354.54 L836 PCL

1161. Dharwadkar, P. P. 1980 "Construction Technology and Management in the National Buildings Construction Corporation." Lok Udyog (New Delhi), V. 14, No. 2, pp. 33-42. /India /Management /Construction industry /Case studies /354.54 L836 PCL

1162. Dharwadker, P. P. 1979 "Management of Construction Industry." Lok Udyog (New Delhi), V. 13, No. 1, pp. 5-8. /Management /Construction industry /India /354.54 L836 PCL

1163. Dhingra, O. P., and J. C. Jhuraney. 1974 "Locating Public Sector Industry in Under Developed Regions - Some Managerial Implications." Lok Udyog (New Delhi), V. 8, No. 9-10, pp. 43-50. /India /Regional development /Management /354.54 L836

1164. Dholakia, Bakul H. 1980 "Trends in the Economic Efficiency of Indian Railways." Lok Udyog (New Delhi), V. 14, No. 1, pp. 51-58. /India /Railway industry /Economic efficiency /Case studies /354.54 L836 PCL

1165. Dholakia, Nikhilesh, and Rakesh Khurana. 1976 "Total Performance Measurement Systems for Public Enterprises - A Framework." Lok Udyog (New Delhi), V. 10, No. 4, pp. 43-56. /India /Economic efficiency /Financial performance

/Methodology /354.54 L836 PCL

1166. Diakite, M. 1969 "Rôle des entreprises publiques dans la planification et l´execution du plan au Mali." Mauritius: UNECA Seminar on Role of Public Enterprises in Planning and Plan Implementation. /Mali /Planning process

1167. Diamand, Marcelo. n.d. *Las empresas conjuntas latinoamericanas: Coincidencias y conflictos de intereses.* Buenos Aires: BID-INTAL. /Law /Multinational corporations /HD 2755.5 D5 LAC

1168. Diamond, W. 1957 *Development Banks.* Baltimore, Md.: Johns Hopkins University Press. /Development banks /HG 4517 D5

1169. Diamond, W. 1968 *Development Finance Companies: Aspects of Policy and Operations.* Baltimore, Md.: Johns Hopkins University Press, for the World Bank. /Development banks /332.3 D49

1170. Diamond, W. 1982 "The Preoccupations and Working Style of Chief Executives of Development Banks." In William Diamond and V. S. Raghavan, ed(s). *Aspects of Development Bank Management.* Baltimore, Md.: The Johns Hopkins University Press. pp. 5-17. /Management /Training /Development banks /HG 3550 A8 PCL

1171. Diamond, W. 1982 "Notes on Purposes and Strategies." In William Diamond and V. S. Raghavan, ed(s). *Aspects of Development Bank Management.* Baltimore, Md.: The Johns Hopkins University Press. pp. 35-55. /Goal setting /Training /Development banks /HG 3550 A8 PCL

1172. Diamond, W. 1982 "The Impact of Development Banks on Their Environment." In William Diamond and V. S. Raghaven, ed(s). *Aspects of Development Bank Management.* Baltimore, Md.: The Johns Hopkins University Press. pp. 116-135. /Training /Development banks /Consumer market /HG 3550 A8 PCL

1173. Diamond, W. 1982 "Training Starts at Home." In William Diamond and V. S. Raghavan, ed(s). *Aspects of Development Bank Management.* Baltimore, Md.: The Johns Hopkins University Press. pp. 257-273. /Development banks /Training /HG 3550 A8 PCL

1174. Diamond, W., and V. S. Raghavan, (eds.). 1982 *Aspects of Development Bank Management.* Baltimore, Md.: Johns Hopkins University Press. /Development banks /Training /HG 3550 A8

1175. Dias, Clarence J. 1976 "Public Corporations in India." *Law and Public Enterprise in Asia.* New York: Praeger Press for the International Legal Center. pp. 49-95. /India /Economic analysis /Law /HD 4283 L32

1176. Diate, Kabamba. 1980 "Une expérience de formateurs dans les entreprises publiques au Zaire." Paper presented at the Séminaire international sur la gestion et la formation dans les enterprises publiques dans le pays en voie de développement, Ljubljana, Yugoslavia, 3-15 March. Ljubljana:

ICPE. /Zaire /Training

1177. Diaz Muller, Luis. 1979 "Las empresas de integración en el desarrollo latinoamericano." Mexico City: Paper presented at the International Seminar on the Regulation of the Public Enterprise. /Latin America /Control process /Economic development /Economic integration / OPSS

1178. Dieck, M. 1968 "Le financement des entreprises publiques dans la Rébublique Fédérale Allemande." Annales de l´Economie Collective No. 1-2, pp. 55-124. /Germany, Federal Rep. of /Public financing

1179. Dieterlen, P. 1962 "L´Entreprise publique dans la Communauté Economique." Annales de l´Economie Collective V. 50, No. 2, pp. 341-356. /European Economic Community

1180. Dimock, Marshall E. 1933 British Public Utilities and National Development. London: Allen & Unwin. /United Kingdom /Public utility industry / 338.8 D5976

1181. Dimock, Marshall E. 1934 Government Operated Enterprises in the Panama Canal Zone. Chicago: University of Chicago Press. /Panama Canal Zone /United States of America / 388.8 D597g

1182. Dimock, Marshall E. 1935 "Principles Underlying Government-Owned Corporations." Public Administration (London), V. 13, pp. 51-66. /Public administration /Economic analysis / 320.5 J826 PCL

1183. Dimock, Marshall E. 1945 "These Government Enterprises." Harpers /United States of America

1184. Dimock, Marshall E. 1949 "Government Corporations: A Focus of Policy and Administration. I." American Political Science Review V. 43, No. 5, pp. 899-921. /Public administration /Economic policy / 320.5 Am31 PCL /J 1 A6 Pub Aff

1185. Dimock, Marshall E. 1949 "Government Corporations: A Focus of Policy and Administration. II." American Political Science Review V. 43, No. 6, pp. 1145-1164. /Public administration /Economic policy / 320.5 Am31 PCL /J 1 A6 Pub Aff

1186. Dimock, Marshall E. 1957 Business and Government. New York: Henry Holt. /Private enterprises / 338.973 D597b PCL

1187. Dince, Robert R., Jr. 1960 The Lending Policy of the Export-Import Bank: A Study in Public Policy. Ithaca, N. Y.: Cornell University Press. /United States of America /Financial institutions / Credit policy

1188. Ding-Mo, Huang. 1981 "Experiences and Viewpoints on Some Aspects of Training Public Enterprise Managers." Paper presented at the Interregional Seminar on Training Management in Public Enterprises in Developing Countries, Ljubljana, Yugoslavia, 19-28 Oct. Ljubljana: ICPE. /Training /Management

1189. Diniz, Eli. 1978 Empresário, estado e capitalismo no Brasil. Rio de Janeiro: Paz e Terra. /Brazil /Economic history /Capitalism /Entrepreneurial activity / HD 3616 B7 D55 LAC

1190. Diniz, J. 1960 "Imunidades fiscais as autarquias." Revista de Financas Públicas (Rio de Janeiro), V. 20, No. 214, pp. 14-17. /Brazil /Public financing /Taxation policy

1191. Dinkelspiel, John R. 1967 "Administrative Style and Economic Development of the Organization and Management of the Guyana Region Development of Venezuela." Ph.D. Dissertation, Harvard University. /Venezuela /Economic development /Public administration /Management /Regional development /FILM 6039 LAC

1192. Diop, Issa. 1980 "Politiques et stratégies de formation: Action et contexte africain: Expérience de la SENELEC au Sénégal." Paper presented at the Séminaire international sur la gestion et la formation dans les entreprises publiques dans les pays en voie de développement, Ljubljana, Yugoslavia, 3-15 March. Ljubljana: ICPE. /Senegal

1193. Directions et contrôle des entreprises publiques. 1956 Troisième colloque des facultés de droit. Paris: Dalloz. /Control process /Financial performance

1194. Diria, Abdulkadir H. 1981 The Role of the Public Enterprise in Somalia. Ljubljana: ICPE. /Somalia

1195. Djamin, Awaloedin. 1963 "The Administration of Public Enterprise in Indonesia." Los Angeles: University of Southern California. /Indonesia /Management /Control process

1196. Djokic, Slobodan. 1978 "Scientific Research and Development in the Transfer of Technology with a Special Emphasis on the Transfer to Developing Countries." Paper presented at the International Workshop on Management of Transfer and Development of Public Enterprises in Developing Countries, Ljubljana, Yugoslavia, 19-25 June. Ljubljana: ICPE. /Technology transfer /Developing nations

1197. Djordjevic, J. 1957 "La autogestión de los productores y la organización política de Yugoeslavia." Le Nouveau Droit Yugoslave (Belgrade), V. 7, No. 2-4. /Yugoslavia /Worker self management

1198. Doerr, Audrey. 1983 "Public Enterprise and Public Policy: A Comparative Study of Vertical Integration in Three State Oil Companies." Paper presented at the 19th International Congress of Administrative Sciences, West Berlin, 19-23 Sept. /Oil industry /Italy /Norway /Canada /Economic analysis / OPSS

1199. Dolguchits, L. A. 1968 "UNESCO: Pre-service and In-service Managerial Training for Industry and Building in the Byelorussion S.S.R." International Social Science Journal (Paris), V. 20, No. 1, pp. 17-27. /Industrial sector /Construction industry /Management /Training

1200. Domancic, Pavao. 1974 "Tourisme et hôtellerie dans les plans sociaux de la commune de Hvar." Paper presented at the International Seminar ´74: Planning in Public Enterprises in Developing Countries, Ljubljana, Yugoslavia, Sept. 23-Oct. 9. Ljubljana: ICPE. /Tourist industry /Hotel industry /Planning process /Case studies

1201. Dominican Republic. Oficina Nacional de Planificación. 1968 Plataforma para el desarrollo económico y social de la República Dominicana. (1968-1985) Santo Domingo. /Dominican Republic /Economic development /Social development /Planning process

1202. Dominican Republic. Centro de Estudios Monetarios y Bancarios. 1983 "Los bancos de desarrollo: Base legal y normas operativas en la República Dominicana." Serie Legal, No. 5 Santo Domingo, D. R.: Centro de Estudios Monetarios y Bancarios. /Dominican Republic /Development banks /Law /Economic development/ Credit policy

1203. Domke, Martin. 1960 "Indonesian Nationalization Measures before Foreign Courts." American Journal of International Law V. 54, pp. 305-323. /Indonesia /International law /Nationalization / Law / 341.05 Am35

1204. Domke, Martin. 1961 "Foreign Nationalizations." American Journal of International Law pp. 585-616. /Nationalization /International law / Law / 341.05 Am35

1205. Donald, Gordon. 1972 "The Role of Development Banks." Development Digest V. 10, No. 4, pp. 3-13. /Development banks

1206. Donald, J. S., and S. Shakraborty. 1976 "A Recovery-Based Approach to Maintenance Management in the Sugar Industry." Lok Udyog (New Delhi), V. 10, No. 7, pp. 47-52. /India /Sugar industry /Management /354.54 L836 PCL

1207. Dorn, Dietmar. 1973 "Marketing in der Staatswirtschaft." Zeitschrift fur Wirtschafts-und Sozialwissenschaften V. 93, No. 1, pp. 21-34. /Marketing / H 5 J

1208. Dorrance, Graeme S. 1974 "A intermediação no mercado financiero e de capitais: O papel das instituições financieras; uma exposição gramática." Revista Brasileira de Mercado de Capitais V. 1, pp. 7-26. /Brazil /Banking system /HG 4503 R45 LAC

1209. Dos Reis, Leonídia G., and Myrian L. Redinger. 1975 "Pesquisa tecnológica em empresas estatais: Um estudo preliminar." Rio de Janeiro: FINEP. /Brazil /Technology

1210. Douer, Joseph. 1973 "State Audit of Government Corporations in Israel: Characteristic Findings, Short-Comings in Matters of Principle, and Their Treatment by State Organs in the Years 1960-1970." /Israel /Budget Auditing /Accounting

1211. Dougonitch, R. 1957 "Les cadres économiques de l´autogestion." Questions Actuelles du Socialisme (Paris),

No. 43, pp. 51-68. /France /Organization behavior /Worker self management

1212. Doyle, L. 1963 "Some problems of State Enterprises in Underdeveloped Nations." California Management Review V. 6, No. 1, pp. 23-32. /Developing Nations / 658.05 C128

1213. Draganu, Tudor, and Ilie Tovanas. 1983 "Le contrôle sur l'Activité des entreprises et des autres organisations économiques d'Etat en droit socialiste roumain." Paper presented at the 19th International Congress of Administrative Sciences, West Berlin, 19-23 Sept. /Romania /Law /Control process / OPSS

1214. Dragicevic, A. 1966 "L'autogestion de la classe ouvrière." Questions Actuelles du Socialisme (Belgrade), No. 82, pp. 83-111. /Yugoslavia /Worker self management

1215. Drago, Roland. 1950 La crise de la notion d'établissement public. Paris: Pedone. /France

1216. Drago, Roland. 1969 "Situation et avenir des entreprises publiques en France." Bulletin de l'Institut International d'Administration Publique (Paris), No. 11, pp. 7-22. /France

1217. Drago, Roland. 1970 "Public Enterprises in France." In Wolfgang G. Friedmann and J. F. Garner, ed(s). Government Enterprise, A Comparative Study. New York: Columbia University Press. pp. 107-122. /France / 350.0092 G746

1218. Dragovic, Dragomir B. 1979 "Production Control: Diagnosis, Design of the New System, Implementation and Servicing, FAT Gear Factory, Yugoslavia Case Study." Paper presented at the Interregional Workship "Developing Problem-Solving Skills in Public Enterprises," Ljubljana, Yugoslavia, 2-17 April. Ljubljana: ICPE. /Yugoslavia /Productivity /Control process /Gear manufacturing industry / Case studies

1219. Drake, C. D. 1970 "The Public Corporation as an Organ of Government Policy." In W. G. Friedmann and J. F. Garner, ed(s). Government Enterprise, A Comparative Study. New York: Columbia University Press. pp. 26-52. /United Kingdom /Control process / 350.0092 G746

1220. Drake, P. J. 1969 "Malaysian Industrial Finance Ltd. - Economic Development Board." Financial Development in Malaysia and Singapore. Canberra: Australian National University Press. /Malaysia /Financial performance

1221. Dresang, Dennis L., and Ira Sharksansky. 1975 "Sequences of Change and the Political Economy of Public Corporations: Kenya." Journal of Politics V. 37, No. 1, pp. 163-186. /Kenya /East Africa / 320.5 J825

1222. Dreyfus, Pierre. 1980 "The Efficiency of Public Enterprise: Lessons of the French Experience." In William J. Baumol, ed(s). Public and Private Enterprise in a Mixed Economy. New York: St. Martin's Press. pp. 198-207. /France /Economic efficiency / HD 3842 P87 PCL

1223. Drobnig, U. 1957 "Soviet Corporations in Eastern Germany." Journal of Central European Affairs V. 17, pp. 150-165. /Germany, Democratic Rep. of /Union of Soviet Socialist Reps.

1224. Du Vignaud, R. G. 1971 "Un IRI européen?" La Vie Française (Paris), No. 1359. /Europe /Economic analysis /Holding company

1225. Dua, B. D. 1966 "Workers Participations in Hindustan Insecticides Limited: A Case Study." A. I. C. C. Economic Review (New Delhi), V. 17, No. 18, pp. 27-32. /India /Worker management participation /Case studies

1226. Dubey, B. L., S. K. Verma, and Padman Dwivedi. 1982 "Personality Profile of Successful Business Executives." Lok Udyog (New Delhi), V. 16, No. 2, pp. 21-24. /India /Management /Entrepreneurial activity /354.54 L836 PCL

1227. Dubey, D. L. 1932 "A Board of National Investments for India." Indian Journal of Economics V. 12, pp. 355-363. /India /Investment /Control process /330.5 In2

1228. Dubhashi, P. R. 1983 "Public Enterprises as an Instrument of State Policies." Paper presented at the 19th International Congress of Administrative Sciences, West Berlin, 19-23 Sept. /India /Economic history /Goal setting /Control process /OPSS

1229. Dublin Institute of Public Administration. 1970 The Devlin Report: A Summary. Dublin: Dublin Institute of Public Administration. /Ireland /Public administration

1230. Ducouloux, Claude. 1963 Les sociétes d'économie mixte en France et en Italie. Paris: R. Pichon et R. Duran-Auzias. /France /Italy /Mixed enterprises

1231. Ducruet, J. 1969 "Secteur publique et planification économique en République Arabe Syrienne." Proche-Orient, Etudes Economiques (Beirut), No. 4, pp. 37-125. /Syria /Planning process

1232. Dudukovic, Boris. 1979 "The Case of Management in the Development of Fermentation Industries in Developing Countries: Yugoslav Case Study." Paper presented at the Interregional Workshop "Developing Problem Solving Skills in Public Enterprises," Ljubljana, Yugoslavia, 2-17 April. Ljubljana: ICPE. /Yugoslavia /Management /Alcohol industry /Case studies

1233. Due, J. F. 1965 "The City of Prineville Railway--Case Study in Government Enterprise." Quarterly Review of Economics and Business pp. 63-81. /United Kingdom /Railway industry /Case studies / 330.5 Q23

1234. Duffau, Jean. 1969 "A Review of the State Economic Enterprises in Turkey." Annals of Public and Cooperative Economy V. 40, No. 4, pp. 469-477. /Turkey /Evaluation /330.5 An73

1235. Duffau, Jean. 1973 Les entreprises publiques. Paris: Editions de l'Actualité Juridique. /France /Evaluation /Law

1236. Duffus, W. M. 1949 "Place of the Government Corporation in Public Utility Industries." Land Economics V. 25, pp. 29-38. /United States of America /Public utility industry /305 J824 PCL

1237. Dugdale, John. 1957 "The Labour Party and Nationalization." Political Quarterly (London), pp. 254-259. /United Kingdom /Nationalization /Labor party / 320.5 P76p

1238. Duggal, V. P. 1962 "Some Observations on the Control of Public Enterprise." Indian Journal of Economics V. 43, No. 169. /India /Evaluation /Control process / 330.5 In2

1239. Duggal, V. P. 1962 "Organisation and Operation of Public Enterprises in the Netherlands." Revue Internationale des Sciences Administratives V. 28, No. 4, pp. 430-434. /Netherlands

1240. Duggal, V. P. 1963 "An Enquiry into the Organization and Operation of Public Enterprises." Annals of Collective Economy V. 34, pp. 530-550. /Netherlands / 330.5 An73

1241. Duggal, V. P. 1964 "Socialist Labour Parties and the Size of the Public Sector in Some Countries." Annals of Public and Cooperative Economy pp. 291-306. /Labor party / 330.5 An73

1242. Duggal, V. P. 1964 "L'Organization et le fonctionnement des entreprises publiques: une enquête aux Pays Bas." Annales de l'Economie Collective V. 52, No. 2, pp. 223-246. /Netherlands

1243. Duggal, V. P. 1965 "The Management of Capital Projects in the Public Sector of India." Annals of Public and Cooperative Economy V. 36, pp. 507-515. /India /Investment /Project management /330.5 An73

1244. Duggal, V. P. 1965 "Efficiency Study of an Indian Public Enterprise." Annals of Public and Cooperative Economy V. 36, pp. 533-536. /India /Evaluation /Economic efficiency /Economic analysis / 330.5 An73

1245. Duggal, V. P. 1966 "A Note on Optimum Extent and Operation of the Public Sector." Economia Internazionale (Genoa, Italy), pp. 285-291. /Economic growth theory

1246. Duggal, V. P. 1970 "Performance of Government Enterprises in Canada." Annals of Public and Cooperative Economy V. 41, No. 4, pp. 339-351. /Canada /Financial performance / 330.5 An73

1247. Duguekar, T. G. 1957 "Management of Nationalized Industry." Indian Journal of Public Administration (New Delhi), pp. 268-276. /India /Management / JA 26 I55 Pub Aff

1248. Dumas, P. 1957 Les entreprises nationalisées et le droit commercial. Bordeaux. /France /Law

1249. Dumic, N. 1978 "Information System Development on Enterprises´ Operations by the Social Accountancy Service: Yugoslav Experience." Paper presented at the Workshop on Information System for the Evaluation of Business Efficiency in Public Enterprises in Developing Countries, Ljubljana, Yugoslavia, 13-18 Nov. Ljubljana: ICPE. /Yugoslavia /Accounting /Information system

1250. Dumic, N., and M. Cvetanovic. 1981 "Financial Profitability and Losses of Yugoslav Organizations of Associated Labour." Paper presented at the International Workshop on Financial Profitability and Losses in Public Enterprises, Ljubljana, Yugoslavia, 1-5 June. Ljubljana: ICPE. /Yugoslavia /Worker management participation /Profits

1251. Dumitrescu, M., et al. 1967 L´Organization des entreprises en Roumanie en comparison avec l´organization des entreprises en Italie. Turin, Italy: International Center for Advanced Technical and Vocational Training. /Italy /Romania /Comparative analysis

1252. Dumoulin, André. 1967 "Le support doctrinal et théorique des subventions publiques aux investissements des entreprises." Revue de Science Financière (Paris), No. 3, pp. 523-563. /France /Financing /Theoretical framework / Subsidization policy

1253. Dumpleton, C. W. 1957 Colonial Development Corporation. London: Fabian Society. /United Kingdom /Development corporation

1254. Dunn, W. N. n.d. Self-Management and the Crisis of Public Organizations in Advanced Industrial Society. Pittsburgh, Pa.: University of Pittsburgh, Graduate School of Public and International Affairs. /Developed Nations /Worker Self management / OPSS

1255. Dupont, P. 1964 "Economie publique et coopérative en Italie." Annales de l´Economie Collective V. 52, No. 1, pp. 3-154. /Italy /Cooperatives

1256. Duprilot, J. P. 1969 La S.N.C.F. Les problèmes du présent et les perspectives d´avenir. Paris: L´Actualité Juridique (Droit Administratif). V. 1. /France /Railway industry

1257. Duprilot, J. P. 1972 La modification du statut des établissements publics et leur conséquences sur le régime juridique de leurs personnels. Paris: Ed. L´Actualité Juridique. /France /Administrative law /Personnel management /Law

1258. Durán Barajas, Guillermo. 1983 Empresas públicas: Enfoque específico al Instituto Mexicano del Seguro Social. Mexico City: IPN, Escuela Superior de Comercio y Administración. /Mexico /Social welfare policy /Social security

1259. Durham, N. C. 1951 "Issue on the Nationalization of British Industries." Law and Contemporary Problems /United Kingdom /Nationalization /Industrial sector

1260. Durish, L. L., and R. E. Lowry. 1953 "The Scope and Content of Administrative Decision: The TVA Illustration." *Public Administration Review* V. 13, No. 4, pp. 219-228. /United States of America /River valley development projects /Public administration /Decision making process

1261. Durish, L. L., and R. E. Lowry. 1956 "L'électricité en France en 1955." *Documentations Politique, Diplomatique et Financière* pp. 27-37. /France /Electrical utility industry

1262. Durupty, Michel, and André G. Delion. 1983 "Chronique des entreprises publiques." *Revue Française d'Administration Publique* (Paris), No. 25, pp. 207-216. /France /Investment /Economic analysis

1263. Durupty, Michel. 1980 "La formation et le perfectionnement des dirigeants d'entreprises publiques: Un impératif du développement économique." Paper presented at the international seminar on management and training in public enterprises in developing countries, Ljubljana, Yugoslavia, 3-15 March. Ljubljana: ICPE. /Training /Management

1264. Durupty, Michel. 1981 "La maîtrise de l'Etat sur les entreprises publiques." *Revue Française d'Administration Publique* (Paris), No. 20, pp. 95-118. /Control process /Public administration

1265. Durupty, Michel. 1982 "L'entreprise publique comme instrument de la politique de l'Etat." Paper presented at the Tokyo Round Table preparatory to the 19th International Congress of Administrative Sciences, 13-17 Sept. /France /Nationalization /Economic analysis /Goal setting /Control process / OPSS

1266. Dutra, Wilson, and Vittoria C. Salles. 1975 "Padrão de financiamento em empresas estatais." Rio de Janeiro: FINEP. /Brazil /Industrial economy /OPSS

1267. Dutt, R. C. 1968 "Financial Control in Public Enterprises." *Lok Udyog* (New Delhi), pp. 11-17. /India /Control process /Financial performance / 354.54 L826

1268. Dutt, R. C. 1973 "Management of Public Enterprises - The Kumaramangalam Model." *Lok Udyog* (New Delhi), V. 7, No. 4, pp. 5-13. /India /Management /Case studies /354.54 L836 PCL

1269. Dutt, R. C. 1975 "The Ethos of the Public Sector." In R. C. Dutt and Raj K. Nigam, ed(s). *Towards Commanding Heights.* New Delhi: Vivek Joshi. pp. 70-81. /India /Private enterprises /Comparative analysis /HD 4293 T63 PCL

1270. Dutt, R. C. 1981 "Principles and Practice of Public Enterprise Management." *Lok Udyog* (New Delhi), V. 15, No. 1, pp. 43-44. /India /Management /Financial performance /354.54 L836 PCL

1271. Dutt, R. C., and Raj K. Nigam. 1975 *Towards Commanding Heights.* New Delhi: Vivek Joshi. /India /HD 4293 T68 PCL

1272. Dutt, S. L. 1981 "Report of the Interregional Seminar on Training Management in Public Ljubljana: ICPE. /Training /Management

1273. Dutt, S. L. 1981 "Training of Public Enterprise Managers in India." Ljubljana: ICPE. /India /Training /Management

1274. Duvall, Raymond D., and John R. Freeman. 1983 "The Techno-Bureaucratic Elite and the Entrepreneurial State in Dependent Industrialization." American Political Science Review V. 77, pp. 569-587. /Bureaucracy /Turkey /Economic theory / Economic history / 320.5 Am31 PCL /J 1 A6 Pub Aff

1275. Dwarkadas, R. 1956 "Accountability of Nationalized Industries." International Journal of Politics V. 17, No. 4, pp. 302-310. /India /Accountability

1276. Dworak, Robert J. 1975 "Economizing in Public Organizations." Public Administration Review V. 35, No. 2, pp. 158-165. /Economic efficiency / JK 1 P85

1277. Dzakpasu, Cornelius K. 1978 "Modern Management Techniques in Public Enterprises and Training in Africa." Paper presented at the International Seminar on Management and Training in Public Enterprises in Developing Countries, Ljubljana, Yugoslavia, Sept.18-Oct.6. Ljubljana: ICPE. /Africa /Training /Management

1278. Dzakpasu, Cornelius K. 1979 "Decision Making in Public Enterprises, a Conceptual Framework and Some Lessons from Experience: Case Study." Paper presented at the Interregional Workshop "Developing Problem Solving Skills in Public Enterprises," Ljubljana, Yugoslavia, 2-17 April. Ljubljana: ICPE. /Decision making process /Case studies

1279. Dzakpasu, Cornelius K. 1980 "Definition and Classification of Public Enterprises in Africa: A Framework for Analysis and Effective Management." Paper presented at the Expert Group Meeting on Concept, Definition and Classification of Public Enterprises, Tangier, Morocco, 15-19 Dec. Ljubljana: ICPE. /Africa /Taxonomy /Evaluation /Management

1280. Dzakpasu, Cornelius K. 1980 "The Process of Managerial Decision Making in Public Enterprises." Paper presented at the Regional Workshop on Development of Training Methodologies for Internal Consultants in African Public Enterprises, Addis Ababa, Ethiopia, 1-6 Dec. Ljubljana: ICPE. /Management /Decision making process

1281. Dzuverovic, Borislav. 1981 "Cultural Pluralism and Self-Management Interests." Socialist Thought and Practice V. 21, No. 1, pp. 49-61. /Yugoslavia /Worker self management /Socialist economy

1282. EEC. 1958 "Economic Planning and Management in Yugoslavia." Economic Bulletin for Europe V. 10. No. 3, pp. 43-62. /Yugoslavia /Planning process /Administrative management /HC 411 U4 A2

1283. East African Airways Corporation. 1975 "Performance Improvement in Public Corporations - A Case Study." Improving Performance in Public Enterprise, Report of an International Conference, Arusha, Tanzania, 2-5 Dec. Arusha, Tanzania: East African Community Management Institute. pp. 110-137. /Economic efficiency /Air transportation industry

1284. Eastham, J. K. 1948 "Compensation Terms for Nationalized Industry." Manchester School of Economics and Social Studies V. 16, pp. 29-45. /United Kingdom /Wages /Nationalization /330.5 M3121 PCL

1285. Echeverría, E. Carlos Manuel, et al. 1980 "Policies and Practices concerning the Decisions Made on Investments of Public Enterprises in Costa Rica." Paper presented at the International Workshop on Investment Criteria and Investment Decision- Making Processes, Ljubljana, Yugoslavia, 20-24 Oct. Ljubljana: ICPE. /Costa Rica /Investment

1286. Economic and Social Studies Conference Board. 1969 "State Economic Enterprises." Paper presented at the International Conference on State Economic Enterprises, Ankara, Turkey. /Turkey

1287. Edgeworth, F. Y. 1911 "Contributions to the Theory of Railway Rates." Economic Journal V. 21, pp. 346-370. /Price policy /Railway industry / 330.5 Ec7

1288. Edgeworth, F. Y. 1912 "Contributions to the Theory of Railway Rates, Pt. II." Economic Journal V. 22, pp. 198-218. /Price policy /Railway industry / 330.5 Ec7

1289. Edgeworth, F. Y. 1913 "Contributions to the Theory of Railway Rates." Economic Journal V. 23, pp. 206-226. /Railway industry /Price policy / 330.5 Ec7

1290. Edwards, R. S. 1961 "The Influence of the Nationalized Industries." Public Administration (London), V. 39, No. 1, pp. 45-58. /Economic analysis /Industrial sector /JA 8 P8 Pub Aff

1291. Edwards, R. S. 1962 "Financial and Economic Aspects of Public Electricity Supply in England and Wales." Annals of Collective Economy V. 33, pp. 207-219. /United Kingdom /Electrical utility industry / 330.5 An73

1292. Edwards, Sir Ronald. 1963 Objectives and Control in Nationalized Industry. London: Electricity Council. /United Kingdom /Electrical utility industry /Control process /Goal setting

1293. Edwards, Sir Ronald. 1964 The Electricity Supply Industry: The Present Position and Aims for the Future. London: Electricity Council. /United Kingdom /Electrical utility industry

1294. Egana, Manuel, et al. 1971 Nacionalización petrolera en Venezuela. Caracas. /Venezuela /Nationalization /Oil industry

1295. Eghtedari, Ali M. 1976 "Coordination of Public Enterprises: Country Study for Iran." Paper presented at the In A. .S. H. K. Sadique, ed(s). Public Enterprise in Asia: Studies on Coordination and Control. Kuala Lumpur: Asian Centre for Development Administration. pp. 307-334. /Iran /Control Process / HD 4276 P8

1296. Egypt. ARAC. 1960 History of Public Sector in the Egyptian Economy. Cairo. /Egypt /Economic history

1297. Egypt. Central Agency of Public Mobilization and Statistics. 1967 Public Corporations and Enterprises. Cairo. /Egypt

1298. Eid Sayed, Hassan. 1978 "Evaluation of Sectorial Studies in Egypt." Paper presented at the International Workshop on Management of Transfer and Development of Technology in Public Enterprises in Developing Countries, Ljubljana, Yugoslavia, 19-25 June. Ljubljana: ICPE. /Egypt /Education system /Training /Management /Technology transfer

1299. Einaudi, M. 1948 "Nationalization in France and Italy." Social Research V. 15, pp. 22-43. /France /Italy /Nationalization / 305 So123 PCL

1300. Einaudi, M. 1950 "Nationalization of Industry in Western Europe, Recent Literature and Debates" American Political Science Review V. 44, No. 1, pp. 177-191. /United Kingdom /Italy /France /Nationalization /JA1 A6 Pub Aff,Law

1301. Einaudi, M., M. Bye, and E. Rossi. 1955 Nationalization in France and Italy. Ithaca, N. Y.: Cornell University Press. /France /Italy /Nationalization / 330.166 Ei61n UGL

1302. Ekbote, Abhay. 1983 "Role of Marketing in Public Sector." Lok Udyog (New Delhi), V. 16, No. 10, pp. 5-12. /India /Marketing /354.54 L836 PCL

1303. El Ashmawy, Yaccout. 1983 "Public Enterprises as Instrument of State Policy." Paper presented at the 19th International Congress of Administrative Sciences, West Berlin, 19-23 Sept. /Egypt /Goal setting /Accountability /Control process /Multinational corporations /OPSS

1304. El Maadawi El-Sayed, Mohamed. 1979 "Management and Training in Public Enterprises: Country Report of Egypt." Paper presented at the International Seminar on Management and Training in Public Enterprises in Developing Countries, Ljubljana, Yugoslavia, 1-13 Oct. Ljubljana: ICPE. /Egypt /Training /Management

1305. El Mallakh, R. 1959 "Some Economic Aspects of the Aswan High Dam Project in Egypt." Land Economics V. 35, pp. 15-23. /Egypt /River valley development projects /Public works policy / 305 J824 PCL

1306. El Mir, Ali. 1980 "Note sur l´identification des besoins en formation de l´entreprise publique." Paper presented at the Séminaire international sur la gestion et la formation dans les entreprises publiques dans les pays en voie de développement, Ljubljana, Yugoslavia, 6-17 Nov. Ljubljana: ICPE. /Training

1307. El Mir, Ali. 1980 "Rapport du séminaire international sur la gestion et la formation dans les pays en voie de développement, Ljubljana, du 3 au 15 Mars, 1980." Ljubljana: ICPE. /Developing nations /Training /Management

1308. El Mir, Ali. 1981 "On the Evaluation of Training." Public Enterprise V. 2, No. 2, pp. 37-48. /Management /Training / OPSS /Paper earlier presented at the Interregional Seminar on Training Management in Public Enterprises in Developing Countries, Ljubljana, Yugoslavia, Oct. 19-28, 1981.

1309. El Mir, Ali. 1981 "On the Assessment of Training Needs." Paper presented at the Interregional Seminar on Training Management in Public Enterprises in Developing Countries, Ljubljana, Yugoslavia, 19-28 Oct. Ljubljana: ICPE. /Training

1310. El Mir, Ali. 1981 "On Implementation of Training." Paper presented at the Interregional Seminar on Training Management in Public Enterprises in Developing Countries, Ljubljana, Yugoslavia, 19-28 Oct. Ljubljana: ICPE. /Training

1311. El Mir, Ali. 1981 "On the Experience of the International Center for Public Enterprises in Developing Countries in Network Building." Paper presented at the Ad Hoc Expert Group Meeting on Network in Public Administration and Finance, Madrid, Spain. Ljubljana: ICPE. /Network analysis /Developing nations

1312. El Mir, Ali. 1981 "On the Evaluation of Public Enterprise Performance." Paper presented at the Expert Group Meeting on Performance Criteria and the Implementation of Performance Evaluation Systems in Public Enterprises in Developing Countries, Ljubljana, Yugoslavia, 23-27 Nov. Ljubljana: ICPE. /Evaluation

1313. El Mir, Ali. 1982 "Government Control Over Public Enterprises: Current and Relevant Forms." Public Enterprise V. 2, No. 4, pp. 45-58. /Control process / OPSS

1314. El Mir, Ali. 1982 "Government Control over Public Enterprises: Current and Relevant Forms." In United Kingdom. Commonwealth Secretariat, ed(s). Government Executive and Supervisory Control over Public Enterprises. London. pp. 101-117. /Control process

1315. El Mir, Ali. 1983 Public Financial Institutions and Their Role in Development. Ljubljana: ICPE. /Financial institutions /Credit policy /Economic development

1316. El Sheikh, Moawia Siddig. 1978 "Science and Technology in Development Agriculture." Paper presented at the International Workshop on Management of Transfer and Development of Technology in Public Enterprises in Developing Countries, Ljubljana, Yugoslavia, 19-25 June. Ljubljana: ICPE. /Agricultural sector /Technology transfer

1317. El Sherif, M., and A. El Ghadban. 1968 Report on Problems and Difficulties of Public Enterprises in Libya. Tunis, Libya: UNECA Seminar. /Libya

1318. El Soued, Ahmed Abu. 1979 "Internal Controls Operated through the Standardized Accounting System in the Public Sector in the Arab Republic of Egypt as Tools for Effective Management." Paper presented at the Interregional Workshop on Control Systems for Public Enterprises in Developing Countries, Ljubljana, Yugoslavia, 9-13 July. Ljubljana: ICPE. /Egypt /Accounting /Management

1319. El-Bachri, A. 1963 Le rôle principal de l´entreprise publique. Cairo: N.I.M.D. /Egypt

1320. El-Badri, A. 1963 Le secteur publique dans la société socialiste. Cairo: N.I.M.D. /Egypt

1321. El-Kocheri, A. S. 1967 "Les nationalisations dans les pays du tiers monde devant le juge occidental." Revue Critique de Droit International Privé (Paris), V. 56, No. 2, pp. 249-275. /France /Nationalization

1322. El-Namaki, M. S. S. 1979 Problems of Management in a Developing Environment: The Case of Tanzania. State Enterprises between 1967 and 1975. New York: North-Holland Publishing Company. /Tanzania /Economic development /Technology transfer /Developing nations /Management /Decision making process /Planning process /Control process /Evaluation /HD 4348.5 N35 PCL

1323. El-Said, M. M. 1968 "On the Many Problems Arising from the Control and Management of Public Enterprises being Established in African Countries." Tunis, Libya: UNECA Seminar. /Africa /Control process /Management

1324. Ellis, C. A. 1953 Public Utilities in Colombia. New York: United Nations. /Colombia /Public utility industry

1325. Ellis, C. A. 1954 Business and Financial Administration and Accounting in Iran. New York: U.N. Technical Assistance Program. /Iran /Accounting /Financing /Private enterprises

1326. Elsayed, S. E. M. 1969 The Role of Public Enterprises in the Sudan in Planning and Plan Implementation. Mauritius: UNECA Seminar on Role of Public Enterprises in Planning and Plan Implementation. /Sudan /Planning process

1327. Eltinay, Ibrahim Omar. 1980 "Some Aspects of Planning in Sudan." Economic Quarterly V. 15, No. 2, pp. 19-27. /Sudan /Planning process

1328. Emmerich, Herbert. 1947 "The Administration of Public Enterprises in the United States." Public Administration (London), V. 35, No. 3, pp. 140-153. /United States of America /Public administration / 320.5 J826 PCL

1329. Encel, S. 1960 "Public Corporations in Australia." Public Administration (Sydney, Australia), pp. 235-252. /Australia

1330. Encel, S. 1965 "Entreprises publiques et cooperatives dans une société libre." Annales d'Economie Collective pp. 151-403. /Capitalism /Cooperatives

1331. Ennis, R. W. 1967 Accountability in Governments, Public Corporation and Public Companies. London: Lyon, Grant and Greer. /Accountability /Public administration /354.42067 En62a

1332. Ennis, R. W., ed. 1967 Accountability in Government Departments, Public Corporations and Public Companies: An Introduction. London: Lyon, Grant, and Greer for Administrative Staff College. /Accountability /United Kingdom /354.42067 En62a

1333. "Les entreprises nationales et le parlement." 1960 Revue du Droit Public et de la Science Politique en France et a L'Etranger (Paris), V. 76, No. 6, pp. 1137-1187. /France /Parliament /Control process

1334. "Les entreprises publiques et coopératives dans une société libre." 1965 Annales de l'Economie Collective V. 53, No. 2-3, pp. 151-403. /Cooperatives

1335. Eorsi, Gyula. 1977 "Two Variants of a Research Project." In Yash Ghai, ed(s). Law in the Political Economy of Public Enterprise. Uppsala: Scandinavian Institute of African Studies. New York: International Legal Centre. pp. 76-80. /Law /Control process /System analysis / Africa 76 L41 Law

1336. Epstein, M. 1910 "Municipal Enterprise in Germany." Economic Journal V. 20, pp. 118-122. /Germany, Federal Rep. of /Germany, Democratic Rep. of / Local government /Decentralized authority / 330.5 Ec7

1337. Erber, Fabio Stefano. 1974 "A empresa estatal e a escolha de tecnologias." Revista Ciencia e Cultura V. 26, No. 12. /Technology / OPSS

1338. Erdman, Howard L. 1973 "Politics and Economic Development in India: The Gujarat State Fertilizers Company as a Joint Sector Enterprise." /India /Economic development / Gujarat, India (State)

1339. Eremyi, E. 1956 "Evolution de la situation économique et financière des entreprises publiques du secteur industriel et comercial de 1952 à 1954." Statistiques et Finances (Paris), pp. 298-341. /France /Industrial sector /Commercial sector /Economic analysis /Financial performance

1340. Escarmelle, J.-F., and A. Dersin. 1980 "Le contrôle économique des entreprises publiques." Administration Publique (Brussels), V. 4, No. 4, pp. 295-303. /Public administration /Control process

1341. Escarmelle, J.-F. 1983 "La crise économique actuelle implique-t-elle un nouvel essor de l'entreprise publique? Le cas de la sidérurgie dans quelques pays européens." Administration Publique (Brussels), No. T2, pp. 105-115.

/Steel industry /European Economic Community

1342. Escobar C., Camilo, and Tomás Nieto T. 1975 "La empresa pública en el Ecuador." Rio de Janeiro: FGV-EIAP. /Ecuador /Directory /Control process / OPSS

1343. Escoto Cruz, José Francisco. 1981 "Informe sobre la planificación de empresas públicas de Honduras." Paper presented at the seminar on public enterprises in development planning for Central America and the Caribbean, San José, Costa Rica, 1-3 July. /Honduras /Planning process /Economic analysis / OPSS

1344. Escuela Nacional de Administración Pública. Instituto de Estudios Administrativos. 1972 Empresas públicas: Bibliografía 1972. Alcalá de Henares, Spain: Escuela Nacional de Administración Pública, Instituto de Estudios Administrativos. /Bibliography

1345. Escuela Nacional de Administración Pública. Instituto de Estudios Administrativos. 1972 Empresas públicas: Bibliografía seleccionada de Mayo, 1966. Alcalá de Henares, Spain: Escuela Nacional de Administración Pública, Instituto de Estudios Administrativos. /Bibliography

1346. Espindola, Oscar A. Camacho. 1975 Organización administrativa y empresas publicas de la República Oriental del Uruguay. Rio de Janeiro: FGV-EIAP. /Uruguay /Management

1347. Espiritu Santo, Benedito Rosa de. 1980 "Sector estatal e desenvolvimento." A empresa pública no Brasil: Uma abordagem multidisciplinar. Brasília: IPEA. pp. 89-140. /Economic history /Brazil

1348. Esseks, J. D. 1971 "Government and Indigenous Private Enterprise in Ghana." Journal of Modern African Studies (London), V. 9, No. 1, pp. 11-31. /Ghana /Evaluation /Private enterprises / 960.5 J828

1349. Esteban Coca, Salvador. 1973 La financiación de las inversiones del INI. La empresa pública industrial en España: El INI. Madrid: Instituto de Estudios Fiscales. /Spain /Industrial sector /Financing /Investment /Holding company

1350. Estefano, M. A. D. 1963 "Las nacionalizaciones del gobierno revolucionario y el derecho internacional." Política International (Havana), No. 3, pp. 41-88. /Cuba /Nationalization /International law

1351. Esteva, Gustavo. 1980 "CONASUPO 1970-1979: The Change of Policies and the Policy of Change." Paper presented in the Workshop held on the Mexican State and the Agricultural Sector. Austin, Texas: ILAS. /Mexico /Food industry /OPSS

1352. Etame, J. T. 1969 The Role of Public Enterprise in Federal Republic of Cameroon, with Particular Reference to West Cameroon. Mauritius: UNECA. Seminar on Role of Public Enterprises in Planning and Plan Implementation. /Cameroon

/Evaluation

1353. European Center for Public Enterprises. 1967 Les entreprises publiques dans la Communauté Economique Européen. Paris: Ed. Dunod. /European Economic Community /Evaluation /HD 4183 C4 Law

1354. European Centre for Public Enterprises. 1969 L'enterprise publique face au dévelopment économique de l'Europe (IV Congrès du CEEP). Paris: Editions Techniques et Economiques. /Europe /Economic development /Evaluation

1355. European Centre for Public Enterprises. 1973 The Evolution of the Public Enterprises in the Community of the Nine. Brussels: CEEP Editions. /European Economic Community /Belgium /Luxemburg /Germany, Federal Rep. of /France /Ireland /Italy /Netherlands /OPSS

1356. European Centre for Public Enterprises. 1978 "The Financing of Public Enterprises in Countries of the European Community." Brussels: CEEP. /European Economic Community /Public financing

1357. European Centre for Public Enterprises. 1978 "Opinion of the European Centre of Public Enterprises concerninng the Economic Behaviour of Public Enterprises in the Market of the European Community." Brussels: CEEP. /European Economic Community /Economic analysis

1358. Evans, Peter. 1977 "Multinationals, State-Owned Corporations and the Transformation of Imperialism: A Brazilian Case Study." Economic Development and Cultural Change V. 26, No. 1, pp. 43-64. /Brazil /Multinational corporations /330.5 Ec66

1359. Evans, Peter. 1979 Dependent Development: The Alliance of Multinational, State and Local Capital in Brazil. Princeton, N.J.: Princeton University Press. /Brazil /Multinational corporations / HC 190 C3 E92 LAC

1360. Evans, Tom. 1980 "Developing Corporate Planning in Public Enterprise." Paper presented at the Regional Workshop on Corporate Planning in Public Enterprises in the Asian and Pacific Region, Kuala Lumpur, Malaysia, 17-21 Nov. Ljubljana: ICPE. /Planning process

1361. Evans, Tom. 1981 Dilemmas in Corporate Planning. Ljubljana: ICPE. /Planning process

1362. FGV-EBAP. n.d. Empresas estatais: Indicador bibliográfico. Rio de Janeiro: FGV-EBAP. /Bibliography /OPSS /Early version of work later published in Spanish.

1363. FGV-EIAP. 1974 "Empresas públicas." Boletim Bibliográfico (Rio de Janeiro), V. 1, No. 3. /Bibliography /OPSS /Irregular serial publication.

1364. FGV-EIAP. 1979 Empresas Públicas: Indicador bibliográfico. Mexico City: Editorial Limusa. /Bibliography /HD 3850 E467

LAC Expanded version of work published in Portuguese by FGV-EBAP.

1365. FIEL. Fundación de Investigaciones Económicas Latinoamericanas. 1976 Las empresas públicas en la economia argentina. Buenos Aires: Consejo Empresario Argentino. /Argentina /Law'/Statistics / OPSS

1366. Fabella, Armand. 1976 "Public Enterprise Policy on Investment, Prices, and Returns." Approaches to the Public Enterprise Policy in Asia on Investment, Prices, and Returns Criteria. Kuala Lumpur: U.N. Asian Centre for Development Administration. pp. 139-142. /Philippines /Price policy /Investment /Profits / HD 4276 A8 1976

1367. Faber, M. L. O., and J. G. Potter. 1971 Towards Economic Independence: Papers on the Nationalization of the Copper Industry in Zambia. Cambridge, England: Cambridge University Press. /Zambia /Copper mining industry /Nationalization /338.2743 F112t

1368. Fabian Society. 1947 "The Nationalization of the Railways." Political Quarterly (London), V. 18, No. 5. /United Kingdom /Railway industry /Nationalization / 320.5 P76p

1369. Fabian Society. 1963 The Future of Public Ownership. London: Fabian Society. /United Kingdom /Evaluation

1370. Fabre, Francis J. 1964 Les societés locales d'économie mixte et leur contrôle. Paris: Ed. Berger Levrault. /France /Mixed enterprises /Control process / 352.044 F114s 1964

1371. Fabre, R. 1945 La nationalisation des houillères du Nord et du Pas de Calais. Paris: Droit Social. /France /Coal mining industry /Nationalization

1372. Fabre, R. 1948 "Les nationalisations en France: le charbon." Societé Belge d'Etudes et d'Expansion (Liège, Belgium), No. 133, pp. 739-742. /France /Coal mining industry /Nationalization

1373. Fabrikant, R. 1975 "PERTAMINA: A Legal and Financial Analysis of a National Oil Company in a Developing Country." Texas International Law Journal V. 10, pp. 495-536. /Indonesia /Oil industry /Economic analysis /Law /Evaluation /Case studies /JX 1 T43 TXC

1374. Fabrikant, R. 1976 "Pertamina: A National Oil Company in a Developing Country." Law and Public Enterprise in Asia. New York: Praeger for the International Legal Center. pp. 192-246. /Indonesia /Oil industry /Control process /Economic efficiency /HD 4283 L32

1375. Faccini, Antonio C. 1969 Working Group on Measures for Improving Performance of Public Enterprises in Developing Countries. (A Case Study of the Early Development of Colombia's Steel Industry.) New York: United Nations. /Colombia /Steel industry /Case studies

1376. Fair, Marvin L. 1961 "Port Authorities in the United States." Law and Contemporary Problems V. 26, No. 4, pp. 703-714. /United States of America /Public Authority /Transportation Industry

1377. Faraco, Francisco. 1975 Reversión petrolera en Venezuela. Caracas: Ediciones Centauro. /Venezuela /Oil industry /Nationalization /Law / HD 9560.7 V42 F372 LAC

1378. Faria, Walter. 1974 "Límites a intervenção do setor público na economia." Revista do Serviço Público (Rio de Janeiro), V. 109, No. 1, pp. 29-39. /Brazil

1379. Farias, T. 1961 "La congestión en una empresa del Estado." Revista de Administración Pública (Buenos Aires), V. 1, No. 2. /Argentina / JA 5 R483 LAC

1380. Farid, S. 1970 Top Management in Egypt--Its Structure, Quality and Problems. Santa Monica: Rand Corporation. /Egypt /Management

1381. Farooqi, Ishrat H. 1983 "Public Enterprise as an Instrument of Economic Change in India." Paper presented at the 19th International Congress of Administrative Sciences, West Berlin, 19-23 Sept. /India /Economic analysis / OPSS

1382. Farooqi, Tariq Zahir. 1981 "Financial Profitability and Losses in Public Sector: Pakistan Experience." Paper presented at the International Workshop on Financial Profitablity and Losses in Public Enterprises, Ljubljana, Yugoslavia, 1-5 June. Ljubljana: ICPE. /Pakistan /Profits

1383. Farrel, M. J. 1968 In Defense of Public Utility Price Theory. Harmondsworth, Middlesex: Penguin Books Ltd. /Public utility industry /Price policy

1384. Farrell, M. J. 1958 "In defence of public-utility price theory." Oxford Economic Papers V. 10, pp. 109-123. /Price policy / 330.6 Ox2 Amended version reprinted in R. Turvey, Public Enterprise, 1968. /338.001 T869e PCL /HD 3850 T89 Pub Aff

1385. Faucher, Philippe. 1981 L´entreprise publique comme instrument de politique économique. Notes de Recherche, No. 2. Montreal: Université de Montréal, Département de Science Politique. /Taxonomy /Autonomy / OPSS

1386. Faulhaber, G. R. 1975 "Cross-Subsidization: Pricing in Public Enterprises." American Economic Review V. 55, No. 5, pp. 966-977. /Price policy /Subsidization policy /330.5 Am312

1387. Faure, Y. A. 1977 "Sénégal: chroniques de droit administratif." Annuaire de Législation Française et Entrangére V. 26, pp. 370-372. /Senegal /Law /Postal service /Education system /Communication industry /Public administration

1388. Favre, H. 1981 "Estado, capitalismo y etnicidad, el caso peruano." Relaciones: Estudios de Historia y Sociedad (Mexico City), No. 6, pp. 82-105. /Peru /Cultural policy

1389. Faya Viesca, Jacinto. 1979 Administración pública federal: La nueva estructura. Mexico City: Editorial Porrúa. /Mexico /Administrative reform / JL 1226 1983 F383 1983 LAC

1390. Fazal, M., and R. K. Nigam. 1967 "Managerial Remuneration and Incentives in Public Undertakings." Lok Udyog (New Delhi), pp. 15-21. /India /Management /Incentive systems /354.54 L836 PCL

1391. Fazal, Mohd. 1964 "Criteria for Measuring Performance of Management in Public Undertakings." Lok Udyog (New Delhi), pp. 903-907. /India /Evaluation /Management /354.54 L836 PCL

1392. Fazal, Mohd. 1972 "Management in Public Enterprises." Lok Udyog (New Delhi), V. 6, No. 5, pp. 5-8. /India /Management /354.54 L836 PCL

1393. Fazal, Mohd. 1973 "Strategic Export Planning at Enterprise Level - Experience of Engineering Projects (I) Ltd." Lok Udyog (New Delhi), V. 7, No. 7, pp. 11-14. /India /Exports /Case studies /354.54 L836 PCL

1394. Fazal, Mohd., and S. S. Das Gupta. 1975 "Tender Engineering for Turn-Key Semi-Integrated Steel Projects." Lok Udyog (New Delhi), V. 9, No. 1, pp. 37-46. /India /Consultant services /Project management /Steel industry /Case studies /354.54 L836 PCL

1395. Federeci, J. L. 1965 Tarifas, entradas y gastos de la empresa de ferrocarriles del Estado de Chile. Santiago: Universidad de Chile. Instituto de Economía. No. 76. /Chile /Railway industry /Evaluation

1396. Fedorowicz, Z. 1966 The Reform of the Financial System of State Owned Enterprises in Poland. Cairo: Inst. of National Planning. No. 646. /Poland /Financial performance

1397. Fedorowicz, Z. 1966 "The Problem of Pricing in a Socialist Economy." Egypte Contemporaine (Cairo), /Egypt /Socialist economy /Price policy / 962.05 Eg98r

1398. Fedorowicz, Z. n.d. Determination and Control of Production Costs in Public Manufacturing Enterprises. Warsaw. p. 22. /Poland /Manufacturing industry /Costs /Control process

1399. Feiwell, George R. 1965 The Economics of a Socialist Enterprise: A Case Study of the Polish Firm. New York: Praeger. /Poland /Management / /658 F329e PCL /HD70 P6 F4 Pub Aff

1400. Feldstein, Martin S. 1964 "Cost-Benefit Analysis and Investment in the Public Sector." Public Administration (London), V. 42, pp. 351-372. /Cost benefit analysis /Investment / JA 8 P8 Pub Aff

1401. Feldstein, Martin S. 1964 "Net Social Benefit and the Public Investment Decision." Oxford Economic Papers V. 16, No. 1, pp. 114-132. /Investment /Cost benefit analysis /330.6 Ox2 PCL

1402. Feletar, Dragutin, et al. 1980 "Women as a Factor of Development: The Composite Organization of Associated Labour (COAL), Podravka, Koprivnica; A Case Study." Paper presented at the International Expert Group Meeting on Women as a Factor of Development and the Responsibilities of Public Sector in This Regard, Ljubljana, Yugoslavia, 14-19 April. Ljubljana: ICPE. /Women's studies /Economic development

1403. Fenet, A. n.d. Le régime juridique des régies de distribution d'énergie électrcité. Amiens, France: Publications de la Faculté de Droit d'Amiens. V. 1. /France /Electrical utility industry /Public services /Law

1404. Fenizio, Ferdinando di. 1965 "Il settore publico d'un sistema economico in transformazione." L'Industria (Milan, Italy), V. 4, pp. 560-580. /Italy / 338.0945 In

1405. Ferencic, Dunja. 1980 "Research on the Status of Women in the Projects of the International Center for Public Enterprises in Developing Countries: An Outline for Methodological Approach." Paper presented at the International Expert Group Meeting on Women as a Factor of Development and the Responsibilities of Public Sector in This Regard, Ljubljana, Yugoslavia 14-19 April. Ljubljana: ICPE. /Women's studies

1406. Fernandes, F. das Chagas. 1981 "Controle financiero das empresas estatais." Revista do Tribunal de Contas da União V. 23, pp. 21-26. /Brazil /Control process /Public financing

1407. Fernandes, J. B. 1966 "Da natureza jurídica das sociedades de economia mista: Aspecto indicativo de personalidade jurídica de direito público." Administracão Paulista (São Paulo), No. 11, pp. 73-90. /Brazil /Mixed enterprises /Law

1408. Fernandes, Praxy J. 1974 "Public Enterprise in India, A Perspective View: National Paper of India." Paper presented at the International Seminar '74 Planning in Public Enterprises in Developing Countries, Ljubljana, Yugoslavia, Sept. 23-Oct. 9. Ljubljana: ICPE. /India /Planning process

1409. Fernandes, Praxy J. 1975 "Report of the International Seminar on Planning in Public Enterprises in Developing Countries, September 23-October 9, 1974." Bulletin of ICPE (Ljubljana), V. 1, No. 1, pp. 5-15. /Developing nations /Planning process

1410. Fernandes, Praxy J. 1976 "Coordination of Public Enterprises: Country Study for India." In A. S. H. K. Sadique, ed(s). Public Enterprise in Asia: Studies on Coordination and Control. Kuala Lumpur: Asian Center for Development Administration. pp. 125-218. /India /Control process / HD 4276 P8

1411. Fernandes, Praxy J. 1977 "Report of the First Meeting of the International Research Project 'The Role of the Public Sector in Developing Countries,' Ljubljana, December 18-20, 1977." Ljubljana: ICPE. /Developing nations

1412. Fernandes, Praxy J. 1978 "Training for Effectiveness: A Multi-Dimensional Approach." Paper presented at the International Seminar on Management and Training in Public Enterprises in Developing Countries, Ljubljana, Yugoslavia, Sept. 18-Oct. 6. Ljubljana: ICPE. /Training / Paper also presented at the Expert Group Meeting on the Research Project on Education and Training in Public Enterprises in Developing Countries, Ljubljana, 17-22 March, 1980.

1413. Fernandes, Praxy J. 1979 "Joint Ventures for Public Enterprises: Why, How, Whither?" Paper presented at the International Seminar on Joint Ventures and Public Enterprises in Developing Countries, Ljubljana, Yugoslavia, 4-12 Dec. Ljubljana: ICPE. /Mixed enterprises /Mixed economy

1414. Fernandes, Praxy J. 1979 "Educating Managers and Managing Educators: Some Reflections on the Interlinkages between Education and Training Processes and Their Absorption and Utilization in Public Enterprises." Paper presented at the International Seminar on Management and Training in Public Enterprises in Developing Countries, Ljubljana, Yugoslavia, 12-17 Feb. Ljubljana: ICPE. /Training /Management Paper also presented to the Expert Group Meeting on the Research Project on Education and Training in Public Enterprises in Developing Countries, Ljubljana, 17-22 March, 1980.

1415. Fernandes, Praxy J. 1979 "Managers for African Public Enterprises: Some Reflections on Problems and Issues Confronting Public Enterprises and Strategies and Approaches for Management Development." Ljubljana: ICPE. /Africa /Training /Management

1416. Fernandes, Praxy J. 1979 "Training Public Enterprise Managers: Some Questions, Issues, Dilemmas." Paper presented at the Expert Group Meeting on the Research Project on Education and Training in Public Enterprises in Developing Countries, Ljubljana, Yugoslavia, March 17-22. Ljubljana: ICPE. /Training /Management

1417. Fernandes, Praxy J. 1979 "The `Technology' of Technology Transfer: Some Thoughts on Licensing Regulations and Technology Transfer Contracts in the Context of Development Planning." Paper presented at the Expert Group Meeting on Structuring of Contractual Relations in Transfer of Technology Transactions of Public Enterprises in Developing Countries (Model Countries/Provisions for Licensing). Ljubljana: ICPE. /Developing nations /Technology transfer /Law /Planning process / Contractual relations

1418. Fernandes, Praxy J. 1979 "Report of the Meeting: Regional Workshop on Planning in Public Enterprises of the African Region, Accra, 10-15 December 1979." Ljubljana: ICPE. /Africa /Planning process

1419. Fernandes, Praxy J. 1979 "Report of the Proceedings of the Second International Meeting on the Role of Public Sector in Developing Countries, 2-7 April, 1979, Ljubljana, Yugoslavia." Ljubljana: ICPE. /Developing nations

1420. Fernandes, Praxy J. 1979 "Report of the Regional Meeting of Arab and Mediterranean Countries on the Role of the Public Sector in Developing Countries, November 19-24, 1979, Ljubljana, Yugoslavia." Ljubljana: ICPE. /Developing nations

1421. Fernandes, Praxy J. 1979 "The Role of the Public Sector in the Industrialization of the Developing Countries: The Issue Paper." Paper presented at the Expert Group Meeting on the Role of the Public Sector in the Industrialization of the Developing Countries, Vienna. Ljubljana: ICPE. /Developing nations /Industrialization

1422. Fernandes, Praxy J. 1979 "The Accountability of Public Enterprises: Some Thoughts on the Rationale and Spirit of External Control Systems." Paper presented at the Interregional Workshop on Control Systems for Public Enterprises in Developing Countries, Ljubljana, Yugoslavia, 9-13 July. Ljubljana: ICPE. /Control process /Accountability

1423. Fernandes, Praxy J. 1979 "Report of the Interregional Workshop on Control Systems for Public Enterprises in Developing Countries, 1979, Ljubljana, July 9-13, 1979." Ljubljana: ICPE. /Developing nations /Control process

1424. Fernandes, Praxy J. 1979 "A Lesson in Agro-Economics: Karnatak Agro-Industries Corporation, Indian Case Study." Paper presented at the Interregional Workshop on Developing Problem Solving Skills in Public Enterprises, Ljubljana, Yugoslavia, 2-17 April. Ljubljana: ICPE. /India /Agricultural sector /Economic efficiency /Case studies /Evaluation

1425. Fernandes, Praxy J. 1979 "Personnel Management and Wage Policy: Hindustan Petroleum Corporation, Indian Case Study." Paper presented at the Interregional Workshop on Developing Problem Solving Skills in Public Enterprises, Ljubljana, Yugoslavia, 2-17 April. Ljubljana: ICPE. /India /Oil industry /Personnel management /Management /Case studies

1426. Fernandes, Praxy J. 1979 "The Problem about Problems." Paper presented at the Interregional Workshop on Developing Problem Solving Skills in Public Enterprises, Ljubljana, Yugoslavia, 2-17 April. Ljubljana: ICPE. /Evaluation /Paper also presented at the Regional Workshop on Development of Training Methodologies for Internal Consultants in African Public Enterprises, Addis Ababa, 1-6 Dec., 1980.

1427. Fernandes, Praxy J. 1979 "Report of the Expert Group Meeting on Development of Methodology for Training Internal Consultants in Public Enterprises in Developing Countries, Ljubljana, December 10-14, 1979." Ljubljana: ICPE. /Training /Methodology /Consultant services /Developing nations

1428. Fernandes, Praxy J. 1979 "Report of the Inter-Regional Workshop "Developing Problem Solving Skills in Public Enterprises," Ljubljana, April 2-17, 1979, Organized Jointly by ICPE, Ljubljana, and U. N. Industrial Development Organization, Vienna." Ljubljana: ICPE. /Evaluation /Consultant services

1429. Fernandes, Praxy J. 1979 "The State Trading Corporation of India, Strategic and Financial Problems: Indian Case Study." Paper presented at the Interregional Workshop on Developing Problem Solving Skills in Public Enterprises, Ljubljana, Yugoslavia, 2-17 April. Ljubljana: ICPE. /India /State trading organizations /Financing /Case studies

1430. Fernandes, Praxy J. 1979 "The `Withering Away´ of the Consultancy Profession." Paper presented at the Expert Group Meeting on Development of Methodologies for Training Internal Consultants in Public Enterprises in Developing Countries, Ljubljana, Yugoslavia, 10-14 Dec. Ljubljana: ICPE. /Consultant services /Paper also presented at the Regional Workshop on the Development of Training Methodologies for Internal Consultants in African Public Enterprises, Addis Ababa, Dec. 1-6, 1980.

1431. Fernandes, Praxy J. 1980 "The Perils, Pitfalls and Perplexities of Public Enterprise Investment: An Empirical View." Paper presented at the International Workshop on Investment Criteria and Investment Decision-Making Processes, Ljubljana, Yugoslavia, 20-24 Oct. Ljubljana: ICPE. /Investment /Evaluation

1432. Fernandes, Praxy J. 1980 "Pricing: Fallacies and Phantasies; Some Thoughts on the Mythology of Public Enterprise Pricing Policies and Practices." Paper presented at the International Workshop on Pricing Policies in Public Enterprises, Ljubljana, Yugoslavia, 26-30 May. Ljubljana: ICPE. /Price policy

1433. Fernandes, Praxy J. 1980 "Corporate Planning." Paper presented at the Regional Workshop on Planning in Public Enterprises in the Latin American and Caribbean Region, Kingston, Jamaica, 11-15 Feb. Ljubljana: ICPE. /Planning process /Paper also presented at the Regional Workshop on Corporate Planning in Public Enterprises in the Asian and Pacific Region, Kuala Lumpur, Malaysia, 17-21 Nov.

1434. Fernandes, Praxy J. 1980 "Final Report of the International Workshop on Preparations and Negotiations of Technology Transfer Agreements for Public Enterprises in Developing Countries, Ljubljana, October 27-31, 1980." Ljubljana: ICPE. /Technology transfer

1435. Fernandes, Praxy J. 1980 "Technology Transfer and Technological Development: (The Public Enterprise Role)." Paper presented at the International Workshop on Preparations and Negotiations of Technology Transfer Agreements for Public Enterprises in Developing Countries, Ljubljana, Yugoslavia, 27-31 Oct. Ljubljana: ICPE. /Technology transfer /Technological change

1436. Fernandes, Praxy J. 1980 "Preliminary and Tentative Draft Report: Regional Workshop on Corporate Planning in Public Enterprises in the Asian and Pacific Region, Kuala Lumpur, Malaysia, 17-21 November, 1980." Ljubljana: ICPE. /Planning process

1437. Fernandes, Praxy J. 1980 "Report of the Regional Workshop on Planning in Public Enterprises in the Latin American and Caribbean Region, Kingston, Jamaica, February 11-15, 1980." Ljubljana: ICPE. /Latin America /Caribbean Region /Planning process

1438. Fernandes, Praxy J. 1980 "Management Culture: Changing Public Policies and Management." Public Enterprise V. 1, No. 1, pp. 11-17. /Management /Public administration / OPSS

1439. Fernandes, Praxy J. 1980 "The Public Enterprise Concept: A Monograph." Three volume monograph presented at the Expert Group Meeting on Concept, Definition and Classification of Public Enterprises, Tangier, Morocco, 15-19 December. Ljubljana: ICPE. /Taxonomy /Part I published as "The Public Enterprise Concept," in Public Enterprise, Vol. 1, No. 2, pp. 54-68.

1440. Fernandes, Praxy J. 1980 "Report of the Expert Group Meeting on Concept, Definition and Classification of Public Enterprises, Tangier, Morocco." Ljubljana: ICPE. /Taxonomy /

1441. Fernandes, Praxy J. 1980 "Report of the International Expert Group Meeting on Women as a Factor of Development and the Responsibilities of Public Enterprises in This Regard, Ljubljana, 14-19 April, 1980." Ljubljana: ICPE. /Women's studies /Economic development

1442. Fernandes, Praxy J. 1980 "Women, Development and Public Enterprises: Some Thoughts on the Integration of Women into National Development and the Role and Responsability of Public Enterprises in This Regard, with a Suggested Action Plan for ICPE." International Expert Group Meeting on Women as a Factor of Development and and Responsibilities of Public Sector in This Regard, Ljubljana, Yugoslavia, 14-19 April. Ljubljana: ICPE. /Women's studies /Economic development

1443. Fernandes, Praxy J. 1980 "Report of the Regional Workshop on Development of Training Methodologies for Internal Consultants in African Public Enterprises, Addis Ababa, December 1-6, 1980." Ljubljana: ICPE. /Africa /Training /Methodology /Consultant services /Evaluation

1444. Fernandes, Praxy J. 1981 "An Approach to Performance Evaluation of Public Industrial Enterprise." Paper presented at the Expert Group Meeting on the Changing Role and Function of the Public Industrial Sector in Development. Ljubljana: ICPE. /Industrial sector /Evaluation

1445. Fernandes, Praxy J. 1981 "`OPTIMA'--An ICPE Approach to Self-Reliant Public Enterprise Management." Public Enterprise V. 2, No. 2, pp. 5-12. /Management / OPSS

1446. Fernandes, Praxy J. 1981 "OPTIMA: An Integrated Package of Instruments Designed for Performance Improvement in Public Enterprises in Developing Countries." Ljubljana: ICPE. /Economic efficiency /Evaluation /System performance

1447. Fernandes, Praxy J. 1981 "Public Enterprises and the Bottom Line: Some Reflections on the Why and How of Profits and Losses in Public Enterprises in Developing Countries." Paper presented at the International Workshop on Financial Profitability and Losses in Public Enterprises, Ljubljana, Yugoslavia, 1-5 June. Ljubljana: ICPE. /Profits

1448. Fernandes, Praxy J. 1981 "Report of the International Workshop on Investment Criteria and Investment Decision-Making Processes, Ljubljana, October 20-24, 1980." Ljubljana: ICPE. /Investment

1449. Fernandes, Praxy J. 1981 "Report of the International Workshop on Financial Profitability and Losses in Public Enterprises, Ljubljana, June 1-5, 1981." Ljubljana: ICPE. /Profits

1450. Fernandes, Praxy J. 1981 "Public Industrial Enterprises in Developing Countries: An Issue Paper." Paper presented at the Expert Group Meeting on the Changing Role and Function of the Public Industrial Sector in Development, Vienna. Ljubljana: ICPE. /Developing nations /Industrial sector /Economic development

1451. Fernandes, Praxy J. 1981 <u>Regional Development: The Role and Contribution of Public Enterprises.</u> Ljubljana: ICPE. /Regional development

1452. Fernandes, Praxy J. 1981 "Promise and Performance: A Search for a Credible System of Evaluating the 'Efficiency' of Public Enterprises." Paper presented at the Expert Group Meeting on Performance Crtiteria and the Implementation of Performance Evaluation Systems in Public Enterprises in Developing Countries, Ljubljana, Yugoslavia, 23-27 Nov. Ljubljana: ICPE. /Evaluation /Economic efficiency

1453. Fernandes, Praxy J. 1981 "Public Enterprise: The Interlinkage Issue." Paper presented at the Expert Group Meeting on the Changing Role and Function of the Public Industrial Sector in Development, Vienna. Ljubljana: ICPE. /Evaluation

1454. Fernandes, Praxy J. 1981 "Enterprise Perspectives and Problem Areas in Mogadishu Milk Factory (Warshadda Caanaha)." Paper presented at the National Workshop of Public Enterprises, Mogadishu, Somalia, 9-13 Aug. Ljubljana: ICPE. /Somalia /Milk processing industry

1455. Fernandes, Praxy J. 1981 "Management Perspectives and Problem Areas in Somaltex (Warshadda Dharka ee Balcad)." Paper presented at the National Workshop of Public Enterprises, Mogadishu, Somalia, 9-13 Aug. Ljubljana: ICPE. /Somalia /Management /Evaluation

1456. Fernandes, Praxy J., ed. 1978 Financing of Public Enterprises in Developing Countries. Ljubljana: ICPE. /Public financing /Developing nations

1457. Fernandes, Praxy J., ed. 1979 Control Systems for Public Enterprises in Developing Countries: Report of the Inter-Regional Workshop 9-13 July, 1979. Ljubljana: ICPE. /Developing nations /Control process

1458. Fernandes, Praxy J., and Pavle Sicherl, eds. 1981 Seeking the Personality of Public Enteprise, An Enquiry into the Concept, Definition and Classification of Public Enterprises: Reports and Papers of an Expert Group Meeting Held in Tangier, Morocco, 15-19 December, 1980. Ljubljana: ICPE. /Taxonomy

1459. Fernandes, Praxy J., ed. 1982 State Trading and Development. Ljubljana: ICPE. /State trading organizations /Economic development

1460. Fernandes, Praxy J., and Vladimir Kreacic. 1982 A Casebook of Public Enterprise Studies. Ljubljana: ICPE. /Case studies /Management

1461. Fernandez Arenas, Jose Antonio. 1978 "El concepto de utilidad y de eficiencia en la empresa pública y en la empresa privada." Paper presented at the Fourth General Assembly of the Latin American Association of Public Administration, Mexico City, 6-11 Nov. /Profits /Economic efficiency /Private enterprises /Comparative analysis /OPSS

1462. Fernandez Carvajal, R. 1950 "Las empresas públicas en Rusia." Revista de Administración Pública (Madrid), No. 3, pp. 435-472. /Union of Soviet Socialist Reps.

1463. Fernandez Chávez, F., et al. 1980 El papel del sector público costarricense en el desarrollo: Un análisis con énfasis en las empresas públicas. Ljubljana: ICPE. /Costa Rica /Economic development

1464. Fernandez Chávez, F., et al. 1981 "El papel del sector público costarricense en el desarrollo: Un análisis con énfasis en las Empresas Públicas." Paper presented at the seminar on public enterprises in development planning for Central America and the Caribbean , San José, Costa Rica, 1-3 July. /Costa Rica /Economic history /Investment /Employment policy /Case studies /Planning process /State trading organizations /Control process /Development banks OPSS

1465. Fernandez Moreno, Hector. 1983 "Experiencias Y Planteamientos Para La Planeacion Y Control De Las Empresas Del Sector Publice." Paper presented at the ECLA seminar: "State Control and Planning of Public Enterprises." Brasília, 15-17 June. Brasília: UNECLA. /Mexico /Control Process /Law /Planning Process OPSS

1466. Fernandez Rodríguez, Tomás Ramón. 1965 "Notas para un planteamiento de los problemas actuales de la empresa pública." Revista de Administración Pública (Madrid), No. 46, pp. 95-122. /Spain /Evaluation

1467. Fernandez Rodríguez, Tomás Ramón. 1966 "El procedimiento previo a la creación o expansión de una empresa nacional." Revista de Administración Pública (Madrid), No. 49, pp. 309-322. /Spain /Administrative law /Economic growth policy

1468. Fernandez Rodríguez, Tomás Ramón. 1970 "La organización y el control del sector público industrial en España." La empresa pública. Zaragoza, Spain: Publicaciones del Real Colegio de España en Bolonia. /Spain /Industrial sector /Control process

1469. Fernandez Zavala, Luis. 1977 "Algunos aspectos metodológicos y empíricos sobre la gestión empresarial del Estado." Lima: Undergraduate thesis, Pontificia Universidad Católica del Perú. /Peru /Evaluation / OPSS

1470. Fernando, Edgar. 1983 "The Ceylon Transport Board: The Role of the Nationalized Transport Board in Passenger Transport with Special Reference to Sri Lanka." Paper presented at the 19th International Congress of Administrative Sciences, West Berlin, 19-23 Sept. /Sri Lanka /Transportation industry /Case studies / OPSS

1471. Ferran, John B. 1947 "State Ownership and the Port of New Orleans". State Government /United States of America /Port authority /State government

1472. Ferrara, Reno. 1961 "Il finanziamiento delle imprese pubbliche in Inghilterra." L´Impresa Pubblica (Rome), pp. 438-440. /United Kingdom /Public financing

1473. Ferrara, Reno. 1961 "The British Nationalizations Experience." L´Impresa Pubblica (Rome), V. 5, No. 8, pp. 518-521. /United Kingdom /Nationalization

1474. Ferrara, Reno. 1961 "State Control of Nationalized Enterprises." L´Impresa Pubblica (Rome), V. 5, No. 2, pp. 127-132. /Italy /Control process

1475. Ferrara, Reno. 1962 "New Trends in Nationalization." L´Impresa Pubblica (Rome), V. 6, No. 6, pp. 388-396. /Italy /Nationalization

1476. Ferrara, Reno. 1968 "Le problemi dell´impresa pubblica. Strumenti, mezzi fini, objetivi." L´Impresa Pubblica (Rome), pp. 3-9. /Italy /Evaluation

1477. Ferreira Neto, Adolfo. 1973 "Empresa pública vem beneficiando a iniciativa particular." Comércio e Mercado (Rio de Janeiro), V. 7, No. 67, pp. 26-28. /Brazil /Economic analysis

1478. Ferreira, Sergio de Andrea. 1976 "Fundações privadas governamentais: Entidades de administração indireta. Arquivos do Ministério da Justica V. 33, pp. 56-79. /Brazil /Public administration /Private foundations /Control process

/G349.81 B7392a LAC

1479. Ferreira, Sergio de Andrea. 1979 "As empresas do Estado no direito brasileiro." Arquivos do Ministério da Justica V. 36, pp. 69-70. /Brazil /Law / G349.81 B7392a LAC

1480. Ferrer Vallés, José. 1979 "Una revisión teórica del problema de la determinación de los precios en el sector de los servicios públicos." In EIAP-FGV, ed(s). Administración de empresas públicas. Mexico: Editorial Limusa. pp. 407-490. /Price policy /Control process / HD 3850 A333 LAC

1481. Ferrer, José Valles. 1974 "Política directa de precios y desarrollo económico." De Economía (Madrid), V. 27, No. 130, pp. 389-404. /Spain /Economic development

1482. Ferri, Luigi. 1970 "Impresiones de un jurista sobre las haciendas con participación estatal predominante y sobre su encuadramiento sindical." La empresa pública. Zaragoza, Spain: Publicaciones del Real Colegio de España en Bolonia. /Spain /Agricultural sector /Labor relations /Law

1483. Ferrier, J. 1961 Statistiques et probabilités dans l'administration des entreprises publiques et privées. Paris: Eyrolles. /Public administration /Statistics /Management

1484. Feuerlein, W. J. 1955 "The Financing of the Electric Power Plant at Chorrera de Guayabo, El Salvador." In A. H. Hanson, ed(s). Public Enterprise. Brussels: IIAS pp. 145-156. /El Salvador /Electrical utility industry /Financing /Case studies /HD 3850 H28 Law

1485. Ficzere, Lajos. 1974 The Socialist State Enterprise. Budapest: Hungarian Academy of Sciences. Institute for Legal and Administrative Science. /Socialist economy /Hungary

1486. Ficzere, Lajos. 1983 "Problems of Public Enterprises: Hungarian National Report." Paper presented at the 19th International Congress of Administrative Sciences, West Berlin, 19-23 Sept. /Hungary /Law /Socialist economy /Control process / OPSS

1487. Field, O. P. 1935 "Government Corporations: A Proposal." Harvard Law Review V. 48, No. 5, pp. 775-796. /Management /340.5 H261

1488. Fiennes, D. E. M. 1965 "The Role of Public Enterprise in the Provision of Capital and Initiative for Industrial Development in the Developing Countries." In R. Robinson, ed(s). Industrialization in Developing Countries. Cambridge: Cambridge University Press. pp. 131-140. /Developing nations /Industrialization

1489. Figueira Barbosa, Antonio L. 1981 "Considerations on Technological Categories and Development Policy." Paper presented at Reunión Regional de Exportos "Estrategias e Instrumentos para Reforza la Negociacíon (SDP) de las Empresas Públicas en los Países en Desarrollo en la

Transferencia Internacional de Transacciones Tecnológicas." San José, Costa Rica, 23-27 Nov. Ljubljana: ICPE. /Technological change /Technology transfer /Development planning

1490. Figueiredo, Lúcia Valle. 1978 Empresas públicas y sociedades de economia mista. São Paulo: Editora Revista dos Tribunais. /Brazil /Mixed enterprises /Law / HD 4093 F538 LAC

1491. Figueroa, E. 1962 El Estado, la empresa pública y el desarrollo económico. Madrid: I.N.I. /Spain /Government authority /Economic development

1492. Figueroa, L., and G. Saberbein. 1978 "Empresas del Estado en el Perú." Paper Prepared for the Seminar on the Planning Process in Latin America and Public Enterprises, Lima, Aug. /Peru / OPSS

1493. Filgueira Penedo, Antonio. 1978 "La Empresa de Navegación Aérea como empresa pública." Paper prepared for the Round Table on the Public Enterprise in Latin America, Mexico City. /Air transportation industry / OPSS

1494. Filgueira Penedo, Antonio. 1978 "Iberia, Líneas Aéreas de España, S.A. y Aviación y Comercio, S.A. como empresas públicas frente a las privadas." Prepared for the IV General Assembly for the Latin American Association for Public Administration. /Spain /Air transportation industry / OPSS

1495. Filho, A. V. 1966 "Organisation and Administration of Public Enterprises in Brazil." New York: United Nations. /Brazil /Structural characteristics /Public administration

1496. "Finance of Large Public Limited Companies, 1976-77." 1978 Lok Udyog (New Delhi), V. 12, No. 4, pp. 47-50. /India /Statistics /Financial performance /354.54 L836 PCL

1497. "Financial Review of Industrial and Commercial Undertakings." 1970 Lok Udyog (New Delhi), V. 4, No. 3, pp. 483-493. /India /Industrial sector /Commercial sector /Financial performance / 354.54 L836

1498. "Financing the Nationalised Industries." 1968 Midland Bank Review (London), /United Kingdom /Industrial sector /Financing / HG11 M5

1499. Fine, S. A. 1970 Role of Job Design in Workers' Participation in Management. 2C-60/SECT. H/C(A) Geneva: International Industrial Relations Association. 2nd World Congress. /Worker management participation

1500. Finer, H. 1947 The Chilean Development Corporation. Montreal: ILO Studies and Reports, New Series. No. 5. /Chile /Development corporation

1501. Finger, N. 1971 The Impact of Government Subsidies on Industrial Management: The Israeli Experience. New York: Praeger. /Israel /Subsidization policy HC 497 P23 S93 Pub Aff

1502. Finnegan, M. 1954 "Ministerial Control of Electricité de France." Public Administration (London), pp. 441-449. /France /Electrical utility industry /Government authority /Control process / 320.5 J826 PCL

1503. Finsinger, J., and I. Vogelsgang. 1982 "Performance Indices for Public Enterprises." In Leroy P. Jones et al., ed(s). Public Enterprise in Less-Developed Countries. New York: Cambridge University Press. pp. 281-296. /Control process /Accountability /Economic efficiency /Financial performance /Price policy /HD 3850 P83 PCL /Also presented at the Second BAPEG Conference, Boston, April 1980 /OPSS

1504. Fischer, K. 1958 Betriebsanalyse in der volkseigenen industrie. Berlin: Verlag die Wirtschaft. /Germany, Federal Rep. of /Industrial sector /Evaluation

1505. Fisera, J., and V. Fisera. 1970 "Les conseils ouvrières tchécoslovaques à la pointe de l'autogestion - un dossier pour le présent et l'avenir." Autogestion et Socialisme (Paris), No. 11-1, pp. 3-23. /Czechoslovakia /Worker self management

1506. Fiszel, H. 1966 Investment Efficiency in a Socialist Economy. Oxford: Pergamon Press. /Socialist economy /Investment / 332.6 F549e PCL

1507. Fitzgerald, G. 1963 State-Sponsored Bodies. Dublin: Institute of Public Administration. /Ireland /Control process

1508. Fitzgerald, G. 1968 "State-sponsored Bodies in Ireland." Revue International des Sciences Administratives V. 34, No. 2, pp. 117-125. /Ireland /Evaluation

1509. Flamme, Maurice-André. 1966 "The Legislation Governing Commercial and Industrial Activity Carried on by Public Authorities in Belgium and in other Countries." Annals of Public and Cooperative Economy V. 37, No. 4, pp. 343-367. /Belgium /Control process /Law / 330.5 An73

1510. Flamme, Maurice-André. 1966 "Le régime des activités commerciales et industrielles des pouvoirs publics en Belgique." Revue de l'Institit de Sociologie (Paris), No. 1, pp. 143-268. /Belgium /Commercial sector /Industrial sector /Law

1511. Flemming, Marcus. 1950 "Production and Price Policy in Public Enterprise." Economica V. 17, pp. 1-22. /Price policy /Productivity / 306 Ec74 n.s.

1512. Fletcher, H. A. 1958 "The Regie-Renault, a Nationalized Enterprise in the French Automobile Industry." In C. J. Friedrich, and E. S. Mason, ed(s). Public Policy. Cambridge, Mass.: Harvard University Press. V. 8, pp. 173-204. /France /Automobile manufacturing industry /JA51 P8 Pub Aff

1513. Fliger, Carlos. 1967 Multinational Public Enterprises. Washington, D. C.: IBRD. /Multinational corporations /International economic relations / HD 350 F553

1514. Florence, P. S. 1955 "Present Problems in the Nationalization of British Industries." Indian Journal of Economics V. 36, No. 140, pp. 13-48. /United Kingdom /Public utility industry / 330.5 In2

1515. Florence, P. S. 1957 Industry and the State. London: Hutchinson. /Planning process / 338.942 F662i

1516. Florence, P. S., and Gilbert Walker. 1952 "Efficiency under Nationalization and Its Management." Political Quarterly (London), pp. 197-208. /Management /Economic efficiency /320.5 P76p

1517. Florence, P. S., and H. Maddick. 1953 "Consumers' Councils in the Nationalized Industries." Political Quarterly (London), V. 24, No. 3, pp. 259-271. /United Kingdom /Consumer relations / 320.5 P76p

1518. Flores Delfin, Edgar. 1981 "An Outline of Training in Bolivia." Paper presented at the International Seminar on Training Management in Public Enterprise in Developing Countries, Ljubljana, Yugoslavia, 29 Sep.-10 Oct. Ljubljana: ICPE. /Bolivia /Training

1519. Flores Delfin, Edgar. 1981 "Proyecto `Mecanismo nacional de transferencia de tecnología en Bolivia.´" Paper presented at the Reunión regional de expertos "Estrategias e instrumentos para forzar la negociación (SDP) de las empresas públicas en los países en desarrollo en la transferencia internacional Ljubljana: ICPE /Bolivia /Technology transfer

1520. Flores Delfin, Edgar. 1981 "Problemas jurídicos en materia de transferencia de tecnología en Bolivia." Paper presented at the Reunión regional expertos de "Estrategias instrumentos para reforzar la negociación (SBP) de las empresas públicas en los países en desarrollo en la transferencia internacional de transacciones Ljubljana: ICPE. /Bolivia /Technology transfer /Law

1521. Flores M., José Francisco, and Rafael Valladares. 1974 "Las empresas públicas en Honduras (Resumen de un diagnóstico)." Rio de Janeiro: FGV-EIAP. /Honduras /Public financing /Control process /Planning process / Public administration /Economic history / OPSS

1522. Floyd, Robert H. 1978 "Some Aspects of Income Taxation of Public Enterprises." IMF Staff Papers V. 25, No. 2, pp. 310-342. /Taxation policy

1523. Floyd, Robert H. 1979 Income Taxation of State Trading Enterprises. Montreal: Ecole des Hautes Etudes Commericales, Les Cahiers du CETAI No. 79-05. /Taxation policy /State trading organizations / OPSS

1524. Floyd, Robert H. 1981 "Income Taxation of State-Trading Enterprises." In M. M. Kostecki, ed(s). State Trading in International Markets. New York: St. Martin's Press. pp. 189-209. /State trading organizations /Taxation policy /HF 1410.5 S7 1981 M

1525. Floyd, Robert H. 1983 Some Topical Issues Concerning Public Enterprises. International Monetary Fund, Fiscal Affairs Department. /Evaluation

1526. Floyd, Robert H. 1983 "Government Relationships with Public Enterprise in Papua New Guinea." In G. Ram Reddy, ed(s). Government and Public Enterprise: Essays in honour of Professor V. V. Ramanadham. Bombay, India: N. M. Tripathi Private Limited. pp. 220-248. /Papua New Guinea /Government authority

1527. Focsaneanu, L. 1953 "Les conséquences internationales des nationalisations." Politique Etranger (Paris), V. 18, pp. 35-50. /Nationalization

1528. Fogarty, M. P., N. Ross, and Gruppo Fabiano. 1966 Problemi e prospettive delle grandi impresse pubbliche e private in Gran Bretagna a cura di A. Brenna. Milan, Italy: Ed. CIRIEC. /United Kingdom /Private sector /Economic analysis

1529. Foldes, L. 1957 "Control of Nationalized Industries." Public Law (London), V. 2, No. 2, pp. 122-138. /United Kingdom /Control process / 350.5 P962

1530. Fontana, Andrés. 1984 "Armed Forces and Neoconservative Ideology: State Shrinking in Argentina (1976-1981)." Paper presented at the conference: "State Shrinking: A Comparative Inquiry into Privatization," Austin, Tex., 1-3 March. /Argentina /Privatization /Political Analysis / OPSS

1531. Fontanesi, Dante, Jr. 1975 "Implantação de um sistema de planejamento, programação e controle de empreendimentos: Uma experiencia de trabalho na Companhia Paulista de Força e Luz." Rio de Janeiro: FGV-EIAP. /Brazil /Electrical utility industry /Control process /Budgetary process /Planning process /OPSS

1532. Fontanesi, Dante, Jr., et al. 1976 "A atividade empresarial do Governo do Estado de S. Paulo (Brasil)." Rio de Janeiro: FGV-EIAP. /Brazil /Sao Paulo, Brazil (State) /Public administration /Directory / Public financing / OPSS

1533. Fontgalland, B. H. de. 1965 L'avenir du chemin de fer." Revue de Defense Nationale (Paris) No. 26, pp. 240-255. /France /Railway industry

1534. Forino, A. 1970 Las empresas del Estado en la República Argentina: Aspectos normativos y económico-financieros en el Estado moderno. Córdoba, Argentina: Ed. Macchi. /Argentina /Economic analysis

1535. Forseto, José Carlos. 1979 "Tarifas de energia eléctrica." In EIAP-FGV, ed(s). Administración de empresas públicas.

Mexico City: Editorial Limusa. pp. 493-519. /Price policy /Electrical utility industry / HD 3850 A333 LAC

1536. Forster, Malcolm, and Donald N. Zillerman. 1982 "The British National Oil Corporation: The State Enterprise as Instrument of Energy Policy." Journal of Energy Law and Policy V. 3, pp. 57-111. /United Kingdom /Oil industry /Energy use policy

1537. Forsthoff, Ernest. 1957 "I limiti costituzionali dell intervento dello Stato nell'economia della Repubblica Federale Tedesca." La Scienza e la Tecnica della Organizacione nella Pubblica Administrazione No. 4, pp. 462-472. /Italy /Constitutional law /Law

1538. Forsyth, P. J. 1974 "The Pricing of Public Enterprise Outputs--A Note." Oxford Economic Papers (Oxford), V. 26, No. 3, pp. 446-449. /Price policy / 330.6 Ox2

1539. Forte, F. 1962 "L'autonomia delle impresa pubbliche." Tempi Moderni (Bari, Italy), pp. 85-87. /Italy /Accountability

1540. Forte, F. 1962 "L'impresa pubblica e la sua funzione nel piano economico." Aggiornamenti Sociali (Milan), V. 13, No. 12, pp. 679-710. /Italy /Evaluation

1541. Forte, F. 1963 "Nationalization of the Electric Power Industry." Aggiornamentti Sociali (Milan), V. 14, No. 3, pp. 167-192. /Nationalization /Electrical utility industry /Italy

1542. Foschini, M. 1960 "L'impresa publica nel trattato della CEE." L'Impresa Pubblica (Rome), pp. 282-285. /Italy /Law /European Economic Community

1543. Foster, C. D. 1960 "The Cost of Financing the Nationalized Industries." Bulletin of Oxford University Institute of Statistics (Oxford), V. 22, No. 2, pp. 93-104. /Financing /Cost benefit analysis

1544. Foster, C. D. 1963 "Finances of Government Companies 1961-1962." Reserve Bank of India Bulletin (Bombay), pp. 1267-1276. /India /Financing

1545. Foster, C. D. 1971 Politics, Finance and the Role of Economics: An Essay on the Control of Public Enterprises. London: Allen & Unwin. /United Kingdom /Financial performance /Public financing /Control process /HD 4147 F66

1546. Fouda, E. K. 1969 The Role of Public Building and Construction Contracting Organizations in Planning and Plan Implementation in U.A.R. Mauritius: UNECA Seminar on Role of Public Enterprise in Planning and Plan Implementation. /Construction industry /Investment /Egypt /Planning process

1547. Fouilloux, G. 1962 La Nationalisation et le Droit International Public. Paris: Librairie générale de droit et de jurisprudence. V. 7. /Law /France /Nationalization /International law

1548. Fournier, H. 1957 "The Bank of France and the Control and Supervision of Credit." *Annals of Collective Economy* V. 28, pp. 228-240. /France /Financial institutions / 330.5 An73

1549. Fowler, H. H. 1900 "Municipal Finance and Municipal Enterprise." *Journal of the Royal Statistical Society* V. 63, pp. 383-407. /United Kingdom /Local government /Public financing

1550. Fox, D. 1977 "Mexico: The Development of an Oil Industry." *BOLSA Review* V. 11, pp. 520-533. /Mexico /Oil industry

1551. Foxley, Alejandro, et al. 1971 "Viabilidad económica del sistema de autogestión." *Chile: Búsqueda de un Nuevo Socialismo.* pp. 66-76. /Chile /Worker self management

1552. Fraeys, W. 1961 "La societé nationale d'investissement." *Socialisme* (Paris), No. 48, pp. 689-708. /France /Evaluation

1553. Fraiture, E. 1958 "The Intermunicipal Flood Control Association for the Communes of the Liège Region." *Annals of Collective Economy* V. 29, pp. 612-616. /Belgium /Cooperatives /Flood control / 330.5 An73

1554. France, C. W. 1978 "Public Enterprises in the United Kingdom." In André Gélinas, ed(s). *Public Enterprise and the Public Interest.* Ontario: The Institute of Public Administration of Canada. pp. 104-118. /United Kingdom /Accountability /Control process /Economic efficiency

1555. France. Direction des Services d'Information et de Presse du MAE. 1963 *Les entreprises publiques nationales.* Paris. /France /Evaluation

1556. France. Ecole Nationale Superieure des Postes et Télécommunications. 1967 "La décision rationelle, étude, participation autorité-rapport et Journées d'Etudes de Sévérac (Loire, Atlantique.)" *Cahiers d'Etudes et d'Information* (Paris), No. 57, pp. 1-79. /France /Evaluation

1557. France. Groupe de Travail du Comité Int. des Entreprises Publiques. 1967 *Rapport sur les entreprises publiques.* Paris: Secréteriat Général du Gouvernement. /France /Government report /Nora Report /OPSS /Known as the Nora Report, after its chairman, Simon Nora

1558. France. National Industrial Nitrogen Office. 1957 "The National Industrial Nitrogen Office." *Annals of Collective Economy* V. 28, pp. 347-359. /France /Chemical industry /330.5 An73

1559. France. Service Central d'Organisation et Methodes. 1962 *L'Etude d'organisation dans le secteur public: Notions sur la méthode.* Paris: Imprimerie Nationale. /France /Evaluation

1560. Francis, O. F. 1975 "Anti-Pollution Steps by Gauhati Refinery." *Lok Udyog* (New Delhi), V. 9, No. 8, pp. 31-34. /India /Pollution /Environmental policy /Case studies /354.54 L836 PCL

1561. Franck, Jacques. 1958 "The Municipal Regies of Saint-Gilles-lez-Bruxelles." Annals of Collective Economy V. 29, pp. 634-637. /Belgium /Cooperatives /Gas utility industry /Electrical utility industry / 330.5 An73

1562. Franco Sobrinho, Manoel de Oliveira. 1970 "A intervenção do Estado na ordem economica." Revista de Direito Público (São Paulo), V. 11, No. 3, pp. 7-12. /Brazil

1563. Franco Sobrinho, Manoel de Oliveira 1970 "As fundações e o direito administrativo." Revista de Direito Administrativo (Rio de Janeiro), No. 100, pp. 1-31. /Brazil /Administrative law

1564. Franco Sobrinho, Manoel de Oliveira. 1970 "Regime jurídico das empresas públicas no Brasil." Revista de Direito Público (São Paulo), V. 12, pp. 14-39. /Brazil /Law

1565. Franco Sobrinho, Manoel de Oliveira. 1970 "Regime jurídico das empresas públicas no Brasil." Ciencias Administrativas (La Plata), V. 13, No. 32, pp. 3-44. /Brazil /Law

1566. Franco Sobrinho, Manoel de Oliveira. 1971 "Organização e mecánica administrativa das empresas públicas." Revista de Direito Administrativo (Rio de Janeiro), No. 104, pp. 49-75. /Brazil /Law /Structural characteristics

1567. Franco Sobrinho, Manoel de Oliveira. 1971 "Regime jurídico das fundações." Revista de Direito Administrativo (Rio de Janeiro), No. 105, pp. 35-69. /Brazil /Law

1568. Franco Sobrinho, Manoel de Oliveira. 1972 "Fundação e empresa pública." Revista de Direito Administrativo (Rio de Janeiro), V. 1, No. 108. pp. 1-27. /Brazil /Administrative law

1569. Franco Sobrinho, Manoel de Oliveira. 1972 Fundações e empresas públicas. Revista dos Tribunais (São Paulo), /Brazil

1570. Franco Sobrinho, Manoel de Oliveira. 1975 Empresas públicas no Brasil: Ação internacional. /Brazil / HD 4093 0548 LAC

1571. François-Marsal, Féderic. 1973 El deterioro de las empresas públicas. Barcelona, Spain: DOPESA. /Economic analysis

1572. François-Marsal, Féderic. 1973 Le déperissement des entreprises publiques. Paris: Calman-Lévy. /Economic analysis

1573. Francony, Michel. 1979 "Theory and Practice of Marginal Cost Pricing: The Experience of `Electricité de France´." Annals of Public and Cooperative Economy V. 50, No. 3, pp. 9-36. /France /Electrical utility industry /Price policy /330.5 An73

1574. Frank, Charles R. 1971 "Public and Private Enterprise in Africa." In Gustav Ranis, ed(s). Government and Economic Development. New Haven: Yale University Press. pp. 88-123.

/Africa /Economic development / 330.9 G746

1575. Frankel, P. H. 1966 Mattei: Oil and Power Politics. New York: Frederick A. Praeger. /Oil industry /Political analysis / Italy / 338.826655 M429Yf PCL

1576. Frankel, P. H. 1980 "The Rationale of National Oil Companies." State Petroleum Enterprises in Developing Countries. New York: Pergamon Press. pp. 3-7. /Oil industry /Goal setting

1577. Frederickson, H. G. 1967 "Human Resources in Public Organization." Revue International des Sciences Administrative V. 33, No. 4, pp. 336-344. /Personnel management

1578. Freedman, L., and G. Hemingway. 1950 Nationalization and the Consumer. London: Fabian Research Series. /Consumer producer conflict /Consumer market / Consumer relations

1579. Freitas do Amaral, Diogo. 1971 Las modernas empresas públicas portuguesas. Madrid: Real Academia de de Legislación y Jurisprudencia. /Portugal

1580. Friedmann, Wolfgang G. 1946 "International Public Corporations." World Unity Booklets, No. 2 London: Herbert Joseph, Ltd. /International economic relations

1581. Friedmann, Wolfgang G. 1951 "The Legal Status and Organization of the Public Corporation." Law and Contemporary Problems V. 16, No. 4, pp. 576-593. /United Kingdom /Law /Structural characteristics / 340.5 L414

1582. Friedmann, Wolfgang G 1954 The Public Corporation: A Comparative Symposium. Toronto: Cecil A. Wright. /Evaluation /Law

1583. Friedmann, Wolfgang G. 1955 "A Theory of Public Industrial Enterprise." In A. H. Hanson, ed(s). Public Enterprise. Brussels: IIAS. pp. 11-23. /Industrial sector /HD 3850 H28 Law

1584. Friedmann, Wolfgang G. 1956 "Some Impacts of Social Organization on International Law: The Government Corporation in International Legal Transactions." American Journal of International Law V. 50, pp. 484-487. /International law / 341.05 Am35

1585. Friedmann, Wolfgang G. 1956 "Introduction générale d'une étude du régime des biens des entreprises nationales." Annales Juridiques, Politiques, Economiques et Sociales (Algiers), pp. 237-271. /Public financing /Law

1586. Friedmann, Wolfgang G. 1959 "Problèmes de la participation ouvrière à la gestion des enterprises- L'International Law." Journées d'Etudes (Brussels), /Worker management participation

1587. Friedmann, Wolfgang G. 1959 "Changing Social Arrangements in State-Trading States and Their Effect on International Law; The Status of the Government-Trading Corporation in International Law." Law and Contemporary Problems V. 24, pp. 350-366. /State trading organizations /International law

1588. Friedmann, Wolfgang G. 1970 "Government Enterprise: A Comparative Analysis." In J. F. Garner and Wolfgang G. Friedmann, ed(s). Government Enterprise, A Comparative Study. New York: Columbia University Press. pp. 303-336. /Comparative analysis / 350.0092 G746 PCL

1589. Friedmann, Wolfgang G., and J. F. Garner, eds. 1970 Government Enterprise: A Comparative Study. New York: Columbia University Press. /Europe /North America /Africa /Israel / Australia / 350.0092 G746 PCL

1590. Friedmann, Wolfgang G., and J. F. Garner. 1970 "The Public Corporation in Italy." In W. G. Friedmann and J. F. Garner, ed(s). Government Enterprise, A Comparative Study. New York: Columbia University Press. pp. 133-153. /Comparative analysis / 350.0092 G746 PCL

1591. Friedmann, Wolfgang G., and J. P. Beguin. 1971 Joint International Business Ventures in Developing Countries: Case Studies and Analysis of Recent Trends. New York: Columbia University Press. /Multinational corporations /Mixed enterprises /Developing nations /Case studies /338.911724 F914j

1592. Friedmann, Wolfgang G. 1971 The State and Rule of Law in Mixed Economy. London: Stevens & Sons. /Law /Mixed enterprises

1593. Friedmann, Wolfgang G., ed. 1974 Public and Private Enterprise in Mixed Economies. New York: Columbia University Press. /Law /Mixed enterprises /Control process /HD 3850 F753 PCL

1594. Friedrich Ebert Stiftung. 1978 "Labour-Management Relations in Public Enterprises in Asia." Bangkok: Proceedings Asian Regional Seminar on Labour-Management. /Labor relations

1595. Friedrich, G. 1959 Aufgaben und Arbeitsweise der Vereinigungem Volksseigner Betriebe. Berlin: Volk und Wiesen. /Germany, Federal Rep. of / Labor relations

1596. Frisch, A. 1957 "Bilanz der Franzosischen Staatsbetriebe." Wirtschaftsdienst pp. 518-520. /France /Industrial sector /Accountability

1597. Frishknecht, Reed L. 1953 "The Commodity Credit Corporation: A Case Study of a Government Corporation." Western Political Quarterly V. 6, No. 3, pp. 559-569. /United States of America /Commercial sector /Credit policy /320.5 W525

1598. Friss, I. 1969 Reform of the Economic Mechanism in Hungary--Nine Studies. Budapest: Akadémiai Kiadó. /Hungary /Economic analysis

1599. Fromont, M. 1968 "Les enterprises publiques, instruments de la planification française." Revue de Science Financière (Paris), V. 60, No. 4, pp. 767-781. /France /Planning process / 336.05 R328

1600. Fromont, M. 1971 "Las fronteras del area de propiedad social." Panorama Económico (Santiago, Chile), V. 2, No. 263, pp. 16-25. /Chile /Worker self management /G330.983 P194 LAC

1601. Frondizi, Arturo. 1963 Petróleo y nación. Buenos Aires: Transición. /Argentina /Oil industry /Nationalism /G338.2 F928p

1602. Fubara, Bedford A. 1984 "Negative Profitability: Performances of Public Enterprises in Developing Countries, A Business Policy Anatomy." Public Enterprise V. 4, No. 3, pp. 61-72. /Management /Economic analysis /Evaluation /Profits /Developing nations /OPSS

1603. Fuentes Quintana, E. 1950 "Perspectivas fiscales de la socialización de la inversión." Revista de Administración Pública (Madrid), No. 3. /Spain /Public administration /Fiscal policy /Investment /Socialization

1604. Fusilier, R. 1955 "Le statut du personnel de l'électricité de France." Revue Politique et Parlementaire (Paris), pp. 246-265. /France /Electrical utility industry /Personnel management

1605. Gaibisso, A. M. 1972 "La ricerca scientifica in Italia: la gestion dei fondi stanziati del settore pubblico." L'Impresa Pubblica (Rome), V. 14, No. 5. /Italy /Management /Research and development

1606. Gaitskell, Hugh. 1956 Socialization and Nationalization. Fabian Tract No. 300 London: Fabian Society. /United Kingdom /Nationalization

1607. Gajl, N. 1961 "Les entreprises d'Etat en France, en Italie et en Pologne." Revue Internationale des Sciences Administratives V. 27, No. 2, pp. 153-167. /France /Italy /Poland /Evaluation /Comparative analysis

1608. Gajl, Natalia. 1984 Problèmes juridiques et financiers des entreprises socialistes. Wroclaw: Laklad Narodowy. /Poland /Law /K 1366 G3414 1984 Law

1609. Galán, Tomás. 1980 "Thoughts on the Role of Public Holdings in Developing Countries: INI's Experience in Spain." In William J. Baumol, ed(s). Public and Private Enterprise in a Mixed Economy. New York: St. Martin's Press. pp. 116-134. /Spain /Industrial sector /Holding company /HD 3842 P87 PCL

1610. Galbraith, John Kenneth. 1961 "Public Administration and the Public Corporation." Indian Journal of Public Administration (New Delhi), V. 7, pp. 438-446. /Public administration /JA 26 I55 Pub Aff

1611. Galenson, W. 1955 Labor Productivity in Soviet and American Industry. New York: Columbia University Press. /Union of Soviet Socialist Reps. /United States of America /Industrial sector /Productivity /Comparative analysis / 338.0947 G1321

1612. Galenson, W. 1964 Wage Structure and Administration in Soviet Industry. Berkeley, California: University of California, Institute of Industrial Relations. /Union of Soviet Socialist Reps. /Industrial sector /Wages

1613. Galeotti, G. 1970 "The Distribution Problem and the Expansion of the Public Sector." Giornale degli Economisti (Padua, Italy), V. 29, No. 1-2, pp. 101-125. /Italy /Resource distribution / 330.5 G433

1614. Galgano, F. 1966 "Public and Private in the Determination of the Legal Entity." Rivista Trimestrale di Diritto Pubblico (Milan, Italy), V. 16, No. 2, pp. 249-302. /Italy /Law /Private enterprises /Taxonomy

1615. Gallardo, Manuel García. 1969 "Bibliografía internacional sobre problemas de la empresa pública." Economía Financiera Española (Madrid), No. 31-2, pp. 205-225. /Bibliography

1616. Gandasegui, Marco A. 1981 "Las empresas públicas en Panamá." Paper presented at the Seminar on Public Enterprises in Development Planning for Central Ameria and the Caribbean, San José, Costa Rica, 1-3 July 1981. /Panama /Planning process /Control process / OPSS

1617. Gangemi, L. 1963 La funzione del controllo in una ordinata. Efficiente conduta della gestion pubblica. /Italy /Control process

1618. Gangemi, L. 1964 "Problemi vechi a nouvi della impresa pubblica." Studi Economici (Naples, Italy), pp. 321-332. /Italy

1619. Gangopadhyay, A. K. 1980 "Research & Development in HMT." Lok Udyog (New Delhi), V. 14, No. 9, pp. 21-34. /India /Case studies /Research and development /Metal manufacturing industry /354.54 L836 PCL

1620. Ganguli, B. C., and R. Lal. 1971 "Railway Administration in India." Indian Journal of Public Administration (New Delhi), V. 17, pp. 481-494. /India /Railway industry /Administrative management / JA 26 I55 Pub Aff

1621. Ganguly, D. S. 1963 Public Corporations in a National Economy. Calcutta: Bookland. /India /Economic system

1622. Gannage, E. 1963 "Finances of Government Companies 1961-1962." Reserve Bank of India Bulletin (Bombay), pp. 1267-1276. /India /Financial performance

1623. Gannage, E. 1965 "Finances of Government Companies 1963-1964." Reserve Bank of India Bulletin (Bombay), pp. 1394-1403. /India /Financial performance

1624. Gantt II, Andrew H., and Guiseppe Dutto. 1968 "Financial Performance of Government Owned Corporations in Less-Developed Countries." IMF Staff Papers V. 15, No. 1, pp. 104-142. /Developing Nations /Financial performance /332.15 In8st

1625. Garces González, Hernán. 1978 "Política y programas de Carbocol (Carbones de Colombia S.A.)." Boletín de Minas y Energía V. 2, No. 5, pp. 23-44. /Colombia /Coal mining industry / TN 45 B628 LAC

1626. García Huidobro, G. 1972 "La experiencia de una empresa del area social, entrevista a Fernando Bustamante." Nueva Economía (Santiago, Chile), No. 2, pp. 110-124. /Chile /HC 191 N84 LAC

1627. García Jimenez, V. 1966 La corporación pública. Mexico: Universidad Nacional Autónoma de México. /Mexico /G380.1622 G1664c

1628. García Madaría, J. M. 1980 "Crónica del XVIII Congreso Internacional de Ciencias Administrativas." Documentación Administrativa. (Madrid), No. 187. /Public administration

1629. García Mata, C. 1967 "The Nationalized Electric Industry." Revista de Economi (Mexico City), V. 24, No. 6, pp. 200-206. /Mexico /Electrical utility industry /Nationalization

1630. García Oviedo, C. 1952 Los servidores del Estado en la empresa pública industrial. Madrid. /Spain /Industrial sector /Personnel management

1631. García Pelayo, Manuel. 1950 "Sobre los supuestos y consecuencias de la socialización " Revista de Administración Publica. (Madrid), No. 3, pp. 13-28. /Spain /Socialization

1632. García Quintana, César A. 1970 "El concepto de empresa pública en las cuentas económicas de 1966." In Spain. Ministerio de Hacienda. Instituto de Estudios Fiscales, ed(s). La empresa pública en España. Madrid: Instituto de Estudios Fiscales, Ministerio de Hacienda. /Spain /Economic analysis /Public financing

1633. García Quintana, César A. 1970 "El concepto de empresa pública en las cuentas economicas de 1966." De Economía (Madrid), V. 23, No. 114, pp. 553-562. /Spain /Evaluation

1634. García Quintana, César A. 1972 "La empresa pública y la socialización económica." De Economía (Madrid), V. 25, No. 123, pp. 587-604. /Socialization

1635. García Ramírez, Sergio. 1979 "Panorama sobre la empresa pública en México." Paper presented at the International Seminar on Regulation of the Public Enterprise in Mexico City. /Mexico /Control process / OPSS

1636. García Tellez, I. 1968 "Hacia la consolidación de la industria petrolera nacionalizada." Justicia (Mexico City),

V. 26, No. 454, pp. 24-28. /Mexico /Oil industry /Nationalization

1637. García Trevijano, J. A. 1953 "Aspectos de la administración económica." Revista de Administración Pública (Madrid), V. 4, No. 12. /Public administration

1638. García Trevijano, J. A. 1970 "Concepción unitaria del sector público." La Empresa Pública. Zaragoza, Spain: Publicaciones del Real Colegio de España en Bolonia. pp. 61-98. /Spain

1639. García de Enterría, E. 1978 "La burocracia de las empresas públicas." Paper presented at the Fourth General Assembly of the Latin American Association of Public Administration, Mexico City, 6-11 Nov. /Organization behavior / OPSS

1640. García de Enterría, E. n.d. "Sobre la naturaleza de la tasa y las tarifas de los servicios públicos." Revista de Administración Pública No. 12. /Public services /Taxation policy

1641. García de Enterría, E. n.d. "La actividad industrial y mercantil de los municipios." Revista de Administración Pública No. 17. /Local government /Industrial sector /Retail trade

1642. García de Enterría, E., and Miguel Sánchez Morán. n.d. "El régimen jurídico de la empresa pública en España." /Spain /Law /OPSS

1643. García, C. 1961 "La industria eléctrica nacionalizada." Revista de Economía (Mexico City). pp. 200-206. /Mexico /Electrical utility industry

1644. García, E. 1969 "Enjuiciamiento económico de la autogestión." Foro sobre la Autogestión en la Empresa. pp. 59-70. /Worker self management

1645. García, Pedro Miguel de. 1974 El intervencionismo y la empresa pública. Madrid: Instituto de Estudios Administrativos. /Control process

1646. García, Pedro Miguel de 1974 "Indice bibliográfico sobre la empresa pública." In Pedro Miguel de García, ed(s). El intervencionismo y la empresa pública. Madrid: Instituto de Estudios Administrativos. /Bibliography

1647. Garcilita Castillo, S., ed. 1980 "Control de empresas públicas en México." Mexico City: Instituto Nacional de Administración Pública. V. 2. /Mexico

1648. Garcilita Castillo, S., and F. J. Rangel. 1981 "Control de empresas públicas en México: El control jurisdiccional de las empresas públicas." pp. 456-504. /Mexico /Control process

1649. Gardellini, R., and P. Cavaillier. 1952 "L'Intervention de l'Etat dans la domaine économique: Les enterprises publiques." Revue Administrative (Paris), V. 5, No. 27, pp.

244-248;354. /France

1650. Gardellini, R., and P. Conailier. n.d. "Les entreprises publiques." Revue Administrative (Paris), No. 27-2. /France

1651. Garduno Pérez, J. 1979 "Los sistemas de control en el funcionamiento de las empresas públicas: responsibilidades legales, administrativas y políticas de sus cuadros directivos." Revista Latinoamericana de Administración Pública (Mexico City), No. 8-9, pp. 205-213. /Mexico /Control process / JL 974 R485 LAC

1652. Garewal, K. S. 1976 "Inter-se Coordination Among Public Sector Enterprises." Lok Udyog (New Delhi), V. 10, No. 5, pp. 9-14. /India /Control process /354.54 L836 PCL

1653. Garfield, P., and F. Wallace. 1964 Public Utility Economics. New Jersey: Prentice Hall. /Public utility industry /Economic theory / 380.16 G18p

1654. Garg, Mahandra Kumar. 1979 "Discussion Paper: Background of the Food Corporation of India." Paper presented at the Interregional Workshop on Developing Problem Solving Skills in Public Enterprises, Ljubljana, Yugoslavia, 2-17 April. Ljubljana: ICPE. /India /Food industry

1655. Garg, P. S. 1981 "Public Sector Performance - Growth Replacing Profit." Lok Udyog (New Delhi), V. 15, No. 3, pp. 17-24. /India /Economic efficiency /Profits /Economic growth policy /354.54 L836 PCL

1656. Garner, J. F. 1966 "New Public Corporations." Public Law (London), V. 44, No. 4, pp. 324-329. /United Kingdom /Law /350.5 P962

1657. Garner, J. F. 1970 "Public Corporations in the United Kingdom." In W. G. Friedmann and J. F. Garner, ed(s). Government Enterprise, A Comparative Study. New York: Columbia University Press. pp. 3-25. /United Kingdom /350.0092 G746 PCL

1658. Garner, Maurice R. 1980 "Some Thoughts Based on Experience in Britain." Paper presented at the International Workshop on Pricing Policies in Public Enterprises, Ljubljana, Yugoslavia, 26 30 May. Ljubljana: ICPE. /United Kingdom /Price policy

1659. Garner, Maurice R. 1983 "The Relationship Between Government and Public Enterprise." In G. Ram Reddy, ed(s). Government and Public Enterprise: Essays in honour of Professor V. V. Ramanadham. Bombay, India: N. M. Tripathi Private Limited. pp. 3-23. /Control process

1660. Garner, Maurice R. 1983 "A Final Reckoning." In G. Ram Reddy, ed(s). Government and Public Enterprise: Essays in honour of Professor V. V. Ramanadham. Bombay, India: N. M. Tripathi Private Limited. pp. 287-299. /Government authority

1661. Garner, Maurice R. 1983 "Autonomy and Control in Relation to the Typology of Public Enterprise." Paper presented at the 19th International Congress of Administrative Sciences, West Berlin, 19-23 Sept. /Autonomy /Control process /Taxonomy /United Kingdom /OPSS

1662. Garreau de Loubresse, G. 1961 "Les nationalisations cubaines." Annuaire Français (Paris), No. 7, pp. 215-226. /Cuba /Nationalization

1663. Garreau, de Loubresse, G. 1965 "Structures et réalités juridiques des nationalisations algériennes." Revue International de Droit Comparé (Paris), V. 17, No. 73-9. /Algeria /Nationalization /Law

1664. Garrido Falla, Fernando. 1950 "La intervención administrativa en materia económica y las corporaciones del gobierno en Norteamérica." Revista de Administración Pública (Buenos Aires), pp. 407-434. /North America /Administrative management

1665. Garrido Falla, Fernando. 1961 "Las empresas públicas." La administración pública y el Estado contemporaneo. Madrid: Instituto de Estudios Políticos. pp. 115-148. /Spain /Public administration

1666. Garrido Falla, Fernando. 1962 Las transformaciones del régimen administrativo. Madrid: Instituto de Estudios Políticos. /Spain /Public administration /Administrative law /Administrative reform

1667. Garrido Falla, Fernando. 1970 "La empresa pública en el derecho español." La empresa pública. Zaragoza, Spain: Publicaciones del Real Colegio de España en Bolonia. pp. 855-876. /Spain /Law

1668. Garrido Valenzuela, Raúl Bernardo. 1966 Las empresas estatales. Santiago, Chile: Editorial Jurídica de Chile. /Chile /Law /Mixed enterprises / G306 Sa59m no. 13 LAC

1669. Garrigou-Lagrange, André. 1953 L'Etat producteur; les entreprises publiques et semipubliques. Paris: Dalloz. /Political economy

1670. Garson, G. David. 1975 "Self-Management and the Public Sector." Prepared for the panel on Self-Management and Public Administration. Second International Conference on Self-Management, Cornell University, Ithaca, New York. /Worker self management /OPSS

1671. Garvy, G. 1963 Planification et gestion de l'économie. Rôle de la banque d'Etat dans la planification soviétique. Spécialisation et coopération des entreprises dans l'économie soviétique. Paris: Institut de Science Economique Appliquée. /Union of Soviet Socialist Reps. /Central banks /Socialist economy / Planning process

1672. Gasch, Albert. 1970 "Public Enterprise and the Economics of Large Scale Production. Critical Comments on Mr. Pryke's

Report." Annals of Public and Cooperative Economy V. 41, pp. 395-400. /United Kingdom /Evaluation / 330.5 An73

1673. Gascon y Marin, José. 1942 "El municipio empresa." Revista de Estudios de la Vida Local (Madrid), No. 1, pp. 22-35. /Spain /Local government /Entrepreneurial activity

1674. Gatchalian, Jose (Jnr.). 1964 "Budgetary Control of Government Corporations." Philippine Journal of Public Administration (Manila), V. 8, No. 1, pp. 46-51. /Philippines /Control process /Budgetary process

1675. Gazier, A. 1953 "Les entreprises publiques sont-elles étatisées?" Revue Banque et Bourse pp. 291-296. /France

1676. Geffaell Gorostegui, José Antonio. 1950 "La socialización en las constituciones de la postguerra." Revista de Administración Pública (Madrid), No. 3, pp. 361-372. /Spain /Constitutional law /Social welfare policy

1677. Gelinas, André (ed.). 1978 L'Entreprise publique et l'intérêt public. Ontario: The Institute of Public Administration of Canada. /Economic analysis /Law

1678. Gelinas, André. 1978 "L'entreprise publique et l'intérêt public: autonomie et tutelle - Un résumé des délibérations." In André Gélinas, ed(s). Public Enterprise and the Public Interest. Ontario: The Institute of Public Administration of Canada. pp. 1-13. /Control process /English translation follows in same volume.

1679. Gendarme, R. 1950 L'expérience française de la nationalisation industrielle et ses enseignements économiques. Charleville, France: J. M. Lemoir. /France /Nationalization /Industrial sector /Economic history

1680. Genoud, R. 1969 Nationalism and Economic Development in Ghana. New York: Frederick A. Praeger. /Ghana /Economic development / 330.9667 G288n PCL

1681. Gentil Nunes, Janari. 1958 Esclarecimentos prestados a Comissão de Inquérito do Petróleo. Rio de Janeiro: Petróleo Brasileiro, S. A. /Brazil /Oil industry

1682. George, P. J. 1975 "Rates of Return and Government Subsidization of the Canadian Pacific Railway: Some Further Remarks." Canadian Journal of Economics V. 8, No. 4, pp. 591-600. /Canada /Railway industry /Subsidization policy /330.5 C16

1683. Georgel, J. 1969 L'Administration générale de l'assistance publique à Paris. /France /Public administration

1684. Gerbart, Paul F. 1976 "Determinants of Bargaining Outcomes in Local Government Labor Negotiations." Industrial and Labor Relations Review V. 29, No. 3, pp. 331-351. /United States of America /Local government /Labor relations /Collective bargaining /331.105 In21

1685. Germain, J. 1962 "L'importance du secteur public dans l'économie française." Revue Social No. 149, pp. 28-38. /France /Economic organization

1686. Gerralda Valcárcel, A. 1970 "La participación del personal en la gestión de las entidades públicas." La Empresa Pública. Zaragoza, Spain: Publicaciones del Real Colegio de España en Bolonia. pp. 443-470. /Worker management participation

1687. Gerskovie, L. 1960 Social and Economic System in Yugoslavia. Belgrade, Yugoslavia. /Yugoslavia /Economic system

1688. Gerwig, Robert. 1961 "Public Authorities in the United States." Law and Contemporary Problems V. 26, No. 4, pp. 591-618. /United States of America /Public Authority / Law

1689. Gerwin, Donald. 1958 La gestion ouvrière des entreprises et relations professionnelles en Yougoslavie. Compte rendu d'une échange de vues non-oficiel tenu le 16 juin 1958 à la 42ème session de la Conférence International du Travail. Série Relations Professionnelles, No. 5. Geneva: ILO. /Yugoslavia /Worker self management

1690. Gerwin, Donald. 1969 "Compensation Decisions in Public Organizations." Industrial Relations V. 8, No. 2, pp. 174-184. /Wages / 331.105 In19

1691. Ghai, Y. 1977 "Control and Management of the Economy: Research Perspectives on Public Enterprise." In Yash Ghai, ed(s). Law in the Political Economy of Public Enterprise. African Perspectives. Uppsala: Scandinavian Institute of African Studies. New York: International Legal Centre. pp. 15-48. /Law /Economic policy / Africa 76 L41 Law

1692. Ghai, Y. 1977 "Law and Public Enterprise in Tanzania." In Yash Ghai, ed(s). Law in the Political Economy of Public Enterprise: African Perspectives. Uppsala: Scandinavian Institute of African Studies. New York: International Legal Centre. pp. 206-266. /Law /Tanzania /East Africa /Africa 76 L41 Law

1693. Ghai, Y. 1981 "The Legislature and Public Enterprises." Paper presented at the Seminar on Relationships between Parliament and Public Enterprises. Ljubljana: ICPE. /Legislature /Control process

1694. Ghai, Y. 1981 "The Legislature and the Public Enterprise." In United Kingdom, Commonwealth Secretariat, ed(s). Relationships between Parliament and Public Enterprises. London. pp. 53-75. /Legislature /Control process

1695. Ghai, Y. 1982 "Alternative Systems of Executive Control." Public Enterprise V. 8, No. 2, pp. 69-75. /Control process /Administrative management / OPSS

1696. Ghai, Y. 1982 "Alternative Systems of Executive Control over Public Enterprises and their Impact on the Performance of Public Enterprises." In United Kingdom, Commonwealth

Secretariat, ed(s). Government Executive and Supervisory Control over Public Enterprises. London. pp. 161-167. /Control process /Administrative management

1697. Ghai, Y. 1983 "Executive Control over Public Enterprises in Africa." In G. Ram Reddy, ed(s). Government and Public Enterprise: Essays in honour of Professor V. V. Ramanadham. Bombay, India: N. M. Tripathi Private Limited. pp. 181-219. /Africa /Control process

1698. Ghai, Y. 1981 "The Legislature and Public Enterprises." In V. V. Ramanadham and Y. Ghai, ed(s). Parliament and Public Enterprise. Ljubljana: ICPE. pp. 23-44. /Parliament /Control process /Management /Accountability /Planning process /OPSS

1699. Ghai, Y., and Susanne Linderos. 1977 "Selective Bibliography." In Yash Ghai, ed(s). Law in the Political Economy of Public Enterprise: African Perspectives. Uppsala: Scandinavina Institute of Africa Studies. New York: International Legal Centre. pp. 327-342. /Bibliography /Africa /Africa 76 L41 Law

1700. Ghana. National Team of Experts. 1979 "Role of the Public Sector in Developing Countries: The Ghanaian Case." Paper presented at the Regional Meeting of African Countries on the Role of the Public Sector in Developing Countries, Arusha, Tanzania, 17-21 Dec. Ljubljana: ICPE. /Ghana

1701. Ghana. State Enterprises Secretariat. 1964 A Report on the Administration and Organisation of State Enterprises. Accra, Ghana: State Enterprises Secretariat. /Ghana /Public administration /Structural characteristics

1702. Gharbaoui, Omar. 1980 "Les entreprises publiques: Gestion et formation." Paper presented at the Séminaire international sur la gestion et la formation dans les entreprises publiques dans les pays en voie de développement, Ljubljana, Yugoslavia, 3-15 March. Ljubljana: ICPE. /Planning process /Developing nations / Management /Training

1703. Ghei, K. L. 1964 "The Collaboration Problem in Steel." Indian Journal of Public Administration (New Delhi), V. 10, No. 3. /India /Steel industry / JA 26 I55 Pub Aff

1704. Ghetti, Giulio. 1970 "Notas sobre los límites generales a la actividad de las empresas públicas." La empresa pública. Zaragoza, Spain: Publicaciones del Real Colegio de España en Bolonia. pp. 1605-1622. /Spain /Control process

1705. Ghezali, Mahfoud, et al. 1980 Le secteur public en Algérie. Ljubljana: ICPE. /Algeria

1706. Ghezali, Mahfoud. 1980 "Le rôle stratégique des entreprises publiques au Maghreb." Algiers, Algeria: ICPE. /Algeria

1707. Ghezali, Mahfoud. 1980 "Le principe de la décentralisation en Algérie: Son application dans les collectivités territoriales et dans l´entreprise socialiste." Public

Enterprise V. 1, No. 2, pp. 26-45. /Algeria /Decentralization /Socialist economy / OPSS

1708. Ghosh, A. P. 1965 Efficiency in Location an Interregional Flows. The Indian Cement Industry during the Five Year Plan 1930-1959. Amsterdam: North Holland Publishing. /India /Cement manufacturing industry / 338.4766694 G346e

1709. Ghosh, Alak, and Amalesh Chandra Banjerjee. 1972 "Public Sector Banks: A Balance Sheet of Their Growth and Performance." Economic Affairs V. 17, No. 9-10, pp. 463-469. /India /Financial institutions / 330.95405 Ec74

1710. Ghosh, B. N., and Roma Ghosh. 1980 "Public Enterprise and Economic Development: Some Observations." Lok Udyog (New Delhi), V. 14, No. 1, pp. 41-44. /Economic development /354.54 L836 PCl

1711. Ghosh, Kumar. 1978 "Price Policy --Its Nature and Problems: The Case of Public Enterprise." In K. R. Gupta, ed(s). Pricing in Public Enterprises. New Delhi, India: Atlantic Publishers and Distributors. pp. 67-88. /India /Price Policy /HB 236 I4 P75

1712. Ghosh, O. K. 1971 "Towards Effective Management Control." Lok Udyog (New Delhi), V. 5, No. 2, pp. 173-179. /India /Information system /Management /354.54 L836 PCL

1713. Ghosh, P. K. 1972 "Holding Company for Public Enterprises." Lok Udyog (New Delhi), V. 6, No. 7, pp. 5-14. /India /Subsidiaries /Holding company /354.54 L836 PCL

1714. Ghosh, Satya Brata. 1971 "Reporting Systems and Company Objectives." Lok Udyog (New Delhi), V. 5, No. 2, pp. 165-172. /India /Information system /354.54 L836 PCL

1715. Ghouse, Ghulam. 1970 "Nationalised Banks and Agricultural Production." Lok Udyog (New Delhi), V. 4, No. 6, pp. 667-670. /India /Agricultural development /354.54 L836 PCL

1716. Ghuge, V. B. 1970 "Nationalized Banks as an Instrument of Economic Growth with Social Justice." Economic Affairs V. 15, pp. 533-41. /India /Financial institutions /Nationalization / 330.95405 Ec74 940.93144 Af89

1717. Giacchi, O. 1967 Il controllo del impresa pubblica. Italy: Il Diritto Parlimentare. /Italy /Control process

1718. Giannini, M. S. 1958 Le imprese pubbliche in Italia. Italy: Riv. Soc. /Italy

1719. Giannini, M. S. 1970 "Actividades económicas públicas y formas jurídicas privadas." La empresa pública. Zaragoza, Spain: Publicaciones del Real Colegio de España en Bolonia. pp. 99-116. /Spain /Private sector /Law

1720. Gignoux, L. 1968 "Nature juridique des statuts des personnels d'Air-France." Revue Française de Droit Aérien /France /Air transportation industry /Personnel management

/Law

1721. Giladi, Dan. 1975 "The Public Sector and the Dilemma of Public Services in the U.S." Annals of Public and Cooperative Economy V. 46, No. 1, pp. 45-60. /United States of America /Public services /330.5 An73

1722. Gilejko, L. 1969 "L'Autogestion ouvrière en Pologne." Perspectives Polonaises (Warsaw), V. 12, No. 6-7, pp. 66-78. /Poland /Worker self management

1723. Gillis, M. 1979 Allocative efficiency and X-efficiency in state-owned enterprises: some Asian and Latin American cases in the mining sector. Austin, Tex.: OPSS Technical Papers Series. No. 13. /Mining industry /Bolivia /Indonesia /Economic efficiency /OPSS

1724. Gillis, M. 1980 The Role of State Enterprises in Economic Development. HIID Development Discussion Paper No. 83. /Economic development /OPSS

1725. Gillis, M. n.d. "Public Enterprise and the Public Interest." Boston: HIID, BAPEG. /Public interest

1726. Gillis, M., Glenn P. Jenkins, and Donald R. Lessard. 1982 "Public Enterprise Finance: Toward a Synthesis." In Leroy P. Jones et al., ed(s). Public Enterprise in Less-Developed Countries. New York: Cambridge University Press. pp. 257-277. /Financing /HD 3850 P83 PCL /Paper earlier presented at the Second BAPEG conference, "Public Enterprise in Mixed Economy LDCs," April 1980 under the title: "Public Enterprise Finance in Developing Countries: Toward a Synthesis." /OPSS

1727. Ginella, E. 1962 "About the Nationalisation of the Electric Power Industry." Stato Sociale (Rome), V. 6, No. 9, pp. 734-749. /Italy /Nationalization /Electrical utility industry

1728. Ginestar, Angel. 1974 "Empresa pública versus empresa privada, un replanteo de la controversia en términos de eficiencia." Revista de la Asociación Interamericana de Presupuesto Público V. 1, No. 4, pp. 31-79. /Latin America /Economic efficiency /OPSS

1729. Giorgetti, A. 1965 "Esigenze e prospettive della contabilitá degli enti pubblici." Risparmio (Rome), V. 13, No. 3, pp. 425-479. /Italy /Accountability /Information system

1730. Giron Tena, José. 1942 Las sociedades de economía mixta. Madrid. /Spain /Mixed enterprises

1731. Giron Tena, José. 1949 "Las empresas públicas." No. 47, pp. 193-216. /Evaluation

1732. Giroux, M., and D. Blain. 1971 "Les entreprises publiques en modeles." Statistiques et Etudes Financières (Paris), /France /Evaluation

1733. Giugni, G. 1949 Las empresas públicas. No. 47, pp. 193-216. /Evaluation

1734. Giugni, G. 1964 L´Evolutione della contrattazione collectiva nelle industrie siderurgica e mineria, 1953-1963. Milan, Italy: A. Giuffré. /Italy /Mining industry /Metal manufacturing industry /Collective bargaining

1735. Glade, William P. 1968 The Latin American Economies: A Study of their Institutional Evolution. London: Van Nostrand. /Latin America /Economic analysis /G330.9806 G4511

1736. Glade, William P. 1973 The Study of State Enterprise in Economic Development. Austin, Tex.: Conference on "Economic Relations between Mexico and the United States." /Economic development /Economic research /Evaluation HD 3850 G55 LAC

1737. Glade, William P. 1973 "Estudio de la empresa pública en el desarrollo económico." Investigación Administrativa No. 10, pp. 16-27. /Economic development

1738. Glade, William P. 1975 "El papel de las empresas del sector público en la integración de la estructura industrial Latino Americana. Algunas observaciones preliminares." Revista de la Integración (Buenos Aires), V. 8, No. 19/2, pp. 7-54. /Latin America /Industrial economy /Economic integration /Multinational corporations /G337.91 R327 LAC

1739. Glade, William P. 1977 "The Role of Public Sector Firms in the Integration of Latin American Industrial Structures: Some Preliminary Observations." Proceedings of the Fourth Congress of the International Economics Association. (Budapest, Aug. 1974). Budapest: Publishing House Academia. /Latin America /Economic integration /Multinational corporations

1740. Glade, William P. 1979 "The Political Economy of Public Enterprise Controls: A Contextual View." Paper presented at the International Seminar on Regulation of the Public Enterprises. /Control process /Political economy /OPSS

1741. Glade, William P. 1979 "Entrepreneurship in the State Sector: CONASUPO of Mexico." In Sidney Greenfield, Arnold M. Strickon, and Robert Aubey, ed(s). Entrepreneurs in Cultural Context. Albuquerque: University of New Mexico Press. pp. 191-222. /Mexico /Entrepreneurial activity /Food industry /Agricultural sector /Retail trade /HB 615 E6 LAC

1742. Glade, William P. 1981 "La política económica de los controles de la empresa pública: Un enfoque contextual." Anuario Jurídico (Mexico City), V. 8, pp. 269-295. /Political economy

1743. Glade, William P. 1983 "The Privatization and Denationalisation of Public Enterprises." In G. Ram Reddy, ed(s). Government and Public Enterprise: Essays in honour of Professor V. V. Ramanadham. Bombay, India: N. M. Tripathi Private Limited. pp. 67-97. /Privatization / Peru

1744. Glade, William P. n.d. "Entrepreneurship in the State Sector: CONASUPO of Mexico." /Mexico /Entrepreneurial activity /Food industry /Agricultural sector /Retail trade /OPSS has typescript copy.

1745. Glaeser, Martin G. 1936 "The TVA Decision of the U S. Supreme Court." Land Economics V. 12, pp. 207-208. /United States of America /River valley development projects /Law / 305 J824 PCL

1746. Glaeser, Martin G. 1952 "The Powers of the Power District Boards." Public Utilities Fortnightly pp. 278-283. /United States of America /Public utility industry

1747. Glaeser, Martin G. 1954 "The St. Lawrence Seaway and Power Project." Land Economics V. 30, pp. 289-300. /Electrical utility industry / 305 J824 PCL

1748. Glentworth, G. 1969 Resource Allocation and Income Distribution in Uganda: the Supply Extension Policies of the Uganda Electricity Board. Nairobi: University Social Sciences Council Conference. /Uganda /Policy analysis /Income distribution /Resource distribution /Electrical utility industry / East Africa

1749. Glentworth, G. 1970 Research Objectives and Para-Statal Bodies. Makerere, Uganda: Institute of Social Research. /Research and development /Development corporation

1750. Glentworth, G. 1970 The Operational Roles of Public Corporations in the Ugandan Environment. Makerere, Uganda: University College. /Uganda /Evaluation

1751. Glentworth, G. 1971 Government Control of Public Enterprises in Developing Countries: Some Suggestions for the Creation, Organization and Control of Public Enterprises in Uganda. Makerere, Uganda: Universities' Social Sciences Council. /Uganda /Organization formation /Structural characteristics /Control process /East Africa

1752. Glentworth, G. 1973 "Public Enterprises in Developing Countries." Journal of Administration Overseas (London), V. 12, No. 3 pp. 190-205. /Developing nations /Control process /Structural characteristics / 352.05 J826

1753. Glentworth, G., and M. Wozei. 1971 "The Role of Public Corporations in National Development in Uganda: Case Studies of the Uganda Development Corporations and the Uganda Electricity Board." Conference in Comparative Administration in East Africa, Arusha, Tanzania. /Uganda /Electrical utility industry /Development corporation / East Africa

1754. Glinski, B. 1966 "The Role of Public Enterprise in Economic Development." Paper presented at the U. N. Seminar on Organization and Administration of Public Enterprises, Geneva, August. /Economic development

1755. Glukman, E. 1969 Las empresas estatales en el proceso ahorro-inversión en Chile. Análisis del período 1901-1964.

Santiago, Chile. /Chile /Savings /Investment /Economic development

1756. Godchot, Jacques E. 1966 Les sociétés d'économie mixte et l'aménagement du territoire. Paris: Ed. Berger-Levrault. /France /Mixed enterprises / Regional development

1757. Goekjian, Samuel V. 1977 "The Role of Arab Public Enterprises in International Transactions." Public Enterprises and Development in the Arab Countries: Legal and Managerial Aspects. New York: Praeger for the International Legal Center for Law and Development. pp. 202-228. /Multinational corporations /Banking system /HD 4334 P8 Law

1758. Gola, Guglielmo. 1970 "Introducción al análisis de los efectos redistributivos (fiscales) de las empresas públicas." La Empresa Pública. Zaragoza, Spain: Publicaciones del Real Colegio de España en Bolonia. pp. 401-422. /Spain /Evaluation

1759. Goldberg, Sidney D., and Harold Seidman. 1953 The Government Corporation: Elements of a Model Charter. Chicago: Public Administration Service. V. 3. /Public administration /Management / 380.162 G564g

1760. Goldenberg, Shirley B. 1973 "Public Sector Bargaining: The Canadian Experience." Monthly Labor Review V. 96, No. 5, pp. 34-36. /Canada /Labor relations /Collective bargaining /HD 8051 A78

1761. Goldman, Marshall I. 1963 Soviet Marketing: Distribution in a Controlled Economy. New York: Free Press of Glencoe. /Union of Soviet Socialist Reps. /Marketing / 658.8 G569s

1762. Goldstein, Sidney. 1961 "An Authority in Action - An Account of the Port of New York Authority and Its Recent Activities." Law and Contemporary Problems V. 26, No. 4, pp. 715-723. /United States of America /Port authority /Transportation Industry

1763. Golembiewski, R. 1969 "Organization Development in Public Agencies: Perspectives on Theory and Practice." Public Administration Review V. 29, No. 4, pp. 367-379. /Public administration /Organization development /Organization theory /JK 1 P85

1764. Gomes, A. Caminha. 1971 A Petrobrás e a pesquisa. Rio de Janeiro: Petróleo Brasileiro S. A., CENPES. /Brazil /Evaluation /Research and development

1765. Gomez Beltran, Fausto. 1963 "El papel de las empresas públicas en INI." Revista de Información del INI Madrid: INI. /Spain /Holding company

1766. Gomez Beltran, Fausto. 1969 La empresa pública en el plan de desarrollo. (Ponencia presentada en las II jornadas de administración financiera). /Spain /Development planning

1767. Gomez Lara, Cipriano. 1978 "Implantación de carrera para los funcionarios de la empresa pública: profesionalismo gerencial y administrativo en la empresa pública." Mexico City. /Mexico /Public administration /Management /OPSS

1768. Gomez Tagle, Silvia. 1978 "La industria eléctrica nacionalizada: bosquejo de un panorama general." Paper presented at the Round Table on Public Enterprise of the Tenth General Assembly of the Latin American Association of Public Administration. Mexico City. /Electrical utility industry /Mexico / OPSS

1769. Gomez Trapala, Ignacio, and Genaro Hernández Villalobos. 1979 "El impacto de las empresas públicas del sector agropecuario y forestal en la economía mexicana." Mexico City. /Mexico /Agricultural sector /Forestry industry /Cattle raising industry /OPSS

1770. González Aguayo, L. A. 1965 _Nationalization in Latin America: International Problems Which Confront the Application of the Institution in the Region._ Mexico City: Escuela Nacional de Ciencias Políticas y Sociales. /Latin America /Nationalization

1771. González Catalán, María Angélica. 1962 _La empresa fiscal como persona jurídica de derecho público._ Santiago, Chile: Editorial Universitaria. /Chile /Law / HD 4098 G688 LAC

1772. González Diáz-Llanos, Antonio Ezequiel. 1971 "Derecho de las comunidades europeas y empresa pública." _Revista de Administración Pública_ (Madrid), No. 65, pp. 493-504. /Western Europe /European Economic Community /International law

1773. González López, Guillermo. 1978 "La empresa pública y la política nacional de empleo y capacitación." Paper presented at the IV General Assembly of ALAP. Mexico City. /Mexico /Employment policy /Training /OPSS

1774. González Muniz, A. J. 1971 "El INI cumple 30 años." _Comercio e Industria_ (Madrid), No. 16. /Spain /Holding company

1775. González Paras, N. 1981 "Control de empresas públicas en México: La reforma administrativa y el control de las empresas públicas." pp. 115-169. /Mexico /Public administration /Administrative reform /Control process

1776. González Pérez, Jesús. 1950 "Las sociedades de economía mixta y las empresas del Estado en la legislación argentina." _Revista de Administración Pública_ (Madrid), No. 3, pp. 495-500. /Argentina /Mixed enterprises /Legislature /Control process

1777. González de León, Anibal. 1976 "La empresa pública en Panamá." Rio de Janeiro: FGV-EIAP. /Panama /Public administration /Directory /OPSS

1778. González-Berenguer Urrutia, J. 1968 "Sobre la crisis del concepto de dominio público." _Revista de Administración_

Pública (Madrid), No. 56, pp. 191-220. /Spain /Administrative management

1779. Goodall, M. R. 1942 "Land and Power Administration of the Central Valley Project of California." Land Economics V. 18, pp. 299-311. /United States of America /California (State) /Public administration / River valley development projects /Electrical utility industry / 305 J824 PCL

1780. Goodhart, A. L. 1952 "Parliamentary Control over the Nationalized Undertakings." In Lord Campion et al., ed(s). Parliament: A Survey. London: Allen & Unwin. /United Kingdom /Parliament /Control process /328.42 P239

1781. Goodman, Edward. 1951 Forms of Public Control and Ownership. London: Christophers. /United Kingdom /Control Process /338.942 G621f

1782. Gopal, M. H. 1946 "A New Basis for Railway Rates: the Social Benefit of Service Principle." Indian Journal of Economics V. 26, pp. 441-451. /Railway industry /Price policy /330.5 In2

1783. Gopal, M. H. 1962 "Public Enterprise and Regional Development." Applied Economic Papers (Hyderabad,India), V. 2, No. 1, pp. 56-59. /Regional development

1784. Gordillo, A. 1965 Empresa del estado, empresas nacionalizadas, sociedades de economía mixta, sociedades del Estado. Buenos Aires: Edic. Macchi. /Argentina /Mixed enterprises

1785. Gordillo, A. 1979 "El control de las empresas públicas en América Latina." Paper presented at the International Seminar on Regulation of the Public Enterprise, Mexico City. /Latin America /Control process /OPSS

1786. Gordillo, A. 1981 Problemas del control de la administración pública en América Latina. Madrid: Editorial Civitas, S.A. /Latin America /Control process

1787. Gordon, Lincoln. 1938 The Public Corporation in Great Britain. New York: Oxford University Press. /United Kingdom /388.8 G656p

1788. Gorenc, Ivan. 1977 "The Concept and the Programme of the School for Managerial Personnel in Economic Enterprises." Paper presented at the Séminaire international sur la gestion et la formation dans les entreprises publiques dans les pays en voie de développement, Ljubljana, Yugoslavia, 3-15 March. Ljubljana: ICPE. /Training /Management /Also presented at the English-language versions of the seminar Oct. 10-28, 1977 and Sept. 18-Oct. 6, 1978. Also Int. Sem. on Training Mgmt. in PEs in Developing Countries, Ljubljana, Sept. 29-Oct. 10, 1980.

1789. Goricar, J. 1957 "La autogestión de los trabajadores a la luz del socialismo cientifico." Le Nouveau Droit Yougoslave (Belgrade), V. 7, No. 2-4. /Yugoslavia /Worker self management

1790. Goricar, J. 1967 "L'autogestion ouvrière en Yougoslavie." Autogestion (Paris), No. 2, pp. 95-103. /Yugoslavia /Worker self management

1791. Gorjan, Bozidar. 1981 "Cooperation Among Banks in Developing Countries." Public Enterprise V. 1 No. 3, pp. 67-74. /Banking agency /International economic relations / OPSS

1792. Gorupic, D. 1969 A Contribution to the Theory of Self-Managed Organization of the Enterprise. Herceg, Novi: U.N. Public Administrative Division. /Worker self management

1793. Gorupic, D., and I. Paj. 1970 Workers' Self Management in Yugoslav Undertakings. 2C-70/Sect. 11/5 Geneva: International Industrial Relations Association, 2nd World Congress. /Yugoslavia /Worker self management

1794. Gorupic, D., and V. Rakic. 1970 "The Development of the Self-Managing Organization of Enterprises in Yugoslavia." Yugoslavia Survey (Belgrade), V. 11, No. 3, pp. 1-16. /Yugoslavia /Worker self management

1795. Gorwala, A. D. 1951 Report on the Efficient Conduct of State Enterprises. New Delhi: Planning Commission. /India /Management /Economic efficiency

1796. Gotlober, V., and V. Ganstak. 1954 "Government Owned Enterprises in India." Business Digest pp. 89-90. /India /Evaluation

1797. Gottinger, H. W. 1983 "Public Failure: Some Reflections on the Management of Large Public Programs." Paper presented at the 19th International Congress of Administrative Sciences, West Berlin, 19-23 Sept. /Management /Efficacy /Economic analysis /OPSS

1798. Govindarjan, P. S. 1980 "Corporate Planning in Public Enterprises: Perspectives and Problems." Lok Udyog (New Delhi), V. 14, No 3, pp. 7-13. /India /Planning process /354.54 L836

1799. Gowda, K. R. S. 1980 "Managerial Personnel Policy - Some Prevailing Practices in H.M.T." Lok Udyog (New Delhi), V. 13, No. 10-1, pp. 23-26. /India /Personnel management /Metal manufacturing industry /Case studies /354.54 L836 PCL

1800. Goyata, C. 1965 "Sobre o principio da continuidade da empresas e do contrato de trabalho." Legislação do Trabalho (São Paulo), No. 29, pp. 221-228. /Brazil /Labor relations /Collective bargaining

1801. Gozard, G. n. d "Le service d'exploitation industrielle des tabacs et des allumettes." Revue Politique et Parlementaire (Paris), pp. 156-169. /France /Tobacco industry /Match manufacturing industry

1802. Grabe, V. 1959 "Le contrôle de l'entreprise publique en Belgique. Pages de documentation et d'histoire." Res Publica (Louvain), No. 1, pp. 38-57. /Belgium /Control process

1803. Gracey, Don. 1978 "Public enterprise in Canada /L'entreprise public au Canada." In André Gélinas, ed(s). Public Enterprise and the Public Interest. Ontario: The Institute of Public Administration of Canada. pp. 25-47. /Canada /Economic history /Accountability /Control process

1804. Grafton, Carl. 1975 "The Creation of Federal Agencies." Administration and Society V. 7, No. 3, pp. 328-365. /United States of America /Organization formation /JA 3 J65 Pub Aff

1805. Graham, Bruce. 1949 "The Administration Structures and Problems of State Owned Utilities in Western Australia." Public Administration (Sydney, Australia), pp. 116-124. /Australia /Administrative management

1806. Graham, G. 1967 "Labour Participation in Management: A Study of the National Coal Board." Political Quarterly (London), V. 38, No. 2, pp. 184-199. /United Kingdom /Coal mining industry /Worker management participation / 320.5 P76p

1807. Graham, Lawrence. 1978 "The Administration of Public Enterprises: Coordination and Control Dilemmas for Contemporary States." Paper presented at the Round Table on Public Enterprise of the Tenth General Assembly of the Latin American Association of Public Administration, Mexico City. /Control process /OPSS

1808. Graham, Lawrence. 1979 "La administración de las empresas públicas: Dilemas de coordinación y control para los estados contemporáneos." Revista Latinoamericana de Administración Pública (Mexico City), No. 8-9, pp. 223-236. /Latin America /Public administration /Control process

1809. Grajil, Natalia. 1961 "Les entreprises d'Etat en France, en Italie,et en Pologne." Revista Internacional de Ciencias Administrativas No. 2, pp. 153-168. /France /Italy /Poland /Evaluation

1810. Granick, David. 1954 Management of the Industrial Firm in the URSS. New York: Columbia University Press. /Union of Soviet Socialist Reps. /Industrial sector /Management /658 G766m

1811. Granick, David. 1960 The Red Executive A Study of the Organization Man in Russian Industry. Garden City, N.Y.: Doubleday. /Union of Soviet Socialist Reps. /Management /658.3124 G766r UGL

1812. Granick, David. 1975 Enterprise Guidance in Eastern Europe: A Comparison of Four Socialist Economies. Princeton, N. J.: Princeton University Press. /Yugoslavia /Romania /Germany, Democratic Rep. of /Hungary /Management /Employment policy /Public administration /Worker self management /Administrative reform /OPSS

1813. Granick, David. 1976 "The Internalizing of Externalities in Socialist Enterprises and in Subunits of Large American Firms." In William G. Shepherd et al., ed(s). Public Enterprise: Economic Analysis of Theory and Practice. Lexington, Ma.: D.C. Heath and Company, Lexington Books. pp. 77-99. /Externalities /Union of Soviet Socialist Reps. /Germany, Democratic Rep. of /HD 3850 P8 PCL

1814. Grant, N. B. 1971 "The Concept of Military Management and Public Enterprises." Lok Udyog (New Delhi), V. 5, No. 9, pp. 887-894. /India /Management /354.54 L836 PCL

1815. Grassini, F. A. 1961 "Appunti sulle imprese publiche." Studi Economici (Naples, Italy), pp. 24-59. /Italy

1816. Grassini, F. A. 1961 "Notes on Public Enterprises." Studi Economici (Naples) V. 16, No. 1-2 pp. 24-59. /Italy

1817. Grassini, Franco. 1981 "The Italian Enterprises: the Political Constraints." In Raymond Vernon and Yair Aharoni, ed(s). State-Owned Enterprises in the Western Economies. New York: St. Martin's Press. pp. 70-84. /Control process /HD 3850 S79 PCL

1818. Gratwick, W. Kenneth. 1951 "Labor Relations in Nationalized Industries with Particular Reference to the Coal Mining Industry." Law and Contemporary Problems V. 16, No. 4, pp. 652-669. /United Kingdom /Coal mining industry /Labor relations / 340.5 L44

1819. Gratwick, W. Kenneth. 1952 "Labour Relations in British Nationalized Industries with Particular Reference to the Coal Mining Industry." Annals of Collective Economy V. 23, pp. 62-80. /United Kingdom /Labor relations / 330.5 An73

1820. Grau, Eros Roberto. 1980 "O controle político sobre as empresas públicas: objetivos, processos, extensão e conceniência." A empresa pública no Brasil: Uma abordagem multidisciplinar. Brasília: IPEA. pp. 205-258. /Control process /Legislature

1821. Gravelle, H. S. E. 1976 "Public Enterprises Under Rate of Return Financial Targets." Manchester School of Economics and Social Studies (Manchester), V. 44, No. 1, pp. 1-16. /Profits /Goal setting 330.5 M3121 PCL

1822. Gray, Clive. 1983 Towards a Conceptual Framework for Macroeconomic Evaluation of Public Enterprise Performance in Mixed Economy. International Monetary Fund, Fiscal Affairs Department. /Mixed economy /Evaluation

1823. Greaves, H. R. C. 1945 "Public Boards and Corporations." Political Quarterly (London), pp. 67-77. /United Kingdom /Management / 320.5 P76p

1824. Greaves, H. R. G. 1964 Democratic Participation and Public Enterprise. London: The Athlone Press. /United Kingdom /Participatory democracy

1825. Greco, Aurélio Marco. 1972 "Aspectos da concessão de servico público." Revista de Direito Público (São Paulo), V. 5, No. 21, pp. 53-88. /Brazil

1826. Greece. Ministry of Co-Ordination. 1965 Public Enterprises in Greece. Athens: Ministry of Co-Ordination. /Greece

1827. Green, J. A. 1966 Policies and Factors Affecting the Development and Operation of Public Enterprises in the African Region. Geneva: U.N. Seminar on Organization and Administration of Public Enterprises. /Africa /Policy analysis

1828. Green, R. H. 1981 "Les entreprises en Argentine face á la nouvelle stratégie économique (1976-1980)." Problemes d'Amérique Latine No. 61, pp. 19-39. /Argentina /Agricultural sector /Banking agency /Energy utility industry

1829. Green, Reginald. 1976 "Public enterprise finance and national development goals: some aspects of coordination, articulation, and efficiency." In UN. DESA., ed(s). Financing of Public Enterprises in Developing Countries: Co-ordination, Forms, and Sources. New York. pp. 1-32. /Financing /Africa

1830. Green, Reginald. 1977 "Law, Laws and Public Enterprise Planning in Africa. Preliminary Analytical Notes towards more Productive Interaction." In Yash Ghai, ed(s). Law in the Political Economy of Public Enterprise: African Perspectives. Uppsala: Scandinavian Institute of African Studies. New York: International Legal Centre. pp. 49-75. /Law /Africa /East Africa /Tanzania /Africa 76 L41 Law

1831. Green, Reginald. 1977 "Public Directly Productive Units/ Sectors in Africa and Political Economy. Some notes on methodological pitfalls." In Yash Ghai, ed(s). Law in the Political Economy of Public Enterprise: African Perspectives. Uppsala: Scandinavian Institute of African Studies. New York: International Legal Centre. pp. 137-148. /Political economy /Africa /System analysis / Africa 76 L41 Law

1832. Green, Reginald. 1977 "Historical, Decision-Taking, Firm and Sectoral Dimensions of Public Sector Enterprise. Some Aspects of and Angles of Attack for Research." In Yash Ghai, ed(s). Law in the Political Economy of Public Enterprise. African Perspectives. Uppsala: Scandinavian Institute of African Studies; New York: International Legal Centre. pp. 92-126. /Law /Africa /Economic efficiency /Economic history /Management /Africa 76 L41 Law

1833. Greenland, R. C. 1950 "Statutory Corporation Finance." Public Administration (Sydney, Australia), pp. 269-280. /Australia /Financing

1834. Greenstreet, D. R. 1973 "Public Corporation in Ghana." African Review (Dar es Salaam, Tanzania), No. 1, pp. 21-23. /Ghana / Africa

1835. Gresh, Hani. 1975 "Les entreprises publiques et la création de filiales." Economie & Statistique (Paris), No. 65, pp. 29-43. /France /Subsidiaries

1836. Grey, R. Y. 1952 "Verdict on Nationalization." Queens Quart Kingston (Ontario, Canada), pp. 427-439. /Canada /Nationalization

1837. Griess, P. R. 1958 "Some Effects of Nationalization on the Bolivian Tin Mining Industry." Association of American Geographical Annals V. 48. /Bolivia /Nationalization /Tin industry / 910.6 As78

1838. Grimond, J. 1959 "Liberalism and Nationalization." New Statesman V. 58. /Nationalization /Political analysis

1839. Grosdidier de Matons, J. 1970 "Dix ans d'évolution des établissements publics en Côte d'Ivoire." Revue de Droit des Pays d'Afrique (Paris), No. 728, pp. 153-180. /Ivory Coast /Economic history /Organization development

1840. Grossman, G. 1967 "Protection of the State's Interest in the Functioning of Socialist Enterprises." Contribution to the 7th World Congress of the International Political Science Association, Brussels, 18-23 Sept. /Socialist economy

1841. Grove, David L. 1955 Política monetaria en países subdesarrollados. Mexico City: CEMLA. /Developing nations /Central banks / G332.401 G919p LAC

1842. Grove, J. W. 1953 "Nationalization in Practice." Public Administration Review V. 13, No. 3, pp. 201-207. /Nationalization / JK1 P85

1843. Grove, J. W. 1956 "British Public Corporations--Some Recent Developments." Journal of Politics V. 18, pp. 651-77. /United Kingdom / JA 1 J6 Law /JA1 J67 Pub Aff

1844. Groves, A. 1970 Pricing, Investment Appraisal and Depreciation Policy. London: Electricity Council. /United Kingdom /Electrical utility industry /Price policy /Investment

1845. Grozdanic, S. 1966 "Administrative Management of Public Enterprises in Yugoslavia." Revue Internationale des Sciences Administratives V. 32, No. 1, pp. 43-57. /Yugoslavia /Administrative management

1846. Grozdanic, Stanislav, and Vesna Smole-Grobovsek. 1981 "Workers' Self-Management and Participation in Developing Countries." Public Enterprise V. 1, No. 2, pp. 47-63. /Developing nations /Worker self management /Worker management participation / OPSS

1847. Grozsman, Robert. 1979 "Current Financing Policies in the Electricity Industry." Annals of Public and Cooperative Economy V. 50, No. 3, pp. 137-149. /Electrical utility Industry /Price policy /330.5 An73

1848. Grujic, Milenko. 1978 "Les cadres et la fonction des cadres dans les entreprises." Paper presented at the Séminaire international sur la gestion et la formation dans les entreprises publiques dans les pays en voie de développement, Ljubljana, Yugoslavia, 6-17 Nov. Ljubljana: ICPE. /Management

1849. Grunwald, K. 1940 "State and Industry in the Middle East." Egypte Contemporaine (Cairo), V. 31, pp. 225-231. /Middle East / Egypt / 962.05 Eg98r

1850. Grunwald, O. 1980 "Steel and the State in Austria." Annals of Public and Cooperative Economy V. 51, No. 4, pp. 477-492. /Austria /Steel industry /330.5 An73

1851. Grunwald, O., and H. Kramer. 1966 Die verstaatliche osterreichische metallindustrie. (The Austrian Nationalized Mining Industry.) Frankfurt: Europaische Verlagsanstalt. /Austria /Mining industry /Nationalization

1852. Guadagni, A. 1963 El marginalismo y la política de precios de las empresas nacionalizadas en Francia: El caso de Electricité de France. Buenos Aires nstituto Torcuato di Tella, Centro de Investigaciones Económicas. /France /Electrical utility industry /Nationalization /Price policy /HD 4168 G834 LAC

1853. Guadagni, Alieto Aldo. 1976 "Análisis económico del financiamiento de las empresas del Estado." Desarrollo Económico (Buenos Aires), V. 15 No. 60, pp. 549-564. /Public financing /Economic analysis / HD 85 S7 D48 LAC

1854. Guadagni, Alieto Aldo. 1977 "Análisis económico de financiamiento de las empresas del Estado. Acerca de un comentario." Desarrollo Económico V. 16, No. 65, pp. 155-158. /Public financing /Economic analysis

1855. Guadement, P. M. 1972 "Le contrôle financier des entreprises publiques." Revue de Droit Public et de la Science Politique (Paris), No. 2. /France /Financing /Control process

1856. Guagliardi, José Augusto. 1977 "A Study of the Application of Social Marketing in a Developing Nation: The Banco Nacional de Habitação in Brazil." Ph.D. dissertation, UT-Austin. /Brazil /Credit policy /Housing industry /Marketing /OPSS

1857. Guanaes, Virginia. 1972 "BADESP financia o desenvolvimento." Industria e Desenvolvimento (São Paulo), No. 5, pp. 17-20. /Brazil /Development banks / Sao Paulo, Brazil (State) /G333.0981 In2 LAC

1858. Guarino, Giuseppe. 1971 "Le ministère italien des participations de l´Etat et les organes de gestion." International Review of Administrative Sciences V. 37, No. 1-2, pp. 68-73. /Italy /Government bureaucracy /Public administration / JA 1 A1 I6 PCL

1859. Gudic, Milenko, and Mirko R. Todorovic. 1980 "Study on the Role of the Public Sector in the Industrialization of Yugoslavia." Ljubljana: ICPE. /Yugoslavia /Industrialization /Economic development

1860. Gudic, Milenko. 1980 "Feasibility Study." Paper presented at the Seminar on Planning, Dar es Salaam, Tanzania, 1-12 December. Ljubljana: ICPE. /Planning process

1861. Gudic, Milenko. 1980 "Marketing." Paper presented at the Seminar on Planning, Dar es Salaam, Tanzania, 1-12 December. Ljubljana: ICPE. /Planning process /Marketing

1862. Gudic, Milenko. 1980 "Regional and National Planning." Paper presented at the Seminar on Planning, Dar es Salaam, Tanzania, 1-12 December. Ljubljana: ICPE.

1863. Gudic, Milenko. 1980 "Strategic Planning." Paper presented at the Seminar on Planning, Dar es Salaam, Tanzania, 1-12 December. Ljubljana: ICPE. /Planning process

1864. Gudin, Eugenio. 1963 _Descalabro-Bras: Un cáncer en la economía brasileña, las empresas nacionalizadas._ Lima: Centro de Documentación Económico-Social. /Brazil /Oil industry / HD 4093 G83 LAC

1865. Guereca Tosantos, L. 1963 _La empresa pública como instrumento de la política industrial de España._ Madrid: ICE. /Spain /Political role

1866. Guerra García, Carlos Domingo, and Frederico José Villanueva Tavares. 1975 "La empresa pública en la República Dominicana." Rio de Janeiro: FGV-EIAP. /Dominican Republic /Economic history /Public administration /OPSS

1867. Guerrero, Maritza Amalia. 1981 "Las empresas públicas en la República Dominicana." Paper presented at the seminar on public enterprises in development planning for Central America and the Caribbean, San José, Costa Rica, 1-3 July. /Caribbean Region /Dominican Republic /OPSS

1868. Guidi, M. 1968 "State Holding in the Italian Economy." _Review of the Economic Condition in Italy_ (Rome), V. 22, No. 5, pp. 339-351. /Italy

1869. Guilherme, Olympio. 1957 _O nacionalismo e a política internacional do Brasil._ São Paulo: Editora Fulgor. /Brazil /Nationalism /International relations

1870. Guilherme, Olympio. 1959 _Roboré: A luta pelo petróleo boliviano._ Rio de Janeiro: Livraria Freitas Bastos, S. A. /Brazil /Bolivia /Oil industry /Policy analysis

1871. Guilherme, Olympio. 1960 _A verdade sobre Roboré._ Rio de Janeiro: Livraria Freitas Bastos. /Brazil /Policy analysis

1872. Guinard, J. 1942 _Le contrôle exercé par l'Etat sur les societés dont il est actionnaire._ Paris. /France /Control process

1873. Guisado, Vicente María G. H. 1971 "La formación permanente de los funcionarios públicos." Documentación Administrativa (Madrid), No. 139. /Spain /Personnel management / Training

1874. Guitian de Lucas, J. María. 1969 "La empresa pública a través de los trabajos de las II Jornadas de Administración Financiera." Economía Financiera Española (Madrid), No. 31-3, pp. 129-135. /Spain /Financial institutions

1875. Guitian de Lucas, J. María. 1969 "Problemática de las empresas públicas desde la perspectiva de su organización y funcionamiento." Economía Financiera Española (Madrid), No. 31-3, pp. 56-81. /Spain /Structural characteristics

1876. Guitian de Lucas, J. María. 1971 "Reforma del régimen jurídico y de la mecánica de actuación financiera del Instituto Nacional de Industria." Revista de Derecho Financiero y Hacienda Pública (Madrid), V. 93. /Spain /Administrative reform /Law /Public financing

1877. Gulbert, Samuel A., and J. Reisel. 1971 "Organization Development: An Applied Philosophy for Managers of Public Enterprise." Public Administration (Sydney, Australia), V. 31, No. 2, pp. 159-169. /Australia /Organization development /Management

1878. Gulick, L., and J. K. Pollock. 1962 Government Reorganization: The United Arab Republic. (A Report Submitted to the Central Committe for the Reorganization of the Machinery of Government). Cairo. /Egypt /Government bureaucracy /Organization change

1879. Gulick, Luther. 1947 "`Authorities´ and How to Use Them." Tax Review pp. 47-52. /United States of America /Local government /State government /Law

1880. Gunther, A. 1960 "The German Railways and Collective Economy." Annals of Collective Economy V. 31, pp. 24-90. /Germany, Federal Rep. of /Railway industry / 330.5 An73

1881. Gupta C. B. 1954 "Role of Costing in Public Enterprise." Indian Journal of Commerce (Allahabad), V. 7, No. 11, pp. 11-16. /Price policy

1882. Gupta, Gouri S. 1976 "Performance Budgeting in Public Sector - A Case Study of State Trading Corporation." Lok Udyog (New Delhi), V. 10, No. 3, pp. 25-37. /India /Control process /State trading organizations /Budgetary process /354.54 L836

1883. Gupta, Janak Raj. 1971 "Comparative Role of Nationalized and Non-Nationalized Banks in Financing Agriculture and Small Scale Industry-A Review of the Pre-Nationalization and the Post-Nationalization Period." Economic Affairs (Calcutta), V. 16, No. 5, pp. 219-228. /India /Financial Institutions /Nationalization / 330.95405 Ec74

1884. Gupta, K. C., J. L. Chadha, and L. N. Agarwal. 1974 "Higher Productivity in Heavy Electricals - A Decade of Intensive Effort." Lok Udyog (New Delhi), V. 7, No. 10, pp. 37-40.

/India /Metal manufacturing industry /354.54 L836 PCL

1885. Gupta, K. R. 1968 "Pricing in Public Enterprises." Annals of Public and Cooperative Economy V. 39, No. 1, pp. 17-32. /India /Price Policy / 330.5 An73

1886. Gupta, K. R. 1968 "Ministerial Control of Public Enterprises." Asian Economic Review (Hyderabad), pp. 35-49. /India /Control process

1887. Gupta, K. R. 1968 "Parliamentary Control of Public Enterprises." Annals of Public and Cooperative Economy V. 39, pp. 573-587. /Parliament /Control process

1888. Gupta, K. R. 1968 "Profit Making in Public Undertakings." Asian Economic Review (Hyderabad), V. 10, No. 2, pp. 113-131. /India /Profits / 330.5 A542

1889. Gupta, K. R. 1969 Issues in Public Enterprise. New Delhi: S. Chand & Co. /India /Control process /Price policy

1890. Gupta, K. R. 1978 "KITCO-Price and Profit Policy." Pricing in Public Enterprises. New Delhi, India: Atlantic Publishers and Distributors. pp. 167-168. /India /Profits /Price policy /HB 236 I4 P75

1891. Gupta. K. R., ed. 1978 Pricing in Public Enterprises. New Delhi, India: Atlantic Publishers and Distributors. /Price Policy /India /HB 236 I4 P75

1892. Gupta, L. N. 1959 "The Organizational Pattern of State Enterprises in India." Indian Journal of Political Science (Lucknow, India), V. 20, No. 3, pp. 216-229. /India /Organization development

1893. Gupta, L. N. 1977 A Study into the Profitability of Government Companies with Reference to Selected Running Concerns. New Delhi: Oxford and IBH Publishing. /India /Profits / HD 4293 G87

1894. Gupta, N. K. 1978 "Optimal Number of Production Runs for Several Products - A Case Study of a Giant Public Sector Engineering Enterprise." Lok Udyog (New Delhi), V. 12, No. 8, pp. 43-48. /India /Metal manufacturing industry /Case studies /Methodology /Economic efficiency /354.54 L836 PCL

1895. Gupta, N. K. 1979 "Operating Control of Inventories - The Selectivity Approach (Part I)." Lok Udyog (New Delhi), V. 13, No. 3, pp. 27-30. /Management /Inventory control /354.54 L836 PCL

1896. Gupta, N. K. 1979 "Selectivity Approach to Inventory Control - A Case Study of a Public Sector (Departmental) Enterprise (Part II)." Lok Udyog (New Delhi), V. 13, No. 4, pp. 13-16. /Management /Case studies /Inventory control /354.54 L836

1897. Gupta. P. S., and G. Sdasyk. 1961 Economic Regionalization of India: Problems and Approaches. New Delhi: Office of the Registrar General. V. 1, No. 8. /India /Economic integration

/Regional development

1898. Gupta, Ravinder Kumar. 1979 "Restructuring of the Organization." Paper presented at the Interregional Workshop "Developing Problem Solving Skills in Public Enterprises," Ljubljana, Yugoslavia, 2-17 April. Ljubljana: ICPE. /Management /Structural characteristics /Organization change

1899. Gupta, S. 1973 "The Role of the Public Sector in Reducing Regional Income Disparity in .Indian Plans." Journal of Development Studies V. 9, No. 2, pp. 243-260. /India /Regional planning /Investment /planning process /Income distribution / 338.9105 J826

1900. Gupta, S. K. 1978 "Development Banking in India - A Case for Post-sanction Appraisals." Lok Udyog (New Delhi), V. 12, No. 6, pp. 19-24. /India /Development banks /Control process /354.54 L836 PCL

1901. Gupta, S. K. Sen. 1979 "Internal Audit in Accountability." Lok Udyog (New Delhi), V. 12, No. 10-1, pp. 13-16. /Accountability /India /Control process /354.54 L836 PCL

1902. Gupta T. K. 1980 "Technology Transfer." Paper presented at the Regional Workshop on Management and Transfer of Technology in Public Enterprises in the ESCAP Region, Bangalore, India, 10-15 November. Ljubljana: ICPE. /Technology transfer

1903. Gupta, V. S. 1975 "Conduct Rules for Public Sector Enterprises." Lok Udyog (New Delhi), V. 9, No. 7, pp. 19-26. /India /Management /354.54 L836 PCL

1904. Gupte, V. R. 1979 "Banking Industry - Some Criteria for Evaluation." Lok Udyog (New Delhi), V. 13, No. 8, pp. 15-20. /India /Banking system /Evaluation /Methodology /354.54 L836

1905. Gustafsson, Hans, Staffan Jacobsson, and Bo Goransson. 1980 "Assessing the Social Benefits from Local Skill Generation: A Preliminary Proposition for a Pilot Study on the Developing Countries' Choice of Technique in the Power Sector." Paper presented at the Expert Group Meeting on Strategies for Energy Development in Developing Countries -Role of Public Enterprises, Ljubljana, Yugoslavia, 19-22 Feb. Ljubljana: ICPE. /Technology transfer /Electrical utility industry

1906. Gustely, Richard D. 1974 Municipal Public Employment and Public Expenditure. Lexington, Mass.: D. C. Heath. /United States of America /Financing /Labor relations /JS 361 G88 Pub Aff

1907. Gutch. G. 1953 "Nationalized Industries and the Public Accounts Committee, 1951-1952." Public Administration (London), V. 31, pp. 255-263. /Australia /Industrial sector /Public administration / JA 8 P8 Pub Aff

1908. Gutierrez Luna, Carlos E. 1981 "Situación y perspectivas de las empresas públicas en Guatemala." Paper presented at the seminar on public enterprises in development planning for Central America and the Caribbean, San José, Costa Rica, 1-3 July. /Guatemala /Planning process /Control process /Economic efficiency /Private enterprises /Comparative analysis /OPSS

1909. Guyana. National Team of Experts. 1979 "Role of the Public Sector: Preliminary National Report of Guyana." Paper presented at the International Meeting on the Role of the Public Sector in Developing Countries, 2nd, Ljubljana, Yugoslavia, 2-7 April. Ljubljana: ICPE. /Guyana

1910. Guyana. National Team of Experts. 1979 "The Role of the Public Sector in Developing Countries, Guyana: International Research Project, Project Outline." Paper presented at the International Meeting on the Role of the Public Sector in Developing Countries, 2nd, Ljubljana, Yugoslavia, 2-7 April. Ljubljana: ICPE. /Guyana /Economic research

1911. Gwilliam, K. M. 1962 "A Report on Consumer Consultation in the Nationalized Industries." Applied Economic Papers (Hyderabad), pp. 11-24. /India /Consumer relations

1912. Haar, Ernst. 1980 "Public Enterprises and Their Employees: Concerning the Control of Public Enterprises by the Workers as Exemplified by the German Federal Railways." Paper presented at the 13th International Congress of Public and Cooperative Economy, Lisbon, 2-4 June. /Germany, Federal Rep. of /Worker self management /Control process /Railway industry /OPSS /Published in Annals of Public and Cooperative Economy, Vol. 52, Nos. 1-2, (1981): pp. 145-156.

1913. Hacker, A. 1955 "Why Nationalize?--British Labour's Unasked Question." Social Research V. 22, pp. 1-24. /United Kingdom /Nationalization /Trade unions / 305 So123 PCL

1914. Hadji Vasileva, Jokica. 1983 "L'entreprise publique et la participation ouvrière en Afrique." Paper presented at the 19th International Congress of Administrative Sciences, West Berlin, 19-23 Sept. /Africa /Worker management participation /OPSS

1915. Hagg, Ingemund. 1971 "Some State-Controlled Industrial Companies in Tanzania: A Case Study." Uppsala: The Scandinavian Institute of African Studies. /Tanzania /Case studies /Industrial sector

1916. Hague, W. 1969 "A Model of Capital Accumulation in the Public Sector." Metroeconomica V. 21, No. 3, pp. 232-242. /Investment

1917. Hahn, Hugo J. 1961 "International and Supranational Public Authorities." Law and Contemporary Problems V. 26, No. 4, pp. 638-665. /Public authority /International economic relations

1918. Haji Othman, Kamaludin bin. 1981 "Management Training and Development in Public Enterprises in Malaysia." Paper presented at the Regional Workshop on Management Training and Development in Public Enterprises of Developing Countries, Karachi, Pakistan, 5-15 Jan. Ljubljana: ICPE. /Malaysia /Training /Management

1919. Haksar, P. N. 1975 "Public Sector: Hope or Despair." In R. C. Dutt and Raj. K. Nigam, ed(s). Towards Commanding Heights. New Delhi: Vivek Joshi. pp. 22-27. /India /Management /HD 4293 T68 PCL

1920. Halim, Abdel Rahman A. 1979 "Successor Planning of Management: The Industrial Research and Consultancy Institute, Sudan Case Study." Paper presented at the Interregional Workshop "Developing Problem Solving Skills in Public Enterprises," Ljubljana, Yugoslavia, 2-17 April. Ljubljana: ICPE. /Sudan /Planning process /Management /Consultant services / Case studies

1921. Hall, Ford P. 1940 The Concept of a Business Affected with a Public Interest. Bloomington, Ind.: Principia Press. /Public interest /Private enterprises

1922. Hallet, Richard M. 1947 The Maine Port Authority State Government. Chicago. /United States of America /Port authority /State government

1923. Halperin, Ricardo. 1977 "Análisis económico del financiamiento de las empresas del Estado, un comentario." Desarrollo Económico V. 16, No. 65, pp. 151-154. /Public financing /Economic analysis

1924. Hamdane, Salah. 1980 "The Process of Identification and Evaluation of Investment Projects of National Enterprises in Algeria." Paper presented at the International Workshop on Investment Criteria and Investment Decision-Making Processes, Ljubljana, Yugoslavia, 20-24 October. Ljubljana: ICPE. /Algeria /Investment

1925. Hamel, J. 1946 "La nouvelle organization des banques françaises." Droit Social (Paris), pp. 310-349. /France /Banking agency /Organization formation

1926. Hamel, J. 1950 "La nationalisation des grandes banques de dépôt." Droit Social (Paris), /France /Nationalization /Financial institutions

1927. Hamilton, N. M. 1971 Picking Pryke. The Facts on State Industry. London: Aims of Industry. /United Kingdom /Industrial sector

1928. Hamilton, Neil. 1982 "Foreward: Symposium on Government of Public Enterprises." Minnesota Law Review V. 67, pp. 179-189. /Public administration /Management

1929. Hamilton, Nora. 1982 "The Limits of State Autonomy: Mexico." Ph.D. dissertation, University of Wisconsin (Madison). /Mexico /Economic development /Economic history /Social development FILM 13,948 LAC

1930. Hamilton, Nora. 1982 The Limits of State Autonomy: Post-Revolutionary Mexico. Princeton, N.J.: Princeton University Press. /Mexico /Economic development /Economic history /Social development /HC 135 H27 1982 LAC

1931. Hamilton, R. E. 1969 "Damodar Valley Corporation: India's Experiment with the T. V. A. Model." Indian Journal of Public Administration (New Delhi), pp. 86-109. /India /River valley development projects / JA 26 I55 Pub Aff

1932. Hamm, W. 1961 Collective Property: The Role of Public Enterprise in the Market Economy. Heidelberg, Germany: Quelle und Meyer. /Germany, Federal Rep. of /Market economy

1933. Hamon, Francis. 1983 "La démocracie dans l'entreprise publique: Nouveaux modes de gestion." Paper presented at the 19th International Congress of Administrative Sciences, West Berlin, 19-23 Sept. /France /Nationalization /Law /Economic history /OPSS

1934. Hamsagar, Ram S. 1980 "Autonomy and Accountability of Public Sector Enterprises in India." Lok Udyog (New Delhi), V. 14, No. 4, pp. 9-12. /India /Accountability /Control process /Autonomy /354.54 L826

1935. Handoussa, Heba Ahmad. 1980 "The Impact of Economic Liberalisation on the Performance of Egypt's Public Sector Industry." Paper presented at the Second BAPEG Conference: Public Enterprises in Mixed Economy LDCs, Boston, April. /Egypt /OPSS

1936. Hannarong, Khajonsak. 1981 "Training for Public Enterprise Management in Thailand." Paper presented at the Interregional Seminar on Training Management in Public Enterprises in Developing Countries, Ljubljana, Yugoslavia, 19-28 October. Ljubljana: ICPE. /Thailand /Training /Management

1937. Hansen, H., et al. 1973 "The Public Enterprises in Germany." The Evolution of the Public Enterprises in the Community of the Nine. Brussels: CEEP Editions. pp. 59-115. /Germany, Federal Rep. of /Statistics /OPSS

1938. Hanson, A. H. 1954 "Parliament and the Nationalized Industries." Yorkshire Bulletin of Economic and Social Research (London), V. 6, pp. 145-161. /United Kingdom /Parliament

1939. Hanson, A. H. 1954 "Labor and the Public Corporation." Public Administration (London), /Labor relations /320.5 J826 PCL

1940. Hanson, A. H. 1955 "Personnel Policy in the State Electricity Commission of Victoria." In A. H. Hanson, ed(s). Public Enterprise. Brussels: IIAS. pp. 503-506. /Personnel management /Electrical utility industry /HD 3850 H28 Law

1941. Hanson, A. H. 1955 "Public Enterprise in the Industrial Field in Puerto Rico." In A. H. Hanson, ed(s). Public

Enterprise. Brussels: IIAS. /Puerto Rico /Industrial sector /HD 3850 H28 Law

1942. Hanson, A. H. 1955 "Public Enterprise in France." In A. H. Hanson, ed(s). Public Enterprise. Brussels: IIAS. pp. 201-224. /France /HD 3850 H28 Law

1943. Hanson, A. H. 1955 "Public Enterprise in New Zealand." In A. H. Hanson, ed(s). Public Enterprise. Brussels: IIAS. pp. 507-514. /New Zealand /HD 3850 H28 Law

1944. Hanson, A. H. 1955 "Public Enterprise in the Union of Burma." In A. H. Hanson, ed(s). Public Enterprise. Brussels: IIAS. pp. 427-442. /Burma / HD 3850 H28 Law

1945. Hanson, A. H. 1955 "Public Enterprise in Ceylon." In A. H. Hanson, ed(s). Public Enterprise. Brussels: IIAS. pp. 443-450. /Sri Lanka / HD 3850 H28 Law

1946. Hanson, A. H. 1955 "Public Enterprise in the German Federated Republic." In A. H. Hanson, ed(s). Public Enterprise. Brussels: IIAS. pp. 225-230. /Germany, Federal Rep. of /HD 3850 H28 Law

1947. Hanson, A. H. 1955 "Public Enterprise in South Africa." In A. H. Hanson, ed(s). Public Enterprise. Brussels: IIAS. pp. 383-395. /South Africa, Rep of /Africa /HD 3850 H28 Law

1948. Hanson, A. H. 1955 "The System of State Banks and Their Role in the Development of Public Enterprise in Turkey." In A. H. Hanson, ed(s). Public Enterprise. Brussels: IIAS. pp. 331-345. /Turkey /Banking agency / HD 3850 H28 Law

1949. Hanson, A. H. 1956 Electricity Reviewed: The Herbert Report. London: Royal Institute of Public Administration. /United Kingdom /Electrical utility industry

1950. Hanson, A. H. 1958 "Public Enterprise in Nigeria." Parts I and II. Public Administration (London), V. 36-37, pp. 366-84;21-3. /United Kingdom /Nigeria / 320.5 J826 PCL

1951. Hanson, A. H. 1959 Public Enterprise and Economic Development. London: Routledge and Kegan Paul. /Economic development / 338.9 H198p

1952. Hanson, A. H. 1959 Some Problems Concerning State Enterprises in Turkey. Ankara: Balkanoglu Matbaasi. /Turkey

1953. Hanson, A. H. 1960 "L'imprensa pubblica in Gran Bretagna." Civilitá della Machine (Milan), pp. 21-26. /United Kingdom

1954. Hanson, A. H. 1960 "Estructura de las empresas públicas en el nivel de la Junta Directiva." Servicios Públicos V. 7, No. 6, pp. 20-25. /Management

1955. Hanson, A. H. 1961 Parliament and Public Ownership. London: The Hansard Society by Cassel. /United Kingdom /Parliament / 338.942 H198p

1956. Hanson, A. H. 1961 "Public Authorities in Underdeveloped Countries." Law and Contemporary Problems V. 26, No. 4, pp. 619-637. /Developing nations /Public authority

1957. Hanson, A. H. 1961 Le secteur public dans une économie en voie de développement. Paris: Presses Universitaires de France. /Developing nations

1958. Hanson, A. H. 1962 Managerial Problems in Public Enterprise. New York: Asia Publishing House. /India /Management /338.74 H198m

1959. Hanson, A. H. 1962 "Parliament and Public Ownership." Annals of Collective Economy pp. 15-19. /United Kingdom /Parliament /330.5 An73

1960. Hanson, A. H. 1962 "Normas para la determinación de la eficiencia administrativa." Servicios Públicos V. 9, No. 3, pp. 34-38. /Evaluation /Public administration

1961. Hanson, A. H. 1962 "El control de la empresa pública." Commerce Exterieur (Ottawa, Canada), V. 12, No. 12, pp. 843-847. /Control process

1962. Hanson, A. H. 1963 Nationalization: A Book of Readings. London: Allen & Unwin. /Nationalization / 338.942 H198n

1963. Hanson, A. H. 1964 Government Organization for Government Enterprise. Paris: OCDE. /France /Management /Organization behavior

1964. Hanson, A. H. 1965 Public Enterprise and Economic Development. London: Routledge & Kegan Paul. /Economic development / Agricultural sector /Agricultural services /Development corporation / Industrialization /Development banks /United Kingdom / 338.9 H198p PCL /HD 3850 H3 1965 Pub Aff /Second edition of 1959 book by same title.

1965. Hanson, A. H. 1965 "L'organisation des entreprises d'Etat." International Review of Administrative Sciences V. 31, No. 2, pp. 107-117. /Organization development / JA 1 A1 I6 PCL

1966. Hanson, A. H. 1966 "Central Administration and the Nationalized Sector." Paper presented at the Seminar on "The Coordination of Departments of Central Government Concerned with Economic Matters." African Training and Research Centre in Administration for Development. /Public administration

1967. Hanson, A. H. 1966 The Management of Public Utilities by Local Authorities. The Hague: Martinus Nijhoff. /Netherlands /Public utility industry /Local government /Management /352.9104 H198m

1968. Hanson, A. H. 1966 The Process of Planning--A Study of India's Five-Year Plans, 1950-1964. London: Oxford University Press. /India /Planning process / 338.954 H198p

1969. Hanson, A. H. 1968 "The Functional Setting of Public Enterprise." Development Digest V. 6, pp. 83-91. /Control process / HC 10 D44 Pub Aff

1970. Hanson, A. H. 1968 "The Creation of Public Enterprises." Development Digest V. 6, No. 3, pp. 71-75. /Developing nations /Planning process / HC 10 D44 Pub Aff

1971. Hanson, A. H. 1968 "Report of Preliminary Study." In United Nations, Department of Economic and Social Affairs, ed(s). Organization and Administration of Public Enterprises. New York: United Nations. pp. 1-111. /Public administration /Organization development

1972. Hanson, A. H. 1968 "Es la junta directiva necesaria en las empresas públicas?" Servicios Públicos pp. 32-37. /Management

1973. Hanson, A. H. 1978 La empresa pública y el desarrollo económico. Mexico City: Ediciones INAP. /Mexico /Economic development /OPSS

1974. Hanson, A. H. n.d. "The Structure and Control of Public Enterprises in Turkey." Ankara, Turkey: Institute of Public Administration. /Turkey /Structural characteristics /Control process / Evaluation

1975. Hanson, A. H., and M. J. Boodhoo. 1969 "A Report on the Administration and Organisation of State Enterprises." Paper presented at the United Nations Seminar, Rome. New York: U.N. /Public administration /Structural characteristics

1976. Hanson, A. H., ed. 1955 Public Enterprise: A Study of Its Organization and Management in Various Countries. Brussels: IIAS. /Structural characteristics /Management /HD 3850 H28 Law

1977. Hanumanthappa, K. 1975 "Cost Control in Road Passenger Transport - A Case Study with Particular Reference to Kerala State Road Transport Corporation (KSRTC)." Lok Udyog (New Delhi), V. 9, No. 9, pp. 39-48. /India /Costs /Kerala, India (State) /354.54 L836 PCL

1978. Hanville, J. 1962 "Le monopole des tabacs et les principales étapes de son évolution." Bulletin Liaison et l'Information de l'Administration Centrale de Finances pp. 50-66. /France /Tobacco industry /Monopoly

1979. Haque Md., Shamsul. 1980 "Controlling Increases in Costs and Prices in Bangladesh: A Management Accounting Approach." Cost and Management V. 8, No. 2-3, pp. 21-24. /Bangladesh /Manufacturing industry /Price control /Cost benefit analysis

1980. Haque Md., Shamsul. 1980 "Resource Allocation in a Regime of Rising Prices, Conventional Accounting and Price Control with Reference to Nationalized Enterprises in Bangladesh." Journal of Management Business and Economics V. 6, No. 3, pp. 262-271. /Bangladesh /Price control /Accounting

1981. Haque, Anwarul. 1979 "System of Internal and External Control of Public Sector Industrial Enterprises in Bangladesh." Paper presented at the Interregional Workshop on Control Systems for Public Enterprises in Developing Countries, Ljubljana, Yugoslavia, 9-13 July. Ljubljana: ICPE. /Bangladesh /Control process /Industrial sector

1982. Harberger, Arnold C. 1970 "Custo marginal e investimento social. Critério aplicável a energia elétrica." Revista de Teoria e Pesquisa Economica (São Paulo), V. 1, No. 2, pp. 15-21. /Brazil /Electrical utility industry /Costs /Investment

1983. Hardern, L. 1952 "Public Relations in the Nationalized Industries." In W. A. Robson, ed(s). Problems of Nationalized Industry. London: Allen & Unwin. /United Kingdom /Industrial sector /Public relations / 338.942 R576p

1984. Hare, Diane M. 1982 "Privatization: What Future for BritOil after the Great Amersham Furor." Company Law V. 3, pp. 229-231. /United Kingdom /Oil industry /Privatization

1985. Harelimana, F. 1980 "Les entreprises publiques au Rwanda: Le cas de la Régie des Transports Publics (RTP)." Paris: Université de Paris-Sud, Faculté de Droit et des Sciences Economiques. /Rwanda /Mass transportation industry

1986. Harlander, H., and D. Mezger. 1971 Development Banking in Africa: Seven Case Studies. Munich: Ifo-Institut fur Wirtschaftsforschung Munchen Afrika-Studienstelle. /Africa /Development banks /Case studies

1987. Haron, Mohd. Suffian. 1980 "Government Executive and Supervisory Controls over Public Enterprises in Developing Countries: Malaysia's Experience." Public Enterprise V. 2, No. 4, pp. 59-68. /Malaysia /Control Process /Public Administration /OPSS

1988. Harris, D. J., and B. C. L. Davies. 1981 "Corporate Planning as a Control System in United Kingdom Nationalized Industries." Long Range Planning V. 14, No. 1, pp. 15-22. /Planning process /United Kingdom

1989. Harris, Mark. 1941 "The Government Corporation in Kentucky." Kentucky Law Journal pp. 285-300. /United States of America /Kentucky (State)

1990. Harris, N. 1972 Competition and the Corporate Society. British Conservatives, the State and Industry, 1945-1964. London: Methuen. /United Kingdom /Competition /Political analysis / HC 256.5 H314

1991. Harris, Shearon. 1975 "What Can Government Do for Utilities." Public Utility Fortnightly V. 95, No. 12. /Public utility industry /Control process

1992. Harrison, J. 1900 "Municipal Trading." Economic Journal V. 10, pp. 251-258. /Local government / 330.5 Ec7

1993. Harvono, Piet. 1980 "Cooperation among State Petroleum Enterprises in Southeast Asian Countries." _State Petroleum Enterprises in Developing Countries._ New York: Pergamon Press. pp. 92-100. /Oil industry /Asia

1994. Hasean, L. F. 1966 _About the Project of Public Enterprises Law: Discussions and Studies._ Cairo: Institute of National Planning. /Egypt /Law /Planning process

1995. Hashmi, Aijaz Ahmad. 1981 "Education and Training in Public Enterprises in Pakistan." Paper presented at the Regional Workshop on Management Training and Development in Public Enterprises of Developing Countries, Karachi, Pakistan, 5-15 January. Ljubljana: ICPE. /Pakistan /Training /Management

1996. Hassan, Babiker El Fadil. 1980 "Price Policy in Public Enterprises in Sudan." Paper presented at the International Workshop on Pricing Policies in Public Enterprises, Ljubljana, Yugoslavia, 26-30 May. Ljubljana: ICPE. /Sudan /Price policy

1997. Hassan, Farouk I. 1981 "Egyptian Sector: Problems, Difficulties and Possible Solutions." Paper presented at the International Workshop on Financial Profitability and Losses in Public Enterprises, Ljubljana, Yugoslavia, 1-5 June. Ljubljana: ICPE. /Egypt /Public financing

1998. Hassan, Farouk I. 1981 "Egyptian Public Sector Training Management." Paper presented at the Interregional Seminar on Training and Management in Public Enterprises in Developing Countries, Ljubljana, Yugosalvia, 19-28 October. Ljubljana: ICPE. /Egypt /Training /Management

1999. Hassan, Mohd. Hashim Bin. 1969 _A General Study of the Muda River Irrigation Project in West Malaysia._ Kuala Lumpur: Faculty of Agriculture, University of Malaysia. /Malaysia /River valley development projects /Economic analysis

2000. Hassumani, A. P. 1964 _Some Problems of Administrative Law in India, with Special Reference to Public Corporations._ London: Asia Publishing House. V. 6. /India /Law

2001. Hausmann, Ricardo. 1984 "Inversión en las empresas del Estado y políticas macroeconómicas de corto plazo." _Cuadernos del CENDES (Centro de Estudios de la Universidad Central de Venezuela)_ (Caracas), V. 2, No. 3, pp. 117-130. /Venezuela /Investment

2002. Haveman, Robert H. 1972 _The Economic Performance of Public Investments: An Ex Post Evaluation of Water Resources Investments._ Baltimore: The Johns Hopkins Press for Resources for the Future, Inc. /United States of America /Water resources development /Cost benefit analysis /HD 1694 A5 H347 PCL, Pub Aff /HG 4936 H3 Law

2003. Haves, R. L., and Carrol V. Kroeger. 1973 "Utility Planning in a Dynamic Environment." _Public Utility Fortnightly_ V. 92, No. 3, pp. 25-30. /United States of America /Public utility industry /Planning process

2004. Hawkesworth, R. I. D. 1976 "Private and Public Sector Pay."" British Journal of Industrial Relations V. 14, No. 2, pp. 206-213. /United Kingdom /Wages / HD6951 B7 Pub Aff

2005. Hawkins, E. K. 1962 "The Political Economy of British Transport." Annals of Collective Economy V. 33, pp. 323-339. /United Kingdom /Transportation industry /Political economy /330.5 An73

2006. Hax, Karl. 1968 "Die offentliche unternehmung in der marktwirtschaft." Finanzarchiv V. 27 pp. 37-48. /Market economy / 336.05 F49

2007. Hayashi, Y. 1956 "Modernization of Japan's Industries and Government Enterprise." Asian Affairs (Tokyo), /Japan /Industrial sector

2008. Hayford, Stephen L., and Anthony V. Sinicropi. 1976 "Bargaining Rights Status of Public Sector Supervisors." Industrial Relations V. 15, No. 1, pp. 44-61. /United States of America /Labor relations /Collective bargaining /331.105 In19

2009. Haynes William W., J. T. Reynolds, and K. S. Varshenya. 1964 "Mahanagar Municipal Dairy." Boston: Harvard Graduate School of Business Administration. /India /Dairy industry /Marketing /Price policy / Case studies

2010. Haynes, William W. 1953 Nationalization in Practice: The British Coal Industry. Cambridge: Harvard University Press; London: Bailey Brothers & Swinfen. /United Kingdom /Coal mining industry / 338.2 H333n

2011. Haynes, William W. 1953 "Does Nationalization Work?" Harvard Business Review V. 31, No. 2, pp. 103-113. /Nationalization /Policy evaluation / HF 5001 H3

2012. Hayward, J. E. S. 1962 "Recent British Nationalization Theory and Practice in Retrospect." Annals of Collective Economy V. 33, pp. 33-49. /United Kingdom /Nationalization

2013. Hayward, J. E. S. 1962 "Theoretical and Practical Aspects of the British Nationalization." Impresa Pubblica (Rome), V. 6, No. 5, pp. 306-314. /United Kingdom /Nationalization

2014. Hazard, John N. 1970 "La empresa pública en los Estados Unidos de América." La Empresa Pública. Zaragoza, Spain: Publicaciones del Real Colegio de España en Bolonia. /United States of America

2015. Hazari, R. K. 1982 "Organizational Structure and Communications Systems." In William Diamond and V. S. Raghavan, ed(s). Aspects of Development Bank Management. Baltimore, Md.: The Johns Hopkins University Press. pp. 236-256. /Organization development /Training /Development banks /HG 3550 A8 PCL

2016. Hazlewood, Arthur. 1950 "Optimum pricing as applied to telephone service." Review of Economic Studies V. 18, pp.

67-78. /Telephone industry /Economic analysis /Price policy /330.5 R326 /Amended version reprinted in R. Turvey, Public Enterprise. /338.001 T869e PCL /HD 3850 T89 Pub Aff

2017. Hazlewood, Arthur. 1953 "The Origin of the State Telephone Service in Britain." Oxford Economic Papers V. 5, No. 1, pp. 13-25. /United Kingdom /Telephone industry / 330.6 Ox2 PCL

2018. Heald, David, and David Steel. 1981 "The Privatisation of UK Public Enterprises." Annals of Public and Cooperative Economy V. 52, No. 3, pp. 351-368. /Privatization /United Kingdom /330.5 An73

2019. Healey, J. M. 1964 "Errors in Project Cost Estimates." Indian Economic Journal (Bombay), V. 12, No. 1. /Costs /Economic analysis /Cost benefit analysis / 330.5 In16

2020. Heath, John B. 1983 "Public enterprise in Britain Today." In G. Ram Reddy, ed(s). Government and Public Enterprise: Essays in honour of Professor V. V. Ramanadham. Bombay, India: N. M. Tripathi Private Limited. pp. 127-139. /United Kingdom /Evaluation

2021. Heath, T. B. 1979 "Control Systems for Public Enterprises in Developing Countries: A Framework for Control Systems." Paper presented at the Interregional Workshop on Control Systems for Public Enterprises in Developing Countries, Ljubljana, Yugoslavia, 9-13 July. Ljubljana: ICPE. /Control process /Developing nations

2022. Hebrew University of Jerusalem. Faculty of Law. 1972 Report of the Committee for the Preparation of a Government Corporation Bill. Jerusalem: Law Faculty, Hebrew University of Jerusalem; Institute for Legislative Research and Comparative Law. /Israel /Law /Planning process

2023. Heeckt, H. 1973 "The Public Enterprises of Denmark." The Evolution of the Public Enterprises in the Community of the Nine. Brussels: CEEP Editions. pp. 25-57. /Denmark /Statistics /OPSS

2024. Heilbroner, R. L. 1952 "Labor Unrest in the British Nationalized Sector." Social Research V. 19, pp. 61-78. /United Kingdom /Labor relations / 305 So123 PCL

2025. Helleiner, G. K. A. 1964 "A Wide Ranging Development Institution: the Northern Nigeria Development Corporation, 1949-1962." Nigerian Journal of Economic and Social Studies (Ibadan, Nigeria), V. 6, pp. 239-257. /Nigeria /Development corporation /Regional development / Case studies

2026. Helleiner, G. K. A. 1964 "The Eastern Nigerian Development Corporation: A Study in Sources and Uses of Public Development Funds, 1949-1962." Nigerian Journal of Economic and Social Studies (Ibadan, Nigeria), V. 6, pp. 98-123. /Nigeria /Development corporation /Regional development /Case studies

2027. Helleiner, G. K. A. 1964 "The Fiscal Role of the Marketing Boards in Nigerian Economic Development 1947-61." Economic Journal V. 74, No. 295, pp. 582-610. /Nigeria /Marketing boards / 330.5 Ec7

2028. Helleiner, G. K. A. 1972 "Socialism and Economic Development in Tanzania." Journal of Development Studies pp. 193-204. /Tanzania /Political analysis / 338.9105 J826

2029. Heller, C. A. 1980 "The Birth and Growth of the Public Sector and State Enterprises in the Petroleum Industry." State Petroleum Enterprises in Developing Countries. New York: Pergamon Press. pp. 8-16. /Oil industry

2030. Heller, Peter S. 1975 Issues in the Costing of Public Sector Outputs: The Public Medical Services of Malaysia. Washington, D. C.: World Bank. /Malaysia /Costs /Economic analysis /Health care system / Case studies

2031. Henderson, A. M. 1947 "The Pricing of Public Utility Undertakings." Manchester School of Economic and Social Studies (London), V. 15, pp. 223-250. /Price policy /Public utility industry / 330.5 M3121 PCL

2032. Henderson, A. M. 1948 "Prices and Profits in State Enterprise." Review of Economic Studies V. 16, No. 39, pp. 13-24. /Price policy /Profits / 330.5 R326

2033. Henderson, H. 1970 "The Highlands and Islands Development Board: A British Experiment in Social Engineering." In W. G. Friedmann and J. F. Garner, ed(s). Government Enterprise. A Comparative Study. New York: Columbia University Press. pp. 91-103. /Scotland /Economic development / 350.0092 G746 PCL

2034. Henderson, P. 1970 "The Social Obligations of Nationalised Industry." New Zealand Journal of Public Administration (Aukland), V. 32, No. 2, pp. 65-72. /New Zealand

2035. Henderson, P. D. 1965 "Notes on Public Investment Criteria in the United Kingdom." Bulletin of the Oxford University Institute of Economics and Statistics V. 27, pp. 55-89. /United Kingdom /Investment /Economic theory /Reprinted in R. Turvey, Public Enterprise. /338.001 T869e PCL /HD 3850 T89 Pub Aff

2036. Henisch, Oskar. 1961 "The Principal Banks in Austria Under Nationalization." Annals of Collective Economy V. 32, pp. 168-181. /Austria /Financial institutions / 330.5 An73

2037. Henry, F. 1966 "Quelques réflexions sur les nationalisations en France. Socialisme (Paris), V. 13, No. 74, pp. 167-195. /France /Nationalization

2038. Hensley, R. J., and S. Boskey. 1967 "Indonesian Development Banking Monograph and Problems and Practices in Development Banks." Djakarta: Jajasan Badan Penerbit, Fakultas Ekinomi Universitas Indonesia. /Indonesia /Development banks

2039. Herbert, Clifford F. 1976 "The Organization and Management of the Public Enterprises in Malaysia." Law and Public Enterprise in Asia. New York: Praeger for the International Legal Center. pp. 294-312. /Malaysia /Management /HD 4283 L32

2040. Herbster de Gusmão, Oswaldo. n.d. Estudios sobre las instituciones autónomas de Costa Rica. San José, Costa Rica: Instituto Centro Americano de Administración Pública e Investigación. No. 304. /Costa Rica

2041. Hernández G., Herberto. 1974 "La organización institucional eléctrica en Colombia." Revista de la Camara de Comercio de Bogotá (Bogotá), V. 4, No. 14, pp. 143-150. /Colombia /Structural characteristics /Electrical utility industry

2042. Hernández Ruiz. 1944 "Municipalización de Servicios." Revista de Estudios de la Vida Local (Madrid), No. 14, pp. 253-270. /Spain /Public services

2043. Herrera, Felipe. 1982 "La banca de fomento latinoamericana y la empresa privada: Perspectiva internacional." San Juan, Puerto Rico: Latin American Association of Development Financing Institutions (ALIDE) XII General Assembly. /Latin America /Development banks / OPSS

2044. Herring, Ronald J. 1984 "Dismantling a Dependent Welfare State: The Case of Sri Lanka." Paper presented at the conference: State Shrinking: A Comparative Inquiry into Privatization, Austin, Texas, 1-3 March. /Privatization /Sri Lanka /OPSS

2045. Hershlag, Z. Y. 1958 Turkey: An Economy in Transition. The Hague: Uitgeverij van Keulen N. V. /Turkey

2046. Hess, Fritz. 1942 "The Swiss Federal Railways from 1926 to 1938." Annals of Collective Economy V. 18, pp. 1-28. /Switzerland /Railway industry /Economic history /330.5 An73

2047. Hetman, F. 1960 "Le secteur publique devant les problèmes de stabilisation et de croissance." Bulletin Sedeis Etude (Paris), No. 34. /Economic policy

2048. Heurtebise, André. 1978 "The Place of Public Enterprises in the Economy." A Report with Discussion and Reply. Annals of Public and Cooperative Economy V. 49, No. 3-4, pp. 309-344. /Economic analysis /330.5 An73

2049. Hexner, J. Tomás. 1970 "The Paradox of the Quasi-Governmental Corporation in East Pakistan." Cambridge, Mass.: Harvard University, Center for International Affairs, Project for Quantitative Research in Economic Development. /Pakistan

2050. Hibden, J. E. 1958 "Flood Control Benefits and the Tennessee Valley Authority." Southern Economic Journal pp. 48-63. /United States of America /River valley development projects /HB 1 S6

2051. Hicks, I. 1963 "Control of Borrowing in the Nationalized Fuel Industries of Great Britain." *Annals of Collective Economy* V. 34, No. 4, pp. 323-529. /United Kingdom /Public utility industry /Financing /Control process / 330.5 An73

2052. Higiro-Semajege, F. 1968 *The Role of the National Trading Corporations in Stimulating African Entrepreneurship.* Makerere, Uganda: Institute of Social Research. /Africa /State trading organizations /Entrepreneurial activity

2053. Hilger, Marye Tharp. 1979 "Marketing Decision-Making in CONASUPO." Paper presented to the Latin American Studies Assoc., Pittsburgh, PA. /Mexico /Marketing /Food industry /Agricultural sector /State trading organizations /OPSS

2054. Hilger, Marye Tharp. 1979 *Consumer Perceptions of a public marketer: the case of CONASUPO in Monterrey, Mexico.* Austin, Tex.: OPSS Technical Papers Series. No. 18. /Mexico /State trading organizations /Marketing /Food industry /Agricultural sector /OPSS

2055. Hilger, Marye Tharp. 1980 "Decision-making in a Public Marketing Enterprise: CONASUPO in Mexico." *Journal of Interamerican Studies and World Affairs* V. 22, No. 4, pp. 471-494. /Marketing /State trading organizations /Mexico /Food industry /Agricultural sector /G 980.605 J826 LAC

2056. Hilie, D. 1969 "L´autogestion industrielle en Algérie." *Autogestion* (Paris), No. 9-10, pp. 37-57. /Algeria /Industrial sector /Worker self management

2057. Hill, Reginald. 1968 "The Formulation and Application of Efficiency Measures in Public Manufacturing Enterprises." Paper presented at the UNIDO Seminar, Rome, 11-15 November. Rome: UNIDO. /Evaluation /Economic efficiency /Manufacturing industry

2058. Hill, Sir Reginald. 1951 "Review of Trade Harbours." *British Transport Review* (London), pp. 383-388. /United Kingdom /Port authority /Marine transportation industry

2059. Hillman, E. 1967 *Essays in Local Government Enterprises.* London: Merlin Press. /United Kingdom /Local government

2060. Hills, T. L. 1959 *The St. Lawrence Seaway.* New York: Praeger. /United States of America /River valley development projects / 627.1 H559s

2061. Hinote, H. 1969 *Benefit-Cost Analysis for Water Resource Projects: A Selected Annotated Bibliography.* Knoxville, Tenn.: University of Tennessee. /Bibliography /Cost benefit analysis /Water resources development /Project management /016.33391 H594b PCL

2062. Hinterhuber, H. 1969 "Der staat als unternechmer." (The State as Entrepreneur) *Weltwirtschaftliches Archiv* (Hamburg), V. 103, No. 1, pp. 58-75. /Germany, Federal Rep. of /330.5 W468 PCL

2063. Hirad, A. H. 1969 Notes on Public Enterprises in Somalia. Mauritius: UNECA Seminar on Role of Public Enterprises in Planning and Plan Implementation. /Somalia

2064. Hirsch, E., et al. 1957 "Various Articles on Public Enterprise in France." Annals of Collective Economy V. 28, pp. 190-364. /France /Evaluation /330.5 An73

2065. Hirsch, H. 1961 Quantity Planning and Price Planning in the Soviet Union Philadelphia, Penn. University of Pennsylvania Press. /Union of Soviet Socialist Reps. /Planning process / 330.947 H6151mTs PCL

2066. Hirschfeld, André. 1973 "The Role of Public Enterprise in the French Economy. Origin and Evolution." Annals of Public and Cooperative Economy V. 44, pp. 255-269. /France /330.5 An73

2067. Hirschman, Albert O. 1967 Development Projects Observed: Discussion about Successes/Failures Based on a Study of a Number of IBRD Development Projects. Washington, D. C.: Brookings Institution. /Development planning / 309.2 H617d

2068. Hirschman, Albert O. 1971 "How to Divest in Latin America and Why." Cross Currents No. 21, pp. 320-333. /Latin America

2069. Hirst, David. 1966 Oil and Public Opinion in the Middle East. New York: Praeger Publishers. /Middle East /Oil industry /Public interest / 338.2728 H618c PCL

2070. Hobbs, Diane. 1980 "Personal Liability of Directors of Federal Government Corporations." Case Western Reserve Law Review V. 30, pp. 733-779. /United States of America /Management /Liability /Law

2071. Hobson, C. R. 1953 "Report on Nationalization." Banker /Nationalization /Policy analysis

2072. Hobson, O. 1955 "The Nationalized Industries in Britain." Institute of Public Administration Review V. 8, No. 1, pp. 23-32. /United Kingdom /Nationalization /Industrial sector

2073. Hodgetts, J. E. 1950 "The Public Corporation in Canada." Public Administration (London), V. 28, pp. 283-294. /Canada /Accountability /Control process /JA 8 P8 Pub Aff

2074. Hodgetts, J. E. 1953 "Responsibility of the Government Corporation to the Governing Body." Paper presented at the Fifth Annual Conference of Public Administration of Canada. pp. 389-399. /Canada /Accountability /Public administration

2075. Hodgetts, J. E. 1954 "The Public Corporation in Canada." In Wolfgang G. Friedmann, ed(s). The Public Corporation. Toronto: Carswell Co., Ltd. pp. 51-92. /Canada

2076. Hodgetts, J. E. 1958 The Control of Public Enterprise in Canada. Rome: I.P.S.A. Congress. /Canada /Control process

2077. Hodgetts, J. E. 1970 "The Public Corporation in Canada." In W. G. Friedmann and J. F. Garner, ed(s). Government Enterprise: A Comparative Study. New York: Columbia University Press. pp. 201-226. /Canada / 350.0092 G746 PCL

2078. Hodson, H. V. 1950 Broadcasting and the Service It Can Render to the Commonwealth. BBC Quarterly (London), No. 1, pp. 1-6. /United Kingdom /Broadcasting industry

2079. Hoens, Robert. 1958 "The Belgium Local Railways Corporation and the Development of Regional Public Transport Services in Belgium." Annals of Collective Economy V. 29, pp. 530-540. /Belgium /Railway industry /Mass transportation industry /330.5 An73

2080. Hoff, Robert K. 1979 "The Role of Public Enterprise in the Economy of São Paulo State, Brazil: 1974-1977." Unpublished M.A. thesis, UT-Austin, Department of Economics. /Brazil /Sao Paulo, Brazil (State) /OPSS

2081. Holland, Stuart, et al. 1971 "Various Articles on Public Enterprise." Public Enterprise (London), No. 2, pp. 1-23. /Evaluation

2082. Holland, Stuart. 1972 The State as Entrepreneur: New Dimensions for Public Enterprise: the IRI State Shareholding Formula. London: Weidenfeld & Nicolson. /Italy /Evaluation /Holding company /HD487 H6 1973 Pub Aff /HD 3616 I83 H65 PCL

2083. Holland, Stuart. 1972 "State Entrepreneurship and State Intervention." In Stuart Holland, ed(s). The State as Entrepreneur. London: Weidenfeld & Nicolson. pp. 5-44. /Economic analysis /Regional development /Financing /Holding company /HD 3616 I83 H65 PCL /HD487 H6 1973 Pub Aff

2084. Holland, Stuart. 1972 "The National Context." In Stuart Holland, ed(s). The State as Entrepreneur. London: Weidenfeld & Nicolson. pp. 56-91. /Italy /Holding company /HD 3616 I83 H65 PCL /HD 487 H6 1973 Pub Aff

2085. Holland, Stuart. 1972 "Delayed Rationalization: Engineering and Shipbuilding." In Stuart Holland, ed(s). The State as Entrepreneur. London: Weidenfeld & Nicolson. pp. 106-126. /Italy /Automobile manufacturing industry /Motor manufacturing industry /Holding company /HD 3616 I83 H65 PCL /HD 487 H6 1973 Pub Aff

2086. Holland, Stuart. 1972 "The Finance Formula." In Stuart Holland, ed(s). The State as Entrepreneur. London: Weidenfeld & Nicolson. pp. 184-201. /Italy /Financing /Holding company /HD 3616 I83 H65 PCL /HD 487 H6 1973 Pub Aff

2087. Holland, Stuart. 1972 "Adoption and Adaptation of the IRI Formula." In Stuart Holland, ed(s). The State as Entrepreneur. London: Weidenfeld & Nicolson. pp. 242-265. /Italy /France /Canada /Australia /Sweden /Germany, Federal Rep. of /Holding company /HD 3616 I83 H65 PCL /HD 487 H6 1973 Pub Aff

2088. Holland, Stuart. 1974 "Meso-Economics, New Public Enterprise and Economic Planning." Annals of Public and Cooperative Economy V. 45, pp. 147-160. /United Kingdom /Planning process / 330.5 An73

2089. Holloway, R. G. 1968 "Public Ownership in Australia." Parliamentary Affairs (London), V. 22, No. 1, pp. 73-76. /Australia 328.4025 P239

2090. Holub, A. 1966 "Some Problems of the State Sector in Developing Countries." International Development Review V. 8, No 4, pp. 17-21. /Developing nations /Evaluation

2091. Holzer, Marc (ed.). 1976 Productivity in Public Organizations. Port Washington, N.Y.: Dunellen, Kennikat Press. /United States of America /Civil service /Productivity / JK 768.4 P76 Pub Aff

2092. Hongsanand, Kesinee. 1981 "Should the Government Seriously Re-Consider the Policies on Public Enterprises?" Paper presented at the Regional Workshop on the Evaluation of Training Packages for Public Enterprise Managers, Bangkok, Thailand, 10-14 August. Ljubljana: ICPE. /Thailand /Policy making process /Policy analysis /OPSS

2093. Hons, André. 1979 "An Attempt at an International Comparison of Electricity Rates." Annals of Public and Cooperative Economy V. 50, No. 3, pp. 37-60. /Electrical utility industry /Price policy /330.5 An73

2094. Hook, Eric. 1980 "Steel and the State in Sweden." Annals of Public and Cooperative Economy V. 51, No. 4, pp. 493-506. /Sweden /Steel industry /330.5 An73

2095. Hope, Kempe R. 1982 "Improving Public Enterprise Management in Developing Countries." Journal of General Management V. 7, No. 3, pp. 72-85. /Developing nations /Management /HD 28 J595 PCL

2096. Hopkins L., Raúl, et al. 1976 Las empresas públicas arequipeñas. Lima: Instituto Nacional de Administración Pública, Universidad Particular Católica Santa María de Arequipa. /Peru /Statistics /Arequipa, Peru /OPSS

2097. Horie, Y. 1939 "Government Industries in the Early Years of the Meiji Era." Kyoto University Economic Review V. 14, No. 1, pp. 67-87. /Japan /Economic history

2098. Horn, Jules. 1951 Essai de théorie générale sur l'entreprise publique. Brussels, Belgium. /Theoretical framework

2099. Horn, Jules. 1956 "How State Industries Should Work." Banker /Industrial sector

2100. Horn, Jules. 1971 "Le gouvernement de l'entreprise publique." Réflets et Perspectives de la Vie Economique (Brussels), No. 2, pp. 121-129. /France /Government authority / 330.5 R258

2101. Horsefield, J. Keith. 1964 "Some Notes on Postal Finance." Bulletin of the Oxford University Institute of Economics and Statistics V. 26, pp. 39-58. /United Kingdom /United States of America /Postal service / Reprinted in R. Turvey, Public Enterprise. 338.001 T869e PCL /HD 3850 T89 Pub Aff

2102. Horvat, B. 1971 "Yugoslavia Economic Policy in the Post-War Period: Problems, Ideas, Institutional Development." American Economic Review V. 61, No. 3, pp. 71-169. /Yugoslavia /Economic history /Economic policy /Economic analysis / 330.5 Am312

2103. Horwitz, B. N. 1968 "Profit Responsibility in Soviet Enterprise." Journal of Business V. 41, pp. 47-55. /Union of Soviet Socialist Reps. /Profits /658.05 J825 PCL

2104. Hotelling, H. 1938 "The General Welfare in Relation to Problems of Taxation and of Railway and Utility Rates." Econometrica V. 6, pp. 242-269. /Price policy /Railway industry /Public utility industry / 330.5 Ec74e

2105. Houin, R. 1957 "Administração das empresas públicas e as normas do direito comercial." Revista de Direito Administrativo (Rio de Janeiro), V. 48, pp. 26-53. /Brazil /Public administration /Law

2106. Houin, R. 1962 "La gestion des entreprises publiques et les méthodes du droit commercial." La distinction du droit privé et du droit publique et l´entreprise publique. Sec. 3/IV-111. pp. 79-109. /France /Commercial sector /Law

2107. Houk, J. T. Dock. 1968 Financing and Problems of Development Banks. London: Pall Mall. /Development banks /Financing

2108. Houk, J. T. Dock. 1969 "Financing and Problems of Development Banks." International Affairs No. 2. /Development banks /Financing

2109. Houldsworth, Hubert. 1952 Efficiency in the Nationalized Industries. London: Allen & Unwin. /United Kingdom /Economic efficiency

2110. Houthakker, H. S. 1951 "Electricity Tariffs in Theory and Practice." Economic Journal V. 61, pp. 1-25. /Electrical utility industry /Price policy / 330.5 Ec7

2111. Howard, John B. 1980 "Law and the Social Accountability of Public Enterprises in New Development Strategies." Paper presented at the Second BAPEG Conference: Public Enterprise in Mixed Economy LDCs, Boston, April. /Law /Accountability /OPSS

2112. Howard, John B. 1982 "Social Accountability of Public Enterprises: Law and Community Controls in the New Development Strategies." In Leroy P. Jones et al., ed(s). Public Enterprise in Less-Developed Countries. New York: Cambridge University Press. pp. 77-99. /Accountability /Law /HD 3850 P83 PCL

2113. Howe, M. 1971 "Financing State Steel: The Irrelevance of Public Dividend Capital." Public Administration (London), V. 49, pp. 309-320. /Australia /Steel industry /Financing /JA 8 P8 Pub Aff

2114. Howes, O., Jr. 1888 "Government Monopoly vs Private Competition." Quarterly Journal of Economics V. 2, pp. 353-361. /Monopoly /Competition / 330.5 Q2

2115. Hsiao, Frank S. T. 1977 "Dual Economic Structure and Factor Markets in Taiwan: The Role of Public Enterprise." Discussion Papers in Economics. Boulder, Colo.: University of Colorado, Department of Economics. No. 114. /China, Rep. of /Taiwan /Mixed enterprises

2116. Hubbard, P. J. 1961 Origins of the TVA: the Muscle Shoals Controversy, 1920-1932. Nashville, Tennessee: Vanderbilt University Press. /United States of America /River valley development projects / 976.8 H861o

2117. Hubka, Bernd. 1976 "Decision-Making on Political Prices: A Process of Compromise between Conflicting Interest Groups." Annals of Public and Cooperative Economy V. 47, No. 2, pp. 143-158. /Price policy /Political analysis /330.5 An73

2118. Hughes, J. 1960 "Nationalized Industries in Mixed Economy." London: Fabian Society. /Nationalization /Mixed enterprises

2119. Hughes, J. 1965 Indemnisation et gestion de l´industrie nationalisée. L´Experience britanique. Paris: R. Inst. Social. /United Kingdom /Industrial sector /Organization behavior

2120. Hughes, Pennethorne. 1952 "How the BBC Trains its Staff." BBC Quarterly (London), pp. 164-168. /United Kingdom /Broadcasting industry /Training

2121. Humba, E. D. B. 1982 "The Public Enterprise as an Instrument of State Policies." Paper presented at the Tokyo Round Table preparatory to the 19th International Congress of Administrative Sciences, 13-17 Sept. /Tanzania /Taxonomy /Goal setting /Profits /Control process /East Africa /OPSS

2122. Humphrey, Don D. 1959 "The Economic Consequences of State Trading." Law and Contemporary Problems V. 24, No. 2, pp. 276-290. /Marketing /State trading organizations

2123. Hunter, A. 1966 "The Indonesian Oil Industry." Australian Economic Papers (Adelaide), V. 5, No. 1, pp. 9-106. /Indonesia /Oil industry / 330.994 Au69

2124. Hunter, Gordon W. 1962 "Financial Control of Crown Corporations." Canadian Chartered Accountant pp. 61-65. /Canada /Control process /Public financing

2125. Hunter, W. D. G. 1962 "The Development of the Canadian Uranium Industry: An Experiment in Public Enterprise." Canadian Journal of Economics and Political Science (Toronto), pp. 329-352. /Canada /Uranium / 305 C16 PCL

2126. Hurcomb, Lord. 1950 "The Development of the Organization of the British Transport Commission." Public Administration (London), pp. 163-175. /United Kingdom /Transportation industry /Organization development / 320.5 J826 PCL

2127. Huret, E., C. Keller, G. Houdre, and J. Rivier. 1972 Les entreprises publiques de 1959 à 1969. Les Collections de L'INSEE, Série Entreprise. No. 11. /France

2128. Husain, V. Rukmini Rao 1980 "Status of Women in Public Enterprises." Human Features V. 3, No. 4, pp. 375-385. /India /Women's studies /Employment policy

2129. Hussain, Zahid. 1980 "Historical Review of Management Education in Bangladesh." Journal of Management Business and Economics V. 6, No. 3, pp. 310-323. /Bangladesh /Management

2130. Hussaint, T. 1967 Financial Resources of Public Enterprises. Lahore, Pakistan: N.I.P.A. Seminar on Problems of Public Enterprises. /Pakistan /Financing

2131. Hussein, A. K. 1966 "Management Problems in Public Corporations in the Sudan." Sudan Journal of Administration and Development (Khartoum, Sudan), V. 11, pp. 92-96. /Sudan /Management

2132. Hussein, Abdul Majid bin. 1981 "Management Training and Development in Malaysian Public Enterprises." Paper presented at the Regional Workshop on Management Training and Development in Public Enterprises of Developing Countries, Karachi, Pakistan, 5-15 January. Ljubljana: ICPE. /Malaysia /Training /Management

2133. Hutoy, Henri. 1958 "The Intercommunal Mechanograph Company." Annals of Collective Economy V. 29, pp. 582-588. /Belgium /330.5 An73

2134. Hyden, Göran. 1977 "The Public Enterprise in African Administrative Research." In Yash Ghai, ed(s). Law in the Political Economy of Public Enterprise. Uppsala: Scandinavian Institute of African Studies. New York: International Legal Centre. pp. 149-158. /Public administration /Africa / Africa 76 L41 Law

2135. Hymans, Max. 1952 "Air France, Service Public." Annales d'Economie Collective pp. 97-112. /France /Public services /Air transportation industry

2136. Hymans, Max. 1957 "`Air France' - A National Company." Annals of Collective Economy V. 28, pp. 311-321. /France /Air transportation industry / 330.5 An73

2137. Hysek, J. 1970 "La gestion professionnelle et la démocratie dans une entreprise industrielle." Autogestion et Socialism (Paris), No. 11-1, pp. 25-48. /France /Industrial sector /Management /Participatory democracy

2138. ICAP. Instituto Centroamericano de Administración Pública. 1978 "La capacitación y el desarrollo del personal de dirección en las entidades públicas autónomas del istmo centroamericano." Paper presented at the Round Table on Public Enterprise of the Tenth General Assembly of the Latin American Association of Public Administration. /Central America /Public administration /Training /Case studies /OPSS

2139. ICPE. 1974 "Financing of Public Enterprises in Developing Countries: Report." Ljubljana: ICPE. /Developing nations /Financing

2140. ICPE. 1974 International Seminar on Planning in Public Enterprises in Developing Countries. Ljubljana: ICPE. /Developing nations /Planning process

2141. ICPE. 1980 "Women as a Factor of Development and the Responsibilities of Public Enterprises in this Regard." Ljubljana: ICPE. /Women´s studies /Developing nations

2142. ICPE. 1980 International Project: Workers Self-Management and Participation in Decision-Making as a Factor of Social Change and Economic Progress in Developing Countries. Ljubljana: ICPE. /Bangladesh /Malta /Peru /Yugoslavia /Economic development / Worker self management

2143. ICPE 1980 "Planning in State-Owned Enterprises in Indonesia." Paper presented at the Regional Workshop on Corporate Planning in Public Enterprises in the Asian and Pacific Region, Kuala Lumpur, Malaysia, 17-21 November. Ljubljana: ICPE. /Indonesia /Planning process

2144. ICPE. 1982 "The Role of Public Enterprises in Regional Development in Developing Countries: Report of an ICPE Expert Group Meeting." Public Enterprise V. 2. No. 4, pp. 5-19. /Agricultural sector /Regional development /Developing nations /OPSS

2145. ICPE. 1984 "The Role of Public Enterprise Joint Ventures among Developing Countries among Developing Countries and Factories Conducive to the Improvement of Their Performance: Conclusions of an Expert Group Meeting." Public Enterprise V. 4, No. 3, pp. 5-9. /Developing nations /Mixed enterprises /Economic development /Economic efficiency /OPSS

2146. ICPE. Information and Documentation Department. 1980 "List of Public Enterprises in Electricity Generation." Paper presented at the expert group meeting on strategies for energy development in developing countries, Ljubljana, Yugoslavia, 19-22 Feb. Ljubljana: ICPE. /Electrical utility industry /Directory

2147. INAD. Instituto Nacional de Administración para el Desarrollo. 1974 Funcionamiento del sector público descentralizado de la República de Guatemala. Guatemala City. /Guatemala /Economic analysis /OPSS

2148. Ianni, Edmond M. 1983 "State Trading: Its Nature and International Treatment." New Journal of International Law and Business V. 5, pp. 46-64. /Law /International trade

/State trading organizations /

2149. Ibarra Aispuro, Fernando. 1978 "Contribución al estudio de los posibles patrones de evolución administrativa de la industria alimentaria en México." Paper presented at the Fourth General Assembly of the Latin American Association of Public Administrators, Mexico City, 6-11 November 1978. /Mexico /Food Industry /OPSS

2150. Ibarra, David. 1976 "Reflexiones sobre la empresa pública en México." Foro Internacional V. 17. No. 2, pp. 141-151. /Mexico /Control process / G056.8 F71 LAC

2151. Ibraheem, Muhamed. 1980 "Summary Research in Manpower Planning: Its Role in Rationalizing the Utilization of Human Resources in Egypt." Paper presented at the Expert Group Meeting on Manpower Planning on Public Enterprises in Developing Countries, Tagaytay, Philippines, 18-22 August. Ljubljana: ICPE. /Egypt /Personnel management / Manpower planning

2152. Ibrahim, R. 1967 Financial Resources of Public Enterprises. Lahore, Pakistan: N.I.P.A. /Pakistan /Public financing

2153. Idachaba, F. S. 1973 "Marketing Boards as Potential Stabilizers of Government Revenues in Developing Countries: The Nigerian Experience." Economic Bulletin of Ghana V. 3, No. 4. /Ghana /Marketing Boards / HG 517 G6 E3136

2154. Iglesias, Gabriel U., and J. A. Carolino. 1976 "Coordination of Public Enterprises: Country Study for the Philippines." In A. S. H. K. Sadique, ed(s). Public Enterprise. Kuala Lumpur: Asian Centre for Development Administration. pp. 489-553. /Philippines /Control process / HD 4276 P8

2155. Iglesias, Gabriel U. 1980 "An Approach in Developing and Training Packages for Public Enterprise Managers: The APDAC Experience." Paper presented at the Interregional Seminar on Training Management in Public Enterprises in Developing Countries, Ljubljana, Yugoslavia, Sept.29-Oct.10. Ljubljana: ICPE. /Training /Management / Also presented at the Regional Workshop on Management Training and Development in Public Enterprises of Developing Countries, Karachi, Pakistan, 5-15 Jan. 1981.

2156. Iglesias, Gabriel U. 1980 "Report of the Expert Group Meeting on the Research Project on Education and Training in Public Enterprises in Developing Countries, March 17-22, 1980, Ljubljana." Ljubljana: ICPE. /Training /Management

2157. Iglesias, Gabriel U. 1981 "A Handbook on Evaluating Effectiveness of Management Training of Public Enterprises in Developing Countries." Paper presented at the Interregional Seminar on Training Management in Public Enterprises in Developing Countries, Ljubljana, Yugoslavia, 19-28 October. Ljubljana: ICPE. /Management /Training /Efficacy /Evaluation

2158. Iglesias, Gabriel U. 1981 "Notes on the Evaluation of Training of Public Enterprise Managers." Paper presented at the Regional Workshop on Management Training and Development in Public Enterprises of Developing Countries, Karachi, Pakistan, 5-15 January. Ljubljana: ICPE. /Management /Training /Evaluation /Also presented at the Regional Workshop on the Evaluation of Training Packages for Public Enterprise Managers, Bangkok, Thailand, 10-14 Aug. 1981.

2159. Iglesias, Gabriel U. 1981 "A Simplified Approach to Manpower Planning for Public Enterprises in Developing Countries." Public Enterprise V. 1, pp. 42-46. /Management /Personnel management /Planning process / Manpower planning /OPSS

2160. Ijose, Abiodun. 1975 "Farm Credit Programs in Western Nigeria: A Problem in Administration and Organization Design." Ph.D. Dissertation, Ohio State University. /Nigeria /Financial institutions /Agricultural sector

2161. Ilic, Stanko. 1980 "Formation et perfectionnement des connaissances des directeurs et d'autre responsables au sein de l'organisation de travail associé dans la RS de Sérbie: Example de PKB (Combinat Agricole de Belgrade)." Paper presented at Séminaire international sur la gestion et la formation dans les entreprises publiques dans les pays en voie de développement, Ljubljana, Yugoslavia, 3-15 March. Ljubljana: ICPE. /Yugoslavia /Trade unions /Management /Agricultural sector

2162. Iloglu, A. S. 1951 "Agricultural Bank of Turkey." Continental Daily Mail--Special Supplement for Turkey /Turkey /Agricultural services /Banking agency

2163. India. 1959 Participation of Workers and Office Employees in the Management of State Enterprises. New Delhi: Indian Government and UNECAFE Seminar on Management of Public Industrial Enterprises, Dec. 1959. /India /Worker management participation

2164. India. Administrative Reforms Commission. 1967 "Report on Public Sector Undertakings." New Delhi. /India /HD 4293 I5

2165. India. Bureau of Public Enterprises. 1970 A Handbook of Information on Public Enterprises, 1969. /India /qHD 4293 A46

2166. India. Bureau of Public Enterprises. 1970 "Report on the Performance Study of Hindustan Shipyard Limited. Visakhapatnam." /India /Marine transportation industry /Case studies /Evaluation

2167. India. Bureau of Public Enterprises. 1977 Performance of Indian Enterprise Sector: Macro Report. New Delhi: Bureau of Public Enterprises. /India /Evaluation /Economic analysis

2168. India. Bureau of Public Enterprises. n.d. "Annual Report on the Working of Industrial and Commercial Undertakings of the Central Government." /India

2169. India. Committee to Review the State Trading Corporation of India. 1969 "Final Report." New Delhi: State Trading Corporation of India. /India /State trading organizations /Evaluation /Case studies / HF 3786.5 A45

2170. India. Department of Expenditure. Projects Coordination Division. 1964 "Annual Report on the Working of Industrial and Commercial Undertakings of the Central Government, 1962/3." New Delhi: India, Department of Expenditure, Projects Coordination Division. /India /Industrial sector /Commercial sector

2171. India. Department of Labor and Employment. 1966 Industrial Relations and Implementation of Labour Enactment in Indian Telephone Industrial Ltd. Bangalore--a Case Study. New Delhi. /India /Telephone industry /Industrial relations /Labor relations /Law / Case studies

2172. India. Department of Labour and Employment. 1968 Labour in the Public Sector Undertakings: Basic Information. /India /Labor relations /HD 8013 L45 L32

2173. India. Directorate General of Employment and Training. 1964 Occupational Pattern in India. (Public Sector) New Delhi. V. 1. /India /Employment characteristics

2174. India. Economic and Scientific Research Foundation. 1967 The Performance of Government Undertakings, 1958-1965. Occasional Paper No. 3 New Delhi: Economic and Scientific Research Foundation. No. 3. /India /Evaluation

2175. India. Estimates Committee. 1955 Sixteenth Report 1954-1955, Organization and Administration of Nationalized Industrial Undertakings. New Delhi: Lok Sabha Secretariat. /India /Administrative management /Industrial sector

2176. India. Estimates Committee. 1960 Eighteenth Report, 1959-1960 (Second Lok Sahba), Public Undertakings - Forms and Organization. New Delhi. /India /Organization formation

2177. India. Hyderabad Institute of Public Enterprise Seminar. 1970 "Pricing and Investment in Public Enterprises." Lok Udyog (New Delhi), V. 3, No. 12, pp. 1453-1465. /India /Investment /Price policy /354.54 L836 PCL

2178. India. Indian Institute of Public Administration. 1958 Administrative Problems of State Enterprises in India: Report of a Seminar, December 1957. New Delhi. /India /Administrative management /Public administration

2179. India. Indian Institute of Public Administration. 1961 A Bibliography on Public Enterprises in India. New Delhi. /India /Bibliography

2180. India. Indian Institute of Public Administration. 1962 Personnel Management in Public Undertakings. New Delhi. /India /Personnel management

2181. India. Indian Institute of Public Administration. n.d. Administration Problems of State Enterprises in India. New Delhi. /India /Administrative management

2182. India. Institute of Public Enterprises. 1973 "Report on the Performance of National Coal Development Corporation Limited: An Abstract." /India /Coal mining industry

2183. India. Kerala (State). Bureau of Economics and Statistics. 1968 "Industrial Undertakings in Kerala State, Owned, Managed and with Shares by the Government of Kerala, 1962-63." /India /Kerala, India (State) /Industrial sector

2184. India. Lok Sabha Secretariat. 1960 Estimates Committee 1959-1960: Seventy-third Report. (Second Lok Sabha) New Delhi. /India /Control process /Government report

2185. India. Management Group. Committee on Plan Projects. 1964 "Management Planning in Public Enterprises." Indian Journal of Public Administration (New Delhi), V. 10, No. 3, pp. 389-411. /India /Management /Planning process /JA26 I55 Pub Aff

2186. India. Ministry of Commerce and Industry. 1959 Public Sector Industries. New Delhi. /India /Industrial sector

2187. India. Ministry of Finance. 1969 "Public Sector Enterprises: A Memorandum." New Delhi. /India

2188. India. Ministry of Finance. 1970 A Handbook of Information on Public Enteprises. New Delhi: Bureau of Public Enterprises. Ministry of Finance. /India

2189. India. Mysore (State). Legislative Assembly. Committee on Estimates. 1969 "Reports, Fourth Assembly, Third Report: Mysore Iron and Steel, Limited." Bangalore. /India /Steel industry

2190. India. Mysore (State). 1973 "Report on Mysore Iron and Steel Ltd." Bangalore. /India /Steel industry

2191. India. National Council of Applied Economic Research. 1978 "Operation of Credit Policies of Nationalized Banks since 1969." New Delhi. /India /Nationalization /Credit policy

2192. India. National Team of Experts. 1979 "Research Proposal on the Role of the Public Sector in India." Paper presented at the International Meeting on the Role of the Public Sector in Developing Countries, Ljubljana, Yugoslavia, 2-7 April. Ljubljana: ICPE. /India /Economic research

2193. India. National Team of Experts. 1979 "The Role of the Public Sector in India." Paper presented at the International Meeting on the Role of the Public Sector in Developing Countries, 2nd, Ljubljana, Yugoslavia, 2-7 April. Ljubljana: ICPE. /India

2194. India. Planning Commission. 1964 Management Planning in Public Enterprises. Management Paper. New Delhi. No. 1. /India /Management /Planning process

2195. India. Planning Commission. Management and Project Evaluation Division. 1969 Bihar: A Study of Bihar State Road Transport Corporation. also Rajasthan: A Study of the Rajasthan State Road Transport Corporation. New Delhi. /India /Bihar, India (State) /Highways and roads /Rajasthan, India (State)

2196. India. Reserve Bank of India 1963 "Finances of Government Companies, 1961-1962." Reserve Bank of India Bulletin (Bombay), V. 17, No. 10, pp. 267-276. /India /Public financing

2197. India. Reserve Bank of India. 1965 "Finances of Government Companies 1963-1964." Reserve Bank of India Bulletin (Bombay), pp. 1394-1403. /India /Financing

2198. India. Reserve Bank of India. 1966 "Finances of Government Companies 1964-1965." Reserve Bank of India Bulletin (Bombay), pp. 1169-1178. /India /Financing

2199. India. Shipping Corporation of India, Ltd. 1971 "Role and Achievements of Public Undertakings in India." /India /Shipping industry

2200. India. Standing Conference of Public Enterprises. 1976 "Public Enterprises in the National Economy: Summary of the Deliberations of the National Convention of Public Enterprises." Bombay. /India

2201. India. State Bank of India. 1967 "Working of the Industrial Development Bank of India." State Bank of India Monthly Review (New Delhi). /India /Development banks /Industrialization

2202. India. Sub-Committee of the Congress Party in Parliament. 1959 Parliamentary Supervision over State Undertakings. /India /Parliament /Control process /Government report

2203. Indonesia. Agency for Industrial Research and Development. 1980 "Management and Transfer of Technology by Public Sectors." Paper presented at the Regional Workshop on Management of Transfer of Technology by Public Enterprises in the ESCAP Region, Bangalore, India, 10-15 November. Ljubljana: ICPE. /Management /Technology transfer

2204. "Indonesian State Oil Company." 1975 Lok Udyog (New Delhi), V. 9, No. 3, pp. 71-76. /Indonesia /Oil industry /354.54 L836 PCL

2205. Ingram, George Mason, IV. 1973 "Nationalization of American Companies in South America: Peru, Bolivia, Chile." Ph.D. dissertation, University of Michigan. V. 1-2. /Peru /Bolivia /Chile /Oil industry /Nationalization /Film 10,776 LAC

2206. Ingram, George Mason, IV. 1974 Expropriation of U.S. Property in South America: Nationalization of Oil and Copper Companies in Peru, Bolivia, and Chile. New York: Praeger Publishers. /Peru /Bolivia /Chile /Nationalization / HD 9579 S6215 1974 LAC

2207. Inostroza Fernández, Luis. 1981 Monografía sobre el papel del sector público y empresas públicas en América Latina. Ljubljana: ICPE. /Latin America

2208. Institute of Public Administration. 1952 Report on the Reports. London. /United Kingdom /Control process

2209. Instituto Americano de Administración de Empresas. 1949 Control interno: Elementos de un sistema coordinado y su importancia para la gerencia y el auditor independiente. Lima. /Peru /Administrative management /Control process

2210. Instituto Nicaragüense de Administración Pública. 1981 "Los problemas de las empresas públicas en un proceso revolucionario." Managua: INAP, Centro de Instrucción para la Dirección Estatal. /Nicaragua /OPSS

2211. Instituto de Estudios Económicos (IDE). 1975 "Diagnóstico general de la empresa pública en Latinoamerica." Proyecto de investigación. Versión preliminar. Madrid. /Latin America /Evaluation

2212. "Los institutos descentralizados y la política partidista." 1973 Coyuntura Económica (Bogotá), V. 3, No. 3, pp. 88-94. /Colombia /Decentralized authority /Political analysis

2213. INTAL. 1973 "Estudio sobre el régimen legal de las empresas públicas latinoamericanas y su acción internacional." Derecho de la Integración (Buenos Aires), V. 6, No. 14, pp. 149-182. /Latin America /Economic integration /Law /International law

2214. INTAL. 1974 Asociación internacional de empresas en América Latina: Aspectos jurídicos. Buenos Aires. /Latin America /Law /Multinational corporations /HD 2810.5 I53 1974 LAC

2215. INTAL. 1974 Proyectos conjuntos y empresas conjuntas en la integración económica de América Latina. Buenos Aires. /Law /Latin America /Multinational corporations /HD 2755.5 I535 LAC

2216. INTAL. 1976 Proyectos conjuntos y empresas conjuntas en la integración latinoamericana. Regímenes nacionales y multinacionales para encauzarlos y estimularlos. Buenos Aires. /Law /Multinational corporations /Latin America /HD 2810.5 I674 1976m LAC

2217. Inter-American Development Bank. 1968 Las inversiones multinacionales, públicas y privadas en el desarrollo y la integración de América Latina: Aspectos jurídicos e institucionales de las inversiones de alcance multinacional. Washington, D.C. /Latin America /International economic relations /Investment /Economic integration /Multinational corporations /Economic development /Law /HC 125 I6924 1968 LAC

2218. International Labour Organization. Asian Advisory Committee. 1966 Labour-Management Relations in Public Industrial Undertakings. Singapore: ILO. /Industrial sector /Labor relations /Management

2219. International Labour Organization. 1966 Background Paper on Aspects of Management Training in Public Enterprises. Geneva: U.N. Seminar on Organization and Administration of Public Enterprises. /Management /Training

2220. International Labour Organization. International Institute for Labour Studies. 1970 "Workers' Participation in Management in Israel." Bulletin International Institute for Labour Studies (Geneva), No. 7, pp. 153-199. /Israel /Worker management participation

2221. International Legal Center. 1976 Law and Public Enterprise in Asia. New York: Praeger. /Asia /Law / HD 4283 L32

2222. Iqbal, Zafar. 1983 Financial Interrelationships between Public Authorities and Public Enterprises: The Pakistan Experience. Ljubljana: ICPE. /Pakistan /Wages /Price policy /Public financing

2223. Irastorza, J. 1973 El INI en el 3er. plan de desarrollo. Empresa industrial en España: El INI. Madrid: Instituto de Estudios Fiscales. /Spain /Industrial sector /Holding company

2224. Ireland. Committee on Industrial Relations in the Electricity Supply Board. 1968 Final Report. Dublin. /Ireland /Industrial relations /Electrical utility industry /Government report

2225. Iristy J., Jorge. 1975 "Relaciones presupuestarias entre el gobierno central y las empresas públicas." Revista de la Asociación Interamericana de Presupuesto Público V. 2, No. 5, pp. 107-145. /Budgetary process /Public financing /OPSS

2226. Iristy J., Jorge. 1978 "Relaciones presupuestarias entre el gobierno central y las empresas públicas." Gobierno y empresas públicas en América Latina. Buenos Aires: SIAP. pp. 185-204. /Budgetary process /Control process /OPSS

2227. Isaza, José Fernando. 1981 "Las empresas públicas." El Estado y el desarrollo. Bogotá: Editorial Dintel. pp. 243-248. /Colombia /Oil industry /HD 3616 C73 E88 1981 LAC

2228. Islam, Sarajul. 1980 "Education and Training in Public Enterprises in Developing Countries: Country Paper on Bangladesh." Paper presented at the Expert Group Meeting on the Research Project on Education and Training in Public Enterprises in Developing Countries, Ljubljana, Yugoslavia, 17-22 March. Ljubljana: ICPE. /Bangladesh /Training /Management

2229. Islam, Sarajul. 1981 "Management Development in Public Enterprises in Bangladesh." Paper presented at the Regional Workshop on Management Training and Development in Public Enterprises of Developing Countries, Karachi, Pakistan, 5-15 January. Ljubljana: ICPE. /Bangladesh /Management /Training

2230. Isofa, Bomolo´oka Nkanga. 1983 "L´entreprise publique comme instrument de la politique économique: Cas de la République du Zaïre." Paper presented at the 19th International Congress of Administrative Sciences, West Berlin, 19-23 Sept. /Zaire /Political economy /Economic history /OPSS

2231. Israel. Assoc. of Political Science. 1965 The Management of State Enterprises. Jerusalem. /Israel /Management

2232. Israel. Institute for Legislative Research and Comparative Law. 1972 Report of the Committee for the Preparation of a Government Corporation Bill. Jerusalem: Faculty of Law, Hebrew University of Jerusalem; Institute for Legislative Research and Comparative Law. /Israel /Law

2233. Italy. Associazione Italiana di Scienze Politiche e Sociali. 1960 Il controlle dell´impresa publica. Milan, Italy: Ed. Vita e Pensien. /Italy /Control process

2234. Italy. Instituto per la Ricostruzione Industriale. (IRI). 1963 An Italian Experiment: State Industry Competes with Private Enterprise. Rome: IRI. /Italy /Industrial economy /Private sector /Competition / Holding company

2235. Italy. Instituto per la Riconstruzione Industriale (IRI). 1971 "L´IRI. Un point de recontre entre les impératifs du dévelopment national et l´initiative privée." Agence Economique et Financière (Paris), No. 119. /Italy /Economic development /Private sector /Economic analysis /Holding company

2236. Ittikul, Pramote. 1981 "Bank for Agriculture and Agricultural Co-Operatives, Thailand." Paper presented at the Regional Workshop on the Evaluation of Training Packages for Public Enterprise Managers, Bangkok, Thailand, 10-14 August. Ljubljana: ICPE. /Thailand /Banking agency /Credit policy /Agricultural sector / Cooperatives

2237. Itzcovich, Samuel, and Heber Camelo. 1983 La empresa pública en la economía, la experiencia argentina: estadísticas para el análisis económico y financiero. Estudios e Informes de la CEPAL, 21 Santiago, Chile: UNECLA. /Argentina /Statistics /Public financing /Economic analysis /Economic system /HD 4083 I89 1983 LAC

2238. Ivanek, L. 1962 Public Corporations in Western Germany. Prague: Statni Nakl. Politicke Literatury. /Germany, Federal Rep. of

2239. Ivanek, L. 1962 "On the Role of Public Enterprises in West German Economy." Wirtschaftwissenschaft (Berlin), V. 10, No. 1, pp. 29-42. /Germany, Federal Rep. of /330.5 W7482 PCL

2240. Iyer, Ramaswamy R. 1979 "Control Systems for Public Enterprises in India." Paper presented at the Interregional Workshop on Control Systems for Public Enterprises in Developing Countries, Ljubljana, Yugoslavia, 9-13 July. Ljubljana: ICPE. /India /Control process

2241. Izquierdo, Jorge Jesús. 1974 "La coordinación del subsector paraestatal: Conferencia nacional de México." Paper presented at the International Seminar ´74: Planning in Public Enterprises in Developing Countries, Ljubljana, Yugoslavia, Sept. 23-Oct. 9. Ljubljana: ICPE. /Mexico /Planning process /Control process

2242. Izquierdo, Jorge Jesús. 1978 "Los órganos de gobierno del sector paraestatal como instrumentos de coordinación y control." in Rosa Luz Alegría et al., *Empresas públicas.* Mexico City: Presidencia de la República. pp. 51-64. /Mexico /Control process /HD 4013 E479 1978 LAC

2243. Jackson, R. 1979 "Optimal Subsidies for Public Transit." *Journal of Transport Economics and Policy* V. 9, No. 111, pp. 3-15. /Mass transportation industry /Subsidization policy /HE 1 J597 Pub Aff

2244. Jackson, Robert G. A. 1959 *The Case for an International Development Authority.* Syracuse, N.Y.: Syracuse University Press. /Development banks /338.91 J137c

2245. Jacob, M. M. 1976 "Specialisation, Diversification and Integration in Public Sector Industries - A Case Discussion on Business Strategy." *Lok Udyog* (New Delhi), V. 10, No. 1, pp. 35-38. /Management /354.54 L836 PCL

2246. Jacomet, R., and M. Buttgenbach. 1947 *Le statut des entreprises publiques, offices a caractère commercial, sociétés d´économie mixte, et entreprises nationalisées.* Paris: Sirey. /France /Law

2247. Jacquignon, L. 1955 "L´Electricité et gaz d´Algerié établissment national." *Annales Juridiques, Politiques, Economiques et Sociales* (Algiers), pp. 87-105. /Algeria /Electrical utility industry /Gas utility industry

2248. Jacquignon, L. 1956 "Introduction générale d´une étude du régime des biens des entreprises nationales." *Annales Juridiques, Politiques, Economiques et Sociales* (Algiers), pp. 237-271. /France /Law /Public financing

2249. Jacquignon, L. 1956 *Le régime des biens des entreprises nationales: contribution au droit des nationalisations.* Paris: Dalloz. /France /Law /Public financing

2250. Jacquignon, L. 1958 *L´Exécution forcée sur les biens des autorités et services publiques. Actualité Juridique* (Paris), /France /Law /Public administration

2251. Jacquignon, L. 1967 "L´Element d´une étude des finances et de la gestion financière des entreprises publiques." *L´Actualité Juridique (Droit Administratif)* (Paris), pp. 436-448. /France /Financing /Management

2252. Jacquignon, L. n.d. "Le régime des entreprises nationalisées." *Jurisclasseur Administratif* Facs. 155 (Paris), No. 155. /France /Law

2253. Jacquignon, L. n.d. "Les entreprises nationalisées." Jurisclasseur Administratif (Paris), pp. 155-159. /France /Nationalization /Law

2254. Jacquignon, L., and Wolfgang G. Friedmann. 1947 "The New Public Corporation and the Law. I." Modern Law Review (London), V. 10, No. 3, pp. 233-254. /Law

2255. Jacquignon, L., and Wolfgang G. Friedmann. 1947 "The New Public Corporation and the Law. II." Modern Law Review (London), V. 10, No. 4, pp. 377-396. /Law

2256. Jacquot, Henri. 1970 La réforme de la SNCF et l´aparition d´une nation nouvelle de l´entreprise publique. Paris: Ed. Droit Social. /France /Railway industry

2257. Jaffarulah, Mohamed. 1980 "Pre-Course Assignment." Paper presented at the Interregional Seminar on Training Management in Public Enterprises in Developing Countries, Ljubljana, Yugoslavia, Sept. 29-Oct. 10. Ljubljana: ICPE. /Management /Training

2258. Jaffe, A. J. 1957 Some Features of the Growth of Private and Public Industries in Planning Development. Washington: International Co-operation Administration, Office of Industrial Resources. /Planning Process /Private sector /Industrial sector

2259. Jagannadham, V., and Laxmi Narain. 1968 "Public Enterprises in India." Annals of Public and Cooperative Economy V. 39, No. 2, pp. 297-298. /India /Evaluation / 330.5 An73

2260. Jaidah, Ali. 1980 "Problems and Prospects of State Petroleum Enterprises in OPEC Countries." State Petroleum Enterprises in Developing Countries. New York: Pergamon Press. pp. 17-22. /Oil industry

2261. Jain, B. 1968 "Personnel Administration and Industrial Democracy in a Growing State." Indian Journal of Labour Economics (Bombay), pp. 295-317. /India /Participatory democracy /Personnel management / 331.0954 In2

2262. Jain, K. K. 1982 "Management Development in Public Sector Iron & Steel Industry." Lok Udyog (New Delhi), V. 16, No. 6, pp. 31-34. /India /Steel industry /Training /354.54 L836 PCL

2263. Jain, L. C. 1958 "Management of Public Enterprises in India." Indian Journal of Commerce (Allahabad, India), V. 11, No. 4. /India /Management

2264. Jain, P. C., and G. Shankar. 1976 "Induced Budget Pressure and its Impact on Job Performance An Empirical Study of Selected Companies." Lok Udyog (New Delhi), V. 10, No. 8, pp. 25-30. /India /Economic efficiency /Financial performance /Budgetary process /354.54 L836 PCL

2265. Jain, R. 1961 "Capital Formation in State Enterprises in India." Indian Journal of Public Administration (New Delhi), V. 7, No. 1. /India /Investment / JA 26 I55 Pub Aff

2266. Jain, R. K. 1967 Management of State Enterprises in India. Bombay: Manaktalas. /India /Management

2267. Jain, R. K. 1969 "Principles of Price Setting in Public Enterprises." Lok Udyog (New Delhi), pp. 487-495. /India /Price policy / 354.54 L836

2268. Jain, S. C. 1969 "Nationalization in Tanzania: Some Legal Aspects." Africa Quarterly (New Delhi), V. 9, No. 2, pp. 141-148. /Tanzania /Nationalization /Law / 960.5 Af835

2269. Jain, S. K. 1974 "Role of Trade Unions in Public Sector Enterprises." Lok Udyog (New Delhi), V. 8, No. 7+8, pp. 27-32. /India /Trade unions /354.54 L836 PCL

2270. Jaiswal, S. L. 1971 The Public Sector in India. New Delhi: S. Chand & Co. /India

2271. Jakhade, V. M. 1967 "Agricultural Production Credit and Institutional Arrangements." Indian Journal of Public Administration (New Delhi), V. 13, No. 3, pp. 540-549. /India /Agricultural production /Credit policy /JA 26 I55 Pub Aff

2272. James, Emili. 1950 "Les résultats des nationalisations en France." Revue de l'Université de Bruxelles (Brussels), No. 2, pp. 138-155. /France /Nationalization /Policy evaluation

2273. Janer y Duran, Enrique de. 1953 "En torno a la municipalización de servicios." Revista de Estudios de la Vida Social (Madrid), No. 69, pp. 351-361. /Spain /Public services /Local government

2274. Janiszewski, Hubert A., and Praxy J. Fernandes. 1981 "What Price Technology?" Public Enterprise V. 1, No. 4, pp. 23-41. /Technology transfer /OPSS

2275. Janjić, Stevo. 1974 "Développement du système d'autogestion de planification au complex 'Jugoplastika'." Paper presented at the International Seminar '74: Planning on Public Enterprises in Developing Countries, Ljubljana, Yugoslavia, Sept.23-Oct.9. Ljubljana: ICPE. /Yugoslavia /Plastic manufacturing industry /Planning process /Case studies /Worker management participation

2276. Jansse, L. 1953 "La politique des nationalisations en France." Economie et Humanisme (Paris), pp. 23-24. /France /Nationalization /Policy analysis

2277. Jansz, S. E. P. 1956 "The Organisational and Administrative Significance of the Public Corporations." Columbo: Central Bank of Ceylon. /Public administration

2278. Japan. Administrative Management Agency. 1982 "The Public Enterprise as the Instrument of State Policies: National Report of Japan." Paper presented at the 19th International Congress of Administrative Sciences, 13-17 Sept. /Japan /Taxonomy /Economic analysis /Goal setting /Profits /OPSS

2279. Jaramillo, Luis Javier. 1976 "El sector público colombiano y su posible papel en la promoción del desarrollo tecnológico nacional." Paper presented at the seminar on Implementation in Latin America's Public Sector: Translating Policies into Action, Austin, Tex., April. Austin, Tex.: ILAS-UT. /Colombia /Technological change /OPSS

2280. Jardim, Manoel Silvino. 1980 "A empresa pública na prestação de serviços municipais: pesquisa junto a algúmas empresas do Estado de São Paulo e perfil econômico-financiero das empresas municipais no Brasil." *A empresa pública no Brasil: Uma abordagem multidisciplinar.* Brasília: IPEA. pp. 497-527. /Sao Paulo, Brazil (State) /Decentralization /Decentralized authority

2281. Jasny, N. 1951 *The Soviet Economy During the Plan Era.* Palo Alto, Calif.: Stanford University Press. /Union of Soviet Socialist Reps. /Economic history

2282. Jaspan, M. A. 1962 "Indonesian Workers' Attitudes in Nationalized Industry." *Science and Society* pp. 257-275. /Indonesia /Labor relations / 305 Sc26 PCL

2283. Jauregui, Jesús, et al. 1980 *Tabamex: un caso de integración vertical de la agricultura.* Mexico City: Nueva Imagen. /Mexico /Tobacco industry / HD 9144 M44 T337 LAC

2284. Jayawardena, A. S. 1981 "The System of Control on Public Enterprises by Executive Departments: A Case Study of Sri Lanka." Ljubljana: ICPE. /Sri Lanka /Control process /Management

2285. Jecht, H. 1966 *Some Observations on Public Enterprises in the Federal Republic of Germany.* Geneva: U.N. Seminar on Organization and Administration of Public Enterprises. /Germany, Federal Rep. of

2286. Jencks, Clinton E. 1966 "A British Coal: Labor Relations Since Nationalism." *Industrial Relations* V. 6, No. 1, pp. 95-110. /United Kingdom /Labor relations /Coal mining industry 331.105 In19

2287. Jenkins, C. 1959 *Power at the Top. A Critical Survey of the Nationalized Industries.* London: McGibbon and Kee. /United Kingdom /Nationalization /Industrial sector /338.942 J415p

2288. Jenkins, Glenn P. 1978 *An Operational Approach to the Performance of Public Sector Enterprises.* Cambridge, Mass: HIID Development Discussion Paper No. 47. /Evaluation /System performance /OPSS

2289. Jenkins, Glenn P. 1978 *Performance Evaluation and Public Sector Enterprises.* Cambridge, Mass.: HIID Development Discussion Paper No. 46. /Evaluation /System analysis /OPSS

2290. Jenkins, Glenn P. 1979 "An Operational Approach to the Performance Evaluation of Public Sector Enterprises." *Annals of Public and Cooperative Economy* V. 50, No. 2, pp. 3-16. /Evaluation /Economic efficiency /Financial performance

/330.5 An73

2291. Jenkins, Glenn P., and Mohamed H. Lahouel. 1981 "Evaluation of Performance of Industrial Public Enterprises: Criteria and Policies." Paper presented at the Expert Group Meeting on Performance Criteria and the Implementation of Performance Evaluation Systems in Public Enterprises in Developing Countries, Ljubljana, Yugoslavia, 23-27 November. Ljubljana: ICPE. /Industrial sector /Evaluation

2292. Jenkins, N. 1970 Electricity: The Alternative to Nationalization. London: Aims of Industry. /United Kingdom /Electrical utility industry /Nationalization /338.4762131 J417e PCL

2293. Jerovsek, J. 1969 Self-Management in Working Organizations from the Point of View of Efficiency and Democracy. Herceg Novi: U.N. Public Administration Division. /Worker self management

2294. Jesús, José P. de. 1983 "Training Courses for Public Management in the Philippines." Public Enterprise V. 3, pp. 85-91. /Philippines /Training /Management /OPSS

2295. Jewkes, J. 1953 "The Nationalization of Industry." The University of Chicago Law Review V. 20, No. 4, pp. 615-645. /Industrial sector /Nationalization

2296. Jewkes, J. 1965 Public and Private Enterprises. London: Routledge & Kegan Paul. /Private sector /Comparative analysis /338.0942 J556p

2297. Jeze, G. 1937 Le Régime juridique des entreprises de fabrication ou de vente de matériel d´armement. Paris: RDP. /France /Law /Arms manufacturing industry

2298. Jha, L. K. 1975 "The Concept of Mixed Economy." In R. C. Dutt and Raj K. Nigam, ed(s). Towards Commanding Heights. New Delhi: Vivek Joshi. pp. 247-259. /India /Mixed economy /HD 4293 T68 PCL

2299. Jha, S. M. 1983 "Indian Railways´ Social Costs." Lok Udyog (New Delhi), V. 16, No. 11, pp. 45-52. /India /Railway industry /Social welfare policy /Cost benefit analysis /354.54 L836 PCL

2300. Jhabvala, Firdaush. 1973 "A Model of Motivation in State Enterprises in Underdeveloped Economies." Indian Economic Review V. 8, No. 2, pp. 172-185. /Economic efficiency /Training /Motivation /330.5 In 18

2301. Jian, Shi. 1981 "Management Training in Public Enterprises within the Municipality of Beijing, China." Paper presented at the Regional Workshop on Management Training and Development in Public Enterprises of Developing Countries, Karachi, Pakistan, 5-15 January. Ljubljana: ICPE. /China, People´s Rep. of /Beijing,People´s Republic of China /Management /Training

2302. Jiménez Castro, Wilberg. 1964 La société publique, instrument important et dilemme dans le processus de développement. /Economic development /Development process

2303. Jiménez Castro, Wilberg. 1965 Los dilemas de la descentralización funcional: Un análisis de la autonomía institucional pública. San José, Costa Rica: E.S.P.A.C. /Costa Rica /Evaluation /Decentralization /G338.74 J564d LAC

2304. Jiménez Castro, Wilberg. 1970 "Los organismos descentralizados funcionalmente en el Istmo Centroamericano." La Empresa Pública. Zaragoza, Spain: Publicaciones del Real Colegio de España en Bolonia. pp. 1859-1880. /Central America /Panama

2305. Jiménez Codinach, María de Lourdes, and Jaime Alvarez Soberanis. 1981 El papel de la empresa pública en el proceso de tanspaso tecnológico. Ljubljana: ICPE. /Technology transfer

2306. Jiménez Nieto, Juan Ignacio. 1974 "Relaciones del gobierno con las empresas públicas: Directorio político y gerencial empresarial." Lima: INAP. /Peru /Political analysis /Accountability /Control process

2307. Jiménez Nieto, Juan Ignacio. 1978 "Directorio politico y gerencia empresarial." Gobierno y empresas públicas en América Latina. Buenos Aires: SIAP. pp. 55-88. /Management /Control process /OPSS

2308. Johnson, Carol. 1972 "Relations with Government and Parliament." In Stuart Holland, ed(s). The State as Entrepreneur. London: Weidenfeld & Nicolson pp. 202-218. /Italy /Control process /Parliament / Holding company /HD 3616 I83 H65 PCL /HD 487 H6 1973 Pub Aff

2309. Johnson, Chalmers. 1978 Japan's Public Policy Companies. Washington, D. C.: American Enterprise Institute for Public Policy Research. /Japan /Taxonomy /Law /Economic history /Control process /Energy use policy /HD 3616 J33 J64 Pub Aff

2310. Johnson, Eldon L. 1952 "Joint Consultation in Britain's Nationalized Industries." Public Administration Review V. 12, No. 3, pp. 181-189. /United Kingdom /Industrial sector /Collective bargaining / JK1 P85

2311. Johnson, Eldon L. 1953 "Consumer 'Control' in British Nationalized Industries." Journal of Politics pp. 88-113. /United Kingdom /Consumer relations /Control process /320.5 J825 PCL

2312. Johnson, Eldon L. 1954 "The Accountability of the British Nationalized Industries." American Political Science Review V. 48, No. 2, pp. 366-385. /United Kingdom /Accountability /320.5 M31

2313. Johnson, Harry G. 1965 "A Theoretical Model of Economic Nationalism in New and Developing States." Political Science Quarterly V. 80, No. 2, pp. 169-185. /Developing nations

/Economic system /Nationalism / 320.5 P75

2314. Johnson, J. 1963 The Economics of Indian Rail Transport. Bombay: Allied Publishers Ltd. /India /Railway industry /Transportation industry /Economic analysis

2315. Joiris, Michel. 1977 "The Renault Régie." Annals of Public and Cooperative Economy V. 49, No. 3, pp. 307-342. /France /Automobile manufacturing industry /Case studies /330.5 An73

2316. Jolly, P. 1930 "The State and Its Subdivisions as Members of Business Corporations." Harvard Business Review V. 9, pp. 18-25. /United States of America /Mixed enterprises /HF 5001 H3

2317. Jones, Arnold R. 1961 "The Financing of the Tennessee Valley Authority." Law and Contemporary Problems V. 26, No. 4, pp. 724-740. /United States of America /Regional development /Public financing /River valley development projects

2318. Jones, Edwin. 1981 "Role of the State in Public Enterprise." Economic and Social Studies (Mona, Kingston, Jamaica), V. 30, No. 1, pp. 17-44. /Caribbean Region /Political analysis /Decision making process /G330.97292 So13 LAC

2319. Jones, Edwin. n.d. "Role of the State in Public Enterprises of the Commonwealth Caribbean." Kingston, Jamaica: Caribbean Public Enterprises Project. /Caribbean Region /OPSS

2320. Jones, H. F. M. 1952 "The Gas Industry." In Sir Hurbert Houldsworth, ed(s). Efficiency in the Nationalized Industries. London: Allen & Unwin. /United Kingdom /Gas utility industry

2321. Jones, Leroy P. 1975 Public Enterprise and Economic Development: The Korean Case. Seoul: Korean Development Institute. /Korea, Rep. of /Economic development /HD 4315.5 J66

2322. Jones, Leroy P. 1979 "Public Enterprise in Less-Developed-Countries." Cambridge, Mass.: HIID. /Developing nations

2323. Jones, Leroy P. 1979 "Evaluating the Performance of Public Enterprise, with Particular Reference to the Oil Producing Countries of the Arabian Peninsula." Cambridge, Mass.: Harvard University. /Middle East /Oil industry /Evaluation

2324. Jones. Leroy P. 1980 "Debt/Equity Ratios in Public Enterprises: Normative Theory, Positive Practice and Prescriptions for Reforms." Paper presented at the International Workshop on Investment Criteria and Investment Decision-Making Processes, Ljubljana, Yugoslavia, 20-24 October. Ljubljana: ICPE. /Debt /Financing

2325. Jones, Leroy P. 1980 "Definition and Taxonomy of Public Enterprise." Paper presented at the Expert Group Meeting on Concept Definition and Classification of Public Enterprises, Tangier, Morocco, 15-19 December. Ljubljana: ICPE. /Taxonomy

2326. Jones, Leroy P. 1981 "The linkage between objectives and control mecahnisms in the public manufacturing sector." Paper presented at the Expert Group Meeting on the Changing Role and Function of the Public Industrial Sector in Development, Vienna, Austria, 5-9 October. Vienna: UNIDO. /Control Process /Goal Setting /OPSS

2327. Jones, Leroy P. 1982 "Introduction." In Leroy P. Jones et al., ed(s). Public enterprise in less-developed countries. New York: Cambridge University Press. pp. 1-13. /Developing nations /HD 3850 P83 PCL

2328. Jones, Leroy P. 1983 "Towards a Performance Evaluation Methodology for Public Enterprises with Special Reference to Pakistan." Paper presented at the ECLA Seminar on State Control and Planning of Public Enterprises, Brasília, 15-17 June. Brasília: UNECLA. /Evaluation /Pakistan /OPSS

2329. Jones, Leroy P., and Il Sakong. 1980 Government, Business, and Entrepreneurship in Economic Development: The Korean Case. Cambridge, Mass.: Harvard University Press. /Korea, Rep. of /Economic history /Economic policy /Private enterprises / Comparative analysis / HC 467 J85 PCL

2330. Jones, Leroy P., and Edward S. Mason. 1982 "Role of economic factors in determining the size and structure of the public-enterprise sector in less-developed countries with mixed economies." In Leroy P. Jones et al., ed(s). Public enterprise in less-developed countries. New York: Cambridge University Press. pp. 17-47. /Economic analysis /HD 3850 P83 PCL /Also presented at BAPEG Conference, Boston, April, 1980 /OPSS

2331. Jones, Leroy P., and Lawrence H. Wortzel. 1982 "Public enterprise and manufactured exports in less-developed countries: institutional and market factors determining comparative advantage." In Leroy P. Jones et al., ed(s). Public enterprise in less-developed countries. New York: Cambridge University Press. pp. 217-242. /Exports /Economic analysis /HD 3850 P83 PCL /Also presented at the Second BAPEG Seminar, April 1980. /OPSS

2332. Jones, Leroy P., and Ingo Vogelsang. 1983 The Effects of Markets on Public Enterprise Conduct, and Vice Versa. Ljubljana: ICPE. /Market economy /Organization behavior

2333. Jones, Leroy P., and Gustav Papanek. 1983 "The Efficiency of Public Enterprise in Less Developed Countries." In G. Ram Reddy, ed(s). Government and Public Enterprise: Essays in honour of Professor V. V. Ramanadham. Bombay, India: N. M. Tripathi Private Limited. pp. 98-112. /Developing nations /Evaluation

2334. Jones, Leroy P., et al. (eds.) 1982 Public enterprise in less-developed countries. New York: Cambridge University Press. /Economic analysis /HD 3850 P83 PCL

2335. Jones, N. S. Carey. 1974 Politics, Public Enterprise and the Industrial Development Agency: Industrialization Policies and Practices. London: Croom Helm. /Industrialization /Political role /Political analysis

2336. Jorba, Juan F., and Israel Wonsewer. 1976 Las empresas públicas en el Uruguay: Su formación y desarrollo. Santiago, Chile: UNECLA. /Uruguay /Economic development /Management /OPSS

2337. Jordana de Pozas, Luis. 1932 "Municipalización de servicios." Estudios Jordana (Pamplona, Spain), No. 1, pp. 745-766. /Spain /City government /Public services

2338. Jordana de Pozas, Luis. 1943 "Algunas consideraciones sobre los servicios municipales de carácter económico." Revista de Estudios de la Vida Social (Madrid), /Economic analysis /City government /Public services

2339. Jorgensen, N. O. 1967 Industrial and Commercial Development Corporation: Its Purpose and Performance. Nairobi: Institute for Development Studies. /Kenya /Industrial sector /Commercial sector /Development corporation

2340. Jorion, E. 1955 "Industrial and Commercial Enterprises under Public Law in Belgium." In A. H. Hanson, ed(s). Public Enterprises. Brussels: IIAS. pp. 515-530. /Belgium /Law /HD 3850 H28 Law

2341. Joseph, Thelma. 1980 "Education and Training in Developing Countries." Paper presented at the Expert Group Meeting on the Research Project on Education and Training in Public Enterprise in Developing Countries, Ljubljana, Yugoslavia, 17-22 March. Ljubljana: ICPE. /Developing nations /Training /Management

2342. Joshi, M. S. 1961 "The Development Banks." Indian Economic Journal pp. 249-357. /India /Development banks / 330.5 In16

2343. Joshi, Navin Chandra. 1979 "Management Information System." Lok Udyog (New Delhi). V. 13, No. 9, pp. 53-56. /India /Information system /354.54 L836 PCL

2344. Juangbhanich, Prakorb. 1980 "Pricing Policy of Public Enterprises: A Case Study on Electricity and Water Supply in Thailand." Paper presented at the International Workshop on Pricing Policies in Public Enterprises, Ljubljana, Yugoslavia, 26-30 May. Ljubljana: ICPE. /Thailand /Price policy /Electrical utility industry

2345. Julliot de la Morandière, L., and M. Bye. 1948 Les nationalisations en France et l'étranger: Les nationalisations en France. Paris: Receuil Sirey. /France /Nationalization / 338.944 J948n v.2

2346. Jungers, Eugene. 1953 "L'Office d'exploitations des transports du Congo Belge: OTRACO." Société Belge d'Etudes et d'Expansion Liège. No. 155. /Zaire /Belgium /Transportation industry

2347. Junguito, Roberto. 1981 "Evolución y comportamiento de las entidades y empresas del Estado, EMPES." El Estado y el desarrollo. Bogotá: Editorial Dintel. pp. 221-240. /Colombia /Taxonomy /Economic analysis /Economic history /HD 3616 C73 E88 1981 LAC

2348. Jurion, F. 1951 "Institut National pour l'Etude agronomique de Congo Belge: INEAC." Société Belge d'Etudes et d'Expansion Liège. No. 147. /Zaire /Agricultural services

2349. Kabaj, M. 1966 "Evolution of the Incentive System in USSR Industry." International Labour Review (Geneva), V. 94, No. 1, pp. 22-38. /Union of Soviet Socialist Reps. /Industrial sector /Incentive systems /331.05 In81 PCL /HD 4811 I65 Pub Aff

2350. Kabra, Kamal Nayan. 1982 "Role of Public Sector in Introducing Technological Change in the Third World." Lok Udyog (New Delhi), V. 16, No. 8, pp. 17-26. /Technology transfer /354.54 L836 PCL

2351. Kacim, Brachemi. 1974 "Planning in Public Enterprises in Developing Countries: National Paper of Algeria." Paper presented at the International Seminar '74: Planning in Public Enterprises in Developing Countries, Ljubljana, Yugoslavia, 23 Sept. - 9 Oct. Ljubljana: ICPE. /Algeria /Planning process

2352. Kacim, Brachemi. 1974 La planificación en las empresas públicas en los países en vías de desarrollo. Ljubljana: ICPE. /Developing nations /Planning process

2353. Kahawita, R. 1951 "Gal Oya Scheme: Facts and Fallacies." Ceylon Economist V. 2. pp. 57-68. /Sri Lanka /Irrigation systems

2354. Kahn, Ellison. 1959 "Public Corporations in South Africa: A Survey." South African Journal of Economics V. 27, pp. 279-92. /South Africa, Rep. of /Africa / 330.968 So87

2355. Kahn, Isabel. 1981 "El rol del sector público en los países en desarrollo." Ljubljana: ICPE. /Developing nations

2356. Kaido, S 1974 "The Financial Plan of the Socialist Industrial Enterprise, I." Kokumin-Kezaizasshi V. 129, No. 2. /Socialist Economy / Financing

2357. Kaido, S. 1976 "The Financial Plan of the Socialist Industrial Enterprise, III." Kokumin-Keizaizasshi V. 133, No. 1. /Socialist Economy /Financing

2358. Kaiser, J. H. 1970 "Public Enterprise in Germany." In W. G. Friedmann and J. F. Garner, ed(s). Government Enterprise: A Comparative Study. New York: Columbia University Press. pp. 154-167. /Germany, Federal Rep. of /350.0092 G746

2359. Kaldor, Nicholas. 1980 "Public or Private Enterprise - The Issues to be Considered." In William J. Baumol, ed(s). Public and Private Enterprise in a Mixed Economy. New York:

St. Martin's Press. pp. 1-12. /Private enterprises /Comparative analysis /HD 3842 P47 PCL

2360. Kalra, G. D. 1982 "Damodar Valley Corporation: Malady and Remedy." Lok Udyog (New Delhi), V. 16, No. 7, pp. 49-54. /India /Case studies /River valley development projects /354.54 L836 PCL

2361. Kalweit, W. 1965 "Le nouveau système de planification et de direction." Democratie Nouvelle pp. 32-38. /France /Administrative reform /Management /Planning process

2362. Kamat, G. S. 1973 "Public Sector Banking and Cooperative Banking in India." Annals of Public and Cooperative Economy V. 44, pp. 159-163. /India /Financial institutions /Cooperatives /330.5 An73

2363. Kambe, M. 1932 "State Monopoly as a Method of Taxing Consumption." Kyoto University Economic Review V. 1, pp. 1-13. /Taxation policy /Price policy /Monopoly

2364. Kamel, Ismail Kamel Ahmed. 1974 "The System of Planning, Its Application and Evaluation, and Follow-Ups of Plans in Economic Units of the General Sector: National Report of Egypt." Paper presented at the International Seminar '74: Planning in Public Enterprises in Developing Countries, Ljubljana, Yugoslavia, 23 Sept. - 9 Oct. Ljubljana: ICPE. /Egypt /Planning process /Evaluation

2365. Kamenister, S. 1953 Organisation und Planung des Sozialistischen Industriebes. Berlin: Verlag die Wirtschaft. /Germany, Democratic Rep. of /Socialist economy /Industrial sector / Organization formation /Planning process

2366. Kamleshwar, D. 1977 "Theoretical Aspect of Price Policy of Coal Industry in the Public Sector in India." Lok Udyog (New Delhi), V. 10, No. 10, pp. 13-20. /India /Price policy /Coal mining industry /354.54 L836 PCL

2367. Kanazawa, Osamu. 1970 "La empresa Japan Air Line como empresa pública." La Empresa Pública. Zaragoza, Spain: Publicaciones del Real Colegio de España en Bolonia. pp. 1881-1890. /Japan /Air transportation industry

2368. Kane, A. R., and P. N. Singh. 1967 "An Exploratory Study of Worker' Participation in Management." Indian Journal of Labour Economics (Bombay), V. 10, No. 12, pp. 116-123. /India /Worker management participation / 331.0954 In2

2369. Kane, Mamadou Lamine, and Serigne Ahmadou Camara. 1983 "Autonomie, contrôle et interférence du gouvernement central dans les entreprises publiques: L'exemple du Sénégal." Paper presented at the 19th International Congress of Administrative Sciences, West Berlin, 19-23 Sept. /Autonomy /Control process /Senegal /Law /OPSS

2370. Kanesalingham, V. 1972 "Pricing Policy of Public Enterprises: A Country Study of Selected Public Enterprises in Ceylon." Colombo, Sri Lanka: Industrial Development

Board, Document and Publications Division. /Sri Lanka /Price policy

2371. Kanuraratne, S. P. R. 1981 "Financial Profitability and Losses in Public Enterprises in Sri Lanka." Paper presented at the International Workshop on Financial Profitability and Losses in Public Enterprises, Ljubljana, Yugoslavia, 1-5 June. Ljubljana: ICPE. /Sri Lanka /Profits

2372. Kaplan, Marcos. 1964 "`Tercer mundo´ y empresa pública." Revista de Ciencias Económicas (Buenos Aires), V. 20, No. 6, pp. 195-222. /Developing nations /G330.5 R327 LAC

2373. Kaplan, Marcos. 1965 Desarrollo económico y empresa pública. Buenos Aires: Ed. Macchi. /Economic development /G338.91 K141d

2374. Kaplan, Marcos. 1966 Países en desarrollo y empresa pública. Buenos Aires: Ed. Macchi, Colección Ciencias Económicas. /Developing nations

2375. Kaplan, Marcos. 1967 Significado y crisis de la empresa pública argentina. Valparaíso, Chile: Ediciones Escuela de Derecho de la Universidad de Chile. /Argentina

2376. Kaplan, Marcos. 1967 La empresa privada y la empresa pública en la integración fronteriza. Valparaíso, Chile: Edeval. /Chile /Private sector /Economic integration /Comparative analysis

2377. Kaplan, Marcos. 1968 Problemas del desarrollo y de la integración en América Latina; ensayo. Caracas: Monte Avila Ed., C. A. /Latin America /Economic integration /G337.91 K141p

2378. Kaplan, Marcos. 1968 "Estado empresario en la Argentina." Aporte (Paris), No. 10, pp. 33-69. /Argentina

2379. Kaplan, Marcos. 1969 El Estado en el desarrollo de la integración de América Latina: Ensayos. Caracas: Monte Avila Ed. C. A. /Latin America /Economic integration /G380.1622 K141e

2380. Kaplan, Marcos. 1969 "El Estado empresario en la Argentina." Trimestre Económico (Mexico City), V. 36, No. 141, pp. 69-111. /Argentina / G330.972 T735 LAC

2381. Kaplan, Marcos. 1970 Corporaciones públicas multinacionales latinoamericana; posibles contribuciones al desarrollo y a la integración de América Latina. ST/ECLA/Conf. 39/L.2 Santiago, Chile: Reunión de Expertos sobre Capacidad Administrativa para el Desarrollo. /Latin America /Multinational corporations / Economic integration

2382. Kapolu, A. 1979 "Workers´ Participation in the Management of Public Enterprises." Committee for the Development of Economic and Social Research in Africa. No. 3. /Africa /Management /Worker management participation

2383. Kapoor, M. C., and J. D. Singh. 1977 "Marketing Planning in Public Enterprises." Lok Udyog (New Delhi), V. 10, No. 12, pp. 17-24. /India /Marketing /Planning process /354.54 L836

2384. Kapp, K. W. 1959 "River Valley Development Projects: Problems of Evaluation and Social Costs." Kyklos V. 12, pp. 589-603. /River valley development projects /Evaluation /305 K983

2385. Kapur, D. V. 1977 "The System Approach to Project Management - Some Thoughts and Experience." Lok Udyog (New Delhi), V. 11, No. 8, pp. 9-14. /India /Project management /354.54 L836

2386. Kapur, D. V. 1980 "Project Management in NTPC - A Total System Approach." Lok Udyog (New Delhi), V. 14, No. 2, pp. 5-20. /India /Project management /Case studies /Management /354.54 L836 PCL

2387. Kapur, D. V. 1982 "If Technology Obsolescence is Dangerous, the Managerial Obsolescence Would be Disastrous: Emphasis on the Matters of Productivity and Project Management." Lok Udyog (New Delhi), V. 16, No. 9, pp. 18-22. /India /Industrial sector /Productivity /Management /Project management /354.54 L836 PCL

2388. Kapustin, E. I. 1970 Soviet Workers´ Participation in Management. Summary. Geneva: International Industrial Relations Association. 2nd World Congress. /Union of Soviet Socialist Reps. /Worker management participation

2389. Karanja, Ngari S. 1980 "Kenya´s Position in the Primary Energy Sector." Paper presented at the Expert Group Meeting on Strategies for Energy Development in Developing Countries, Ljubljana, Yugoslavia, 19-22 Feb. Ljubljana: ICPE. /Kenya /Energy utility industry

2390. Karavastev, Sémo, and Ivan Voutchev. 1983 "Le problème de la rentabilité des entreprises d´Etat en République Populaire de Bulgarie et l´intérêt public." Paper presented at the 19th International Congress of Administrative Sciences, West Berlin, 19-23 Sept. /Bulgaria /Profits /Public interest /OPSS

2391. Kardelj, Edward. 1955 "La démocratie socialiste dans la pratique yougoslave." Annales de l´Economie Collective pp. 185-220. /Yugoslavia

2392. Kardelj, Edward. 1956 "Evolution in Yugoslavia." Foreign Affairs V. 34, No. 4, pp. 580-602. /Yugoslavia /Economic analysis /341.705 F761

2393. Kardelj, Edward. 1975 "The Integration of Labor and Social Capital Under Workers´ Control." In Ichak Adizes and Elisabeth Mann Borgese, ed(s). Self-Management: New Dimensions to Democracy Santa Barbara, Cal.;Oxford, England: American Bibliographical Center; Clio Press. pp. 39-48. /Yugoslavia /Worker self management /Socialist economy /OPSS

2394. Karehnke, H. 1980 "Zum Berichtszyklus uber die Haushalts-und Wirtschaftsfuhrng des Bundes." Verwaltungs Archiv No. 4, pp. 384-404. /Public financing /Control process /Budget record /Cost benefit analysis

2395. Karikurubu, Charles. 1980 "Le cas du centre de perfectionnement et de formation des cadres en cours d'emploi en République du Burundi (C.P.F.)." Paper presented at the Séminaire international sur la gestion et la formation dans les entreprises publiques dans les pays voie de développement, Ljubljana, Yugoslavia, 3-15 March. Ljubljana: ICPE. /Burundi /Management /Training

2396. Karim, Bazle, and S. R. Bahadur. 1978 , "Spare Parts Management in Public Enterprises." (Part 1) Lok Udyog (New Delhi), V. 12, No. 4, pp. 5-13. /India /Management /354.54 L836 PCL

2397. Karim, Bazle, and S. R. Bahadur. 1978 "Spare Parts Management in Public Enterprises." (Part 2) Lok Udyog (New Delhi), V. 12, No. 5, pp. 5-12. /Management /354.54 L836 PCL

2398. Karim, Bazle. 1980 "Experiences of Setting Up a Thermal-Power Station in the Himalayas in India as an Indo-Yugoslav Collaboration Project (1960-71): A Case Study." Paper presented at the Expert Group Meeting on Strategies for Energy Development in Developing Countries--Role of Public Enterprises, Ljubljana, Yugoslavia, 19-22 February. Ljubljana: ICPE. /India /Yugoslavia /Electrical utility industry /Case studies

2399. Karmoul, Akram-Jamil. 1980 "Case Study of a Proposed Joint-Venture among a Company from Jordan and Foreign Supplier of Technology." Paper presented at the International Workshop on Preparations and Negotiations of Technology Transfer Agreements for Public Enterprises in Developing Countries, Ljubljana, Yugoslavia, 27-31 Oct. Ljubljana: ICPE. /Jordan /Technology transfer /Case studies

2400. Kartadjoemena, H. S. 1980 State Enterprises and Commodity Policy in Indonesia: Towards a Framework of Analysis. Geneva: CEI. /International relations

2401. Karunananda, Vimal Chandra. 1974 "Planning in Relation to Public Sector Enterprises: Sri Lanka." Paper presented at the International Seminar '74: Planning in Public Enterprises in Developing Countries, Ljubljana, Yugoslavia, 23 Sept.-9 Oct. Ljubljana: ICPE. /Sri Lanka /Planning process

2402. Karunatilake, H. N. S. 1968 Banking and Financial Institutions in Ceylon. Colombo: Central Bank of Ceylon. /Sri Lanka /Banking agency / HG 188 C4 K36 PCL

2403. Karunatilake, H. N. S. 1971 "Industrial Expansion in the Public Sector." Economic Development in Ceylon. London: Praeger. /Sri Lanka /Industrialization /Economic growth policy / 330.95493 K149e

2404. Kaser, M., and J. G. Zielinski. 1970 Planning in East Europe, Industrial Management by the State--A Background Paper. London: Bodley Head. /Eastern Europe /Industrial sector /Management / HC 244 K36

2405. Kassab, M. S. 1963 Nature juridique des entreprises publiques. Cairo: N.I.M.D. /Egypt /Law

2406. Katorobo, James, et al. 1978 Public Enterprises in Botswana, Lesotho and Swaziland. Gaborone, Botswana: Institute of Development Management, Occasional Paper No.2. /Botswana /Lesotho /Swaziland /Africa /Economic history /OPSS

2407. Katzarov, C. 1950 "L'Etat commerçant et les nationalisations." Revue Trimestrielle de Droit Commercial (Paris), V. 3, pp. 20-35. /Nationalization

2408. Katzarov, K. 1957 "Les entreprises d'Etat continuent elles la personne juridique des anciens enterprises?" Revue Trimestrelle Droit Comparé (Paris), V. 10, pp. 313-322. /France /Law

2409. Katzarov, K. 1957 "Le problème du contrôle en matière de nationalisation." Droit Social (Paris), V. 22. /Nationalization /Control process

2410. Katzarov, K. 1960 "Théorie de la nationalisation." La Baconniére (Neuchatel, Switzerland), /Nationalization /Theoretical framework

2411. Kaufman, E. 1954 "Subjects and Forms of Public Economic Activity in Germany." International Institute of Administrative Sciences Round Table, The Hague, Netherlands. Brussels: IIAS. /Germany, Federal Rep. of

2412. Kaul, P. N. 1970 "Escalated Gestation - Lags in Public Sector Undertakings." (Part 1) Lok Udyog (New Delhi), V. 3, No. 12, pp. 1403-1413. /India /Management / 354.54 L836

2413. Kaul, P. N. 1970 "Escalated Gestation - Lags in Public Sector Undertakings." (Part 2) Lok Udyog (New Delhi), V. 4, No. 1, pp. 21-28. /India /Management /354.54 L836 PCL

2414. Kaushal, Om. P. 1964 Management, Organization and Control in Public Enterprise. Bombay, India: Allied Publishers Private Ltd. /India /Management /Organization formation /Control process

2415. Kavcic, Bogdan. 1980 "Self-Management in Yugoslavia." Public Enterprise V. 1, No. 4, pp. 69-72. /Yugoslavia /Worker self management /OPSS

2416. Kavran, Dragoljub. 1976 "Personnel Management in Enterprises." Paper presented at the International Seminar on Management and Training in Public Enterprises in Developing Countries, Ljubljana, Yugoslavia, Sept. 21-October 2. Ljubljana: ICPE. /Personnel management / /Also presented at similar seminars in Ljubljana, Yugoslavia, Oct. 10-28, 1977 and Sept. 18-Oct. 6, 1978.

2417. Kazim, Husein Ramzy. 1980 "Training and Development in Public Enterprises." Paper presented at the Expert Group Meeting on the Research Projects on Education and Training in Public Enterprises in Developing Countries, Ljubljana, Yugoslavia, 17-22 March. Ljubljana: ICPE. /Training

2418. Kazmierczak, L. 1955 L'Application du droit commercial aux entreprises nationalisées. Lille, France. /France /Law /

2419. Kelf-Cohen, Reuben. 1958 Nationalization in Britain; the End of a Dogma. London: Macmillan; New York: St. Martin's Press /United Kingdom / 338.942 K277n

2420. Kelf-Cohen, Reuben. 1969 Twenty Years of Nationalization; The British Experience. London: Macmillan; New York: St. Martin's Press /United Kingdom /Nationalization /338.942 K277t UGL,Pub Aff

2421. Kelf-Cohen, Reuben. 1973 British Nationalization, 1945-1973. London: Macmillan /United Kingdom /Nationalization /HD 4148 K39

2422. Keller, P. 1972 "Action syndicale et co-gestion au niveau multinational." Problèmes Economiques (Paris), No. 1266. /Trade unions /International negotiation

2423. Kelly Escobar, Janet. 1980 "The Comparison of State Enterprise Across International Boundaries: The Corporación Venezolana de Guayana and the Companhia Vale do Rio Doce." Prepared for the 2nd BAPEG Conference on Public Enterprises in Mixed Economy LDC's, April. /Venezuela /Brazil /Comparative analysis /OPSS

2424. Kelly Escobar, Janet. 1981 "Empresas del Estado, Negociación y el Balance del poder económico." Argos (Caracas, Venezuela), No. 2, pp. 69-95. /Mining industry

2425. Kelly Escobar, Janet. 1982 "Comparing state enterprises across international boundaries: the Corporación Venezolana de Guayana and the Companhía Vale do Rio Doce." In Leroy P. Jones et al., ed(s). Public Enterprise in less-developed countries. New York: Cambridge University Press. pp. 103-127. /Decision making process /Steel Industry /Venezuela /Brazil /HD 3850 P83 PCL

2426. Kelly, D. W. 1953 "The Administration of the National Coal Board." Public Administration (London), No. 1, pp. 1-11. /United Kingdom /Coal mining industry /Administrative management / 320.5 J826 PCL

2427. Kelly, M. A. 1950 "Socialization of German Industry." American Journal of Economics and Sociology /Germany, Federal Rep. of / 330.5 Am311 PCL /H 1 A48 Pub Aff

2428. Kendall, Walter. 1972 "Labour Relations." In Stuart Holland, ed(s). The State as Entrepreneur. London: Weidenfeld & Nicolson. pp. 219-233. /Italy /Labor relations / Holding company /HD 3616 I83 H65 PCL /HD 487 H6 1973 Pub Aff

2429. Kendrick, John W. 1963 "Exploring Productivity Measurement in Government." Public Administration Review V. 23, No. 2, pp. 59-66. /Productivity / JA1 P67 Pub Aff

2430. Kennedy, Peter. 1983 Food and Agricultural Policy in Peru, 1960-1977. Austin, Tex.: OPSS Technical Papers Series, No. 39. /Peru /Financial institutions /OPSS

2431. Kennedy, Peter. 1984 "State Shrinkage: The Jamaican Experience." Paper presented at the conference: State Shrinking: A Comparative Inquiry into Privatization, Austin, Texas, 1-3 March. /Jamaica /Privatization /OPSS

2432. Kent, Calvin A. 1974 "As taxas de servicos nos Estados Unidos." Revista de Administração Municipal (Rio de Janeiro), V. 21, No. 127, pp. 57-69. /United States of America /Price policy / JS 41 R484 LAC

2433. Kesari, V. G. 1978 "Report of the Workshop on Information System for the Evaluation of Business Efficiency in Public Enterprises in Developing Countries, Ljubljana, 13-18 November, 1978." Ljubljana: ICPE. /Evaluation /Economic efficiency /Information system

2434. Kesary, V. G. 1976 "Working Results of Public Enterprises - 1974-75." Lok Udyog (New Delhi), V. 10, No. 1, pp. 61-64. /India /Statistics /Economic history /354.54 L836 PCL

2435. Kesary, V. G. 1976 "Matching Corporate Goals to Social Objectives." Lok Udyog (New Delhi), V. 9. No. 12, pp. 9-10. /India /Goal setting /354.54 L836 PCL

2436. Kesary, V. G. 1977 "Exports and the Public Enterprises." Lok Udyog (New Delhi), V. 11, No. 3, pp. 3-6. /India /Exports /354.54 L836 PCL

2437. Keshava, G. P. 1967 "Price Policy in Public Enterprises." Asian Economic Review V. 10, pp. 30-50. /India /Price policy /330.5 As42

2438. Keshava, G. P. 1967 "Appraisal of Management's Performance in Public Enterprises." Arthanti (New Delhi), No. 10, pp. 34-55. /Management /Evaluation

2439. Keshava, G. P. 1970 Readings in the Operational Problems of Public Enterprises. New Delhi: S. Chand & Co. /Case studies

2440. Keshava, G. P. 1971 "Price Fixation of Insecticides in the Public Sector: A Study of Decision Making." Economic Affairs V. 16, No. 5, pp. 207-218. /India /Pesticide industry /Price policy / 330.95405 Ec74

2441. Kessols, S. H. 1951 "Some Legal Aspects of Port Working: Liabilities and Rights of Dock Authorities." Dock and Harbour Authority (London), pp. 181-182. /United Kingdom /Port authority /Law

2442. Keutgen, Rene. 1971 "The Vereinigte Industrie-Unternehmen AG: A German Public Enterprise." Annals of Public and Cooperative Economy V. 42, pp. 303-346. /Germany, Federal Rep. of / Case studies / 330.5 An73

2443. Kewley, T. H. 1955 "Commonwealth Enterprises." In A. H. Hanson, ed(s). Public Enterprise. Brussels: IIAS. pp. 469-481. /British Commonwealth / Law / HD 3850 H28 Law

2444. Kewley, T. H. 1958 "The Control of Public Enterprise in Australia." Congress of the International Political Science Association, Rome. /Australia /Control process

2445. Kewley, T. H., and Joan Rydon. 1949 "The Joint Coal Board." Public Administration (Sydney, Australia), pp. 58-69. /Australia /Coal mining industry /Management

2446. Kewley, T. H., and Joan Rydon. 1950 "The Australian Commonwealth Government Corporations a Statutory Analysis." Public Administration (Sydney, Australia), pp. 200-221. /Australia /Law

2447. Kewley, T. H., and Joan Rydon. 1957 "Some General Features of the Statutory Corporation in Australia." Public Administration (Sydney, Australia), V. 16, No. 3, pp. 3-28. /Australia /Law

2448. Kewley, T. H., et al. 1957 "Public Enterprise in Australia." Public Administration (Sydney, Australia), pp. 3-104. /Australia

2449. Key, V. D. 1959 "Government Corporations." In Fritz Morstein Marx, ed(s). Elements of Public Administration. Englewood Cliffs, N. J.: Prentice Hall. /Evaluation

2450. Keyes, L. S. 1955 "Some Controversial Aspects of the Public Corporation." Political Science Quarterly V. 70, pp. 28-56. /Evaluation / 320.5 P75

2451. Keyser, W., R. Windle, and A. Jacquemin. 1978 In W. Keyser and R. Windle, ed(s). Belgium/Luxembourg. Volume 1 in Public Enterprise in the EEC. Leiden: Sijthoff and Noordhoof. /Belgium /Luxemburg /Economic analysis /Employment /Financial performance /JX 1982 P85 F4 Law

2452. Keyser, W., R. Windle, H. P. Myrup, and B. Fog. 1978 In W. Keyser and R. Windle, ed(s). Denmark, Volume 2 in Public Enterprise in the EEC. Leiden: Sijthoff and Noordhoff. /Denmark /Economic analysis /Control process /Price policy /JX 1982 P85 F4 Law

2453. Keyser, W., R. Windle, and P. Eichhorn. 1978 In W. Keyser and R. Windle, ed(s). Federal Republic of Germany, Volume 3 in Public Enterprise in the EEC. Leiden: Sijthoff and Noordhoff. /Germany, Federal Rep. of /Law /Goal setting /City government /JX 1982 P85 F4 Law

2454. Keyser, W., R. Windle, and J. Virole. 1978 In W. Keyser and R. Windle, ed(s). France, Volume 4 in Public Enterprise in the EEC. Leiden: Sijthoff and Noordhoff. /France /Law /City government /Economic analysis /Control process /JX 1982 P85 F4 Law

2455. Keyser, W., R. Windle, and C. M. Guerci. 1978 In W. Keyser and R. Windle, ed(s). Italy, Volume 5 in Public Enterprise in the EEC. Leiden: Sijthoff and Noordhoff. /Italy /Law /Economic analysis /City government /JX 1982 P85 F4 Law

2456. Keyser, W., R. Windle, and H. Van de Kar. 1978 In W. KEyser and R. Windle, ed(s). The Netherlands, Volume 6 in Public Enterprise in the EEC. Leiden: Sijthoff and Noordhoff. /Netherlands /Economic analysis /Law /Employment /Investment /Financial performance /JX 1982 P85 F4 Law

2457. Keyser, W., and R. Windle. 1978 In W. Keyser and R. Windle, ed(s). United Kingdom and Ireland, Volume 7 in Public Enterprise in the EEC. Leiden: Sijthoff and Noordhoff. /United Kingdom /Ireland /Economic history /Control process /Law /JX 1982 P85 F4 Law

2458. Keyser, William, and Ralph Windle, eds. 1978 Public Enterprise in the EEC. Leiden: Sijthoff & Noordhoff. /European Economic Community /JX 1982 P85 K4 Law

2459. Khadka, Narayan. 1981 "The Development of Public Sector Enterprises." Lok Udyog (New Delhi), V. 15, No. 2, pp. 67-76. /India /Economic history /354.54 L836 PCL

2460. Khalfina, E. 1959 "The State Enterprise under the New Conditions of Industrial Management." Problems of Economics V. 3, pp. 39-43. /Union of Soviet Socialist Reps. /Management / 330.5 V899T

2461. Khalil, K. H. 1965 "Incentives and Productivity in the Public Sector." Egypte Contemporaine (Cairo), /Egypt /Incentive systems /Productivity / 962.05 Eg98r

2462. Khalil, K. H. 1967 "Contrôle des projets et organismes publiques dans les économies socialistes." Egypte Contemporaine (Cairo), No. 329, pp. 73-132. /Egypt /Socialist economy /Control process / 962.05 Eg98r

2463. Khamis, Shafiq. 1979 "Management and Training in Public Enterprises: Country Report of Jordan." Paper presented at the International Seminar on Management and Training in Public Enterprises in Developing Countries, Ljubljana, Yugoslavia, 1-13 October. Ljubljana: ICPE. /Jordan /Management /Training

2464. Khan, A. F. 1971 "Social Responsibilities of Public Enterprises." Lok Udyog (New Delhi), V. 5, No. 5, pp. 453-456. /India /Social welfare policy /Goal setting /354.54 L836 PCL

2465. Khan, Irshad H. 1980 "An Overview of the System and Problems of Management Development in Public Enterprises in Pakistan: Country Report." Paper presented at the Expert Group Meeting on the Research Projects on Education and Training in Public

Enterprises in Developing Countries, Ljubljana, Yugoslavia, 17-22 March. Ljubljana: ICPE. /Pakistan /Training /Management

2466. Khan, Irshad H. 1981 "Management Training and Development in Public Enterprises." Public Enterprise V. 1, pp. 68-71. /Management /Training /OPSS

2467. Khan, Irshad H. 1981 "Training Trainers." Paper presented at the Regional Workshop on Management Training and Development in Public Enterprises of Developing Countries, Karachi, Pakistan, 5-15 January. Ljubljana: ICPE. /Training /Management

2468. Khan, Irshad H., Shahiruddin Alvi, and Stane Mozina, eds. 1982 Management Training and Development in Public Enterprises. Ljubljana: ICPE. /Training /Management

2469. Khan, M. Y. 1981 "Development Banking - The Indian Experience." Lok Udyog (New Delhi), V. 15, No. 4, pp. 17-32. /India /Development banks /354.54 L836 PCL

2470. Khan, M. Y. 1981 "Life Insurance Corporation of India and Capital Market." Lok Udyog (New Delhi), V. 14, No. 10, pp. 35-48. /India /Insurance industry /Case studies /354.54 L836 PCL

2471. Khan, Mohd. Asif Ali. 1979 "Pricing Policy of Public Enterprises vis-a-vis their Social Responsibilities." Lok Udyog (New Delhi), V. 13, No. 9, pp. 43-46. /India /Price policy /Social welfare policy /354.54 L836 PCL

2472. Khan, Mohd. Asif Ali. 1980 "Pattern of Investment in Public Enterprises." Lok Udyog (New Delhi), V. 14, No. 7, pp. 45-52. /India /Investment /354.54 L836 PCL

2473. Khan, Mohd. Asif Ali. 1981 "Role of Public Enterprises vis-a-vis Growth with Stability." Lok Udyog (New Delhi), V. 15, No. 1, pp. 3-10. /India /Economic growth policy /Economic history /354.54 L836 PCL

2474. Khan, Mohmood Ali. 1980 "Pricing Policy in the Public Enterprises." Paper presented at the International Workshop on Pricing Policies and Public Enterprises, Ljubljana, Yugoslavia, 26-30 May. Ljubljana: ICPE. /Price policy

2475. Khan, Nurul Islam. 1980 "A Case Experience of Bangladesh in Acquiring Foreign Technology." Paper presented at the International Workshop on Preparations and Negotiations of Technology Transfer Agreements for Public Enterprises in Developing Countries, Ljubljana, Yugoslavia, 27-31 October. Ljubljana: ICPE. /Bangladesh /Technology transfer /Case studies

2476. Khandelwal, N. M. 1979 "Human Resource Accounting - A Case Study of Bharat Heavy Electricals Ltd." Lok Udyog (New Delhi), V. 13, No. 9, pp. 7-10. /India /Personnel management /Case studies /354.54 L836 PCL

2477. Khandwalla, Pradip N. n.d. "Managerial and Organizational Determinants of the Performance of Indian Corporate Public Sector Enterprises." Ahmedabad: Indian Institute of Management. /India /Financial performance /Evaluation /Management /OPSS

2478. Khanna, K. C. 1980 "Kudremukh Iron Ore Project - Challenge in Construction Management." Lok Udyog (New Delhi), V. 14, No. 2, pp. 21-32. /India /Project management /Mining industry /Construction industry /Case studies /354.54 L836

2479. Kharchi, Djamel. 1983 "L'entreprise publique peut-elle être le champ d'expérimentation de nouveaux rapports sociaux?" Paper presented at the 19th International Congress of Administrative Sciences, West Berlin, 19-23 Sept. /Algeria /Organization behavior /OPSS

2480. Khatian, K. M. 1981 "Experience in Management Training and Development in Public Enterprises in Pakistan." Paper presented at the Regional Workshop on Management Training and Development on Public Enterprises in Developing Countries, Karachi, Pakistan, 5-15 January. Ljubljana: ICPE. /Pakistan /Training /Management

2481. Khedr, Y. 1968 Management and Organization of Public Organizations in UAR. Cairo: Institute of National Planning. /Egypt /Management /Organization formation

2482. Khera, Sucha Singh. 1960 "Delegation and Accountability." Indian Journal of Public Administration (New Delhi), V. 7, No. 1. /India /Accountability / JA 26 I55 Pub Aff

2483. Khera, Sucha Singh. 1961 "Government and Public Enterprises: Problems in Communication and Control." Indian Journal of Public Administration (New Delhi), V. 7, No. 3, pp. 331-344. /India /Control process /JA 26 I55 Pub Aff

2484. Khera, Sucha Singh. 1963 Government in Business. London: Asia Publishing House; New Delhi: Indian Institute of Public Administration. /India /Public administration / 338.954 K528

2485. Khera, Sucha Singh. 1964 Management and Control in Public Enterprise. New York: Asia Publishing House. /India /Management /Control process / 338.954 K528g PCL

2486. Khera, Sucha Singh. 1968 "Legal and Organizational Forms of Public Enterprise." Organization and Administration of Public Enterprises. New York: United Nations, Department of Economic and Social Affairs. pp. 146-156. /Law /Structural characteristics

2487. Khera, Sucha Singh. 1975 "The Public Sector and National Objectives." In R. C. Dutt and Raj K. Nigam, ed(s). Towards Commanding Heights. New Delhi: Vivek Joshi. pp. 46-70. /India /Goal setting /HD 4293 T68 PCL

2488. Khera, Sucha Singh. 1981 "Socio-Economic Indicators for Performance Evaluation of Public Enterprises." Paper presented at the Expert Group Meeting on Performance

Criteria and the Implementation of Performance Evaluation Systems in Public Enterprises in Developing Countries, Ljubljana, Yugoslavia, 23-27 November. Ljubljana: ICPE. /Evaluation

2489. Kiapi, A. 1971 The Parastatal Bodies in Uganda: Types, Characteristics, Classifications and Functions. Makerere. Uganda: Institute of Social Research. /Uganda /Taxonomy /East Africa

2490. Kibria, M. G. 1980 "Investment Criteria and Investment Decision-Making Processes: Country Paper of Bangladesh." Paper presented at the International Workshop on Investment Criteria and Investment Decision-Making Processes, Ljubljana, Yugoslavia, 20-24 October. Ljubljana: ICPE. /Bangladesh /Investment

2491. Kicks, L. 1963 "La réglementation des emprunts dans les industries des énergétiques en Grande Bretagne." Annals de Finances Publiques (Paris), pp. 563-572. /United Kingdom /Energy utility industry /Law

2492. Kidwai, Waris R. 1976 "Public Enterprises in West European Countries." Lok Udyog (New Delhi), V. 10, No. 8, pp. 61-68. /European Economic Community /354.54 L836 PCL

2493. Killick, Tony. 1981 "The Role of the Public Sector in the Industrialization of African Developing Countries." Paper presented at the Expert Group Meeting on the Changing Role and Function of the Public Industrial Sector in Development, Vienna, Austria, 5-9 October. Vienna: UNIDO. /Africa /Industrialization

2494. Kimble, D. 1969 Memorandum on the Organization and Management of Public Enterprises in Africa. Tangier: CAFRAD. /Africa /Organization formation /Management

2495. Kimble, E. 1933 "The Tennessee Valley Project." Land Economics V. 9, pp. 325-339. /United States of America /River valley development projects / 305 J824 PCL

2496. King, J. A. 1967 Economic Development Projects and Their Appraisal. London: Oxford University Press. /Economic development /Evaluation /Economic analysis / 332.15 K583e

2497. Kinze, W. 1960 "Public Undertakings Administered by Municipal and Rural Communities." Annals of Collective Economy V. 31, pp. 437-445. /Austria /Management /Local government /330.5 An73

2498. Kirschen, E. S. n.d. Conduite financière des entreprises privées et publiques. Amiens, France: Les Editions Scientifiques et Littéraires /France /Private sector /Financing

2499. Kirtiputra, Pharani. 1980 "Pre-Course Assignment." Paper presented at the Interregional Seminar on Training Management in Public Enterprises in Developing Countries, Ljubljana, Yugoslavia, Sept. 29-Oct. 10. Ljubljana: ICPE.

/Training /Management

2500. Kirtiputra, Pharani. 1981 "NIDA's Experience in Training of Public Enterprise Managers." Paper presented at the Regional Workshop on the Evaluation of Training Packages for Public Enterprise Managers, Bangkok, Thailand, 10-14 August. Ljubljana: ICPE. /Training /Management

2501. Kishore, Braj. 1978 "Working Capital Policy - A General Framework for Analysis." Lok Udyog (New Delhi), V. 11, No. 11, pp. 9-16. /India /Financial performance /Working capital /354.54 L836 PCL

2502. Kishore, Kamal. 1980 "Progress in Partnership: A Case Study of Labour Participation in Bhilai Steel." Lok Udyog (New Delhi), V. 14, No. 6, pp. 47-54. /India /Worker management participation /Steel industry / 354.54 L836 PCL

2503. Kita, K. 1961 Public Enterprise. Tokyo: Ooyokeizai Shino-Sha. /Japan

2504. Kiyohiko, Yoshitake. 1973 An Introduction to Public Enterprise in Japan. Tokyo: Nippon Hyoron SHA. /Japan

2505. Klatzmann, J. 1957 "Originalité de l'économie Yougoslave." Revue Economique (Paris), No. 3. /Yugoslavia /Economic system / 330.5 R3282 PCL

2506. Kleber, Klaus. 1974 "Bom crédito para as empresas nacionais." Industria e Desenvolvimento (São Paulo), V. 7, No. 9, pp. 19-20. /Credit policy / G333.0981 In2 LAC

2507. Kleindorfer, Paul R., and Murat R. Sertel. 1980 "Labor-Management and Co-determination in Regulated Monopolies." In Bridger M. Mitchell and Paul R. Kleindorfer, ed(s). Regulated Industries and Public Enterprise. Lexington, Ma.: D.C. Heath and Company, Lexington Books. pp. 139-167. /Labor relations /Economic theory /OPSS

2508. Kleingarner, Archie. 1973 Collective Bargaining Between Salaried Professionals and Public Sector Management. Los Angeles: UCLA, Institute of Industrial Relations. /United States of America /Labor relations /Collective bargaining /Management /KF 3409 P77 K5 Law

2509. Klemencic, Vlado. 1977 "Socio-Economic Development in Yugoslavia." Paper presented at the International Seminar on Management and Training in Public Enterprises in Developing Countries, Ljubljana, Yugoslavia, 10-28 October. Ljubljana: ICPE. /Yugoslavia /Training /Management

2510. Kliemt, Walter. 1979 "Current Electricity Pricing Peculiarities in Federal Republic of Germany." Annals of Public and Cooperative Economy V. 50, No. 3, pp. 61-80. /Germany, Federal Rep. of /Electrical utility industry /Price policy /330.5 An73

2511. Kliksberg, Bernardo. 1975 "Propuesta de un modelo metodológico para la investigación sistemática del complejo de empresas públicas en países de América Latina." Revista de la Asociación Interamericana de Presupuesto Público V. 2, No. 7, pp. 119-141. /Latin America /Methodology /Comparative analysis /OPSS

2512. Klindera, Ferdinand. 1935 "The Czechoslovak Grain Company, Prague: Its Functions, Its Work and the Results." Annals of Collective Economy V. 11, No. 1, pp. 56-63. /Czechoslovakia /Agricultural sector / Case studies / 330.5 An 73

2513. Knapp, V. 1961 "Quelques remarques au sujet des entreprises nationales en Tchécoslovaquie." Revue du Droit Public et de la Science Politique en France et a l´Etranger (Paris), V. 77, No. 4, pp. 737-753. /Czechoslovakia / Law

2514. Knauss, Fritz. 1977 "Federal Enterprises as a Boost to the Economy?" Annals of Public and Cooperative Economy V. 49, No. 4, pp. 429-434. /Germany, Federal Rep. of /330.5 An73

2515. Knàuthe, E. 1957 Der Finanzplan des Volkseignen Industriebetriebes. Berlin: Verlag die Wirtschaft. /Germany, Federal Rep. of /Industrial sector /Financing

2516. Knezevic, Radovan. 1979 "Introduction of Marketing into Iron and Steel Company: Steel Industry, Yugoslav Case Study." Paper presented at the Interregional Workshop "Developing Problem Solving Skills in Public Enterprises," Ljubljana, Yugoslavia, 2-17 April. Ljubljana: ICPE. /Yugoslavia /Steel industry /Marketing /Case studies

2517. Kock, Karin. 1950 "L´Entreprise d´Etat Belge." Societé Belge d´Etudes et d´Expansion (Liège, Belgium), No. 144, pp. 124-129. /Belgium /Economic analysis

2518. Kohli, U. K. 1969 "Criteria for Project Evaluation." Lok Udyog (New Delhi), V. 3, No. 4, pp. 357-363. /India /Evaluation / 354.54 L836

2519. Kohli, U. K. 1979 "Monitoring, Evaluation, and Control." Lok Udyog (New Delhi), V. 13, No. 4, pp. 5-12. /India /Evaluation /Control process /354.54 L836 PCL

2520. Kolaja, Jiri Thomas. 1965 Workers´ Councils: The Yugoslav Experience. London: Tavistock. /Yugoslavia /Worker self management / 658.3152 K83p

2521. Kolm, Serge-Christophe. 1971 Prix publiques optimaux. Paris: CNRS-DUNOD. /France / Price policy

2522. Konopnicki, Maurice. 1971 "The Public and Cooperative Sectors in Israel." Annals of Public and Cooperative Economy V. 42, pp. 47-71. /Israel /Cooperatives / 330.5 An73

2523. Konvalinka, Vojan, Dusan Bilandzic, and Ivan Maksimovic. 1979 "Preliminary Yugoslav National Report on the Role of the Public Sector." Paper presented at the International Meeting on the Role of the Public Sector in Developing Countries, 2nd, Ljubljana, Yugoslavia, 2-7 April. Ljubljana: ICPE. /Yugoslavia

2524. Konvalinka, Vojan. 1977 "Proposed Statistical Tables and Introduction to the Tables." Paper presented at the Meeting of the International Research Project `The Role of the Public Sector in Developing Countries,´ 1st, Ljubljana, Yugoslavia, 7-11 December. Ljubljana: ICPE. /Statistics

2525. Kornai, J. 1959 Overcentralization in Economic Administration: A Critical Analysis Based on Experience in Hungarian Light Industry. London: Oxford University Press. /Hungary /Centralization /Management /Manufacturing industry /Evaluation / Public administration / 338.94391 K842gTk

2526. Koromo, Francis A. 1974 "Systems of Planning and Planning Machinery in the Public Enterprises: National Paper of Tanzania." Paper presented at the International Seminar ´74: Planning in Public Enterprises in Developing Countries, Ljubljana, Yugoslavia, 23 Sept. - 9 Oct. Ljubljana: ICPE. /Tanzania /Planning process

2527. Koromo, Francis A. 1974 Sistemas de planificación en las empresas públicas. Ljubljana: ICPE. /Planning process

2528. Kosakul, Nonglak. 1980 "Policies and Practices of Public Enterprise Planning in Thailand." Paper presented at the Regional Workshop on Corporate Planning in Public Enterprises in the Asian and Pacific Region, Luala Lumpur, Malaysia, 17-22 November. Ljubljana: ICPE. /Thailand /Planning process

2529. Kosakul, Nonglak. 1981 "Financial Profitability and Losses in Thailand." Paper presented at the International Workshop on Financial Profitability and Losses in Public Enterprises, Ljubljana, Yugoslavia, 1-5 June. Ljubljana: ICPE. /Thailand /Profits /Public financing

2530. Koshal, Rajindar K. 1971 "Marginal Cost Analysis of a Nationalized Passenger Road Transport System." Land Economics V. 47, No. 2. /India /Highways and roads /Costs /305 J824 PCL

2531. Kostecki, M. M. 1979 International Implications of State Trading by the Advanced Countries. Les Cahiers du CETAI, No. 79-04 Montreal: Ecole des Hautes Etudes Comerciales. /State trading organizations /OPSS

2532. Kostecki, M. M. 1981 "State Trading." In Raymond Vernon and Yair Aharoni, ed(s). State-Owned Enterprise in the Western Economies. New York: St. Martin´s Press. pp. 170-183. /State trading organizations /HD 3850 S79 PCL

2533. Kostecki, M. M. 1981 "State Trading by the Advanced and Developing Countries: The Background." In M. M. Kostecki, ed(s). State Trading in International Markets. New York: St. Martin´s Press. pp. 6-21. /State trading organizations /Comparative analysis /HF 1410.5 S7 1981 M

2534. Kostecki, M. M. 1981 "State Trading in Agricultural Products by the Advanced Countries." In M. M. Kostecki, ed(s). State Trading in International Markets. New York: St. Martin´s

Press. pp. 22-54. /State trading organizations /Agricultural services /HF 1410.5 S7 1981 M

2535. Kostecki, M. M. (ed.). 1981 State Trading in International Markets: Theory and Practice of Industrialized and Developing Countries. New York: St Martin's Press. /International trade /Agricultural sector /State trading organizations /Oil industry /Mining industry /Food industry /HF 1410.5 S7 1981 M

2536. Kotany, L. 1924 "The Socialization of Industries." American Economic Review V. 14, pp. 127-139. /Industrial sector /330.5 Am312

2537. Koulytvhizky, S. 1971 "Worker's Management in Algeria." Cooperative Information (Geneva), No. 1, pp.'31-37. /Algeria /Worker management participation

2538. Kovak, P. 1957 "Siete años de experiencia de los organos de autogestión de los trabajadores." Le Nouveau Droit (Belgrade), V. 7, No. 2-4. /Worker self management

2539. Kowalska, H. 1957 "Productivity in the Planned Economies of Eastern Europe." Far Eastern Economic Review V. 22, pp. 513-517. /Eastern Europe /Socialist economy /Productivity /330.95 F223

2540. Kozminski, A. K. 1970 "Le rôle du manager en économie socialiste." Economies et Sociétés (Paris), V. 4, No. 1, pp. 241-261. /Socialist economy /Management

2541. Kralj, Janko. 1976 "Decision-Making Simulation as a Means of Management Training." Paper presented at the International Seminar on Management and Training in Public Enterprises in Developing Countries, Ljubljana, Yugoslavia, Sept. 21-Oct. 2. Ljubljana: ICPE. /Decision making process /Training /Management /Simulation

2542. Kralj, Janko. 1977 "Management Development and Training of Managers for Public Enterprises." Paper presented at the International Seminar on Management and Training in Public Enterprises in Developing Countries, Ljubljana, Yugoslavia, 10-28 October. Ljubljana: ICPE. /Training /Management / Also presented at the International Seminar on Management and Training in Public Enterprises in Developing Countries, Ljubljana, Yugoslavia, Sep. 18- Oct. 6, 1978.

2543. Kralj, Janko. 1978 "Information Design for Efficiency Control of Organizational Units in a Public Enterprise." Paper presented at the Workshop on Information Systems for the Evaluation of Business Efficency in Public Enterprises in Developing Countries, Ljubljana, Yugoslavia, 13-18 Nov. Ljubljana: ICPE. /Information system /Economic efficiency /Control process /Management

2544. Kramer, Fred Allen. 1969 "The Food Corporation of India; A Study of Administrative Development." Ph.D. Dissertation, Syracuse University. /India /Food industry

2545. Krausucki, H. 1969 Syndicats et lutte de classes. Paris: Editions Sociales. /France /Trade unions

2546. Krbec, I. 1957 "La gestión obrera y el sistema constitutional." Le Nouveau Droit (Belgrade), V. 7, No. 2-4. /Worker management participation /Constitutional law

2547. Kreacic, Vladimir. 1977 "Training of Internal Consultants in Public Enterprises." Paper presented at the International Seminar on Management and Training in Public Enterprises in Developing Countries, Ljubljana, Yugoslavia, 10-28 October. Ljubljana: ICPE. /Training /Management / Also presented at the International Seminar on Management and Training in Public Enterprises in Developing Countries, Sep. 18- Oct. 6, 1978, Ljubljana, Yugoslavia.

2548. Kreacic, Vladimir. 1979 "An Approach towards Performance Improvement through Internal Consultancy in Public Enterprises in Developing Countries." Paper presented at the Expert Group Meeting on Development of Methodologies for Training Internal Consultants in Public Enterprises in Developing Countries, Ljubljana, Yugoslavia, 10-14 December. Ljubljana: ICPE. /Evaluation /Management /Economic efficiency /Also presented at the International Seminar on Management and Training in Public Enterprises in Developing Countries, Ljubljana, OCt. 1-13, 1979.

2549. Kreacic, Vladimir. 1979 "Identification of the System's Bottleneck, Analysis, Design of New Methods and Implementation: Iron and Steel Industry, Yugoslav Case Study." Paper presented at the Interregional Workshop "Developing Problem Solving Skills on Public Enterprises," Ljubljana, Yugoslavia, 2-17 April. Ljubljana: ICPE. /Yugoslavia /Steel industry /Case studies /Evaluation /System analysis

2550. Kreacic, Vladimir. 1981 "`OPTIMA´ in Somalia." Public Enterprise V. 2, No. 2, pp. 13-15. /Somalia /Management /Economic efficiency /OPSS

2551. Kreacic, Vladimir. 1981 "Possible Courses for Internal Management Action in Cigarette and Match Factory (Warshadda Sigaarka iyo Taraqua)." Paper presented at the National Workshop of Public Enterprises, Mogadishu, Somalia, 9-13 Aug. Ljubljana: ICPE. /Cigarette manufacturing industry /Match manufacturing industry / Management /Somalia / Later published in Public Enterprise. Vol. 2, No. 2, pp. 17-24. /OPSS

2552. Kremser, Miha. 1980 "Licensee Evaluation of Payments in Pharmaceutical Industry." Paper presented at the International Workshop on Preparations and Negatiations of Technology Transfer Agreements for Public Enterprises in Developing Countries, Ljubljana, Yugoslavia, 27-31 October. Ljubljana: ICPE. /Pharmaceutical industry /Technology transfer

2553. Kreuzberger, Hans. 1961 "Oil in Austria." Annals of Collective Economy V. 32, pp. 190-203. /Austria /Oil industry / 330.5 An73

2554. Krishnamacharyulu, C. S. G., and H. Lajipathi Rai. 1982 "Pollution Control by Public Enterprises." Lok Udyog (New Delhi), V. 15. No. 10, pp. 49-54. /Pollution /Environmental policy /354.54 L836 PCL

2555. Krishnaswamy, K. S. 1958 "The Hindustan Housing Factory." Indian Journal of Public Administration (New Delhi), V. 4, No. 2. /Hindustan, India /Housing industry /Case studies /JA 26 I55 Pub Aff

2556. Krishnaswamy, K. S. 1981 "What Ails the Public Sector?" Eastern Economist V. 76, No. 2, pp. 70-75. /India

2557. Kristjanson, K. 1954 "Institutional Arrangements in Water Resource Development." Land Economics V. 30, pp. 347-362. /Planning process /Water resources development /305 J824 PCL

2558. Kristjanson, K. 1958 "Organization for River Basin Development: The Columbia River." Journal of Farm Economics V. 40, pp. 1705-1716. /United States of America /Public works policy / River valley development projects

2559. Kristjanson, K. 1968 "Crown Corporations: Administrative Responsability and Public Accountability." Canadian Public Administration (Ontario), V. 11, No. 4, pp. 454-459. /Canada /Administrative management /Accountability / 350.5 C16

2560. Kroeger, Carroll V., and James R. Rawls. 1975 "Managerial Attitudes towards Government Roles in Electricity and Gas." Public Utilities Fortnightly V. 96, No. 4. /United States of America /Electrical utility industry /Gas utility industry /Management /388.9 P97

2561. Kruger, A. 1974 "Bargaining in the Public Sector: Some Canadian Experiments." International Labour Review (Geneva), V. 109, No. 4, pp. 319-31. /Canada /Labor relations /Collective bargaining /331.05 In81 PCL /HD4811 I65 Pub Aff

2562. Kruijt, Dirk. 1982 "State, State Enterprise and Labor in Peru. CENTROMIN and the Peruvian Mining Sector During the Military Junta (1968-1980)." Utrecht, Netherlands: Center for Comparative Socioeconomic Studies. /Peru /Mining industry /Labor relations /Economic history /OPSS

2563. Krutilla, J. V. 1958 "River Basin Development: Planning and Evaluation." Journal of Farm Economics V. 40, pp. 1674-1689. /United States of America /Public works policy

2564. Krutilla, J. V. 1958 "Water Resources Development: The Regional Incidence of Costs and Gains." Proceedings of the Regional Science Association V. 4, pp. 273-300. /Water resources development /Regional development /Cost benefit analysis

2565. Krutilla, J. V. and Otto Eckstein. 1958 Multiple Purpose River Development: Studies in Applied Economic Analysis. Baltimore, Md.: Johns Hopkins University Press. /River valley development projects /Economic analysis /333.91 R312m

2566. Ksontini, Ezzedine. 1979 "Systems of Information and Control in Public Enterprises in Tunisia." Paper presented at the Interregional Workshop on Control Systems for Public Enterprises in Developing Countries, Ljubljana, Yugoslavia, 9-13 July. Ljubljana: ICPE. /Tunisia /Control process /Information system

2567. Kuchhal, Suresh Chandra. 1966 The Industrial Economy of India. Allahabad, India: Chatanya Publishing House. /India /Industrial economy / 330.954 K952i

2568. Kuhn, Arthur K. 1945 "Extension of Sovereign Inmunity to Government Owned Comercial Corporations." American Journal of International Law pp. 772-775. /International law /Law /341.05 Am35

2569. Kuhn, Tillo E. 1962 Public Enterprise Economics and Transport Problems. Berkeley, Cal.: University of California Press. /United States of America /Public utility industry /Highways and roads /338.74 K955p

2570. Kuhn, Tillo E. 1962 Empresas públicas, planificación de proyectos y desarrollo económico. Tegucigalpa, Honduras: Banco Central de Honduras. /Honduras /Planning process /Economic development /Economic analysis /G380.1622 K955pS LAC

2571. Kuiper, E. T. 1972 "The Promotional Role and Managerial Responsibilities of a Development Finance Company." Development Digest V. 10, No. 4, pp. 14-24. /Marketing /Management /Development financing

2572. Kukovica, Anton, and Stane Mozina, eds. 1980 La gestion de la formation dans les entreprises publiques dans les pays en voie de développement: compte rendu d´un séminaire du 3 au 15 mars, 1980. Ljubljana: ICPE. /Planning process /Developing nations

2573. Kukovica, Anton. 1978 "Le rôle, le système et les méthodes d´éducation et de formation des cadres dans les entreprises publiques." Paper presented at the Séminaire international sur la gestion et la formation dans les entreprises publiques dans les pays en voie de développement, Ljubljana, Yugoslavia, 6-17 November. Ljubljana: ICPE. /Training

2574. Kukovica, Anton. 1980 "Les aspects financiers de la formation." Paper presented at the Séminaire international sur la gestion et la formation dans les entreprises publiques dans les pays en voie de développement, Ljubljana, Yugoslavia, 6-17 November. Ljubljana: ICPE. /Financing /Training

2575. Kukovica, Anton. 1980 "L´Education orientée en Yugoslavie." Paper presented at the Séminaire international sur la gestion et la formation dans les entreprise publiques dans les pays en voie de développement, Ljubljana, Yugoslavia, 6-17 November. Ljubljana: ICPE. /Training /Management

2576. Kukovica, Anton. 1980 "L'Evaluation de la formation." Paper presented at the Séminaire international sur la gestion et la formation dans les entreprises publiques dans les pays en voie de développement, Ljubljana, Yugoslavia, 6-17 November. Ljubljana: ICPE. /Training /Efficacy /Management /Evaluation

2577. Kukovica, Anton. 1980 "Les politiques et stratégies éducatives." Paper presented at the Séminaire international sur la gestion et la formation dans les entreprises publiques dans les pays en voie de développement, Ljubljana, Yugoslavia, 6-17 November. Ljubljana: ICPE. /Training

2578. Kulkarni, G. R. 1979 "Evaluating Public Sector Performance and the STC." Lok Udyog (New Delhi), V. 13, No. 8, pp. 35-40. /India /Economic efficiency /Financial performance /Evaluation /Case studies /354.54 L836 PCL

2579. Kulkarni, Govind Manik. 1963 "The Development of Government Corporation: A Comparative Study in the United States and India." Ph.D. Dissertation, Washington University /India /United States of America /United Kingdom

2580. Kull, Donald C. 1949 "Decentralized Budget Administration in the Tennessee Valley Authority." Public Administrative Review V. 1, No. 1, pp. 30-35. /United States of America /Decentralized authority /Budgetary process /River valley development projects /Public administration

2581. Kumar, G. 1949 "A Note on Some Problems Arising Out of Payment of Compensation." Indian Journal of Economics V. 29, pp. 399-402. /Public financing /Wages / 330.5 In2

2582. Kumar, Krishna. 1982 "Problems in Designing Information System for Commercial Banks." Lok Udyog (New Delhi), V. 16, No. 9, pp. 41-48. /India /Information system /Banking system /354.54 L836 PCL

2583. Kumar, Krishna. 1982 "Motivational Strategies in Indian Corporate Sector." Lok Udyog (New Delhi), V. 16, No. 2, pp. 3-12. /India /Management /Motivation /354.54 L836 PCL

2584. Kumar, Lav Raj. 1980 "Pricing and Performance Evaluation in Public Enterprises." Paper presented at the International Workshop on Pricing Policies in Public Enterprises, Ljubljana, Yugoslavia, 26-30 May. Ljubljana: ICPE. /Price policy /Evaluation /Also published in Public Enterprise, Vol. 1, No. 2(1980), pp. 46-53.

2585. Kumar, N. 1969 Bank Nationalization in India: A Symposium. Bombay: Lalvani Publishing House. /India /Nationalization /Financial institutions / HG 3284 K85

2586. Kumar, P. 1966 "State Small Industries Corporations in India: A Comparative Factual Review." Atha Vijñana (India), pp. 259-270. /India /Industrial sector /Evaluation

2587. Kumaramangalam, S. Mohan. 1975 "New Model for Governmental Administration of Industry." In R. C. Dutt and Raj K. Nigam, ed(s). Towards Commanding Heights. New Delhi: Vivek Joshi.

pp. 1-21. /India /Control process /Holding company /Parliament /HD 4293 T68 PCL

2588. Kunkuta, Musesha C. J. 1980 "Experience of Republic of Zambia in Acquiring Foreign Technology." Paper presented at the International Workshop on Preparations and Negotiations of Technology Transfer Agreements for Public Enterprises in Developing Countries, Ljubljana, Yugoslavia, 27-31 October. Ljubljana: ICPE. /Zambia /Technology transfer

2589. Kushawa, D. S. 1963 "Indian Industrial Policy and Public Enterprise." Indian Journal of Economics V. 43, No. 171. /India /Industrial sector /Policy analysis / 330.5 In2

2590. Kuspilic, Ivo. 1974 "Planification par voie de développement de `Lavcevic´ depuis 1966." International Seminar ´74: Planning in Public Enterprises in Developing Countries, Ljubljana, Yugoslavia, Sept. 23-Oct. 9. Ljubljana: ICPE. /Planning process / Case studies

2591. Kyesimira, Y. 1968 The Public Sector and Development in East Africa. Makerere, Uganda: Institute of Social Research. /East Africa /Economic development /Kenya /Tanzania /Uganda

2592. L´Heriteau, Marie-France. 1972 Pourquoi des entreprises publiques? Paris: Presses Universitaires de France. /Economic analysis /France /European Economic Community /Nationalization /OPSS

2593. L´Huillier, J. 1949 La propriété des biens transférés aux établissements publiques de gaz et des combustibles mineraux. V. 129. /Law /France /Public utility industry /Nationalization

2594. Labaíde Otermín, Francisco. 1958 "EL INI, ese gran desconocido." Revista de Información del Instituto Nacional de Industria (Madrid), /Spain /Holding company

2595. Labaíde Otermín, Francisco. 1962 "Problemática de la empresa pública." La Empresa (Madrid), pp. 141-188. /Spain

2596. Labra, Armando. 1980 "Public Enterprise in an Underdeveloped and Dependent Economy." In William J. Baumol, ed(s). Public and Private Enterprise in a Mixed Economy. New York: St. Martin´s Press. pp. 36-40. /Economic analysis /HD 3842 P87

2597. Labrum, J. Harry. 1952 "Delaware River Port Authority." The Authority pp. 14-18. /United States of America /Port authority

2598. Labys, Walter C. 1981 "The Role of State Trading in Mineral Commodity Markets." In M. M. Kostecki, ed(s). State Trading in International Markets. New York: St. Martin´s Press. pp. 78-102. /State trading organizations /HF 1410.5 S7 1981 M. /Also found in Les Cahiers du Cetai, no. 79-06, April, 1979 /OPSS

2599. Laca, Ivan. 1981 "The League of Communists and Self-Management." In ed(s). Socialist Thought and Practice

V. 21, No. 1, pp. 38-48. /Yugoslavia /Political party program /Worker self management / 335.05 So136 PCL

2600. Lacina, Ferdinand. 1976 In ed(s). The Development of the Austrian Public Sector Since World War II. Austin, Tex.: OPSS Technical Papers Series, No. 7. /Austria /OPSS

2601. Lacombe, Américo, and L. Masset. 1966 "A imunidade tributária das sociedades de économie mista." Revista de Administracão de Empresas (Rio de Janeiro), V. 6, No. 21. pp. 129-158. /Brazil /Mixed enterprises /Taxation policy /G350.5 R3261 LAC

2602. Lacson, T. V. 1967 "Tax Exemptions of Government Corporations." Philippine Journal of Public Administration (Manila), V. 11, No. 2, pp. 174-185. /Philippines /Taxation policy

2603. Ladhari, N. 1983 "Labour-management relations in Tunisian public enterprises." Labour-management relations in public enterprises in Africa. Geneva: ILO. pp. 57-84. /Labor relations /Personnel management /Tunisia /Africa /OPSS

2604. Lafer, Celso. 1973 "Estado e sociedade no Brasil: problemas de planejamento." Argumento (São Paulo), No. 3, pp. 33-44. /Brazil /Planning process

2605. Lagarde, G. n.d. "De la société anonyme a l´entreprise publique." Le droit privé français au milieu du XX Siècle /France /Law

2606. Lagos, G. 1968 "Empresas multinacionais: aspectos socioeconomicos, jurídicos e institucionais." Las inversiones multinacionales, públicas y privadas en el desarrollo y la integración de América Latina: aspectos jurídicos e institucionales de las inversiones de alcance multinacional. Washington, D. C.: Inter-American Development Bank. pp. 211-247. /Latin America /Multinational corporations / HC 125 I6924 1968 LAC

2607. Lagunilla, A. 1969 "Neocapitalismo, fiducia de gestión y planeamiento." Comercio Exterior (Mexico City), V. 19, No. 6, pp. 449-451. /Mexico /HF 3238 C658 LAC

2608. Lahaya, R. 1961 Les entreprises publiques au Maroc. Essai d´analyse des forme d´action de la puissance publique. Paris: Librairie de Medicis. /Morocco

2609. Laid, A. 1969 Le rôle des entreprises publiques en Algérie. Mauritius: UNECA. /Algeria

2610. Laidin, Ahmad Zaidee bin. 1981 "In-House Management Training in the National Electricity Board, Malaysia." Paper presented at the Regional Workshop on Management Training and Development in Public Enterprises of Developing Countries. Karachi, Pakistan, 5-15 January. Ljubljana: ICPE. /Malaysia /Training /Management /Electrical utility industry /Business regulation policy

2611. Lakdawala, D. T. 1960 "Contribution of Public Enterprises." Indian Economic Journal (Bombay), V. 7, No. 4, pp. 395-404. /India /Evaluation / 330.5 In16

2612. Lakhera, M. K. 1968 "Production Functions for Public Sector Manufacture in India." Indian Economic Review (New Delhi), V. 3, No. 2, pp. 149-155. /India /Econometric model /Productivity /Manufacturing industry / 330.5 In18

2613. Lakhera, M. L. 1969 "Capital Formation in the Public Sector in India." Indian Journal of Economics V. 49, No. 194, pp. 223-235. /India /Investment / 330.5 In2

2614. Lakz, M. 1970 Autogestion ouvrière et pouvoir politique en Algérie, 1962-1965. Paris: Etudes et Documentation Internationales. /Algeria /Worker self management

2615. Lal, Deepak. 1976 "Basic Issues in Public Enterprise Policy and Tentative Framework for Individual Country Studies in Asia." Approaches to the Public Enterprise Policy in Asia on Investment, Prices and Returns Criteria. Kuala Lumpur: Asian Centre for Development Administration. pp. 162-167. /Asia /India /Planning process / HD 4276 A8 1976

2616. Lal, L. 1979 "A Study of Managerial Behaviour and Performance." Lok Udyog (New Delhi), V. 13, No. 3, pp. 17-26. /Organization behavior /India /354.54 L836 PCL

2617. Lal, R. N. 1956 "The Problem of Administration and Management in the Public Sector." Modern Review (Calcutta), V. 99, No. 6, pp. 463-466. /Public administration /Management / 059.54 M72 PCL

2618. Lal, R., and S. N. Srivastrava. 1970 "Profit Strategy in Public Sector." Lok Udyog (New Delhi), V. 3, No. 11, pp. 1281-1289. /India /Profits / 354.54 L836

2619. Laleye, Mouftaou. 1983 "Notes sur les objectifs des entreprises publiques en République Fédérale du Nigeria." Paper presented at the 19th International Congress of Administrative Sciences, West Berlin, 19-23 Sept. /Nigeria /Goal setting /Financial performance /OPSS

2620. Lambert, Paul. 1966 "Some Problems Facing a Public Undertaking." Annals of Public and Cooperative Economy V. 37, pp. 339-342. /Belgium /Cooperatives / 330.5 An73

2621. Lambert, Paul. 1968 "Survey of Public and Co-operative Economy throughout the World." Annals of Public and Cooperative Economy V. 39, No. 3, pp. 315-330. /Economic analysis / 330.5 An73

2622. Lamizana Sangou´é, El Hadj Aboubacar. 1977 "Statuts de la caisse nationale des dépots et des investissements." /Upper Volta /Savings /Law /Case studies

2623. Lamont, Douglas F. 1973 "Joining Forces with Foreign State Enterprises." Harvard Business Review V. 51, No. 4, pp. 68-79. /Mixed enterprises / HF 5001 H3

2624. Lamont, Douglas F. 1979 Foreign State Enterprises, A Threat to American Business. New York: Basic Books. /Foreign policy / HD 3850 L33 Pub Aff

2625. Land, James W. 1971 "The Role of Public Enterprise in Turkish Economic Development." In Gustav Ranis, ed(s). Government and Economic Development. New Haven: Yale University Press. pp. 53-79. /Turkey /Economic development /330.9 G746

2626. Lange, O., et al. 1960 La fuzione delle imprese pubbliche nello sviluppo economico. Milan, Italy: CIRIEC. /Italy

2627. Langendonckt Van, L. 1961 "El sector público de la electricidad en Bélgica." Revista de los Servicios Públicos /Belgium /Electrical utility industry

2628. Langer, E. 1960 "General Survey of Collective Economy in Austria." Annals of Collective Economy V. 31, pp. 382-436. /Austria /Socialist economy / 330.5 An73

2629. Langer, E. 1961 "The Dangers of Denationalization to Freedom, Security and Welfare." Annals of Collective Economy V. 32, pp. 27-75. /Nationalization

2630. Langer, E. 1964 Les nationalisations en Autriche. Liège: Faculté de Droit. /Austria /Nationalization /Law /338.9436 L262n

2631. Langer, E. 1964 "Nationalizations in Austria." Annals of Public and Cooperative Economy V. 35, No. 2-3, pp. 115-163. /Austria /Nationalization /Law / 330.5 An73

2632. Langer, E. 1964 "Le cas autrichien dans les discussions de principes relatives à la nationalisation." Annales de l´Economie Collective V. 52, No. 3, pp. 343-363. /Nationalization /Austria

2633. Langer, E. 1970 "Comentario sobre el artículo del profesor Weber." La Empresa Pública. Zaragoza, Spain: Publicaciones del Real Colegio de España en Bolonia. /Spain

2634. Langer, E., and A. Ingenito. 1966 "The Economic Importance of Public Enterprise in Belgium." Annals of Public and Cooperative Economy V. 37, pp. 65-76. /Belgium / 330.5 An73

2635. Langford, J. W. 1980 "The Identification and Classification of Federal Public Corporations: A Preface to Regime Building." Canadian Public Administration (Ontario), V. 23, No. 1, pp. 76-104. /Canada /Control process /Administrative reform /Public administration / Taxonomy / 350.5 C16

2636. Lanversin, J. de. 1962 "Le ministère des participations de l´Etat en Italie." Revue de Droit Publique et de la Science Politique en France et a l´Etranger (Paris), V. 78, No. 4, pp. 629-645. /Italy /Control process

2637. Lapajne, Ivo. 1978 "The Basis of the Self-Management System of Societal Planning and Some Practical Experiences of

Planning in Ljubljana: Theses." Paper presented at the International Workshop on Planning in Public Enterprises in Developing Countries, Ljubljana, Yugoslavia, 20-25 November. Ljubljana: ICPE. /Yugoslavia /Planning process /Worker self management

2638. Lapie, P. Q. 1925 *Les entreprises d'économie mixte.* Paris. /France /Mixed enterprises

2639. Laporte, Robert Jr. 1967 "An Analysis of a Development Strategy: Public Corporations and Resource Development in South Asia." *International Review of Administrative Sciences* V. 33, No. 4. /South Asia /Economic development /Economic analysis / JA 1 A1 I6 PCL

2640. Laporte, Robert, Jr. 1967 "Public Corporations and Resource Development in South Asia: A Comparative Analysis." Ph. D. dissertation: Syracuse University. /India /Pakistan /Sri Lanka /Natural resource policy

2641. Laporte, Robert, Jr. 1968 "Intergovernmental Change in India: Politics and Administration of the Damodar Valley Scheme." *Asian Survey* pp. 748-760. /India /River valley development projects /Public administration / Policy analysis /Case studies / DS 1 A4923

2642. Laroia, M. L. 1982 "Standardisation in Steel Industry." *Lok Udyog* (New Delhi), V. 16, No. 5, pp. 5-10. /India /Steel industry /354.54 L836 PCL

2643. Larra, Raúl. 1981 "El General Baldrich y la nacionalización del petróleo argentino." *Todo es Historia* No. 164, pp. 8-14;16-22. /Argentina /Oil industry /Nationalization /Economic history / G982.005/T569

2644. Larraz del Rio, F. 1965 *La industria siderúrgica, empresa pública.* ICE. /Steel industry

2645. Larrondo, René Labrana, and Raúl Díaz Sanhueza. 1975 *Diagnóstico general de la empresa pública en latinoamerica.* Madrid: Proyecto de Investgación. Versión Preliminar. Instituto de Estudios Economicos. /Latin America /Evaluation

2646. Lasserre, G. 1967 "Profit, the Enterprises and the General Interest." *Annals of Public and Cooperative Economy* V. 38, pp. 343-373. /Evaluation /Profits /Public interest /330.5 An73

2647. Latham, J. 1954 "Common Services in a Public Corporation." *Public Administration* (London), V. 32, pp. 274-283. /United Kingdom /Public services / 320.5 J826 PCL

2648. Latham, Lord. 1952 "London Transport." In Sir Hurbert Houldsworth, ed(s). *Efficiency in the Nationalized Industries.* London: Allen & Unwin. /United Kingdom /Mass transportation industry

2649. Lau, Alan W., and Cynthis M. Pavett. 1980 "The Nature of Managerial Work: A Comparison of Public- and Private-sector

Managers." Group and Organization Studies V. 5, No. 4, pp. 453-466. /Management /Comparative analysis /HM 134 G73

2650. Laubadére, André de. 1959 "La notion et le régime juridique des services publiques sociaux." Droit Social (Paris), No. 22. /Law /Social welfare policy /Public services

2651. Laubadére, André de. 1964 Grands services publiques et entreprises nationales. Paris: Ed. Les Cours de Droit. /France /Law

2652. Laufenberger, H. 1939 L´Intervention de l´Etat en matière économique. Paris: Librairie générale de droit et de jurisprudence. /France / 330.1 L366i

2653. Laufenberger, H. 1945 Intervención del Estado en la vida económica. Mexico City: Fondo de Cultura Económica. /France

2654. Laufenberger, H. 1951 "Peut-on indéfiniment élargir le sécteur publique? L´Expérience française." Revue Suisse d´Economie Politique et de Statistique No. 1, pp. 20-28. /France /Policy analysis

2655. Laufenberger, H. 1952 "Entreprise privée et entreprise publique." L´Actualité Economique (Montreal, Canada), pp. 293-299. /Canada /Comparative analysis /HB 3 A 185

2656. Lauger, E. 1965 "L´importance économique des entreprises publiques belges." Annales d´Economie Collective pp. 587-598. /Belgium /Evaluation

2657. Laurent, Alfred. 1950 "Les méthodes actuelles de gestion de l´Electricité de France." L´Année Politique, Economique et Cooperative (Paris), /France /Electrical utility industry /Case studies /Management

2658. Lauterbach, Albert. 1960 Las actitudes administrativas en Chile. Publicaciones del Instituto de Economía. Santiago, Chile. No. 32. /Chile /Administrative management

2659. Lauterbach, Albert. n.d. "The Austrian Public Sector in International Perspective: A Socio-Historical Evaluation. " /Austria /Economic history /Comparative analysis /OPSS

2660. Lavergne, Bernard. 1946 Le problème des nationalisations. Paris: Presses Universitaires de France. /France /Nationalization

2661. Lavergne, Nestor, and Dante Caputo. 1979 "Para una revalorización de las políticas de comercio exterior." Paper presented at the First Latin American seminar on Public Policies, São Paulo, 3-5 December. /State trading organizations /Peru /OPSS

2662. Lavez, Frederick A. 1962 "West Germany Unscrambles Its Socialist Omelette." Public Utilities Fortnightly V. 69, No. 12, pp. 822-833. /Germany, Federal Rep. of / 388.9 P97

2663. Lavigne, P. 1959 "Aspects juridiques de la dotation en capital des entreprises nationales." Revue de Science Financière (Paris), /France /Law /Public financing

2664. Lavigne, P. 1970 "Problemas jurídicos planteados por el cese de empresas en la URSS." La empresa pública. Zaragoza, Spain: Publicaciones del Real Colegio de España en Bolonia. /Union of Soviet Socialist Reps.

2665. Lavigne, P., and Roger Pollet. 1952 "Les institutions d'économie mixte." Jurisclasseur Administratif (Paris), No. 150. /France /Mixed enterprises

2666. Lavigne, P., and Roger Pollet. 1952 "Les modalités du contrôle étatique des institutions d'économie mixte." Jurisclasseur Administratif (Paris), /France /Control process /Mixed enterprises

2667. Layton, Cristopher. 1972 "State Entrepreneurship in a Market Environment." In Stuart Holland, ed(s). The State as Entrepreneur. London: Weidenfeld & Nicolson. pp. 45-55. /Nationalization /Control process /Profits / Holding company /HD 3616 I83 H65 PCL /HD 487 H6 1973 Pub Aff

2668. Layton, Cristopher. 1972 "IRI's Future in Europe." In Stuart Holland, ed(s). The State as Entrepreneur. London: Weidenfeld & Nicolson pp. 234-241. /Italy /Europe / Holding company /HD 3616 I83 H65 PCL /HD 487 H6 1973 Pub Aff

2669. Lazard, F. 1965 "Les nationalisations." Economie et Politique (Paris), No. 136, pp. 21-39. /Nationalization /France

2670. Le Besnerais. 1942 "The National Railroad Company and the Financial Amendment of the French Railroads." Annals of Collective Economy V. 18, No. 1, pp. 29-33. /France /Railway industry / 330.5 An73

2671. Le Brun, Pierre. 1948 "Le problème du statut des entreprises publiques." Revue Politique et Parlamentaire (Paris), No. 577, pp. 15-23. /France /Law / 305 R329

2672. Le Gall, P. 1957 "Evolution des relations collectives entre les chemins de fer d'intérêt général et leur personnel." Paris: Unpublished Thesis. /France /Railway industry /Collective bargaining / Personnel management

2673. Le Grand, R. 1970 L'interprétation jurisprudentielle du statut national du personnel des industries électriques et gazières. C.J.E.G. /France /Electrical utility industry /Gas utility industry / Personnel management /Law

2674. Le Guellec, Jean. 1957 "The French Gas Company, 1946-1956." Annals of Collective Economy V. 28, pp. 265-283. /France /Gas utility industry / 330.5 An73

2675. LeMay, G. H. L. 1954 "Some Aspects of Nationalized Industries in Great Britain." South African Journal of Economics (Pretoria), V. 22, pp. 350-352. /United Kingdom

/Nationalization

2676. Leach, Richard M. 1961 "Interstate Authorities in the United States." Law and Contemporary Problems V. 26, No. 4, pp. 666-681. /United States of America /Public authority /Law

2677. Leaes, L. G. P. de B. O. 1965 "O conceito jurídico de sociedade de economia mista." Revista de Direito Administrativo (Rio de Janeiro), No. 79, pp. 1-22. /Law /Mixed enterprises

2678. Leal de Meireles, Gilson Luis. 1979 "Administración de materiales para empresas de servicios públicos - un enfoque sistematico." In EIAP-FGV, ed(s). Administración de empresas. Mexico: Editorial Limusa. pp. 295-376. /Management /HD 3850 A333 LAC.

2679. Leason, Walter J. 1974 "Capitalism´s Greatest Test. The Electric Utilities." Public Utility Fortnightly V. 94, No. 4. /United States of America /Electrical utility industry

2680. Lebois, R. 1957 "Charbonnages de France, General Studies and Common Market: The State and Nationalized Power Undertaking in France, Coordination in the Power Field." Annals of Collective Economy V. 28, pp. 256-264. /France /Energy utility industry /Price policy /Investment /Control process /Case studies /330.5 An73

2681. Leclercq, Joseph. 1953 "Une intercommunale pure. L´association liègoise d´électricité." Annales d´Economie Collective pp. 103-135. /Belgium /Electrical utility industry

2682. Leclercq, Joseph. 1958 "The Belgium Public Electricity Companies Coordinating Committee (Interpublic)." Annals of Collective Economy V. 29, pp. 604-608. /Belgium /Cooperatives /Electrical utility industry /330.5 An73

2683. Leclercq, Joseph. 1958 "Liège Cooperative Electric Company (Socoliè)." Annals of Collective Economy V. 29, pp. 600-603. /Belgium /Cooperatives /Electrical utility industry /330.5 An73

2684. Ledey, P. 1953 Le régime financier des entreprises publiques. Lyon, France. /France /Law /Financing

2685. Lee, C. 1966 "Mexican State Enterprises and Management Controls." Mexican American Review V. 4, No. 34, pp. 27-33. /Mexico /Management /Control process

2686. Lee, H. 1967 Current Status and Development of Local Public Enterprises. Seoul, Korea: Ministry of Home Affairs Local Government Research Committee. /Korea, Rep. of /Local government

2687. Lee, L. 1971 La publicidad en una empresa del area social. Santiago, Chile. /Chile /Advertising

2688. Lee, Soo Ann. 1974 *Economic Growth and the Public Sector in Malaya and Singapore 1948-1960.* New York: Oxford University Press. /Malaysia /Singapore / HC 445.5 L442 Ma

2689. Lefaucheux, L. 1954 "Une entreprise nationalisé française. La régie nationale des usines Renault." *Revue Universitaire* (Brussels), pp. 242-259. /France /Automobile manufacturing industry /Nationalization

2690. Leff, Nathaniel H. 1968 *The Brazilian Capital Goods Industry, 1929-1964.* Cambridge, Mass.: Harvard University Press. /Brazil /Economic history /Economic development /Economic growth policy / G338.0981 L521b

2691. Lefranc, G. 1959 "Los orígenes de la idea de la nacionalización industrializada." *La Información Histórica* /Nationalization /Economic history

2692. Leibenstein, Harvey 1980 "X-Efficiency Theory and the Analysis of State Enterprises." paper presented at the Second BAPEG Conference: Public Enterprises in Mixed Economy LDCs, Boston, April. /Economic theory /OPSS

2693. Leighton, Eric A. 1975 "Accounting and the Determination of Revenue Requirements." *Public Utility Fortnightly* /United States of America /Public utility industry /Accounting

2694. Leleux, P. 1954 *Autonomía y control de los organismos paraestatales.* /Control process /Administrative management

2695. Lemass, S. F. 1952 "Les participations de l´Etat dans les entreprises en Italie." *Problèmes Economiques* (Paris), pp. 15-19. /Italy /Entrepreneurial activity

2696. Lemass, S. F. 1958 "The Role of the State Sponsored Bodies in the Economy." *Administration* (Dublin, Ireland), pp. 277-295. /Ireland

2697. Lenoudia, Pella. 1963 "Public Enterprises in Greece." *Public Finance* V. 18, No. 3-4, pp. 287-306. /Greece / 336.05 Op2

2698. Leon, Paolo. 1971 "Reflections on Public Enterprise in Italy." *Annals of Public and Cooperative Economy* V. 42, pp. 385-397. /Italy /Evaluation / 330.5 An73

2699. Leoni, B. 1960 "Una critica delle nazionalizzazione." *Político* (Padua, Italy), /Italy /Nationalization

2700. Lermer, Arthur, and Balbir S. Sabhni. 1967 "The Public Sector in Canada." *Annals of Public and Cooperative Economy* V. 38, pp. 291-323. /Canada / 330.5 An73

2701. Lerner, Salomón. 1978 *La comercialización externa, 1970-1977.* Lima: EPCHAP. /Peru / State trading organizations /Cotton industry /Fishing industry /OPSS

2702. Lescuyer, G. 1962 *Le contrôle de l´Etat sur les entreprises nationalisées.* Paris: Pichon & Durand-Auzias. /France /Control process

2703. Lescuyer, G. 1971 Le contrat de programme d'Electricité de France. C.J.E.G. /France /Electrical utility industry /Planning process / Contractual relations

2704. Lescuyer, G. 1974 "La responsabilité civile des dirigeants d'entreprises publiques." Revue de Droit Publique et de la Science Politique (Paris), No. 4, pp. 975-990. /Management

2705. Lesourne, J. 1958 Technique économique et gestion industrielle. Paris: Dunod. /Spain /Technology /Industrialization /330 L565t

2706. Lesourne, J. 1964 Técnica económica y gestión industrial. Madrid: Aguilar. /France /Technology /Industrialization

2707. Lessa, Gustavo de Sá. 1954 As corporações públicas na Gran-Bretanha. FGV/SPB. (Cuadernos de Administração Pública. Administração Geral 11). Rio de Janeiro. /United Kingdom

2708. Lessona, Silvio. 1970 "Líneas generales sobre la empresa pública." La empresa pública. Zaragosa, Spain: Publicaciones del Real Colegio de España en Bolonia. /Spain

2709. Letia, C. 1967 Managerial Problems of the Public Sector in India. Bombay: Ed. Manaktalas. /India /Management

2710. Levert, J. 1961 "Les rapports d'ensemble de la Commission de Verification des entreprises publiques." Bulletin de Liaison et d'Information de l'Administration Centrale des Finances (Paris), V. 11, pp. 29-37. /France /Control process

2711. Levi, I. 1953 "A propos de nationalisation." Egypte Contemporaine (Cairo), No. 272, pp. 35-42. /Egypt /Nationalization / 962.05 Eg98R

2712. Levia Hita, F. V. 1954 "Unidad de gobierno y división administrativa. Caracterización de la empresa pública frente a la administración central." Revista de la Facultad de Ciencias Económicas (University of Cuyo), pp. 23-33. /Argentina /Public administration

2713. Levick, B. 1967 "Wages and Employment Problems in the New System of Planned Management in Czechoslovakia." International Labour Review (Geneva), V. 95, No. 4, pp. 299-314. /Czechoslovakia /Management /Employment characteristics /Wages /331.05 In82 PCL /HD4811 I65 Pub Aff

2714. Levy, D. G. M. 1970 "Control of Public Enterprises in France." In W. G. Friedmann and J. F. Garner, ed(s). Government Enterprise: A Comparative Study. New York: Columbia University Press. pp. 123-132. /France /Control process / 350.0092 G746

2715. Lewin, David. 1973 "Public Employment Relations: Confronting the Issues." Industrial Relations V. 12, No. 3, pp. 309-321. /United States of America /Labor relations /Collective bargaining /331.105 In19

2716. Lewis, Ben W. 1952 British Planning and Nationalization. New York: The Twentieth Century Fund. /United Kingdom /Planning process /Nationalization / 338.942 L585b

2717. Lewis, Ben W. 1965 "British Nationalization and American Private Enterprise: Some Parallels and Contrasts." American Economic Review V. 55, No. 2, pp. 50-64. /United Kingdom /Nationalization /United States of America / Private enterprises /Comparative analysis /330.5 Am312

2718. Lewis, E. G. 1957 "Parliamentary Control of Nationalized Industry in France." American Political Science Review V. 51, pp. 669-683. /France /Control process /Parliament /320.5 Am31

2719. Lewis, W. Arthur. 1950 "The Price Policy of Public Corporations." Political Quarterly V. 21, pp. 184-197. /United Kingdom /Price Policy / 320.5 P76p

2720. Li Chiu-Tse. 1954 "State Department Store in Shanghai." People's China No. 14, pp. 29-31. /China, People's Rep. of /Retail trade

2721. Li Tsung-Huang. 1967 Public Utilities and Economic Development in the Republic of China. Chinese Institute of Local Self-Government. /China, Rep. of /Economic development /Public utility industry

2722. Liberman, E. G. 1966 "Profitability of Socialist Enterprises." Problems of Economics V. 8, No. 11, pp. 3-10. /Union of Soviet Socialist Reps. /Planning process /Profits /330.5 V899T

2723. Liekens, C. 1962 "La empresa de participación estatal, sociedades de economía mixta." Rev. Itat No. 17, pp. 43-149. /Mixed enterprises

2724. Liet-Veaux, G. 1952 Structure interne de l'établissment public industriel ou commercial. Paris: Ed. Jurisclasseur Administratif. /France /Industrial sector /Commercial sector /Law

2725. Lijadu, Yinka. 1980 "Problem of Developing and Retaining to Cope with the Onerous Responsibilities of Managing a National Insurance Institution." Paper presented at the Regional Workshop on Development of Training Methodologies for Internal Consultants in African Public Enterpriese, Addis Ababa, Ethiopia, 1-6 Dec. Ljubljana: ICPE /Insurance industry

2726. Lilienthal, D. 1944 TVA--Democracy on the March. New York: Harper. /United States of America /River valley development projects / 627.1 L627t

2727. Lilienthal, D., and Robert H. Marquis. 1941 "The Conduct of Business Enterprises by the Federal Government." Harvard Law Review V. 54, No. 4, pp. 545-601. /Public administration / 340.5 H261

2728. Lim Jiam Hoo. 1969 "Development Finance Institutions and Economic Development in Malaysia." Ekonomi (Kuala Lumpur), V. 10, pp. 48-52. /Malaysia /Development financing

2729. Lima, Griovaldo P. 1972 A Petrobrás e a distribuição de produtos de petróleo. Rio de Janeiro: Petróleo Brasileiro, S.A. /Brazil /Oil industry

2730. Lindgren, G. S. 1949 "The Role of Joint Consultation in Nationalized Industries." Personnel Management pp. 133-139. /Consultant services

2731. Lindsay, Cotton M. 1976 "A Theory of Government Enterprise." Journal of Political Economy V. 84, No. 5, pp. 1061-1077. /United States of America /Economic theory /Management /HB1 J7 Pub Aff

2732. Line, R. J. 1965 "The Role of Development Banks in Assisting Industrialization in Developing Commonwealth Countries." In Richard D. Robinson, ed(s). Industrialisation in Developing Countries. Cambridge, England: Cambridge University Overseas Study Committee. pp. 141-152. /British Commonwealth /Development banks

2733. Linsel, H., and K. Sack. 1964 "The Role of Semi-State Enterprises in National Economy." Cairo: Institute of National Planning. No. 494. /Egypt /Mixed enterprises

2734. Lipton, Joan. 1979 Bauxite in Jamaica: Ownership and Control in a Partially Nationalized Industry. Austin, Tex.: OPSS Technical Papers Series, No. 21. /Mining industry /Jamaica /Control process /OPSS

2735. Lipton, Michael. 1976 "What is Nationalization For?" Lloyds Bank Review V. 121, pp. 33-38. /Nationalization /330.5 L779

2736. Litner, John. 1981 "Economic Theory and Financial Management." In Raymond Vernon and Yair Aharoni, ed(s). State-Owned Enterprises in the Western Economies. New York: St. Martin's Press. pp. 23-53. /Financial management /HD3850 S79 PCL

2737. Little, Ian M. D. 1949 "Welfare and Tariffs." Review of Economic Studies V. 16, No. 2, pp. 65-70. /Price policy /Social welfare policy / 330.5 R326

2738. Little, Ian M. D. 1951 "Electricity Tariffs: A Comment." Economic Journal V. 61, pp. 875-882. /Electrical utility industry /Price policy / 330.5 Ec7

2739. Little, Ian M. D. 1957 A Critique of Welfare Economics. London: Oxford University Press. /Social welfare policy /Economic policy / 330.1 L724c

2740. Little, Ian M. D., and James A. Mirrlees. 1969 Manual of Industrial Project Analysis in Developing Countries. Paris: Development Centre, Organisation for Economic Co-Operation and Development. /Mexico /Pakistan /Case studies /Evaluation /Wages / Private enterprises /Price policy /Financing

/Industrial sector / 338.4 Or14m PCL

2741. Llamas, Virginia B. 1981 "Training Management in Public Enterprises." Paper presented at the Interregional Seminar on Training Management in Public Enterprises in Developing Countries, Ljubljana, Yugoslavia, 19-28 October. Ljubljana: ICPE. /Training /Management

2742. Lleonart y Amselen, Alberto J. 1967 "Las nacionalizaciones en el derecho internacional." Revista de Derecho Español y Americano (Madrid), V. 12, No. 16. /Nationalization /International law

2743. Lloyd, P. J. 1981 "State Trading and the Theory of International Trade." In M. M. Kostecki, ed(s). State Trading in International Markets. New York: St. Martin's Press. pp. 117-141. /State trading organizations /Economic theory /HF 1410.5 S7 1981 M. Also found in Les Cahiers du Cetai, no 79-08, April, 1979 /OPSS

2744. Lloyd, Selwyn. 1951 "The Future of (British) Broadcasting." National and English Review (London), pp. 340-344. /United Kingdom /Broadcasting industry

2745. Lockwood, W. 1970 The State and Economic Enterprise in Japan. Princeton, N.J.: Princeton University Press. /Japan /HC 462 L78 Pub Aff,UGL

2746. Loeber, D. 1968 "Zur vertragsfreiheite von staatsunternehmen in einer planwirtschaft." (Contractual Liberty of State Enterprises in a Planned Economy.) Osteuropa Recht (Stuttgart, F.R.G.), V. 14, No. 4, pp. 221-238. /Germany, Federal Rep. of /Control process /Law /Contractual relations

2747. Loganathan, Chelliah. 1972 "A New Deal in Development Banking." Development Digest V. 10, No. 4, pp. 25-36. /Development banks

2748. Lokanathan, P. S. 1957 "The Public Sector in India." Indian Journal of Public Administration (New Delhi), pp. 9-15. /India / JA 26 I55 Pub Aff

2749. Lombardini, S. 1963 "L'impresa publica e il piano economico." In Lombardini, S., and F. Archibugi, ed(s). Piano economico e impresa publica. Turin, Italy: Boringhieri. /Italy /Planning process

2750. Lombardo, I. M. 1960 "L'impresa publica di fronte alla produttivitá." L'Impresa Pubblica (Rome), pp. 64-68. /Italy /Productivity

2751. Lombroni, M., and Claudio Martín Viale. 1976 "La empresa pública en la República Argentina." Rio de Janeiro: FGV-EIAP. /Argentina /Directory /OPSS

2752. Lombroni, M. 1976 "El control de gestión en las empresas públicas argentinas." Rio de Janeiro: FGV-EIAP. /Argentina /Control process /OPSS

2753. Lomelín, José Luis. 1978 Las empresas eléctricas privadas y públicas en México. Mexico City: Comisión Federal de Electricidad. Mimeo. /Mexico /Electrical utility industry /Private sector /HD 9685 M62 L653 1980 LAC

2754. Loncke, K. H. P., and J. H. Van Der Meide. 1965 Administrative Management of Public Enterprise. Paris: 12th Congress, IIAS. /Administrative management

2755. Long, M. 1980 "La diversification des entreprises publiques françaises." Révue Française d'Administration Publique (Paris), No. 15, pp. 17-31. /France /Control process

2756. Long, Ngo Van. 1975 "Resource Extraction under the Uncertainty about Possible Nationalization." Journal of Economic Theory V. 10, No. 1, pp. 42-53. /Nationalization /Natural resource policy / 330.5 J8265

2757. Longhurst, John. 1950 Nationalization in Practice: The Civil Aviation Experience. London. /United Kingdom /Air transportation industry

2758. Longley, J. 1969 "Cost Control of Training--Does It Make Sense?" Industrial Training International (Oxford), V. 4, No. 11, pp. 471-474. /Training /Costs /Accounting

2759. Lopera Eusse, B. 1955 "TVA, un portento de planificación." Revista de Ciencia Económica (Antioquía), pp. 133-152. /United States of America /River valley development projects /Planning process

2760. Lopez Escalera, Mario. 1978 Relaciones de trabajo en las empresas públicas y su situación jurídico e laboral. Mexico City: mimeo. /Labor relations /Law /OPSS

2761. Lopez Escutia, Luiz A. 1974 "Estado, economía mixta y desarrollo nacional." Pensamiento Político (Mexico City), V. 15, No. 58, pp. 211-226. /Mexico /Management /Mixed enterprises /Economic development / G320.5 P387

2762. Lopez Guerra, Jaime. 1976 "Organización de los servicios de acueducto y alcantarillado en Colombia-- Estudio de caso: Bogotá." Rio de Janeiro: FGV-EIAP. /Colombia /Bogota, Colombia /Water resources development /Case studies /Sanitation industry /OPSS

2763. Lopez Mateos, A. 1960 "Nationalization of Petroleum and the Electric Power Industry." Justicia (Mexico), V. 20, No. 367, pp. 13-21. /Mexico /Oil industry /Electrical utility industry /Nationalization

2764. Lopez Rodó, L. 1950 "Las empresas nacionalizadas en Inglaterra." Revista de Administración Pública (Madrid), No. 3, pp. 373-406. /United Kingdom /Nationalization

2765. Lopez Rodó, L. 1954 El intervencionismo administrativo en materia de subsistencias. Ed. Coimbra. /Administrative management /Subsidization policy

2766. Lopez, A. 1963 La empresa portuaria de Chile. Santiago, Chile: Editorial Universitaria. /Chile

2767. Lopez, Lerroy, and José J. Villamil. 1981 "Corporaciones públicas y desarrollo en Puerto Rico." Paper presented at the seminar on public enterprises in development planning for Central America and the Caribbean, San José, Costa Rica, 1-3 July. /Puerto Rico /Economic analysis /Investment /Profits /Economic efficiency /OPSS

2768. Losada Lora, Rodrigo. 1973 Los institutos descentralizados de carácter financiero: Aspectos políticos del caso colombiano. Bogotá: Fedesarrollo. /Colombia /Banking system /HG 1798 C7 L665 LAC

2769. Losenbeck, H. D. 1963 Price Formation in Public Enterprises. Berlin: Duncker und Humbolt. /Price policy

2770. Lotia, C. 1958 "Management of State Entreprises in India." Indian Journal of Commerce (Allahabad), pp. 69-170. /India /Management

2771. Lotia, C. 1967 Managerial Problems of the Public Sector in India. Bombay: Manaktalas. /India /Management / 354.54 L914m

2772. Loucks, William N. 1958 "Workers´ Self-Government in Yugoslav Industry." World Politics pp. 68-82. /Yugoslavia /Worker self management / 909.8205 W893 PCL

2773. Louit, Christian. 1974 "L´actionnariat dans les entreprises publiques; l´expérience de la régie Renault et des societes nationales de banques et d´assurances." Bulletin de l´Institit Internationale d´Administration Publique (Paris), No. 29. /France /Automobile manufacturing industry /Banking agency /Insurance industry

2774. Louit, Christian. 1974 Les finances des entreprises publiques. Paris: Librarie générale de droit et de jurisprudence. /France /Financing

2775. Love, Thomas M., and George T. Sulzner. 1972 "Political Implications of Public Employee Bargaining." Industrial Relations V. 11, No. 1, pp. 18-33. /United States of America /Labor relations /Collective bargaining /331.105 In19

2776. Low, Sir Toby. 1962 "The Select Committee on the Nationalized Industry." Public Administration V. 40, pp. 1-15. /Parliament /Control process / 320.5 J826

2777. Loxley, John, and John S. Saul. 1972 The Political Economy of the Parastatals. Dar es Salaam, Tanzania: University of Dar es Salaam. /Tanzania /Political economy

2778. Loy, Michael. n.d. "L´Entreprise publique dans le Marché Commun." Réflets et Perspectives de la Vie Economique (Brussels), V. 9, No. 1, pp. 51-58. /France /European Economic Community / 330.5 R328

2779. Loyo, G. 1967 "Los organismos descentralizados y las empresas de participación estatal en el desarrollo económico." Economía Política (Mexico City), V. 40, No. 12, pp. 133-144. /Mexico /Decentralized authority /Economic development

2780. Lozada, Faustino R. 1954 "Supervising and Executive Development: Its relevance to Government Corporations." Philippine Journal of Public Administration (Manila), V. 14, No. 1. /Philippines /Personnel management /Training

2781. Lozada, Juan C., and Ricardo E Gerardi. 1981 "La nacionalización del petróleo en Venezuela: Análisis y perspectivas." Realidad Económica V. 43, pp. 86-112. /Venezuela /Nationalization /Oil industry /Investment /HC 171 R424 LAC

2782. Lozano Irueste, and José Maria. 1971 "Control de la empresa pública." Revista de Economia Política (Madrid), pp. 23-37. /Public administration /Control process / HC186 R484

2783. Lubell, Harold. 1961 "The Public and Private Sectors and Investment in Israel." Middle Eastern Affairs pp. 98-111. /Israel /Investment /Private sector /Mixed enterprises

2784. Luce, Charles F. 1961 Power for Progress. Portland, Ore.: Bonneville Power Administration. /United States of America /Oregon (State) /Electrical utility industry / Public works policy

2785. Luchaire, François. 1947 "Le statut des entreprises publiques." Droit Social (Paris), V. 10, No. 7-8. /Law

2786. Lueso, José Joaquín. 1978 "Estructura jurídica de la empresa pública: Tipología?" Paper presented at the IV General Assembly of the Asociación Latinoamericana de Administración Pública, Mexico. /Law /Taxonomy /OPSS

2787. Lueso, José Joaquín 1978 "El papel de las empresas públicas en los programas de gobierno." Paper presented at the Fourth General Assembly of the Latin American Association of Public Administrators, Mexico City, 6-11 November. /Planning process /Goal setting /Control process /OPSS

2788. Lukaszevicz, Aleksander. 1978 "The Financing of Public Enterprises: The Polish Experience." Paper presented at the Interregional Workshops on Financing of Public Enterprises in Developing Countries, Ljubljana, Yugoslavia, 22-26 May. Ljubljana: ICPE. /Poland /Public financing

2789. Lukens, Matthias F. 1955 "Controls, Accountability and Administration in the Port of New York Authority." In A. H.Hanson, ed(s). Public Enterprise. Brussels: IIAS. pp. 49-70. /United States of America /Port authority /Control process /Accountability /Public administration /HD 3850 H28 Law

2790. Lukic, R. 1957 "Propiedad social y autogestión de los trabajadores." Le Nouveau Droit (Belgrade), V. 7, No. 2-4.

/Yugoslavia /Worker self management

2791. Lulla, L. S. 1962 "Corporation Pattern of Nationalized Road Transport Undertakings." Indian Journal of Public Administration (New Delhi), V. 8, No. 2, pp. 210-214. /Land transportation industry / JA 26 I55 Pub Aff

2792. Lund, R. 1970 Employees' Participation in the Management of Municipal Institutions in Denmark. Geneva: International Industrial Relations Association, 2nd World Congress. /Denmark /Worker management participation

2793. Lyakurwa, W., et al. 1979 "Preliminary Tanzanian National Report: The Role of the Public Sector in Developing Countries." Paper presented at the Regional Meeting of African Countries on the Role of the Public Sector in Developing Countries, Arusha, Tanzania, 17-21 December. Ljubljana: ICPE /Tanzania

2794. Lyon-Caen, A. 1979 "Le contrôle des concentrations: Etude de loi française et de la Revue Trimestrielle de Droit Européen (Paris), No. 1-2, pp. 1-31. /Europe /France /Law /Control process / Europe 05 R328 LAW

2795. Lyon-Caen, G. 1945 "Les diverses formules de nationalisation." Droit Social (Paris), No. 2. /Law /Nationalization

2796. Lyra, João Filho. 1963 Regime do contrôle das empresas públicas. Rio de Janeiro: Pongetti. /Brazil /Public Administration /Control process

2797. Ma, R., and P. C. K. Tan. 1970 "The Public Sector Accounts of Singapore, 1966." Malayan Economic Review (Singapore), V. 15, No. 1, pp. 17-65. /Singapore /Public financing /Accounting

2798. Mabert, Vincent A., and Michael J. Showalter. 1974 "Managing Productivity in the United States Postal Service." Paper No. 488, West Lafayette, Indiana: Krannert Graduate School of Industrial Administration Purdue University. /United States of America /Postal service /Productivity /OPSS

2799. MacKenzie, N. 1955 "Lessons from the Railways." Economist V. 174, pp. 165-167. /United Kingdom /Railway industry /330.5 Ec74

2800. Macchiavello Contreras, Guido. 1968 Colaboración y cogestión en las empresas. Santiago, Chile: Editorial Jurídica de Chile. /Chile /Mixed enterprises / G658.3152 M131c

2801. Macdougall, D. 1958 "The Government Financing of Development: Bold or Cautious?" Social and Economic Studies (Kingston, Jamaica), V. 3, No. 4, pp. 75-84. /Public financing /Development banks /Development corporation /G330.97292 So13 LAC

2802. Mackie, J. A. C. n.d. "Indonesia's Government Estates and Their Masters." Public Affairs V. 34, No. 4, pp. 337-360.

/Indonesia /Agricultural sector

2803. Macmahon, W. 1961 Delegation and Autonomy. (Part 3: Problems of Autonomy in the Conduct of Public Enterprises). New Delhi: Asia Publishing House. pp. 139-170. /India /Evaluation / 351 M227d

2804. Macmahon, W., and W. R. Dittmar. 1940 "Autonomous Public Enterprises: the German Railways." Political Science Quarterly /Germany, Federal Rep. of /Railway industry /320.5 P75

2805. Macmahon, W., and W. R. Dittmar. 1941 "The Mexican Railways under Workers Administration." Public Administration Review V. 1, No. 11. /Mexico /Railway industry /Worker management participation

2806. Macmahon, W., and W. R. Dittmar. 1942 "The Mexican Oil Industry Since Expropriation." Political Science Quarterly /Mexico /Oil industry /Nationalization

2807. Macus, Rasto. 1978 "Role of Public Enterprises in Developing Countries in the Field of Management of Transfer and Development of Technology." Paper presented at the International Workshop on Management of Transfer and Development of Technology in Public Enterprises in Developing Countries, Ljubljana, Yugoslavia, 19-25 June. Ljubljana: ICPE. /Technology transfer

2808. Macus, Rasto. 1981 "The Bargaining Position of Public Enterprises of Developing Countries in Acquisition of Foreign Technology." Paper presented at the Reunión regional de expertos "Estrategias e instrumentos para reforzar la negociación (SBP) de las empresas públicas en los países en desarrollo en la transferencia internacional de transacciones tecnológicas," San José, Costa Rica, 23-27 November. Ljubljana: ICPE /Technology transfer

2809. Madan, G. S. 1980 "Accountability of Public Enterprises to Parliament." Lok Udyog (New Delhi), V. 14, No. 4. /India /Parliament /Accountability /354.54 L836 PCL

2810. Maeyer, Joseph M. M. 1970 "Las empresas públicas en los países bajos." La Empresa Pública. Zaragosa, Spain: Publicaciones del Real Colegio de España en Bolonia. pp. 1375-1398. /Netherlands

2811. Magalhães, Celso de 1965 "Sociedades de economia mista." In John F. Rood, ed(s). Administração Federal, antología. Rio de Janeiro: FGV/SPB. pp. 115-123. /Brazil /Mixed enterprises

2812. Maggs, P. B. 1965 "Soviet Corporation Law: The New Statute on the Socialist State Production Enterprise." American Journal of Comparative Law V. 14, No. 3, pp. 478-489. /Union of Soviet Socialist Reps. /Law

2813. Magtolis, Leanor M. 1969 "Public Enterprise in the Philippines, Structure and Problems." Philippine Journal of Public Administration (Manila), V. 13, No. 4, pp. 415-423.

/Philippines / 350.5 P538

2814. Maier, L. 1960 "On the Return to the Private Sector of State Enterprises in West Germany." Wirtschafts Wissenschaft (Bonn), V. 8, No. 7, pp. 1011-1029. /Germany, Federal Rep. of /Privatization

2815. Mailángil, J. L. 1970 "Cuestiones institucionales de las empresas públicas en Espana." La empresa pública. Zaragosa, Spain: Publicaciones del Real Colegio de España en Bolonia. pp. 1375-1398. /Spain /Public administration /Structural characteristics

2816. Maillet-Chassagne, M. 1959 "Influence de la nationalisation sur la gestion des entreprises publiques." Econometrica V. 27, pp. 322-323. /France /Nationalization /Management /330.5 Ec74e

2817. Maisch von Humbolt, Lucrecia. 1973 Sociedades de economía mixta. Lima: Universidad Nacional Mayor de San Marcos. /Peru /Law /Peru 76 M2864 Law

2818. Majer, Boris. 1981 "Self-Management and Philosophy." Socialist Thought and Practice V. 21, No. 2, pp. 55-68. /Yugoslavia /Worker self management

2819. Malagon y de Parees, J. F. 1970 La participación de los trabajadores en la propiedad de los bienes de producción. Mexico City: Escuela Libre de Derecho. /Mexico /Worker management participation

2820. Malan, Pedro Sampaio. 1980 "O debate sobre `estatização´ no Brasil." Dados, Revista de Ciencias Sociais V. 24, No. 1, pp. 25-36. /Brazil /Economic history / G305 D127 LAC

2821. Malaysia. Ministry of Public Enterprises. 1976 "Public Enterprise Policy on Investment, Prices, Costs, and Returns." Kuala Lumpur: U.N. Asian Center for Development Administration. pp. 187-199. /Malaysia /Investment /Price policy /Profits / HD 4276 A8 1976

2822. Malegam, Y. H. 1970 "Performance Evaluation of Public Enterprise." Lok Udyog (New Delhi), V. 4, No. 3, pp. 417-425. /Evaluation /Economic efficiency / 354.54 L836

2823. Malenbaum, Wilfred. 1968 "A Different Entrepreneurial Role for Government." Development Digest V. 6, No. 3, pp. 105-109. /Public administration /Management

2824. Maleville, G. 1970 "L´Autorité de l´Etat sur les services nationaux: Electricité de France et Gaz de France." Cahiers Juridiques de l´Electricité et du Gaz (Brussels), V. 1. /France /Public utility industry /Electrical utility industry / Gas utility industry /Control process

2825. Malhotra, R. L. 1978 "Public Relations in a Development Bank - Effective Communication is a Key to Corporate Profits." Lok Udyog (New Delhi), V. 11, No. 12, pp. 7-12. /India /Development banks /Public relations /354.54 L836 PCL

2826. Malik, M. 1959 "Relative Role of Private and Public Sector." Pakistan Economic Journal V. 9, No. 2-3, pp. 195-200. /Private sector /Comparative analysis

2827. Mallikarjanayya, G. 1974 "The Organisation and Working of Andhra Pradesh State Financial Corporation." Lok Udyog (New Delhi), V. 8, No. 6, pp. 55-60. /India /Andhra Pradesh, India (State) /Development corporation /354.54 L836 PCL

2828. Mallon, Richard D. 1980 "Public Enterprise as an Instrument for the Redistribution of Ownership: The Malaysian Case." Paper presented at the Second BAPEG Conference in Boston, Public Enterprise in Mixed Economy LDCs, Boston, April. /Malaysia /OPSS

2829. Mallon, Richard D. 1981 "Performance Evaluation and Compensation of the Social Burdens of Public Enterprise in Less Developed Countries." Annals of Public and Cooperative Economy V. 52, No. 3, pp. 281-300. /Evaluation /Economic efficiency /Financial performance /Social welfare policy /330.5 An73

2830. Mallon, Richard D. 1982 "Public enterprise versus other methods of state intervention as instruments of redistribution policy: the Malaysian experience." In Leroy P. Jones et al., ed(s). Public enterprise in less-developed countries. New York: Cambridge University Press. pp. 313-325. /Malaysia /Income distribution /Economic policy /HD 3850 P83 PCL

2831. Mallya, N. N. 1971 Public Enterprises in India: Their Control and Accountability. New Delhi: National Publishing House. /India / HD 4294 M34

2832. Malpede, Ernesto Miguel. 1973 "La política, las empresas estatales y la política exterior." Función del estado en la economía. Buenos Aires: Cuenca Ed. /Political analysis /Evaluation /Foreign policy

2833. "Management of Public Enterprises in India." 1974 Lok Udyog (New Delhi), V. 8, No. 1, pp. 35-44. /India /Management /354.54 L836 PCL

2834. "Management of Public Corporations in Bangladesh." 1974 Lok Udyog (New Delhi), V. 8, No. 1, pp. 45-52. /Bangladesh /Management /354.54 L836 PCL

2835. Mandel, E. 1970 Contrôle ouvrier, conseils ouvriers, autogestion. Anthologie. Paris: François Maspero. /Worker self management / 331.1 M312c

2836. Maneschi, Andrea. 1972 "The Brazilian Public Sector" In Riordan Roett, ed(s). Brazil in the Sixties. Nashville, Tenn.: Vanderbilt University Press. pp. 185-230. /Brazil /F 2538.2 B75 LAC

2837. Maniatis, George C. 1964 "State Control over Public Enterprise: The Case of Italy." Ph.D. dissertation, University of California-Berkeley. /Italy /Control process

/Holding company

2838. Maniatis, George C. 1966 "Appraising Managerial Efficiency in Public Enterprises." Revista Internazionale di Scienza Economiche e Commerciale (Milan, Italy), V. 8, No. 12, pp. 1101-1125. /Evaluation /Management /330.5 R526

2839. Maniatis, George C. 1966 "Executive Control over State Holding Companies and their Subsidiaries in Italy." Indian Journal of Public Administration (New Delhi), V. 12, No. 4, pp. 743-756. /Italy /Control process /Holding company /JA 26 I55 Pub Aff

2840. Maniatis, George C. 1967 "Evaluation of Operating Efficiency in Italian Public Undertakings." Economia Internazionale (Genoa), V. 20, No. 1, pp. 111-119. /Italy /Evaluation /Economic efficiency / 330.5 Ec74i

2841. Maniatis, George C. 1967 "Quantitative vs. Qualitative Standards for Evaluating Managerial Efficiency in Public Undertakings." Indian Economic Journal (Bombay), No. 14, pp. 576-589. /Evaluation /Management / 330.5 In16

2842. Maniatis, George C. 1967 "Private Minority Shareholding Interest in Italian Mixed Companies." Land Economics No. 43, pp. 116-120. /Italy /Mixed enterprises /305 J824 PCL

2843. Maniatis, George C. 1968 "Managerial Autonomy vs. State Control in Public Enterprise: Fact and Antifact." Annals of Public and Cooperative Economy V. 39, No. 4, pp. 513-530. /Switzerland /Autonomy /Control process /330.5 An73

2844. Maniatis, George C. 1969 "The Impromptu Establishment of State Ownership in Italian Industry." Weltwirtschaftliches Archiv (Hamburg), V. 102, No. 1, pp. 97-113. /Italy /Industrial sector / 330.5 W468 PCL

2845. Maniatis, George C. 1970 "Social Calculus, Profitability, and the Conduct of Public Corporations." American Journal of Economics and Sociology V. 29, No. 3, pp. 225-239. /Evaluation / 330.5 Am311

2846. Mann, P. 1970 "Publicly-Owned Electric Utility Profits and Resource Allocation." Land Economics V. 46, No. 4, pp. 478-84. /United States of America /Public utility industry /305 J824 PCL

2847. Mann, P., and E. J. Seifried. 1972 "Pricing in the Case of Public Owned Electric Utilities." Economic and Business No. 2. /United States of America /Electrical utility industry /Price policy

2848. Manne, A. S. 1952 "Multiple-Purpose Public Enterprises, Criteria for Pricing." Economica (London), V. 19, pp. 322-326. /Price Policy / 306 Ec74 n.s.

2849. Manove, Michael. 1982 "Public enterprise versus regulation when costs are uncertain." In Leroy P. Jones et al., ed(s). Public enterprise in less-developed countries. New York:

Cambridge University Press. pp. 297-310. /Control process /Economic policy /Economic theory /HD 3850 P83 PCL

2850. Manuelli, E. 1949 *La nationalisation en Italie: Théorie générale expériences et pourcentage d'intervention étatique. Société Belge d'Etudes et d'Expansion* (Liège, Belgium), No. 138. /Italy /Nationalization

2851. Manzocchi, B. 1960 "Nationalization of the Electric Power Industry." *Cronache Meridionali* (Naples), V. 7, No. 4, pp. 165-180. /Electrical utility industry /Nationalization /Italy

2852. Mapolu, Henry. 1976 "Workers and Management." Tanzanian Studies Series. Dar es Salaam, Tanzania: Tanzania Publishing House. No. 4. /Worker management participation /Tanzania

2853. Maranhão, Jarbas. 1959 "O petróleo no senado." *Revista do Servico Público* No. 83. /Brazil /Oil industry

2854. Marathe, Sharad S. 1981 "Financial Profitability and Losses in the Public Sector: Some Reflections on the Indian Experience." Paper presented at the International Workshop on Financial Profitability and Losses in Public Enterprises, Ljubljana, Yugoslavia, 1-5 June. Ljubljana: ICPE. /India /Profits /Public financing

2855. Marberger, Glen A, ed. 1963 *The Authority.* Harrisburg, Pa.: Pennsylvania Municipal Authorities Association. /United States of America /Public authority /Local government

2856. Marcantonio, Arnoldo. 1956 *La gestion delle imprese pubblique schemi e appunti.* Milan, Italy: Dott. A. Giuffré Editore. /Italy /Management

2857. Marchal, Jean. 1964 "Investment Decisions in French Public Undertakings" *Annals of Public and Cooperative Economy* V. 35, No. 4, pp. 264-275. /France /Investment /Decision making process

2858. Marchal, Jean. 1964 "Les entreprises publiques françaises et la décision d'investir." *Annales de l'Economie Collective* V. 52, No. 3, pp. 321-335. /France /Investment /Decision making process

2859. Marchal, Philippe. 1971 *L'économie mixte.* Paris: Presses Universitaires de France. /France /Mixed enterprises

2860. Marchand, Maurice, and Henry Tulkens. 1979 "What Should be the Significance of Public Tariffs?" *Annals of Public and Cooperative Economy* V. 50, No. 3, pp. 3-8. /Price policy /Electrical utility industry /330.5 An73

2861. Marchand, Maurice, and Pierre Ppestieau. 1979 "Price Setting and Divergent Anticipations." *Annals of Public and Cooperative Economy* V. 50, No. 3, pp. 111-136. /Price policy /330.5 An73

2862. Marclay, A. 1971 "Workers Participation in Management: Selected Bibliography, 1950-1970." International Educational Materials Exchange, Geneva, July 1, 1971. Geneva: International Institute for Labour Studies. /Worker management participation /Bibliography

2863. Marcos, Ernesto. 1980 "Design of a Development Policy for Mexico: Industry and Oil." In William J. Baumol, ed(s). Public and Private Enterprise in a Mixed Economy. New York: St. Martin's Press. pp. 57-65. /Oil industry /Mexico /HD 3842 P87 PCL

2864. Marcus, George. 1931 "The Nationalization of the Hungarian Regional Railways" Annals of Collective Economy V. 7, pp. 383-384. /Hungary /Railway industry /Nationalization /330.5 An73

2865. Marek, E. 1970 "Workers Participation in Planning and Management in Poland." International Labour Review (Geneva), V. 101, No. 3, pp. 271-290. /Poland /Worker management participation /Planning process /331.05 In81 PCL /HD 4811 I65 Pub Aff

2866. Marel, J. H. Van der. 1968 "Some Considerations on Cost, Tariffs and Finance in the Netherlands State Owned P.T.T. Undertaking." Annals of Public and Cooperative Economy V. 39, No. 2, pp. 195-214. /Netherlands /Costs /Price policy /Telephone industry / 330.5 An73

2867. Marfan, A. 1961 Corporación de Fomento de la Producción de Chile. Santiago, Chile. /Chile /Development corporation /Productivity

2868. Marga Institute. 1981 "Issues in the Relationships between Parliament and Public Enterprise." Paper presented at the Seminar on Relationships between Parliament and Public Enterprise, Columbo, Sri Lanka, 15-19 June. Ljubljana: ICPE /Legislature /Control process

2869. Marga Institute. 1981 "Report of the Seminar on Relationships between Parliament and Public Enterprise, Colombo, Sri Lanka, 15-19 June, 1981." Ljubljana: ICPE /Legislature /Control process

2870. Marga Institute. 1981 "Issues in the Relationship between Parliament and Public Enterprise." In United Kingdom, Commonwealth Secretariat, ed(s). Relationship between Parliament and Public Enterprises. London. pp. 37-52. /Parliament /Control process

2871. Marglin, Stephen A. 1968 "Pricing Policy for Public Enterprise." Development Digest V. 6, No. 3, pp. 99-104. /Price policy /

2872. Margolis, J., and H. Guitton. 1969 Public Economics. London: Macmillan. /Economic analysis

2873. Marinho, Ilmar Penna Jr. 1970 Petróleo, soberania e desenvolvimento. Rio de Janeiro: Editora Saga S.A. /Brazil

/Oil industry

2874. Marini, Caio Marcio,and Jorge Luiz de Barros Nóbrega. 1979 "Teoría de sistemas aplicada a empresas públicas." In EIAP-FGV, ed(s). Administración de empresas públicas. Mexico: Editorial Limusa. pp. 89-120. /Planning process /System analysis /HD 3850 A333 LAC

2875. Marione, E. 1947 Les sociétés d'économie mixte en Belgique. Brussels: Etablissements Emile Bruylant. /Belgium /Mixed enterprises

2876. Mark, Louis, Jr. 1959 "The Favored Status of the State Entrepreneur in Economic Development Programs." Economic Development and Cultural Change V. 7, No. 4, pp. 422-430. /Entrepreneurial activity / 330.5 Ec66

2877. Markham, J. 1983 "The Provision of Public Transport Service in Ireland Relies on an On-going Reconciliation of the Political, Social, and Economic Objectives of the States." Paper presented at the 19th International Congress of Administrative Sciences, West Berlin, 19-23 Sept. /Ireland /Mass transportation industry /Goal setting /Economic history /OPSS

2878. Markides, Nicos Markou. 1979 "Management and Training in Public Enterprises: Country Report of Cyprus." Paper presented at the International Seminar on Management and Training in Public Enterprises in Developing Countries, Ljubljana, Yugoslavia, 1-13 October. Ljubljana: ICPE. /Sri Lanka /Training /Management

2879. Markovcic, T. 1969 The New Productive Forces, Modern Methods and Techniques, and Workers' Self- Management in SFR of Yugoslavia. Herceg Novi: U.N. Public Administrative Division. /Yugoslavia /Productivity /Technology /Worker self management

2880. Markovth, M. 1959 "La rémunération dans le système d'autogestion." Questions Actuelles du Socialisme (Paris), No. 55, pp. 79-102. /Worker self management

2881. Marlett, D. L. 1939 "The TVA Investigation (Report of the Joint Congressional Committee)." Land Economics V. 15, pp. 212-24; 360. /United States of America /River valley development projects / 305 J824 PCL

2882. Marsan, V. A. 1969 Financing of Manufacturing Companies in a State Shareholding System. Rome: UNIDO, Seminar on Financial Aspects of Manufacturing Enterprises in the Public Sector. /Financing /Industrial sector / Holding company

2883. Marsan, V. A. 1978 "L'entreprise publique en Italie." In André Gélinas, ed(s). Public Enterprise and the Public Interest. Ontario: The Institute of Public Administration of Canada. pp. 186-199. /Italy /Law /Control process

2884. Marsan, V. A. 1981 "The State Holding System in Italian Development." In William J. Baumol, ed(s). Public and

Private Enterprise in a Mixed Economy. New York: St. Martin's Press. pp. 138-157. /Italy /Control Process / Holding company / HD 3842 T87 PCL

2885. Marschak, T. A. 1960 Theory and Policy in the French Nationalized Industries. Santa Monica, California: The Rand Corporation. /France /Industrial sector /Nationalization /Policy analysis

2886. Marsden, R. P. 1973 Bibliography of Public Enterprise with Special Reference to the Developing Countries. (Leeds, England), University of Leeds. /Bibliography /OPSS

2887. Marsh, H. J. 1948 "Nationalized Industries and Industrial Relations." Personnel Management (London), pp. 53-64. /Industrial relations

2888. Marshall, Jorge. 1984 "Privatización económica: Lecciones de la Chilena." Paper presented at the conference, "State Shrinking: A Comparative Inquiry into Privatization," Austin, Texas, 1-3 March. /Chile /Privatization /OPSS

2889. Martelliti, José Angel, et al. 1973 "Las empresas del Estado en la economía Argentina." Buenos Aires: Universidad Argentina de la Empresa. Instituto de Investigaciones Económicas. /Public Financing

2890. Martelliti, José Angel, et al. 1973 Empresas estatales en la economía argentina. B Universidad Argentina de la Empresa, Institute de Investigaciones Económicas. /Argentina /Economic analysis /HD 4083 U567 1973 LAC

2891. Martin Mateo, Ramón. 1975 "Relaciones entre gobierno y empresa a través de instituciones." Revista de Administración Pública (Madrid), No. 76, pp. 401-417. /Spain /Private enterprises

2892. Martin Mateo, Ramón. 1978 "Relaciones entre el gobierno y la empresa pública a través de instituciones especializadas." Gobierno y empresas públicas en América Latina. Buenos Aires: SIAP. pp. 89-130. /Management /Control process /OPSS

2893. Martin Retordillo, Sebastían. 1966 "Organización administrativa de las empresas públicas en España." Revista Internacional de Ciencias Administrativas No. 1, pp. 1-15. /Spain /Administrative management

2894. Martin Retordillo, Sebastián. 1970 "La empresa pública como alternativa (Un análisis del sistema español)." La empresa pública. Zaragosa, Spain: Publicaciones del Real Colegio de España en Bolonia. pp. 877-906. /Spain /Evaluation

2895. Martin-Pannetier, A. 1966 Eléments d'analyse comparative des établissements publiques en droit français et en droit anglais. Paris: Librairie générale de droit et de jurisprudence. /France /United Kingdom /Administrative law /Comparative analysis / Law

2896. Martinelli, Alberto. 1981 "The Italian Experience: A Historical Perspective." In Raymond Vernon and Yair Aharoni, ed(s). State-Owned Enterprise in the Western Economies. New York: St. Martin's Press. pp. 85-99. /Italy /Economic history /HD 3850 S79 PCL

2897. Martinez Caro, S. 1970 "Problemas de inmunidad de la empresa estatal en derecho internacional." La empresa pública. Zaragoza, Spain: Publicaciones del Real Colegio de España en Bolonia. pp. 687-734. /International law /Law

2898. Martinez Esteruelas, C. 1964 "La empresa pública y mixta." Reforma de la empresa. Madrid. /Spain /Evaluation /Mixed enterprises

2899. Martinez Hurtado, José Luis. 1979 "Information over Public Sector Control in Mexico." Paper presented at the Interregional Workshop on Control Systems for Public Enterprises in Developing Countries, Ljubljana, Yugoslavia, 9-13 July. Ljubljana: ICPE. /Mexico /Control process

2900. Martinez Najera, Julio. 1980 "Public Enterprises in Mexico." Paper presented at the International Workshop on Pricing Policies in Public Enterprises, Ljubljana, Yugoslavia, 26-30 May. Ljubljana: ICPE. /Mexico /Public financing

2901. Martinez Nogueira, Roberto. 1974 "Los procesos de formulación e implementación de políticas y sus consecuencias sobre las empresas públicas." Revista Latinoamericana de Administración Pública (Bogotá), No. 2, pp. 29-36. /Policy development /Evaluation /Control process

2902. Martinez Pujana, A., and T. Mendes Reyes. 1964 "Evolución del sector público de la economía española." Anales de Economía V. 2, No. 6, pp. 327-446. /Spain /Economic history

2903. Martinez Saccarello, Julio. 1976 "Estudio de los recursos financieros de la Corporación de Obras Sanitarias del Paraguay." Rio de Janeiro: FGV-EIAP. /Paraguay /Sanitation industry /Public financing /Case studies /OPSS

2904. Martinez Serratos, Patricia. 1975 "La función de la Secretaría del Patrimonio Nacional en materia de control y vigilancia de los organismos descentralizados y empresas de participación estatal en México." Rio de Janeiro: FGV-EIAP. /Mexico /Control process /Law /Public administration /OPSS

2905. Martinez Serratos, Patricia, and Porfirio Solís Chávez. 1976 "La empresa pública en México." Rio de Janeiro: FGV-EIAP. /Mexico /Control process /Law /OPSS

2906. Martini, Gianfranco. 1969 "Il 'Rapporto Nora' sulle imprese publiche in Francia." L'Impresa Púbblica (Rome), pp. 12-23. /France /Evaluation

2907. Martins, Carlos Estevam. 1977 Capitalismo de estado e modelo político no Brasil. Rio de Janeiro: Edições do Graal Ltds. /Brazil /Political economy /Political analysis /HB 501 M37 LAC

2908. Martins, Luciano. 1968 Industrializacão, burguesia nacional e desenvolvimento. Rio de Janeiro: Editora Saga S.A. /Brazil /Industrialization /Economic development /G330.981 M367i LAC

2909. Martins, Luciano. 1976 Pouvoir et développement économique, formation et évolution des structures politiques au Brésil. Paris: Editions anthropos. /Brazil /Steel industry /Oil industry /Development banks /Political economy /JL 2424 M378 LAC

2910. Martinson, H. M. 1954 "T.V.A. Improves Its Communications." Public Administration Review V. 14, No. 1, pp. 52-54. /United States of America /River valley development projects /Public relations

2911. Marus, J. J. 1952 "Structura e funcionamento delle industrie nazionalizzate." Ponte pp. 588-595. /Italy /Industrial sector

2912. Marzola, P. L. 1975 "Polivalenza dell´impresa pubblica e productività: Il contributo di una recente ricerca" Giornale delgi Economisti e Annali dé Economia V. 34, No. 5-6, pp. 305-333. /Productivity / 330.5 G438 n.s.

2913. Mascarenhas, R. C. 1964 "A General Law for Public Enterprise in India." Revue Internationale des Sciences Administratives V. 30, No. 4, pp. 397-403. /India /Law /Administrative law

2914. Mascarenhas, R. C. 1964 "Recent Developments in Public Enterprises." Indian Journal of Public Administration (New Delhi), pp. 535-546. /India /Evaluation / JA 26 I55 Pub Aff

2915. Mascarenhas, R. C. 1968 "The Bureau of Public Enterprises in India." Revue Internationale des Sciences Administratives V. 34, No. 3, pp. 246-264. /India /Evaluation /Control process

2916. Mascarenhas, R. C. 1975 "A Systems View of the Performance of Public Enterprises." In R. C. Dutt and Raj K. Nigam, ed(s). Towards Commanding Heights. New Delhi: Vivek Joshi. pp. 142-175. /India /Economic efficiency /Financial performance /HD 4293 T68 PCL

2917. Maseda, J. L. 1969 "La empresa pública y los criterios para evaluar la gestión gerencial de la misma." Paper presented at the Reunión de expertos en administración de empresas públicas en América Latina y el Caribe, Santiago, Chile, 17-22 November. ST/ECLA/Conf. 35/L. 5 Santiago, Chile: UNECLA /Evaluation /Management

2918. Massé, P. 1956 "Les entreprises nationalisés et le bien public." Coopération pp. 18-21. /Evaluation

2919. Massera, A. 1974 "La riforma dello stato e degli enti pubblici in Francia." Rivista Trimestrale di Diritto Publico (Rome), No. 1, pp. 200-214. /France /Administrative law

2920. Masseron, J. P. 1969 Les établissements publics au Sénegal. Bulletin de l´Institut International d´Administration Publique (Paris), No. 11. /Senegal

2921. Mateega, E. L. K. 1970 The Uganda Development Corporation. Makerere, Uganda: Makerere Economic Seminar Programmme. /Uganda /Development corporation

2922. Matejka, Harriet. 1981 "Trade Policy Instruments, State Trading and First-Best Intervention." In M. M. Kostecki, ed(s). State Trading in International Markets. New York: St. Martin's Press. pp. 142-160. /State trading organizations /Economic policy /HF 1410.5 S7 1981 M. Also found in Les Cahiers du Cetai, no 79-12, June,1979 /OPSS

2923. Mateo, F. 1977 El papel del sector público y de las empresas públicas en la integración económica de América Latina. Austin, Tex.: OPSS Technical Papers Series, No. 6. /Economic integration /OPSS

2924. Mateo, F., and E. White. 1974 "Las empresas públicas como instrumentos de distribución de costos y beneficios en un marco de integración." Revista de la Integración (Buenos Aires), V. 8, No. 16, pp. 71-112. /Economic integration /Cost benefit analysis /Multinational corporations /G337.91 R327 LAC

2925. Mathew, M. O., and D. Amarchand. 1974 "Nominee Directors on the Boards of Joint Sector Companies." Lok Udyog (New Delhi), V. 7, No. 12, pp. 29-32. /Management /Control process /354.54 L836 PCL

2926. Mathew, P. M 1982 "Government and Development Bank Relations." In William Diamond and V. S. Raghaven, ed(s). Aspects of Development Bank Management. Baltimore, Md.: The Johns Hopkins University Press. pp. 277-294. /Development banks /Control process /HG 3550 A8 PCL

2927. Mathijsen, Pierre. 1972 "State Aids, State Monopolies, and Public Enterprises in The Common Market." Law and Contemporary Problems V. 37, No. 2, pp. 376-391. /European Economic Community / 340.5 L414

2928. Mathiot, A. 1961 Grands services publics et entreprises nationales. Paris: Faculté de Droit. /France /Public services /Evaluation

2929. Mathur, A. B. L. 1979 "Training in Export Marketing." Lok Udyog (New Delhi), V. 13, No. 6, pp. 41-52. /India /Exports /Marketing /Training /354.54 L836 PCL

2930. Mathur, B. L. 1978 "Evaluation of a New Pricing Policy for Steel." Lok Udyog (New Delhi), V. 12, No. 7, pp. 29-30. /India /Steel industry /Price policy /354.54 L836 PCL

2931. Mathur, B. L., and R. K. Mishra. 1981 "Working Capital Management- A Case Study." Lok Udyog (New Delhi), V. 14, No. 12, pp. 47-50. /India /Financial performance /Financing /Case studies /Working capital /354.54 L836 PCL

2932. Mathur, Birendra Prased. 1969 "Accountability of Public Undertakings in India." Lok Udyog (New Delhi), pp. 1125-1133. /India /Accountability / 354.54 L836

2933. Mathur, Birendra Prased. 1969 "The Role of Financial Adviser in Public Enterprises." Lok Udyog (New Delhi), pp. 1049-1057. /India /Financing / 354.54 L836

2934. Mathur, Birendra Prased. 1969 "The Financing of Public Enterprises in India and the Question of Private Equity Participation." Indian Journal of Economics pp. 55-75. /India /Mixed enterprises / 330.5 In2

2935. Mathur, Birendra Prased. 1973 Public Enterprise in Perspective; Aspects of Financial Administration and Control in India. Bombay: Orient Longman. /India /Financing /Control Process / HD 4293 M38

2936. Mathur, K. B. 1964 "Collaboration in Heavy Electricals and Railways." Indian Journal of Public Administration (New Delhi), V. 10, No. 3. /India /Electrical utility industry /Railway industry / JA 26 I55 Pub Aff

2937. Mathur, N. D. 1979 "Profitability of Public Enterprise." Lok Udyog (New Delhi), V. 13, No. 1, pp. 25-28. /India /Profits /Financial performance /354.54 L836 PCL

2938. Mathur, N. D. 1980 "Pricing Policy in Hindustan Machine Tools Limited-Amjer Unit." Lok Udyog (New Delhi), V. 14, No. 4, pp. 53-57. /Price policy /India Case studies / /354.54 L836

2939. Mathur, P. C. 1964 "Surpluses from Public Enterprises." Indian Journal of Public Administration (New Delhi), pp. 524-532. /India /Evaluation / Profits

2940. Matkovic, Z. 1965 "Réalites de l´autogestion yugoslave." Temps Moderns (Paris), V. 20, No. 229, pp. 2187-2203. /Yugoslavia /Worker self management

2941. Matuzita, Myoci. 1975 "Sistema de controle patrimonial nas empresas de energia elétrica." Rio de Janeiro: FGV-EIAP /Brazil /Electrical utility industry /Control process /OPSS

2942. Mayo-Smith, Ian. 1975 "Barriers to Effective Performance in Public Enterprises." Improving Performance in Public Enterprise, Report of the International Conference, Arusha, Tanzania, 2-5 December. Arusha, Tanzania: East African Community Management Institute. pp. 25-37. /Economic efficiency /East Africa

2943. Maza Zavala, Domingo Felipe. 1974 Hacia el dominio nacional de la actividad petrolera. Caracas: Universidad Central de Venezuela, Facultad de Ciencias Económicas y Sociales. /Venezuela /Nationalization /Oil industry /HD9574 V42 M3 LAC

2944. Mazari, A. M. K. 1967 Problems of Public Enterprises. Proceedings of Seminar Held by NIPA, Lahore, Pakistan. /Evaluation /Economic analysis

2945. Mazzolini, R. 1979 Government Controlled Enterprises: International Strategic and Policy Decisions. New York: John Wiley and Sons. /United Kingdom /France /Italy /Control

Process /Comparative Analysis / HD 4140.5 M39

2946. Mbewe, Nathan Jackson. 1979 "Management and Training in Public Enterprises: A Country Report of Zambia." Paper presented at the International Seminar on Management and Training in Public Enterprises in Developing Countries, Ljubljana, Yugoslavia, 1-13 October. Ljubljana: ICPE. /Zambia /Training /Management

2947. Mbewe, Nathan Jackson. 1980 "Management Planning and Development in Public Enterprises: The Case of Zambia." Paper presented at the Expert Group Meeting on Manpower Planning in Public Enterprises in Developing Countries, Tagaytay, Philippines, 18-22 August. Ljubljana: ICPE. /Zambia /Personnel management / Manpower planning

2948. Mbowe, George F. 1979 "Project Implementation and Control: A Critical Problem in Public Enterprises in Tanzania." Paper presented at the Regional Workshop on Planning in Public Enterprises of the African Region, Accra, Ghana, 10-15 December. Ljubljana: ICPE /Tanzania /Planning process /Control process /Project management /Also published in Public Enterprise, Vol. 1, No. 1(1980), pp. 57-65. /OPSS

2949. Mbowe, George F. 1979 "System of Information and Control in Public Enterprises in Developing Countries with Particular Reference in Tanzania." Paper presented at the Interregional Workshop on Control Systems for Public Enterprises in Developing Countries, Ljubljana, Yugoslavia, 9-13 July. Ljubljana: ICPE. /Tanzania /Control process /Information system / East Africa

2950. Mbowe, George F. 1980 "Decision Structure in Public Enterprises." Paper presented at the International Workshop on Investment Criteria and Investment Decision-Making Processes, Ljubljana, Yugoslavia, 20-24 Oct. Ljubljana: ICPE. /Decision making process /Management /Public administration

2951. Mbowe, George F. 1980 "Pricing Policies in Public Enterprises with Special Reference to Experience in Tanzania." Paper presented at the International Workshop on Pricing Policies in Public Enterprises, Ljubljana, Yugoslavia, 26-30 May. Ljubljana: ICPE. /Tanzania /Price policy / East Africa

2952. Mbowe, George F. 1980 "Investment Criteria in Manufacturing Industry." Paper presented at the International Workshop on Investment Criteria and Investment Decision-Making Processes, Ljubljana, Yugoslavia, 20-24 Oct. Ljubljana: ICPE. /Investment /Manufacturing industry /Tanzania /East Africa

2953. McBain, Helen. 1981 "External Financing of the Water Commission of Jamaica." Economic and Social Studies (Mona, Kingston, Jamaica), V. 30, No. 1, pp. 171-196. /Caribbean Region /Jamaica /Water resources development /G330.97292 So13 LAC

2954. McCalla, Alex F., and Andrew Schmitz. 1981 "State Trading in Grain." In M. M. Kostecki, ed(s). State Trading in International Markets. New York: St. Martin's Press. pp. 55-77. /State trading organizations /Agricultural services / /HF 1410.5 S7 1981 M. /Also found in Les Cahiers du Cetai, no 79-07, April, 1979 /OPSS

2955. McCawley, P. 1970 "The Price of Electricity." Bulletin of Indonesia Economic Studies (Canberra, Australia), pp. 61-86. /Indonesia /Electrical utility industry /Price policy

2956. McCusker, Neal. 1958 "Administration of the New South Wales Government Railways." Public Administration (Sydney, Australia), pp. 229-237. /Australia /New South Wales, Australia(State) /Railway industry /Management

2957. McDermontt, D. E. 1967 "Salary Fixation for Top Management Personnel." Journal of Industrial Relations (Sydney, Australia), V. 9, No. 2, pp. 107-118. /Australia /Wages /Policy analysis

2958. McDiarmid, John. 1938 Government Corporations and Federal Funds. Chicago: University of Chicago Press. /Public financing / 388.8 M144g

2959. McDiarmid, John. 1940 "California Uses the Government Corporation." American Political Science Review V. 34, No. 2, pp. 300-306. /United States of America /California (State) / 320.5 Am31

2960. McDonald, J. A. 1951 "Some Notes on the Economics of Transportation." Canadian Journal of Economics and Political Science (Toronto), V. 17, pp. 515-522. /Economic analysis /Transportation industry / 305 C16

2961. McGuire, O. R. 1937 "Some Problems Arising from Government Corporations." University of Pennsylvania Law Review V. 85, No. 8, pp. 778-794. /United States of America

2962. McIntire, John A. 1936 "Government Corporations as Administrative Agencies: An Approach." George Washington Law Review pp. 161-210. /Public administration

2963. McKinley, Charles. 1952 Uncle Sam in the Pacific Northwest: Federal Management of Natural Resources in the Columbia River Valley. Berkeley, Calif.: University of California Press. /United States of America /Management / River valley development projects / Natural resource policy / 333.7 M215u

2964. McNeely, J. H. 1964 The Railways of Mexico. A Study in Nationalization. El Paso, Tex.: Texas Western College Press. /Mexico /Railway industry /Nationalization / HE 2817 M3 LAC

2965. McQuown, Omega Ruth. 1961 "From National Agency to Regional Institution: A Study of TVA in the Political Process." Ph.D. dissertation, Florida University. /United States of America /River valley development projects

2966. McVey, G. L. 1960 "The Public Accountability of Industry." Political Quarterly (London), V. 31, No. 4, pp. 495-508. /United Kingdom /Industrial sector /Accountability /320.5 P76p

2967. Mcleod, Thomas H. 1960 "Public Enterprise in Saskatchewan. The Development of Public Policy and Administrative Controls" Cambridge, Mass.: Unpublished Thesis, Harvard University. /Canada /Control Process

2968. Mdaghri, Driss Alaoui. 1981 "The Limits of State Control over Public Enterprises in Morocco." Public Enterprise V. 2, No. 1, pp. 41-52. /Morocco /Control process /OPSS

2969. Meade, J. E., and J. M. Flemming. 1944 "Price and Output Policy of State Enterprise, a Symposium." Economic Journal V. 44, pp. 321-339. /Price policy / 330.5 Ec7

2970. Medel Cámara, Braulio. 1972 "Notas históricas sobre la empresa pública en España." La Empresa Pública en España. Madrid: Instituto de Estudios Fiscales. /Spain

2971. Medel Camara, Braulio. 1973 "Análisis sectorial de la financiación de las empresas del INI." La empresa pública industrial en España: El INI. Madrid: Instituto de Estudios Fiscales. /Spain /Financing /Holding company

2972. Medina Ortega, Manuel. 1963 "Nacionalizaciones y acuerdos globales de indemnización." Revista de Administración Pública (Madrid), No. 40, pp. 79-120. /Nationalization

2973. Medling, C. T. 1963 Long Term Planning for Electricity Supply. London: Electricity Council. /United Kingdom /Electrical utility industry /Planning process

2974. Meher, M. R. 1971 "Problems of Public Enterprises." Lok Udyog (New Delhi), V. 5, No. 8, pp. 777-780. /India /354.54 L836 PCL

2975. Mehta, Asoka. 1975 "Seminal Role of Public Enterprises." In R. C. Dutt and Raj K. Nigam, ed(s). Towards Commanding Heights. New Delhi: Vivek Joshi. pp. 28-25. /India /Industrial sector /HD 4293 T68 PCL

2976. Mehta, B. 1958 "Public Enterprises and Parliamentary Control." Indian Journal of Public Administration (New Delhi), V. 4, No. 2. /India /Parliament /Control process /JA 26 I55 Pub Aff

2977. Meilan Gil, José Luis. 1967 Empresas públicas y turismo. Colegio de Estudios Administrativos Serie. Madrid: Boletín Oficial del Estado. No. 34. /Spain /Tourist industry

2978. Meireles, Heli Lopes. 1963 "Autarquias e entidades paraestatais." Revista Forense (Rio de Janeiro), V. 204, No. 724/, pp. 26-38. /Brazil /Public administration

2979. Meister, A. 1970 "Oú va l'autogestion yugoslave?" Homme et la Société (Paris), No. 17, pp. 91-96. /Yugoslavia /Worker self management

2980. Mejía Alarcón, Pedro Esteban. 1971 El ingreso fiscal y la industria petrolera. Santiago, Chile. /Chile /Oil industry

2981. Mejía Alarcón, Pedro Esteban. 1972 La industria del petróleo en Venezuela. Caracas: Instituto de Investigaciones Económicas, Facultad de Economía, Universidad Central de Venezuela. /Venezuela /Oil industry /Economic history /HD 9574 V42 M465 LAC

2982. Melin, Ingvar S. 1958 "The Control of Public Enterprises in Finland." Paper presented at the Congress of the International Political Science Association, Rome, September. /Finland /Control process

2983. Melin, Ingvar S. 1959 "Possibilities for Controlling State Business Activities in the Forms of Joint-Stock Companies." Politika V. 1, No. 3-4, pp. 126-139. /Control process /Mixed enterprises

2984. Melin, Ingvar S. 1963 "State Enterprise in Finland." Annals of Collective Economy V. 34, pp. 572-576. /Finland /330.5 An73

2985. Mello e Souza, Nelson. 1967 "Tecnocracia e nacionalismo." Revista de Administração Pública (Rio de Janeiro), V. 1, No. 2, pp. 72-112. /Public administration /Economic development /Nationalism / G350.5 R3261 LAC

2986. Mello, D. L. de 1967 The Management of Public Utilities--Brazil. Bangkok: I.U.L.A. Congress. /Brazil /Public utility industry /Management

2987. Mello, Pedro Carvalho de. 1978 "Bancos estaduais de desenvolvimento: Conflitos de objetivos e a estratégia de atuação regional." Revista Brasileira de Mercado de Capitais V. 4, No. 12, pp. 337-358. /Brazil /Development banks /Regional development / HG 4503 R45 LAC

2988. Membiela Guitian, Antonio. 1950 La municipalización de servicios públicos especialmente referida al abastecimiento de agua de las poblaciones. Madrid. /Spain /Public utility industry /Water supply industry

2989. Mendes France, P., and P. Cassese. 1960 "Note sulle imprese pubbliche in Francia e sulla misura dell'efficienza." Milan, Italy: Editora CIRIEC. /Evaluation /Economic efficiency /France

2990. Mendez G., Juan Carlos. 1981 "Un intento de medición del tamaño del sector público y de la presencia empresarial del Estado en Chile." Santiago, Chile: Unpublished. /Chile /Management /OPSS

2991. Mendez-Arocha, Alberto. 1974 Bases para una política energética venezolana. Caracas: Banco Central de Venezuela. /Venezuela /Energy use policy /Economic development /Oil industry / HD 9574 V42 M452 LAC

2992. Mendieta Zapata, Carlos. 1976 "El sistema de ventas de CONASUPO, organismo descentralizado del gobierno mexicano." Rio de Janeiro: FGV-EIAP. /Mexico /Decentralized authority /Food industry /Marketing /Case studies /OPSS

2993. Mendoza Oliván, V. 1972 "La configuración jurídica de la empresa pública." La empresa pública en España. Madrid: Instituto de Estudios Fiscales. /Spain /Law

2994. Menegazzi, Guido. 1970 "Las características fundamentales del mercado y de la empresa en una economía mixta." La Empresa Pública. Zaragoza, Spain: Publicaciones del Real Colegio de España en Bolonia. pp. 33-40. /Mixed enterprises

2995. Menemkis, P. R., Jr. 1937 "The Public Authority: Some Legal and Practical Aspects." Yale Law Review pp. 14-33. /United States of America /Public authority /Law

2996. Menon, T. M. C. 1976 "Policy Regarding Investment, Prices and Returns in Public Sector Companies." Approaches to the Public Enterprise Policy in Asia on Investment, Prices and Returns Criteria. Kuala Lumpur, Malaysia: U.N. Asian Center for Development Administration. pp. 168-187. /India /Price policy /Investment /Profits / HD 4276 A8 1976

2997. Menon, T. M. C., and Prem Shankar Jha. 1980 Management of Public Enterprises in Developing Asian Countries: A Guide. Kuala Lumpur: UN. Asian and Pacific Development Administration Centre. /Asia /Management /Control process

2998. Menon, V. K. R. 1955 "Role of Management in a Welfare State--Stress on Productivity of Labour." Major Industries of Asia V. 5, pp. 249-259. /Productivity /Management /Social welfare policy /Socialist economy / Labor relations

2999. Menthon, F. de. 1945 "La nationalisation du crédit." Droit Social (Paris), /France /Banking system /Nationalization

3000. Menzler, F. A. A. 1950 "London and Its Passenger Transport System." Journal of the Royal Statistical Society (London), V. 93, pp. 229-345. /United Kingdom /Transportation industry

3001. Merewitz, Leonard. 1972 "Public Transportation: Wish Fulfillment and Reality in the San Francisco Bay Area." American Economic Review V. 62, No. 2, pp. 78-86. /United States of America /Mass transportation industry /330.5 Am312

3002. Merewitz, Leonard. 1977 "On Measuring the Efficiency of Public Enterprises: Bus Operating Companies in the San Francisco Bay Area." Transportation V. 6, pp. 45-55. /United States of America /Mass transportation industry

3003. Merino-Manon, J. 1981 "Control de empresas públicas en México." pp. 419-455. /Mexico

3004. Merlot, Joseph, and Joseph Haverland. 1958 "The Public Services Mutual Insurance Company (S.M.A.P.)." Annals of Collective Economy V. 29, pp. 571-581. /Belgium /Cooperatives /Insurance industry /Financial institutions

/330.5 An733

3005. Merrett, A. J. 1964 A Consideration of Investment and Pricing Criteria in the Nationalized Industries. Manchester: School of Economic and Social Studies. pp. 261-288. /Investment /Price policy

3006. Merrett, A. J., and Allen Sykes. 1962 "Financial Control of State Industry. II." Banker V. 112, No. 434, pp. 227-234. /United Kingdom /Public financing /Control process /332.05 B224

3007. Merrett, A. J., and Allen Sykes. 1962 "Financial Control of State Industry. I." Banker V. 112, No. 433, pp. 156-161. /United Kingdom /Control process /Public financing /332.05 B224

3008. Merusi, Fabio. 1962 "Osservazioni in tema di privatizzazione di imprese di stato nella República Federale." Tedesca (Milan). /Italy /Privatization

3009. Merusi, Fabio. 1970 "La participación de la empresa pública en la elaboración del plan." La Empresa Pública. Zaragoza, Spain: Publicaciones del Real Colegio de España en Bolonia. pp. 1589-1604. /Spain /Planning process

3010. Mesa Cock, Luis Alfonso. 1975 "El Instituto Colombiano de los Seguros Sociales,`ICSS´." Rio de Janeiro: FGV-EIAP. /Colombia /Social security /Public financing /Control process /Law /Public administration /Case studies /OPSS

3011. Meschini, Pietro. 1957 "Alcune considerazioni in torno alta natura giuridica degli enti publici economici nell´ordinamento italiano." Rivista Trimestrale di Diretto Pubblico (Rome), pp. 858-907. /Italy /Law

3012. Meschini, Pietro. 1961 "Entes públicos econômicos na Italia." Revista de Direito Administrativo (Rio de Janeiro), V. 63, pp. 355-381. /Italy /Evaluation

3013. Mestre, A. 1980 "Les problèmes juridiques posés par les entreprises publiques tunisiennes." Revue Francaise d´Administration Publique and Bulletin de l´Institut International d´Administration Publique (Paris), No. 15, pp. 33-43. /Tunisia /Law

3014. Mesuri, Fabio. 1964 Il potere di indirizzo del Ministero delle Partecipazioni Statali sugli enti di gestione. Milan: Ed. CIRIEC. /Italy /Management

3015. Metz, M. 1964 Evaluación económica del subsidio de la empresa de Ferrocarriles del Estado de Chile. Santiago, Chile: Ministerio de Hacienda, Dirección de Presupuestos. /Chile /Railway industry /Subsidization policy /Economic analysis

3016. Mexico. Centro Nacional de Productividad. 1981 La empresa pública en México: Factor de desarrollo económico y social del país. Mexico City. /Mexico /Economic development /Social development

3017. Mexico. Fondo de Garantía y Fomento a la Indústria Mediana y Pequeña. FOGAIN. 25 Años. Mexico City: Nacional Financiera. /Mexico /Development corporation /Development planning /Economic history /Industrial sector /OPSS

3018. Mexico. Instituto Nacional de Administración Pública. 1976 Las empresas públicas en México. Su importancia en el sector industrial y comercial: Bases jurídicas de su acción. Mexico City. /Mexico /Industrial sector /Law /Control process /Planning process / HD 4013 E475 LAC

3019. Mexico. Instituto de Desarrollo Económico. 1964 Problemas relativos a la organización y administración de empresas públicas en el sector industrial. Mexico City. /Mexico /Industrial sector /Organization behavior /Administrative management

3020. Mexico. National Team of Experts. 1980 The Role of the Public Sector in the Mexican Economy. Ljubljana: ICPE. /Mexico

3021. Mexico. Secretaría de Programación y Presupuesto. 1979 La industria petrolera en México. Mexico City. /Mexico /Oil industry /Wages /Export policy /Statistics /HD 9574 M62 I528 LAC

3022. Meyer, H. R. 1905 "Municipal Ownership in Great Britain." Journal of Political Economy V. 13, pp. 481-505. /United Kingdom /Local government / 330.5 J82 PCL

3023. Meyer, Monique. 1966 L'entreprise industrielle d'Etat en Union Soviétique. Paris: Cujas. /Union of Soviet Socialist Reps. /Industrial sector

3024. Meyers, Charles A. 1956 "Labor Problems of Rationalization: The Experience of India." International Labor Review V. 73, pp. 431-50. /India /Labor relations

3025. Meyers, Frederic. 1958 "Nationalization, Union Structures, and Wages Policy in the British Coal Mining Industry." Southern Economics Journal V. 24, pp. 421-433. /United Kingdom /Wages /Trade unions /Coal mining industry /Nationalization

3026. Meyers, Frederic. 1971 The State and Government Employee Unions in France. Ann Arbor: Institute of Labor and Industrial Relations, University of Michigan, Wayne State University. /France /Labor relations /Trade unions /HD 8013 F6 M48

3027. Meyers, Frederic. 1973 "Public Employee Unions: The French Experience." Industrial Relations V. 12, No. 1. /France /Labor relations /Trade unions / 331.105 In19

3028. Meynaud, Jean. 1957 Aspectos actuais da empresa pública na França: o estatuto jurídico, o aspecto economico, o aspecto político-social. Rio de Janeiro: FGV-EIAP. /France /Economic analysis /Political analysis /Law

3029. Meynaud, Jean. 1959 "Etudes et documents sur l´entreprise publique." Revue Economique (Paris), V. 10, No. 4, pp. 609-623. /Evaluation / 330.5 R3282

3030. Meynaud, Jean. 1961 "Aspects of Public Enterprise Today: A Bibliographical Study." Annals of Collective Economy V. 32, pp. 239-260. /Bibliography / 330.5 An73

3031. Meynaud, Jean. 1961 Bilan de l´entreprise publique en France. Milan, Italy: ENI, Scuola di Studi Sugli Idrocarburi. /France

3032. Meza Hidalgo, Horacio. 1981 El papel de la banca de desarrollo en la nueva economía sandinista. Managua, Nicaragua: Banco Nacional de Desarrollo. /Nicaragua /Development banks /Economic development /Mixed enterprises

3033. Meza San Martin, W. 1963 "Consolidation of the Public Sector in Chile and Alternative Method with Planning Ends." Economía (Chile), V. 21, No. 80-8, pp. 35-48. /Chile /Planning process

3034. Meza, Scott. 1980 "Two Interpretations of Immunity from Prejudgment Attachment under the Foreign Sovereign Immunities Act." North Carolina Journal of International Law and Comparative Regulation V. 6, pp. 151-162. /Law /International trade /United States of America

3035. Mezzocapo, V. 1966 Enti pubblici dell´ordinamento creditizio. Milan: CIRIEC. /Italy /Credit policy

3036. Miah, Uttam Ali. 1981 "Financial Profitability and Losses in Public Enterprises in Bangladesh." Paper presented at the International Workshop on Financial Profitability and Losses in Public Enterprises, Ljubljana, Yugoslavia, 1-5 June. Ljubljana: ICPE. /Bangladesh /Profits

3037. Michael, Mesfin Gabre. 1983 "Labour-Management Relations in Public Enterprises in Africa." Labour Management Relations in Public Enterprises in Africa, Labour-Management Relations Series No. 60. Geneva: ILO. pp. 3-31. /Labor relations /Personnel management /Africa /OPSS

3038. Midoun, Mohamed. 1982 "L´entreprise publique comme instrument des politiques de l´Etat." Paper presented at the Tokyo Round Table preparatory to the 19th International Congress of Administrative Sciences, 13-17 Sept. /Tunisia /Goal setting /Accountability /Policy analysis /OPSS

3039. Mier, Mariano J. 1982 "Palabras del Sr. Mariano J. Mier, presidente de la Asociación de Bancos de Puerto Rico, ante los delegados de la Asociación Latinoamericana de Instituciones de Desarrollo Económico." San Juan, Puerto Rico: Asociación Latinoamericana de Instituciones Financieras de Desarrollo (ALIDE), XII Asamblea General Ordinaria. /Puerto Rico /Development planning /OPSS

3040. Mifsud, Francis. 1980 "Case Study of Transfer of Technology through a Joint Venture among Malta Development Corporation (MDC) and a Foreign Corporation." paper presented at the International Workshop on Preparations and Negotiations of Technology Transfer Agreements for Public Enterprises in Developing Countries, Ljubljana, Yugoslavia, 27-31 October. Ljubljana: ICPE. /Malta /Technology transfer

3041. Miguel García, Pedro de. 1970 "The Tennessee Valley Authority." Documentación Administrativa (Madrid), No. 149. /United States of America /River valley development projects

3042. Milisavljevic, M. 1969 Latest Planning Tendencies of Yugoslav Enterprise. Herceg Novi, Yugoslavia: U.N. Public Administrative Division. /Yugoslavia /Planning process

3043. Militerno, A. A. 1976 "Sull'equilibrio dell'impresa pubblica." Rassegna Economica V. 40, No. 1, pp. 97-114. /Evaluation

3044. Milivojevic, Bogoljub, and Sinisa Kalapasev. 1979 "Capital Project Management: Danube Oil and Gas Enterprise-DOG: Yugoslav Case Study." Paper presented at the Interregional Workshop "Developing Problem Solving Skills in Public Enterprises," Ljubljana, Yugoslavia, 2-17 April. Ljubljana: ICPE. /Yugoslavia /Oil industry /Case studies / Project management

3045. Millaruelo, Jesús. 1950 "Las nacionalizaciones y el derecho internacional." Revista de Administración Pública (Madrid), No. 3, pp. 213-254. /Nationalization /International law

3046. Milligan, Frank C. 1951 "Ministerial Control of the British Nationalized Industries." Canadian Journal of Economics and Political Science (Toronto), V. 17, pp. 164-183. /United Kingdom /Control process / 305 C16

3047. Milligan, Frank C., and H. R. Bolls. 1955 "The Crown Corporations." In A. H. Hanson, ed(s). Public Enterprise. Brussels: IIAS. pp. 79-109. /United Kingdom /HD 3850 H28 Law

3048. Mills, G. E., and M. Howe. 1960 "Consumer Representation and the Withdrawal of Railway Services." Public Administration (Sydney, Australia), V. 38. /Australia /Railway industry /Public services /Consumer producer conflict

3049. Mills, Gladstone E. 1974 "Public Policy and Private Enterprise in the Commonwealth Caribbean." Social and Economic Studies (Mona, Kingston, Jamaica), pp. 216-241. /British Caribbean /Private sector / G330.97292 So13 LAC

3050. Mills, Gladstone E. 1980 "Definitions and Classification of Public Enterprises." Paper presented at the Expert Group Meeting on Concept, Definition and Classification of Public Enterprises, Tangier, Morocco, 15-19 December. Ljubljana: ICPE. /Taxonomy

3051. Mills, Gladstone E. 1981 "The Administration of Public Enterprise: Jamaica and Trinidad-Tobago." Economic and

Social Studies (Mona, Kingston, Jamaica), V. 30, No. 1, pp. 45-74. /Caribbean Region /Jamaica /Trinidad and Tobago /Management /Accountability /Parliament /Goal setting /Price policy /G330.97292 So13 LAC

3052. Millward, R. 1973 "Price Restraint, Anti-Inflation Policy and Public and Private Industry in the United Kingdom, 1949-1973." Economic Journal V. 86, No. 342, pp. 226-242. /United Kingdom /Price policy /Inflation /Industrial sector /330.5 Ec7

3053. Milne, R. S. 1956 "Control of Government Corporations in the United States." Public Administration (London), V. 34, No. 4, pp. 355-364. /United States of America /Control process /320.5 J826

3054. Milne, R. S. 1967 "Government Corporations in the Philippines. In Chandrasekhar and Hultman, ed(s). Problems of Economic Development. Boston: D.C. Heath. pp. 155-170. /Philippines /Evaluation

3055. Milosavljevic, Ljubisa. 1978 "L´entraînement des consultants internés pour l´amélioration de la productivité dans les entreprises publiques." Paper presented at the Séminaire international sur la gestion et la formation dans les entreprises publiques dans les pays en voie de dévelopement, Ljubljana, Yugoslavia, 3-15 March. Ljubljana: ICPE. /Training /Productivity /Consultant services

3056. Milward, A. S. 1970 The New Order and the French Economy. (The Exploitation of the French Coal Industry) Oxford: Clarendon Press. /France /Coal mining industry /Economic analysis / 330.944 M648n

3057. Mimica, Milos. 1962 "How Means of Production in Yugoslavia Became Social Property." Yugoslav Trade Unions pp. 19-24. /Yugoslavia /Socialist economy

3058. Minces, J. 1965 "Autogestion et lutte de classe en Algerie." Temps Modernes (Paris), V. 20, No. 229, pp. 2204-2231. /Algeria /Worker self management / 054 T249 PCL

3059. Minelli, A. R. 1973 "Il controllo político sugli enti di intervento economico-sociale in Inghilterra." Rivista Trimestrale di Scienza della Administrazione (Rome), V. 2, No. 3, pp. 195-224. /United Kingdom /Control process

3060. Minervini, Gustavo. 1970 "La empresa pública y el estatuto del gran empresario." La empresa pública. Zaragoza, Spain: Publicaciones del Real Colegio de España en Bolonia. pp. 231-244. /Law /Entrepreneurial activity

3061. Minervini, Gustavo. 1982 "Societa a participazione pubblica." Giurisprudenza Commerciale V. 1982, No. 2. /Italy /Law /Mixed enterprises

3062. Minguet, L. R. 1968 "Public Undertakings in the Economic Community; A Note on Recent Publication by the European Center for Public Enterprise." Annals of Public and

Cooperative Economy V. 39, No. 1, pp. 98-101. /Evaluation / /European Economic Community /Case studies / 330.5 An73

3063. Minocha, O. P. 1979 "A Critical Assessment of Staffing Managerial Positions in Public Undertakings." Lok Udyog (New Delhi), V. 13, No. 6, pp. 1-14. /Management /Personnel management /354.54 L836 PCL

3064. Minocha, O. P. 1981 "Remunerating Managerial Positions in Public and Private Sectors in India: A Comparative Analysis." Lok Udyog (New Delhi), V. 15, No. 4, pp. 7-16. /India /Private enterprises /Comparative analysis /Wages /354.54 L836 PCL

3065. Minsic, D. 1959 "Le revenu de l´entreprise et son répartition." Annales de l´Economie Collective pp. 110-124. /Profits

3066. Mintz, J. M. 1980 "Mixed Enterprises and State Equity Financing of Industry." Paper presented at the Second BAPEG Conference: Public Enterprises in Mixed Economy LDCs, at Boston, April. /OPSS

3067. Mintz, J. M. 1982 "Mixed enterprises and risk sharing in industrial development." In Leroy P. Jones et al., ed(s). Public enterprise in less-developed countries. New York: Cambridge University Press. pp. 327-348. /Economic theory /HD 3850 P83 PCL

3068. Miranda, S. 1968 Estructura financiera de las empresas estatales de producción y su evolución en el período 1962-1966. Santiago, Chile. /Chile /Financing

3069. Mircev, Dimitar, Anka Tominsk, and Tanja Dobrin. 1983 The Role of Public Enterprises in the Advancement of Women in Yugoslavia. Ljubljana: ICPE. /Yugoslavia /Women´s studies /Social development

3070. Mirza, Ghafoor A. 1978 "Report of the International Seminar on Management and Training in Public Enterprises, Ljubljana, September 18-October 6, 1978." Ljubljana: ICPE. /Training /Management

3071. Mishan, E. J. 1967 "A Proposed Normalization Procedure for Public Investment Criteria." Economic Journal pp. 777-796. /Investment / 330.5 Ec7

3072. Mishra, M. 1958 "Price Policy of Public Enterprises in Underdeveloped Economies with Special Indian Journal of Commerce (Allahabad, India), V. 11, No. 38. /India /Price policy

3073. Mishra, N. D. 1966 "Public Sector Enterprises; Some Problem Areas in the Administration of Industrial Undertakings." Monthly Commentary on Indian Economic Conditions pp. 13-20. /Industrial sector /Public administration /Evaluation /Control process

3074. Mishra, R. K. 1974 "Profitability of Public Enterprises in India." *Lok Udyog* (New Delhi), V. 8, No. 2, pp. 53-62. /India /Profits /354.54 L836 PCL

3075. Mishra, R. K. 1975 *Problems of Working Capital with Reference to Selected Public Undertakings in India.* Bombay: Somaiya Publications Pvt., Ltd. /Accounting /India /Financial performance /Working capital

3076. Mishra, R. K. 1980 "Bank Financing of Working Capital in Public Enterprises." *Institute of Public Enterprises Journal* V. 3, No. 1-2, pp. 7-18. /India /Financing /Commercial banks /Working capital

3077. Mishra, R. K. 1980 "Pricing in Public Enterprises." *Indian Journal of Public Administration* (New Delhi), V. 26, pp. 987-1008. /India /Price policy / JA 26 I55 Pub Aff

3078. Mishra, R. K. 1980 "Pricing and Returns in Public Enterprises." *Lok Udyog* (New Delhi), V. 14, No. 8, pp. 29-40. /India /Price policy /Profits /Financial performance /354.54 L836 PCL

3079. Mishra, R. K., and Shri S. Ravishankar. 1982 "Public Enterprises in India: The Problem of Organization Development." *Lok Udyog* (New Delhi), V. 16, No. 4, pp. 23-28. /India /Organization development /354.54 L836 PCL

3080. Mishra, R. N. 1979 "Technology Transfer - A Systems Approach." *Lok Udyog* (New Delhi), V. 13, No. 7, pp. 15-20. /Technology transfer /354.54 L836 PCL

3081. Misra, A. C. 1979 "Worker's Management Participation in Industry: Conditions for its Success." *Lok Udyog* (New Delhi), V. 13, No. 4, pp. 37-42. /India /Worker management participation /354.54 L836 PCL

3082. Misra, P. N. 1980 "Industrial Finance Corporation of India in the Promotion of New International Class." *Lok Udyog* (New Delhi), V. 13, No. 10-1, pp. 55-62. /India /Financial institutions /Development corporation /Case studies /354.54 L836 PCL

3083. Mitchell, Bridger M., and Paul R. Kleindorfer. 1980 "Public Enterprise and Regulation in International Perspective." In Bridger M. Mitchell and Paul R. Kleindorfer, ed(s). *Regulated Industries and Public Enterprise.* Lexington, Ma.: D.C. Heath and Company, Lexington Books. pp. 3-6. /Economic analysis /OPSS

3084. Mitchell, Bridger M., and Paul R. Kleindorfer, eds. 1980 *Regulated Industries and Public Enterprises: European and United States Perspectives.* Lexington, Mass.: Lexington Books. /United States of America /United Kingdom /Price policy /Business regulation policy /Public utility regulation policy /Airline regulation policy /Electrical utility industry /OPSS

3085. Mitra, M. S. 1972 "A Design for Public Sector Holding Company." Lok Udyog (New Delhi), V. 6, No. 7, pp. 15-20. /India /Subsidiaries /Holding company /354.54 L836 PCL

3086. Mitsufuji, T. 1969 Industrial Relations in the Public Sector in Japan. (Asian Regional Conference on Industrial Relations). Tokyo. /Japan /Industrial relations

3087. Mittal, Dutt Kumar. 1982 "Pricing by Public Enterprises - An Orientation to Suit all Interests." Lok Udyog (New Delhi), V. 16, No. 2, pp. 25-30. /India /Price policy /354.54 L836

3088. Mittal, Sharad K. 1980 "An Experience of Technology Transfer." Paper presented at the International Workshop on Preparations and Negotiations of Technology Transfer Agreements for Public Enterprises in Developing Countries, Ljubljana, Yugoslavia, 27-31 October. Ljubljana: ICPE. /Technology transfer

3089. Moch, J. 1953 "Nationalization in France." Annals of Collective Economy V. 24, No. 2, pp. 97-117. /France /Nationalization / 330.5 An73

3090. Modeen, T. 1965 "Théorie sur la notion d'établissement publique indépendent en droit finlandais." Revue Internationale des Sciences Administratives V. 31, No. 3, pp. 217-221. /Finland /Law

3091. Modeen, T. 1965 Les établissements publics indépendents dans l'organisation administrative de Finlande. Abo: Abo Akademi. /Finland /Public administration

3092. Modeen, T. 1966 Le régime des activités commerciales et industrielles des pouvoirs publics en Finlande. Helsinki: Institutum Jurisprudentiae Comparativae Universitatis Helsingiensis. /Finland /Commercial sector /Industrial sector / K 555 I507 F5 Law

3093. Moggi, Antonio S. 1971 A investigação tecnológica. Rio de Janeiro: Petróleo Brasileiro S.A. /Brazil /Oil industry /Technology /

3094. Mohamed, A. R. 1969 The Role of Financial Intermediaries in Public Enterprises. Mauritius: UNECA. Seminar on Role of Public Enterprise in Planning and Plan Implementation. /Planning process /Financing

3095. Mohamed, I., and Hersi M. Hersi. 1979 "Role of Public Sector in Developing Countries: Somali Country Report." Paper presented at the Regional Meeting of African Countries on the Role of the Public Sector in Developing Countries, Arusha, Tanzania, 17-21 Dec. Ljubljana: ICPE. /Somalia

3096. Mohan, Manendra. 1982 "Life Insurance Corporation of India - A Conceptual Analysis." Lok Udyog (New Delhi), V. 16, No. 5, pp. 17-26. /India /Case studies /Insurance industry /354.54 L836 PCL

3097. Mohsin, Mohammad. 1973 "Public Financial Corporations and the Problem of Equity Financing." Lok Udyog (New Delhi), V. 6, No. 11, pp. 41-46. /India /Financing /354.54 L836 PCL

3098. Mohtadullah, Khalid. 1981 "Organizational Commitment to Management Training in Public Enterprises (Utilities)." Paper presented at the Regional Workshop on Management Training and Development in Public Enterprises in Developing Countries, Karachi, Pakistan, 5-15 Jan. Ljubljana: ICPE. /Training /Management /Public utility industry

3099. Molina Lopes, Guillermo E. 1972 Empresas públicas: Proyectos de esquema de manual del analista. Rio de Janeiro: FGV-EIAP. /Planning process

3100. Molina Lopes, Guillermo E. 1972 Metodologia para programación presupuestoria de las empresas públicas. Rio de Janeiro: FGV-EIAP. /Budgetary process

3101. Moll, Klaus. 1979 "Performance Improvement of Public Sector Industries in Mixed Economy Countries." Paper presented at the Interregional Worshop on Control Systems for Public Enterprises in Developing Countries, Ljubljana, Yugoslavia, 9-13 July. Ljubljana: ICPE. /Economic efficiency /Control process /Industrial sector /Mixed enterprises

3102. Molle, Giacomo. 1970 "En materia de empresas públicas." La empresa pública. Zaragoza, Spain: Publicaciones del Real Colegio de España en Bolonia. pp. 1649-1654. /Law

3103. Mombach, M. 1958 "A Brief Historical Account of the Work of the National Housing Society." Annals of Collective Economy V. 29, pp. 550-557. /Belgium /Housing industry /Urban development / Case studies / 330.5 An73

3104. Mommer, D. 1971 El Estado venezolano y la industria petrolera. Santiago, Chile. /Venezuela /Oil industry /Nationalization

3105. Mon Santos, Pablo. 1979 "Control Mechanism of Public Enterprises in Latin America." Paper presented at the Interregional Workshop on Control Systems for Public Enterprises in Developing Countries, Ljubljana, Yugoslavia, 9-13 July. Ljubljana: ICPE. /Latin America /Control process

3106. Moncayo, Eduardo Pascual. 1978 "La programación y las empresas públicas." In Rosa Luz Alegría et al., Empresas públicas. Mexico City: Presidencia de la República. pp. 65-76. /Mexico /Planning process /HD 4013 E479 1978 LAC

3107. Moncayo, G. R. 1959 "The Nationalization of Enterprises in France." Revista Jurídica (Tucumán, Argentina), No. 6, pp. 97-121. /France /Nationalization

3108. Moneim, Abdel Salam Abdel. 1974 "Public Industries in the Sudan Industrial Production Corporation (IPC): A National Paper of Sudan." Paper presented at the International Seminar '74: Planning in Public Enterprises in Developing Countries, Ljubljana, Yugoslavia, Sept.23-Oct.9. Ljubljana:

ICPE. /Sudan /Industrial sector

3109. Mongia, M. L., and B. T. Bhide. 1973 "Import Procedures and Public Enterprises." Lok Udyog (New Delhi), V. 6, No. 11, pp. 27-36. /India /Imports /Control process /354.54 L836 PCL

3110. Monnier, Lionel. 1979 "Comments on Marginal Cost Pricing in the EDF." Annals of Public and Cooperative Economy V. 50, No. 3, pp. 149-156. /France /Electrical utility industry /Price policy /330.5 An73

3111. Monteiro, Antonio Rodrigues. 1951 O problema da eletricidade no Brasil. Rio de Janeiro. /Brazil /Electrical utility industry

3112. Montel, M. 1958 "L´Etat et les entreprises nationalisées." Annales de l´Economie Collective pp. 84-104. /France /Nationalization

3113. Monteverde Bussaleu, Juan-José. 1979 "Informe preliminar sobre la regulación de la empresa pública en el Perú." Paper presented at the International Seminar on Regulation of the Public Enterprise, Mexico City. /Law /Peru /Control process /OPSS

3114. Montias, J. M. 1965 The Economics of a Socialist Enterprise. New York: Praeger. /Socialist economy /Economic analysis

3115. Moorthy, V. K. 1981 "The Malaysian National Oil Corporation--Is It a Government Instrumentality?" International Law and Comparative Law Quarterly V. 30, pp. 638-659. /Malaysia /Oil industry

3116. Moortlz, K. Krishna. 1960 "The `Public or Private´ Debate--People´s Shares?" Far Eastern Economic Review V. 30, No. 11, pp. 587-590. /India /Comparative analysis /Private sector / 330.95 F223

3117. Moos, S. 1964 "An Experiment in Mixed Enterprise." Bulletin of the Oxford University Institute of Economics and Statistics V. 26, No. 2, pp. 195-204. /Italy / 310.5 OX2b

3118. Morais, Antao de. 1960 "Autarquia. Autonomia." Revista de Direito Administrativo (Rio de Janeiro), No. 59, pp. 497-504. /Brazil /Law

3119. Moran, Theodore. 1972 "América Latina después de las nacionalizaciones: Problemas e incógnitas." Panorama Económico (Santiago, Chile), No. 270. /Latin America /Nationalization / G330.983 P194 LAC

3120. Moreno Paez, Leocadio Manuel. 1958 "Notas para un estudio sobre la municipalización de servicios públicos." Revista de Estudios de la Vida Social (Madrid), V. 17, No. 98, pp. 211-232. /Spain /Decentralization /Public services /Local government

3121. Moreno, Xavier. 1983 "Conciliação dos orçamentos das empresas estatais com os orçamentos e os imperativos financieros nacionais." Paper presented at the ECLA seminar on state control and planning of public enterprises, Brasília, 15-17 June. Brasília: UNECLA. /Control Process /Financing /OPSS

3122. Morrison, Herbert. 1933 Socialization and Transport. London: Constable. /United Kingdom /Nationalization /Transportation industry / HD 4145 M6 HRC

3123. Morrison, Herbert. 1950 Public Accountability. Public Administration. London. pp. 176-178. /Public Administration /Accountability

3124. Morrison, Herbert. 1950 "Public Control of the Socialized Industries." Public Administration (London), V. 28, pp. 3-9. /United Kingdom /Control process /JA 8 P8 Pub Aff

3125. Morrison, Herbert. 1952 Efficiency in the Nationalised Industries. London: Institute of Public Administration; Allen & Unwin. /United Kingdom /Economic efficiency /Evaluation

3126. Morrison, Lord. 1959 Government and Parliament. A Survey from the Inside. London: Oxford University Press. /United Kingdom /Government authority /Parliament /Control process /354.42 M834g

3127. Moscovici, S. 1960 "Les mineurs jugent la nationalization." Sociologie du Travail (Paris), V. 2, No. 3, pp. 216-229. /France /Mining industry /Nationalization / 331.05 So14 PCL

3128. Moshi, H. P. B. 1980 "Financial Performance of Public Corporations: A Case of District Development Corporations (DDCc)." Utafiti V. 5, No. 1, pp. 1-25. /Tanzania /East Africa /Financial performance /Profits /Regional development /OPSS

3129. Motta, Paulo Roberto. 1979 "Control of Public Enterprises in Brazil." Paper presented at the Interregional Workshop on Control Systems for Public Enterprises in Developing Countries, Ljubljana, Yugoslavia, 9-13 July. Ljubljana: ICPE. /Brazil /Control process

3130. Motta, Paulo Roberto. 1980 "Management Development and Training: Inference from the Experience of Brazilian Public Enterprises." Paper presented at the Expert Group Meeting on the Research Projects on Education and Training in Public Enterprises in Developing Countries, Ljubljana, Yugoslavia, 17-22 March. Ljubljana: ICPE. /Brazil /Training /Management

3131. Motta, Paulo Roberto. 1980 "Management Development and Training: Inference from the Experience of Brazilian Public Enterprises." Public Enterprise V. 1, No. 2, pp. 18-25. /Brazil /Training /Management

3132. Motta, Paulo Roberto. 1981 "Report of the Expert Group Meeting on Performance Criteria and the Implementation of Performance Evaluation Systems in Public Enterprises in Developing Countries, Ljubljana, November 23-27, 1981."

Ljubljana: ICPE. /Evaluation

3133. Motta, Paulo Roberto. 1981 "Evaluation of Public Enterprises: The Public Dimension and the Quest for Responsiveness." Paper presented at the Expert Group Meeting on Performance Criteria and the Implementation of Performance Evaluation Systems in Public Enterprises in Developing Countries, Ljubljana, Yugoslavia, 23-27 November. Ljubljana: ICPE. /Evaluation

3134. Motta, Paulo Roberto. 1982 "Government Control of Public Enterprises." Public Enterprise V. 2, No. 4, pp. 9-75. /Control process / OPSS

3135. Motta, Paulo Roberto. 1982 "Rationale for Government Control over Public Enterprises." In United Kingdom, Commonwealth Secretariat, ed(s). Government Executive and Supervisory Control over Public Enterprises. London. pp. 181-194. /Control process

3136. Motta, Paulo Roberto 1983 "Avaliação de empresas públicas nos países em desenvolvimento: A Perspective Social." Paper presented at the ECLA seminar:State Control and Planning of Public Enterprises, Brasília, 15-17 June. Brasília: UNECLA. /Goal setting /Economic efficiency /Profits /OPSS

3137. Moulin, L. 1959 "Note sur le principe du contrôl des organismes d´intérêt publique." Res Publica (Louvain), pp. 28-37. /France /Public interest /Control process

3138. Mourad, Ahmed F., and Sadiq Al-Ayoubi. 1977 "Syria." Public Enterprises and Development in the Arab Countries: Legal and Managerial Aspects. New York: PRaeger for the International Center for Law in Development. pp. 124-155. /Syria /Law /Economic analysis /Control process /HD 3850 P8 PCL

3139. Mozina, S. 1976 "Methods and Programmes of Management Training." Paper presented at the International Seminar on Management and Training on Public Enterprises in Developing Countries, Ljubljana, Yugoslavia, Sept. 21-Oct. 2. Ljubljana: ICPE. /Training /Management /Also presented at similar seminars in Ljubljana, Oct. 10-28, 1977 and Sept. 18-Oct. 6, 1978 and at the French-language version in Ljubljana, 5-15 Mar. 1978.

3140. Mozina, S. 1978 "The Design of Sociologically Relevant Information for Assessing the Achievement of the Public Enterprise." Paper presented at the Workshop on Information System for the Evaluation of Business Efficiency in Public Enterprises in Developing Countries, Ljubljana, Yugoslavia, 13-17 November. Ljubljana: ICPE. /Information system /Evaluation

3141. Mozina, S. 1979 "Management Education and Training in Yugoslavia." Paper presented at the International Workshop on Education and Training in Public Enterprises in Developing Countries, Ljubljana, Yugoslavia, 12-17 February. Ljubljana: ICPE. /Yugoslavia /Training /Management /

3142. Mozina, S. 1979 "Training in Public Enterprises: Purpose, Concepts, Topics and Problems." Paper presented at the International Seminar on Management and Training in Public Enterprises in Developing Countries, Ljubljana, Yugoslavia, 12-17 February. Ljubljana: ICPE. /Training / Also presented at the French-language seminar version under the title, "La formation dans les entreprises publiques: But, concepts, sujets et problèmes," Ljubljana, Yugoslavia, 5-15 Mar. 1980.

3143. Mozina, S. 1980 "Management Training and Development in Public Enterprises of Developing Countries: Some Problems and Recommendations." Paper presented at the Interregional Seminar on Training Management in Public Enterprises in Developing Countries, Ljubljana, Yugoslavia, Sept. 29-Oct.10. Ljubljana: ICPE. /Developing nations /Management /Training

3144. Mozina, S. 1981 "Training of Trainers." _Public Enterprise_ V. 1, No. 4, pp. 79-80. /Training /Management /OPSS

3145. Mozina, S. 1981 "Why Research in Management Training?" Paper presented at the Interregional Seminar on Training Management in Public Enterprises in Developing Countries, Ljubljana, Yugoslavia, 19-28 October. Ljubljana: ICPE. /Training /Management / Economic research

3146. Mozina, S., and Anton Kukovica, eds. 1979 _La gestion et la formation dans les entreprises publiques dans les pays en voie de développement._ Ljubljana: ICPE. /Developing nations /Planning process

3147. Mozina, S., and Aubrey B. Armstrong. 1976 "Report of the International Seminar on Management and Training in Public Enterprises, Ljubljana, September 21-October 2, 1976." Ljubljana: ICPE. /Training /Management

3148. Mozina, S., and Marija Oblak. 1980 "Education and Training of Managers in Yugoslavia in 1945-1980." Paper presented at the Expert Group Meeting on the Research Projects on Education and Training in Developing Countries, Ljubljana, Yugoslavia, 17-22 March. Ljubljana: ICPE. /Training /Economic history /Yugoslavia /Management

3149. Mozina, S., and Marija Oblak. 1981 "Handbook on Manpower Planning in Public Enterprises in Developing Countries." Paper presented at the Interregional Seminar on Training Management in Public Enterprises in Developing Countries, Ljubljana, Yugoslavia, 19-28 October. Ljubljana: ICPE. /Personnel management /Developing nations /Training /Manpower planning

3150. Mozina, S., ed. 1979 _Management and Training in Public Enterprises._ Ljubljana: ICPE. /Training /Management

3151. Mozoomadar, Ajit. 1976 "Suggested Outline of ACDA Project on Investment and Pricing Policies for _Approaches to the Public Enterprise Policy in Asia on Investment, Prices, and Returns Criteria._ Kuala Lumpur: U. N. Asian Center for Development Administration. pp. 107-112. /Asia /Price policy /Investment

/HD 4276 A8 1976

3152. Mramba, B. 1981 "Holding Companies in Tanzania: The Pros and Cons." Lok Udyog (New Delhi), V. 15, No. 1, pp. 33-38. /Tanzania /Subsidiaries /Holding company /354.54 L836 PCL

3153. Mrambe, B. P., and B. U. Mwansasu. 1971 Management for Socialist Development in Tanzania: the Case of the National Development Corporations. Arusha, Tanzania: Conference of Comparative Administration in East Africa. /Tanzania /East Africa /Management /Development corporation /Case studies

3154. Muchelembra, Josephine B. 1978 "National Development Planning in Zambia with Special Reference to Planning in Public Enterprises." Paper presented at the International Workshop on Planning in Public Enterprises in Developing Countries, Ljubljana, Yugoslavia, 20-25 Nov. Ljubljana: ICPE. /Zambia /Planning process /Economic development

3155. Muchtarundin, S. 1966 Management Problems of Public Enterprise in Indonesia. Nashville, Tennessee: M.A. Thesis, Vanderbilt University. /Indonesia /Management

3156. Muhammad Idris, Sahibzadah. 1966 "The Role of the PIDC and the Industrial Development Bank of Pakistan in the Industrialization of the Northwest Frontier Region." Peshawar. /Pakistan /Development banks /Regional development /Case studies

3157. Muhammad, Faqir. 1978 "Public Enterprise and National Development in the 1980's: An Agenda for Research and Action." Paper presented at the Round Table on Public Enterprise of the Tenth General Assembly of the Latin American Assoc. of Pub. Adm. /Economic development /Taxation policy /OPSS

3158. Muhar, P. S. 1965 "Corruption in the Public Services in India." Indian Journal of Political Science (Lucknow, India), pp. 1-18. /India /Public services

3159. Muir, Valerie. 1953 "The Emergence of State Enterprise in New Zealand in the 19th Century." Explorations in Entrepreneurial History V. 5, pp. 186-197. /New Zealand /Economic history

3160. Mukerjee, B. K. 1955 "Mixed Economy in Theory and Practice." Indian Journal of Economics V. 36, pp. 223-229. /Economic analysis /Mixed enterprises / 330.5 In2

3161. Mukharji, B. C. 1964 "The Role of the Managing Director." Indian Journal of Public Administration (New Delhi), V. 10, No. 3. /India /Management / JA 26 I55 Pub Aff

3162. Mukherjee, G. 1980 "Research and Development Centre for Iron and Steel." Lok Udyog (New Delhi), V. 14, No. 9, pp. 43-50. /India /Case studies /Research and development /Steel industry /354.54 L836 PCL

3163. Mukherjee, J. 1976 "Breakthroughs in Equipment Self-Sufficiency at Steel Plants." Lok Udyog (New Delhi), V. 10, No. 5, pp. 15-16. /India /Steel industry /354.54 L836 PCL

3164. Mukherjee, P. K. 1975 "Productivity in the Manufacturing Public Sector." Lok Udyog (New Delhi), V. 9, No. 7, pp. 43-48. /India /Productivity /Economic efficiency /354.54 L836 PCL

3165. Mukherjee, Pranab Kumar. 1982 "Capacity Utilization is the Most Important Priority in our Economy Today, if the Public Sector Enterprises are to Achieve a Commanding Position." Lok Udyog (New Delhi), V. 16, No. 9, pp. 8-11. /India /Economic efficiency /Productivity /354.54 L836 PCL

3166. Muller, A. O. 1955 Die verstaatlichung des britischen kohlemberghaus. Zurich: Nu. St. Gallen Polygraphischer Verlag. /United Kingdom /Coal mining industry /Nationalization

3167. Muñoz Ledo, P. 1965 "La nationalisation du pétrole au Mexique." Révue Française de Science Politique (Paris), V. 15, No. 6, pp. 1145-1153. /Mexico /Oil industry /Nationalization

3168. Munby, D. L. 1959 "Finance of the Nationalized Industries." Bulletin of the Oxford University Institute of Economics and Statistics V. 21, pp. 73-84. /United Kingdom /Public financing / 310.5 Ox2b

3169. Munby, D. L. 1959 "Investing in Coal: Investment Policies in the Nationalized Coal Industry." Oxford Economic Papers V. 2, No. 3, pp. 242-269. /United Kingdom /Coal mining industry / 330.5 Ox2 n.s. PCL

3170. Mund, Vernon A., and H. Ronald Wolf. 1971 "Public Enterprise as an Alternative to Government Control." Industrial Organization and Public Policy. New York: Appleton Century Crofts. pp. 384-400. /United States of America /Government authority /Control process

3171. Munier, B. 1967 La Banque Nationale pour le Développement Economique (B.N.D.E.) et l'industrialisation au Maroc. Paris: Editions du Centre de la Recherch Scientifique. /Morocco /Central banks /Economic development /Industrialization / Case studies

3172. Muniz, Alvaro A. 1972 Caminha: A empresa pública no direito brasileiro. Rio de Janeiro: Trabalhistas, S. A. /Brazil /Law

3173. Munkonge, G. M. 1978 "Paper on the Zambian Experience." Paper presented at the Interregional Workshop on Financing of Public Enterprises in Developing Countries, Ljubljana, Yugoslavia, 22-26 May. Ljubljana: ICPE. /Zambia /Public financing

3174. Mupeso, Rose D., and Shushil Chandra. 1980 "Final Report of the Interregional Seminar on Training Management in Public Enterprises in Developing Countries, September 29 - October

10, 1980, Ljubljana, Yugoslavia." Ljubljana: ICPE. /Training /Management

3175. Mupeso, Rose D., and Sanford N. Mulundika. 1980 "Pre-Course Assignments." Paper presented at the Interregional Seminar on Training Management in Public Enterprises in Developing Countries, Ljubljana, Yugoslavia, 19-28 October. Ljubljana: ICPE. /Training /Management

3176. Murant, D. 1969 L'intervention de l'Etat dans le secteur pétrolier en France. Paris: Technip. /France /Oil industry /Control process

3177. Murao, Bahadur. 1975 Inflation Accounting as a Tool to Fight Inflation. Calcutta: Institute of Cost and Works Accountants of India. /India /Accounting /Inflation / HF 5657 M87

3178. Murdeshwar, A. K. 1957 Administrative Problems Relating to Nationalization: With Special Reference to Indian State Enterprises. Bombay, India: Popular Book Depot. /India /Nationalization /Administrative management / 338.954 M94a

3179. Murillo Ferrol, F. 1950 "El poder económico." Revista de Administración Pública No. 3, pp. 255-270. /Economic analysis

3180. Murphy, M. E. 1952 "Nationalization of British Industry." Canadian Journal of Economics and Political Science (Toronto), V. 18, pp. 146-162. /United Kingdom /Nationalization /Industrial sector / 305 C16

3181. Murray, D. J. 1970 Studies in Nigerian Administration. (Essays from University of Ife). London: Hutchinson. /Nigeria /Public administration / 354.669 M962s

3182. Murray, Michel A. 1975 "Comparing Public and Private Management: An Exploratory Essay." Public Administration Review No. 4, pp. 364-371. /Private sector /Management /Comparative analysis

3183. Murthy, K. R. S. 1980 "Strategic Management of Public Enterprise: A Framework for Analysis." Paper presented at the Second BAPEG Conference: Public Enterprise in Mixed Economy LDCs, Boston, April. /India /Goal Setting /Management /OPSS

3184. Musolf, Lloyd D. 1956 "Canadian Public Enterprise, a Character Study." American Political Science Review V. 50, pp. 405-421. /Canada / 320.5 Am31

3185. Musolf, Lloyd D. 1959 Public Ownership and Accountability: The Canadian Experience. Cambridge, Mass.: Harvard University Press. /Canada /Accountability / 380.162 M974p

3186. Musolf, Lloyd D. 1963 "Public Enterprise and Development Perspectives in S. Vietnam; Public Enterprise and Developed Organizational Forms: S. Vietnam." Reprint Series No. 1. Davis, Cal.: University of California, Institute of Governmental Affairs. /Vietnam, Rep. of /Economic development /Organization development

3187. Musolf, Lloyd D. 1963 "Public Enterprise and `Developed' Organizational Forms: South Vietnam." Revue Internationale des Sciences Administratives V. 29, No. 3, pp. 261-266. /Vietnam, Rep. of /Evaluation /Organization behavior

3188. Musolf, Lloyd D. 1965 Government and the Economy. Chicago: Scott Foresman. /Government authority /Economic development /Economic theory /338.973 M974g

3189. Musolf, Lloyd D. 1966 "Public Enterprise and Economic Planning: A Comparative Perspective." George Washington Law Review V. 35, No. 2, pp. 362-377. /United States of America /Developing nations /Planning process /Financial institutions /Comparative analysis

3190. Musolf, Lloyd D. 1966 Public Enterprise and National Development. New York: United Nations. /Evaluation /Economic development /Economic theory

3191. Musolf, Lloyd D. 1967 El gobierno y la economía. Mexico City. /Mexico /Government authority /Economic development

3192. Musolf, Lloyd D. 1971 "American Mixed Enterprise and Government Responsibility." Western Political Quarterly V. 24, No. 4, pp. 789-806. /United States of America /Mixed enterprises / 320.5 W525

3193. Musolf, Lloyd D. 1971 "Mixed Enterprise in a Developmental Perspective: France, Italy and Japan." Journal of Comparative Administration No. 3, pp. 131-168. /France /Italy /Japan /Mixed enterprises /Comparative analysis

3194. Musolf, Lloyd D. 1972 Mixed Enterprise: A Development Perspective. Lexington, Mass.: D. C. Heath. /Economic development /Mixed enterprises / HD 3850 M87 M

3195. Musolf, Lloyd D. 1972 American Mixed Enterprise and Government Responsibility. Davis: University of California, Institute of Government Affairs. /United States of America /Management /Control process / Mixed enterprises

3196. Musolf, Lloyd D. 1976 "Coordination of Public Enterprises: Now More Essential but More Complex." In A. S. H. K. Sadique, ed(s). Public Enterprises in Asia: Studies in Coordination and Control. Kuala Lumpur: Asian Centre for Development Administration. pp. 77-102. /Asia /Control process /HD 4296 P8

3197. Musolf, Lloyd D. 1978 "Public Enterprise and Public Interest in the United States." In André Gélinas, ed(s). Public Enterprise and the Public Interest. Ontario: The Institute of Public Administration of Canada. pp. 148-169. /United States of America /Accountability /Control process

3198. Musolf, Lloyd D. 1982 "Public Enterprises as Instruments of Public Policy in the United States," Paper presented as the Tokyo Round Table preparatory to the 19th International

Congress of Administrative Sciences, 13-17 Sept. /United States of America /Economic analysis /Goal setting /Accountability /Control process /OPSS

3199. Musolf, Lloyd D. 1983 Uncle Sam's Private, Profitseeking Corporations. Lexington, Mass.: D.C. Heath and Company, Lexington Books. /United States of America /Railway industry /Financial institutions /Communication industry /Economic analysis /HD 3888 M87

3200. Musolf, Lloyd D. 1983 "Employing U.S.A. Public Enterprises as Instruments of Public Policy: Techniques and Limitations." Paper presented at the 19th International Congress of Administrative Sciences, West Berlin, 19-23 Sept. /United States of America /Goal setting /Management /Accountability /OPSS

3201. Musolf, Lloyd D., and Harold Seidman. 1980 "The Blurred Boundaries of Public Administration." Public Administration Review V. 40, pp. 124-130. /Public administration /Management

3202. Mussowir, M. Abdul. 1980 "Pricing Policies in Public Enterprises in Bangladesh." Paper presented at the International Workshop on Pricing Policies in Public Enterprises, Ljubljana, Yugoslavia, 26-30 May. Ljubljana: ICPE. /Bangladesh /Price policy

3203. Mussowir, M. Abdul. 1980 "Pricing Policies in Public Enterprises in Bangladesh." The Cost and Management V. 8, No. 2-3, pp. 17-20. /Price policy /Bangladesh

3204. Muthuramalingam, U. M. 1963 "The State as Entrepreneur in Low Income Countries." Indian Journal of Economics V. 43, No. 170. /Developing nations /Government authority /Entrepreneurial activity / 330.5 In2

3205. Mwabulambo, Wilfred. 1981 "Performance Criteria and Implementation of Performance Evaluation Systems in Developing Countries: Tanzanian Experience." Paper presented at the Expert Group Meeting on Performance Criteria and the Implementation of Performance Evaluation Systems in Public Enterprises in Developing Countries, Ljubljana, Yugoslavia, 23-27 November. Ljubljana: ICPE. /Tanzania /Control process /Evaluation /Information system

3206. Mwambene, Nkundwe K. 1980 "Shortcomings in Training National Counter-Parts." Paper presented at the Regional Workshop on Development of Training Methologies for Internal Consultants in African Public Enterprises, Addis Ababa, Ethiopia, 1-6 Dec. Ljubljana: ICPE. /Training /Management

3207. Mwambene, Nkundwe K. 1981 "Management Training Needs of Parastatal Organizations in Tanzania." Paper presented at the Interregional Seminar on Training Management in Public Enterprises in Developing Countries, Ljubljana, Yugoslavia, 19-28 October. Ljubljana: ICPE. /Tanzania /Training /Management / East Africa

3208. Mwanza, A. M., et al. 1980 "The Role of the Public Sector in Developing Countries: The Zambian National Report." Ljubljana: ICPE. /Zambia / Africa

3209. Mwapachu, H. Bakari. 1975 "The Restructuring of Public Enterprises for Improved Performance." Paper presented at Improving Performance of Public Enterprise, Report of an International Conference, Arusha, Tanzania, 2-5 December. Arusha, Tanzania: East African Community Management Institute. pp. 54-69. /Tanzania /State trading organizations /Case studies /Management / East Africa

3210. Mwapachu, H. Bakari. 1978 "Holding Corporations in Tanzania: Factors Affecting Performance." Lok Udyog (New Delhi), V. 12, No. 2, pp. 17-20. /Tanzania /Financial performance /Economic efficiency /Holding company /354.54 L836 PCL

3211. Mwapachu, Juma Volter. 1977 "Public Sector Commercial Bank Lending and Investment Policy: Case of Tanzania." Lok Udyog (New Delhi), V. 11, No. 4, pp. 37-52. /Tanzania /Banking system /354.54 L836 PCL

3212. Mwapachu, Juma Volter. 1983 Management of Public Enterprises in Developing Countries (The Tanzania Experience). New Delhi: Oxford & IBH Publishing Co. /Management /Tanzania /Accountability /Control process /Political economy / Industrial relations / East Africa

3213. Myers, C. A. 1956 "Labour Problems of Nationalization: The Experience of India." International Labour Review V. 73, pp. 431-450. /India /Nationalization /Labor relations /331.05 In81 PCl /HD 4811 I65 Pub Aff

3214. Myers, John. 1981 "Privatized Concerns." National Law Journal V. 131. /United Kingdom /Privatization

3215. Myers, Robert J. 1972 "Note on Funding Procedures and Investments of Government Employee Retirement Systems." Journal of Risk and Insurance V. 39, No. 1. /United States of America /Retirement systems /Investment / 368.05 J827

3216. Nacionalización del hierro en Venezuela. 1975 Caracas: Ediciones Centauro. /Venezuela /Nationalization /Steel industry / HD 9514 V42 N235 LAC

3217. Nagrath, Anita. 1980 "A Peep into the Performance and Role of State Financial Corporations." Lok Udyog (New Delhi), V. 14, No. 7, pp. 53-60. /India /Financial institutions /Financial performance /354.54 L836 PCL

3218. Naharro, J. M. 1970 "Consideraciones en torno a la planificación económica y la empresa pública." La Empresa Pública. Zaragoza, Spain: Publicaciones del Real Colegio de España en Bolonia. /Planning process

3219. Nair, C. S. B. 1981 "Research and Development at FACT." Lok Udyog (New Delhi), V. 14, No. 9, pp. 35-42. /India /Case studies /Research and development /354.54 L836 PCL

3220. Nair, D. P. 1980 "Efficacy of State Enterprises Investment in Kerala." Lok Udyog (New Delhi), V. 14, No. 5, pp. 33-40. /India /Investment /Efficacy /Kerala, India (State) /354.54 L836 PCL

3221. Nair, G. K. 1960 "The Rural and Industrial Development Authority." Ekonomi (Kuala Lumpur), No. 1, pp. 56-60. /Malaysia /Rural development /Industrial sector /Government authority / Case studies

3222. Nair, Krishnadas. 1976 "Management of Research & Development in an Industry." Lok Udyog (New Delhi), V. 9, No. 12, pp. 45-52. /Research and development /India /354.54 L836 PCL

3223. Nair, N. K. 1973 "Cost of Steel Production in India." Lok Udyog (New Delhi), V. 7, No. 4, pp. 47-58. /India /Steel industry /Costs /354.54 L836 PCL

3224. Nair, N. K. 1973 "Productivity Ratios in Indian Iron and Steel Industry." Lok Udyog (New Delhi), V. 7, No. 7, pp. 43-50. /India /Productivity /Steel industry /354.54 L836 PCL

3225. Nakajima, H., and K. Yamamura. 1959 Management of Public Industrial Enterprises in Japan. /Japan

3226. Nakra, D. S. 1968 "Pricing Policy and Public Sector Undertakings." Lok Udyog (New Delhi), pp. 11-23. /India /Price policy / 354.54 L836

3227. Nakra, D. S. 1971 "Financial Management in Public Enterprises." Lok Udyog (New Delhi), V. 5, No. 3, pp. 245-256. /India /Financial performance /Financial management /354.54 L836 PCL

3228. Nakra, D. S. 1972 "Problems in Financial Management in Steel Industry." Lok Udyog (New Delhi), V. 6, No. 5, pp. 21-28. /India /Steel industry /Financial management /354.54 L836

3229. Nakra, D. S. 1973 "Performance Evaluation of Public Undertakings." Lok Udyog (New Delhi), V. 7, No. 5, pp. 23-26. /India /Evaluation /354.54 L836 PCL

3230. Nakra, D. S. 1974 "Some Suggestions for Improving the Profitability of H.S.L." Lok Udyog (New Delhi), V. 8, No. 2, pp. 51-52. /India /Steel industry /Profits /Productivity /354.54 L836 PCL

3231. Nakra, D. S. 1975 "Macro-financial Management in the Public Sector." In R. C. Dutt and Raj K. Nigam, ed(s). Towards Commanding Heights. New Delhi: Vivek Joshi. pp. 232-244. /India /Financial management /HD 4293 T68 PCL

3232. Nakra, D. S. 1976 "Industrial Sickness - Causes and Remedies." Lok Udyog (New Delhi), V. 10, No. 8, pp. 13-18. /India /Environmental policy /Personnel management /354.54 L836 PCL

3233. Nakra, D. S. 1977 "Pricing for Export." Lok Udyog (New Delhi), V. 10, No. 11, pp. 25-26. /India /Exports /Price policy /354.54 L836 PCL

3234. Narain, Iqbal. 1956 "Some Aspects of the Management of Public Enterprises." Indian Journal of Political Science (New Delhi), V. 17, No. 4, pp. 360-377. /Management /302.05 In2

3235. Narain, Iqbal. 1957 "Some Aspects of the Management of Public Enterprises." Indian Journal of Political Science (New Delhi), V. 18, No. 2, pp. 119-134. /Management

3236. Narain, Iqbal. 1958 "The Management of Public Enterprises." Indian Journal of Public Administration (New Delhi), V. 4, pp. 302-318. /India /Management / JA26 I55 Pub Aff

3237. Narain, Iqbal. 1959 The Management of Public Enterprises. (Seminar on Management of Public Industrial Enterprises). New Delhi: Government of India and United Nations. /India

3238. Narain, Laxmi. 1962 "Constitution of the Governing Boards of Public Enterprises." Indian Journal of Public Administration (New Delhi), V. 8, No. 1, pp. 18-39. /India /Management /Law /JA 26 I55 Pub Aff

3239. Narain, Laxmi. 1963 "The Comtroller and Auditor-General and Public Enterprise in India." Indian Journal of Public Administration (New Delhi), V. 9, No. 1, pp. 74-87. /India /Budget auditing / JA 26 I55 Pub Aff

3240. Narain, Laxmi. 1967 "The Establishment of the Fertilizer Corporation of India: A Case Study." New Delhi: Indian Institute of Public Administration, Committee on Case Studies. /India /Fertilizer industry / Case studies

3241. Narain, Laxmi. 1967 Public Enterprises in India: A Study of Public Relations and Annual Reports. New Delhi: S. Chand. /India / 354.54092 N164p

3242. Narain, Laxmi. 1970 "The Law of Public Enterprise Audit in India." Chartered Accountant (London), pp. 449-455. /India /Accounting /Law

3243. Narain, Laxmi. 1971 "Managerial Motivation in Public Enterprises." Lok Udyog (New Delhi), V. 5, No. 9, pp. 861-876. /India /Management /Motivation /354.54 L836 PCL

3244. Narain, Laxmi. 1972 "Efficiency Audit of Public Enterprises in India." New Delhi: Planning Commission, Research Programmes Committee. /Budget Auditing /India

3245. Narain, Laxmi. 1972 "Managerial Turnover in Public Enterprises." Lok Udyog (New Delhi), V. 6, No. 2, pp. 11-16. /India /Management /354.54 L836 PCL

3246. Narain, Laxmi. 1973 "Managerial Compensation and Motivation in Public Enterprises." New Delhi: Planning Commission. Research Programmes Committee. /India /Wages / Motivation

3247. Narain, Laxmi. 1974 "Top Management Organization of the British Steel Corporation." Lok Udyog (New Delhi), V. 7, No. 10, pp. 5-12. /United Kingdom /Management /Steel industry /354.54 L836 PCL

3248. Narain, Laxmi. 1975 "Public Enterprises in India: A Study of Public Relations and Annual Reports." New Delhi: Planning Commission, Research Programmes Committee. /India

3249. Narain, Laxmi. 1975 "Social Objectives and the Accountability of Public Enterprises." In R. C. Dutt and Raj K. Nigam, ed(s). Towards Commanding Heights. New Delhi: Vivek Joshi. pp. 82-91. /India /Social welfare policy /Accountability /HD 4293 T68 PCL

3250. Narain, Laxmi. 1978 "Management of Public Enterprises in Italy - The Trail Blazing Example of IRI." Lok Udyog (New Delhi), V. 12, No. 8, pp. 5-10. /Italy /Holding company /354.54 L836 PCL

3251. Narain, Laxmi. 1978 "Parliamentary Committee on Public Undertakings - The British Experience." Lok Udyog (New Delhi), V. 12, No. 7, pp. 11-18. /Control process /Parliament /United Kingdom /354.54 L836 PCL

3252. Narain, Laxmi. 1979 Parliament and Public Enterprise in India. Report of a Seminar on the Parliamentary Committee on Public Undertakings. New Delhi: S. Chand & Company, Ltd. /India /Parliament /Control process

3253. Narain, Laxmi. 1979 "Public Enterprise in India. An Overview." Annals of Public and Cooperative Economy V. 50, No. 4, pp. 59-80. /India /330.5 An73

3254. Narain, Laxmi. 1980 Principles and Practice of Public Enterprise Management. New Delhi: S. Chand. /Public administration /Management

3255. Narain, Laxmi. 1981 "Managing Public Enterprise: Reflections on Three Decades of Indian Experience." Public Enterprise V. 1, No. 3, pp. 23-37. /Management /Public administration /India /OPSS

3256. Narain, Laxmi. 1981 "Yugoslavia's Self-management: Setting the World on a New Course?" Lok Udyog (New Delhi), V. 14, No. 10, pp. 19-26. /Yugoslavia /Worker self management /354.54 L836 PCL

3257. Narain, Laxmi. 1982 "Public Enterprises in Canada - Some Perspectives." Lok Udyog (New Delhi), V. 16, No. 7, pp. 43-49. /Canada /354.54 L836 PCL

3258. Narain, Laxmi. 1983 "Parliament and Public Enterprise in India." In G. Ram Reddy, ed(s). Government and Public Enterprise: Essays in honour of Professor V. V. Ramanadham. Bombay, India: N. M. Tripathi Private Limited. pp. 264-286. /India /Parliament

3259. Narain, Laxmi. 1983 "Some Thoughts on Making Public Enterprise an Effective Instrument of State Policy." Paper presented at the 19th International Congress of Administrative Sciences, West Berlin, 19-23 Sept. /Autonomy /Goal setting /India /OPSS

3260. Narang, R. C. 1980 "The Case for Job Evaluation." Lok Udyog (New Delhi), V. 13, No. 10-1, pp. 27-30. /India /Personnel management /Evaluation /354.54 L836 PCL

3261. Narayanaswamy, P. K. 1980 "Autonomy and Accountability of Public Sector Enterprises." Lok Udyog (New Delhi), V. 14, No. 4, pp. 13-16. /Financing /India / 354.54 L836

3262. Narayanaswamy, P. K. 1980 "Autonomy and Accountability of Public Sector Enterprises." Lok Udyog (New Delhi), V. 14, No. 4, pp. 13-16. /India /Accountability /Autonomy /Control process /354.54 L836 PCL

3263. Nash, J. 1972 "The Devil in Bolivia's Nationalized Tin Mines." Science and Society V. 36, No. 2. /Bolivia /Tin industry /Nationalization / 305 Sc26 PCL

3264. Natarajan, K. 1968 "Subsidiaries of the State Bank of India." State Bank of India Monthly Review (New Delhi), /India /Central banks /Subsidization policy

3265. Nath, Arun K. 1975 "Public Sector in the Fertilizer Industry." Lok Udyog (New Delhi), V. 9, No. 2, pp. 27-32. /India /Fertilizer industry /354.54 L836 PCL

3266. Nath, Ashok. 1977 "Study of Corporate Sector Development in India During 1965-1976: Government and Non-Government Companies." Lok Udyog (New Delhi), V. 11, No. 9, pp. 33-36. /India /Private enterprises /Comparative analysis /354.54 L836 PCL

3267. Nava Negrete, A. 1965 "Empresa pública y sociedad anómina del Estado." Revista de la Facultad de Derecho de México (Mexico City), V. 15, No. 57, pp. 161-188. /Mexico

3268. Navarrete, A. 1957 "El sector público en el desarrollo económico." Investigación Económica pp. 43-49. /Economic development

3269. Naville, P., J. P. Bardou, P. Brachet, and C. Levy. 1971 L'Etat entrepreneur: le Cas de la Régie Renault; une enquête sur les fonctions sociales du secteur publique industrielle en France. Paris: Editions Anthropos. /France /Management /Entrepreneurial activity /Automobile manufacturing industry /Case studies

3270. Nayak, P. R. 1964 "Collaboration in Oil: Some Operational Aspects." Indian Journal of Public Administration (New Delhi), V. 10, No. 3. /India /Oil industry /JA26 I55 Pub Aff

3271. Nayar, G. K., and V. G. Kamath. 1979 Inter-Firm Comparison for Public Sector Industries. Bangalore, India: Indian Institute of Management. /India /Evaluation /Comparative analysis

3272. Naylor, G. W. 1966 "Report of Reconnaissance Mission to Ceylon in Connection with State Industrial Corporations." Colombo, Sri Lanka: Ministry of Planning and Economic Affairs. /Sri Lanka /Industrial sector

3273. Ndegwa, Philip. 1964 The Role of Development Banks in Underdeveloped Countries. Makerere, Uganda: Institute of Social Research. /Developing nations /Development banks

3274. Ndegwa, Philip. 1979 Review of Statutory Boards. Nairobi, Kenya: Government Printer. /Kenya /Control process /Evaluation /Law /OPSS

3275. Ndulu, Benno. 1979 "Report of the Regional Meeting of African States on the Role of the Public Sector in Developing Countries, 1979, Arusha, Tanzania." Ljubljana: ICPE. /Africa

3276. Negrus, Mariana. 1978 "Romania's Experience as a Developing Country in the Establishment, Running and Organization of Joint Ventures." Paper presented at the Interregional Workshop on Financing of Public Enterprises in Developing Countries, Ljubljana, Yugoslavia, 22-26 May. Ljubljana: ICPE. /Romania /Mixed enterprises

3277. Nelson, H. P. 1968 Financial Aspects of Manufacturing Enterprises in the Public Sector. /Manufacturing industry /Financing

3278. Nelson, H. P. 1968 Organization and Administration of Public Enterprises. The Experience of Ghana. Accra, Ghana: U.N. Seminar. /Ghana /Public administration /Organization formation

3279. Nelson, J. R. 1965 "The Fleck Report and the Area Organisation of the National Coal Board." Public Administration (London), pp. 41-58. /United Kingdom /Coal mining industry /Public utility regulation policy / JA 8 P8 Pub Aff

3280. Nelson, J. R. 1976 "Public Enterprise: Pricing and Investment Criteria." In William G. Shepherd et al., ed(s). Public Enterprise: Economic Analysis of Theory and Practice. Lexington, Ma.: D.C. Heath and Company, Lexington Books. pp. 49-76. /Price policy /Investment / /HD 3850 P8 PCL

3281. Nemekiroh, G. 1970 La cooperación en la economía del interés general, la cooperació creciente de las empresas públicas, cooperativas y libres del sector de la economía de interés general. Frankfurt, Main: Bank fur Germiniwinstochoftf. /Private sector /Cooperatives /Economic integration

3282. Ness, Walter L., Jr. 1978 "A empresa estatal no mercado de capitais." Revista Brasileira de Mercado de Capitais V. 4, pp. 359-377. /Brazil /Stock market / HG 4053 R45 LAC

3283. Netter, Klaus. 1981 "Cooperation among State-Trading Organizations of Developing Countries." In M. M. Kostecki, ed(s). _State Trading in International Markets._ New York: St. Martin's Press. pp. 210-220. /State trading organizations /HF 1410.5 S7 1981 M. /Also found in Les Cahiers du Cetai, no 79-15, June, 1979. /OPSS

3284. Neuman, Andrew M. 1944 "Private Profits and Extra-Budgetary Revenue." _Oxford University: Institute of Statistics Bulletin_ V. 6, pp. 178-183. /Profits /Accounting

3285. Neuman, Andrew M. 1950 "Consumers' Representation in the Public Sector of Industry." _Manchester School of Economic and Social Studies_ V. 18, pp. 143-162. /United Kingdom /Industrial sector /Consumer market /Control process /330.5 M3121 PCL

3286. Neuman, Andrew M. 1951 "Some Economic Aspects of Nationalization." _Law and Contemporary Problems_ V. 16, No. 4, pp. 702-751. /United Kingdom /Nationalization /Economic analysis / 340.5 L44

3287. Neuman, Andrew M. 1952 _The Economic Aspects of Nationalization in Great Britain._ Cambridge: Students' Bookshops. /United Kingdom /Nationalization /Economic analysis

3288. Neuman, Henri. 1977 "The `Société Nationale d'Investissement': Its Role and New Mission on Public Economic Initiative." _Annals of Public and Cooperative Economy_ V. 49, No. 4, pp. 407-428. /France /Financial institutions /Case studies /Goal setting /330.5 An73

3289. "A New Report from the Nationalised Industries Committee." 1959 _Parliamentary Affairs_ (London), V. 13, No. 1, pp. 95-99. /United Kingdom /Industrial sector /Parliament /Control process

3290. Newfarmer, Richard. 1977 "Multinational Conglomerates and the Economics of Dependent Development A Case Study of the International Electrical Oligopoly and Brazil's Electrical Industry." Madison, Wis.: Ph.D. dissertation, University of Wisconsin. /Brazil /Electrical utility industry /Multinational corporations / Economic development /Economic dependency / FILM 14,739 LAC

3291. Newfarmer, Richard. 1981 _State Elites in Power: State Control of the Electric Power Industry in Latin America._ Mexico City: ILET. /Venezuela /Peru /Mexico /Brazil /Electrical utility industry /Price policy /Control process /Comparative analysis /OPSS

3292. Nezam-Mafi, M. 1980 "Cooperation among State Petroleum Enterprises." _State Petroleum Enterprises in Developing Countries._ New York: Pergamon Press. pp. 61-76. /Oil industry

3293. Ng'Amilo, Adam Oswald. 1980 "Technology Transfer Agreements for Public Enterprises in Tanzania." Paper presented at the

International Workshop on Preparations and Negotiations of Technology Transfer Agreements for Public Enterprises in Developing Countries, Ljubljana, Yugoslavia, 27-31 October. Ljubljana: ICPE. /Tanzania /Technology transfer

3294. Niakou, Joseph. 1980 "Les principales actions de formation conduites par l'OPEI (Office National de Promotion de l'Entreprise Ivoirienne)." Paper presented at the Séminare international sur la gestion et la formation dans les entreprises publiques dans les pays en voie de développement, Ljubljana, Yugoslavia, 3-15 March. Ljubljana: ICPE. /Ivory Coast /Development corporation

3295. Niaz, Aslam. 1962 "Public Corporations in India and Pakistan." Los Angeles: International Public Administration Center, University of Southern California. /India /Pakistan

3296. Nicosia, M. F. 1960 Tecnica administrativa dello impreso de servizi pubblici. Rome. /Italy /Public administration /Public services

3297. Nieto Terán, Tomás. 1975 "Ecuador: Administración del Fondo Nacional de Saneamiento Ambiental." Rio de Janeiro: FGV-EIAP. /Ecuador /Environmental policy /Case studies /OPSS

3298. Nigam, R. K. 1967 "Structure Pattern of Boards of Directors of Public Enterprises." Lok Udyog (New Delhi), pp. 19-24. /India /Evaluation /Structural characteristics /Management

3299. Nigam, R. K. 1967 "State Enterprises in India: Measurement of Profitability." Commerce (Bombay, India), No. 339, pp. 336-337. /India /Profits

3300. Nigam, R. K. 1968 "Concept of Efficiency Audit and Its Application to Public Enterprises." Lok Udyog (New Delhi), pp. 11-15. /Accounting /Economic efficiency /Evaluation /354.54 L836

3301. Nigam, R. K. 1969 "New Financial Discipline for Public Undertakings for Improving their Performance." Lok Udyog (New Delhi), V. 3, No. 7, pp. 907-915. /India /Law /Financial performance /354.54 L836

3302. Nigam, R. K. 1969 "Profit Criterion and the Public Sector Enterprises." Indian Management (New Delhi), pp. 39-42. /India /Profits

3303. Nigam, R. K. 1973 "The Quinquennial Review of Public Enterprises." Lok Udyog (New Delhi), V. 7, No. 1, pp. 47-58. /India /354.54 L836 PCL

3304. Nigam, R. K. 1975 "People's Investment in Public Enterprises." Lok Udyog (New Delhi), V. 8, No. 12, pp. 3-6. /India /354.54 L836 PCL

3305. Nigam, R. K. 1975 "Ten Years of the Bureau of Public Enterprises." Lok Udyog (New Delhi), V. 9, No. 1, pp. 3-8. /India /Control process /Case studies /354.54 L836 PCL

3306. Nigam, R. K. 1975 "A Test Situation in the British Steel Corporation." Lok Udyog (New Delhi), V. 9, No. 3, pp. 3-9. /United Kingdom /Steel industry /354.54 L836 PCL

3307. Nigam, R. K. 1976 "Catalyst's Role of Bureau of Public Enterprises." Lok Udyog (New Delhi), V. 10, No. 6, pp. 49-54. /India /Control process /354.54 L836 PCL

3308. Nigam, R. K. 1976 "New Facets of Management Development." Lok Udyog (New Delhi), V. 9, No. 12, pp. 11-16. /Training /354.54 L836 PCL

3309. Nigam, R. K. 1981 "Eighties for the Public Sector - Some Central Issues." Public Enterprise Management: Constraints and Autonomy. New Delhi: Documentation Centre for Corporate & Business Policy Reasearch. pp. 39-56. /India /Management /HD 4293 P77 1981 PCL

3310. Nigam, R. S. 1980 Issues in Public Enterprise. New Delhi: Pragati Publications. /India /Control process /Price policy /HD 4293 I83

3311. Nigam, R. S., and G. Sundaram. 1976 "Public Enterprises and Exports." Lok Udyog (New Delhi), V. 10, No. 6, pp. 21-34. /Exports /India /354.54 L836 PCL

3312. Nigeria. Ahmadu Bello University. 1970 "Conference on Public Enterprises in Nigeria." Nigeria. Ahmadu Bello University. /Nigeria

3313. Nigeria. Federal Department of Commerce and Industries. 1957 "Industrial Development: Public Agencies and Private Enterprises." Nigeria Handbook of Commerce and Industry. Lagos, Nigeria. /Nigeria /Industrialization /Private enterprises /Investment /Development banks

3314. Nigeria. Nigerian Economic Society. 1974 Public Enterprises in Nigeria: Proceedings of the Annual Conference of the Nigerian Economic Society, Enugu, 1974. /Nigeria

3315. Nigeria. Nigerian Government. 1957 The Capital Structure of the Electricity Corporation of Nigeria. Sessional Paper. Lagos: Government Printing. No. 3. /Nigeria /Electrical utility industry /Investment

3316. Niksic, Sefko. 1974 "Planification a l'entreprise Dalmacijacement." Paper presented at the International Seminar '74: Planning in Public Enterprises in Developing Countries, Ljubljana, Yugoslavia, 23 Sept. - 9 Oct. Ljubljana: ICPE. /Yugoslavia /Planning process /Case studies

3317. Nimkar, Balkrishna. 1977 "Rural Branch Expansion of Banks: Problem of Viability." Lok Udyog (New Delhi), V. 11, No. 8, pp. 35-38. /India /Banking system /Rural development /354.54 L836 PCL

3318. Niosi, Jorge. 1974 Los empresarios y el Estado argentino, 1955-1969. Buenos Aires: Publicaciones Siglo Veintiuno. /Argentina /Economic history /Planning process /Private sector /F 2849.2 N565 LAC

3319. Niyogi, S. P. 1954 "Management and Finance of Public Enterprises." Indian Economic Journal (Bombay), V. 2, No. 3, pp. 274-280. /Management /Public financing /Public administration

3320. Njoroge, John M. 1980 "Kenya Management Training and Advisory Centre." Paper presented at the Regional Workshop on Development of Training Methodologies for Internal Consultants in African Public Enterprises, Addis Ababa, Ethiopia, 1-6 December. Ljubljana: ICPE. /Kenya /Training /Management

3321. Nogueira, P. 1969 Autogestão-participação dos trabalhadores na empresa. Rio de Janeiro: José Olympio. /Worker self management /Worker management participation /G658.3152 N689a

3322. Nogueira, P. 1970 "Função da lei na vida dos entes paraestateis." Revista Direito Administrativo (Rio de Janeiro), No. 99, pp. 33-43. /Law

3323. Nogueira, Roberto Martínez. 1974 "Los procesos de formulación e implementación de políticas y sus consecuencias sobre las empresas públicas." Ciencias Administrativas (Buenos Aires), No. 45, pp. 37-55. /Argentina /Policy analysis

3324. Nogueira, Rubem Rodrigues. 1977 "Estadualização e municipalização de empresa pública e sociedade de economia mista." Revista de Informação Legislativa V. 14, pp. 115-126. /Brazil /Mixed enterprises /Nationalization /G340.05 R3251 LAC

3325. Nokdhes, Sribang-orn. 1981 "Management Training in EGAT." Paper presented at the Interregional Seminar on Training Management in Public Enterprises in Developing Countries, Ljubljana, Yugoslavia, 19-28 October. Ljubljana: ICPE. /Training /Management

3326. Non, Jesus V. 1980 "Pricing Policies and Practices of Philippine Public Enterprises." Paper presented at the International Workshop on Pricing Policies in Public Enterprises, Ljubljana, Yugoslavia, 26-30 May. Ljubljana: ICPE. /Philippines /Price policy

3327. Noori, Shiekh-Hosseini. 1965 "A Study of the Nationalization of the Oil Industry in Iran." Greeley, Colo.: Ph.D. dissertation, University of Northern Colorado. /Iran /Nationalization /Oil industry

3328. Nora, Simon. 1963 "Note résumant le rapport du groupe de travail des entreprises publiques." Promotions (Paris), No. 85, pp. 9-19. /France

3329. Nora, Simon. 1979 "Bien gérer, c'est choisir." Revue Française de Gestion No. 20, p. 51. /France

3330. Noreng, Øystein. 1981 "State-owned Oil Companies: Western Europe." In Raymond Vernon and Yair Aharoni, ed(s). State-Owned Enterprise in the Western Economies. New York: St. Martin's Press. pp. 133-144. /Petroleum industry /HD 3850 S79 PCL

3331. Normanton, E. L. 1966 "Public Accountability and the Nationalized Industries, the Government Corporations of the USA. British Nationalized Industries: A Continuing Crisis of Accountability. France, Germany State Shareholdings in Industry." The Accountability and Audit of Government. Manchester: Manchester University Press. /Government bureaucracy /Accountability / 657.835 N789a

3332. Normanton, E. L. 1981 "Accountability and Audit." In Raymond Vernon and Yair Aharoni, ed(s). State-Owned Enterprise in the Western Economies. New York: St. Martin's Press. pp. 157-169. /Accountability /Control process /HD 3850 S79 PCL

3333. Norris, H. 1947 "State Enterprise Price and Output Policy and the Problem of Cost Imputation." Economica (London), V. 14, pp. 54-62. /Price policy /Productivity /306 Ec74 PCL

3334. Nottage, Raymond. 1951 "Report of the Broadcasting Committee, 1949." Public Administration (London), pp. 173-178. /United Kingdom /Broadcasting industry /320.5 J826

3335. Nottage, Raymond. 1955 "O and M in the Nationalized Industries." Public Administration (London), V. 33, No. 4, pp. 395-400. /United Kingdom /Management /320.5 J826

3336. Nottage, Raymond. 1957 "Reporting to Parliament on the Nationalized Industries." Public Administration (London), V. 35, No. 2, pp. 143-167. /United Kingdom /Parliament /Control process / 320.5 J826 PCL

3337. Nottidge, Doris E. 1974 "Public Enterprises in Nigeria, Some Problems of Planning: National Paper of Nigeria." Paper presented at the International Seminar '74: Planning in Public Enterprises in Developing Countries, Ljubljana, Yugoslavia, 23 Sept. - 9 Oct. Ljubljana: ICPE. /Nigeria /Planning process

3338. Nour, M. 1969 Aide-mémoire sur l'organisation et la gestion des entreprises publiques en Afrique. Tangier: CAFRAD. /Africa /Organization formation /Management

3339. Nove, Alec. 1958 "The Problem of Success Indicators in Soviet Industry." Economica (London), V. 25, pp. 1-13. /Union of Soviet Socialist Reps. /Evaluation / 306 Ec74 n.s.

3340. Nove, Alec. 1968 The Soviet Economy: An Introduction. London: George Allen & Unwin. /Union of Soviet Socialist Reps. /Economic system / HC 336.2 N62 Pub Aff

3341. Nove, Alec. 1969 "The Piecemeal Economics of Nationalized Firms." New Society V. 13, No. 334, pp. 275-277. /Economic efficiency /Economic analysis /Evaluation

3342. Nove, Alec. 1973 Efficiency Criteria for Nationalized Industries. London: Allen & Unwin. /Economic efficiency /HD 3850 N68

3343. Nove, Alec. 1977 "State Capitalism and the Third World - A Discussion." Development and Change V. 8, No. 4, pp. 539-541. /Political analysis /Political economy (See Petras, 1977) /HD 82 D387

3344. Nove, Alec. 1977 "A Reply to a Reply." Development and Change V. 8, No. 4, pp. 544-546. /Political economy /Political analysis (See Petras, 1977) /HD 82 D387

3345. Nove, Alec. 1981 "Public Enterprises: Performance Evaluation." Paper presented at the Expert Group Meeting on Performance Criteria and the Implementation of Performance Evaluation Systems in Public Enterprises in Developing Countries, Ljubljana, Yugoslavia, 23-27 November. Ljubljana: ICPE. /Evaluation /Economic efficiency

3346. Novoa Monreal, E. 1978 "Las empresas públicas y el estado." Paper presented at the Round Table on Public Enterprise of the Tenth General Assembly of the Latin American Association of Public Administration, Mexico City. /Mexico /OPSS

3347. Nowrojee, Pheroze. 1977 "Public Enterprise in Kenya." In Yash Ghai, ed(s). Law in the Political Economy of Public Enterprise, African Perspectives. Uppsala: Scandinavian Institute of African Studies. New York: International Legal Centre. pp. 161-205. /Kenya /East Africa /Case studies /Africa 76 L41 Law

3348. Nsiah, D. K. 1980 "Pricing Policy in Public Enterprises: The Ghanaian Case." Paper presented at the International Workshop on Pricing Policies in Public Enterprises, Ljubljana, Yugoslavia, 26-30 May. Ljubljana: ICPE. /Ghana /Price policy

3349. Nucete, Diego. 1974 "Las compañías estatales de petróleo." Comercio Exterior (Mexico City), V. 24, pp. 1259-1262. /Mexico /Oil industry / HF 3238 C658 LAC

3350. Nudelman, Pablo. 1980 "Relation between National Planning and Planning in Public Enterprises." Paper presented at the Regional Workshop on Planning in Public Enterprises in the Latin American and Caribbean Region, Kingston, Jamaica, 11-15 February. Ljubljana: ICPE /Planning process

3351. Nugent, Jeffrey B. 1984 "International Instability and the Survival Capabilities of Inter-Arab Public Enterprise Joint Ventures." Public Enterprise V. 4, No. 3, pp. 11-21. /Middle East /International economic relations /Syria /Jordan /Iraq /Egypt /Libya Multinational corporations

3352. Numan, Andrew M. de. 1952 The Economic Aspects of Nationalization in Great Britain. Cambridge. /United Kingdom /Nationalization /Economic analysis

3353. Nunes, Janary. 1959 Defesa dos programas da Petrobrás. Rio de Janeiro: Petróleo Brasileiro. /Brazil /Oil industry

3354. Nunez Miñana, Horacio, and Alberto Porto. 1976 "Análisis de la evolución de precios de empresas públicas en la Argentina." Desarrollo Económico (Buenos Aires), V. 16, No. 63, pp. 307-332. /Argentina /Price policy /Economic history /Economic analysis / HD 85 S7 D48 LAC

3355. Nunez, L. n.d. "Area del conflicto: Cómo, por qué y para qué se estatiza." Ahora (Santiago, Chile), V. 1, No. 5, pp. 26-29. /Chile /Nationalization

3356. Nunome, M. 1962 Study in Nationalized Industries in England. Tokyo: Toyo Keizai Shinpo-Sha. /United Kingdom /Nationalization /Industrial sector

3357. Nutter, G. Warren. 1967 "Pricing Policy for State-Owned Enterprises." Il Politic V. 32, No. 2, pp. 383-387. /Price Policy

3358. Nwanwene, O. 1970 Public Corporations and State-Owned Companies. Ife, Nigeria: Institute of Administration. /Nigeria

3359. Nwanwene, O. 1970 "Public Corporations and State-Owned Companies." Quarterly Journal of Administration (Ibadan, Nigeria), V. 5, No. 1, pp. 53-75. /Nigeria

3360. Nwanwene, O., and E. O. Kowe. 1970 The Progress of Nigerian Public Administration: A Report of Research. Ife, Nigeria: University of Ife, Institute of Administration. /Nigeria /Public administration

3361. Nyers, R. 1966 "The Comprehensive Reform of Managing the National Economy in Hungary." Acta Oeconomica (Budapest), V. 1, No. 1-2, pp. 19-37. /Hungary /Socialist economy /Management /Administrative reform / 330.5 Ac81

3362. Nyers, R., and Márton Tardos. 1980 "Enterprises in Hungary before and after the Economic Reform." In William J. Baumol, ed(s). Public and Private Enterprise in a Mixed Economy. New York: St. Martin's Press. pp. 161-193. /Hungary /Economic history /HD 3842 P87 PCL

3363. Nyhart, J. D. 1959 The Uganda Development Corporation and the Promotion of Entrepreneurship. Makerere, Uganda: East African Institute of Social Research. /Uganda /Development corporation /Entrepreneurial activity /Case studies /East Africa

3364. Nyhart, J. D., and Edmond F. Janssens. 1967 A Global Directory of Development Finance Institutions in Developing Countries. Paris: Development Centre of the Organization for Economic Cooperation and Development. /Development banks /Developing nations /Directory / HG4509 N92 Pub Aff

3365. Nyhart, J. Daniel. 1962 "African Development Banks: Public, Private or Mixed?" Industrial Management Review V. 4, No. 1, pp. 59-78. /Africa /Development banks /Financing /HD28 I538

3366. Nyres, R. 1969 La réforme du mecanisme de l´économie en Hongrie. Vingt-cinq questions et vingt-cinq résponses. Budapest: Ed. Panorama. /Hungary /Economic policy /Economic analysis

3367. O´Brien, Patrick. 1966 The Revolution in Egypt´s Economic System. From Private Enterprise to Socialism. London: Oxford University Press. /Egypt /Economic development /Nationalization / 338.962 Ob6r

3368. O´Brien, Peter. 1980 "Report of the Expert Group Meeting on Strategies for Energy Development in Developing Countries--Role of Public Enterprises, 1980." Ljubljana: ICPE. /Energy utility industry /Energy resources /Developing nations

3369. O´Brien, Peter. 1980 "Towards an Energy Strategy for Developing Countries: Some Preliminary Notes." Paper presented at the Expert Group Meeting on Strategies for Energy Development in Developing Countries--Role of Public Enterprises, Ljubljana, Yugoslavia, 19-22 Feb. Ljubljana: ICPE. /Developing nations /Energy resources /Energy use policy Energy utility industry

3370. O´Brien, Peter. 1981 "Self-Reliance through Cooperation - The Power Sector and Public Enterprises." Public Enterprise V. 1, No. 4, pp. 18-22. /Energy utility industry /Energy resources /Energy use policy /OPSS

3371. O´Brien, Peter. 1981 "La empresa pública en la encrucijada: Posibilidades y problemas de desarrollo tecnológico en América Latina." Paper presented at the Reunión regional de expertos "Estrategias e instrumentos para reforzar la negociación (SBP) de las empresas públicas en los países en desarrollo en la transferencia internacional de transacciones tecnológicas," San José, Costa Rica, 23-27 November. Ljubljana: ICPE. /Latin America /Technology transfer

3372. O´Brien, T. H. 1937 British Experiments in Public Ownership and Control. (A Study of the CEB, BBC, and LPTB). London: Allen & Unwin. /United Kingdom /Control process /388.8 Ob61b

3373. O´Connell, Donald W. 1972 Public Sector Labor Relations in Maryland: Issues and Prospects. College Park, Maryland: Public Sector Labor Relations Conference Board. /United States of America /Labor relations

3374. O´Halpin, P. 1979 The Chief Executive in State Enterprise. Dublin: Irish Productivity Centre. /Ireland /Government authority /Evaluation

3375. Oakeshott, Michael. 1951 "The BBC." Cambridge Journal pp. 543-544. /United Kingdom /Broadcasting industry

3376. Oatman, Miriam E. 1946 "The Nationalization Program in Czechoslovakia." Department of State Bulletin pp. 1027-1031.

/Czechoslovakia /Nationalization

3377. Obando Correa, Federico J. 1975 "El Instituto de Crédito Territorial de Colombia: Un análisis de experiencias." Rio de Janeiro: FGV-EIAP. /Colombia /Economic development /Evaluation /Credit policy /Regional development /OPSS

3378. Obiyan, A. I. 1966 Organization and Administration of Public Enterprise in Nigeria. Geneva: U.N. Seminar on Organization and Administration of Public Enterprises. /Nigeria /Public administration /Organization formation

3379. Oblak, Marija. 1980 "L'évolution de la formation dans les entreprises de l'électricité de Slovenie (E. D. S.)." Paper presented at the Séminaire international sur la gestion et la formation dans les entreprises publiques dans les pays en voie de développement, Ljubljana, Yugoslavia, 3-15 March. Ljubljana: ICPE. /Economic history /Yugoslavia /Electrical utility industry

3380. Oblak, Marija. 1980 "Training of Personnel in Electrical Utilities of Slovenia with Examples in Two Enterprises: The Coal Mines Velenje and the Thermal Plant Sostanj; Case Study." Paper presented at the Interregional Seminar on Training Management in Public Enterprises in Developing Countries, Ljubljana, Yugoslavia, Sept.29-Oct.10. Ljubljana: ICPE. /Yugoslavia /Electrical utility industry /Coal mining industry / Thermal energy industry /Case studies

3381. Obradovic, J. 1970 "Participation and Work Attitudes in Yugoslavia." Industrial Relations V. 9, No. 2, pp. 161-169. /Yugoslavia /Worker management participation

3382. Ochoa Campos, Moisés. 1978 La municipalización de empresas de servicios públicos. Mexico City: Paper presented at the Round Table Meeting on Public Enterprises in Latin America. /Decentralized authority /Local government /OPSS

3383. Odle, Maurice A. 1975 "Conflicting Attitudes Towards Public Enterprises: The Commonwealth Caribbean." Lok Udyog (New Delhi), V. 9, No. 6, pp. 75-82. /Caribbean Region /354.54 L836 PCL

3384. Oettle, Karl. 1978 "Public Enterprises in West Germany." In Andeŕ Gélinas, ed(s). Public Enterprise and the Public Interest. Ontario: The Institute of Public Administration of Canada. pp. 170-185. /Germany, Federal Rep. of

3385. Oettle, Karl. 1982 "The Public Enterprise as an Instrument of State Policies." Paper presented at the Tokyo Round Table preparatory to the 19th International Congress of Administrative Sciences, 13-17 Sept. /Germany, Federal Rep. of /Goal setting /Accountability /Taxonomy / OPSS

3386. Oftering, H. 1953 "The Participation of the German Federal State in Economic Enterprise." Annales de l'Economie Collective pp. 271-288. /Germany, Federal Rep. of

3387. Okabe, S. 1955 "Public Corporations in Japan." Indian Journal of Public Administration (New Delhi), V. 1, No. 3, pp. 217-223. /Japan / JA 26 I55 Pub Aff

3388. Okafor, Francis O. 1979 "Planning Process of Public Enterprises in Nigeria." Paper presented at the Regional Workshop on Planning in Public Enterprises of the African Region, Accra, Ghana, 10-15 December. Ljubljana: ICPE. /Nigeria /Planning process

3389. Okoumou, Victor, and Ion Niculescu. 1974 "La trilogie déterminante organes de gestion dans l´entreprise d´Etat congolaise." Paper presented at the International Seminar ´74: Planning in Public Enterprises in Developing Countries, Ljubljana, Yugoslavai, 23 Sept. - 9 Oct. Ljubljana: ICPE. /Congo, People´s Rep. of /Planning process

3390. Okuthe-Oyugi, Francis C. 1981 "The Public Corporation in Kenya: Economic Nationalism and Social Change." Unpublished doctoral thesis, Centre d´Etudes d´Afrique Noire, Institut d´Etudes Politiques de Bordeaux. /Kenya /East Africa /Political analysis

3391. Okyar, Osman. 1965 "The Concept of Statism." Economic Journal V. 75, pp. 98-111. /Turkey / 330.5 Ec7

3392. Olea Baudoin, Antonio, and Humberto Torrico Pacheco. 1975 "Bolivia: Empresas públicas." Rio de Janeiro: FGV-EIAP. /Bolivia /Public administration /Public financing /Directory /OPSS

3393. Olea, Manuel Alonso. 1955 "The Organisation and Administration of Public Enterprises in Spain." In A. H. Hanson, ed(s). Public Enterprise. Brussels: IIAS. pp. 269-274. /Spain /Public administration /Organization formation / HD 3850 H28 Law

3394. Oliva de Castro, Andrés de la. 1978 "Las empresas públicas: Apuntes para su caracterización con particular referencia a España." Mexico City: Paper presented at the Round Table on Public Enterprises in Latin America. /Spain / OPSS

3395. Oliveira Franco Sobrinho, Manoel de. 1970 Regime jurídico das empresas públicas no Brasil. La Plata, Argentina: Universidad Nacional. /Brazil /Law

3396. Oliveira Franco Sobrinho, Manoel de. 1972 Fundações e empresas públicas. Revista dos Tribunais (São Paulo), /Brazil /Directory

3397. Oliveira Franco Sobrinho, Manoel de. 1975 Empresas públicas no Brasil: Ação internacional. São Paulo: Editora Resenha Universitária. /Brazil /Law / HD 4093 O548 LAC

3398. Oliveira d´Almeida, Paulo Cesar. 1976 "Saneamento básico no Brasil, as empresas prestadores do servico: O PLANASA." Rio de Janeiro: FGV-EIAP. /Brazil /Sanitation industry /Public financing /Law / OPSS

3399. Oliveira, A. 1969 "As atividades empresariais do Governo Federal no Brasil." Revista Brasileira de Economia (Rio de Janeiro), V. 23, No. 3, pp. 89-108. /Brazil /Federal government /Entrepreneurial activity / G330.5 R326 LAC

3400. Oliveira, F. del. 1981 "Etat et science économique: La contribution de l'économie pour une théorie de l'Etat." Revue de l'Institut de Sociologie No. 1-2, pp. 141-151. /Latin America

3401. Olivencia Ruiz, M. 1968 Organos de poder y sujetos responsables de la empresa pública y privada. Madrid. /Spain /Organization behavior /Comparative analysis

3402. Oliver, J. 1967 "The Application of TVA Experience to Underdeveloped Countries." In Moore, J. R., ed(s). The Economic Impact of TVA. Knoxville, Tenn.: University of Tennessee Press. pp. 25-40. /United States of America /River valley development projects / 333.91 T256Ym UGL

3403. Olivier, J. P. 1969 "Public and Co-operative Economy in Sweden." Annals of Public and Cooperative Economy V. 40, pp. 435-455. /Sweden /Cooperatives / 330.5 An73

3404. Ollig, Gerhard. 1980 "Steel and the State in Germany." Annals of Public and Cooperative Economy V. 51, No. 4, pp. 423-438. /Germany, Federal Rep. of /Steel industry /330.5 An73

3405. Oluoch, J. N. 1968 "The Administration of Public Enterprises in Kenya." Paper presented at the UNECA Seminar, Tunis, 9-20 Dec. /Kenya /Management /Control process

3406. Oluwasanmi, H. A., and J. A. Alao. 1965 "The Role of Credit in the Transformation of Traditional Agriculture: the Nigerian Experience." Nigerian Journal of Economic and Social Studies (Ibadan, Nigeria), V. 7, pp. 31-50. /Nigeria /Agricultural development /Credit policy

3407. Olvarría, Jorge. 1967 "La desnacionalización de las empresas del Estado." Espejo (Mexico City), V. 8, No. 64, pp. 35-36. /Mexico /Privatization / 330.5 Es64 LAC

3408. Omar, Abdel Gawad Gad. 1978 "Transfer and Management of Technology: Egyptian Iron Ores Problems and Its Relation of Technology." Paper presented at the International Workshop on Management of Transfer and Development of Technology in Public Enterprises in Developing Countries, Ljubljana, Yugoslavia, 19-25 June. Ljubljana: ICPE. /Egypt /Steel industry /Technology transfer

3409. Ommati, Fides Angelica. 1980 "O controle administrativo da empresa pública e sociedade de economia mista no direito brasileiro." Revista de Informação Legislativa V. 17, pp. 201-238. /Brazil /Law /Control process /Mixed enterprises /G340.05 R3251 LAC

3410. Onar, S. S. 1954 "The Analysis and the Criticism of the Causes of Appearance of the Public Corporation in Turkey and the Legal and Administrative Structure of These Corporations." International Review of Administrative Sciences V. 20, No. 1, pp. 23-65. /Turkey /Public administration /Law /Economic analysis / JA 1 A1 I6 PCL

3411. Ondarts, Guillermo, and Carlos Correa. 1982 Compras Estatales e Integración Económica. Buenos Aires: INTAL-BID. /State trading organizations /Latin America /Economic integration /OPSS

3412. "Operational Control and Performance Reporting in HSL." 1971 Lok Udyog (New Delhi), V. 5, No. 2, pp. 197-198. /India /Information system /Steel industry /354.54 L836 PCL

3413. "The Organization and Financing of Public and Cooperative Enterprise." 1968 Annals of Public and Cooperative Economy V. 39, pp. 313-409. /Cooperatives /Organization formation /Financing /330.5 An73

3414. "The Organization and Financing of Public and Cooperative Enterprise." 1969 Annals of Public and Cooperative Economy V. 40, No. 1-2, pp. 1-206. /Cooperatives /Mixed enterprises /Structural characteristics /Financing /330.5 An73

3415. Organization for Economic Cooperation and Development. 1964 Part 1, Government Organization and Economic Development. Part 2, the Public Corporation and the Private Sector. Paris: O.E.C.D. Conference, September 7-11, 1964. /Economic development /Management

3416. "The Organization of Self-Management in Enterprises." 1971 Yugoslav Survey (Belgrade), V. 12, No. 1, pp. 131-150. /Yugoslavia /Worker self management / 949.70 Yu89 PCL

3417. Orozco, R. 1964 Economía de empresas cubanas. Havana: Ed. Financiera Económica. /Cuba

3418. Orrenius, Jan. 1978 "Public Enterprise and Public Interest in Sweden." In André Gélinas, ed(s). Public Enterprise and the Public Interest. Ontario: The Institute of Public Administration of Canada. pp. 200-209. /Sweden

3419. Ortiz de Zevallos M., Felipe. 1982 The Entrepreneurial Role of the Peruvian State. Lima: Intercampus. /Peru /Economic development /Development corporation /Public financing /Public administration /Entrepreneurial activity /OPSS

3420. Ortiz de Zevallos M., Felipe. 1982 El rol empresarial del Estado. Lima: Intercampus. /Peru /Economic development /Development corporation /Public financing /Public administration /Entrepreneurial activity /OPSS

3421. Ortiz de Zevallos M., Felipe 1984 "The Case of Peru: An Insider View." Paper presented at the conference: State Shrinking: A Comparative Inquiry into Privatization, Austin, Texas, 1-3 March. /Peru /Portugal /Economic analysis /OPSS

3422. Osculati, F. 1972 "Gli investimenti delle imprese pubbliche del l'ultimo decennio." Economia Pubblica No. 4. /Italy

/Investment

3423. Osman, Dina Sheikh El Din. 1977 "Notes toward the Study of Public Enterprise in Sudan." In Yash Ghai, ed(s). Law in the Political Economy of Public Enterprise. Uppsala: Scandinavian Institute of African Studies. New York: International Legal Centre. pp. 295-305. /Sudan /Economic history /Africa / Africa 76 L41 Law

3424. Osorio, D. 1967 La empresa pública en Chile. Santiago, Chile. /Chile

3425. Osorio, Jorge. 1981 "Informe de la reunión regional de expertos "Estrategias e instrumentos para reforzar la posición de negociación (SBP) de las empresas públicas en los países en desarrollo en la transferencia de transacciones tecnolgicas." San José, Costa Rica, 23-27 November. Ljubljana: ICPE /Developing nations /Technology transfer

3426. Ospina, Antonio. 1981 "Las empresas públicas." El Estado y el desarrollo. Bogotá: Editorial Dintel. pp. 251-256. /Colombia /HD 3616 C73 E88 1981 LAC

3427. Ossa, R. 1971 "Análisis económico-financiero y otros pormenores del gran holding público." Información (Bilbao, Spain), V. 239, No. 1. /Economic analysis /Financial performance /Holding company

3428. Ostergaard, G. N. 1954 "Labour and the Development of the Public Corporation." Manchester School of Economic and Social Studies V. 22, pp. 199-226. /Trade unions /330.5 M3121 PCL

3429. Osterkamp, K. 1963 "Réflexions sur le Congrès de Rome: L'utilité des services publics." Annales de l'Economie Collective No. 2-3, pp. 443-449. /Europe /Public utility industry /Public services

3430. Ostrum, Elinor. 1965 "Public Entrepreneurship: A Case Study in Ground Water Basin Management." Los Angeles: Unpublished Ph.D. dissertation, UCLA. /United States of America /Water resources development /Water supply industry

3431. Oswal, B. E. 1968 The Management of Public Enterprises in Uganda. Tunis: UNECA Seminar. /Uganda /Management /East Africa

3432. Oszlak, Oscar. 1978 "Capitalismo de Estado: forma acabada o transición?" Gobierno y empresas públicas en América Latina. Buenos Aires: SIAP. pp. 15-54. /Political economy /Political analysis /Latin America /OPSS

3433. Ottaviano, Vittorio. 1970 "Sometimiento de la empresa pública al derecho privado y exigencias conexas con los fines públicos que mediante el ejercicio de la empresa se quieran conseguir." La empresa pública. Zaragoza, Spain: Publicaciones del Real Colegio de España en Bolonia. /Law

3434. Ottonello, N. J. 1966 "Una posible solución para nuestras empresas estatales." Boletín del Museo Social Argentino (Buenos Aires), V. 43, No. 328, pp. 117-121. /Argentina

3435. Ottonello, N. J. 1968 "Empresas del Estado, mesa redonda celebrada el 5 de Abril de 1963." Boletín del Museo Social Argentino (Buenos Aires), V. 45, No. 336, pp. 194-196. /Argentina

3436. Ottou-Abanda, Ambroise. 1980 "Efforts du government de la République Unie du Cameroun pour l'encadrement technique des populations et la perfectionnement des cadres." Paper presented at the Séminaire international sur la gestion et la formation dans les entreprises publiques dans les pays en voie de développement, Ljubljana, Yugoslavia, 3-15 March. Ljubljana: ICPE. /Cameroon /Training

3437. Ouamba-Awola, Joseph. 1980 "La formation dans la République Populaire du Congo: Example du Centre National de Gestion (CENAGES)." Paper presented at the Séminaire international sur la gestion et la formation dans les entreprises publiques dans les pays en voie de développement, Ljubljana, Yugoslavia, 3-15 March. Ljubljana: ICPE. /Congo, People's Rep. of /Planning process

3438. Owen, Glenville H. 1980 Management Development and Training in Public Enterprises in Jamaica. Kingston: Jamaican Institute of Management. /Jamaica /Management

3439. Owen, Glenville H. 1980 "Management Development and Training in Public Enterprises in Jamaica." Paper presented at the Expert Group Meeting on the Research Project on Education and Training in Public Enterprises in Developing Countries, Ljubljana, Yugoslavia, 17-22 March. Ljubljana: ICPE. /Jamaica /Training /Management

3440. Oyugi, Walter Ouma. 1980 "The African Public Services: Challenges and Prospects." Indian Journal of Public Administration (New Delhi), V. 26, No. 3, pp. 792-813. /Africa /Public services / JA 26 I55 Pub Aff

3441. Pacek, Joze. 1975 "Self-Management: The Experience and the Results." In Ichak Adizes and Elisabeth Mann Borgese, ed(s). Self-Management: New Dimensions to Democracy. Santa Barbara, Cal.; Oxford, England: American Bibliographical Center; Clio Press. pp. 67-70. /Yugoslavia /Worker self management /OPSS

3442. Pacho, Arturo G., and Gabriel U. Iglesias. 1981 "The Role of Public Enterprises in Regional Development, the Philippine Experience: Country Paper." Paper presented at the Expert Group Meeting on the Role of Public Enterprises in Regional Development in Developing Countries, Ljubljana, Yugoslavia, 7-11 December. Ljubljana: ICPE. /Philippines /Regional development

3443. Padmanathen, Chelliah, and Piyadasa Ranasinghe. 1980 "Corporate Planning in Public Enterprises in Sri Lanka." Paper presented at the Regional Workshop on Corporate Planning in Public Enterprises in the Asian and Pacific

Region, Kuala Lumpar, Malaysia, 17-21 November. Ljubljana: ICPE /Sri Lanka /Planning process

3444. Page, Alan C. 1980 "The New Directive on Transparency of Financial Relations between Member States and Public Undertakings." European Law Review V. 5, pp. 492-500. /European Economic Community /Financing /Law

3445. Pagliano, Gary J., et al. 1978 "A Draft Report on Mexico's Oil and Gas Policy." Washington, D.C.: Library of Congress, Congressional Research Service. /Mexico /Oil industry /Gas utility industry /OPSS

3446. Paine, C. L. 1937 "Some Aspects of Discrimination by Public Utilities." Economica (London), V. 4, pp. 425-439. /Price policy /Public utility industry / 306 Ec74

3447. Paiva, Alfredo de Almeida. 1960 "As sociedades de economia mista e as empresas públicas como instrumentos jurídicos a servico do Estado." Revista de Direito Administrativo (Rio de Janeiro), No. 60, pp. 1-55. /Mixed enterprises /Law /Planning process

3448. Pakistan. Industrial Development Bank of Pakistan. 1970 Nine Years of the Industrial Development Bank of Pakistan. Karachi: Elite Publishers. /Pakistan /Development banks /Industrial sector /HG 3290.5 A8 I5

3449. Pakistan. Investment Advisory Centre of Pakistan. 1976 In Reza H. Syed, ed(s). Role and Performance of Public Enterprises in the Economic Growth of Pakistan. /Pakistan /Economic growth policy

3450. Pakistan. Ministry of Finance. 1967 Government Sponsored Corporations. Rawalpindi. /Pakistan

3451. Pakistan. Ministry of Finance. 1970 Government Sponsored Corporations, 1969-70. Islamabad. /Pakistan

3452. Pakistan. Ministry of Finance. 1971 Government Sponsored Corporations (1970-1971). Islamabad. /Pakistan

3453. Pakistan. Office of the Economic Adviser. 1965 Government Sponsored Corporations. Rawalpindi. /Pakistan

3454. Pakistan. Pakistan Administrative Staff College. 1979 In Anwar H. Siddiqui, ed(s). Management of Public Enterprises in Pakistan. /Pakistan /Management

3455. Pandit, A. D. 1961 Commercial Policies of Public Enterprises. Cambridge, Mass.: Harvard University, Center for International Affairs. /Evaluation /Policy analysis /Price policy

3456. Pandit, Shrikrishna A. 1973 "Nationalization of Banks in India." Finance and Development V. 10, No. 1, pp. 32-36. /India /Nationalization /Banking system /HG 3881 F857

3457. Pangadharan Pillai, V. 1970 State Enterprises in Kerala. Trivandrum, India: Kerala Academy of Political Science. /India /Evaluation /Public administration /Management /Legislature /Kerala, India (State) /HD 3616 I44 K45

3458. Panglaykim, J. 1963 "Some Aspects of State Enterprises in Indonesia." Ekonomi dan Keunngan Indonesia (Djakarta), V. 16, No. 3. /Indonesia /Evaluation

3459. Panglaykim, J. 1965 "Some Notes on the Administrative Aspects of the Indonesian State Trading Corporations." Economie (Tilburg), V. 30, No. 1, pp. 25-37. /Indonesia /State trading organizations /Administrative management

3460. Panglaykim, J., and Ingrid Palmer. 1969 State Trading Corporations in Developing Countries, with Special Reference to Indonesia and Selected Asian Countries. Rotterdam: Rotterdam University Press. /Asia /Indonesia /State trading organizations / 381.0991 P193s

3461. Panicker, A. R. 1980 "Transfer of Technology by Indian Public Sector Enterprises to the Developing Countries of the ESCAP Region with Particular Reference to Pesticides Industry." Paper presented at the Regional Workshop on Management of Transfer of Technology by Public Enterprises in the ESCAP Region, Bangalore, India, 10-15 November. Ljubljana: ICPE /India /Technology transfer /Pesticide industry

3462. Panigrahi, S. N. 1955 "Profit and Loss in Public Enterprises." Indian Taxation (New Delhi), V. 6, No. 2, pp. 49-52. /India /Profits

3463. Panigrahi, S. N. 1956 "Profit and Loss in Public Enterprises." Indian Merchants' Chamber V. 50, No. 2, pp. 55-57. /India /Profits

3464. Papi, Guiseppe Ugo. 1970 "La función del Estado en las economías mixtas." La Empresa Pública. Zaragoza, Spain: Publicaciones del Real Colegio de España en Bolonia. pp. 13-32. /Spain /Mixed enterprises /Management

3465. Papic, A. 1959 "Le financement des investissements en Yougoslavie." Annales de l'Economie Collective V. 47, No. 550, pp. 84-109. /Yugoslavia /Investment /Financing

3466. Paramanathan, Velupillai. 1979 "Control Systems for Public Enterprises in Developing Countries: Sri Lanka." paper presented at the Interregional Workshop on Control Systems for Public Enterprises in Developing Countries, Ljubljana, Yugoslavia, 9-13 July. Ljubljana: ICPE. /Sri Lanka /Control process

3467. Parames Montenegro, Carlos. 1978 "Las empresas públicas y las empresas privadas ante el desafio de la rentabilidad y la participación." Paper presented at the Fourth General Assembly of the Latin American Association of Public Administration, Mexico City, 6-11 Nov. /Worker management participation /Profits /Private enterprises /Comparative analysis /OPSS

3468. Parameswaran, N. 1978 "Cash Management in Public Sector Undertakings." Lok Udyog (New Delhi), V. 12, No. 9, pp. 15-18. /India /Financial management /354.54 L836 PCL

3469. Paranjape, H. K. 1953 "`Measurement of Productivity': Comparative Productivity in State-Owned and Privately-Owned Enterprises." Indian Journal of Economics V. 33, pp. 375-394. /Productivity /Evaluation /Economic analysis /Comparative analysis /330.5 In2

3470. Paranjape, H. K. 1954 "Organization of State Enterprise in India." Indian Economic Journal (Bombay), V. 2, No. 2, pp. 131-141. /India /Structural characteristics

3471. Paranjape, H. K. 1960 "Measurement of Management in the Public Sector." Indian Journal of Public Administration (New Delhi), V. 6, No. 2, pp. 159-176. /Evaluation /Management /JA 26 I55 Pub Aff

3472. Paranjape, H. K. 1961 "State Enterprises: Co-Ordination and Control." Indian Journal of Public Administration (New Delhi), V. 7, pp. 528-542. /India /Public administration /Control process /Evaluation / JA 26 I55 Pub Aff

3473. Paranjape, H. K. 1963 "Evolving Pattern in the Organization and Administration of Public Enterprises." Indian Journal of Public Administration (New Delhi), V. 14, pp. 396-418. /India /Structural characteristics /Economic history /Control process / JA 26 I55 Pub Aff

3474. Paranjape, H. K. 1964 "The Flight of Technical Personnel in Public Undertakings: A Study Report for the Government of India, Ministry of Commerce and Industry, on Behalf of the Indian Institute of Public Administration." New Delhi: Indian Institute of Public Administration. /India /Labor relations /Personnel management / 351.10954 P212f

3475. Paranjape, H. K. 1964 "Public Sector Projects: Difficulties of Efficient Execution." Economic Weekly (Bombay), pp. 269-276. /Project management

3476. Paranjape, H. K. 1966 A Regional Report on India, Iran, Iraq, Pakistan, and the Philippines. Geneva: U.N. Seminar on Organization and Administration of Public Enterprises, Sept. 1966. /India /Iran /Iraq /Pakistan /Philippines

3477. Parappa, H. C. 1961 "Parliamentary Control and Accountability of Public Undertakings." Indian Journal of Public Administration (New Delhi), V. 7, No. 3. /India /Parliament /Control process /Accountability /JA26 I55 Pub Aff

3478. Pardigon, Vladimir. 1966 "Recent Developments in the Soviet Union's Experiments with Autonomous Enterprises Operated on a Profit-Earning Basis." Annals of Public and Cooperative Economy V. 37, pp. 133-144. /Union of Soviet Socialist Reps. /Profits /

3479. Parekh, Vinod. 1976 "Profitability and Social Objectives in the Public Sector." Lok Udyog (New Delhi), V. 10, No. 7, pp. 9-12. /India /Goal setting /354.54 L836 PCL

3480. "Parliamentary Control of Nationalised Industries." 1958 Parliamentary Affairs (London), /United Kingdom /Parliament /Industrial sector /Control process /

3481. Parmeswaran, N. 1978 "Project Costing." Lok Udyog (New Delhi), V. 12, No. 3, pp. 17-18. /India /Project management /Costs /354.54 L836 PCL

3482. Parris, Carl D. 1981 "Joint Venture I: The Trinidad-Tobago Telephone Company 1968-1972." Economic and Social Studies (Mona, Kingston, Jamaica), V. 30, No. 1, pp. 108-126. /Caribbean Region /Trinidad and Tobago /Case studies /Telephone industry /Mixed enterprises /Multinational corporations /G330.97292 So13 LAC

3483. Parris, Carl D. 1981 "Joint Venture II: The National Flour Mill of Trinidad-Tobago 1972-1979." Economic and Social Studies (Mona, Kingston, Jamaica), V. 30, No. 1, pp. 127-145. /Caribbean Region /Trinidad and Tobago /Case studies /Mixed enterprises /Multinational corporations /Food industry /G330.97292 So13 LAC

3484. Parti Communiste Francais. 1971 "La Régie Nationale des Usines Renault et l´industrie automobile." Economie et Politique (Paris), No. 209. /France /Automobile manufacturing industry

3485. Pashev, A. 1967 "The New System of Management: An Important Stage in the Development of the Bulgarian Economy." Eastern European Economics V. 5, No. 3, pp. 3-8. /Bulgaria /Management /Administrative reform / 330.5 Ea79

3486. Pasic, Najdan. 1970 "L´intégration d´autogestion et le système politique." Questions Actuelles du Socialism (Belgrade), V. 98, No. 12-3. /Yugoslavia /Worker self management /Political analysis

3487. Pasic, Najdan. 1975 "Self-Management in Yugoslavia: Some Impending Problems." In Ichak Adizes and Elisabeth Mann Borgese, ed(s). Self-Management: New Dimensions to Democracy. Santa Barbara, Cal.; Oxford, England: American Bibliographical Center; Clio Press. pp. 57-66. /Yugoslavia /Worker self management /OPSS

3488. Pass, Y. P. 1972 "Flight of Technical Personnel and Managerial Morale in Public Enterprises." New Delhi: Bureau of Public Enterprises. /India /Working Conditions

3489. Passeron, S. 1968 L´autonomie de gestion des établissements publics nationaux. Paris: Librairie générale de droit et de jurisprudence. /France /Management /Accountability

3490. Passeron, S. 1972 La Réforme des établissements publics. Rapport adopté par l´Assemblee Générale du Conseil d´Etat et remis au Président de la République le 4 mars 1971. Paris:

Documentation Française. /France /Organization change /Government report

3491. Pastor, C. Vanrell. 1980 "Latin American State Petroleum Enterprises and their Association in ARPEL." State Petroleum Enterprises in Developing Countries. New York: Pergamon Press. pp. 82-91. /Oil industry /Latin America

3492. Pastuovic, Nikola. 1977 "The Training Cycle in the Enterprise." Paper presented at the International Seminar on Management and Training in Public Enterprises in Developing Countries, Ljubljana, Yugoslavia, 10-28 October. Ljubljana: ICPE. /Training /Management / Also presented at the same seminars in Ljubljana, Yugoslavia, Sept. 21-Oct 2, 1976 and Sept. 18-Oct. 6, 1978.

3493. Patankar, S. M. 1979 "Evaluation of Financial and Physical Performance." Lok Udyog (New Delhi), V. 13, No. 8, pp. 51-54. /India /Economic efficiency /Financial performance /Evaluation /354.54 L836 PCL

3494. Patankar, Shreenivas Mahdav. 1980 "Pricing Policy in Public Enterprises: Some Aspects of Indian Experience." Paper presented at the International Workshop on Pricing Policies in Public Enterprises, Ljubljana, Yugoslavia, 26-30 May. Ljubljana: ICPE. /India /Price policy

3495. Patel, H. M. 1978 "National Seminar on Corporate Planning in Public Enterprises." Lok Udyog (New Delhi), V. 11, No. 12, pp. 3-6. /India /Planning process /Management /354.54 L836

3496. Patel, H. M. 1978 "Public Enterprise in Indian Economy - Problems of Management." Lok Udyog (New Delhi), V. 11, No. 11, pp. 5-8. /India /Management /354.54 L836 PCL

3497. Pathak, H. N. 1954 "Central Banking in Relation to the Problem of Economic Development." Indian Economic Journal (Bombay), V. 1, No. 4, pp. 395-406. /India /Central banks

3498. Pathak, Mahesh T. 1972 "Significance of Public Investment for Backward Regions: A Case Study, Flourspar Project in Gujarat." Kaira, Gujarat, India: Sardar Patel University. Department of Economics. /India /Gujarat, India (State)

3499. Patil, S. M. 1971 "Participative Management; Mechanics of Workers' Participation." Indian Journal of Industrial Relations (New Delhi), V. 7, No. 1, pp. 111-117. /India /Worker management participation / 331.105 In22

3500. Patil, S. M. 1981 "Experiences of a Public Sector Chief Executive: Constraints, Disappointments & Fulfillments." Public Enterprise Management: Constraints and Autonomy. New Delhi: Documentation Centre for Corporate & Business Policy Research. pp. 1-37. /India /Management /HD 4293 P77 1981 PCL

3501. Patil, S. S. 1971 "Choosing Chief Executives (for Government Undertakings): Ideologists, Specialists or Generalists." Indian Journal of Public Administration (New Delhi), V. 18, No. 1, pp. 7-35. /India /Management / JA 26 I55 Pub Aff

3502. Patnaik, Jyotiprakash. 1978 "Theory of Price Policy of Public Enterprises." In K. R. Gupta, ed(s). Pricing in Public Enterprises. New Delhi, India: Atlantic Publishers and Distributors. /Price Policy / HB 236 I4 P75

3503. Patnaik, R. C. 1951 "Port Organizations and Finance." Dock and Harbour Authority. London. pp. 211-216. /United Kingdom /Port authority /Financial performance

3504. Patnaik, R. C. 1954 "Public Enterprise in India." Indian Economic Journal (Bombay), pp. 281-288. /India /Evaluation

3505. Patnaik, R. C. 1956 "Management of Nationalized Industry in India." Indian Journal of Political Science (New Delhi), V. 17, No. 4, pp. 331-340. /India /Management

3506. Paul, James C. N. 1977 "Law, Lawyers, and Decision-Making in State Enterprise." In Yash Ghai, ed(s). Law in the Political Economy of Public Enterprise. Uppsala: Scandinavian Institute of African Studies. New York: International Legal Centre. pp. 81-91. /Law /Management / Africa 76 L41 Law

3507. Pauwels, Jean-Pierre. 1980 "Steel and the State in Belgium." Annals of Public and Cooperative Economy V. 51, No. 4, pp. 393-404. /Belgium /Steel industry /330.5 An73

3508. Pavez, Guillermo. 1976 "Las empresas públicas y otros organismos descentralizados en la República de Nicaragua." Paper presented at ICAP, San José, Costa Rica, 1978. /Nicaragua /Economic Analysis /OPSS

3509. Pavlin, Igor. 1983 "Training of Trainers: Survey of the Results of an Interregional Seminar on the Implementation of Training of Management for Industrial Public Enterprises in Developing Countries." Public Enterprise V. 3, pp. 67-70. /Developing nations /Personnel management /Training /Efficacy /OPSS

3510. Pearce, John Edward. 1962 "The Creeping Conservatism of TVA." Reporter pp. 31-35. /United States of America /River valley development projects / Public administration

3511. Peco, Franco. 1980 "Steel and the State in Italy." Annals of Public and Cooperative Economy V. 51, No. 4, pp. 459-476. /Italy /Steel industry /330.5 An73

3512. Peconick, Jayme de Andrade. 1980 "Brief Comments on the Brazilian Situation concerning Investment Criteria and Investment Decision-Making Processes." Paper presented at the International Workshop on Pricing Policies in Public Enterprises, Ljubljana, Yugoslavia, 26-30 May. Ljubljana: ICPE. /Brazil /Investment

3513. Pedini, M. 1960 "State Participations and Economic Organizations." Lavaro e Sicurezza Sociale (Rome), V. 4, No. 1, pp. 29-40. /Italy /Mixed enterprises

3514. Pedregal y Fernandez, Manuel. 1930 "Municipalización comparada de servicios." Revista de Ciencias Jurídicas y

Sociales (Mexico City), No. 13, pp. 245-300. /Mexico /Public services

3515. Pedroza, Arturo. 1973 "Las cuentas de las empresas estatales." Espejo (Mexico City), V. 14, No. 102, pp. 22-26. /Mexico /Accounting / 330.5 Es64 LAC

3516. Pegrum, D. F. 1940 "The Public Corporation as a Regulatory Device." Land Economics V. 16, pp. 335-343. /Business regulation policy / 305 J824 PCL

3517. Peirson, C. G. 1963 "Financing of Australian Government Business Undertakings Capital Formation 1956-57 to 1959-60." Economic Record (Melbourne, Australia), V. 39, No. 86, pp. 214-221. /Australia /Financing /Investment / 330.99305 Ec74

3518. Peirson, David. 1974 The Major Public Corporations: A Statutory Analysis. London: Royal Institute of Public Administration. /United Kingdom /Law

3519. Pejovich, S. 1966 The Market-Planned Economy of Yugoslavia. Minneapolis, Minn.: University of Minnesota Press. /Yugoslavia /Mixed enterprises / 330.9497 P359m PCL

3520. Pelaez, Carlos Manuel. 1968 "The State, the Great Depression, and the Industrialization of Brazil." New York: Unpublished Ph.D. dissertation, Columbia University. /Brazil /Industrial sector /Economic history / Cement manufacturing industry / FILM 8754 LAC

3521. Pelikan, P., and R. Kocanda. 1967 "The Socialist Enterprise as a Participant in the Market." Czechoslovak Economic Papers (Prague), V. 9, pp. 49-64. /Socialist economy /330.9437 C995

3522. Peltosalo, Arthur E. 1974 "New Challenges in Planning Distribution Systems." Public Utilities Fortnightly V. 94, No. 3. /Planning process /Resource distribution / 388.9 P97

3523. Peltzman, Sam. 1971 "Pricing in Public and Private Enterprises: Electric Utilities in the United States." Journal of Law and Economics V. 14, No. 1, pp. 109-148. /United States of America /Price policy /Electrical utility industry / Comparative analysis /330.5 J827

3524. Pena Soto, Carlos. 1978 "Semejanzas y diferencias entre las empresas públicas y las empresas privadas en cuanto a sus motivaciones económicas y sociales." Paper presented at the Fourth General Assembly of the Latin American Association of Public Administration, Mexico City, 6-11 Nov. /Organization behavior /Private enterprises /Comparative analysis /OPSS

3525. Pendleton, Edwin C. and Paul D. Staudohar. 1974 "Arbitration and Strikes in Hawaii Public Employment." Industrial Relations V. 13, No. 3, pp. 299-307. /United States of America /Labor relations / 331.105 In19

3526. Penney, Freeland F. 1946 Governmental Use of the Corporate Device. New York: Universal Books. /Control process /Policy analysis

3527. Penz, Philippe. 1979 "Planning and Price Setting: Theoretical and Practical Calculation of Marginal Production Costs within `Electricité de France´." Annals of Public and Cooperative Economy V. 50, No. 3, pp. 81-110. /France /Electrical utility industry /Price policy /330.5 An73

3528. People´s Democratic Republic of Korea. 1980 "Experiences on Unified and Detailed Planning in Self-Reliance National Economic Construction: Democratic People´s Republic of Korea." Paper presented at the Regional Workshop on Corporate Planning in Public Enterprises in the Asian and Pacific Region, Kuala Lumpur, Malaysia, 17-21 November. Ljubljana: ICPE. /Korea, People´s Democratic Rep. of /Planning process

3529. Perampalam, V. 1966 Organization and Administration of Public Enterprises in Ceylon. Geneva: U.N. Seminar on Organization and Administration of Public Enterprises. /Sri Lanka /Public administration /Organization formation

3530. Peregrín Puga, F. 1970 "Las fábricas de la Real Hacienda. Un prototipo de empresa pública en la España del siglo XVIII." La Empresa Pública. Zaragoza, Spain: Publicaciones del Real Colegio de España en Bolonia. pp. 1239-1288. /Spain /Economic history

3531. Pereira, Jesus Soares. 1975 Petróleo, energia elétrica e siderurgia: A luta pela emancipação, um depoimento de Jesus Soares Pereira sobre a política de Vargas. Rio de Janeiro: Paz e Terra. /Brazil /Oil industry /Steel industry /Electrical utility industry / HD 9574 B82 P36 LAC

3532. Perera, B. C. 1971 Public Enterprise in Ceylon. Leeds: Seminar Essay, Social Studies Department. /Sri Lanka /Evaluation

3533. Peres, L. 1968 "The Resurrection of Autonomy: Organization Theory and the Statutory Corporation." Public Administration (Sydney, Australia), pp. 360-370. /Australia /Public administration /Organization theory

3534. Perez Alfonzo, J. P. 1967 "El camino de Mossadegh." (Oil Nationalization in Iran). Política pp. 15-43. /Iran /Oil industry /Nationalization

3535. Perez Baltodno, Andrés. 1980 "Development of New Didactic Material for Training Programs in Public Enterprises for Latin America and the Caribbean." Public Enterprise V. 1, No. 1, pp. 67-76. /Latin America /Caribbean Region /Training /OPSS

3536. Perez Botija, Eugenio. 1970 "Problemas fundamentales de los entes públicos económicos en relación con su personal." La Empresa Pública. Zaragoza, Spain: Publicaciones del Real Colegio de España en Bolonia. pp. 423-442. /Spain /Labor relations

3537. Perez Creus, J. 1964 "El sistema de la autogestión en Yugoslavia." Revista de Trabajo (Madrid), No. 6, pp. 11-137. /Yugoslavia /Worker self management

3538. Perez Moreno, A. 1969 La forma jurídica de las empresas públicas. Sevilla. /Spain /Law

3539. Perez, Arturo del Castillo. 1980 "Investment and Financing Aspects of State Petroleum Enterprises." State Petroleum Enterprises in Developing Countries. New York: Pergamon Press. pp. 141-150. /Oil industry /Investment /Financing

3540. "Performance of Public Enterprises During 1976-77." 1978 Lok Udyog (New Delhi), V. 11, No. 12, pp. 63-68. /India /Statistics /Economic efficiency /Financial performance /354.54 L836 PCL

3541. "Performance of Public Enterprises during 1977-78." 1979 Lok Udyog (New Delhi), V. 12, No. 12. /India /Financial performance /Statistics /354.54 L836 PCL

3542. Perouse, Maurice. 1957 "The French National Credit Council." Annals of Collective Economy V. 28, pp. 201-205. /France /Financial institutions / 330.5 An73

3543. Perpar, Gabriel, and Janez Jereb. 1974 "Bibliography of Socio-Economic Planning in Yugoslavia." Paper presented at the International Seminar '74: Planning in Public Enterprises in Developing Countries, Ljubljana, Yugoslavia, Sept.23-Oct 9. Ljubljana: ICPE. /Yugoslavia /Planning process /Bibliography

3544. Perrot, F. R. 1971 Industry in the Public Sector. London: Ginn (Manchester Economics Project). /United Kingdom /Industrial sector

3545. Perroux, F. 1953 "Le secteur public industriel et les conditions de cohérence." Economie et Humanité (Paris), pp. 3-12. /France /Industrial sector

3546. Perry, Guillermo. 1981 "Empresas públicas: Donde está el problema?" El Estado y el desarrollo. Bogotá: Editorial Dintel. pp. 211-217. /Colombia /Evaluation /Goal setting /HD 3616 C73 E88 1981 LAC

3547. Pershpance, R. A. 1962 "Pricing Policy of Public Enterprises." Indian Journal of Public Administration (New Delhi), V. 8, No. 1. /India /Price policy /JA26 I55 Pub Aff

3548. Personnaz, J. 1947 "La nationalisation des houillères françaises." Droit Social (Paris), /France /Coal mining industry /Nationalization

3549. Personnaz, J. 1952 "La mise en application de la nationalisation des houillères." Droit Social (Paris), /France /Coal mining industry /Nationalization

3550. Persons, Warren M. 1934 Government Experimentation in Business. New York: John Wiley & Sons. /Industrial sector

/Law

3551. Peru. Corporación Financiera de Desarrollo. 1979 "COFIDE: Evolución de sus operaciones y su resultado económico, 1975-77." Lima. /Peru /Development banks /Investment / Holding company

3552. Peru. INAP. 1975 Empresas públicas por sector de la administración pública. Lima. /Peru /Directory

3553. Peru. INAP. 1975 "Proyecto de ley de bases de la actividad empresarial del Estado." Lima. /Peru /Law /Mixed enterprises /OPSS

3554. Peru. MITI. Oficina Sectorial de Planificación. 1981 Evaluación económica de la Empresa Siderúrgica del Perú (SIDERPERU). Lima: Ministerio de Industria, Turismo e Integración, Oficina Sectorial de Planificación, Sector Industria. /Peru /Steel industry /Evaluation /OPSS

3555. Peru. National Team of Experts. 1979 "Outline for a Study of the Role of the State in Developing Countries." Paper presented at the International Meeting on the Role of the Public Sector in Developing Countries, 2nd, Ljubljana, Yugoslavia, 2-7 April. Ljubljana: ICPE. /Peru

3556. Peru. National Team of Experts. 1980 Peruvian National Report: The Role of the Public Sector in Developing Countries. Ljubljana: ICPE. /Peru

3557. Peru. National Team of Experts. 1980 The Role of the State in the Industrialization Process in Peru. Ljubljana: ICPE. /Industrialization /Peru

3558. Perulles Bassas, J. J. 1970 La empresa pública y su normativa. Barcelona, Spain: Librería Bosch. /Law /Spain

3559. Perulles, Juan José. 1970 "Perfiles de la empresa pública." La Empresa Pública. Zaragoza, Spain: Publicaciones del Real Colegio de España en Bolonia. pp. 189-202. /Spain /Evaluation

3560. Pesakovic, M. 1970 Deux décennies d'autogestion en Yugoslavie. Belgrade: Medunarodna Politika. /Yugoslavia /Worker self management

3561. Peselj, B. M. 1959 "International Aspects of the Recent Yugoslav Nationalization Law." American Journal of International Law V. 53, pp. 428-432. /Yugoslavia /Nationalization /Law /International economic relations /341.05 Am35

3562. Pesenti, A. 1969 "Imprensa pubblica e sviluppo." Critica Marxixta (Rome), V. 7, No. 1, pp. 72-90. /Italy

3563. Peterson, S. 1932 "Highway Policy on a Commercial Basis." Quarterly Journal of Economics V. 46, pp. 417-443. /Highways and roads /Public financing / 330.5 Q2

3564. Petitat, Paul. 1942 "The Administration of the Swiss State Railways under the Influence of the Crisis (1930-1939)." Annals of Collective Economy V. 18, No. 2, pp. 150-157. /Switzerland /Railway industry /Economic history /330.5 An73

3565. Petras, James. 1977 "A Reply to Nove." Development and Change V. 8, No. 4, pp. 542-543. /Political economy /Political analysis (See Nove, 1977) /HD 82 D387

3566. Petras, James. 1977 "The Last Word?" Development and Change V. 8, No. 4, pp. 547-548. /Political analysis /Political economy (See Nove, 1977) /HD 82 D387

3567. Petric, Ivo. 1974 "Planning at the Level of the Region and the Commune with Special Reference to Planning in the Enterprise: Case Study of Yugoslavia." Paper presented at the International Seminar ´74: Planning in Public Enterprises in Developing Countries, Ljubljana, Yugoslavia, Sept.23-Oct. 9. Ljubljana: ICPE. /Yugoslavia /Planning process /Regional development /Local development

3568. Petrilli, Giuseppe. 1962 "The Institute for Industrial Reconstruction (I.R.I.)." Annals of Collective Economy V. 33, pp. 15-19. /Italy /Development corporation /Holding company /330.5 An73

3569. Petrilli, Giuseppe. 1964 L´IRI nell´economia italiana. Milan: Univ. de Messina. /Italy /Development corporation /Economic analysis / Holding company

3570. Petrilli, Giuseppe. 1967 Lo stato imprenditore: Validitá e attualita di uma formula. Bologna, Italy: Capelli Editore. /Italy /Government authority /Entrepreneurial activity /

3571. Petrilli, Giuseppe. 1971 L´Etat entrepreneur. Paris: Robert Lafont. /Italy /Government authority

3572. Petrilli, Giuseppe. 1972 El Estado empresario. Madrid: Ediciones y Publicaciones Españolas. /Italy /Government authority

3573. Petros, Laiketsion. 1980 "Preliminary Case Study of Transfer of Technology for Glass Products´ Manufacture in Ethiopia." Paper presented at the International Workshop on Preparations and Negotiations of Technology Transfer Agreements for Public Enterprises in Developing Countries, Ljubljana, Yugoslavia, 27-31 October. Ljubljana: ICPE. /Ethiopia /Glassware manufacturing industry /Technology transfer

3574. Petrovic, Marko. 1978 "Authorities for the Assessment of the Efficiency of Public Enterprises Particularly with Regard to the Type of Enterprises and the Type of Socio-Economic Systems." Paper presented at the Workshop on Information System for the Evaluation of Business Efficiency in Public Enterprises in Developing Countries, Ljubljana, Yugoslavia, 13-18 Nov. Ljubljana: ICPE. /Evaluation /Economic efficiency

3575. Petrovic, Marko. 1978 "The Role and Foundation of a Uniform Accounting System with General Chart of Accounts, Scheme of Cost Price Calculation and Final Accounts as a Basis for Measurement of the Efficiency of Public Enterprises." Paper presented at the Workshop on Information System for the Evaluation of Business Efficiency in Public Enterprises in Developing Countries, Ljubljana, Yugoslavia, 13-18 Nov. Ljubljana: ICPE. /Evaluation /Economic efficiency /Accounting

3576. Petrovic, Marko. 1978 "The Shaping of Information from the Viewpoint of Accountants´ Ethical Conduct and of Basic Accounting Principles." Paper presented at the Workshop on Information System for the Evaluation of Business Efficiency in Public Enterprises in Developing Countries, Ljubljana, Yugoslavia, 13-18 Nov. Ljubljana: ICPE. /Information management /Accounting

3577. Petrovic, R. 1955 _L´autoadministration locale en Yugoslavie. (La Commune)._ Belgrade. /Yugoslavia /Local government

3578. Pevc, Ema. 1977 "The Development of Training in Sava, Kranj: A Case Study." Paper presented at the International Seminar on Management and Training in Public Enterprises in Developing Countries, Ljubljana, Yugoslavia, 10-28 October. Ljubljana: ICPE. /Yugoslavia /Training /Management /Case studies / Also presented at the Expert Group Meeting on the Research Project on Education and Training in Public Enterprises in Developing Countries, Ljubljana, Yugoslavia, March 17-22, 1980.

3579. Pezdek, Robert V. 1973 _Public Employment: Bibliography._ Ithaca, N.Y.: Cornell University Press. /United States of America /Labor relations /Bibliography /Z7164 A2 P48 Pub Aff /HD 8001 P493 PCL,UGL

3580. Phatak, A. 1969 "Governmental Interference and Management Problems of Public Sector Firms. (Factors causing top management and staffing problems--Public sector firms in India)." _Annals of Public and Cooperative Economy_ V. 40, No. 3, pp. 337-351. /India /Personnel management /Control process / 330.5 An73

3581. Phegan, C. S. 1980 "Damage for Improper Exercise of Statutory Powers." _Sydney Law Review_ V. 9, pp. 93-120. /Australia /Liability /Law

3582. Philip, George. 1978 _Oil and Politics in Latin America: Nationalist Movements and State Companies._ New York: Cambridge University Press. /Nationalization /Oil industry /Latin America /Peru /Argentina /Brazil /Mexico /Ecuador /Venezuela /HD 9574 L3 1982 LAC

3583. Philippines. Board of Investment. 1969 _Annual Report: 1969-1970._ Rizal, Philippines: Board of Investment. /Philippines /Investment /Government report

3584. Philippines. Comm. on Reorg. of Government-owned or -Controlled Corporations. 1950 _Report of the Committee on_

Reorganization of Government-owned or -controlled Corporations. Manila. /Philippines /Administrative reform /Public administration

3585. Phillipe, M. 1970 Rôle de l'Etat dans le financement des entreprises. Paris: Dunod. /France /Financing

3586. Phillips, J. V. L. 1967 "Administrative Problems of Public Industrial Enterprises in Africa." Paper presented at the Seminar on Organisation and Administration of Industrial Services in Africa, Tangier, Morocco, 14-30 August. /Africa /Industrial sector /Management

3587. Picarelli, A. 1975 "Sulla gestione delle imprese di pubblici servizi." Rossegna Economica V. 39, No. 1, pp. 107-146. /Management

3588. Piccoli, F. 1971 Le partecipazioni statali. Milan, Italy: Etas Kompass. /Italy

3589. Pickstock, F. 1950 British Railways--The Human Problem. London: Fabian Society. /United Kingdom /Railway industry /Personnel management

3590. Pidgeon, G. W. F. 1971 Financial Control in Developing Countries with Particular Reference to State Corporations. London: Longman Group Limited. /Developing nations /Control process / Financial performance / HJ 9768 P5

3591. Pierandrei, F. 1960 Libertá sindicale e imprese "a prevalente participazione statale." Giur, Italy. /Italy /Trade unions

3592. Pigou, A. C. 1913 "Railway Rates and Joint Cost." Quarterly Journal of Economics V. 27, pp. 535-538. /Price policy /Railway industry / 330.5 Q2

3593. Pimentel, J. 1971 "La empresa pública en los países de economía mixta: Presencia y problemas." Economía Industrial No. 95. /Mixed enterprises /Evaluation

3594. Pincus, William. 1945 "Shall We Have More TVA." Public Administration Review V. 5, No. 2, pp. 149-152. /United States of America /River valley development projects /JK1 P85

3595. Pinelo, Adalberto. 1973 The Multinational Corporation as a Force in Latin American Politics: A Case Study of the International Petroleum Company in Peru. New York: Praeger Publishers. /Peru /Oil industry /Nationalization /Case studies / HD 9574 P54 I55 1973 LAC

3596. Pini, José A. 1978 "Las empresas públicas en el Uruguay: Medidas necesarias para desarrollar su eficiencia y eficacia." Paper presented at the General Assembly of the Latin American Association of Public Administration, 10th, Mexico City, Mexico. /Uruguay /Economic efficiency /Control process /Personnel management /OPSS

3597. Pinkney, David H. 1950 "Nationalization on Trial. France." Yale Review No. 1, pp. 94-110. /France /Nationalization

3598. Pinochet, C. 1970 Análisis de la política de fomento de ENAMI. Santiago, Chile. /Chile /Evaluation /Copper industry

3599. Pinto, Aluizio Loureiro. 1974 "O estudo das organizações públicas." Revista de Administração Municipal (Rio de Janeiro), V. 21, No. 123, pp. 46-56. /Brazil /Evaluation /JS 41 R484 LAC

3600. Pinto, Bilac. 1953 "O declíno das sociedades de economia mista e o advento das modernas empresas públicas." Revista de Direito Administrativo (Rio de Janeiro), No. 32, pp. 1-15. /Brazil /Mixed enterprises

3601. Pirnazar, H. 1966 Public Enterprises in Iran (An Historic Review). Tehran: State Organization for Administration and Employment Affairs. /Iran /Evaluation /Economic history

3602. Pivato, G. 1967 L'efficienza delle imprese publiche. Milan, Italy: Dott. A. Diuffe, Ed. /Evaluation /Economic efficiency

3603. Pizza, Célio Toledo., and Almeida Filho. 1968 "Banco do Estado destinatá maiores recursos para financiar produção." Indústria e desenvolvimiento (São Paulo), V. 1, No. 6, pp. 32-34. /Brazil /Banking agency /Financing /G333.0981 In2 LAC

3604. Platt, John. 1968 British Coals: A Review of the Industry, Its Organization and Management. London: Lyon, Grant and Green. /United Kingdom /Coal mining industry /Management

3605. Please, S. 1941 "The Paradox of the Government Corporation." Public Administration Review V. 1, No. 4, pp. 381-399. /Mixed enterprises / JK1 P85

3606. Please, S. 1955 "Government Control of the Capital Expenditure of the Nationalized Industries." Public Administration (London), V. 33, No. 1, pp. 31-41. /Control process /Public financing / 320.5 J826

3607. Please, S. 1959 "How Autonomous is Public Investment?" Kyklos (Zurich), V. 12, pp. 167-182. /Investment /Control process / 305 K983

3608. Please, S. 1959 "The Counter-Cyclical Behavior of Public Investment in the United Kingdom since the War." Public Finance (The Hague), No. 3-4, pp. 269-280. /United Kingdom /Investment / 336.05 Op2

3609. Pluta, Joseph E. 1981 "Real Public Sector Growth and Decline in Developing Countries." Public Finance/Finances Publiques (The Hague), V. 36, No. 3. /Developing nations /Economic growth policy / 336.05 Op2

3610. Pluta, Joseph E., and Peter C. Frederiksen. 1980 Nationalization of Industry and Other Factors Affecting the Growth and Centralization of Public Expenditures in Pakistan. Austin, Tex.: OPSS Technical Papers Series,

/Nationalization /Pakistan /Economic policy /OPSS

3611. Poelofs, J. M., and B. V. Berenschot-Bosboom. 1976 "Politics, Policy and Effective Planning." Paper presented at the International Seminar ´74: Planning in Public Enterprises in Developing Countries, Ljubljana, Yugoslavia, 23 Sept. - 9 Oct. Ljubljana: ICPE. /Planning process /Political influence

3612. Poklemba, John, and Peter Crusco. 1982 "Public Enterprises and RICO: The Aftermath of United States vs. Turkette." Criminal Law Bulletin V. 18, pp. 197-203. /United States of America /Law

3613. Polak, Kenneth. 1970 "Las empresas públicas en Gran Bretaña." La Empresa Pública. Zaragoza, Spain: Publicaciones del Real Colegio de España en Bolonia. pp. 1339-1354. /United Kingdom /Evaluation

3614. Polanyi, George. 1968 Contrasts in Nationalized Transport since 1947. London: Institute of Economic Affairs. /United Kingdom /Transportation industry

3615. Polaschek, R. J. 1958 Government Administration in New Zealand. London: Oxford University Press. /New Zealand /Public administration / 354.931 P757g

3616. Poltier, Etienne. 1982 "L´entreprise publique comme instrument des politiques de l´Etat." Paper presented at the Tokyo Round Table preparatory to the 19th International Congress of Administrative Sciences, 13-17 Sept. /Switzerland /Economic history /Law /Goal setting /Control process / Multinational corporations /OPSS

3617. Poltier, Etienne. 1983 "L´entreprise publique comme instrument des politiques de l´Etat." Paper presented at the 19th International Congress of Administrative Sciences, West Berlin, 19-23 Sept. /Switzerland /Economic history /Taxonomy /Goal setting /Autonomy /Law /Control process /Multinational corporations /OPSS

3618. Ponchelet, Daniéle. 1981 "Las empresas públicas en el Caribe Françes. Paper presented at the seminar on public enterprises in development planning for Central America and the Caribbean, San José, Costa Rica, 1-3 July. /Caribbean Region /France /French West Indies /Guadeloupe /Martinique /OPSS

3619. Poncio, J. A. 1960 "La gestión financiera de las empresas del Estado y su proyección en el tesoro nacional." Revista de Ciencia Económica pp. 277-282. /Argentina /Financial management

3620. Pondaven, P. 1969 "Les organes dirigeants des entreprises publiques." Revue Française d´Energie (Paris), /France /Management

3621. Ponsoldt, James F., and Jesse Stone. 1981 "The Liability of Foreign Governments under the United States Anti-Trust Law."

Georgia Journal of International and Comparative Law V. 11, pp. 103-132. /United States of America /International law /International trade / Liability /Monopoly

3622. Poom, E. 1956 "Public Sector Industries in Second Plan." Indian Journal of Trade pp. 816-818. /India /Industrial sector

3623. Popopo, Roy P. 1979 "National Report of Zambia." Paper presented at the Regional Workshop on Planning in Public Enterprises of the African Region, Accra, Ghana, 10-15 December. Ljubljana: ICPE /Zambia /Planning process

3624. Popopo, Roy P. 1981 "Sectoral Economic Co-Ordination through Public Enterprises: A Case Study of the Zambia Industrial and Mining Corporation Limited (ZIMCO)." Ljubljana: ICPE. /Zambia /Industrial sector /Mining industry

3625. Popov, G., and V. Ozira. 1968 Soviet Public Enterprise: the Planning Process and Measurement of Performance. Moscow: University of Moscow. /Union of Soviet Socialist Reps. /Evaluation /Planning process

3626. Popov, M. G. 1966 "The Organization, Management and General Evaluation of Operations of State Industrial Enterprises in USSR." Paper presented at the U.N. Seminar on Organization and Administration of Public Enterprises, Geneva, September. /Union of Soviet Socialist Reps. /Evaluation /Management

3627. Popovitch, M. 1958 "Planification et autogestion." Questions Actuelles du Socialism (Paris), No. 46, pp. 3-18. /Planning process /Management

3628. Por, Odon. 1937 "The Italian Corporations at Work." Annals of Collective Economy V. 13, No. 2, pp. 346-373. /Italy /Agricultural sector / 330.5 An73

3629. Porcari, Massimo. 1981 "O sistema italiano das participações do Estado." Paper presented a the First International Seminar on Public Enterprises in Economic Development, Brasília, 27-31 July. /Italy /Mixed enterprises /OPSS

3630. Portes, R. D. 1969 "The Enterprise under Central Planning." Review of Economic Studies V. 36, No. 106, pp. 197-212. /Planning process / 330.5 R326

3631. Portugal. Instituto das Participações do Estado. 1980 "The Criteria used by the Public Authorities to Control Public Enterprises." Paper presented at the 13th International Congress of Public and Co-operative Economy, Lisbon, 2-5 June. /Portugal /Control process /OPSS

3632. Porwal, B. L., and B. Singh. 1980 "MBO for Public Sector Units." Lok Udyog (New Delhi), V. 14, No. 5, pp. 49-53. /India /Management / 354.54 L836

3633. Posada, F. J. Antonio, and Jeanne de Posada. 1966 "La CVC: un reto al subdesarrollo y al tradicionalismo." Colección "Aventuras del Desarrollo". No. 9. /Development process

3634. Posner, Michael V. 1962 "The National Coal Board, 1947-1962." Annals of Collective Economy V. 33, pp. 339-383. /United Kingdom /Coal mining industry / 330.5 An73

3635. Posner, Michael V. 1962 "Les charbonnages nationalisées en Grande Brétagne." Annales de l'Economie Collective V. 50, No. 4, pp. 603-657. /United Kingdom /Coal mining industry /Nationalization

3636. Posner, Michael V. 1962 "Old Problems and New Policies in Nationalized Industries." District Bank Review (Manchester), pp. 3-18. /United Kingdom /Evaluation

3637. Posner, Michael V. 1962 "The Financial Aims of Nationalized Industries." London and Cambridge Bulletin (London), /United Kingdom /Industrial sector /Financing

3638. Posner, Michael V. 1970 "Pricing and Investment Policies of Nationalized Industries." In A. Cairncross, ed(s). The Managed Economy. Oxford: Basil Blackwell. /Price policy /Investment / 338.9 B777m

3639. Posner, Michael V. 1979 "Public Enterprise in the Market Place." NICG Occasional Papers. London: Nationalized Industries' Chairmen's Group. No. 1. /United Kingdom

3640. Posner, Michael V. 1980 "Running Public Enterprises: Theory and Practice." Paper presented at the International Congress of Public and Co-Operative Economy, XIII, Lisbon, 2-4 June. /Management /OPSS /Published in Annals of Public and Cooperative Economy, Vol. 52, Nos. 1-2, (1981): pp. 17-26.

3641. Posner, Michael V., and R. Pryke. 1966 New Public Enterprise. London: Fabian Society. /United Kingdom /Evaluation / 335 F112re no.254

3642. Posner, Michael V., and S. J. Woolf. 1967 Italian Public Enterprise. Cambridge, Mass.: Harvard University Press. /Italy /Economic history /Profits /Control process /Financing /Investment /338.945 P843i

3643. Postan, M. M. 1969 "Quelle est la mission du secteur public?" Droit Social (Paris), No. 1, pp. 6-18. /France /Evaluation / France 05 D835 Law

3644. Postel, Claude, Claude Collet, and Jean Bonnefont. 1979 "Trois exemples de relations contractuelles: Air France, S.N.C.F. et C.D.F." Revue Française de Gestion (Paris), No. 20, pp. 86-95. /Financing /Management /Control process /Air transportation industry / Railway industry /Coal mining industry / Contractual relations

3645. Potter, D. C., and S. J. Woolf. 1959 "Public Enterprises: Parliamentary Control or Accountability?" Indian Journal of Public Administration (New Delhi), V. 5, No. 3, pp. 320-332. /India /Parliament /Control process /Accountability /JA 26 I55 Pub Aff

3646. Poulin, F. 1980 "Notas sobre las empresas públicas en Québec: El caso de la Société Nationale d'Amiante." Revista Latinoamericana de Administración Pública (Bogotá), No. 10-1, pp. 531-533. /Canada

3647. Pozen, Robert C. 1976 Legal Choices for State Enterprises in the Third World. New York: New York University Press. /Law /Developing nations / HD 3850 P694 PCL

3648. Prabhakar, Rohit K. 1980 "Magnitude of Marketing Concepts in Public Sector Banks." Lok Udyog (New Delhi), V. 14, No. 3, pp. 51-54. /India /Marketing /Banking system /354.54 L836

3649. Pradeep, Prem, et al. 1980 A Review of the Role of Public Enterprises in India's Development. New Delhi: Public Enterprise Centre for Continuing Education. /India /Economic development / HD 4294 R48

3650. Pradhan, P. C. 1978 "Future Prospects in Iron & Steel Industry in India." Lok Udyog (New Delhi), V. 11, No. 11, pp. 17-24. /India /Steel industry /354.54 L836 PCL

3651. Pradhan, P. C., and P. S. Marwah. 1975 "Indian Steel Industry vis-a-vis Energy Crisis." Lok Udyog (New Delhi), V. 9, No. 7, pp. 27-32. /India /Steel industry /Energy use policy /354.54 L836 PCL

3652. Prakash, Om. 1957 "Industrial Development Corporations in India and Pakistan." Economic Journal V. 67, pp. 40-48. /Pakistan /India /Development banks /Development corporation /Industrial sector /FILM 9093 Micro 330.5 Ec7

3653. Prakash, Om. 1958 "The Problem of Entrepreneurship in Socialist Economy." Indian Journal of Economics V. 39, pp. 59-70. /Socialist economy /Entrepreneurial activity /330.5 In2

3654. Prakash, Om. 1962 The Theory and Working of State Corporations, with Special Reference to India. London: Allen & Unwin. /India /Case studies /Steel industry /State trading organizations / Insurance industry /Control process /Personnel management /Profits /338.9 P884t /Second edition revised and expanded. Pub. by Orient Longman Ltd., New Delhi. /HD 3850 P7 1971 PCL

3655. Prakash, R. 1979 "Unused Inventories in Central Government Enterprises - Case for Credit Squeeze." Lok Udyog (New Delhi), V. 12, No. 10-1, pp. 21-24. /India /Management /Inventory control /354.54 L836 PCL

3656. Prasad, A. 1958 "The Railways Rates Tribunal." Indian Journal of Public Administration (New Delhi), V. 4, No. 1. /India /Railway industry /Price policy /JA 26 I55 Pub Aff

3657. Prasad, A. 1960 Indian Railways: A Study of Public Utility Administration. London: Asia Publishing House. /India /Railway industry /Public administration / 385.0954 P886i

3658. Prasad, A. 1960 "The Theory and Practice on the Public Corporation in a Democracy." Indian Journal of Public Administration (New Delhi), pp. 27-51. /Evaluation /Democratic government / JA 26 I55 Pub Aff

3659. Prasad, J. 1956 "Organizational Problems of the State Enterprises in India." Economic Papers V. 1, No. 2, pp. 71-88. /India /Structural characteristics

3660. Prasad, J. 1956 "Nationalization of Road Transport in Uttar Pradesh." Indian Journal of Public Administration (New Delhi), V. 4, No. 2, pp. 333-336. /India /Transportation industry /Nationalization / JA 26 I55 Pub Aff

3661. Prasad, J. 1965 "Training Facilities in Public Sector Undertakings in India." Indian Worker (New Delhi), V. 13, No. 17, pp. 49-50. /India

3662. Prasad, Parmanand. 1957 Some Economic Problems of Public Enterprises in India. Leiden, Holland: Stenfert Krosse. /India

3663. Prasad, Parmanand. 1961 "Efficiency and Its Evaluation in Public Enterprises." Indian Journal of Public Administration (New Delhi), V. 7, No. 1. /Evaluation /Economic efficiency /JA 26 I55 Pub Aff

3664. Prasad, S. Bishwanath. 1958 "Productivity Measurement in Manufacturing Industries in India's Public Sector." Indian Journal of Economics /India /Evaluation /Productivity /Manufacturing industry / 330.5 In2

3665. Prasad, S. Bishwanath. 1962 "Mixed and Composite Enterprises in Indian Industries." Modern Review (Calcutta), pp. 108-116. /India /Mixed enterprises /Industrial sector /059.54 M72 PCL

3666. Prasetya, Rudhi, and Neil Hamilton. 1976 "The Regulation of Indonesian State Enterprises." Law and Public Enterprise in Asia. New York: Praeger for the International Legal Center. pp. 147-191. /Indonesia /Law /Control process /HD 4283 L32

3667. Prat, J. A. 1956 "Las corporaciones públicas en el Reino Unido." Revista de la Facultad de Derecho e Ciencias Sociales (Montevideo), pp. 555-579. /United Kingdom

3668. Pratten, C. F. 1965 Steel: To Nationalize or not to Nationalize. London: Moorgate & Wall. pp. 67-84. /United Kingdom /Steel industry /Nationalization

3669. Pray, K. L. 1947 "Financial Status of Federal Corporations." Harvard Business Review V. 25, No. 2, pp. 158-168. /Public financing /Accounting /Profits /HF 5001 H3

3670. Premchand, A. 1969 "Performance Budgeting in Public Sector." Economic and Political Weekly (Bombay), pp. 13-17. /Public administration /Budgetary process

3671. Premchand, A. 1983 "Government and Public Enterprise: The Budget Link." In G. Ram Reddy, ed(s). *Government and Public Enterprise: Essays in honour of Professor V. V. Ramanadham.* Bombay, India: N. T. Tripathi Private Limited. pp. 24-47. /Government authority /Budgetary process

3672. Prest, A. R. 1968 *Public Utilities in Nigeria: Economic and Financial Aspects.* Ife, Nigeria: Institute of Administration. /Nigeria /Public utility industry /Financial performance /Economic efficiency /Evaluation

3673. Presthus, R. 1949 "British Public Administration: The National Coal Board." *Public Administration Review* pp. 200-210. /United Kingdom /Coal mining industry /Public administration

3674. Presthus, R. 1950 "Financial Aspects of Britain's National Coal Board." *Journal of Politics* V. 12, No. 2, pp. 348-370. /United Kingdom /Coal mining industry /Financial performance / 320.5 J825 PCL

3675. Preston, M. H. 1968 "Reflections on Public Authority Investment." In A. R. Prest, ed(s). *Public Sector Economics.* Manchester: Manchester University Press. /United Kingdom /Investment / 354.420072 B777p

3676. Preston, Nathaniel S. 1961 "Public Authorities Today." *State Government* pp. 205-211. /United States of America /Public authority / JK 2401 S7 Pub Aff

3677. Pretnar, Stojan. 1978 "Les aspects économiques de la propriété industrielle." Paper presented at the Séminaire international sur la gestion et la formation dans les entreprises publiques dans les pays en voie de développement, Ljubljana, Yugoslavia, 3-15 March. Ljubljana: ICPE. /Economic analysis /industrial sector

3678. Prieur, Michel. 1969 *Les entreprises publiques locales.* Paris: Berger-Levrault. /France /Local development /Evaluation

3679. Prieur, Michel. 1971 "L'évolution recente de entreprises publiques locales." *Revue d'Administration Publique* (Paris), No. 17, pp. 7-21. /France /Public administration /Evaluation

3680. Prieur, R. 1971 "Les entreprises publiques." *Les Cahiers Françaises* (Paris), No. 150. /France /Evaluation

3681. Prince, E. A. 1974 "The Development of Public Enterprises in Guyana." *Social and Economic Studies* (Mona, Kingston, Jamaica), V. 23, No. 2, pp. 204-215. /Guyana /G330.97292 So13 LAC

3682. Pritchard, E P. 1964 "The Responsibility of the Nationalized Industries to Parliament." *Parliamentary Affairs* (London), V. 17, No. 4, pp. 439-449. /United Kingdom /Parliament /Industrial sector /Control process

3683. Pritchett, C. Herman. 1944 The Tennessee Valley Authority. Chapel Hill, N. C.: University of North Carolina. /United States of America /River valley development projects /309.973 T256Yp

3684. Pritchett, C. Herman. 1946 "Lessons of the TVA Power Program." Public Affairs (Halifac, Nova Scotia), pp. 98-103. /United States of America /River valley development projects

3685. Pritchett, C. Herman. 1946 "The Government Corporation Control Act of 1945." American Political Science Review pp. 495-509. /United States of America /Law /Control process /320.5 Am31

3686. Pritchett, C. Herman. 1947 "The Transplantability of the TVA." Iowa Law Review V. 32, No. 2, pp. 327-338. /United States of America /River valley development projects

3687. Proaño, Alexis. 1966 "Las empresas públicas." Boletín de Información (Quito), No. 7, pp. 35-67. /Ecuador /Evaluation

3688. Probsting, Karl. 1967 "The Public and Cooperative Economy in Austria." Annals of Public and Cooperative Economy V. 38, pp. 25-31. /Austria / 330.5 An73

3689. Probsting, Karl. 1973 "Austria's Collective Economy and European Integration." Annals of Public and Cooperative Economy V. 44, pp. 211-217. /Austria /Europe /Economic integration / 330.5 An73

3690. Probsting, Karl. 1977 "Thoughts about a Public Service Balance Sheet." Annals of Public and Cooperative Economy V. 48, No. 1, pp. 45-54. /Accounting /Public services /330.5 An73

3691. Pryke, Richard. 1965 "Why Steel?" Fabian Research Series (London: Fabian Society), No. 248. /United Kingdom /Steel industry /Nationalization

3692. Pryke, Richard. 1970 "Public Enterprise and the Economics of Large Scale Production." Annals of Public and Cooperative Economy V. 41, pp. 43-61. /United Kingdom /Evaluation /330.5 An73

3693. Pryke, Richard. 1970 "Are Nationalized Industries Becoming More Efficient?" Moorgate and Wall St. Review (London), /United Kingdom /Evaluation /Economic efficiency

3694. Pryke, Richard. 1971 "Strategy for Steel." Public Enterprise (London), No. 2, pp. 23-24. /United Kingdom /Steel industry /Planning process

3695. Pryke, Richard. 1972 Public Enterprise in Practice: The British Experience of Nationalization over Two Decades. London: Macmillan and Kee, 1971; NY: St. Martin's, 1972. /United Kingdom /Economic history /HD4145 P75 1972 Pub Aff

3696. Pryke, Richard. 1980 "Public Enterprise in Practice: The British Experience of Nationalization During the Past

Decade." In William J. Baumol, ed(s). Public and Private Enterprise in a Mixed Economy. New York: St. Martin's Press. pp. 215-229. /United Kingdom /Productivity /Economic efficiency /Profits /Price policy /Subsidization policy /HD 3842 P87 PCL

3697. Pryor, Frederic L. 1976 "Public Ownership: Some Quantitative Dimensions." In William G. Shepherd et al., ed(s). Public Enterprise: Economic Analysis of Theory and Practice. Lexington, Ma.: D.C. Heath and Company, Lexington Books. pp. 3-22. /Economic analysis /HD 3850 P8 PCL

3698. Psacharopoulous, George. 1981 "Education, Employment and Inequality in LDCs." World Development V. 9, No. 1, pp. 37-54. /Developing nations /Income distribution /Education system /Employment policy

3699. Psaros, D. C. 1955 "Two Greek Power Corporations: The Public Power Corporation and the Copais Estate Corporation." In A. H. Hanson, ed(s). Public Enterprise. Brussels: IIAS. pp. 241-252. /Greece /Electrical utility industry /HD 3850 H28 Law

3700. Psaros, D. C. 1958 "Public Corporations in Greece." Annals of Collective Economy V. 29, pp. 275-290. /Greece /Law /330.5 An73

3701. "Public Corporations and their Developmental Role in Asia." 1974 Lok Udyog (New Delhi), V. 8, No. 1, pp. 33-34. /Asia /354.54 L836 PCL

3702. Public Enterprise and Development in the Arab Countries: Legal and Managerial Aspects. 1977 New York: Legal Center for Law and Development. /Asia /HD 4334 P8 Law

3703. "Public Enterprises in India-A Study of Public Relations and Annual Reports." 1968 Lok Udyog (New Delhi), pp. 97-100. /India /Public relations / 354.54 L826

3704. "Public Enterprises in the United Kingdom." 1973 The Evolution of the Public Enterprises in the Community of the Nine. Brussels: CEEP Editions. pp. 291-311. /United Kingdom /Statistics /OPSS

3705. "Public Enterprises in Indonesia - Some Management Aspects." 1974 Lok Udyog (New Delhi), V. 8, No. 2, pp. 41-46. /Indonesia /354.54 L836 PCL

3706. "Public Sector Enterprises and the National Economy." 1983 Lok Udyog (New Delhi), V. 16, No. 11. /India /Economic analysis /Economic history /354.54 L836 PCL

3707. "Public and Cooperative Enterprises in a Free Society." 1965 Annals of Public and Cooperative Economy V. 36, No. 2-3. /Cooperatives /330.5 An73

3708. Puget, H. 1958 Les nationalisations en France et á l'étranger: II, les nationalisations à l'étranger. Paris: Sirey. Travaux et Recherches de l'Institut de Droit Comparé de l'Université de Paris. /Nationalization / 338.944 J948n

3709. Puget, H. 1969 Les institutions administratives étrangères. Paris: Fondation Nationale des Sciences Politiques. /Administrative management

3710. Pugliese, Francesco, and Stelio Valentini. 1982 "The Public Enterprise as an Instrument of National Policies." Paper presented at the Tokyo Round Table preparatory to the 19th International Congress of Administrative Sciences, 13-17 Sept. /Italy /Control process /Law /OPSS

3711. Puiseux. 1969 "Neutralité tarifaire et entreprises publiques." Bulletin d'Institut Internationale d'Administration Publique (Paris), No. 12, pp. 109-121. /Price policy

3712. Pume, Salum Omari. 1979 "Management and Training in Public Enterprises: Country Report of Tanzania." Paper presented at the International Seminar on Management and Training in Public Enterprises in Developing Countries, Ljubljana, Yugoslavia, 1-13 October. Ljubljana: ICPE. /Tanzania /Training /Management

3713. Punnett, R. M. 1966 "State Management of the Liquor Trade." Public Administration (London), V. 44, No. 2, pp. 193-211. /Australia /Alcohol industry /Management / JA 8 P8 Pub Aff

3714. Punta, V. del. 1971 "Il sistema delle participazioni statali: Una grave incognita per l'economia italiana." Richerche Economiche (Venice, Italy), /Italy /Public administration /System analysis

3715. Pupovic, Zoran. 1980 "Price Policy in the Yugoslav Enterprises." Paper presented at the International Workshop on Pricing Policies in Public Enterprises, Ljubljana, Yugoslavia, 26-30 May. Ljubljana: ICPE. /Yugoslavia /Price policy

3716. Puranik, S. N. 1978 "The Problem of Autonomy and Control in Public Enterprises in India." Indian Journal of Public Administration V. 24, No. 4, pp. 1044-1059. /India /Control process / JA 26 I55 Pub Aff

3717. Puri, Y. P. 1969 "Managing Capital Expenditure in Public Undertakings." Lok Udyog (New Delhi), V. 3, No. 7, pp. 763-772. /India /Investment /Management / 354.54 L836

3718. Puri, Y. P. 1970 "In Quest of a Rational Capital Structure for Public Undertakings." Lok Udyog (New Delhi), V. 3, No. 10, pp. 1167-1173. /India /Investment / 354.54 L836

3719. Puri, Y. P. 1971 "The Riddle of Inventory Control in Public Undertakings." Lok Udyog (New Delhi), V. 5, No. 1, pp. 13-27. /Management /India /Inventory control /354.54 L836

3720. Purohit, G. B. 1977 "Status of Fertilizer Industry and Technology in India - A Review." (Part 2) Lok Udyog (New Delhi), V. 11, No. 6, pp. 19-24. /India /Fertilizer industry /Technology /Case studies /354.54 L836 PCL

3721. Purohit, G. B. 1977 "Status of Fertilizer Industry and Technology in India - A Review." (Part 1) Lok Udyog (New Delhi), V. 11, No. 5, pp. 21-26. /India /Fertilizer industry /Technology /Case studies /354.54 L836 PCL

3722. Purohit, G. B. 1978 "Investment Appraisal of Capital Projects." Lok Udyog (New Delhi), V. 11, No. 12, pp. 13-22. /India /Investment /Project management /354.54 L836 PCL

3723. Puthucheary, M. E. 1976 "Coordination of Public Enterprises: Country Study for Malaysia." In A. S. H. K. Sadique, ed(s). Public Enterprises in Asia: Studies on Coordination and Control. Kuala Lumpur: Asian Center for Development Administration. pp. 417-448. /Malaysia /Control process /HD 4276 P8

3724. Pylee, M. V. 1961 "Accountability of Public Enterprises." In J. S. Bains, ed(s). Studies in Political Science pp. 354-380. /India /Evaluation /Accountability

3725. Pylee, M. V. 1963 "Some Aspects of the Management of India's State Enterprises." Indian Journal of Political Science (Lucknow), V. 24, No. 1, pp. 1-13. /India /Public administration /Management / 320.5 In2

3726. Pylee, M. V. 1968 "Faulty Management of Public Sector Enterprises Retards Economic Development." Capital pp. 119-127. /Management /Economic development

3727. "Que se passe-t-il dans les sociétés du secteur publique?" n.d. Syrie et monde Arabe (Damascus), No. 216. /Syria

3728. Quijano Torres, M. 1978 "Los órganos administrativos deconcentrados." Paper presented a the Round Table on Public Enterprise of the Tenth General Assembly of the Latin American Association of Public Administration, Mexico City. /Mexico /OPSS

3729. Quillot, R. 1957 "Dix ans de nationalisation des houillères." Revue Social pp. 18-28. /France /Coal mining industry /Nationalization

3730. Quochi, M. Redditi. 1958 "Investimenti nelle aziendi di Stato." Política e Economía (Rome), pp. 15-21. /Investment

3731. Quoilin, Josette. 1976 "Marginal Cost Selling in ELectricité de France." Annals of Public and Cooperative Economy V. 47, No. 2, pp. 115-142. /France /Electrical utility industry /Price policy /330.5 An73

3732. Qurashi, Muzaffar Mahmood. 1979 "Experience of Developing Countries with Joint Ventures with Centrally Planned and Market Economies." Paper presented at the International Seminar on Joint Ventures and Public Enterprises in Developing Countries, Ljubljana, Yugoslavia, 4-12 December. Ljubljana: ICPE. /Developing nations /Planning process /Mixed enterprises /Also published in Public Enterprise, V. 1, No. 1(1981), pp. 19-36. /OPSS

3733. Qurashi, Muzaffar Mahmood. 1980 "Report of the International Workshop on Pricing Policies in Public Enterprises, Ljubljana, May 26-30, 1980." Ljubljana: ICPE. /Price policy

3734. Qurashi, Muzaffar Mahmood. 1980 "Pricing Policies in Public Enterprises." Paper presented at the International Workshop on Pricing Policies in Public Enterprises, Ljubljana, Yugoslavia, 26-30 May. Ljubljana: ICPE. /Price policy

3735. Qureshi, Zafar Iqbal. 1977 Industrial Culture in Pakistan: Lessons for State Enterprises. Lahore, Pakistan: Progressive Books. /Pakistan / HD 31 Q73

3736. Rabhi, Mohammed. 1983 "Planning in Public Enterprises in the Arab Countries--Problems and Perspectives." Public Enterprise V. 3, pp. 33-47. /Middle East /Planning process /OPSS

3737. Rabska, Teresa. 1982 "The Public Enterprise as an Instrument of State Policies." Paper presented at the Tokyo Round Table preparatory to the 19th International Congress of Administrative Sciences, 13-17 Sept. /Poland /Taxonomy /Law /Goal setting /Accountability /Control process /OPSS

3738. Rachid, A. 1970 "The Emergence and Development of Public Enterprise in the U.A.R." Egypte Contemporaine (Cairo), No. 340, pp. 201-244. /Middle East /Evaluation / 962.05 Eg98r

3739. Radeva, Vaska. 1980 "Women as a Factor of Development: ´Astibo,´ Stip, Case Study." Paper presented at the International Expert Group Meeting on Women as a Factor of Development and the Responsibilities of the Public Sector in this Regard, Ljubljana, Yugoslavia, 14-19 April. Ljubljana: ICPE. /Women´s studies /Economic development /Case studies

3740. Radice, Hugo. 1978 "The Scottish Development Agency and the Contradictions of State Entrepreneurship." University of Stirling Discussion Papers in Economics, Finance and Investment Scotland. No. 59. /Scotland /Economic development

3741. Rafiquddin, Mohammad. 1981 "Management Training and Development in Public Enterprises in Pakistan." Paper presented at the Regional Workshop on Management Training and Development in Public Enterprises in Developing Countries, Karachi, Pakistan, 5-15 January. Ljubljana: ICPE /Pakistan /Management /Training

3742. Rahman, H. 1952 "Public Enterprise in Pakistan." Pakistan Economic Journal V. 3, No. 2, pp. 206-216. /Pakistan

3743. Rai, Khemraj. 1981 "Worker Participation in Public Enterprise in Guyana." Economic and Social Studies (Mona, Kingston, Jamaica), V. 30, No. 1, pp. 209-244. /Caribbean Region /Guyana /Worker management participation /G330.97292 So13 LAC

3744. Raiffa, Howard. 1981 "Decision Making in the State-Owned Enterprises." In Raymond Vernon and Yair Aharoni, ed(s). State-Owned Enterprises in the Western Economies. New York:

St. Martin's Press. pp. 54-62. /Management / HD 3850 S79 PCL

3745. Rainford, Roderick E. 1979 "Joint Ventures in Jamaica: A General Review of the Policy and Experience of Jamaica." Paper presented at the International Seminar on Joint Ventures and Public Enterprises in Developing Countries, Ljubljana, Yugoslavia, 4-12 December. Ljubljana: ICPE. /Jamaica /Mixed Enterprises

3746. Raj, Mulakh. 1978 "Pricing Strategy in Housing Undertakings." In K. R. Guyta, ed(s). Pricing in Public Enterprises. New Delhi: Atlantic Publishers & Distributors. pp. 145-160. /India /Housing industry /Price policy / HB 236 I4 P75

3747. Raj, Mulk. 1975 "Pricing Policy - An Alternative for Public Housing Agencies." Lok Udyog (New Delhi), V. 9, No. 8, pp. 25-30. /India /Price policy /Housing industry /354.54 L836

3748. Raj, Mulkh. 1979 "Information System for Housing Agencies in Public Sector." Lok Udyog (New Delhi), V. 13, No. 2, pp. 5-12. /Information system /India /Housing industry /354.54 L836 PCL

3749. Raja Mohd, Affandi bin Raja Halim. 1976 "Coordination of Public Enterprises: Country Study for Malaysia." In A. S. H. K. Sadique, ed(s). Public Enterprises in Asia: Studies on Coordination and Control. Kuala Lumpur: Asian Centre for Development Administration. pp. 363-416. /Malaysia /Control process / HD 4276 P8

3750. Raja, S. T. 1965 "Middle and Higher Management Personnel in Public Sector." Indian Journal of Public Administration (New Delhi), pp. 19-25. /India /Personnel management /Management /JA 26 I55 Pub Aff

3751. Rajagopalan, D. 1972 "The Financial and Economic Objectives of Public Sector Undertakings." Lok Udyog (New Delhi), V. 6, No. 7, pp. 35-40. /India /Goal setting /354.54 L836 PCL

3752. Rajagopalan, N. 1977 "The New Frontiers of Information Technology." Lok Udyog (New Delhi), V. 11, No. 7, pp. 13-18. /India /Information system /354.54 L836 PCL

3753. Rajan, J. S. Sundara. 1965 "Limits and Potentials of Public Enterprise." International Development /Evaluation

3754. Rajan, N. 1976 "Asian Development Strategies and the Role of Public Enterprises." Lok Udyog (New Delhi), V. 10, No. 8, pp. 55-60. /Asia /Economic development /354.54 L836 PCL

3755. Rajkovic, Velimir. 1978 "The Financing of Public Enterprises: The Yugoslav Experience." Paper presented at the Interregional Workshop on Financing of Public Enterprises in Developing Countries, Ljubljana, Yugoslavia, 22-26 May. Ljubljana: ICPE. /Yugoslavia /Public financing

3756. Rajkovic, Velimir. 1979 "On Joint Ventures between Foreign and Domestic Enterprises in Yugoslavia." Paper presented at the International Seminar on Joint Ventures and Public Enterprises in Developing Countries, Ljubljana, Yugoslavia, 4-12 December. Ljubljana: ICPE. /Yugoslavia /Mixed enterprises /Multinational corporations

3757. Rajkovic, Velimir. 1980 "Project Implementation and Management." Paper presented at the International Workshop on Investment Criteria and Investment Decision-Making Processes, Ljubljana, Yugoslavia, 20-24 October. Ljubljana: ICPE. /Project management /Planning process

3758. Raju, C. S. N. 1979 "The Chief Executive." Lok Udyog (New Delhi), V. 13, No. 6, pp. 35-40. /Management /354.54 L836

3759. Rajwar, L. S. M. 1970 "The Shipping Corporation of India: A Profile." Lok Udyog (New Delhi), V. 4, No. 2, pp. 161-166. /India /Shipping industry /354.54 L836 PCL

3760. Rakouth, Siméon Wilson. 1980 "La formation dans la Société Pétrolière de l'Etat "SOLIMA" au Madagascar." Papre presented at the Séminaire international sur la gestion et la formation dans les entreprises publiques dans les pays en voie de développement, Ljubljana, Yugoslavia, 3-15 March. Ljubljana: ICPE. /Madagascar /Oil industry /Training

3761. Ramachandra, B. 1980 "Accountability and Autonomy." Lok Udyog (New Delhi), V. 14, No. 4. /Accountability /Control process /Autonomy /354.54 L836

3762. Ramachandra, B. 1980 "HMT's Role in Fostering Ancillaries." Lok Udyog (New Delhi), V. 13, No. 12, pp. 3-8. /India /Case studies /Metal manufacturing industry /Private enterprises /Subsidiaries /354.54 L836 PCL

3763. Ramadier, P. 1960 "Nationalisations et programmes socialistes." Année Politique et Economique (Paris), V. 33, No. 155-, pp. 181-208. /France /Nationalization

3764. Ramamurti, Ravi. 1978 "Control and Evaluation of State Owned Enterprises by External Agencies." Cambridge, Mass.: HIID and BAPEG. /Control process

3765. Ramanadham, V. V. 1945 "Road-Owners and Road-Haulers." Indian Journal of Economics V. 25, pp. 520-532. /India /Highways and roads /Land transportation industry /330.5 In2

3766. Ramanadham, V. V. 1954 "The Capitalization of Public Corporations." Indian Economic Journal (Bombay), V. 2, No. 3, pp. 289-298. /Investment

3767. Ramanadham, V. V. 1959 Problems of Public Enterprise: Thoughts on British Experience. Chicago: Quadrangle Books; London: Frank Cass. /India /Price policy /Management /Accountability /Nationalization /Control process /338.942 R141p

3768. Ramanadham, V. V. 1961 The Structure of Public Enterprise in India. New York: Asia Publishing House. /India / 338.954 R141s

3769. Ramanadham, V. V. 1961 A Study of the Operation of State Economic Enterprises in Turkey. Ankara: Government of Turkey. /Turkey /Evaluation

3770. Ramanadham, V. V. 1963 The Finances of Public Enterprises. New York: Asia Publishing House; New Delhi: Indian Institute of Public Administration. /India /Public financing /338.74 R141f

3771. Ramanadham, V. V. 1963 The Efficacy of Public Enterprise: Proceedings of the 2nd Seminar on Public Enterprise. London: Allen & Unwin; Bombay: Allied Publishers. /Economic efficiency

3772. Ramanadham, V. V. 1964 The Control of Public Enterprise in India. New York: Asia Publishing House. /India /Control process / 338.954 R141c

3773. Ramanadham, V. V. 1964 "Tax and Subsidy Elements in Public Enterprise Prices." Review of Economics and Statistics V. 46, No. 4, pp. 392-397. /Taxation policy /Subsidization policy / 330.5 R325

3774. Ramanadham, V. V. 1964 "The Role of the Financial Adviser in Indian Enterprises." Management International Review (Wiesbadan, Germany), No. 2, pp. 119-123. /India /Financing

3775. Ramanadham, V. V. 1967 Financial Organisation in Public Enterprise. Bombay: N. M. Tripathi. /India /Public financing

3776. Ramanadham, V. V. 1968 "Pricing System in Public Enterprises in India." Developing Economies (Tokyo), V. 6, No. 1, pp. 3-26. /India /Price policy / 338.915 D485

3777. Ramanadham, V. V. 1971 "Regulation of Pricing by Public Enterprises." International Review of Administrative Sciences No. 3, pp. 212-224. /Price policy / JA 1 A1 I6 PCL

3778. Ramanadham, V. V. 1972 "Substantive Working Document." Prepared for the Meeting of Consultants on Administration of Public Enterprises Santiago, Chile, 27-29 Nov., UNECLA. /Latin America /Caribbean Region /Public administration /OPSS

3779. Ramanadham, V. V. 1978 "The Financing of Public Enterprises." Paper presented at the International Workshop on Financing of Public Enterprises in Developing Countries, Ljublajana, Yugoslavia, 22-6 May. Ljubljana: ICPE. /Financing

3780. Ramanadham, V. V. 1979 "A Control System for Public Enterprise." Paper presented at the International Workshop on Control Systems for Public Enterprises in Developing Countries, Ljubljana, Yugoslavia, 9-13 July. Ljubljana: ICPE. /Control process

3781. Ramanadham, V. V. 1980 "Under-Pricing in Public Enterprise." Paper presented at the International Workshop on Pricing Policies in Public Enterprises, Ljubljana, Yugoslavia, 26-30

May. Ljubljana: ICPE. /Price policy

3782. Ramanadham, V. V. 1980 "The National Economic Context of Corporate Planning in Public Enterprise." Paper presented at the Regional Workshop on Corporate Planning in Public Enterprises in the Asian and Pacific Region, Kuala Lumpur, Malaysia, 17-21 November. Ljubljana: ICPE /Planning process

3783. Ramanadham, V. V. 1981 "Public Enterprise Losses and Public Policy Options." Paper presented at the International Workshop on Financial Profitability and Losses in Public Enterprises, Ljubljana, Yugoslavia, 1-5 June. Ljubljana: ICPE. /Profits

3784. Ramanadham, V. V. 1981 The Yugoslav Enterprise. ICPE monograph series 2 Ljubljana: ICPE. /Yugoslavia

3785. Ramanadham, V. V. 1981 "Parliament and Public Enterprise: Some Basic Concerns." Paper presented at the Seminar on Relationships between Parliament and Public Enterprises, Columbo, Sri Lanka, 15-19 June. Ljubljana: ICPE. /Parliament /Control process

3786. Ramanadham, V. V. 1981 "Parliament and Public Enterprise: A Technical Note." In V. V. Ramanadham and Yash Ghai, Parliament and Public Enterprise. Ljubljana: ICPE Monograph Series No. 1. pp. 9-22. /Parliament /OPSS

3787. Ramanadham, V. V. 1981 "Parliamant´s Basic Concerns vis-à-vis Public Enterprise." In V. V. Ramanadham and Yash Ghai, Parliament and Public Enterprise. Ljubljana: ICPE Monograph Series No. 1. pp. 45-56. /Parliament /OPSS

3788. Ramanadham, V. V. 1984 "Privatisation in the African Context." Paper presented at the conference State Shrinking: A Comparative Inquiry into Privatization, Austin, Texas, 1-3 March. /Privatization /Kenya /Ethiopia /Sudan /Egypt /OPSS

3789. Ramanadham, V. V., and K. K. Nangea. 1960 "Corporation versus Departmental Form in Road Transport." Indian Journal of Public Administration (New Delhi), V. 6, pp. 52-60. /Highways and roads /Economic efficiency /Public works policy /JA 26 I55 Pub Aff

3790. Ramanadham, V. V., and Bazle Karim. 1979 "Report of the International Seminar on Joint Ventures and Public Enterprises in the Developing Countries, Ljubljana, 4-12 December, 1979." Ljubljana: ICPE. /Developing nations /Mixed enterprises

3791. Ramanadham, V. V., and Yash Ghai. 1981 Parliament and Public Enterprise. Ljubljana: ICPE. /Parliament /Control process /Management /Accountability /Planning process /OPSS

3792. Ramanadham, V. V., ed. 1980 Joint Ventures and Public Enterprises in Developing Countries: Proceedings of an International Seminar Held in Ljubljana, 4-12 December, 1979. Ljubljana: ICPE. /Mixed enterprises

3793. Ramanathan, K. V. 1979 "Some Thoughts on the Criteria for Evaluation of the Performance of Public Sector Fertilizer Enterprises." Lok Udyog (New Delhi), V. 13, No. 8, pp. 7-14. /India /Economic efficiency /Fertilizer industry /Evaluation /Case studies /354.54 L836 PCL

3794. Ramasastri, J. V. S. 1954 "The Managers of Nationalized Industries." Indian Journal of Economics V. 35, No. 137. /India /Industrial sector /Management / 330.5 In2

3795. Ramasastri, J. V. S. 1955 "The Industrial Development Corporation: A Pioneering Enterprise." Indian Journal of Economics V. 36, No. 140. /India /Industrial sector /Development corporation / 330.5 In2

3796. Ramasastri, J. V. S. 1955 "Managerial Implications of Nationalization in India and Great Britain." India Quarterly (New Delhi), V. 11, No. 1, pp. 55-64. /India /United Kingdom /Management

3797. Ramasastri, J. V. S. 1957 Nationalization and Managerial Role, a Theoretical Study. Bombay, India: Popular Book Depot. /Management / 658 R141n

3798. Ramaswamy, K. 1971 "Integrated Project Control at BSL." Lok Udyog (New Delhi), V. 5, No. 2, pp. 159-164. /India /Information system /Project management /354.54 L836 PCL

3799. Ramaswamy, N. S., and Raj K. Nigam. 1977 "Performance of Public Enterprises in Asia: Project." New Delhi: Bureau of Public Enterprises; Ottowa: IDRC. /India /Korea, Rep. of /Sri Lanka /Fertilizer industry /Management /Pharmaceutical industry /Cement manufacturing industry /Steel industry /Shipbuilding industry

3800. Ramaswamy, N. S., and V. Kesarv. 1978 "Performance of Indian Public Enterprises." New Delhi: SCOPE, Standing Conference of Public Enterprises. /India /Control process /Personnel management /Management

3801. Ramaswamy, S. 1973 "Management Information System." Lok Udyog (New Delhi), V. 6, No. 11, pp. 33-38. /Information system /India /354.54 L836 PCL

3802. Ramaswamy, S. 1978 "Pricing Policy in Hindustan Organic Chemicals Limited." In K. R. Gupta, ed(s). Pricing in Public Enterprises. New Delhi, India: Atlantic Publishers & Distributors. pp. 164-166. /India /Chemical industry /Price policy /HB 236 I4 P75

3803. Ramaswamy, T. 1972 Public Enterprise of India: Objectives and Performance. Meerut: Meenakshi Singhri. /India /Evaluation / HD 4294 R34 PCL

3804. Ramayya, S. V. 1961 "Profit and Pricing Policies of Public Enterprises." Rural India (Bombay), pp. 133-136. /India /Evaluation /Price policy /Profits

3805. Ramic, Dusan. 1974 "Système et mécanisme de planification au Chantier Naval et a la fabrique de Moteurs Diesel." Paper presented at the International Seminar '74: Planning in Public Enterprises in Developing Countries, Ljubljana, Yugoslavia, 23 Sept. - 9 Oct. Ljubljana: ICPE. /Yugoslavia /Planning process /Motor manufacturing industry / Marine transportation industry

3806. Ramirez Gómez, Manuel. 1973 Cambio tecnológico en la industria de energía eléctrica de Colombia. Bogotá: Centro de Estudios sobre Desarrollo Económico, Facultad de Economía, Universidad de los Andes. /Colombia /Electrical utility industry / T 58.8 R35 LAC

3807. Ramlogan, Vishnu. 1980 "Organisation and Control of Public Enterprises in Trinidad and Tobago." Lok Udyog (New Delhi), V. 14, No. 8, pp. 3-18. /Trinidad and Tobago /Control process /Economic history /354.54 L836 PCL

3808. Ramon-Luca, Jesús de. 1983 "Fijación de precios y tarifas de las empresas públicas." Paper presented at the ECLA seminar "State Control and Planning of Public Enterprises." Brasília, 15-17 June. Brasília: UNECLA. /Price Policy /Spain /OPSS

3809. Ramos, José Nabantino. 1971 "Empresas públicas." Revista de Direito Público (São Paulo), V. 17, No. 4, pp. 99-110. /Brazil

3810. Rand, Adam. 1981 "Public Enterprises and Consumers." Annals of Public and Cooperative Economy V. 52, No. 1-2. /Consumer relations /330.5 An73

3811. Randall, Maury R., and Conway L. Lackman. 1982 "The Incentives Encouraging State and Local Takeovers of Utilities." Public Utilities Fortnightly V. 109, pp. 31-35. /Public utility industry /United States of America /Nationalization / 388.9 P97

3812. Ranganadha, Sripati. 1982 "Practices in Management." Lok Udyog (New Delhi), V. 16, No. 5, pp. 11-16. /India /Management /354.54 L836 PCL

3813. Rangarajan, D. 1954 "Organizational Forms of Public Enterprises and Their Effect on Management." Indian Economic Journal (Bombay), V. 2, No. 3, pp. 299-306. /Management /Structural characteristics

3814. Rangarajan, S. 1976 "Public Corporations in India: Their Structuring and Legal Control." Law and Public Enterprise in Asia. New York: Praeger for the International Legal Center. pp. 96-146. /India / Control process /Legislature /HD 4283 L32

3815. Rangnekar, D. K. 1963 Bokaro: A Story of Bungling. New Delhi: The International Institute of Public Affairs. /India / 338.9173 R163b

3816. Ransmeier, J. S. 1951 "Government Action or Private Enterprise in River Valley Development: Discussion." American Economic Association Papers and Proceedings V. 41, pp. 299-306. /River valley development projects / Private enterprises /Comparative analysis

3817. Rao, A. N., R. N. Das, and N. S. Datar. 1975 "Energy Planning for Indian Steel Industry." Lok Udyog (New Delhi), V. 9, No. 4, pp. 43-46. /India /Steel industry /Energy use policy /354.54 L836 PCL

3818. Rao, B. Anand. 1980 "Chairman-cum-Managing Director: The COncept and Implications Revisited." Lok Udyog (New Delhi), V. 14, No. 7, pp. 29-34. /India /Management /354.54 L836 PCL

3819. Rao, B. Gopal. 1972 "Maintenance and Operation of Integrated Steel Plant." Lok Udyog (New Delhi), V. 5, No. 10, pp. 981-984. /India /Steel industry /Case studies /354.54 L836

3820. Rao, B. Satyanarayana. 1981 "Reporting Practices of Tamilnadu Industrial Development Corporation Limited - A Retrospective Study." Lok Udyog (New Delhi), V. 15, No. 7+8, pp. 47-52. /India /Information management /Case studies /354.54 L836 PCL

3821. Rao, B. Satyanarayana. 1981 "Tools for Measurement of Efficiency in State Passenger Road Transport Corporations." Lok Udyog (New Delhi), V. 14, No. 11, pp. 47-52. /India /Economic efficiency /Methodology /Transportation industry /354.54 L836 PCL

3822. Rao, C. R. Ananda. 1980 "Autonomy and Accountability of the Public Enterprises in India Vis-a-Vis the Committee on Public Undertakings." Lok Udyog (New Delhi), V. 14, No. 4, pp. 25-33. /India /Accountability /Control process /Autonomy /354.54 L836

3823. Rao, C. S. S. 1980 "Ancillary Development in ITI." Lok Udyog (New Delhi), V. 13, No. 12, pp. 9-14. /Private enterprises /India /Case studies /Subsidiaries /354.54 L836 PCL

3824. Rao, G. R. S. 1982 "Balancing the Corporate Boards in the State Sector." Lok Udyog (New Delhi), V. 16, No. 3, pp. 11-18. /India /Management /354.54 L836 PCL

3825. Rao, G. V.Chelapathi. 1982 "Is Audit an Impediment to Materials Management?" Lok Udyog (New Delhi), V. 16, No. 4, pp. 3-10. /India /Control process /354.54 L836 PCL

3826. Rao, H. R. S. 1970 "Hindustan Steel, A Growing Force in the Steel World." Lok Udyog (New Delhi), V. 3, No. 10, pp. 1179-1199. /India /Steel Industry /354.54 L836 PCL

3827. Rao, K. L. 1972 "Recent Issues in Water Resources Administration in India." Indian Journal of Public Administration (New Delhi), V. 18, No. 2, pp. 170-185. /India /Water resources development / JA 26 I55 Pub Aff

3828. Rao, K. Rajeshwar, and S. P. Vijaya Saradhi. 1980 "Management of Advances in Public Enterprises in India." Lok Udyog (New Delhi), V. 14, No. 3, pp. 39-45. /Management /Public financing /India / 354.54 L836

3829. Rao, K. Rajeshwar, and M. Subrahmanya Sarma. 1982 "Some Aspects of Capital Financing in Public Enterprises." Lok Udyog (New Delhi), V. 15, No. 12, pp. 17-32. /India /Financing /354.54 L836 PCL

3830. Rao, K. Rajeshwar. 1982 "Management Effectiveness in Transport Operations - A Case Study of Delhi Transport Corporation." Lok Udyog (New Delhi), V. 16, No. 4, pp. 11-22. /India /Transportation industry /Case studies /354.54 L836 PCL

3831. Rao, Rampalli Visweswar. 1949 "Mixed Economy in Theory and Practice, with Special Reference to India." Indian Journal of Economics V. 30, pp. 193-196. /India /Mixed enterprises / 330.5 In2

3832. Rao, S. Kishan. 1978 "Capacity Utilisation in Indian Railways vis-a-vis Manufacturing Industries." Lok Udyog (New Delhi), V. 12, No. 4, pp. 13-16. /India /Economic efficiency /Railway industry /Industrial sector /354.54 L836 PCL

3833. Rao, S. P. Ranga, and V. Madanmohan Reddy. 1972 "Governing Boards of State Corporations - A Study of Their Composition in Andhra Pradesh." Lok Udyog (New Delhi), V. 6, No. 9, pp. 17-28. /India /Management /Andhra Pradesh, India (State) /354.54 L836 PCL

3834. Rao, S. P. Ranga, and V. Madanmohan Reddy. 1973 "Governing Boards of State Corporations - A Case Study of their Composition in Andhra Pradesh - Part II." Lok Udyog (New Delhi), V. 6, No. 10, pp. 35-42. /India /Management /Andhra Pradesh, India (State) /354.54 L836 PCL

3835. Rao, T. V. 1982 "HRD Practices in Indian Industry." Lok Udyog (New Delhi), V. 15, No. 12, pp. 5-16. /India /Training /Industrial sector /354.54 L836 PCL

3836. Rao, T. V. S. R., S. Sriraman, and S. P. Palaniswamy. 1981 "Disequilibrium in the Supply of Rail Freight Services." Lok Udyog (New Delhi), V. 15, No. 7+8, pp. 13-20. /India /Railway industry /354.54 L836 PCL

3837. Rao, V. K. R. V. 1964 "The Role of Public Enterprises in the Indian Economy." Indian Journal of Public Administration (New Delhi), V. 10, No. 3, pp. 412-426. /India / JA 26 I55 Pub Aff

3838. Rao, V. Lakshmana. 1978 "Some Ad Hoc Rules for Price Fixation in Public Enterprises." In K. R. Gupta, ed(s). Pricing in Public Enterprises. New Delhi, India: Atlantic Publishers & Distributors. pp. 103-115. /India /Price Policy /HB 236 I4 P75

3839. Raquejo, Alonso. 1966 "El juego de poderes en el control de la administración económica." Documentación Administrativa (Madrid), No. 106. /Public administration /Control process /Political analysis

3840. Rascetti, A. 1959 "Lo stato e l'iniziativa economica dell'esperienza italiana." Notizie IRI (Rome), /Italy

3841. Rashid, A. 1967 Administration of Public Enterprises. Cairo: Dar El-Maaref. /Egypt /Control process

3842. Rasidi. 1980 "Investment Policies and Practice of Public Enterprises in Indonesia." Paper presented at the International Workshop on Investment Criteria and Investment Decision-Making Processes, Ljubljana, Yugoslavia, 20-24 October. Ljubljana: ICPE. /Indonesia /Investment

3843. Ratchford, B. U. 1951 "Government Action or Private Enterprise in River Valley Development: An Economist's View." American Economic Association Papers and Proceedings V. 41, pp. 307-312. /River valley development projects / Private enterprises / Comparative analysis

3844. Rathsman, B. G., Arne Sjoberg, and S. I. Sjosedt. 1955 "Public Enterprise in Sweden." In A. H. Hanson, ed(s). Public Enterprise. Brussels: IIAS. pp. 275-285. /Sweden /HD 3850 H28 Law

3845. Ratnam, T. S. 1980 "The Construction Division of the Bureau of Public Enterprises - A Study." Lok Udyog (New Delhi), V. 14, No. 2, pp. 65-70. /India /Construction industry /Control process /Case studies /354.54 L836 PCL

3846. Ratnam, V. S. 1980 "Appropriate Technology: Policy, Plans and Criteria for Selection." Paper presented at the Regional Workshop on Management of Transfer of Technology by Public Enterprises in the ESCAP Region, Bangalore, India, 10-15 November. Ljubljana: ICPE /Technology transfer

3847. Raventos Noguer, Manuel. 1970 "Régimen jurídico del Banco de España, entidad de derecho público." La Empresa Pública. Zaragoza, Spain: Publicaciones del Real Colegio de España en Bolonia. /Spain /Law /Administrative law /Central banks

3848. Ravizzini, Alberto. 1981 "Current Practices in the Negotiation, Drafting and Enforcement of Guarantee Clauses in Transfer of Technology Transactions by Public Enterprises: Case Study on Argentina." Ljubljana: ICPE /Argentina /Technology transfer /Case studies

3849. Rawin, S. J. 1965 "The Manager in the Polish Enterprise--A Study of Accommodation under Conditions of Role Conflict." British Journal of Industrial Relations (London), V. 3, No. 1, pp. 1-16. /Poland /Management /331.105 B777 PCL

3850. Ray, Anandarup. 1975 Cost Recovery Policies for Public Sector Projects. Washington, D. C.: World Bank. /Costs /Public financing /Control process

3851. Ray, H. N. 1965 Public Enterprises in India--Strategy, Objective and Control. Cambridge, Mass.: Harvard University, Center for International Affairs. /India /Evaluation

3852. Ray, H. N. 1967 "Public Enterprises in India: Harmonization of Commercial Interests with the Public Interest." Lok Udyog (New Delhi), pp. 11-76. /India /Control process

3853. Ray, H. N. 1977 "Corporate Planning by Public Enterprises - Its Linkage with National Resources Planning." Lok Udyog (New Delhi), V. 11, No. 1, pp. 23-28. /India /Planning process /354.54 L836 PCL

3854. Razafindrasoava, J. 1969 Le rôle des entreprises publiques à Madagascar. Mauritius: UNECA Seminar on Role of Public Enterprises in Planning and Plan Implementation, September 16-26, 1969. /Madagascar /Evaluation

3855. Reagan, M. M. 1958 "Sharing Financial Responsibility of River Basin Development." Journal of Farm Economics V. 40, pp. 1690-1704. /Public financing /River valley development projects

3856. Reati, A. 1963 "La concorrenza fra sectore pubblico e sectore privato nella Comunitá Economica Europea." Rivista Internazionale di Scienze Sociale (Milan, Italy), pp. 605-609. /European Economic Community /Private sector /Competition /305 R525 PCL

3857. Reati, A. 1965 "Responsabilité matérielle des Etats en matière de nationalisation." Revue de Droit Contemporain (Brussels), pp. 78-101. /Nationalization / Law

3858. Reati, A. 1965 "Impresa pubblica e integrazione europea." Revista Internazionale di Scienze Sociali (Milan, Italy), V. 73, No. 1, pp. 62-72. /European Economic Community

3859. Reddaway, W. B. 1975 "Pricing Policy for State Enterprise in Bangladesh." Bangladesh Development Studies (Dacca), V. 3, No. 1, pp. 77-82. /Bangladesh /Price Policy

3860. Reddaway, W. B. 1975 "Pricing Policy for Public Enterprises in Bangladesh." Lok Udyog (New Delhi), V. 9, No. 4, pp. 79-84. /Bangladesh /Price policy /354.54 L836 PCL

3861. Reddy, K. C. 1954 "Management of State Enterprises--Some Aspects Outlined." Major Industries of India V. 4, pp. 81-85. /India /Management

3862. Reddy, V. Madan Mohan, and P. Ranga Rao. 1974 "Boards of Public Enterprises." Lok Udyok (New Delhi), V. 8, No. 5, pp. 23-32. /India /Management /354.54 L836 PCL

3863. Redford, E. S. 1961 "L'impresa pubblica negli stati uniti." Civiltá della Machina (Milan, Italy), pp. 29-31. /United States of America

3864. Redwood, John. 1976 "Government and the Nationalized Industries." Lloyds Bank Review No. 120. /United Kingdom

/330.5 L779 PCL

3865. Redwood, John. 1976 "The Future of the Nationalized Industries." Lloyds Bank Review No. 122, pp. 33-44. /Nationalization / 330.5 L779 PCL

3866. Reed, P. W. 1973 The Economics of Public Enterprise. London: The Butterworth Group. /United Kingdom /Public utility industry /HD 4147 R28 Pub Aff,PCL

3867. Rees, Merlyn. 1973 The Public Sector in a Mixed Economy. New York: Harper & Row Publishers. /United Kingdom /Control process / HD 4145 R38 PCL

3868. Rees, R. 1968 "Second-Best Roles for Public Enterprise Pricing." Economica (London), V. 48, No. 139, pp. 260-273. /Price Policy / 306 Ec74 n.s.

3869. Reesley, M. E., and G. M. White. 1973 "The Industrial Reorganization Corporation." Public Administration (London), pp. 61-89. /United Kingdom /Development corporation 320.5 J826 PCL

3870. Rehman, A., A. K. Roy, and K. D. Sharma. 1969 "Management Attitude to Research and Development in Iron and Steel Industry: A Case Study." Lok Udyog (New Delhi), pp. 557-571. /India /Management /Research and development /Steel industry /354.54 L836

3871. Reichard, Cristoph. 1975 "The Lessons of Experience in Applying Management by Objectives to Public Enterprises - A German Perspective." Improving Performance in Public Enterprise Report of an International Conference, Arusha, Tanzania, 2-5 Dec. Arusha, Tanzania: East African Community Management Institute. pp. 70-91. /Management /Germany, Federal Rep. of

3872. Reichstul, Henri Philippe, and Luciano G. Coutinho. 1979 "Tendencias recentes do investimento empresarial do Estado." Prepared for the First Latin American Seminar on Public Policies, São Paulo, Brazil. /Brazil /Investment /OPSS

3873. Reid, Graham L., and Kevin Allen. 1970 Nationalized Industries. Baltimore, Md.: Penguin Books. /United Kingdom /HD 9145 R4

3874. Reis, Fernando Antonio Roquette. 1980 "A administração federal direta e as empresas públicas: análise de suas relações, recomendações e alternativas para seu aprimoramento." A empresa pública no Brasil: Uma abordagem multidisciplinar. Brasília: IPEA. pp. 143-167. /Control process /Accountability

3875. Reis, O. P. 1970 "Os preços nas empresas públicas." Sudam Documenta (Belém), V. 1, No. 2-3, pp. 151-167. /Price policy

3876. Reith, Lord. 1956 "Public Corporations: Need to Examine Control and Structure." Public Administration (London), V. 34, No. 4, pp. 351-354. /Control process /Evaluation /320.5

J826

3877. Rejec, Emil, and Bojan Mozina. 1981 "Maintenance Planning Manual." Paper presented at the Seminar on Maintenance Management, Mogadishu, Somalia, Nov.28-Dec.3. Ljubljana: ICPE. /Management

3878. Remili, Abdul Rahman. 1977 "Algeria." Public Enterprises and Development in the Arab Countries: Legal and Managerial Aspects. New York: Praeger for the International Legal Center. pp. 156-179. /Algeria /Economic history /Economic efficiency /Control process /Financing /Law /Management /HD 4334 P8 Law

3879. Renne, R. R. 1948 "An Economist's Appraisal of the Missouri River Development Program." Journal of Farm Economics V. 31, pp. 1017-1023. /United States of America /Economic analysis /Public works policy

3880. Report of the 8th Int'l. Cong. of Pub. and Coop. Ec., Liège, Oct. 14-17. 1968 "The Organization and Financing of Public and Cooperative Enterprises." Annals of Public and Cooperative Economy V. 34, No. 3, pp. 315-505. /Cooperatives /Financing / 330.5 An73

3881. Republic of China. Industrial Development Commission. 1955 "Public Enterprise in the Republic of China (Formosa)." In A. H. Hanson, ed(s). Public Enterprise. Brussels: IIAS. pp. 451-462. /China, Rep. of / HD 3850 H28 Law

3882. Republic of Korea. Korean Industrial Development Research Institute. 1972 "Survey of Government Enterprises in Korea." Seoul: Korean Industrial Development Institute. /Korea, Rep. of /Directory

3883. Retortillo, M. 1966 "Organización administrativa de las empresas públicas en España." International Review of Administrative Sciences V. 32, No. 1, pp. 1-15. /Spain /Public administration / JA 1 A1 I6 PCL

3884. Reuter, P. 1936 Les participations financières. La société anonyme au service des collectivités publiques. Paris: Sirey. /France

3885. Revollo Bravo, Alberto. 1960 "The Nationalization of Petroleum." Universitas (Stuttgart), V. 18, pp. 193-200. /Oil industry /Nationalization

3886. Revollo Bravo, Alberto. 1974 "Régimen legal de la explotación del petróleo en Colombia." Revista de la Cámara de Comercio de Bogotá V. 44, No. 14, pp. 31-55. /Colombia /Oil industry /Law

3887. Reyes Heroles, J. 1962 "La nacionalización de la industria eléctrica en México." Cuadernos Americanos (Mexico City), V. 21, No. 6, pp. 7-14. /Mexico /Nationalization /Electrical utility industry

3888. Reza, Sadrel. 1980 "An Appraisal of Development Objectives & Policies with Reference to Bangladesh." Journal of Management Business & Economics V. 6, No. 3, pp. 236-261. /Bangladesh /Developing nations /Planning process

3889. Rezende, F. 1971 "A evolução das funçoes do governo e a expansão do setor público brasileiro." Pesquisa e Planejamento Economico (Rio de Janeiro), V. 1, No. 4, pp. 235-282. /Brazil /Management

3890. Rezende, F. 1978 "Las empresas públicas en la economía brasileña." Prepared for the ECLA Seminar on Public Enterprise and the Planning Process in Latin America, Lima, August. /Brazil /OPSS

3891. Rezende, F. 1980 "A Empresa Pública e a intervenção do Estado no economia: Ação suplementar à iniciativa privada - perspectivas em face da conjuntura atual." A empresa pública no Brasil: Uma abordagem multidisciplinar. Brasília: IPEA. pp. 35-85. /Brazil /Goal setting /Investment /Financing /Private enterprises

3892. Rezende, F. 1983 O crescimento (descontrolado) da intervenção governamental na economia brasileira." Paper presented at the ECLA seminar "State control and planning of public enterprises," Brasília, 15-17 June. /Brazil /Economic analysis /Control process /OPSS

3893. Rezende, F., et al. 1976 "Aspectos da participação do governo na economia." Monografias No. 26. Rio de Janeiro: IPEA. /Brazil

3894. Riad, F. A. 1966 "Le statut des entreprises publiques en droit international privé." Egypte Contemporaine (Cairo), No. 323, pp. 169-196. /Law / 962.05 Eg98r

3895. Ribicki, Zygmunt. 1962 "La empresa pública en el sistema polaco de la economía planificada." Revista Internacional Ciencias Administrativas No. 3, pp. 312-319. /Poland /Socialist economy

3896. Ricf, A. K. 1968 "Management and the Nationalized Industries." New Society (London), V. 11, No. 280, pp. 189-191. /Management /United Kingdom

3897. Richardson, J. J. 1971 "The Administration of Denationalization: The Case of Haulage." Public Administration (London), V. 49, pp. 385-402. /Australia /Public administration /Case studies /Privatization /JA 8 P8 Pub Aff

3898. Richman, Barry M. 1963 "Employee Motivation in Soviet Industry." Annals of Collective Economy V. 34, No. 4, pp. 551-571. /Union of Soviet Socialist Reps. /Industrial sector /Employment policy / Motivation / 330.5 An73

3899. Richman, Barry M. 1965 Soviet Management, with Significant American Comparison. Englewood Cliffs, N.J.: Prentice-Hall, Inc. /Union of Soviet Socialist Reps. /Management /United

States of America /Comparative analysis / 658 R411s

3900. Richman, Barry M. 1967 "Capitalists and Managers in Communist China." Harvard Business Review pp. 57-58. /China, People's Rep. of /Management

3901. Richman, Barry M. 1967 Management, Industry and Ideology in Communist China. London: Random House. /China, People's Rep. of /Industrial sector /Management

3902. Richman, Barry M. 1967 Management Development and Education in the Soviet Union. East Lansing, Mich.: Institute for International Business and Economic Development Studies, Michigan State University. /Union of Soviet Socialist Reps. /Management / HD 70 R9 R48

3903. Richman, Barry M. 1971 "Ideology and Management: The Soviet Evolution." Columbia Journal of World Business V. 6, No. 2, pp. 62-72. /Union of Soviet Socialist Reps. /658.05 C723 PCL

3904. Rico Ramírez, Miguel. 1978 "El presupuesto federal y las empresas públicas." In Rosa Luz Alegría et al. Empresas públicas. Mexico City: Presidencia de la República. pp. 95-107. /Mexico /Budgetary process /HD 4013 E474 1978 LAC

3905. Ridley, F. 1964 "The German Federal Railways--A State Administered System." Parliamentary Affairs (London), V. 17, No. 2, pp. 182-194. /Germany, Federal Rep. of /Railway industry

3906. Ridley, T. M. 1951 "Note on the Extent of the Public Sector of the Economy in Recent Years." Journal of the Royal Statistical Society V. 114, No. 2, pp. 207-213. /United Kingdom /Statistics

3907. Rienstock, G., S. A. Schawartz, and A. Yugow. 1944 Management in Russian Industry and Agriculture. New York: Oxford University Press. /Union of Soviet Socialist Reps. /Management /Industrial sector / Agricultural sector

3908. Riethmayer, L. C. 1955 "Government Corporations." Public Administration in the Philippines. Manila, Philippines: Institute of Public Administration. pp. 289-318. /Philippines

3909. Rio de Janeiro Group. 1967 Public Utilities. (Centennial Study and Training Program on Metropolitan Problems). Rio de Janeiro, Brazil: Rio de Janeiro Group. /Brazil /Public utility industry

3910. Rios Gamboa, Walter. 1976 "La Corporación Boliviana de Fomento (CBF) como instrumento de desarrollo nacional." Rio de Janeiro: FGV-EIAP. /Bolivia /Development banks /Directory /Holding company /OPSS

3911. Rippy, M. 1957 "Nationalized Oil Industry of Mexico: 1938-1955." South West Social Science Quarterly V. 38, pp. 6-18. /Mexico /Oil industry /Economic history

3912. Risk, W. W. 1950 "Efficiency in Nationalized Industries." Accountant (London), pp. 56-58. /United Kingdom /Evaluation /Economic efficiency

3913. Ristic, Slobodan. 1979 "Problem Solving as a Factor in Social and Economic Prosperity of Developing Countries." Paper presented at the Interregional Workshop "Developing Problem Solving Skills in Public Enterprise," Ljubljana, Yugoslavia, 2-17 April. Ljubljana: ICPE. /Developing nations /Economic development /Social development /Decision making process

3914. Ristmaki, Juhani. 1962 "The Financing of Capital Formation by the Public Sector in Finland." Bank of England Monthly Bulletin pp. 18-22. /Finland /Public financing /Investment

3915. Ristuccia, Sergio. 1983 "The Crisis of Public Enterprises: The Political Reasons." Paper presented at the 19th International Congress of Administrative Sciences, West Berlin, 19-23 Sept. /Europe /Political analysis /OPSS

3916. Ritchie, Sir Douglas. 1949 "The Constitution and Functions of a Port Authority." Journal of the Institute of Transport (London), pp. 211-214. /United Kingdom /Port authority

3917. Ritschl, Hans. 1955 "La empresa pública en la economía de mercado." Die Offentliche Wirtschaft No. 5. /Market economy

3918. Ritschl, Hans. 1963 "The Taxation of Public Undertakings." Annals of Collective Economy V. 34, No. 4, pp. 440-442. /Taxation policy / 330.5 An73

3919. Rittenberg, S. N. 1935 "Legality of the Federal Tennessee Valley Program." Land Economics V. 11, pp. 210-213. /United States of America /River valley development projects /Law /305 J824 PCL

3920. Rittig, G. 1965 "Public Enterprise in a Growing Economy." Annals of Public and Cooperative Economy V. 36, pp. 349-357. /Economic analysis

3921. Rivero, J. 1949 "Le nouveau statut de la compagnie Air-France." Droit Social (Paris), V. 12, No. 6, pp. 204-208. /France /Law /Air transportation industry

3922. Rivero, J. 1952 "Essai d'un bilan des nationalisations françaises," Revue de l'Université de Bruxelles (Brussels), No. 1, pp. 5-26. /France /Nationalization

3923. Rivero, J. 1952 "Le régime des entreprises nationalisées et l'évolution du droit administratif." La distinction du droit privé et du droit public et l'entreprise publique. Paris: Sirey. /France /Law

3924. Rivero, J. 1955 "Le fonctionement des entreprises nationalisées." Droit Social (Paris), pp. 533-538. /Public administration /Organization behavior /System performance

3925. Rivero, J. 1956 "Il funzionamento delle imprese nazionalizzate." *Nowva Rivista di Diritto Comerciale* pp. 277-283. /Italy /Management

3926. Rivero, J. 1962 "Action économique de l'Etat et évolution administrative." *Revue Economique* (Paris), pp. 986-996. /Administrative reform 330.5 R3282 PCL

3927. Rivero, J. 1967 *Rapport sur le droit français des sociétés et l'entreprise publique.* Paris: Dalloz. /France /Law

3928. Rivier, M. Jacques. 1970 "La place des entreprises publiques dans l'économie française." *Problèmes Economiques* (Paris), No. 1148, pp. 2-8. /France /Evaluation

3929. Roberts, C. A. 1957 "The National Coal Board and the Fleck Report." *Public Administration* (London), V. 35, No. 1, pp. 1-14. /United Kingdom /Coal mining industry /Control process / Evaluation /Economic analysis / JA 8 P8 Pub Aff

3930. Roberts, C. A. 1966 "The Reorganization of the National Coal Board's Management Structure." *Public Administration* (London), V. 44, pp. 283-294. /Coal mining industry /Organization change / JA 8 P8 Pub Aff

3931. Roberts, E. 1955 *One River-Seven States; TVA--State Relations in the Development of the Tennessee River.* Knoxville, Tenn.: Bureau of Public Administration, University of Tennessee. /United States of America /River valley development projects / State government

3932. Roberts, H. S., and J. B. Ferguson. 1970 *Collective Bargaining and Dispute Settlement in the Public and Private Sectors, A Review and Evaluation Proceeding of Conference.* Honolulu: University of Hawaii, Industrial Relations Center. /United States of America /Private sector /Collective bargaining

3933. Roberts, Paul E. 1971 "Development Banking: The Issue of Public and Private Development Banking." *Economic Development and Cultural Change* V. 19, No. 3, pp. 424-437. /Development banks /Comparative analysis /330.5 Ec66

3934. Roberts, Paul E. 1974 "The Issue of Public and Private Development Banking: Reply." *Economic Development and Cultural Change* V. 22, No. 2, pp. 351-352. /Financial institutions /Development banks /330.5 Ec66

3935. Robin, M. 1957 "Essai sur la representation des intèrets dans l'organisation des entreprises publiques." *Revue de Droit Publique et de la Science Politique en France et a l'Etranger* (Paris), V. 73, No. 5. /Evaluation /Organization formation

3936. Robinson, Howard. 1948 *The British Post Office.* Princeton, N. J.: Princeton University Press. /United Kingdom /Postal service / Case studies / 383 R562b

3937. Robinson, James W. 1967 "A Note on the Wage and Employment Decision in Public Enterprises Institutions." Quarterly Review of Economics and Business V. 7, No. 1, pp. 71-74. /Employment policy /Wages / 330.5 Q23

3938. Robinson, Richard D. 1961 "State Enterprise in Turkey." New Outlook pp. 8-12. /Turkey

3939. Robinson, Richard D. 1979 "Major Issues in Joint Ventures between Developed and Developing Countries." Paper presented at the International Seminar on Joint Venture and Public Enterprises in Developing Countries, Ljubljana, Yugoslavia, 4-12 December. Ljubljana: ICPE. /Multinational corporations

3940. Robinson, W. C. 1959 "Financing of Federal Authorities." American Journal of Economics and Sociology V. 19, pp. 45-63. /United States of America /Public financing / 330.5 Am311 PCL /H 1 A48 Pub Aff

3941. Roblot, R. 1946 "La nationalisation du gaz et de électricité." Droit Social (Paris), No. 5. /France /Gas utility industry /Electrical utility industry

3942. Robock, Stefan H. 1970 "Desenvolvimento integrado e industrialização de Bacia Fluvial. A experiencia do Valley Tennessee." Revista Economica (Fortaleza), V. 1, No. 4, pp. 24-42. /Brazil /Water resources development /River valley development projects

3943. Robson, William A. 1937 Public Enterprise. London: Allen & Unwin. /United Kingdom / 388.8 R576p

3944. Robson, William A. 1947 "The Administration of Nationalized Industries in Britain." Public Administration Review V. 7, No. 3, pp. 161-169. /United Kingdom /Management / JK1 P85

3945. Robson, William A. 1950 "The Governing Board of the Public Corporation." Political Quarterly (London), V. 21, pp. 135-149. /United Kingdom /Control process /Management /320.5 P76p

3946. Robson, William A. 1950 "Nationalized Industries in Britain and France." American Political Science Review V. 44, No. 2, pp. 299-322. /United Kingdom /France /Comparative analysis /320.5 Am31

3947. Robson, William A. 1955 "Forms and Directions of Public Enterprise." Indian Journal of Public Administration (New Delhi), V. 1, No. 1, pp. 14-24. /Structural characteristics /JA 26 I55 Pub Aff

3948. Robson, William A. 1957 "La corporación pública en Gran Bretaña." Revista de Administración Pública (Madrid), pp. 11-128. /United Kingdom

3949. Robson, William A. 1960 "Mixed Enterprise." In ed(s). National Westminister Bank Quarterly Review /Europe /Mixed enterprises / 332.10942 N214q

3950. Robson, William A. 1960 Nationalized Industry and Public Ownership. Toronto, Canada: Toronto University. /Nationalization /Mixed enterprises / 338.942 R576n

3951. Robson, William A. 1964 Industria nacionalizada y propiedad pública. Madrid: Editorial Tecnos S. A. /Spain /Industrial sector

3952. Robson, William A. 1965 Report on the State Investment Bank and Its Relations with State Economic Enterprises, the State Planning Organization and the Ministries concerned with Investment, Programmes of the State Economic Enterprises. Paris: OECD. /Development banks /Planning process /Control process

3953. Robson, William A. 1970 "Ministerial Control of the Nationalized Industries." In W. G. Friedmann and J. F. Garner, ed(s). Government Enterprise, a Comparative Study. New York: Columbia University. pp. 79-90. /United Kingdom /Control Process / 350.0092 G746

3954. Robson, William A. 1973 "Public Enterprise as a Function of Economic and Social Development." Annals of Public and Cooperative Economy V. 44, pp. 313-320. /Economic Development / 330.5 An73

3955. Robson, William A., ed. 1952 Problems of Nationalized Industry. London: Allen & Unwin. /United Kingdom /Industrial sector / 338.942 R576p

3956. Roca T., Santiago, and Efraín Salas C. 1982 "The Organization of Workers for Self-Management." Public Enterprise V. 2, No. 4, pp. 89-96. /Worker self management /Management /OPSS

3957. Roca T., Santiago, ed. 1978 La autogestión en América Latina. Lima: Escuela de Administración de Negocios para Graduados. /Latin America /Worker self management /OPSS

3958. Rocco, L. 1956 "Imprese pubbliche e politica della spesa." Nord e Sud (Milan, Italy), pp. 58-64. /Italy

3959. Rodríguez Gómez. 1953 "La municipalización de servicios en el municipio antiguo de Alcalá de Henares." Revista de Estudios de la Vida Social (Madrid), /Spain /Local government /

3960. Rodriguez Fernández, G. 1966 "El control de la empresa pública." Economía Industrial /Control process

3961. Rodriguez Rodriguez, Federico. 1950 "Aspectos sociales de la nacionalización." Revista de Administración Pública (Madrid), No. 3, pp. 173-212. /Spain /Nationalization

3962. Rodriguez, Alvaro A. 1981 "Los estudios de factibilidad como elementos de juicio para la toma de decisión - Estudio comparativo de quatro estudios de factibilidad para la electrificación de las vias bananeras del Atlantico." San José, Costa Rica: Ferrocarriles de Costa Rica, S.A. /Costa

Rica /Railway industry /Case studies /OPSS

3963. Rodriguez, G. 1965 "La información de precios en las empresas del Estado." Cuadernos de la Corporación Venezolana de Fomento (Caracas), V. 2, No. 4, pp. 69-75. /Venezuela /Price policy / G330.987 C817cua

3964. Rodriguez, Policarpo. 1974 Características y evolución de las inversiones petroleras en Venezuela. Caracas: Facultad de Ciencias Económicas y Sociales, Universidad Central de Venezuela. /Venezuela /Oil industry /Investment /Economic development / Economic history / HD 9574 V42 R637 LAC

3965. Rodriguez, Q. 1964 "La flexibilidad en la administración pública y en la conducción de las empresas del Estado." Ciencias Administrativas (Buenos Aires), V. 8, No. 17, pp. 5-31. /Control process /Organization development

3966. Rodrik, Dani. 1982 "Changing patterns of ownership and integration in the international bauxite-aluminum industry." In Leroy P. Jones et al., ed(s). Public enterprise in less-developed countries. New York: Cambridge University Press. pp. 189-215. /Mining industry /HD 3850 P83 PCL Also presented at the Second BAPEG conference, April, 1980. /OPSS

3967. Roessler, Frieder. 1981 "State Trading and Trade Liberalization." In M. M. Kostecki, ed(s). State trading in International Markets. New York: St. Martin's Press. pp. 261-284. /State trading organizations /Economic policy /HF 1410.5 S7 1981 M

3968. Rofman, Alejandro. 1981 "Role of Public Enterprises in Regional Development in Latin America." Paper presented at the Expert Group Meeting on the Role of Public Enterprises in Regional Development in Developing Countries, Ljubljana, Yugoslavia, 7-11 December. Ljubljana: ICPE. /Latin America /Regional development

3969. Rogan, E. P., M. R. Stradwick, and R. L. Wettenhall. 1968 "Government Department or Statutory Authority?" Public Administration (Sydney, Australia), V. 27, No. 4, pp. 328-359. /Australia /Public administration /Government authority /Structural characteristics

3970. Rogissart, G. 1978 "Les entreprises publiques dans la CEE." In André Gélinas, ed(s). Public Enterprise and the Public Interest. Ontario: The Institute of Public Administration of Canada. pp. 210-214. /European Economic Community

3971. Rogissart, G., and André Dumoulin. 1962 "Problems of Public Undertakings Within the Common Market." Annals of Collective Economy V. 33, pp. 234-250. /European Economic Community /330.5 An73

3972. Roldan Confesor, Maria Nieves. 1980 "Approaches to Training Needs Assessment." Paper presented at the Interregional Seminar on Training Management in Public Enterprises in Developing Countries, Ljubljana, Yugoslavia, Sept.29-Oct.10. Ljubljana: ICPE. /Training

3973. "Role of Industrial Development Corporations." 1962 National and Grindlays Bank Review (London), /Industrialization /Development banks

3974. Rolland, L. 1912 "La personnification des services publiques." Rassegna di Diritto Público (Naples, Italy), /Italy /Public services

3975. Rollet, H. 1948 "Les nationalisations françaises." Revue Nouvelle No. 4, pp. 372-379. /France /Nationalization

3976. Romac, P. and J. Franic. 1962 Obreros como gestores de las fábricas. Belgrade. /Yugoslavia /Worker self management

3977. Roman, Zoltán. 1970 "Factors of Productivity Growth." Budapest: Hungarian Academy of Sciences, Institute for Industrial Economics. /Hungary /Productivity

3978. Roman, Zoltán. 1980 "Productivity Appraisal at Public Enterprises." Paper presented at the Second BAPEG Conference: Public Enterprises in Mixed Economy LDCs, Boston, Mass., April. /Productivity /Economic efficiency /OPSS

3979. Roman, Zoltán. 1981 "Government Control and Performance Evaluation of Public Enterprises in the Hungarian Industry." Ljubljana: ICPE. /Hungary /Evaluation

3980. Romero, Elena V. 1980 "Integrated Report of the Expert Group Meeting on Manpower Planning in Public Enterprises held in DAP Conference Center, Tagaytay City, on August 18-22, 1980." Ljubljana: ICPE /Personnel management /Planning process / Manpower planning

3981. Ronson, G. 1958 A Suggested Manual of Management and Cost Accounting for the Government Cotton Spinning Weaving Factory. Rangoon, Burma: UN. TAA. /Burma /Textile industry /Management /Cost accounting

3982. Roseman, Herman G. 1974 "Utility Financing Problems and National Energy Policy." Public Utilities Fortnightly V. 94, No. 6. /Public utility industry /Financing / 388.9 P97

3983. Rosen, George. 1958 Industrial Change in India: Industrial Growth, Capital Requirements and Technical Change, 1937-1955. Glencoe, Ill.: Free Press. /India /Industrialization /Economic history / 338.954 R722i

3984. Rosete, Nievelene V. 1979 "Management and Training in Public Enterprises: Country Report of the Philippines." Paper presented at the International Seminar on Management and Training in Public Enterprises in Developing Countries, Ljubljana, Yugoslavia, October 1-13. Ljubljana: ICPE. /Philippines /Management /Training

3985. Rosete, Nievelene V. 1980 "Research Approaches in Management Training and Development in the Philippines." Paper presented at the Expert Group Meeting on the Research Project in Education and Training in Public Enterprises in

Developing Countries, Ljubljana, Yugoslavia, 17-22 March. Ljubljana: ICPE. /Philippines /Economic research /Training /Management

3986. Rosete, Nievelene V., et al. 1980 "Management Manpower Planning in the Philippines: The Philippine Experience." Paper presented at the Expert Group Meeting on the Research Project in Education and Training in Public Enterprises in Developing Countries, Ljubljana, Yugoslavia, 17-22 March. Ljubljana: ICPE. /Philippines /Personnel management /Training /Manpower planning

3987. Rosete, Nievelene V. 1981 "Behind Profits and Losses: The Experiences of Selected Philippine Public Enterprises." Public Enterprise V. 2, No. 2, pp. 69-91. /Philippines /Public financing /Financial performance /Profits /OPSS

3988. Roseveare, R. W. 1977 "Public Enterprise Boards in the United Kingdom and Worker Participation (with Some Reference to Practice in Western Europe Generally." Paper presented at the International Seminar on Management and Training in Public Enterprises in Developing Countries, Ljubljana, Yugoslavia, 10-28 October. Ljubljana: ICPE. /United Kingdom /Western Europe /Control process /Worker management participation /Management

3989. Rosner, J. 1956 "Management by the Workers in Poland." International Labour Review (Geneva), V. 76, No. 3. /Poland /Worker self management /331.05 In81 PCL /HD4811 I65 Pub Aff

3990. Roson, H., M. Durupty, and M. Debenne. 1980 "La formación y el perfeccionamiento de dirigentes de empresas públicas." Revista Latinoamericana de Administración Pública No. 10-1, pp. 557-570. /Training

3991. Ross, G. W. 1965 The Nationalization of Steel. London: MacGibbon and Kee. /United Kingdom /Steel industry /Nationalization

3992. Ross, N. 1965 "Workers, Participation and Control." Scientific Business (Reading), V. 2, No. 8, pp. 352-359. /Worker management participation /Control process

3993. Rossi, A. 1982 "Le societa a partecipazione statale e la nuova procedura di administrazione." Giurisprudenza Commerciale No. 2. /Italy /Mixed enterprises /Public administration / Administrative reform

3994. Rossi, Giampaolo. 1960 "Soviet State Enterprise." Politica delgi Scambi (Milan, Italy), V. 1, No. 4, pp. 5-44. /Union of Soviet Socialist Reps.

3995. Rossi, Giampaolo. 1970 "I criteri di economicitá nella gestione delle imprese pubbliche." Rivista Trimestrale di Diritto Pubblico (Rome), No. 1, pp. 237-270. /Italy /Evaluation /Management

3996. Rossi, V. 1962 "About the Nationalization of the Electric Power Industry." Studi Economici (Naples), V. 17, No. 6, pp.

556-562. /Electrical utility industry /Nationalization /Italy

3997. Rothchild, D. 1970 "Kenya's Africanization Program - Priorities of Development and Equity." American Political Science Review V. 64, No. 3, pp. 735-753. /Kenya /320.5 Am31

3998. Rothrock, Van Edwin. 1969 "The Autonomous Entities of the Peruvian Government in Perspective." D.B.A. dissertation, University of Indiana. /Peru /Economic history /Public administration /Control process /Management /FILM 8980 LAC

3999. Roubier, P., and R. Maspetiol. 1952 La distinction du droit privé et du droit publique et l'entreprise publique. Paris: Sirey. /France /Law /Private sector

4000. Rougeau, D. 1979 "Una medida de la eficiencia de la empresa pública: El excedente de productividad." Revista Latinoamericana de Administración Pública No. 8-9, pp. 311-317. /Economic efficiency /Productivity /Control process

4001. Roulac, Stephen E. 1980 "Structuring the Joint Venture." AMA Management Digest V. 3, No. 6, pp. 25-28. /Mixed enterprises

4002. Rousseau, Stephen H., and Philip Chong-Seng. 1980 "Un aperçu sur la formation au niveau ministère et dans l'entreprise électrique aux Seychelles." Paper presented at the Séminaire international sur la gestion et la formation dans les entreprises publiques dans les pays en voie de développement, Ljubljana, Yugoslavia, 3-15 March. Ljubljana: ICPE. /Seychelles /Planning process /Electrical utility industry

4003. Roversi Monaco, Fabio. 1970 "Consideración sobre los entes `autónomos´ de gestión de las participaciones estatales." La Empresa Pública. Zaragoza, Spain: Publicaciones del Real Colegio de España en Bolonia. /Spain /Management

4004. Rowley, C. K. 1968 Monopoly in Britain---Private Vice but Public Virtue? Reprint Series, Economics, No.64 York University, Institute of Social and Economic Research. No. 64. /United Kingdom /Private sector /Comparative analysis

4005. Rowley, C. K., and J. Cubitt. 1975 The British Steel Corporation. Lexington, Mass.: D.C. Heath & Company. /United Kingdom /Steel industry /354.42 R797b

4006. Roww, Walt W., et al. 1974 Empresa pública versus empresa privada en economías en proceso de desarrollo. Barcelona, Spain: DOPESA. /Developing nations /Private sector /Comparative analysis

4007. Roy, P. C. 1957 "Pricing Policy Under Public Enterprise." Indian Journal of Commerce (Allahabad, India), V. 10, No. 4. /India /Price policy

4008. Roy, P. C. 1958 "Management of Public Enterprises in India." Indian Journal of Commerce (Allahabad, India), V. 11, No. 4. /India /Management

4009. Roychowdhury, A. K., et al. 1980 Role of the Public Industrial Enterprises in India. New Delhi: Bureau of Public Enterprises. /India /Industrial sector

4010. Roychowdhury, A. K., et al. 1981 Role of Public Sector in India. Ljubljana: ICPE. /India

4011. Rozas Zornoza, Manuel. 1969 "Consideraciones acerca de las empresas públicas españolas." Economía Financiera Española (Madrid), No. 31-3. /Spain /Evaluation

4012. Rozman, Rudi. 1976 "The Training of Planning Specialists." Paper presented at the International Seminar on Management and Training in Public Enterprises in Developing Countries, Ljubljana, Yugoslavia, Sept.21-Oct.2. Ljubljana: ICPE. /Training /Management / Also presented at the same seminar Sept. 18-Oct. 6, 1978 and the French version Nov. 6-17, 1978, both in Ljubljana, Yugoslavia.

4013. Rozman, Rudi. 1978 "Indicators of Achievement in Production." Paper presented at the Workshop on Information System for the Evaluation of Business Efficiency in Public Enterprises in Developing Countries, Ljubljana, Yugoslavia, 13-18 November. Ljubljana: ICPE. /Evaluation /Productivity /Also presented at the Seminar on Production Planning, Mogadishu, Feb. 26 - Mar. 3, 1979 and the Regional Wkshp. on Planning in PEs in the Latin American and Caribbean Region, Feb. 11-15, 1980, Kingston, Jamaica.

4014. Rozman, Rudi. 1979 "The Managing and Planning of Projects." Paper presented at the Seminar on Production Planning, Mogadishu, Somalia, Feb.26-March 3. Ljubljana: ICPE. /Project management /Planning process / Also presented at the Seminar on Production Planning, Mogadishu, Somalia, Nov. 24 - Dec. 3, 1980.

4015. Rozman, Rudi. 1979 "Project Planning." Paper presented at the Seminar on Production Planning, Mogadishu, Somalia, Feb.26-March 3. Ljubljana: ICPE. /Planning process / Also presented at the Seminar on Production Planning, Mogadishu, Somalia, Nov. 24 - Dec. 3, 1980.

4016. Rozman, Rudi. 1979 "Planning in Working Organizations in SFRY." Paper presented at the Regional Workshop on Planning in Public Enterprises of the African Region, Accra, Ghana, 10-15 December. Ljubljana: ICPE /Planning process

4017. Rozman, Rudi. 1980 "Different Kinds of Plans and Certain Shortcomings of the Planning in Organizations of Associated Labour." Paper presented at the Seminar on Planning, Dar es Salaam, Tanzania, 1-12 December. Ljubljana: ICPE. /Planning process /Worker self management /Worker management participation / Also presented at the Regional Workshop on Planning in PEs in the L. American and Caribbean Region, Kingston, Jamaica, Feb. 11-15, 1980, under the title "Planning in Enterprises: Meaning, Importance, and Kinds of Plans."

4018. Ruggles, Nancy. 1949 "Recent Developments in the Theory of Marginal Cost Pricing." Review of Economic Studies V. 17, No. 43, pp. 107-126. /Price policy / 330.5 R326 /Reprinted in R. Turvey, Public Enterprise. /338.001 T869e PCL /HD 3850 T89 Pub Aff

4019. Ruggles, Nancy. 1949 "The Welfare Basis of the Marginal Cost Pricing Principle." Review of Economic Studies V. 17, No. 42, pp. 29-46. /Price policy /Social welfare policy /330.5 R326

4020. Ruiz Duenas, J. 1983 "The Public Enterprise and the Economic Stabilization Processes: A Comparative Approach to the Mexican Case." Paper presented at the 19th International Congress of Administrative Sciences, West Berlin, 19-23 Sept. /Mexico /Economic policy /Latin America /Privatization /OPSS

4021. Ruiz Jiméniz, J. 1921 Nacionalización y municipalización de servicios colectivos. Madrid. /Spain /Public services /Nationalization

4022. Ruiz Massieu, José Francisco. 1979 "La empresa pública en México: Bases constitucionales y formas de organización jurídica y administrativa." Mexico City: Seminario sobre Empresas Públicas. /Mexico /Law /Public administration /OPSS

4023. Ruiz Massieu, José Francisco. 1979 "Una aproximación al control jurisdiccional de las empresas públicas." Mexico City: Universidad Autónoma Metropolitana, Seminario Internacional de la Regulación Jurídica de la Empresa Pública. /Mexico /Control process /Law /OPSS

4024. Ruiz Pina, Silvia. 1962 "Empresas del sector paraestatal en el derecho administrativo." Mexico City: Thesis presented to obtain the Licentiate in Law at the Universidad Nacional Autonoma de México. /Mexico /Law /G380.1622 R859e LAC

4025. Ruiz Zubiaurre, Antonio. 1979 "Joint Venture's Mechanisms among Public and Private Enterprises in Mexico." Paper presented at the International Seminar on Joint Ventures and Public Enterprises in Developing Countries, Ljubljana, Yugoslavia, 4-12 December. Ljubljana: ICPE. /Mexico /Mixed enterprises

4026. Ruiz Zubiaurre, Antonio. 1980 Public Industrial Enterprises in Mexico. Ljubljana: ICPE. /Mexico /Industrial sector

4027. Ruiz, J. 1951 "The Fomento Production Corporation in Chile." Social Science No. 26, pp. 221-225. /Chile /Development corporation

4028. Ruiz, S. 1963 "Las empresas del sector paraestatal en México y su reglamentación." Rev. Itat No. 18-9, pp. 39-98. /Mexico /Law /Control process

4029. Rukeyser, William S. 1968 "Creeping Capitalism in Government Corporations." Fortune V. 78, No. 4, pp. 124-127. /Management /Economic Efficiency /AP2 F6 Pub Aff

4030. Ruky, Saiful M. 1981 "A Case Study on the Assessment of Training Needs." Paper presented at the Interregional Seminar on Training Management in Public Enterprises in Developing Countries, Ljubljana, Yugoslavia, 19-28 October. Ljubljana: ICPE. /Training /Evaluation

4031. Ruozi, R. 1968 "L'Autofinanziamento." In G. Stefani, ed(s). Studi sul finanziamento delle imprese pubbliche in Europe. Milan: CIRIEC. pp. 144-145. /Europe /Financing

4032. Rus, V. 1970 "Influence Structure in Yugoslav Enterprise." Industrial Relations V. 9, No. 2, pp. 148-160. /Yugoslavia /Administrative management /331.105 In19

4033. Russell, D. 1951 "Government Action or Private Enterprise in River Valley Developments: Discussion." American Economic Association Papers and Proceedings V. 41, pp. 312-314. /River valley development projects /Comparative analysis

4034. Russo, G. 1965 "Impresa pubblica e piano." Stato Sociale (Rome), V. 9, No. 6, pp. 521-541. /Italy

4035. Rutega, S. B. 1978 "Co-operation among State Trading Organizations of Developing Countries in English-speaking Africa." (Geneva: UNCTAD). TB/B/C.7/18/Add.1 /State trading organizations /Africa /Tanzania /Kenya /Zambia /Nigeria /Ghana /OPSS

4036. Rutherford, George R. D., V. T. Kale, and Leo Marsan Chileshe. 1978 "Report of the International Workshop on Management and Transfer and Development of Technology in Public Enterprises in Developing Countries Jointly Organised by UNIDO and ICPE, Ljubljana, June 19-24, 1978." Ljubljana: ICPE. /Technology transfer

4037. Rutherford, L. A. 1980 "The Consumer Voice in Nationalized Industry." National Law Journal V. 130. /United Kingdom /Consumer relations /Control process

4038. Rutledge, P. 1980 "Las empresas públicas: su identidad y su utilización como instrumentos promotores del desarrollo económico." Revista Latinoamericana de Administración Pública No. 10-1, pp. 571-579. /Economic development /Policy analysis

4039. Rutman, Gilbert. 1966 "State Trading in Tanganyika." The South African Journal of Economics (Pretoria), V. 32, No. 4, pp. 148-157. /Tanzania /State trading organizations /Africa /330.968 So87

4040. Rwegasira, Kami S. P. n.d. "Financial Impact of Inflation on the Business Parastatal Sector in an L.D.C. - Tanzania." Journal of Eastern African Research & Development pp. 9-31. /Tanzania /East Africa /Inflation /Financial performance

4041. Rybicki, Zygmunt. 1962 "L'entreprise publique dans le système polonais de l'économie planifiée." International Review of Administrative Science No. 3, pp. 312-319. /Poland /Planning process

4042. Rydon, Joan. 1952 "The Australian Broadcasting Corporation: 1932-1942. The Study of a Public Corporation." Public Administration (Sydney, Australia), pp. 12-25. /Australia /Broadcasting industry

4043. Saad Eddine, I. 1969 Contrôle sur le secteur publique: Le cadre intellectual et les bases d'application. Khartoum, Sudan: Institute of Public Administration. /Sudan /Personnel recruitment /Personnel management /Control process

4044. Sabato, Jorge, et al. 1978 Energía atómica e industria nacional. Washington, D. C.: OAS, General Secretariat. /Argentina /Nuclear power

4045. Sabato, Jorge. 1971 SEGBA: Cogestión y Banco Mundial. Buenos Aires: Juárez. /Argentina /Transportation industry /World Bank /HD 9685 A74 S46 LAC

4046. Sabato, Jorge. 1971 Empresas del Estado. San Carlos de Bariloche: Fundación Bariloche. /Argentina /HD 4083 S217

4047. Sabato, Jorge. 1974 Rol de las empresas del sector público en el desarrollo cientifico tecnológico. San Carlos de Bariloche: Fundación Bariloche. /Argentina /Technology /T177 L29 S2 LAC

4048. Sachica, Luis Carlos. 1979 "Regulación de la empresa pública en Colombia." Paper presented at the Seminario de empresa pública, Mexico. /Colombia /Control process /Law /OPSS

4049. Sachs, I. 1959 "Patterns of Public Sector in Underdeveloped Economies." Indian Economic Review V. 4, No. 3, pp. 76-82. /Developing nations /Taxonomy

4050. Sachs, I. 1959 "A Note on Polish Industrialization: Its Results and Prospects." Indian Economic Journal (Bombay), V. 6, pp. 332-341. /Poland /Industrialization / 330.5 In16

4051. Sachs, I. 1964 Patterns of Public Sector in Underdeveloped Economies. London: Asia Publishing House. /Developing nations /Taxonomy /Economic history /330.5 In18

4052. Sack, K., and H. Linsel. 1965 Management in Socialist Industry and Enterprises. (Part 1: Economic Basis and Main Features of Socialist Management). (Part 2: Structure of Management in Socialist Industry and Enterprises.) Cairo: Institute of National Planning. Nos. 561 and 562. /Egypt /Socialist economy /Public administration /Management

4053. Sackey, James A. 1981 "The Case of Guyana Electricity Corporation." Economic and Social Studies (Mona, Kingston, Jamaica), V. 30, No. 1, pp. 146-170. /Caribbean Region /Guyana /Case studies /Electrical utility industry /G330.97292 So13 LAC

4054. Sacraceno, Pasquale. 1960 L'Imprensa pubblica nell'esperienza italiana. Milan, Italy. /Italy /Evaluation

4055. Sacraceno, Pasquale. 1970 "El fin del beneficio en las empresas públicas de producción." La Empresa Pública. Zaragoza, Spain: Publicaciones del Real Colegio de España en Bolonia. pp. 357-372. /Spain /Cost benefit analysis /Profits

4056. Sacristán Roy, Emilio. 1980 "Some Considerations on the Role of Public Enterprise." In William J. Baumol, ed(s). Public and Private Enterprise in a Mixed Economy. New York: St. Martin's Press. pp. 44-52. /Investment /Technology transfer /Monopoly /HD 3842 P87 PCL

4057. Saddux, R. 1968 "L'Institut pour la Reconstruction Industrielle (I.R.I.) et l'économie italienne." Problèmes Economiques (Paris), V. 31, pp. 28-31. /Italy /Economic research /Economic analysis

4058. Sadik, Muhamad. 1977 "Bahrain, Kuwait, Qatar, the United Arab Emirates and Saudi Arabia." Public Enterprises and Development in the Arab Countries: Legan and Managerial Aspects. New York: Praeger for the Intertional Legal Centre for Law in Development. pp. 9-62. /Bahrain /Kuwait /Qatar /United Arab Emirates /Saudi Arabia /Economic analysis /Economic efficiency /Financial performance /Management /Law /HD 4334 P8 Law

4059. Sadique, Abu Sharaf H. K. ed. 1976 Public Enterprise in Asia: Studies on Coordination and Control. Kuala Lumpur: Asian Centre for Development Administration. /Asia /Control process / HD 4276 P8

4060. Sadique, Abu Sharaf H. K. 1976 "Coordination and Control of Public Enterprises: An Overview of the Asian Situation." Public Enterprise in Asia: Studies on Coordination and Control. Kuala Lumpur: Asian Centre for Development Administration. pp. 3-76. /Asia /Control process /HD 4276 P8

4061. Sadique, Abu Sharaf H. K. 1978 "Coordination and Control of Public Enterprises: An Overview of the Asian Situation." Bulletin of ICPE (International Center for Public Enterprises in Developing Countries V. 4, No. 1, pp. 12-16. /Asia /Control process

4062. Sadli, Mohammad. 1960 "Structural and Operational Aspects of Public Enterprises in Indonesia." Economics and Finance in Indonesia pp. 227-253. /Indonesia /Management /Structural characteristics

4063. Sadli, Mohammad. 1965 "The Public Sector, Private Sector and Economic Growth of Indonesia." Ekonomi dan Keuangan Indonesia /Indonesia /Private sector /Economic growth policy / Comparative analysis

4064. Sagardoy Bengoechea, Juan Antonio. 1968 "Anotaciones sobre las empresas públicas." Revista de Derecho Español y Americano (Madrid), No. 19, pp. 135-143. /Evaluation /Law

4065. Sagnardoy Bengoechea, Juan Antonio. 1967 "La cogestión en las empresas públicas." Diecisiete lecciones sobre participación de los trabajadores en la empresa. Madrid. pp.

211-239. /Spain /Management /Worker management participation

4066. Sahni, B. 1972 "A Public Sector Holding Company: The Swedish Experience." Annals of Public and Cooperative Economy V. 43, pp. 161-168. /Sweden /Nationalization /Holding company /330.5 An73

4067. Saias, Maurice, and Michel Montebello. 1979 "Quand les usagers deviennent des clients." Revue Française de Gestion (Paris), No. 20, pp. 77-81. /France /Consumer producer conflict

4068. Said-Amer, Tayeb. 1978 "L'Industrialization en Algérie: L'entreprise Algérienne dans le développement." Paris Anthropos. /Algeria /Industrialization /Economic development

4069. Saint-Geours, J. 1953 L'Etat et les entreprises publiques. Paris: Droit Social. /France /Government authority

4070. Salama, A. A. 1962 A Study About the Participation of Workers in Management of Public Enterprises in UAR with a Comparison with England, France and Germany. Cairo: Institute of National Planning. /United Kingdom /Germany, Federal Rep. of /France /Worker management participation /Egypt

4071. Salama, A. A. 1962 Public Enterprises. Cairo: Institute of National Planning. /Egypt

4072. Salazar, Melito. 1981 "Integrated Report of the Regional Workshop on the Evaluation of Training Packages for Public Enterprise Managers, Bangkok, August 10-14, 1981." Ljubljana: ICPE. /Evaluation /Training

4073. Salgado, I. P. 1969 "Capacitación del personal superior de las empresas públicas." Santiago, Chile: UNECLA Meeting of Experts on Administration of Public Enterprises in Latin America and Caribbean. /Personnel management

4074. Salim, P. B. A. 1949 "Irrigation and Power Development in Pakistan." Pakistan Economic Journal V. 1, pp. 33-39. /Pakistan /Irrigation systems /Electrical utility industry

4075. Salinas de Gortari, Carlos. 1978 "Algunas consideraciones respecto a la importancia de la política de empresas públicas." Paper presented at the fourth Latin American Association of Public Administrators, Mexico City, 6-11 November. /Planning process /OPSS

4076. Salisheva, Nadezda-Georgievna. 1969 "La autonomía de las empresas públicas ante la planificación centralizada." Perspectivas del derecho público en la segunda mitad del siglo XX. Madrid. /Spain /Planning process

4077. Salmonson, Roland F., ed. 1971 "Public Utility Accounting: Models, Mergers, and Information Systems." MSU Public Utilities Papers. East Lansing, Mich.: Institute of Public Utilities, Graduate School of Business Administration, Michigan State University. /Public utility industry

/Accounting / HF 5686 P93 P8

4078. Salter, Sir Arthur. 1950 "The Crux of Nationalization." Political Quarterly (London), V. 21, No. 2, pp. 209-217. /Nationalization / 320.5 P76p

4079. Salwa, Z. 1967 "La participation des travailleurs à la gestion des entreprises en Pologne." Revue de Droit Contemporain (Brussels), V. 14, No. 1, pp. 131-141. /Poland /Worker management participation

4080. Samonte, A. G. 1962 "The Sale or Disposal of Philippine Government Corporations." Philippine Journal of Public Administration pp. 211-214. /Philippines /Privatization

4081. Samonte, A. G. 1967 "The Role of Public Enterprise in the Philippines' National Development." Revue Internationale des Sciences Administratives pp. 139-144. /Philippines /Economic development

4082. Samonte, A. G. 1976 "Problems and Pitfalls in the Coordination of Public Enterprise." In A. S. H. K. Sadique, ed(s). Public Enterprise in Asia: Studies on Coordination and Control. Kuala Lumpur: Asian Centre for Development Administration. pp. 103-124. /Asia /Control process /HD 4276 P8

4083. Samukawa, T. 1967 "The Public Sector in Financial Flow Statement: Japan's Case." Review of Income and Wealth V. 13. /Japan /Public financing

4084. Sanchez Albavera, Fernando, and J. Esteves Ostolaza. 1978 "Cooperation between State Trading Organizations in Latin America." Geneva: UNCTAD. /State trading organizations /Latin America /OPSS

4085. Sanchez Albavera, Fernando. 1983 "Perú: Política de desarrollo y empresas públicas." Paper presented at the ECLA seminar "State Control and Planning of Public Enterprises, Brasília, 15-17 June. Brasília: UNECLA. /Peru /Goal setting /Planning process /Control process /OPSS

4086. Sanchez Calero, Fernando. 1970 "Manifestaciones del empresario público de seguros." La Empresa Pública. Zaragoza, Spain: Publicaciones del Real Colegio de España en Bolonia. pp. 1015-1048. /Spain /Insurance industry

4087. Sandesara, J. C. 1975 "Joint Sector: Alternatives and Implications." In R. C. Dutt and Raj K. Nigam, ed(s). Towards Commanding Heights. New Delhi: Vivek Joshi. pp. 386-401. /India /Mixed enterprises /HD 4293 T68 PCL

4088. Sandoval, Francisco. 1975 "La administración pública descentralizada en Costa Rica." Rio de Janeiro: FGV, Area de Administración de Empresas Públicas. /Costa Rica /Public administration /Decentralized authority /Directory /OPSS

4089. Sanga, Raymond K. 1979 "Management and Training in Public Enterprises: Country Report of Tanzania." Paper presented at the International Seminar on Management and Training in Public Enterprises in Developing Countries, Ljubljana, Yugoslavia, 1-13 October. Ljubljana: ICPE. /Tanzania /Training /Management

4090. Sankin, D. 1964 La planificación de la actividad económico-productiva de las empresas industriales. Havana, Cuba: Publicaciones Económicas. /Cuba /Industrial sector /Planning process

4091. Sanmuganathan, M. 1976 "Public Corporations in Sri Lanka." Law and Public Enterprise in Asia. New York: Praeger for the International Legal Center. pp. 380-390. /Sri Lanka /Control process /Legislature /HD 4283 L32

4092. Sant, Alfred. 1978 "Structure and Financing of Maltese Public Enterprises." Paper presented at the Interregional Workshop on Financing of Public Enterprises in Developing Countries, Ljubljana, Yugoslavia, 22-26 May. Ljubljana: ICPE. /Malta /Financing

4093. Santaniello, Giuseppe. 1965 "Profili giuridici dell´impresa pubblica." RDPN No. 1, pp. 1-34. /Italy /Law

4094. Santhanam, K. 1958 "Management of Public Enterprises. AICC." Economic Review (Helsinki), V. 9, No. 21. /Finland /Management

4095. Santoro, Francesco. 1968 "La gestione econnomico-finanziaria delle ferrovie dello state nel quadro generale della polítíco dei trasporti." Impressa Publica (Rome), pp. 3-16. /Italy /Management /Financing /Transportation industry /Policy analysis / Railway industry

4096. Santos, Edison de Souza Leao. 1982 Banco do Nordeste: Uma experimentação de fomento a la empresa privada. Fortaleza, Brazil: Banco de Nordeste, XII Reunión de la Asamblea General de la Asociación Latinoamericana de Instituciones Financieras de Desarrollo (ALIDE). /Brazil /Banking agency /Private enterprises /Financing /OPSS

4097. Santos, Rui Cezar dos. 1977 "State Enterprises and Peripheral Capitalism: The Case of Brazil." /Brazil /Mixed enterprises

4098. Santos, Theophilo de Azeredo. 1964 As sociedades de economia mista no direito brasileiro; doutrina, jurisprudencia, legisição. Rio de Janeiro: Forense. /Brazil /Mixed enterprises /Law / HD 4092 S3 LAC

4099. Sanyal, A. 1980 "Maintenance Management in Rashtriya Chemicals & Fertilizers Ltd." Lok Udyog (New Delhi), V. 14, No. 7, pp. 11-20. /India /Management /Chemical industry /Case studies /354.54 L836 PCL

4100. Sanz Hurtado, Emílio. 1969 Economía y política de petróleo. Madrid: Guardiana de Publicaciones S. A. /Spain /Economic development /Oil industry /Policy analysis

4101. Sapru, Radhakrishnan. 1979 "Public Enterprise - Improving its Performance for Socio-Economic Development." Lok Udyog (New Delhi), V. 13, No. 9, pp. 11-18. /Economic development /Efficacy /354.54 L836 PCL

4102. Sarabhai, V. 1969 Control and Management of Public Sector Undertakings. Hyderabad, India: Administration Staff College of India. /India /Control process /Management

4103. Sarabhai, V. 1970 "Control and Management of Public Sector Enterprises." (Part 1) Lok Udyog (New Delhi), V. 4, No. 9, pp. 905-914. /India /Control process /Management /354.54 L836 PCL

4104. Sarabhai, V. 1970 "Control and Management of Public Enterprises." (Part 2) Lok Udyog (New Delhi), V. 4, No. 9, pp. 1033-1040. /India /Control process /Management /354.54 L836 PCL

4105. Saraceno, Pasquale. 1961 Public Enterprises in Turkey. Paris: OEEC. /Turkey

4106. Saraceno, Pasquale. 1962 "Public Enterprise in the Market Economy." In A. Winsemius and J. A. Pincus, ed(s). Methods of Industrial Development. Paris: OECD. /Market economy

4107. Saraceno, Pasquale. 1963 "Planning in Public Undertakings." Annals of Collective Economy V. 34, No. 2-3, pp. 169-181. /Planning process / 330.5 An73

4108. Saraceno, Pasquale. 1980 El sistema de las empresas con participación del estado en Italia. Rome: IFAP, Centro IRI per lo Studio Delle Funzioni Direttive. /Italy /Management /Autonomy /Goal setting /Holding company /OPSS /Translation of "The Italian System of State Held Enterprises," Journal of International Law and Economics Vol. 2, No. 3(1977).

4109. Saraceno, Pasquale. 1981 "Gli interventi del primo iri: Dallo smobilizzo delle grandi banche alla proposta de legge bancaria (1933-1936)." Banca, Borsa, Titoli di Credito No. 3. /Italy /Central banks /Economic history /Law /Holding company

4110. Saradhi, S. P. Vijaya, and K. Rajeshwar Rao. 1980 "Cash Management in a Multi-Division Enterprise - A Case Study." Lok Udyog (New Delhi), V. 14, No. 7, pp. 35-38. /India /Financial management /Case studies /354.54 L836 PCL

4111. Saradhi, S. P. Vijaya. 1981 "The Planning Process in Public Sector Enterprises." Lok Udyog (New Delhi), V. 15, No. 3, pp. 11-16. /India /Planning process /354.54 L836 PCL

4112. Saraiya, R. G. 1956 "Administration of Nationalized Undertakings." Indian Journal of Public Administration (New Delhi), V. 2, No. 2, pp. 111-120. /India /Management /Control process / JA 26 I55 Pub Aff

4113. Saran, T. K. 1979 "Scheduling and Monitoring of Projects Under Construction." Lok Udyog (New Delhi), V. 13, No. 7, pp. 11-14. /Project management /354.54 L836 PCL

4114. Saran, T. K. 1980 "Management of Cost and Time in Public Sector Project Construction." Lok Udyog (New Delhi), V. 14, No. 2, pp. 61-64. /India /Project management /Construction industry /Costs /354.54 L836 PCL

4115. Sarathi, Parth. 1983 "Effectiveness of Management Services in Public Sector Enterprises - Some Barriers." Lok Udyog (New Delhi), V. 16, No. 12, pp. 39-46. /India /Management /Information system /354.54 L836 PCL

4116. Saravia, Enrique J. 1974 "Argentina: Corporación de Empresas Nacionales, legislación." Derecho de la Integración V. 1, No. 15, pp. 285-299. /Argentina /Law /Control process /OPSS

4117. Saravia, Enrique J. 1976 Aspectos generales sobre el comportamiento de las empresas públicas brasileñas y su acción internacional. Rio de Janeiro: FGV-EIAP. /Brazil /International trade /State trading organizations /HD 4093 S27 LAC

4118. Saravia, Enrique J. 1977 "Las empresas públicas binacionales de energía eléctrica en América Latina. Aspectos jurídicos y administrativos." Derecho de la Integración (Buenos Aires), V. 10, No. 25/2, pp. 39-52. /Latin America /Electrical utility industry /Administrative management /Multinational corporations /Law

4119. Saravia, Enrique J. 1977 "El régimen legal de las empresas públicas en el Brasil y su acción internacional." In BID-INTAL, ed(s). El régimen legal de las empresas públicas latinoamericanas y su acción internacional. Buenos Aires. /Brazil /Multinational corporations /Law /HD 4010.5 I524 LAC

4120. Saravia, Enrique J. 1977 "Aspectos gerais das empresas públicas brasileiras e sua açao internacional." Revista de Administração Pública (Rio de Janeiro), V. 11, No. 1. /Brazil /Law /Multinational corporations

4121. Saravia, Enrique J. 1979 "Regimen jurídico de las empresas gubernamentales brasileñas." Paper presented at the International Seminar on Regulation of the Public Enterprise, Mexico City. /Brazil /Control process /Law /OPSS

4122. Saravia, Enrique J. 1981 "Management Development in Public Enterprises." Paper presented at the Interregional Seminar on Training Management in Public Enterprises in Developing Countries, Ljubljana, Yugoslavia, 19-28 October. Ljubljana: ICPE. /Training /Management

4123. Sardjono. 1976 "Coordination of Public Enterprises: Country Study for Indonesia." In A. S. H. K. Sadique, ed(s). Public Enterprise in Asia: Studies on Coordination and Control. Kuala Lumpur: Asian Centre for Development Administration. pp. 277-306. /Indonesia /Control Process / HD 4276 P8

4124. Sarkar, J. B. 1982 "Depreciation and Working Capital Financing in Central Government Companies - An Overview."

Lok Udyog (New Delhi), V. 15, No. 11, pp. 17-22. /India /Financing /Working capital /354.54 L836 PCL

4125. Sarkozy, Tamás. 1977 "The Legal Status of State Enterprises in Socialist Countries, with special Reference to Hungary." In Yash Ghai, ed(s). Law in the Politicl Economy of Public Enterprise: African Perspectives. Uppsala: Scandinavian Institute of African Studies. New York: International Legal Centre. pp. 306-323. /Hungary /Law / Africa 76 L41 Law

4126. Sarma K., Rama Krishna. 1981 "Regional Development and the Role of Public Sector: The Indian Experience." Paper presented at the Expert Group Meeting on the Role of Public Enterprises in Regional Development in Developing Countries, Ljubljana, Yugoslavia, 7-11 Dec. Ljubljana: ICPE. /India /Regional development

4127. Sarma, K. S. 1980 "R&D in the Fertilizer Industry." Lok Udyog (New Delhi), V. 14, No. 9, pp. 7-10. /India /Fertilizer industry /Case studies /Research and development /354.54 L836 PCL

4128. Sarraute, R. and P. Tager. 1952 "Hier et aujourd'hui: Les effets en France des nationalisations étrangères." Journal de Droit pp. 1138-1191. /France /Nationalization

4129. Sartori, R. 1957 Le partecipazioni economiche dello stato. Rome: Universale Studium. /Italy / 338.945 Sa77p

4130. Sasaki, Hiroshi. 1971 "Recent Developments in American Public Utility Economics." Kokumin-Keizai-Zasshi V. 124, No. 2. /United States of America /Public utility industry

4131. Sasaki, Hiroshi. 1974 "Local Public Enterprise." Kokumin-Keizai-Zasshi V. 130, No. 1. /Japan

4132. Sasaki, Hiroshi. 1976 "Behavior of the Public Utility Firm under Regulatory Constraint." Kokumin-Keizai-Zasshi V. 133, No. 1. /Japan /Public utility industry /Public utility regulation policy

4133. Sastri, J. V. S. R. 1954 "The Managers of Nationalized Industries." Indian Journal of Economics V. 35, pp. 99-106. /India /Management / 330.5 In2

4134. Sastri, J. V. S. R. 1955 "The Industrial Development Corporation: A Pioneering Enterprise." Indian Journal of Economics V. 36, pp. 101-109. /Development corporation /Industrial sector / 330.5 In2

4135. Sastri, V. V. 1980 "Research and Training in State Petroleum Enterprises." State Petroleum Enterprises in Developing Countries. New York: Pergamon Press. pp. 123-140. /Oil industry /Research and development /Training

4136. Satch, Khchiro. 1970 Utilización de técnicas modernas de gestión administrativa de los ministerios, empresas públicas y sector privado del Japon. EAS/PA/MMTS/10 Washington. /Japan /Private sector /Administrative management

4137. Satyamurthi, Y. 1972 "Image of Public Sector." Lok Udyog (New Delhi), V. 6, No. 2, pp. 17-22. /India /Public relations /354.54 L836 PCL

4138. Sau, R. K. 1963 "Pricing Policy in Public Enterprises in the Context of Development Planning." Indian Journal of Economics V. 44, pp. 81-94. /Price policy /Planning process /330.5 In5

4139. Saulniers, Alfred. 1980 State Trading Organizations: A Bias Decision Model and Applications. Austin, Tex.: OPSS Technical Papers Series, No. 28. /Peru /State trading organizations /OPSS

4140. Saulniers, Alfred. 1980 "ENCI: Peru´s Bandied Monopolist." Journal of Inter-American Studies and World Affairs V. 22, No. 4, pp. 441-462. /Peru /Case studies /State trading organizations / G980.605 J826 LAC

4141. Saulniers, Alfred. 1980 "Public Enterprises in Latin America: An Annotated Bibliography." Journal of Inter-American Studies and World Affairs V. 22, No. 4, pp. 463-470. /Latin America /Bibliography / G980.605 J826 LAC

4142. Saulniers, Alfred. 1980 "Public Enterprises in Latin America: An Overview." Paper presented at the conference: "Preparing the University Community for International Development." /Latin America /Economic analysis /OPSS

4143. Saulniers, Alfred. 1980 "State Trading Organizations: A Bias Decision Model and Applications." Paper presented at the Second BAPEG Conference: Public Enterprise in Mixed Economy LDCs, Boston, Massachusetts, April. /OPSS

4144. Saulniers, Alfred. 1981 "State Trading Organizations: A Bias Decision Model and Applications." World Development V. 9, No. 7, pp. 679-694. /Peru /State trading organizations / qHC 4 W66 PCL

4145. Saulniers, Alfred. 1981 "Public Enterprises." Discovery V. 5, No. 4, pp. 20-24. /Mexico /OPSS

4146. Saulniers, Alfred. 1982 "Shifting Strategies and Implementation: Public Enterprises in Peru, 1968-1980." Paper presented at the 10th National Meeting of the Latin American Studies Association, Washington, D.C., 4-6 March. /Peru /Economic analysis /Planning process /OPSS

4147. Saulniers, Alfred. 1983 "Public Enterprises in Latin America: The New Look?" Paper presented a the ECLA Seminar, State Control and Planning of Public Enterprises, Brasília, 15-17 June. /Economic analysis /Mixed economy /Comparative analysis /OPSS

4148. Saunders, Robert J., and Jeremy J. Warford. 1976 Village Water Supply Economies and Policy in the Developing World. Baltimore and London: The Johns Hopkins University Press. /Developing nations /Water resources development /Policy analysis

4149. Sauriol, P. 1962 The Nationalization of Electric Power. Montreal: Harvest House. /Canada /Electrical utility industry /Nationalization / 380.16 Sa87nTb

4150. Sauvel, J. 1949 Les administrateurs représentants de l'Etat dans les conseils d'administration des sociétés d'économie mixte. Paris. /France /Mixed enterprises /Management

4151. Savas, E. S. 1977 The Organization and Efficiency of Solid Waste Collection. Lexington, Mass.: D.C. Heath and Company, Lexington Books. /Garbage collection /United States of America / Private enterprises /Comparative analysis

4152. Savas, E. S. 1977 "Policy Analysis for Local Government: Public vs. Private Refuse Collection." Policy Analysis V. 3, No. 1, pp. 49-74. /United States of America /Garbage collection / Private enterprises /Comparative analysis

4153. Savas, E. S. 1980 "Comparative Costs of Public and Private Enterprise in a Municipal Service." In William J. Baumol, ed(s). Public and Private Enterprise in a Mixed Economy. New York: St. Martin's Press. pp. 253-264. /Garbage collection /United States of America / Private enterprises /Comparative analysis / /HD 3842 P87 PCL

4154. Savic, V. 1963 "The Public Sector of the Economy in Some Countries of South and South-West Asia." Medunarodni Problemi V. 15, No. 2, pp. 85-109. /South Asia

4155. Sawyerr, Akilagpa. 1977 "Multinational Corporations and Development: The Case of the Rubber Industry in Ghana." In Yash Ghai, ed(s). Law in the Political Economy of Public Enterprise: African Perspectives. Uppsala: Scandinavian Institute of African Studies. New York: International Legal Centre. pp. 267-294. /Mixed enterprises /Multinational corporations /Rubber industry /Ghana /Africa /Case studies /Africa 76 L41 Law

4156. Saxena, S. K. 1955 Nationalization and Industrial Conflict: Example of British Coal-Mining. The Hague: M. Nijhoff. /Nationalization /Industrial relations /Coal mining industry /United Kingdom

4157. Sayagues Laso, Enrique. 1956 "Les établissements publiques économiques en Uruguay." Revue Internationale de Sciences Administratives No. 1. /Uruguay

4158. Sayers, Richard S. 1976 The Bank of England: 1891-1944. Cambridge: Cambridge University Press. /United Kingdom /Financial institutions / HG 2994 S29 1976

4159. Saynor, P. J. 1950 Accountability to Parliament. London: Acton Society Trust. /United Kingdom /Parliament /Accountability

4160. Sayre Steeves, J. 1971 The Role of the Kenya Tea Development Authority in the Introduction of Tea on a Smallholder Basis in Kenya. Arusha, Tanzania: Conference on Comparative Administration. /Kenya /East Africa /Agricultural development /Tea industry

4161. Scalabrini Ortiz, Raúl. 1964 Historia de los ferrocarriles argentinos con un apéndice de la Ley Mitre. Buenos Aires: Plus Ultra. /Argentina /Railway industry /Economic history /Law / G385.982 Sca42h

4162. Scammell, E. H. 1952 "Nationalization in Legal Perspective." Current Legal Problems (London), /Nationalization /Law

4163. "La scelta dei prezzi delle imprese pubblique in relazione el costo di produzione." 1962 Giornale delgi Economisti e Anali di Economia (Padua). pp. 96-147. /Italy /Price policy /Costs

4164. Schachter, G. 1967 "Regional Development in the Italian Dual Economy." Economic Development and Cultural Change V. 15, No. 4, pp. 398-407. /Italy /Private sector /Regional development / 330.5 Ec66

4165. Schachter, G., and Bruce Cohen. 1973 "The Efficiency of State Economic Enterprises in Forging Development in Turkey." Annals of Public and Cooperative Economy V. 44, pp. 165-179. /Turkey /Planning process / 330.5 An73

4166. Schatz, Sayre P. 1964 Development Bank Lending in Nigeria, the Federal Loans Board. Ibadan: Nigerian Institute of Economic and Social Research, Oxford University Press. /Nigeria /Financial institutions /332.31 Sch18d

4167. Schatz, Sayre P. 1968 "Government Lending to African Businessmen: Inept Incentives." Journal of Modern African Studies (London), V. 6, No. 4, pp. 519-529. /Africa /Commercial sector /Credit policy / 960.5 J828

4168. Schatz, Sayre P. 1970 Economics, Politics and Administration in Government Lending: The Regional Loans Boards of Nigeria. Ibadan, Nigeria: Oxford University Press. /Nigeria /Financial institutions / 343.669074 Schl 8e

4169. Schenker, A., and L. D. Musolf. 1964 Statutory Accountability to California Transportation, Authorities and Districts. Davis, Calif.: Institute of Governmental Affairs. /United States of America /Transportation industry /Accountability / Government authority

4170. Schenker, E. 1963 "Nationalization and Denationalization of Motor Carriers in Great Britain." Land Economics V. 39, No. 3, pp. 219-230. /United Kingdom /Motor manufacturing industry /Nationalization /Privatization /305 J824 PCL

4171. Scheving, Dieter H. n.p. "Rapport préliminaire sur le régime des entreprises publiques dans le droit de la République Fédérale d'Allemagne." /Germany, Federal Rep. of /Law /OPSS

4172. Schiesari, Nélson. 1970 "Fundações de direito público." Administração Paulista (São Paulo), No. 19, pp. 105-110. /Brazil /Public administration

4173. Schindeler, Fred. 1980 "Make or Buy: Internal or External Consultants for Small Enterprises?" Paper presented at the Regional Workshop on Development of Training Methodologies for Internal Consultants in African Public Enterprises, Addis Ababa, Ethiopia, 1-6 December. Ljubljana: ICPE /Consultant services

4174. Schippers, H. L. 1979 "The Developmental Role of Indian Public Enterprises in the Context of the International Economic Order." Ph.D. dissertation, State University, Groningen. /India

4175. Schloss, Henry H. 1970 "Productivity in Public Enterprise." Annals of Public and Cooperative Economy V. 41, pp. 317-323. /Productivity / 330.5 An73

4176. Schloss, Henry H. 1977 "Public Enterprise as a Form of Business Enterprise: Role, Purpose and Performance." Annals of Public and Cooperative Economy V. 40, No. 3, pp. 299-307. /Goal setting /Economic analysis /Financial performance /Economic efficiency /330.5 An73

4177. Schloss, Henry H. 1978 "The Rationale for and the Effectiveness of Public Enterprise." Lok Udyog (New Delhi), V. 12, No. 7, pp. 3-6. /Goal setting /Economic analysis /Economic efficiency /Taxonomy /354.54 L836 PCL

4178. Schmidt, G. 1955 "Economics of T.V.A." Indian Journal of Economics V. 36, pp. 231-233. /United States of America /River valley development projects / 330.5 In2

4179. Schmidt, G. 1956 "Government Corporations in the U.S.A." Indian Journal of Economics V. 37, pp. 197-204. /United States of America / 330.5 In2

4180. Schmitthoff, Clive M. 1951 "The Nationalization of Basic Industries in Great Britain." Law and Contemporary Problems V. 16, No. 4, pp. 557-575. /United Kingdom /Nationalization /340.5 L414

4181. Schneider, Hans K., and Walter Schulz. 1980 "Market Structure and Market Organization in the Electricity and Gas Public Utility Sector of the FRG." In William J. Baumol, ed(s). Public and Private Enterprise in a Mixed Economy. New York: St. Martin's Press. pp. 71-90. /Germany, Federal Rep. of /Electrical utility industry /Gas utility industry /HD 3842 P87 PCL

4182. Schnettler, Albert. 1956 Establecimientos públicos. Essen, Germany. /Germany, Federal Rep. of

4183. Schoenfeld, Benjamin N. 1970 "The Politics and Administration of Hydro-electric Power Development in India." Studies in Comparative Federalism Reprints. Philadelphia, Pa.: Temple University Center for the Study of Federalism. No. 26. /India /Hydroelectric power

4184. Schonberg, H. 1970 "On the Development of Semi-State Enterprises in the German Democratic Republic."

Wissenschaftliche Beitrage (Berlin), No. 1, pp. 54-66. /Germany, Democratic Rep. of /Mixed enterprises

4185. Schregle, Johannes. 1970 "Workers Participation in Management." Industrial Relations V. 9, No. 2, pp. 117-122. /Worker management participation

4186. Schregle, Johannes. 1974 "Labour Relations in the Public Sector." International Labour Review (Geneva), V. 110, No. 5, pp. 381-404. /Labor relations /Collective bargaining /HD4811 I65 Pub Aff

4187. Schrenk, Martin. 1981 "Managerial Structures and Practices in Public Manufacturing Enterprises: A Yugoslav Case Study." Washington, D.C.: World Bank. /Yugoslavia /Management /Manufacturing industry /Case studies /OPSS

4188. Schuchman, A. 1957 "Economic Rationale of Codetermination." Industry and Labor Relations Review V. 10, pp. 270-283. /Labor relations

4189. Schwartz, D. S. 1947 "Investigations of the Columbia Basin Project and Their Procedural Significance." Land Economics V. 23, pp. 83-86. /United States of America /River valley development projects /305 J824 PCL

4190. Scimone, G. S. 1963 "The Italian State in Big Business." Federation of British Industries Review pp. 47-48. /Italy

4191. Scott, M. F. 1950 "Investment Policy in a Nationalized Industry." Review of Economic Studies V. 17, No. 3, pp. 179-188. /Investment / 330.5 R326

4192. Scully, M. 1954 "Parliamentary Control of Public Corporations in Eire." Public Administration (London), V. 32, No. 4, pp. 455-462. /Ireland /Control process /Parliament / 320.5 J826

4193. Scurrah, Martin, and Bruno Podestá. 1984 "The Experience of Worker Self-Management in Peru and Chile." Grassroots Development V. 8, No. 1, pp. 12-23. /Chile /Peru /Worker self management

4194. Sefer, B. 1968 "Income Distribution in Yugoslavia." International Labour Review (Geneva), V. 97, No. 47, pp. 371-389. /Yugoslavia /Income distribution /331.05 In81 PCL /HD 4811 I65 Pub Aff

4195. Sehgal, K. L. 1981 "Productivity Measurement System and Practices." Lok Udyog (New Delhi), V. 15, No. 3, pp. 5-10. /India /Productivity /Methodology /354.54 L836 PCL

4196. Seidel, G. 1960 "The Nationalized Industry of Austria." Wirtschaftsaissenschaft (Berlin), V. 8, No. 6, pp. 904-918. /Austria /Industrial sector

4197. Seidman, Harold. 1952 "The Theory of the Autonomous Government Corporation, A Critical Appraisal." Public Administration Review V. 12, No. 2, pp. 89-96.

/Decentralized authority /United States of America /JK1 P85

4198. Seidman, Harold. 1954 "The Government Corporation: Organization and Controls." Public Administration Review V. 14, No. 3, pp. 183-192. /Management /Control process /Structural characteristics /JK 1 P85

4199. Seidman, Harold. 1955 "A Theory of Public Industrial Enterprise." In A. H. Hanson, ed(s). Public Enterprise. Brussels: IIAS. pp. 41-48. /Industrial sector /HD3850 H28 Law

4200. Seidman, Harold. 1955 "The Government Corporation, its Place in the Federal Structure." In A. H. Hanson, ed(s). Public Enterprise. Brussels: IIAS. /United States of America /Federal government /HD 3850 H28 Law

4201. Seidman, Harold. 1958 "The Control of Public Enterprise." Paper presented at the Congress of the International Political Science Association, Rome, September. /Control process

4202. Seidman, Harold. 1959 "The Government Corporations in the United States." Public Administration pp. 106-110. /United States of America

4203. Seidman, Harold. 1964 "Public Enterprise in Turkey." Enterprise in the Emerging Socialist Societies of the Near East: Princeton University Conference. Princeton, N. J.: Princeton University Press. /Turkey

4204. Seidman, Harold. 1966 "Organizational Relationships and Control of Public Enterprises." Paper presented at the U.N. Seminar on Organization and Administration of Public Enterprises, Geneva. /Public administration /Control process

4205. Seidman, Harold. 1970 Politics, Position and Power: The Dynamics of Federal Organization. New York: Oxford University Press. /Federal government /Political analysis /JK 421 S44

4206. Seidman, Harold. 1975 "Government-Sponsored Enterprise in the United States." In Bruce L. R. Lee, ed(s). The New Political Economy: The Public Use of the Private Sector. London: The Macmillan Press Ltd. /United States of America /Private sector /Planning process / Political economy

4207. Seidman, Harold. 1977 "Report on the International Association of Schools and Institutes of Administration, Working Group on Public Enterprise." /Public administration /Training

4208. Self, H. 1947 "The Public Accountability of the Corporation." Public Administration (Sydney, Australia), /Australia /Accountability

4209. Self, H. 1949 "Organization of the British Electricity Authority." Public Administration (Sydney, Australia), pp. 10-12. /United Kingdom /Electrical utility industry /Public authority / Organization behavior

4210. Self, H., and Elizabeth M. Watson. 1952 Electricity Supply in Great Britain. London: Allen & Unwin. /United Kingdom /Electrical utility industry

4211. Selznick, Philip. 1949 T.V.A. and the Grass Roots. Berkeley and Los Angeles: University of California Press. /United States of America /River valley development projects /306 C127c V.3

4212. Semenza, G. 1961 "On the Proposed Bianchi Bill for the Socialization of the Electric Power Industry." Rivista di Politica Economica (Rome), V. 51, No. 1, pp. 91-107. /Italy /Law /Nationalization /Electrical utility industry

4213. Sempe Minvielle, Carlos. 1981 "The Role of Public Enterprise in Mexico´s Regional Development." Paper presented at the Expert Group Meeting on the Role of Public Enterprises in Regional Development, Ljubljana, Yugoslavia, 7-11 December. Ljubljana: ICPE. /Mexico /Regional development

4214. Sen, S. C. 1971 The New Frontiers of Company Law. Calcutta: Eastern Law House. /India /Law

4215. Senna, Homero, and Clovis Zobaran Monteiro. 1970 Fendações no direito na administração. Rio de Janeiro: FGV. /Brazil /Public administration /Law / JA 40 B5 no.15 LAC

4216. Senna, Homero, and Clóvis Zobaran Monteiro. 1970 "Empresas públicas." Fundações no direito na administração. Rio de Janeiro: FGV/SPB. No. 15, pp. 37-48. /Brazil /JA 40 B5 no.15 LAC

4217. Senna, Homero, and Clóvis Zobaran Monteiro. 1970 "Sociedades de economia mista." Fundaçọes no direito na administração. Rio de Janeiro: FGV. pp. 23-36. /Brazil /Mixed enterprises /Administrative management / JA 40 B5 no.15 LAC

4218. Serour, Mohamed Abdel Moneim. 1980 "Main Features of Pricing Policies in Public Enterprises in Egypt." Paper presented at the International Workshop on Pricing Polocies in Public Enterprises, Ljubljana, Yugoslavia, 26-30 May. Ljubljana: ICPE. /Egypt /Price policy

4219. Serrano Migallon, Fernando. 1978 "Los objetivos de comercialización de las empresas públicas y de las empresas privadas." Paper presented at the fourth general assembly of the Latin American Association of public administration, Mexico City, 6-11 Nov. /Air transportation industry /Marketing /Planning process /Comparative analysis /Private enterprises /OPSS

4220. Seshadri, T. R. 1980 "Construction of Dry Dock and Wet Basin at Hindustan Shipyard Ltd." Lok Udyog (New Delhi), V. 14, No. 2, pp. 51-60. /India /Construction industry /Case studies /Shipping industry /354.54 L836 PCL

4221. Sestakova, M. 1967 "The Firm in the Czechoslovak Economy." Journal of Industrial Economics V. 26, No. 1, pp. 23-33. /Czechoslovakia / 330.5 J81 PCL

4222. Setai, Bethuel. 1979 "Management and Training in Public Enterprises: Country Report of Namibia." Paper presented at the International Seminar on Management and Training in Public Enterprises in Developing Countries, Ljubljana, Yugoslavia, 1-13 October. Ljubljana: ICPE. /Namibia /Training /Management

4223. Seth, K. L. 1967 "The Technique of Planning in Pakistan, Japan and India--A Comparison." Asian Economic Review V. 9, No. 3, pp. 292-301. /Pakistan /Japan /India /Planning process /Comparative analysis

4224. Seth, R. P. 1969 "The Pricing Policies of the Nationalized Industries in Britain." Canadian Public Administration (Ontario), V. 12, No. 2, pp. 261-280. /United Kingdom /Industrial sector / 350.5 C16

4225. Sethi, Krishan C. 1977 "Public Enterprises and Government of India." Bulletin of ICPE V. 3, No. 2, pp. 4-8. /India /Government authority

4226. Sethi, Krishan C., and Jacob Mankidy, eds. 1983 Workers' Self-Management and Participation: Comparative Analysis and Recent Developments. Ljubljana: ICPE /Worker self management /Case studies

4227. Sethi, Narendra K. 1978 Managerial Dynamics: A Multi-Dimensional View. New Delhi: Sterling. /India /Management

4228. Sethi, S. K. 1973 "House Journals inn Public Enterprises: An Analysis." Lok Udyog (New Delhi), V. 7, No. 9, pp. 21-30. /Public relations /354.54 L836 PCL

4229. Sethuraman, T. V. 1970 Institutional Financing of Economic Development in India. London: UBS Publishers' Distributors. Delhi: Vikas Publications. /India /Economic development /Industrialization /Public financing / HG 188 I4 S48

4230. Sevillano, Martin A. 1966 "Planes, proyectos y expropiación forzosa." Documentación Administrativa (Madrid), No. 103, pp. 55-66. /Spain / Nationalization

4231. Shaffer, H. G. 1964 "The Enterprise Director and the New Economic Model in Czechoslovakia." Journal of Industrial Economics V. 15, pp. 44-53. /Czechoslovakia /Management /Administrative reform / 330.5 J81 PCL

4232. Shah, A. K. 1954 "Cost Accounting and Management in Public Enterprise." Indian Journal of Commerce (Allahabad), V. 7, No. 1, pp. 41-48. /Cost accounting /Management

4233. Shah, Hashmukh S. 1980 "Investment Criteria and Investment Decision-Making Processes in India." Paper presented at the International Workshop on Investment Criteria and Investment

Decision-Making Processes, Ljubljana, Yugoslavia, 20-24 October. Ljubljana: ICPE. /India /Investment

4234. Shah, M 1958 "Role of the Private and Public Sectors in Economic Development." AICC Economic Review (New Delhi), V. 9, No. 21. /Private sector /Economic development

4235. Shamanna, K. 1961 "Price and Profit in Indian Public Enterprises." AICC Economic Review (New Delhi), No. 22. /India /Evaluation

4236. Shamanna, K. 1972 "Changing Technology: Implications for Marketing Process." Lok Udyog (New Delhi), V. 6, No. 7, pp. 41-46. /India /Technology /Marketing /354.54 L836 PCL

4237. Shamsul, Islam. 1975 "Public Corporations in Bangladesh." Dacca, Bangladesh: Local Government Institute. /Bangladesh

4238. Shankaaraiah, A. 1983 Financial Management of Public Enterprises: A Study of Budgeting in State Undertakings of Andhra Pradesh. New Delhi: Seema Publications. /Financial management /Management /India /Andhra Pradesh, India (State) /HD 4295 A5 S5 1983 PCL

4239. Shankar, V. 1975 "The Need for Professionalism in Managing State Enterprises." In R. C. Dutt and Raj K. Nigam, ed(s). Towards Commanding Heights. New Delhi: Vivek Joshi. pp. 190-207. /India /Management /HD 4293 T68 PCL

4240. Shankar, V. 1979 "Public Enterprises & Employee Participation." Lok Udyog (New Delhi), V. 13, No. 5. /India /Worker management participation /354.54 L836 PCL

4241. Shanks, Michael, ed. 1963 The Lessons of Public Enterprise, Fabian Society Study. London: Jonathan Cape. /United Kingdom /335.5 Sh181

4242. Shapiro, S. 1965 A Review of Public Enterprise in Israel. Jerusalem: Ministry of Finance. /Israel

4243. Sharda, H. M., and B. Nimkar. 1977 "Regional Rural Banks: Exploring New Economic Dimensions." Lok Udyog (New Delhi), V. 11, No. 5, pp. 37-40. /India /Rural development /Financial institutions /354.54 L836 PCL

4244. Shariff, Z. 1971 "Social Information and Government-Sponsored Development: A Case Study from West Pakistan." The Annals of American Academy of Political and Social Sciences V. 393, pp. 92-108. /Pakistan /Management /Case studies / 305 An7

4245. Sharkansky, Ira, and Dennis L. Dresang. 1974 "International Assistance: Its Variety, Coordination and Impact among Public Corporations in Kenya and the East African Community." International Organization V. 28, No. 2, pp. 207-232. /Africa /Kenya /East Africa /Foreign aid /Tanzania /Uganda / 341.05 Int86

4246. Sharma, A. K. 1978 "Some Issues in Management Development: The Experience of British Public Enterprise." Lok Udyog (New Delhi), V. 12, No. 1, pp. 13-22. /United Kingdom /Training /354.54 L836 PCL

4247. Sharma, A., and H. Issarani. 1972 "Recruitment of Managerial Personnel to Public Undertakings in India: A Diagnosis of Ideas and Issues." International Review of Administrative Sciences /India /Personnel management / JA 1 A1 I6 PCL

4248. Sharma, Atul, and Kewal Ram. 1982 "Pricing Problems of Public Enterprises." Lok Udyog (New Delhi), V. 16, No. 4, pp. 35-40. /India /Price policy /354.54 L836 PCL

4249. Sharma, B. P. 1977 "A Case Study of Efficiency-cum Propriety Audit in Public Sector Banking." Lok Udyog (New Delhi), V. 11, No. 7, pp. 19-26. /India /Banking system /Accountability /Economic efficiency /354.54 L836 PCL

4250. Sharma, B. P. 1978 "Professionalisation of Management in Public Sector Banking: Management Consultancy Service Vital." Lok Udyog (New Delhi), V. 12, No. 8, pp. 19-24. /India /Consultant services /Banking system /354.54 L836 PCL

4251. Sharma, Baldev R., and S. K. Warrier. 1981 "Organizational Determinants of Employer - Employee Relations in an Indian Factory: Bharat Metals Ltd." Lok Udyog (New Delhi), V. 15, No. 9, pp. 7-18. /India /Labor relations /Metal manufacturing industry /354.54 L836 PCL

4252. Sharma, Bheem Sain. 1968 Financing of Public Enterprises in India Heavy Industry.(Summary of Findings of Ph. D. Dissertation) Jodhpur, India. /India /Industrial sector /Financing

4253. Sharma, C. L. 1979 "Criteria for Evaluation of Financial and Physical Performace of Air India." Lok Udyog (New Delhi), V. 13, No. 8, pp. 31-34. /India /Economic efficiency /Financial performance /Case studies /Air transportation industry /354.54 L836 PCL

4254. Sharma, G. D. 1970 "Public Enterprises in Medieval India." Lok Udyog (New Delhi), V. 4, No. 3, pp. 441-446. /India /Economic history /354.54 L836 PCL

4255. Sharma, G. D. 1975 Working of State Enterprises in Rajasthan. New Delhi: Sterling Publishers. /India /HD 4295 R3 S47

4256. Sharma, H. C. 1970 Nationalization of Banks in India: Retrospect and Prospect. Agra, India: Sahutya Bhawan. /India /Nationalization /Financial institutions / HG 3284 S4842

4257. Sharma, Inderjit. 1979 "Career Satisfaction Among Public Sector Managers - A Survey." Lok Udyog (New Delhi), V. 12, No. 10-1, pp. 25-32. /Management /Organization behavior /India /354.54 L836 PCL

4258. Sharma, Inderjit. 1980 "Career Mobility Among Public Sector Managers." Lok Udyog (New Delhi), V. 13, No. 12, pp. 55-64. /India /Management /354.54 L836 PCL

4259. Sharma, J. P. 1965 "Estimates Committee Reports on Public Enterprises." Indian Journal of Public Administration (New Delhi), V. 11, No. 1, pp. 83-114. /India /Evaluation /JA 26 I55 Pub Aff

4260. Sharma, K. K. 1957 "Price Policy of Public Enterprises." Indian Journal of Commerce (Allahabad), V. 10, No. 4. /India /Price policy

4261. Sharma, S. L. 1958 "Pricing Policy of State Undertakings." Indian Journal of Commerce (Allahabad), V. 11, No. 38. /India /Price policy

4262. Sharma, T. R., and D. S. Chanhan. 1957 "The State Industrial Enterprise in India: Organization and Management." Agra. Univ. J. Res. Letters pp. 35-43. /India /Organization formation /Management

4263. Sharma, Tirth R. 1961 Working of State Enterprises in India. Bombay: Vora. /India / 338.954 Sh23w

4264. Sharp, M. 1938 "Another Victory for TVA." Land Economics V. 14. /United States of America /River valley development projects / 305 J824 PCL

4265. Sharpe, M. E. 1966 "Planning Profit Incentives in the U.S.S.R." The Liberman Discussion: a New Phase of Soviet Economic Thought. White Plains New York. International Arts and Sciences Press. V. 1. /Union of Soviet Socialist Reps. /Incentive systems / Planning process

4266. Sheahan, John B. 1960 "La concurrence d'une entreprise nationalisée et les réalisations de l'industrie automobile française." Bulletin Sédeis Etude (Paris), No. 763. /France /Automobile manufacturing industry /Nationalization

4267. Sheahan, John B. 1976 "Public Enterprise in Developing Countries." In William G. Shepherd et al., ed(s). Public Enterprise: Economic Analysis of Theory and Practice. Lexington, Mass.: D.C. Heath and Company, Lexington Books. pp. 205-233. /Developing nations / HD 3850 P8 PCL

4268. Sheahan, John B. 1976 "Experience with Public Enterprise in France and Italy." In William G. Shepherd et al., ed(s). Public Enterprise: Economic Analysis of Theory and Practice. Lexington, Mass.: D.C. Heath and Company, Lexington Books. pp. 123-184. /France /Italy /HD 3850 P8 PCL

4269. Shenfield, A. A. 1961 "The Public Sector versus the Private Sector in Britain." Modern Age pp. 43-58. /United Kingdom /Mixed enterprises / Comparative analysis

4270. Shepherd, William G. 1964 "Cross-Subsidizing and Allocation in Public Firms." Oxford Economic Papers V. 16, No. 1, pp. 132-160. /United Kingdom /Subsidization policy /Price policy

/330.6 Ox2 n.s. /Abridged version printed in R. Turvey, Public Enterprise. /338.001 T869e PCL /HD 3850 T89 Pub Aff

4271. Shepherd, William G. 1964 "British Nationalized Industry: Performance and Policy." Yale Economic Essays V. 4, No. 1, pp. 183-224. /United Kingdom /Evaluation /Policy analysis /330.5 Y12

4272. Shepherd, William G. 1964 "Public Corporations and Public Action." Political Quarterly (London), pp. 58-68. /United Kingdom / 320.5 P76p

4273. Shepherd, William G. 1965 Economic Performance under Public Ownership: British Fuel and Power. New Haven, Conn.: Yale University Press. /United Kingdom /Evaluation /Energy utility industry / 330.6 y12 v.18

4274. Shepherd, William G. 1966 "Residence Expansion in the British Telephone System." Journal of Industrial Economics V. 14, pp. 263-274. /United Kingdom /Telephone industry /Reprinted in R. Turvey, Public Enterprise. /338.001 T869e PCL /HD 3850 T89 Pub Aff

4275. Shepherd, William G. 1975 The Treatment of Market Power: Antitrust, Regulation, and Public Enterprise. New York: Columbia University Press. /United States of America /Business regulation policy /Market economy /Monopoly /Law /HD 2795 S48

4276. Shepherd, William G., et al. 1976 Public Enterprise: Economic Analysis of Theory and Practice. Lexington, Mass.: D. C. Heath & Co. /Political economy /Evaluation /Economic analysis /Control process /Comparative analysis /HD 3850 P8 /Draft version of the book manuscript in OPSS files.

4277. Shepherd, William G. 1976 "Objectives, Types, Accountability." In William G. Shepherd et al., ed(s). Public Enterprise: Economic Analysis of Theory and Practice. Lexington, Mass.: D.C. Heath and Company, Lexington Books. pp. 33-48. /Goal setting /Taxonomy /Economic analysis /HD 3850 P8 PCL

4278. Shepherd, William G. 1976 "British and United States Experience." In William G. Shepherd et al., ed(s). Public Enterprise: Economic Analysis of Theory and Practice. Lexington, Mass.: D.C. Heath and Company, Lexington Books. pp. 103-122. /United Kingdom /United States of America /HD 3850 P8 PCL

4279. Shepherd, William G. 1976 "Public Enterprise in Financial Sectors." In William G. Shepherd et al., ed(s). Public Enterprise: Economic Analysis of Theory and Practice. Lexington, Mass.: D.C. Heath and Company, Lexington Books. pp. 185-204. /Financial institutions /HD 3850 P8 PCL

4280. Shepherd, William G. 1978 "British and United States Experience." Paper presented at the Interregional Workshop on Financing of Public Enterprises in Developing Countries, Ljubljana, Yugoslavia, 22-26 May. Ljubljana: ICPE. /United

States of America /United Kingdom /Public financing Comparative analysis

4281. Sheppard, Harold L., Bennett Harrison, and William J. Spring. 1972 The Political Economy of Public Service Employment. Lexington, Mass.: D.C. Heath & Co. /United States of America /Employment policy /Public services /Political economy /HD 5724 P57

4282. Sheremetiaev, I. 1969 El capitalismo de Estado en México. Mexico City: Fondo de Cultura Popular. /Mexico

4283. Sherif, Ahmed. 1979 "The Role of Public Sector in Developing Countries: Country Paper of Ethiopia." Paper presented at the Regional Meeting of African Countries on the Role of the Public Sector in Developing Countries. Arusha, Tanazania, 17-21 December. Ljubljana: ICPE. /Ethiopia

4284. Sherif, Fouad. 1957 Economie du secteur publique. Cairo: Dar-Al-Maaref. /Egypt /Economic analysis

4285. Sherif, Fouad. 1972 "Perfectionnement des directeurs des entreprises du secteur publique: quelques leçons tirées de la experience de la République Arabe d´Egypte." Cahiers Africains d´Administration Publique (Tangier, Morroco), No. 8, pp. 19-31. /Egypt /Management / Training

4286. Sherif, Fouad. 1973 Measures for improving performance of public enterprises in developing countries. New York: UN. DESA. /Management /Economic efficiency /OPSS

4287. Sherif, Fouad. 1974 "Planning for Improved Performance of Public Enterprises in Developing Countries, Some Lessons of International Experience: Background of the UNDP." Paper presented at the International Seminar ´74: Planning in Public Enterprises in Developing Countries, Ljubljana, Yugoslavia, 23 Sept.-9 Oct. Ljubljana: ICPE. /Planning process /Developing nations /System performance

4288. Sherif, Sammi. 1980 "Activities and Technical Capabilities of State Petroleum Enterprises." State Petroleum Enterprises in Developing Countries. New York: Pergamon Press. pp. 48-60. /Oil industry /Iraq

4289. Sherman, R. 1970 "The Design of Public Utility Institutions." Land Economics V. 46, No. 1, pp. 51-58. /United States of America /Public utility industry /305 J824

4290. Sherman, Roger. 1980 "Pricing Policies of the U.S. Postal Service." In Bridger M. Mitchell and Paul R. Kleindorfer, ed(s). Regulated Industries and Public Enterprise. Lexington, Ma.: D.C. Heath and Company, Lexington Books. pp. 95-117. /Price policy /United States of America /Postal service /OPSS

4291. Sherrard, H. M., and L. V. Smith. 1961 "Statutory corporation." Public Administration (Sydney, Australia), pp. 246-258. /Australia /Law

4292. Sherwood, Frank P. 1970 "The Problem of the Public Enterprise." In Fred Riggs, ed(s). Frontiers of Development Administration. Durham, N. C.: Duke University Press. pp. 348-372. /Developing nations / JF 60 F7

4293. Shihata, Ibrahim F. I. 1977 "Inter-Arab Equity Joint Ventures." Public Enterprises and Development in the Arab Countries: Legal and Managerial Aspects. New York: Praeger for the International Legal Center for Law in Development. pp. 180-201. /Multinational corporations /HD 4334 P8 Law

4294. Shinde, A. P. 1968 "Relationship Between Cooperatives and Public sector Undertaking in the Supply of Agricultural Inputs." Review of International Cooperation pp. 455-459. /Cooperatives /Agricultural sector /Retail trade

4295. Shirima, P. S. P. 1978 "A Talk on Marketing Planning in Public Enterprises in Developing Countries." Paper presented at the International Workshop on Planning in Public Enterprises in Developing Countries, Ljubljana, Yugoslavia, 20-25 November. Ljubljana: ICPE. /Marketing /Planning process

4296. Shirley, Mary M. 1983 Managing State-Owned Enterprises. World Bank Staff Working Papers. No. 577. Washington, D.C. /Management / HC 59.7 W655 Pub Aff

4297. Shita, M. A. 1963 Managerial and Practical Studies about Public Enterprises and Public Sector Corporation. Cairo. /Egypt /Management

4298. Shonfield, A. 1965 Modern Capitalism, the Changing Balance of Public and Private Power. London: Oxford University Press. /Capitalism /Private sector /Comparative analysis /330.904 Sh75m

4299. Short, J. A. 1949 "An Engineer's Appraisal of the Missouri Basin Development Program." Journal of Farm Economics V. 31, pp. 1030-1034. /United States of America /Public works policy /Economic analysis /River valley development projects

4300. Short, R. P. 1983 The Role of Public Enterprises: An International Statistical Comparison. Washington: IMF. /Evaluation /Comparative analysis /Statistics

4301. Shrinagesh, J. M. 1964 "Organization for Top Management." Indian Journal of Public Administration (New Delhi), V. 10, No. 3. /India /Management /JA 26 I55 Pub Aff

4302. Shrivastava, N. C. 1961 "Management for State Industrial Undertakings." Indian Journal of Public Administration (New Delhi), V. 7, No. 3. /India /Industrial sector /Management /JA 26 I55 Pub Aff

4303. Shulka, M. C. 1959 Administrative Problems of Public Enterprises in India. New Delhi: S. Chand. /India /Public administration /Management

4304. Shwe U, Tin. 1981 "Methods of Evaluation of Training in Public Enterprises on the Level of a Public Enterprise." Paper presented at the Interregional Seminar on Training Management in Public Enterprises in Developing Countries, Ljubljana, Yugoslavia, 19-28 October. Ljubljana: ICPE. /Training /Evaluation

4305. Sicherl, P. 1977 "Proposal for an International Research Project on the Role of the Public Sector in Developing Countries." Paper presented at the Meeting of the International Research Project "The Role of the Public Sector in Developing Countries," 1st, Ljubljana, Yugoslavia, 7-11 December. Ljubljana: ICPE. /Developing nations /Economic research / /Also presented at the International Meeting on the Role of the Public Sector in Developing Countries, Ljubljana, Yugoslavia, 2-7 April, 1979.

4306. Sicherl, P. 1978 "Goals in Public Enterprises in Developing Socio-Economic Systems." Paper presented at the International Workshop on Planning in Public Enterprises in Developing Countries, Ljubljana, Yugoslavia, 20-25 Nov. Ljubljana: ICPE. /Planning process /Developing nations /Goal setting /Also presented at the Workshop on Information System for the Evaluation of Business Efficiency in Public Enterprises in Developing Countries, Ljubljana, 13-18 Nov. 1981.

4307. Sicherl, P. 1979 "Role of the Public Sector in Promoting the Economic and Industrial Development of Developing Countries." Paper presented at the Expert Group Meeting on the Role of the Public Sector in the Industrialization of the Developing Countries. Ljubljana: ICPE /Developing nations /Economic development /Industrialization

4308. Sicherl, P. 1980 "The Role Assigned to Public Industrial Enterprises in Different Development Strategies." Ljubljana: ICPE. /Developing nations /Industrial sector /Economic development / Goal setting

4309. Sicherl, P. 1980 "Studies on the Role of the Public Sector in the Industrialization of the Developing Countries: Summary of Findings." Ljubljana: ICPE. /Developing nations /Industrialization /Industrial sector

4310. Sicherl, P. 1983 The Role of Public Enterprises in National Development. Ljubljana: ICPE /Developing nations /Economic development

4311. Sicherl, P., and Praxy J. Fernandes. 1980 "The Identity and Character of Public Enterprises: A Building Blocks Approach." Paper presented at the Expert Group Meeting on Concept, Definition and Classification of Public Enterprises, Tangier, Morocco, 15-19 December. Ljubljana: ICPE /Taxonomy /OPSS

4312. Sickler, B. J. 1928 "A Theory of Telephone Rates." Land Economics V. 4, pp. 175-188. /Price policy /Telephone industry / 305 J824 PCL

4313. Siddiqui, Anwar H. 1979 Management of Public Enterprises in Pakistan. Lahore, Pakistan: Wajidalis. /Pakistan /Management /HD 4295.5 N37

4314. Sijan, D. 1959 "The Trade Unions Place in Workers' Management." Annals of Collective Economy V. 30, pp. 318-331. /Trade unions /Worker management participation /330.5 An73

4315. Sik, O. 1965 "La gestion économique en Tchecoslovaquie." Temps Modernes (Paris), V. 20, No. 229, pp. 2113-2135. /Czechoslovakia /Management / 054 T249 PCL

4316. Silberston, Aubrey. 1972 "The British Steel Corporation." Annals of Public and Cooperative Economy V. 43, pp. 107-112. /United Kingdom /Steel industry /Case studies /330.5 An73

4317. Silcock, T. H. 1967 "The Structure of Thai Government Enterprises as Shown in the Thai Budget Documents." In T. H. Silcock, ed(s). Thailand: Social and Economic Studies in Development. Canberra: Australian National Universities Press. pp. 308-316. /Thailand /Evaluation

4318. Silva Munoz, Federico. 1970 "La propiedad de la empresa pública." La Empresa Pública. Zaragoza, Spain: Publicaciones del Real Colegio de España en Bolonia. pp. 221-230. /Spain

4319. Silva Rojas, Leoni. 1979 "Country Report: Peru." Paper presented at the Interregional Workshop on Control Systems for Public Enterprises in Developing Countries, Ljubljana, Yugoslavia, 9-13 July. Ljubljana: ICPE. /Peru /Control process

4320. Silva, L. I. J. 1970 "Accountability in Public Enterprise." Journal of the Academy of Administrative Studies (Colombo, Sri Lanka), V. 2, No. 4, pp. 3-11. /Sri Lanka /Accountability

4321. Silva, Maria da Conceição. 1976 A dívida do setor público brasileiro. Rio de Janeiro: IPEA/INPES. /Brazil /Debt /OPSS

4322. Silva, Sebastião de Sant'Anna. 1973 "O controle financeiro das empresas estatais." Revista do Servico Público (Brasília), V. 108, No. 3, pp. 39-49. /Brazil /Financing /Control process

4323. Silveira, V. 1962 "Les mésures récentes relatives au régime juridique des dirigents des entreprises publiques. La Revue Administrative (Paris), V. 15, No. 89, pp. 508-510. /Administrative law /Administrative management /351.05 R328

4324. Silverman, A. D. 1961 "Select Aspects of Administration of Public-Owned Housing: Great Britain, Netherlands and Sweden." Public Housing Administration Washington, D. C.: Housing and Home Finance Agency. /United Kingdom /Netherlands /Sweden /Housing industry /Comparative analysis /Public administration

4325. Simai, Mihaly. 1979 "International Joint Companies of Centrally Planned Economies Countries." Paper presented at the International Seminar on Joint Ventures and Public Enterprises in Developing Countries, Ljubljana, Yugoslavia, 4-12 December. Ljubljana: ICPE. /Planning process /International economic relations /Mixed enterprises /Multinational corporations

4326. Simha, S. L. N., ed. 1973 "Reform of the Indian Banking System: Proceedings of a Seminar Organized in Madras on December 1-2, 1972" Madras: Orient Longman Ltd., for the Institute for Financial Management and Research. /India /Financial institutions / HG 3284 S44 1972

4327. Simmons, R. H. 1961 "The Role of the Select Committe on Nationalized Industry in Parliament." Western Political Quarterly pp. 741-747. /Parliament /320.5 W525

4328. Simon of Wythenshawe, Lord. 1957 The Boards of Nationalised Industries. London: Longmans Green. /United Kingdom /Control process /Public administration

4329. Simon, C. 1971 "Quelques problèmes de la mise en marche des reformes économiques en Europe de l´est: Exemples de la Pologne et de l´Allemagne Orientale." Revue de l´Est (Paris), V. 2, No. 2, pp. 157-174. /Poland /Germany, Democratic Rep. of /Eastern Europe / Planning process

4330. Simonyi, I. 1972 "Hungarian Management Systems and Methods as Functions of Economic Reform." International Review of Management (Cambridge), V. 12, No. 1, pp. 3-16. /Hungary /Management

4331. Simpson, J. R. 1949 "Organizing the Larger Units, Government Departments and Nationalized Industries." British Management Review (London), /United Kingdom /Public administration /Control process

4332. Simpson, J. R. 1955 "Some Problems in the Organization and Administration of Public Enterprise in the Industrial Field." Annales de l´Economie Collective pp. 144-204. /United Kingdom /Public administration /Control process

4333. Singer, J. 1960 "Le nouveau statut des régies a caractère industriel et commercial." Revue Administrative (Paris), V. 13, No. 76, pp. 420-422. /France /Law /Commercial sector /Industrial sector / 351.05 R328

4334. Singh, B. B. 1979 "Report of the International Workshop on ICPE´s International Research Project Education and Training in Public Enterprises, Ljubljana, February 12-17, 1979." Ljubljana: ICPE. /Training /Management

4335. Singh, C. D., and R. D. Sharma. 1972 "Indian Banking Nationalisation and After." Lok Udyog (New Delhi), V. 6, No. 5, pp. 29-38. /India /Nationalization /Banking system /354.54 L836 PCL

4336. Singh, C. D., and R. D. Sharma. 1974 "The State Bank of India - An Assessment." Lok Udyog (New Delhi), V. 8, No. 4, pp. 55-62. /India /Central banks /354.54 L836 PCL

4337. Singh, D. B. 1954 "Problems of the Motor Transport Industry in India." Indian Journal of Economics V. 35, No. 136. /India /Motor manufacturing industry / 330.5 In2

4338. Singh, D. P. N., C. D. Singh, and S. K. Verma. 1983 "Job Satisfaction of Graduate Engineers and Superintendents in Bhilai, Durgapur, Rourkela and Bokaro Steel Plants." Lok Udyog (New Delhi), V. 16, No. 11, pp. 21-36. /India /Management /Steel industry /354.54 L836 PCL

4339. Singh, Frank C. 1980 "Frame Work of Accountability of State Trading Corporation of India Ltd." Lok Udyog (New Delhi), V. 14, No. 1, pp. 45-50. /India /Accountability /Case studies /State trading organizations /354.54 L836 PCL

4340. Singh, I. 1964 "Measurement of Efficiency." Indian Journal of Public Administration (New Delhi), V. 10, No. 3. /Evaluation /Economic efficiency / JA 26 I55 Pub Aff

4341. Singh, J. B. 1955 "The National Small Industries Corporation." Eastern Economist (New Delhi), V. 25, pp. 751-752. /India /Small business

4342. Singh, J. D. 1981 "Marketing Planning Practices of Public Sector Enterprises in India." Lok Udyog (New Delhi), V. 14, No. 12, pp. 25-34. /India /Marketing /Management /354.54 L836 PCL

4343. Singh, Jaginder. 1976 "Public Enterprises and their Legal Structure in Malaysia." Law and Public Enterprise in Asia. New York: Praeger for the International Legal Center. pp. 247-293. /Economic analysis /Law /Control process /Malaysia /HD 4283 L32

4344. Singh, L. P. 1960 Public Control of National Enterprises in India. Cambridge, Mass.: Harvard University, Center for International Affairs. /India /Public administration /Control process

4345. Singh, N. K. 1972 "Industrial Relations in the Bhilai Steel Plant." Lok Udyog (New Delhi), V. 6, No. 5, pp. 9-14. /India /Labor relations /Steel industry /354.54 L836 PCL

4346. Singh, N. K. 1974 "Labour Productivity and Industrial Peace for Increasing Productivity - Experience of Bhilai Steel Plant." Lok Udyog (New Delhi), V. 7, No. 10, pp. 21-28. /India /Steel industry /354.54 L836 PCL

4347. Singh, Narinder Kumar. 1980 "Country Paper on India on Management Education and Training in Public Enterprises in India." Paper presented at the Expert Group Meeting on the Research Project on Education and Training in Public Enterprises in Developing Countries, Ljubljana, Yugoslavia, 17-22 March. Ljubljana: ICPE. /India /Training /Management

4348. Singh, Narinder Kumar. 1981 "Training and Development in India Steel Industry: Concepts and Issues." Paper presented at the Regional Workshop on Management Training and Development in Public Enterprises in Developing Countries, Ljubljana, Yugoslavia, 19-28 Oct. Ljubljana: ICPE. /India /Steel industry /Training

4349. Singh, Preeti. 1978 "Savings Through Life Insurance Corporation in India: An Evaluation During the Post-Nationalised Period (1956-1977)." Lok Udyog (New Delhi), V. 12, No. 3, pp. 41-45. /India /Nationalization /Insurance industry /Case studies /354.54 L836 PCL

4350. Singh, Sarup. 1981 "Training by Objectives: The Behl Experience." Paper presented at the Interregional Seminar on Training Management in Public Enterprises in Developing Countries, Ljubljana, Yugoslavia, 19-28 October. Ljubljana: ICPE. /Training

4351. Singleton, F. and A. Topham. 1963 Workers Control in Yugoslavia. London: Fabian Society. /Yugoslavia /Worker management participation / 335 F112re no.233

4352. Sinha, D. K. 1957 "The State and Industrial Enterprises in India." Indian Journal of Political Science (New Delhi), pp. 98-104. /India /Control process /Industrial sector

4353. Sinha, D. K. 1966 Working of Public Corporations in India. Allahabad: Lokbharti Publications. /India / 354.54092 Si64w

4354. Sinha, D. K. 1969 "Determinants of Profitability in Public Enterprises." Lok Udyog (New Delhi), pp. 1143-1149. /India /Evaluation /Profits / 354.54 L836

4355. Sinha, Jai B. P. 1973 "Some Problems of Public Sector Organizations." Bombay: Planning Commission, Research Programmes Committee. /Public Administration /India

4356. Sinha, R. K. 1970 "Ministerial Control and the Nationalised Industries in India." Lok Udyog (New Delhi), V. 4, No. 1, pp. 37-42. /India /Control process /354.54 L836 PCL

4357. Sinha, Raghuvir K. 1971 "Parliamentary Control and Nationalized Industries in India." Economic Affairs (Calcutta), V. 16, No. 6. /India /Control Process /330.954 Ec73

4358. Sinha, Raj Kishore. 1970 "Comsumers' Interests and the Nationalised Industries." Lok Udyog (New Delhi), V. 3, No. 12, pp. 1423-1426. /India /Consumer relations /354.54 L836

4359. Sinha, S. N. 1962 "Price Policy in Public Undertakings and Development Planning." AICC Economic Review (New Delhi), V. 11, No. 38. /India /Price policy /Development planning

4360. Sipic, Gorana, ed. 1980 Women as a Factor of Development and Responsibilities of Public Enterprises in This Regard: International Expert Group Meeting, Ljubljana, April 14-19, 1980. Ljubljana: ICPE. /Women's studies /Economic development

4361. Sipkov, L. 1958 "Postwar Nationalizations and Alien Property in Bulgaria." American Journal of International Law V. 52, pp. 469-494. /Bulgaria /Nationalization /341.05 Am35

4362. Siregar, Astar. 1976 "State Enterprises in Indonesia: Some Pricing, Investment and Retained Earnings Aspects." Approaches to the Public Enterprise Policy in Asia. Kuala Lumpur: Asian Centre for Development Administration. pp. 113-121. /Indonesia /Price policy /Investment /Profits /HD 4276 A8 1976

4363. Sirghi, Silviu. 1980 "Certains Aspects Concernant la Formation et le Perfectionnement du Personnel des Entreprises en Roumanie." Paper presented at the Séminaire international sur la gestion et la formayion dans les entreprises publiques dans les pays en voie de développement, Ljubljana, Yugoslavia, 3-15 March. Ljubljana: ICPE. /Romania /Training /Personnel management

4364. Sirotkevic, J. 1967 Self-Management and the Planning System in Yugoslavia with Special Reference to Industry. (UNIDO/ID/CONF. 1/G.25) /Yugoslavia /Industrial sector /Worker self management /Planning process

4365. Sirvent, José. 1970 "El Instituto Nacional de Industria." La Empresa Pública. Zaragoza, Spain: Publicaciones del Real Colegio de España en Bolonia. pp. 969-980. /Spain /Industrial sector

4366. Sishtla, Vijaya Saradhi P. 1982 Working Capital Management in Public Enterprises. Ljubljana: ICPE. /Financial management /Working capital

4367. Siswohardjono, Mursono. 1981 "Government Policy to Overcome Losses in State Enterprises." Paper presented at the International Workshop on Financial Profitability and Losses in Public Enterprises, Ljubljana, Yugoslavia, 1-5 June. Ljubljana: ICPE. /Public financing /Profits

4368. Sivaraman, B. 1982 "Development of Backward Areas: Role of Public Sector Industries in India." Public Enterprise V. 2, No. 4, pp. 37-43. /India /Japan /Regional development /Development planning /Developing nations /OPSS

4369. Skafar, Leopold. 1979 "Programme and Organization of Service for Development and Acceleration of Agricultural Production." Paper presented at the Seminar on Production Planning, Mogadishu, Somalia, Nov.24-Dec.3. Ljubljana: ICPE. /Agricultural sector /Agricultural development /Also at the same seminar in Mogadishu, Nov. 24-Dec. 3, 1980.

4370. Skafar, Leopold. 1980 "Cost Accounting." Seminar on Planning, Dar es Salaam, Tanzania, 1-12 December. Ljubljana: ICPE. /Cost accounting

4371. Skafar, Leopold. 1980 "Planning in the Enterprises." Paper presented at the Seminar on Planning, Dar es Salaam,

Tanzania, 1-12 December. Ljubljana: ICPE. /Planning process

4372. Skafar, Leopold. 1980 "Production Cost Analysis, Following of Execution of Plan and Replanning." Paper presented at the Seminar on Planning, Dar es Salaam, Tanzania, 1-12 December. Ljubljana: ICPE. /Planning process /Accounting /Evaluation

4373. Skafar, Leopold. 1980 "Time and Work Study." Paper presented at the Seminar on Planning, Dar es Salaam, Tanzania, 1-12 December. Ljubljana: ICPE. /Economic efficiency

4374. Skafar, Leopold. 1980 "Programme and Organization of Service for Development and Acceleration of Agricultural production." Paper presented at the Seminar on Production Planning, Mogadishu, Somalia, Nov.24-Dec.3. Ljubljana: IPCE. /Planning process /Agricultural sector

4375. Skendzic, V. 1964 "Trade Unions, Workers Management and the Struggle for the Development of Direct Democracy in Production." Yugoslav Trade Unions (Belgrade), V. 5, No. 14, pp. 12-19. /Yugoslavia /Trade unions /Worker self management

4376. Skuse, Allen. 1968 State Ownership. London: Heineman Educational Books. /United Kingdom

4377. Sleeman, J. F. 1953 British Public Utilitites. London: Pitman. /United Kingdom /Public utility industry

4378. Slejka, D. 1969 "Le modèle d'autogestion et ses conditions en Tchécoslovaquie après janvier 1969." Homme et la Société (Paris), No. 14, pp. 157-178. /Czechoslovakia /Worker self management /

4379. Smah, M. G. 1968 "Management of Public Undertakings in India." Indian Journal of Public Administration (New Delhi), V. 95, No. 2, pp. 308-321. /India /Management /JA 26 I55 Pub Aff

4380. Smart, W. 1895 "Glasgow and Its Municipal Industries." Quarterly Journal of Economics V. 9, pp. 188-194. /United Kingdom /Glasgow, Scotland /Local government /Scotland /330.5 Q2 PCL

4381. Smart, W. 1901 "Municipal Industries and the Ratepayer." Economic Journal V. 11, pp. 169-179. /Local government /Consumer market / 330.5 Ec7

4382. Smith, Bruce L. R. 1967 "The Future of the Not-For-Profit Corporations." Public Interest No. 8, pp. 127-142. /United States of America /Nonprofit corporations /Consultant services /H 1 P86

4383. Smith, G. W. Q. 1952 "Road Haulage as a National Service." British Transport Review (London), pp. 199-210. /United Kingdom /Public services

4384. Smith, Hadley Edwin. 1963 An International Comparison of the Role Government in the Economic Development of Developed and Emerging Economies with Particular Reference to Government

Corporations. Los Angeles: University of Southern California. V. 1. /Developed nations /Developing nations /Comparative analysis

4385. Smith, Hadley Edwin. 1964 Public Enterprise and Economic Development, an International Bibliography. Los Angeles: University of Southern California, International Public Administration. /Bibliography / G016.3801622 Sm58p

4386. Smith, J. H., and T. H. Chester. 1951 "The Distribution of Power in Nationalised Industries." British Journal of Sociology (London), pp. 275-293. /United Kingdom /Industrial sector / 305 B777

4387. Smith, Peter Seaborn. 1969 "Petroleum in Brazil: A Study in Economic Nationalism." University of New Mexico: Unpublished Ph. D. Dissertation. /Brazil /Oil industry /Nationalism /Film 8910 LAC

4388. Smith, Peter Seaborn. 1971 "Bolivian Oil and Brazilian Economic Nationalism." Journal of Interamerican Studies and World Affairs V. 13, pp. 166-181. /Bolivia /Oil industry /Brazil /Nationalism / G980.605 J826 LAC

4389. Smith, Peter Seaborn. 1972 "Petrobás: The Politicizing of a State Company, 1953-1964." Business History Review V. 46, pp. 182-201. /Brazil /Oil industry /Evaluation /HF 5001 B8262

4390. Smith, Peter Seaborn. 1976 Oil and Politics in Modern Brazil. Toronto: The MacMillan Company of Canada Limited. /Brazil /Oil industry /Political analysis /HD 9574 B82 S637 LAC

4391. Smith, Robert Gillen. 1964 Public Authorities, Special Districts and Local Government. Washington, D.C.: National Association of Counties. /Public authority /Local government /Regional development /United States of America /JS 425 S6 Pub Aff

4392. Smith, Selwyn P. 1980 "Planning, Developing, Implementing and Evaluating a Regional Management Development and Training Capability: The Case of the Caribbean Centre for Development Administration (CARICAD)." Paper presented at the Interregional Seminar on Training Management in Public Enterprises in Developing Countries, Ljubljana, Yugoslavia, Sept.29-Oct.10. Ljubljana: ICPE. /Caribbean Region /Regional development /Training / Management / /Also presented at the Regional Workshop on Management Development and Training in the English-speaking Caribbean "Training of Trainers," Bridgetown, Barbados, Oct. 13-18, 1980.

4393. Smith, Sir Harold. 1958 "Responsibility and Efficiency in a Nationalized Industry." Personnel Management pp. 225-230. /Accountability /Economic efficiency

4394. Smith, T. C. 1955 Political Change and Industrial Development in Japan: Government Enterprise, 1868-1880. Stanford, Cal.: Stanford University Press. /Japan

/Industrialization /Economic history / 305 L539h v.10

4395. Smith, Victor B. 1978 "Management of Transfer and Development of Technology in Public Enterprises in Developing Countries." Paper presented at the International Workshop on Management of Transfer and Development of Technology in Public Enterprises in Developing Countries, Ljubljana, Yugoslavia, 19-25 June. Ljubljana: ICPE. /Technology transfer /Developing nations

4396. Smock, Ray F. 1952 "Pennsylvania's `Rental' Method of Financing Needed Highway Improvement." American Highways pp. 8-9; 18. /United States of America /Pennsylvania (State) /Highways and roads / Public financing /Modernization

4397. Smole-Grobovsek, Vesna. 1979 "Education and Training of Public Enterprise Managers in Developing Countries." Paper presented at the International Seminar on Management and Training in Public Enterprises in Developing Countries, Ljubljana, Yugoslavia, Sept.21-Oct.2. Ljubljana: ICPE. /Developing nations /Training /Management

4398. Snoeck, J. 1950 "Les entreprises d'électricité nationalisées." Union des Exploitations Electriques en Belgique No. 1, pp. 36-43. /Belgium /Electrical utility industry

4399. Snyder, W. 1971 "L'investissement de l'entreprise publique et la stabilité économique." Annales de l'Economie Collective pp. 21-23. /Investment /Economic policy

4400. Snyder, W. 1971 "Public Enterprise Investment and Economic Stability: A Six Country Comparison." Annals of Public and Cooperative Economy V. 42, No. 1, pp. 37-46. /Investment /Economic policy /Comparative analysis / 330.5 An73

4401. Sobhan, R. 1959 "Role of Private and Public Sector in Economic Development of Pakistan." Pakistan Economic Journal V. 9, No. 2-3, pp. 157-168. /Pakistan /Economic development

4402. Sobhan, R. 1981 "Public Enterprise and Regional Development: The Asian Experience." Paper presented at the Expert Group Meeting on the Role of Public Enterprises in Regional Development in Developing Countries, Ljubljana, Yugoslavia, 7-11 December. Ljubljana: ICPE. /Asia /Regional development

4403. Sobhan, R. 1981 "Report of the Expert Group Meeting on the Role of Public Enterprises in Regional Development in Developing Countries, Ljubljana, December 7-11, 1981." Ljubljana: ICPE. /Developing nations /Regional development

4404. Sobhan, R., and Muzaffer Ahmad. 1980 Public Enterprise in an Intermediate Regime: A Study in the Political Economy of Bangladesh. Dacca, Bangladesh: Bangladesh Institute of Development Studies. /Bangladesh /Policy making process /Management /Price policy / HD 4295.6 S62

4405. Soboleva, C. D. 1970 "The New Soviet Incentive Scheme: A Study of Its Operations in Kiev." International Labour

Review (Geneva), pp. 15-34. /Union of Soviet Socialist Reps. /Incentive systems /331.05 In81 PCL /HD 4811 I65 Pub Aff

4406. Social Science Research Council. Committee on Public Administration. 1940 Research in the Use of the Government Corporation. An outline of suggested research topics. New York: unpublished. /Bibliography /Public administration /HD 3853 S6 Law

4407. Sohet, G. 1958 "Intermunicipal Union for the Study and Management of Public Industrial and Commercial Services (I.E.G.S.P.)." Annals of Collective Economy V. 29, pp. 626-633. /Belgium /Cooperatives / 330.5 An73

4408. Sokol, M. 1967 "Changes in Economic Management in Czechoslovakia." Czechoslovak Economic Papers. Prague, Czechoslovakia: Academia. No. 8, pp. 7-18. /Czechoslovakia /Economic policy making

4409. Sol, Hugo. 1969 "El control oficial de las empresas." Espejo (Mexico City), V. 10, No. 77, pp. 34-35. /Mexico /Control process / 330.5 Es64 LAC

4410. Solaiman, M. 1959 "Public Sector and Developmental Policy." Pakistan Economic Journal V. 9, No. 2-3, pp. 187-194. /Development process

4411. Solano, R. V. 1970 Labor Relations Source Book: A Guide to Resources in Management Employee Relations in the Public Sector. Chicago: Public Employee Relations Library. No. 30. /Labor relations /Personnel management / HD 8008 A1 P8 no.3

4412. Solares Mendiola, Alfonso. 1973 "Las empresas públicas en el proceso de desarrollo mexicano." Pensamiento Político (Mexico City), V. 14, No. 55, pp. 361-368. /Mexico /Development process / G320.5 P387 LAC

4413. Solari, A., and R Franco. 1978 "La inserción de las empresas públicas en el aparato estatal uruguayo." Paper presented at the Seminar on the Planning Process in Latin America and Public Enterprises, Lima, August. /Uruguay /Economic history /OPSS

4414. Solari, L. 1966 "L'entreprise publique." Annales d'Economie Collective pp. 309-336. /Evaluation

4415. Solari, L. 1968 "L'impresa pubblica in una politica comunitaria." Nord e Sud (Milan), V. 15, No. 107, pp. 118-128. /Italy /Political analysis

4416. Solari, L. n.d. L'imprensa pubblica nel trattato institutivo della CEE. Milan: Giuffré. /European Economic Community

4417. Solís Chávez, Porfirio. 1975 "La función de la Companía Nacional de Subsistencias Populares-- CONASUPO--en México." Rio de Janeiro: FGV-EIAP, Area de Administración de Empresas Públicas. /Mexico /Food industry /Retail trade /State trading organizations /OPSS

4418. Solís Fallas, Ottón. 1979 "El papel del sector público en el desarrollo de Costa Rica." Ljubljana: ICPE /Costa Rica /Economic development

4419. Solomon, J. 1962 "Public Enterprise Abroad: Concept, Organization, Structure and Control Systems." Cairo: Institute of National Planning. No. 257. /Control process /Organization development

4420. Solomovie, J. A. 1954 "Some Commercial and Economic Aspects of Public Enterprise in Certain Asian Countries." Economic Bulletin Asia Far East V. 5, No. 1, pp. 29-35. /Asia /Economic analysis / HC411 U4 A2

4421. Somalia Somali Institute of Development Administration and Management. 1973 "Public Agencies in Somalia." /Somalia /Directory

4422. Somasundram, Magalingam. 1981 "Report on the Role of Public Enterprises in Developing Countries: Sri Lanka." Ljubljana: ICPE. /Sri Lanka

4423. Somasundram, Magalingam. 1984 "From Watchdog to `Watchgod´ The Transformation of Relationships between Democratically Elected Legislature and Public Enterprises--The Sri Lanka Experience." Public Enterprise V. 4, No. 3, pp. 49-60. /Sri Lanka /Parliament /Control process /Accountability /Economic efficiency /Public administration /Management /OPSS

4424. Sombatsiri, Krit. 1976 "Government Policy Relating to Public Enterprises in Thailand." Approaches to the Public Enterprise Policy in Asia on Investment, Prices, and Returns Criteria. Kuala Lumpur: U.N. Asian Centre for Development Administration. pp. 122-138. /Thailand /Price Policy /Investment / HD 4276 A8 1976

4425. Sonachalam, K. S. 1962 "Economic and Social Benefits of Public Enterprise." Applied Economic Papers (Hyderabad), V. 2, No. 1, pp. 30-39. /Cost benefit analysis

4426. Sonnet, Jean. 1957 "The National Insurance Board and the Nationalization of Insurance in France." Annals of Collective Economy V. 28, pp. 206-211. /France /Insurance industry /Nationalization / 330.5 An73

4427. Sorj, Bernardo. 1976 "The Structure of the Peruvian Public Enterprise Sector." Manchester: mimeo. /Peru /OPSS

4428. Sorj, Bernardo. 1976 "The State in Peripheral Capitalism, with a Case Study of Peru after 1968." Ph.D. dissertation, University of Manchester. /Peru /Political economy /Capitalism /Economic dependency /FILM 14,438 LAC

4429. Sorj, Bernardo. 1983 "Public Enterprise and the Question of the State Bourgeoisie, 1968-1976." In David Booth and Bernardo Sorj, ed(s). Military Reformism and Social Classes: The Peruvian Experience, 1968-1980. New York: St. Martin's Press. pp. 72-93. /Management / HN 350 Z9 S626 1983b LAC

4430. Sosa Wagner, F. 1971 Organización y control del sector empresarial público en España. Madrid: Instituto de Estudios Administrativos. /Spain /Organization formation /Control process

4431. Sotgia, Sergio. 1970 "El INI: Empresa pública." La Empresa Pública. Zaragoza, Spain: Publicaciones del Real Colegio de España en Bolonia. pp. 1623-1648. /Spain /Holding company /Industrial sector

4432. Soto, Jean de. 1971 Grands services publiques et entreprises nationales. Paris: Montchrestien. /France /Public services

4433. Soto-Krebs, Luis. 1980 "Project `Development of Disaggregation Methodologies for the Energy Sector and Their Introduction to the Users.´" Ljubljana: ICPE. /Energy use policy /Methodology /Developing Nations

4434. Soto-Krebs, Luis. 1980 "Development of National Technological Capabilities and the Energy Sector." Paper presented at the Expert Group Meeting on Strategies for Energy Development in Developing Countries--Role of Public Enterprises, Ljubljana, Yugoslavia, 19-22 Feb. Ljubljana: ICPE. /Technology transfer /Energy utility industry

4435. Soupek, R. 1957 "L´humanisation du travail et l´autogestion ouvière." Questions Actuelles du Socialisme (Paris), No. 43, pp. 141-162. /Worker self management

4436. Soysal, Mumtag, and Gulgun Gonanc 1959 The Structure and Control of State Enterprises in Turkey. Ankara, Turkey: Institute of Public Administration. /Turkey /Control process

4437. Spagnoulo Vigorita, Vicenzo. 1959 L´iniziativa economica privata nel diritto pubblico. Naples, Italy: Casa Editrice Dottore Eugenio Yovene. /Italy /Law /Private sector

4438. Spagnoulo Vigorita, Vincenzo. 1970 "Las empresas nacionalizadas." La Empresa Pública. Zaragoza, Spain: Publicaciones del Real Colegio de España en Bolonia. pp. 1427-1454. /Spain /Nationalization

4439. Spain. Instituto de Estudios Fiscales. 1970 La empresa pública en España. Madrid: Ministerio de Hacienda. /Spain

4440. Spain. Instituto de Estudios Fiscales. 1973 La empresa pública industrial en España: El INI. Madrid: Ministerio de Hacienda. /Spain /Industrial sector /Holding company HC 381 I63 A4

4441. Span, R. N. 1950 "Reith and BBC." Public Administration (London) pp. 211-218. /United Kingdom /Broadcasting industry / 320.5 J826 PCL

4442. "Special Issue on the Nationalised Industries." 1950 Political Quarterly (London), /United Kingdom /Industrial sector /Control process

4443. Spencer, Daniel L. 1955 "Mixed Enterprise as a Tool of Development: India's Contribution." American Journal of Economics and Sociology V. 14, No. 2, pp. 139-158. /India /Economic development /Mixed enterprises /330.5 Am311 PCL /H 1 A48 Pub Aff

4444. Spencer, Daniel L. 1959 India, Mixed Enterprise and Western Business: Experiments in Controlled Change for Growth and Profit. The Hague: M. Nijhoff. /India /International economic relations /Mixed enterprises /338.954 Sp33i

4445. Spero, S. 1955 Labor Relations in British Nationalized Industry. New York: New York University Press. /United Kingdom /Labor relations / 331.1 Sp361

4446. Spiliotopoulos, Epaminondas. 1959 Distinction des institutions publiques et des institutions privées en droit français." Paris. /France /Law /Taxonomy

4447. Spiliotopoulos, Epaminondas. 1966 "The Nature of the Public Undertaking." Annals of Public and Cooperative Economy V. 37, No. 2, pp. 273-298. /Nationalization / 330.5 An73

4448. Spiliotopoulos, Epaminondas. 1966 "L'entreprise publique." Annales de l'Economie Collective V. 54, No. 3, pp. 309-336. /France /Law /Taxonomy

4449. Spiliotopoulos, Epaminondas. 1970 "La empresas públicas en Grecia." La Empresa Pública. Zaragoza, Spain: Publicaciones del Real Colegio de España en Bolonia. /Greece /Evaluation

4450. Spiliotopoulos, Epaminondas. 1983 "L'entreprise publique (E.P.) comme instrument des politiques de l'Etat." Paper presented at the 19th International Congress of Administrative Sciences, West Berlin, 19-23 Sept. /Greece /Autonomy /Control process /OPSS

4451. Spinetti, G. 1959 Service Economy: Community of Interests, Private Initiative and State Participations. Milan: A. Giuffre. /Italy /Public services

4452. Spiteri, Lewis. 1979 "Management and Training in Public Enterprises: A Country Report of Malta." Paper presented at the International Seminar on Management and Training in Public Enterprises in Developing Countries, Ljubljana, Yugoslavia, 1-13 October. Ljubljana: ICPE. /Malta /Training /Management

4453. Splawn, Walter M. W. 1928 Government Ownership and Operation of Railroads. New York: Macmillan. /Railway industry T22 385.1 Sp51g

4454. Sporn, Philip. 1971 The Social Organization of Electric Power Supply in Modern Societies. Cambridge, Mass.: MIT Press. /United States of America /Electrical utility industry / 363.62 Sp67s

4455. Spulber, N. 1962 The Soviet Economy: Structure, Principles, Problems. New York: W. W. Norton. /Union of Soviet Socialist

Reps. /Economic system / 338.947 Sp92s

4456. Sri Lanka. 1966 "State Industrial Corporation." Colombo, Sri Lanka. /Sri Lanka /Industrial sector /

4457. Sri Lanka. Commission on Government Commercial Undertakings. 1953 Report of the Commission on Government Commercial Undertakings. Sessional Paper XIX. Colombo, Sri Lanka: Government Publications Bureau. /Sri Lanka /Public administration

4458. Sri Lanka. National Team of Experts. 1979 "Research Proposal on the Role of the Public Sector in Sri Lanka." Paper presented at the International Meeting on the Role of the Public Sector in Developing Countries, 2nd, Ljubljana, Yugoslavia, 2-7 April. Ljubljana: ICPE. /Sri Lanka /Economic research

4459. Srinivasan, V. R. 1974 "Grievance Procedure in Public Enterprises." Lok Udyog (New Delhi), V. 8, No. 4, pp. 39-44. /India /Labor relations /354.54 L836 PCL

4460. Srinivasan, V., et al. 1979 "A Technique for the Analysis of Corporate Objectives in the Public Sector." Lok Udyog (New Delhi), V. 13, No. 1, pp. 19-24. /India /Evaluation /Goal setting /354.54 L836 PCL

4461. Srisuchart, Valai. 1980 "Policies and Practices on Investment Decision Affecting Public Enterprises in Thailand." Paper presented at the International Workshop on Investment Criteria and Investment Decision-Making Processes, Ljubljana, Yugosalvia, 20-24 Oct. Ljubljana: ICPE. /Investment /Public financing

4462. Srivastava, J. P., and B. R. Choyal. 1982 "Financial Appraisalof State Warehousing Corporation." Lok Udyog (New Delhi), V. 16, No. 6, pp. 5-14. /India /Evaluation /Financial performance /Case studies /354.54 L836 PCL

4463. Srivastava, Mukesh. 1974 "Export Performance of Hindustan Steel Ltd." Lok Udyog (New Delhi), V. 7, No. 10, pp. 33-36. /India /Steel industry /Exports /354.54 L836 PCL

4464. Srivastava, S. N. 1970 "Pricing Policy of Public Enterprises." Lok Udyog (New Delhi), pp. 425-433. /India /Price policy / 354.54 L836

4465. Stafani, A. de. 1962 "The Early Stages of State Petroleum in Italy." Stato Sociale (Rome), V. 6, No. 12, pp. 1011-1026. /Italy /Oil industry

4466. Staller, G. J. 1968 "Czechoslovakia--The New Model of Planning and Management." American Economic Review V. 58, No. 2, pp. 559-567. /Czechoslovakia /Planning process /Worker management participation / 330.5 Am312

4467. Stammati, Gaetano. 1961 "The Public Sector and the Achivement of Freedom, Security and Welfare." Annals of Collective Economy V. 32, pp. 119-131. /Evaluation /330.5

An73

4468. Stammati, Gaetano. 1970 "La impresa pública en el marco de la acción del Estado." In Euelio Verdera y Tuells, ed(s). La Empresa Pública. Zaragoza, Spain: Publicaciones del Real Colegio de España en Bolonia. V. 2, pp. 41-59. /Goal setting /Control process

4469. Stanini, G. 1972 "L'Impresa publica nei paesi d'Europa." Sucesso No. 2. /Europe /Comparative analysis / Italy /Germany, Federal Rep. of /France /Belgium /United Kingdom / Switzerland

4470. Stanojcic, L. 1957 "La gestion ouvrière en Yugoslovie." Archives Internationales de Sociologie et de la Coopération (Paris), No. 2, pp. 166-182. /Yugoslavia /Worker self management

4471. Stanovick, Janez. 1962 "Planning through the Market: The Yugoslav Experience." Foreign Affairs pp. 252-263. /Yugoslavia /Planning process /Market economy / 341.705 F761

4472. Stanovick, Janez. 1977 International Financial Cooperation as an Essential Factor of World Security. Dubrovnik, Yugoslavia: International Financing of Economic Development Seminar. /International economic relations /Economic development

4473. Stassen, Jacques. n.d. "Aperçcu du contrôle des entreprises publiques en Belgique." Estudios en Homenaje al Profesor López Rodó. V. 2, pp. 239-263. /Belgium /Evaluation /Control process

4474. Stead, William H. 1958 Fomento: The Economic Development of Puerto Rico. Washington, D. C.: National Planning Association. /Puerto Rico /Economic development /330.973 P693 no.103

4475. Steel, David, and David Heald. 1982 "The Public Enterprise as the Instrument of State Policies: United Kingdom National Report." Paper presented at the Tokyo Round Table preparatory to the 19th International Congress of Administrative Sciences, 13-17 Sept. /United Kingdom /Taxonomy /Economic analysis /Goal setting /Accountability /Control process /OPSS

4476. Steel, David, and David Heald. 1984 "Privatizing Public Enterprise: The Record of the UK Conservative Government, 1979-83." Paper presented at the conference: State Shrinking: A Comparative Inquiry into Privatization, Austin, Texas, 1-3 March. /Privatization /United Kingdom /OPSS

4477. Steele, H. A. 1949 "The Missouri River Development Program." Journal of Farm Economics V. 31, pp. 1010-1016. /Public works policy /United States of America /River valley development projects

4478. Stefani, Giorgio. 1958 "La imprese pubbliche e la pressione fiscale." Stato Social (Rome), pp. 1071-1081. /Italy /Fiscal policy

4479. Stefani, Giorgio. 1961 "Prices and Production Costs in Public Enterprises." Annals of Collective Economy V. 32, pp. 417-437. /Price policy / 330.5 An73

4480. Stefani, Giorgio. 1961 "Les tarifs et les coûts de production dans les entreprises publiques." Annales de l'Economie Collective V. 49, No. 2, pp. 333-352. /Price policy /Accounting /Costs /Productivity

4481. Stefani, Giorgio. 1965 "L'Evoluzione delle impresa pubbliche in Italia e lo sviluppo programmato." Stato Sociale (Milan), V. 9, No. 3-4, pp. 250-272. /Italy / Planning process

4482. Stefani, Giorgio. 1966 "Public Undertakings in Italy and the Prospects for Economic Programming." Annals of Public and Cooperative Economy V. 37, pp. 43-63. /Italy /Planning process / 330.5 An73

4483. Stefani, Giorgio. 1968 Studi sul finanziamento delle imprese pubbliche in Europa. Milan, Italy: Etas Kompass. /Europe /Financing

4484. Stefani, Giorgio. 1968 Finanziamento e tassazione delle impresa pubblica in Italia, Francia, Gran-Bretagna. Italia, Padova: Cedam. /Italy /France /United Kingdom /Financing /Taxation policy

4485. Stefani, Giorgio. 1968 "C.I.R.I.E.C. International Committee for the Study of the Financing of Public Undertakings in European Countries." Annals of Public and Cooperative Economy V. 39, No. 3, pp. 353-406. /Europe /Financing /330.5 An73

4486. Stefani, Giorgio. 1969 "La financiación de la empresa pública." Economía Financiera Española (Madrid), No. 31-2, pp. 17-55. /Spain /Public financing

4487. Stefani, Giorgio. 1970 "La política tarifaria y la gestión de las empresas públicas en relación a la persecución de los fines estatutarios." La Empresa Pública. Zaragoza, Spain: Publicaciones del Real Colegio de España en Bolonia. pp. 373-401. /Spain /Evaluation /Price policy

4488. Stefani, Giorgio. 1973 "The Productivity of Public Enterprises." Annals of Public and Cooperative Economy V. 44, No. 1, pp. 13-58. /Productivity / 330.5 An73

4489. Stefani, Giorgio. 1980 "Machinery for the Control of Public Enterprises by the Public Authorities." Paper presented at the the 13th International Congress of Public and Cooperative Economy, Lisbon, 2-4 June. /Public administration /Control process /OPSS /Published in Annals of Public and Cooperative Economy, V. 52, Nos. 1-2, (1981): pp. 49-72. /330.5 An73

4490. Stefano, de, and Coltelli. 1959 Condice delle participazioni e delle azienda patrimoniali dello stato. Milano: Giuffré.

/Italy

4491. Stefanovic, J. 1957 "El derecho de autogestión de los productores en la economía y su protección constitucional." Le Nouveau Droit Yougoslave (Belgrade), V. 7, No. 2-4. /Yugoslavia /Law /Worker self management

4492. Stegemann, Klaus. 1981 "State Trading and Domestic Distortions in a Mixed World Economy." In M. M. Kostecki, ed(s). State Trading in International Markets. New York: St. Martin's Press. pp. 161-188. /State trading organizations / /HF 1410.5 S7 1981 M. /Also found in Les Cahiers du Cetai, no 79-13, June,1979 /OPSS

4493. Stendaidi, G. G. 1965 Libertá di stabilimento e imprese pubbliche nel settore dell'energia. Italy. /Italy /Energy utility industry

4494. Stepanovic, Nicola. 1955 "Organisation and Management of an Industrial Enterprise in the Federated People's Republic of Yugoslavia." In A. H. Hanson, ed(s). Public Enterprise. Brussels: IIAS. pp. 287-297. /Yugoslavia /Management /HD 3850 H28 Law

4495. Stepanovic, Nikola. 1969 "Legal Status of Yugoslav Enterprises with a Special Review of the Control of Constitutioality and Legality of their Rule-Making." Paper presented at the Herceg Novi Seminar, 13-25 Oct. New York: United Nations. /Yugoslavia /Law

4496. Stephan, C. 1979 "Administración por objetivos en las empresas públicas." In EIAP-FGV, ed(s). Administración de empresas públicas. Mexico City: Editorial Limusa. pp. 219-261. /Management / HD 3850 A333 LAC

4497. Stephan, C., and Paul F. Simas P. de Abreu. 1979 "La toma de decisiones en el sistema público: problemas principales y una introducción a la utilización de las técnicas de análisis de criterios multiples." In EIAP-FGV, ed(s). Administración de empresas públicas." Mexico City: Editorial Limusa. pp. 263-293. /Management /Cost benefit analysis /HD 3850 A333 LAC

4498. Stephen, Frank H. 1977 "Bank Credit and Investment by the Yugoslav Firm." Discussion Papers. Strathclyde: University of Strathclyde, Department of Economics. V. 77. No. 1. /Yugoslavia /Worker self management

4499. Stephens, Elvis C. 1976 "Resolution of Impasses in Public Employee Bargaining." Monthly Labor Review V. 99, No. 1, pp. 57-58. /United States of America /Labor relations /Collective bargaining / FILM 7161 UGL HD 8051 A78

4500. Sterling, R. 1972 "Hacia la reforma del sistema de monopolio estatal del comercio exterior en los países del Comecon?" Información Comerical Española (Madrid), No. 1323, pp. 2-167. /Spain /Imports /Exports /Policy analysis /State trading organizations

4501. Sterpi, S. 1971 "Imprese pubbliche e fini stato. Una nota intepretativa." Rivista Internazionale di Scienze Sociale (Milan), pp. 507-526. /Italy / 305 R525 PCL

4502. Sterpi, S. 1973 "Congiuntura e sviluppo della politica di espasione delle impresse pubbliche." Rivista Internazionale di Scienza Sociali (Milan), V. 4, No 5, pp. 443-448. /Italy /Evaluation / 305 R525 PCL

4503. Stieber, Jack. 1973 Public Employee Unionism: Structures, Growth, Policy. Washington, D. C.: Brookings Institution. /United States of America /Trade unions /HD8008 S74 Pub Aff

4504. Stillmann, James Peter. 1975 "Foreign Aid, Ideology and Bureaucratic Politics: The Bollaro Steel Mill and Indian-American Relations." Unpublished Ph.D. dissertation, Columbia University. /India /Steel industry

4505. Stimpson, J. R. 1949 "Organizing the Larger Units: Government Departments and Nationalized Industries." British Management Review (London), /United Kingdom /Public administration /Management

4506. Stock, W. 1960 Die Investitions Politik in Nationalisierten Industrieunternehmengen Frankreichs seit iherer Nationalsierung. Cologne: Westdeustcher Verlag. /France /Industrial sector /Investment /338.944 St621

4507. Stoddart, C. 1960 The Histadrut Plan for Worker Participation in Management. New York: Brooklyn College. /Worker management participation

4508. Stoffaes, Christian, and Pierre Gadonneix. 1980 "Steel and the State in France." Annals of Public and Cooperative Economy V. 51, No. 4, pp. 405-422. /France /Steel industry /330.5 An73

4509. Stoffaes, Christian. 1979 "Les instruments d´une stratégie industrielle." Revue Française de Gestion (Paris), No. 20, pp. 58-63. /France /Management /Industrial sector

4510. Stokes, W. S. 1959 "Revolución Nacional and the MNR in Bolivia." Inter-American Economic Affairs V. 12, pp. 28-53. /Bolivia /Nationalization /Political history /HC 161 I585 LAC

4511. Stout, Sir R. 1892 "State Experiments in New Zealand." Royal Statistical Society Journal V. 55, pp. 388-414. /New Zealand

4512. Strauch, Volkmar. 1981 "Guarantee Clauses in Transfer of Technology Transactions of Public Enterprises in Developing Countries." Ljubljana: ICPE. /Developing nations /Technology transfer /Law

4513. Strauss, Robert P., and Kenneth L. Wertz. 1976 "The Impact of Municipal Electric Profits on Local Public Finance." National Tax Journal V. 29, No. 1. /United States of America /Electrical utility industry /Profits / 336.205 N213

4514. Streich, R. 1968 "Statut juridique des entreprises industrielles nationalisées." Revue de Droit et de Législation R.D.A. (Berlin), No. 1, pp. 34-45. /Germany, Democratic Rep. of /Law

4515. Stroganov, K. V. 1959 Management of State Industrial Enterprise. New Delhi: U. N. Seminar on Management of Industrial Enterprises. Industrial sector /Management /India

4516. Stromberg, Hokan. 1970 "The Public Corporation in Sweden." In W. G. Friedmann, and J. F. Garner, ed(s). Government Enterprise: A Comparative Study. New York: Columbia University Press. pp. 168-177. /Sweden / 350.0092 G746

4517. Struyf, E. 1958 "The Belgium Post Office." Annals of Collective Economy V. 29, pp. 498-508. /Belgium /Postal service / 330.5 An73

4518. Stuna, S. 1956 "La loi sur les entreprises nationales et quelques autres organisations économiques." Bulletin de Droit Tchécoslovaque (Prague), pp. 293-300. /Czechoslovakia /Law

4519. Sturmthal, Adolf. 1952 "The Structure of Nationalized Enterprises in France." Political Science Quarterly V. 67, No. 3, pp. 357-377. /France /Structural characteristics /320.5 P75

4520. Sturmthal, Adolf. 1953 "Nationalization and Workers' Control in Britain and France." Journal of Political Economy V. 61, pp. 43-79. /United Kingdom /France /Worker self management /330.5 J82 PCL

4521. Sturmthal, Adolf. 1964 Workers Councils: A Study of Workplace Organization on Both Sides of the Iron Curtain. Cambridge, Mass.: Harvard University Press. /Worker management participation /658.3152 St97w PCL

4522. Sturmthal, Adolf. 1967 La participation ouvrière a l'est et a l'ouest. Paris: Editions Economie et Humanisme. /Worker management participation

4523. Subbaramaiah, S. 1962 "Consumers and Public Enterprise: The Divisional Railway Users' Consulative Council." Indian Journal of Public Administration (New Delhi), V. 8, No. 3. /India /Railway industry /Consumer relations /Control process /JA26 I55 Pub Aff

4524. Subbaraman, K. N. 1967 "Performance Evaluation in Industries." Lok Udyog (New Delhi), pp. 29-37. /Evaluation /354.54 L836 PCL

4525. Subrahmanyam, V. V. 1976 "Management and Accounting of Research & Development." Lok Udyog (New Delhi), V. 9, No. 10, pp. 25-30. /Research and development /India /Accounting /354.54 L836 PCL

4526. Subramanian, R. P. 1980 "Research & Development in ITI in the Telecommunications Field." Lok Udyog (New Delhi), V. 14,

No. 9, pp. 19-20. /India /Case studies /Research and development /Communication industry /354.54 L836 PCL

4527. Subramony, V., and J. C. Madan. 1980 "Development of Ancillary and Small Scale Industries around Steel Plants under SAIL." Lok Udyog (New Delhi), V. 13, No. 12, pp. 35-40. /India /Private enterprises /Subsidiaries /354.54 L836 PCL

4528. Sufrin, Sidney C., and Edward E. Palmer. 1957 The New Saint Lawrence Frontier. Syracuse, N. Y.: Syracuse University Press. /United States of America /River valley development projects / 338.97 Su29n

4529. Suman, H. N. P. S. 1974 "SAIL and the Management of Steel Industry." Lok Udyog (New Delhi), V. 7, No. 10, pp. 13-20. /India /Steel industry /354.54 L836 PCL

4530. Sumar, A. K. 1957 "Our Industrial and Commercial Policies." Pakistan Economist V. 9, pp. 13-14; 24. /Pakistan /Industrialization /Commercial sector

4531. Summers, Clyde W. 1974 "Public Employee Bargaining: A Political Perspective." Yale Law Journal V. 83, No. 6, pp. 1156-1201. /United States of America /Collective bargaining / KF 1 y3 Pub Aff

4532. Sundaram, S. 1972 "National Objectives and the Manager's Role." Lok Udyog (New Delhi), V. 6, No. 7, pp. 31-34. /India /Goal setting /Accountability /Management /354.54 L836 PCL

4533. Sundaram, S. 1974 "A Thought on the Objectives of the Public Sector Management." Lok Udyog (New Delhi), V. 8, No. 7+8, pp. 39-42. /India /Goal setting /354.54 L836 PCL

4534. Sundaram, S. 1978 "Cost of Training." Lok Udyog (New Delhi), V. 12, No. 8, pp. 25-32. /India /Training /Costs /354.54 L836 PCL

4535. Sunderam, V. S. 1954 "Management of Public Enterprises." Indian Economic Journal (Bombay), V. 2, No. 3, pp. 312-318. /Management

4536. Sundjaswadi, S., J. B. Sumarlin, and B. Tjokroamidjojo. 1969 "Industrial Financing of Public Manufacturing Enterprises in Indonesia." Paper presented at the Seminar on Financial Aspects of Manufacturing Enterprises in the Public Sector, Rome, December. Rome: UNIDO. /Indonesia /Industrialization /Manufacturing industry

4537. Sundstrom, Zacharias G. O. 1972 Public International Utility Corporations: Case Studies of Public International Institutions in Corporations. Leiden, Holland: A.W. Sijthoff International Publishing Company. /Public utility industry /HD 2763 S953 PCL

4538. Suonoja, Kyosti, and Karl Vahatalo. 1969 "The Public and Co-operative Sectors in Finland." Annals of Public and Cooperative Economy V. 40, No. 4. /Finland / 330.5 An73

4539 Supranowitz, Stephen. 1961 "The Law of State-Owned Enterprises in a Socialist State." Law and Contemporary Problems V. 26, No. 4, pp. 794-801. /Germany, Democratic Rep. of /Law

4540. Surbiguet, M. 1970 Les sociétés d'économie mixte dans les pays en voie de developement a partir de l'exemple Malgache. Paris: Librairie générale de droit et de jurisprudence. V. 2. /Madagascar /Mixed enterprises

4541. Suri, Prakash Chandra. 1957 "Some Problems of Organization of Public Enterprise in India." Annals of Collective Economy V. 28, pp. 81-87. /India /Structural characteristics /Management / 330.5 An73

4542. Suwanabol, Issara. 1980 "Management Manpower Planning in Public Enterprises in Thailand." Paper presented at the Expert Group Meeting on Manpower Planning in Public Enterprises in Developing Countries, Tagaytay, Philippines, 18-22 August. Ljubljana: ICPE. /Thailand /Personnel management /Training / Manpower planning

4543. Suwanabol, Issara. 1980 "Pre-Course Assignment, Public Enterprise Institute, Chulalongkorn University." Paper presented at the Interregional Seminar on Training Management in Public Enterprises in Developing Countries, Ljubljana, Yugoslavia, Sept.29-Oct.10. Ljubljana: ICPE. /Training /Management /Personnel management

4544. Svetlicic, Marjan. 1982 "Joint Ventures among Developing Countries--With Special Emphasis on the Role of Public Enterprises." Public Enterprise V. 3, pp. 85-96. /Developing nations /Multinational corporations /Mixed enterprises

4545. Svetlicic, Marjan. 1982 "Joint Ventures among Developing Countries with Special Emphasis on the Role of Public Enterprises." Paper presented at the ECA/OAU Regional Conference on the Role of the Public Sector in National and Regional Development in the Context of the Implementation of the Lagos Plan of Action, Addis Ababa, Ethiopia, 22-27 Nov. /E/ECA/PAMM/PS/82/4 New York: United Nations Economic and Social Council. /Developing nations /Multinational corporations /Mixed enterprises /OPSS

4546. Swaby, Raphael A. 1981 "The Rationale for Ownership of Public Utilities in Jamaica." Economic and Social Studies (Mona, Kingston, Jamaica), V. 30, No. 1, pp. 75-107. /Caribbean Region /Jamaica /Case studies /Telephone industry /Mass transportation industry /Electrical utility industry /G330.97292 So13 LAC

4547. Sweden. Statsforetag Group. 1974 "Statsforetag Group of Sweden." Paper presented at the International Seminar '74: Planning in Public Enterprises in Developing Countries, Ljubljana, Yugoslavia, 23 Sept. - 9 Oct. Ljubljana: ICPE. /Sweden /Planning process

4548. Sweet, Morris L., and S. George Walters. 1976 Mandatory Housing Finance Programs: A Comparative International

Analysis. New York: Praeger. /Housing industry /Financing /HD7289.5 A2 S94 Pub Aff

4549. Sy, Ibrahim. 1978 "Co-operation among State Marketing Companies in French-Speaking Africa South of the Sahara." (Geneva: UNCTAD). TD/B/C.7/18/Add.2. /State trading organizations /Africa /Goal setting /Mali /Niger /Senegal /Chad /Congo, People's Rep. of /OPSS

4550. Syed, Reza H. ed. 1977 Role and Performance of Public Enterprises in the Economic Growth of Pakistan. Islamabad: Investment Advisory Centre of Pakistan. /Pakistan /Economic development /Evaluation /Economic efficiency /Financial performance /HD 4295.5 I58 1977 PCL

4551. Sylvester, E. 1951 The Management and Control of Public Corporations. London: Institute of Municipal Treasures and Accountants. /United Kingdom /Management /Control process

4552. Synder, Wayne W. 1971 "Public Enterprise Investment and Economic Stability: A Six Country Comparison." Annals of Public and Cooperative Economy V. 42, No. 1, pp. 37-45. /Belgium /France /Italy /Sweden /United Kingdom /Economic policy /United States of America /330.5 An73

4553. Szamel, L. 1966 "L'Aspect politique du fonctionnement des entreprises." Paper presented at the International Political Science Association. Documentation of the Jablonna Round Table Meetings, 19-24 Sept. Paris. /Political analysis

4554. Sznich, Valdir. 1974 "Fundação pública, uma contradição." Revista de Direito Administrativo (Rio de Janeiro), No. 118, pp. 34-48. /Brazil /Law

4555. Szwawlowski, Richard. 1962 "Le contrôle étatique en Union Soviétique." Revista International de Ciencias Administrativas No. 3, pp. 325-332. /Union of Soviet Socialist Reps. /Government bureaucracy / Control process

4556. Tabb, J. Y., and A. Goldfarb. 1970 Workers' Participation in Management - Expectations and Experience. Oxford: Pergamon Press. /Worker management participation /658.3152 T112w PCL

4557. Taccone, Juan C. 1971 La empresa de Estado. San Carlos de Bariloche: Fundación Bariloche. /Argentina /HD 4083 T327

4558. Tacito, Caio. 1964 "Sociedades comerciais e fundações do Estado." Revista Forensa (Rio de Janeiro), No. 205. /Brazil /Commercial sector

4559. Tacito, Caio. 1965 "As empresas públicas do Brasil." Agora (Rio de Janeiro), V. 1, No. 1, pp. 13-22. /Brazil

4560. Tacito, Caio. 1973 "Controle das empresas do Estado (públicas e mistas)." Revista de Direito Administrativo (Rio de Janeiro), No. 11, pp. 1-9. /Brazil /Mixed enterprises /Public administration /Control process

4561. Tagand, Roger. 1969 Le régime juridique de la société d'économie mixte. Paris: Librairie générale de droit et de jurisprudence. /France /Mixed enterprises /Law

4562. Taha, Akila Ezz El Din. 1980 "Problems and Evaluation of Transfered Technology: (A Point of View from the United Arab Republic of Egypt)." Paper presented at the International Workshop on Preparations and Negotiations of Technology Transfer Agreements for Public Enterprises in Developing Countries, Ljubljana, Yugoslavia, 27-31 October. Ljubljana: ICPE. /Egypt /Technology transfer

4563. Taher, A. H. 1980 "The Role of State Petroleum Enterprises in Developing Countries: The Case of Saudi Arabia." State Petroleum Enterprises in Developing Countries. New York: Pergamon Press. pp. 23-27. /Oil industry /Case studies /Saudi Arabia

4564. Taher-Zahed, Mohamed. 1979 "Management and Training in Public Enterprises: Country Report of Afghanistan." Paper presented at the International Seminar on Management and Training in Public Enterprises in Developing Countries, Ljubljana, Yugoslavia, 1-13 October. Ljubljana: ICPE. /Afghanistan /Training /Management

4565. Taib, Bin Haji Andak. 1967 Land Development in Malaysia under the Federal Land Development Authority-- Description of Programme and Techniques of Development Implementation. Kuala Lumpur: Malaysian Center for Development Studies. /Malaysia /Land use policy

4566. Taira, K. 1966 "Participation by Workers and Employers Organizations in Economic Planning in Japan." International Labour Review (Geneva), V. 94, No. 6, pp. 511-534. /Japan /Planning process /Participatory democracy /331.05 In81 PCL /HD 4811 I65 Pub Aff

4567. Tall, Maki. 1974 "Financement des sociétés et entreprises d'Etat au Mali." Paper presented at the International Seminar '74: Planning in Public Enterprises in Developing Countries, Ljubljana, Yugoslavia, 23 Sept. - 9 Oct. Ljubljana: ICPE. /Mali /Financing

4568. Tamagna, Frank. 1965 Central Banking in Latin America. Mexico City: CEMLA. /Latin America /Central banks /Economic history /G332.11 T15bTS

4569. Tamames, R. 1972 "Una nueva estrategia para las empresas públicas." La Empresa Pública en Espana Madrid: Instituto de Estudios Fiscales. /Spain

4570. Tamayo, J. J. 1963 "The Role of the Public Sector in the Process of Accumulation of Capital in a Less Developed Economy. The Case of Mexico." Investigación Económica (Mexico City), V. 23, No. 92. /Mexico /Investment

4571. Tamburrini, Ugo, Elvina Devetag, and Luisa Bravetti. 1973 "Italian Public Enterprises." The Evolution of the Public Enterprises in the Community of the Nine. Brussels: CEEP

Editions. pp. 184-264. /Italy /Statistics /OPSS

4572. Tamburrino, L. 1966 Industria pubblica e mezzogiorno. Rome: Ed. Sindicale Italiana. /Italy /Industrial sector /Regional development

4573. Tan, Chwee-Huat. 1966 Transfer of Public Enterprise to Private Ownership. An Experience in the Republic of China. Taiwan: U. N. Seminar on Organization and Administration of Public Enterprises. /China, Rep. of /Privatization

4574. Tan, Chwee-Huat. 1972 "Selected Bibliography on Public Enterprise." (Madison, Wis.: unpublished). /Bibliography /OPSS

4575. Tan, Chwee-Huat. 1975 "The Public Enterprise as a Development Strategy: The Case of Singapore." Annals of Public and Cooperative Economy V. 46, No. 1, pp. 61-86. /Singapore /Economic development /330.5 An73

4576. Tan, Chwee-Huat. 1979 "Domestic Joint Ventures between the Public and Private Sectors: The Case of Singapore." Paper presented at the International Seminar on Joint Ventures and Public Enterprises in Developing Countries, Ljubljana, Yugoslavia, 1-13 October. Ljubljana: ICPE. /Singapore /Mixed enterprises

4577. Tan, Chwee-Huat. 1983 "Public Enterprise and the Government in Singapore." In G. Ram Reddy, ed(s). Government and Public Enterprise: Essays in honour of Professor V. V. Ramanadham. Bombay, India: N. M. Tripathi Private Limited. pp. 249-263. /Singapore /Control process

4578. Tandon, B. B. 1982 "Financial Institutions and Backward Areas." Lok Udyog (New Delhi), V. 16, No. 6, pp. 15-20. /India /Regional development /Financial institutions /354.54 L836 PCL

4579. Tandon, B. N. 1954 "Cost Accounting and Public Enterprise." Indian Journal of Commerce (Allahabad), V. 7, No. 1, pp. 35-59. /Cost accounting

4580. Tandon, Pankaj. 1982 "Hierarchical structure and attitudes toward risk in state-owned enterprises." In Leroy P. Jones et al., ed(s). Public enterprise in less-developed countries. New York: Cambridge University Press. pp. 245-255. /Decision making process /HD 3850 P83 PCL Also presented at the Second BAPEG Conference, Boston, April, 1980 /OPSS

4581. Tandon, Prakash. 1979 "Control Systems and Accountability in the Public Enterprise." Paper presented at the Interregional Workshop on Control Systems for Public Enterprises in Developing Countries, Ljubljana, Yugoslavia, 9-13 July. Ljubljana: ICPE. /Accountability /Control process

4582. Tang, Yinghong. 1980 "Some Experiences of People's Republic of China in Acquiring Foreign Technology." Paper presented at the International Workshop on Preparations and

Negotiations of Technology Transfer Agreements for Public Enterprises in Developing Countries, Ljubljana, Yugoslavia, 27-31 October. Ljubljana: ICPE. /China, People's Rep. of /Technology transfer

4583. Tanic, Z. 1967 "Social Composition of Workers Councils in Yugoslavia." Indian Journal of Industrial Relations (New Delhi), V. 3, No. 1, pp. 19-40. /Yugoslavia /Worker self management

4584. Tanzania. National Team of Experts. 1979 "International Research on the Role of Public Enterprises in Developing Countries: A Preliminary Tanzanian National Report." Paper presented at the International Meeting in the Role of the Public Sector on Developing Countries, 2nd, Ljubljana, Yugoslavia, 2-7 April. Ljubljana: ICPE. /Tanzania

4585. Tanzer, M. 1969 The Political Economy of International Oil and the Underdeveloped Countries. Boston: Beacon Press. /Developing nations /Multinational corporations /Oil industry / Political economy / HD 9560.5 T35

4586. Tapía-Videla, Jorge Juan. 1969 "Bureaucratic Power in a Developing Country: The Case of the Chilean Social Security Administration." Ph.D. dissertation, UT-Austin. /Chile /Social security / TD1969 T16L

4587. Taussig, F. W. 1891 "A Contribution to the Theory of Railway Rates." Quarterly Journal of Economics V. 5, pp. 438-465. /Railway industry /Price policy / 330.5 Q2 PCL

4588. Taussig, F. W. 1913 "Railway Rates and Joint Cost Once More." Quarterly Journal of Economics V. 27, pp. 378-384. /Railway industry /Price policy / 330.5 Q2 PCL

4589. Tautscher, A. 1952 "Les fonctions économiques des entreprises publiques." Revue de Science et Legislation Financière (Paris), pp. 339-348. /Economic analysis

4590. Tawfik, Hassan, Ali Abdul Majeed, and Atef Obeid. 1977 "Egypt." Public Enterprises and Development in the Arab Countries: Legal and Managerial Aspects. New York: Praeger for the International Center for Law in Development. pp. 63-122. /Egypt /Law /Goal setting /Personnel management /HD 4334 P8 Law

4591. Taylor, A. J. 1948 "Staff Organization of the Railways Department." Journal of Public Administration (Wellington), pp. 28-44. /New Zealand /Railway industry /Structural characteristics

4592. Teck, Ng. 1980 "Personnel Planning in Public Enterprises: A Malaysian Experience." Paper presented at the Regional Workshop on Corporate Planning in Public Enterprises in the Asian and Pacific Region, Kuala Lumpur, Malaysia, 17-21 November. Ljubljana: ICPE. /Malaysia /Personnel management

4593. Tedeschi, Guido Uberto. 1970 "Los entes públicos económicos en el derecho concursal italiano." La Empresa Pública.

Zaragoza, Spain: Publicaciones del Real Colegio de España en Bolonia. /Italy /Law

4594. Tedeschini, F. 1973 "Le aziende autonome dello stato." Nuova Rassegna (Rome), No. 5-6, pp. 524-566. /Italy

4595. Teilac, J. 1965 Autogestion en Algérie. Paris, Université Centre de Hautes Etudes Administratives sur L'Afrique et L'Asie Modernes. "Recherches et Documents." Paris: J. Peyronne. No. 2. /Algeria /Worker self management

4596. Temmar, H. 1971 "L'Organisation de l'autogestion dans l'agriculture algerienne." Developpement et Civilisations (Paris), No. 43, pp. 56-96. /Algeria /Agricultural sector /Worker self management

4597. Tendler, Judith. 1958 Electric Power in Brazil: Entrepreneurship in the Public Sector. Cambridge, Mass.: Harvard University Press. /Brazil /Electrical utility industry /Entrepreneurial activity / G621 30981 T253e LAC

4598. Tennessee Valley Authority. 1956 TVA: The First Twenty Years. Tuscaloosa, Ala. and Knoxville, Tenn.: University of Alabama and University of Tennessee Press. /United States of Amenica /River valley development projects / TK 1425 M8 A54

4599. Terceiro, José B. 1972 "La empresa pública en la estructura económica de España; un análisis cuantitativo de su ámbito y tendencia." La empresa en España. Madrid: Instituto de Estudios Fiscales. /Spain /Economic analysis

4600. Teriba, O. 1966 "Development Strategy, Investment Decisions and Expenditure Patterns of a Public Development Institution: The Case of the Western Nigeria Development Corporations." Nigerian Journal of Economic and Social Studies (Ibadan, Nigeria), V. 8, pp. 235-258. /Nigeria /Development corporation /Development planning /Investment /Case studies

4601. Teriba, O. 1967 "Some Organizational Problems of West Nigerian Public Corporations." Administration (Ibadan, Nigeria), /Nigeria /Structural characteristics

4602. Teriba, O. 1969 "Parliamentary Control of West Nigerian Public Corporations: A Critical Appraisal." Administration (Ibadan, Nigeria), V. 3, No. 1, pp. 111-121. /Nigeria /Evaluation /Parliament /Control process

4603. Tersman, Rune. 1959 Statsmakterna och de statliga aktiebolagen. Stockholm: Nordiska bokhanden. /Sweden /Management /Control process /380.16 T279s

4604. Tersman, Rune. 1959 Management and Control of the State Joint-Stock Company. Stockolm: Studieforbundet Narinsliv Och Samhall. /Sweden /Management /Control process

4605. Thaiarry, Phiphat. 1980 "Country Paper on Thailand on Management and Training in Public Enterprises." Paper presented at the Expert Group Meeting on the Research

Projects on Education and Training in Public Enterprises in Developing Countries, Ljubljana, Yugoslavia, 17-22 March. Ljubljana: ICPE. /Thailand /Training /Management

4606. Thaiarry, Phiphat. 1981 "Management Training and Development in Public Enterprises in Thailand." Paper presented at the Regional Workshop on Management Training and Development in Public Enterprises in Developing Countries, Karachi, Pakistan, 5-15 January. Ljubljana: ICPE. /Thailand /Training /Management

4607. Thailand. Ministry of Science, Technology and Energy. National Energy Administration. 1979 <u>Oil and Thailand.</u> Bangkok. /Thailand /Oil industry

4608. Thamm, J. 1957 "Zur Discussion Uber die Witere Verbesserung der Leitung der Volkseigenen Industrie." <u>Wirtschafts Wissenschaft</u> (Berlin, F.R.G.), pp. 346-361. /Germany, Federal Rep. of /Management /Industrial sector

4609. Thammavong, Kadam, and Sang Koumpholphakdi. 1980 "Quelques idées sur la formation dans l´entreprise Syviengkham Tobaco et dans le cadre du Centre de Formation en Céramique au Laos." Paper presented at the Séminaire international sur la gestion et la formation dans les entreprises publiques dans les pays en voie de développement, Ljubljana, Yugoslavia, 3-15 March. Ljubljana: ICPE. /Laos /Tobacco industry /Ceramics industry

4610. Thapa, Ajit N. 1980 "Performance of Public Enterprises in Nepal: A Managerial Analysis." Kathmandu: His Majesty´s Government of Nepal Corporation Coordination Council, Industrial Services Centre. /Nepal /Management /Marketing /Financing /Economic efficiency / Evaluation

4611. Thavaraj, M. J. K. 1975 "Investment Decisions in Government." In R. C. Dutt and Raj K. Nigam, ed(s). <u>Towards Commanding Heights.</u> New Delhi: Vivek Joshi. pp. 120-141. /India /Investment /HD 4293 T68 PCL

4612. Thibault, P. 1961 "Raisons, formes et conséquences d´une politique de nationalisation." <u>Revue Socialiste</u> (Paris), No. 145, pp. 126-139. /Nationalization /Policy analysis

4613. Thiel, E. 1951 "The Power Industry in the Soviet Union." <u>Economic Geography</u> V. 27, No. 2. /Union of Soviet Socialist Reps. /Energy utility industry / 380.5 Ec74

4614. Thiemeyer, T. 1962 "Theories Concerning the Problem of Price Setting in Public Undertakings." <u>Annals of Collective Economy</u> V. 33, pp. 251-281. /Price policy / 330.5 An73

4615. Thiemeyer, T. 1962 "Thèses relatives a la formation des prix dans les entreprises publiques." <u>Annales de l´Economie Collective</u> pp. 311-326. /Price policy

4616. Thiemeyer, T. 1964 <u>Marginal Cost Prices in Public Undertakings.</u> Cologne: Westdeutscher Verlag. /Costs /Price policy

4617. Thietart, Raymond-Alain. 1979 "Public-privé: Une guerre de frontières." Revue Française de Gestion (Paris), No. 20, pp. 72-76. /France /Private enterprises /Economic analysis

4618. Thomas, K. D., and B. Glassburner. 1965 "Arrogation, Takeover and Nationalization: The Elimination of Dutch Economic Domination from the Republic of Indonesia." Australian Outlook (Camberra), V. 19, No. 2, pp. 158-179. /Indonesia /Nationalization / 994.005 Au78

4619. Thompson, A. E. 1957 "Organization in Two Nationalized Industries; Fleck versus Herbert." Scottish Journal of Political Economy (Edinburg), pp. 81-100. /United Kingdom /Organization formation /Coal mining industry

4620. Thompson, Carl D. 1925 Public Ownership. New York: Thomas Y. Crowell. /United States of America / 338.8 T372

4621. Thomson, L. R. 1930 "The St. Lawrence Navigation and Power Project." Journal of Political Economy V. 38, pp. 86-107. /United States of America /River valley development projects /330.5 J82 PCL

4622. Thornhill, C. 1983 "The Malfunctioning of Traditional Control Methods and Bodies." Paper presented at the 19th International Congress of Administrative Sciences, West Berlin, 19-23 Sept. /Control process /South Africa, Rep. of /OPSS

4623. Thornhill, W. 1968 The Nationalized Industries: An Introduction. London: Thomas Nelson. /United Kingdom /354.42092 T393n

4624. Thornton, R. H. 1947 "Nationalization: Administrative Problems Inherent in a State-Owned Enterprise." Public Administration (London), V. 35, No. 1, pp. 10-21. /Nationalization /Public administration / JA 8 P8 Pub Aff

4625. Thurston, John. 1937 Government Proprietary Corporations in English Speaking Countries. Cambridge, Mass.: Harvard University Press. /British Commonwealth / 388.8 T427g

4626. Thurston, John. 1960 "Government Economic Enterprises: Review Article." Public Administration Review V. 20, pp. 165-169. /Bibliography

4627. Thusing, Rolf. 1972 "Productivity under Codetermination." Lok Udyog (New Delhi), V. 5, No. 12, pp. 1189-1201. /India /Worker management participation /Productivity /354.54 L836

4628. Tiano, A. 1968 "L´Expérience du secteur publique de production au Maghreb depuis l´indépendence." Annales de l´Economie Collective pp. 567-610. /Maghreb /Algeria /Morocco /Tunisia

4629. Tierno, A. 1979 "El Estado y las empresas públicas, una propuesto de cambio para su organización y sus relaciones con el Estado: Caso de la Administración Nacional de Combustibles, Alcohol y Portland de Uruguay." Revista

Latinoamericana de Administración Pública No. 8-9, pp. 345-359. /Uruguay /Public administration /Administrative reform /Oil industry / Control process /Cement manufacturing industry

4630. Tikku, R. K., and P. P. Ramanathan. 1980 "Role of Government in Selecting Top Executives in Public Sector." Lok Udyog (New Delhi), V. 13, No. 10-1, pp. 7-22. /India /Management /Control process /Personnel recruitment /354.54 L836 PCL

4631. Tilakaratna, W. M. 1964 Agricultural Credit in a Developing Economy: Ceylon. Colombo: Central Bank of Ceylon. /Sri Lanka /Agricultural sector /Credit policy /Agricultural services /332.71 T45a

4632. Tinbergen, J. 1962 "Organization and Operation of Public Enterprises in the Netherlands." International Review of Administrative Sciences No. 4, pp. 430-434. /Netherlands /Management /Organization behavior /Control process /JA 1 A1 I6 PCL

4633. Tinbergen, J. 1964 "Welfare Economics and Management of Public Enterprises." Annals of Public and Cooperative Economy pp. 99-106. /Management /Social welfare policy

4634. Tinbergen, J. 1964 "La théorie du bien-être et la gestion des entreprises publiques." Annales de l´Economie Collective /Management

4635. Tinguy du Pouet, L. De. 1955 "Les entreprises nationalisées et le Parlement." Rev. Pol. Adm. Inst. /France /Nationalization /Parliament

4636. Tintic, N. 1957 "El derecho al trabajo dentro del sistema de autogestión de los trabajadores." Le Nouveau Droit Yugoslave (Belgrade), No. 2-4. /Yugoslavia /Worker self management

4637. Tiourine, I. 1960 Comment les ouvriers soviétiques participent à la gestion de la production. Moscow. /Union of Soviet Socialist Reps. /Worker management participation

4638. Tiraspolsky, A. 1971 "La participation des travailleurs a la gestion de l´entreprise industrielle." Revue de l´Etat (Paris), V. 2, No. 2, pp. 75-130. /Industrial sector /Worker management participation

4639. Tivey, L. J. 1966 Nationalization in British Industry. London: Cape. /United Kingdom /Nationalization /Industrial sector / HD 4145 T5 PCL

4640. Tivey, L. J., ed. 1972 The Nationalized Industries since 1960. London: George Allen & Unwin. /United Kingdom /Economic history /Evaluation /HD 4148 T55 PCL

4641. Tiwari, Narayan Datt. 1982 "Industry Must Address Itself to the more Challenging Task of Improving Productivity which is the Ultimate Task of Success." Lok Udyog (New Delhi), V. 16, No. 9, pp. 14-15. /India /Industrial sector /Economic efficiency /Productivity /354.54 L836 PCL

4642. Tiwary, K. N. 1954 "Some Aspects of the Management of State Enterprises in India." *Indian Economic Journal* (Bombay), V. 2, No. 3, pp. 319-327. /India /Management

4643. Tobias, Thomas J. 1947 "South Carolina State Ports Authority." *State Government* pp. 252-256. /United States of America /Port authority

4644. Tobin, Austin J. 1947 "The Port of New York Authority." *State Government* pp. 234-239. /United States of America /Port authority

4645. Todorovic, M. 1965 "Les tâches actuelles dans le développement du systeme économique et des rapports socio-économiques." *Questions Actuelles du Socialisme* (Belgrade), No. 78, pp. 15-57. /Development process /Economic system

4646. Toledo, G. 1979 "Las empresas públicas en Ecuador: Una perspectiva de acción." *Revista Latinoamericana de Administración Pública* No. 8-9, pp. 361-384. /Ecuador /Planning process /Control process /Public financing /Economic development

4647. Tomasevic, Dusan. 1978 "Organisation de l'activité de formation dans les entreprises (méthodologie)." Paper presented at the Séminaire international sur la gestion et la formation dans les entreprises publiques dans les pays en voie de développement, Ljubljana, Yugoslavia, 6-17 November. Ljubljana: ICPE. /Training

4648. Tomsic, Vida. 1980 "General Approach." Paper presented at the International Expert Group Meeting on Women as a factor of development and the Responsibilities of the Public Sector in this Regard, Ljubljana, Yugoslavia, 14-19 April. Ljubljana: ICPE. /Women's studies

4649. Tonioll, M. A. 1962 "Prezzo delle imprese pubbliche a costi crescenti e rendita del produttore." *Giornale desgli Economisti e Anali di Economie* (Padua, Italy), No. 11-2, pp. 742-771. /Costs /Productivity / Price policy

4650. Tonkovic, Stripe. 1976 "Training in Enterprises." Paper presented at the International Seminar on Management and Training in Public Enterprises in Developing Countries, Ljubljana, Yugoslavia, Sept.21-Oct.2. Ljubljana: ICPE. /Training /Also presented at the same seminars in Ljubljana, Yugoslavia, Oct. 10-28, 1977 and Sept. 18-Oct. 6, 1978.

4651. Topik, Stephen. 1979 *The evolution of the economic role of the Brazilian State, 1889-1930.* Austin, Tex.: OPSS Technical Papers Series, No. 15. /Brazil /Financial institutions /Railway industry /Economic history /OPSS

4652. Topik, Stephen. 1980 "State Enterprise in a Liberal Regime: The Banco do Brasil, 1905-1930." *Journal of Interamerican Studies and World Affairs* V. 22, No. 4, pp. 395-422. /Economic history /Financial institutions /Brazil /G 980.605 J826 LAC

4653. Tornblom, Lars. 1977 "The Swedish State Company Limited Statsföretag AB: Its Role in the Swedish Economy." Annals of Public and Cooperative Economy V. 49, No. 4, pp. 451-462. /Sweden /Economic analysis /Industrial sector /330.5 An73

4654. Torrealba Alvarez, Raúl. 1974 El petróleo en la economía venezolana. Caracas: Tallares Gráficas de Editorial. /Venezuela /Oil industry /Economic development /Economic history / HD 9574 V42 T627 LAC

4655. Torres Goitia, Hugo. 1979 "Las empresas públicas en Bolivia." Paper presented at the International Seminar on Regulation of the Public Enterprise, Mexico City. /Bolivia /Control process /OPSS

4656. Torres de Freitas, Byron. 1953 "Planejamento e controle da produção de energia elétrica no Estado do Rio: Comissao Estadual de Energia Elétrica." Revista do Servico Público (Rio de Janeiro), V. 1, No. 1, pp. 39-45. /Brazil /Electrical utility industry /Planning process /Control process / G354.81005 B739r

4657. Torres, José Garrido. 1974 "O papel da empresa privada e da empresa pública no desenvolvimento sócio- econômico." Digesto Econômico (São Paulo), V. 31, No. 235, pp. 131-140. /Brazil /Private sector /Comparative analysis /G330.981 D569 LAC

4658. Torres, Lorenzo Thomas. 1980 "Transfer of Technology in Public Enterprises: (Mexico)." Paper presented at the International Workshop on Preparations and Negotiations of Technology Transfer Agreements for Public Enterprises in Developing Countries, Ljubljana, Yugoslavia, 27-31 October. Ljubljana: ICPE. /Mexico /Technology transfer

4659. Tovias, A. 1979 State Trading and Preferential Trading. Les Cahiers du CETAI, No. 79-10. Montreal: Ecole des Hautes Etudes Commerciales. /State trading organizations /OPSS

4660. Townshend-Rose, H. 1960 The British Coal Industry. London: Allen & Unwin. /United Kingdom /Coal mining industry

4661. Train, J. C. L. 1951 "A Review of the Railways Under Nationalization." Journal of the Permanent Way Institute (London), pp. 43-48. /United Kingdom /Railway industry /Evaluation

4662. Trapeznikov, V. 1964 "Pour une direction économique souple des entreprises." Annales de l'Economie Collective V. 52, No. 4, pp. 450-458. /Planning process

4663. Traves, Giuseppino. 1958 "The Control of Public Enterprise in Italy." Paper presented at the Congress of the International Political Science Association, Rome, Sept. /Italy /Control process

4664. Trebat, Thomas J. 1979 "An Evaluation of the Economic Performance of Large Public Enterprises in Brazil, 1965-1975." Paper presented at the Eighth National Meeting of the Latin American Studies Association, Pittsburgh, Pa. /Brazil /Evaluation /Economic development /OPSS

4665. Trebat, Thomas J. 1980 An Evaluation of the Economic Performance of Large Public Enterprises in Brazil, 1965-1975. Austin, Tex.: OPSS Technical Papers Series, No. 24. /Brazil /Evaluation /Economic history /HD 4093 T73 LAC

4666. Trebat, Thomas J. 1981 "Public Enterprises in Brazil and Mexico: A Comparison of Origins and Performance." In Thomas Bruneau and Phillipe Faucher, ed(s). Authoritarian Capitalism: Brazil´s Contemporary Economic and Political Development. Boulder, Colo.: Westview Press. pp. 41-58. /Economic analysis /Brazil /Mexico /HC 187 A798 LAC

4667. Trebat, Thomas J. 1983 Brazil´s State-Owned Enterprises: A Case Study in the State as Entrepreneur. New York: Cambridge University Press. /Brazil /Economic analysis /HD 4093 T727

4668. Trebat, Thomas J., and Jan Peter Wogart. 1980 "Introduction." Journal of Interamerican Studies and World Affairs V. 22, No. 4, pp. 395-399. /Economic analysis /Latin America / G 980.605 J826 LAC

4669. Trehan, V. R. 1977 "Indian Technique for Higher Productivity: Transcendental Meditation." Lok Udyog (New Delhi), V. 11, No. 8, pp. 39-46. /India /Organization behavior /Transcendental meditation /354.54 L836 PCL

4670. Trehan, V. R. 1977 "Managing Confusion - An Overview of Management Information Systems." Lok Udyog (New Delhi), V. 10, No. 10, pp. 37-40. /India /Information system /354.54 L836 PCL

4671. Treillard, J. 1953 "La notion juridique d´entreprise des nationalisations." Revue Trimestrale Droit Commercial V. 6, pp. 605-616. /France /Law /Nationalization

4672. Treppo, R. 1966 "Le parti communiste et le problème des nationalisations." Cahiers du Communisme (Paris), V. 42, No. 10, pp. 15-30. /France /Communist party /Nationalization

4673. Trescott, P. B. 1958 "Louisville and Portland Canal Company, 1825-1874." Mississippi Valley Historical Review V. 44, pp. 686-708. /United States of America /Economic history / River valley development projects

4674. Treves, Giuseppino. 1966 "Las empresas públicas en Italia." Documentación Administrative (Madrid), No. 100, pp. 215-225. /Italy

4675. Treves, Giuseppino. 1970 "The Public Corporation in Italy." In W. P. Friedmann and J. F. Garner, ed(s). Government Enterprise, A Comparative Study New York: Columbia University Press. pp. 133-153. /Italy / 350.0092 G746 PCL

4676. Triebenstein, Olaf. 1958 La empresa industrial estatal y la posibilidad y necesidad de su utilización instrumental en las economías organizadas bajo el sistema de la economía de mercado. Berlin. /Market economy /Industrial sector / Policy analysis

4677. Tripathi, B. N. 1982 "The Concept of Public Enterprise." Lok Udyog (New Delhi), V. 15, No. 12, pp. 33-36. /Structural characteristics /Taxonomy /Economic history /354.54 L836 PCL

4678. Tripathi, P. C. 1956 "Public Enterprises in India." Modern Review (Calcutta), V. 99, No. 5, pp. 370-374. /India /059.54 M72

4679. Tripathi, S. D. 1971 "Tasks before Nationalised Banks." Lok Udyog (New Delhi), V. 4, No. 11, pp. 1273-1280. /Goal setting /Banking system /India /354.54 L836 PCL

4680. Tripathi, S. D. 1981 "Perspectives in Indian Public Sector Banking and Insurance." Lok Udyog (New Delhi), V. 14, No. 12, pp. 17-24. /India /Banking system /Insurance industry /354.54 L836 PCL

4681. Tripathy, R. N. 1964 "Criteria for the Choice of Investment Projects in Development Planning." Indian Journal of Economics pp. 69-81. /India /Development planning /Investment / 330.5 In2

4682. Trist, Eric. 1970 Management and Organization Development in Government Agencies and Public Enterprises. Washington, D. C. /Organization development /Management

4683. Troxel, E. 1948 "Demand Elasticity and Control of Public Utility Earnings." American Economic Review V. 38, pp. 372-382. /Public utility industry /Public financing /Price policy /Control process / Demand analysis

4684. Truong-Nguyen. 1974 "The Role of Public Enterprise in National Development in South Vietnam: Problems and Prospects." Singapore: Regional Institute of Higher Education and Development. /Vietnam, Rep. of

4685. Truong-Nguyen. 1976 "The Role of Public Enterprise in National Development in Southeast Asia: Problems and Prospects." Singapore: Regional Institute of Higher Education and Development. /Southeast Asia

4686. Tucker, W. H. 1954 "Public Control of Statutory Corporations." Public Administration (Sydney, Australia), V. 13, No. 1, pp. 19-24. /Control process /Public administration

4687. Tulkens, Henry. 1976 "The Publicness of Public Enterprise." In William G. Shepherd et al., ed(s). Public Enterprise: Economic Analysis of Theory and Practice. Lexington, Mass.: D.C. Heath and Company, Lexington Books. pp. 23-32. /Mixed enterprises /Economic analysis /HD 3850 P8 PCL

4688. Tunisia. National Team of Experts. 1979 "Rôle du secteur publique dans les pays en voie de développement: rapport préliminaire présenté par la Tunisie." Paper presented at the International Meeting on the Role of the Public Sector in Developing Countries, 2nd, Ljubljana, Yugoslavia, 2-7 April. Ljubljana: ICPE. /Tunisia

4689. Tunisia. National Team of Experts. 1981 "Rôle des entreprises publiques dans le développement économique et social du pays: Tunisie." Ljubljana: ICPE. /Tunisia /Economic development

4690. Turk, Ivan. 1976 "The Improvement of Specialists for the Requirements of Public Enterprises." Paper presented at the International Seminar on Management and Training on Public Enterprises in Developing Countries, Ljubljana, Yugoslavia, Sept.21-Oct.2. Ljubljana: ICPE. /Training /Management / Also presented at the same seminar in Ljubljana, Oct. 10-28, 1977.

4691. Turk, Ivan. 1976 "Improvement of Specialists for Work in the Field of Accounting Information." Paper presented at the International Seminar on Management and Training in Public Enterprises in Developing Countries, Ljubljana, Yugoslavia, Sept.21-Oct.2. Ljubljana: ICPE. /Training /Accounting / Also presented at the same seminars in Ljubljana, Yugoslavia, from 10-28 Oct., 1977 and from Sept. 18 to Oct. 6, 1978.

4692. Turk, Ivan. 1978 "Accounting Information Needed in Assessing the Efficiency of the Public Enterprise." Paper presented at the Workshop on Information System for the Evaluation of Business Efficiency in Public Enterprises in Developing Countries, Ljubljana, Yugoslavia, 13-18 Nov. Ljubljana: ICPE. /Accounting /Economic efficiency /Evaluation / Also published in Public Enterprise, Vol 1, No.2(1980), pp. 7-17. /OPSS

4693. Turk, Ivan. 1978 "Analysis of the Differences between the Achieved Financial Result and the Planned One." Paper presented at the Workshop on Information System for the Evaluation of Business Efficiency in Public Enterprises in Developing Countries, Ljubljana, Yugoslavia, 13-18 Nov. Ljubljana: ICPE. /Budget auditing /Accounting /Economic efficiency /Evaluation

4694. Turk, Ivan. 1978 "Analysis of Efficiency by Means of Interrelated Indicators." Paper presented at the Workshop on Information System for the Evaluation of Business Efficiency in Public Enterprises in Developing Countries, Ljubljana, Yugoslavia, 13-18 Nov. Ljubljana: ICPE. /Economic efficiency /Evaluation

4695. Turk, Ivan. 1979 "Theoretical Considerations on Data, Information and Control in Public Enterprises." Paper presented at the Interregional Workshop on Control Systems for Public Enterprises in Developing Countries, Ljubljana, Yugoslavia, 9-13 July. Ljubljana: ICPE. /Control process /Information system

4696. Turk, Ivan. 1983 "Efficiency Analysis Through Interrelated Indicators: The Yugoslav Approach." In G. Ram Reddy, ed(s). Government and Public Enterprise: Essays in honour of Professor V. V. Ramanadham. Bombay, India: N. M. Tripathi

Private Limited. pp. 140-156. /Yugoslavia /Economic efficiency

4697. Turkey. Institute of Administrative Sciences. 1959 Bibliography on Public Administration in Turkey, 1928-1957. Ankara. /Turkey /Public administration /Bibliography

4698. Turkey. Ministry of Industry. 1958 A Law Relating to the Organization and Supervision of Economic Corporations Established by Means of Capital Wholly Provided by the State. Ankara. /Turkey /Law /Management /Public administration /Public financing /Structural characteristics

4699. Turkey. Public Administration Institute. 1954 The Structure and Control of State Enterprises in Turkey. Ankara. /Turkey /Control process

4700. Turner, S. H. 1904 "Depreciation and Sinking Funds in Municipal Undertakings." Economic Journal V. 14, pp. 47-56. /Local government /Public financing / 330.5 Ec7

4701. Turot, P. 1970 Les entreprises publiques en Europe. Paris: Dunod. /Europe

4702. Turot, P. 1971 Les entreprises publiques en Grande-Bretagne. Paris: La Documentation Française. /United Kingdom

4703. Turvey, R. 1968 Public Enterprises: Selected Readings. Baltimore: Penguin Books Inc. /Economic theory /338.001 T869e PCL /HD 3850 T89 Pub Aff

4704. Turvey, R. 1968 Optimal Pricing and Investment in Electricity Supply. An Essay in Welfare Economics. London: Allen & Unwin. /United Kingdom /Electrical utility industry /Price policy /Investment / 621.3002 T869o

4705. Turvey, R. 1971 Economic Analysis and Public Enterprise. London: George Allen & Unwin. /Economic analysis /Evaluation /338.001 T869c

4706. Turvey R., and D. Anderson. 1976 Electricity Economics: Essays and Case Studies. Baltimore: The Johns Hopkins University Press. /Electrical utility industry /Economic theory /Case studies / HD 9685 A2 T85

4707. Tyler, William. 1969 "Performance of Hindustan Steel and Other Running Concerns during 1967-68." Lok Udyog (New Delhi), V. 3, No. 3, pp. 291-301. /India /Steel industry /Case studies /Evaluation / 354.54 L836

4708. Tyler, William. 1970 "Desenvolvimento de indicadores de eficiencia do complexo governamental." Revista de Administração Pública (Rio de Janeiro), V. 4, No. 2, pp. 115-131. /Evaluation /Economic efficiency /Economic analysis /G350.5 R3261 LAC

4709. Tyrrell, S. C. 1948 "Nationalization and Cost Accountancy." Cost Accountant pp. 67-71. /Nationalization /Accountability /Cost benefit analysis

4710. Udo-Aka, Udo. 1979 "Government Policies towards Joint Ventures for Promoting Economic Development." Paper presented at the International Seminar on Joint Ventures and Public Enterprises in Developing Countries, Ljubljana, Yugoslavia, 4-12 December. Ljubljana: ICPE. /Economic development /Mixed enterprises /Planning process /Control process

4711. Udo-Aka, Udo. 1980 "Management Development and Training in Public Enterprises: An Overview of the Nigerian Experience." Paper presented at the expert group meeting on the research project on education and training in public enterprises in developing countries, Ljubljana, Yugoslavia, 17-22 March. Ljubljana: ICPE. /Nigeria /Training

4712. Udo-Aka, Udo. 1980 "Development of Training Methodologies for Internal Consultants in Nigerian Public Enterprises: The CMD Experience." Paper presented at the Regional Workshop on Development of Training Methodologies for Internal Consultants in African Public Enterprises, Addis Ababa, Ethiopia, 1-6 December. Ljubljana: ICPE. /Nigeria /Training /Methodology /Consultant services / Case studies

4713. Udoji, J. O. 1970 "Reforming the Public Enterprises in Africa." <u>Quarterly Journal of Administration</u> (Ibadan, Nigeria), V. 4, No. 3, pp. 217-234. /Africa /Evaluation /Administrative reform

4714. Ugalde, Alberto J. 1983 "Las empresas públicas en Argentina." Paper presented at the ECLA seminar, "State Control and Planning of Public Enterprises," Brasília, 15-17 June. /Argentina /Economic History /OPSS

4715. Uganda. Institute of Public Administration. 1970 "The Role of the Parastatal Bodies in the Implementation of the Common Man´s Charter." Paper presented at the Seminar on the Role of Public Officials in the Implementation of the Common Man´s Charter. Kampala, Uganda: Ministry of Public Services and Cabinet Affairs. /Uganda /Social development

4716. Uganda. Makerere University. 1970 <u>Papers of Working Party in Comparative Administration: Para-Statal Bodies in Uganda.</u> Kampala, Uganda: Makerere University. /Uganda

4717. Uganda. Uganda Development Corporation Ltd. 1955 <u>Legislation Relating to the Creation and Running of the Uganda Development Corporation Ltd.</u> Kampala. /Uganda /Law /Organization formation /Management /Development corporation

4718. Ugoh, S. U. 1964 "The Nigerian Cement Company." <u>Nigerian Journal of Economic and Social Studies</u> (Ibadan, Nigeria), V. 6, pp. 72-91. /Nigeria /Cement manufacturing industry /Case studies

4719. Ulkmen, I. H. 1956 "Les entreprises industrielles et minières de l´Etat en Turquie." <u>Annales de l´Economie Collective</u> pp. 377-394. /Turkey /Industrial sector /Mining industry

4720. Ullmann, Friedrich. 1979 The Austrian Model of Its Nationalized Industrial Sector. Vienna: UNIDO. /Austria /Industrial sector /OPSS

4721. Ulosch, H. Vater, and W. Schmidt, E. 1957 Organisation und Planung der volkseigenen artlichen Industrie. Berlin: Ed. Verlag Die Wirtschaft. /Germany, Federal Rep. of /Planning process /Organization development

4722. Umex, Manca, and Matjaz Musek, eds. 1982 Bibliography of ICPE, 1974-1981. Ljubljana: ICPE. /Bibliography

4723. United Kingdom. 1967 A Review of Economic and Financial Objectives. London: Command Paper 3437. /United Kingdom /Economic research /Financial performance /Government report

4724. United Kingdom. Acton Society Trust. 1950 Accountability to Parliament. Claygate. No. 1. /United Kingdom /Parliament /Control process

4725. United Kingdom. Acton Society Trust. 1950 A Series of 12 Research Booklets on Nationalized Industry. London. /United Kingdom /Industrial sector /Accountability /Government bureaucracy /Management /Organization formation

4726. United Kingdom. Acton Society Trust. 1951 The Powers of the Minister. London. /United Kingdom /Control process

4727. United Kingdom. Acton Society Trust. 1951 "Promotion Policy in the Nationalized Industries." Personnel Management (London), pp. 17-22. /United Kingdom /Personnel management

4728. United Kingdom. Acton Society Trust. 1951 Studies in Nationalized Industry, No. 4: The Men the Boards. London. /United Kingdom /Management /Control process

4729. United Kingdom. Acton Society Trust. 1953 Relations with the Public. London. /United Kingdom /Public relations

4730. United Kingdom. Acton Society Trust. 1953 Studies in Nationalized Industry, No. 9: Patterns of Organization. London. /United Kingdom /Industrial sector /Organization formation

4731. United Kingdom. Acton Society Trust. n.d. Management under Nationalization and the Extent of Centralization. London. /United Kingdom /Public administration /Management /Centralization

4732. United Kingdom. Acton Society Trust. n.d. (I) The Miner´s Pensions; (II) The Workers Point of View; (III) Training and Promotion in Nationalized Industry; (IV) Problems of Promotion Policy; (V) The Future of the Unions; (VI) The Framework of Joint Consultation. London. /United Kingdom /Industrial sector /Trade unions /Policy development / Worker management participation /Mining industry

4733. United Kingdom. Administrative Staff College. 1963 The Accountability of Public Corporations. /United Kingdom

/Accountability

4734. United Kingdom. British Productivity Council. 1965 Capital Investment for Technological Development, Papers Given at the Industry 65 Exibition Conference on Productivity, Technology, Change. London. /United Kingdom /Technology /Investment /Productivity

4735. United Kingdom. British Consumer Council. 1968 Consumer Consultive Machinery in the Nationalized Industries. London: HMSO. /Public relations /Consumer relations

4736. United Kingdom. Broadcasting Committee. 1950 Report of the Broadcasting Committee. London: HMSO. /United Kingdom /Broadcasting industry

4737. United Kingdom. Bureau of Railway Economics. 1953 Nationalized Transport Operations in Great Britain. London. /United Kingdom /Nationalization /Transportation industry

4738. United Kingdom. Central Office of Information. 1964 Nationalized Industries in Britain. London. /United Kingdom /Industrial sector

4739. United Kingdom. Chancellor of the Exchequer. 1960 Public Investment in Great Britain: Report to Parliament. London: HMSO. /United Kingdom /Investment

4740. United Kingdom. Chancellor of the Exchequer. 1961 Public Investment in Great Britain. London: HMSO. /United Kingdom /Investment

4741. United Kingdom. Chancellor of the Exchequer. 1961 "The Financial and Economic Obligations of the Nationalized Industries." Public Administration (London), pp. 263-269. /United Kingdom /Debt / 320.5 J826 PCL

4742. United Kingdom. Chancellor of the Exchequer. 1961 The Financial and Economic Obligations of the Nationalized Industries. London: HMSO. /United Kingdom /Economic analysis / Financial performance

4743. United Kingdom. Chancellor of the Exchequer. 1967 Nationalized Industries--A Review of Economic and Financial Objectives. London: HMSO. /United Kingdom /Industrial sector /Economic analysis /Financial performance

4744. United Kingdom. Commonwealth Secretariat. 1982 Relationships between Parliament and Public Enterprises.(Report of a Seminar held at Colombo, Sri Lanka, 15-19 June, 1981. London. /Parliament /Control process

4745. United Kingdom. Commonwealth Secretariat. 1982 Government executive and Supervisory Control over Public Enterprise: Report of a Workshop held in New Delhi, India, 4-8 June, 1982. London. /Control process

4746. United Kingdom. District Bank. 1968 Management Training in the Public Sector. District Bank Review (Manchester),

/United Kingdom /Management /Training

4747. United Kingdom. Electricity Council. 1971 The Organization and Development of the Electricity Supply Industry in England and Wales. (Reference papers) London. /United Kingdom /Electrical utility industry /Public services /Organization development

4748. United Kingdom. Federation of British Industries. 1952 Coal: The Price Structure. London: Federation of British Industries. /United Kingdom /Coal mining industry /Price policy

4749. United Kingdom. Federation of British Industries. 1959 Report on Nationalization. London. /United Kingdom /Nationalization

4750. United Kingdom. Fleck Committee. 1955 Report of the Advisory Committee on Organization. London: National Coal Board. /United Kingdom /Coal mining industry /Management

4751. United Kingdom. I.E.A. 1968 Comparative Returns from Investment in Nationalized Industries. London. /United Kingdom /Industrial sector / Comparative analysis /Profits

4752. United Kingdom. Labour Party. 1946 Nationalization of Coal. London. /United Kingdom /Coal mining industry /Nationalization / Labor party

4753. United Kingdom. Labour Party National Executive Committee. 1946 Post-War Organization of British Transport. London. /United Kingdom /Transportation industry /Organization change /Labor party

4754. United Kingdom. Labour Party National Executive Committee. 1953 "Labour Party and Public Ownership. Challenge to Britain." Annales de l´Economie Collective pp. 118-167. /United Kingdom /Labor party

4755. United Kingdom. Labour Party. 1957 Industry and Society: Labour´s Policy on Future Public Ownership. London. /United Kingdom /Labor party

4756. United Kingdom. Labour Party. 1957 Labour´s Review of the Nationalised Industries. London. /United Kingdom /Industrial sector /Labor party

4757. United Kingdom. Labour Party. 1957 Public Enterprise. London. /United Kingdom / Labor party

4758. United Kingdom. Ministry of Power. 1965 Steel Nationalization. London: HMSO. /United Kingdom /Steel industry /Nationalization

4759. United Kingdom. Ministry of Overseas Development. Library. 1967 Public Administration--A Select Bibliography. London. /Bibliography /Public administration

4760. United Kingdom. National Coal Board. 1955 Report of the Advisory Committee on Organisation. London. /United Kingdom /Coal mining industry

4761. United Kingdom. National Board for Prices and Incomes. 1968 Top Salaries in the Private Sector and Nationalized Industries. London: HMSO, Cmnd. 3970. No. 107. /United Kingdom /Private sector /Wages /Comparative analysis

4762. United Kingdom. Parliament. Select Committee on Nationalized Industries. 1953 Report. London: HMSO. /United Kingdom /Parliament /Evaluation

4763. United Kingdom. Parliament. Select Committee on Nationalized Industries. 1957 1st Report. House of Commons Paper 304. London: HMSO. /United Kingdom /Parliament / Evaluation

4764. United Kingdom. Parliament. Select Committee on Nationalized Industries. 1957 2nd Report. House of Commons Papers 187 and 187-I. London: HMSO. /United Kingdom /Parliament / Evaluation

4765. United Kingdom. Parliament. Select Committee on Nationalized Industries. 1962 Reports of Former Select Committees on Nationalised Industries: Outcome of Recommendations and Conclusions. London: HMSO. /United Kingdom /Parliament

4766. United Kingdom. Parliament. Select Committee on Nationalized Industries. 1971 Second Report from the Select Committee on Nationalized Industries. (Session 1970/1971: Relations with the Public). London: HMSO. /United Kingdom /Industrial sector /Public relations

4767. United Kingdom. Royal Institute of Public Administration. 1960 Administrative Organization for Economic Development. London. /United Kingdom /Economic development /Administrative management Organization behavior

4768. United Kingdom. The Air Corporation. 1959 Report from the Select Committee on Nationalized Industry: Reports and Accounts. London: HMSO. No. 213. /United Kingdom /Nationalization /Industrial sector

4769. United Kingdom. Trade Union Congress. 1946 Interim Report on Post-War Reconstruction. London. /United Kingdom /Trade unions

4770. United Kingdom. Trade Union Congress. 1951 "Public Ownership Review."(Five Articles). Labour (London), /United Kingdom

4771. United Kingdom. Treasury. 1961 The Financial and Economic Obligations of the Nationalized Industries, Cmnd. 1337. London: HMSO. /Industrial sector /Financing /Economic efficiency

4772. United Nations. 1956 "Economic Development of Under-Developed Countries, Evolution and Functioning of Development Corporations: Working Paper." New York. /Developing nations /Economic development /Development corporation

4773. United Nations. 1956 "United Nations Economic Development of Underdeveloped Countries: Survey of Current Work on Industrialization and Productivity." New York: United Nations. /Economic development /Developing nations /Industrialization /Productivity

4774. United Nations. 1959 "Administrative Problems of State Enterprise in India." Paper presented at the Seminar on Management of Public Industrial Enterprises. Seminar Paper No. 46. New Delhi: United Nations. /India /Public administration /Industrial sector

4775. United Nations. 1959 "Industrial Enterprises in the Public Sector in India." Paper presented at the Seminar on Management of Public Industrial Enterprises. Seminar Paper No. 26. New Delhi: United Nations. /India /Industrial sector

4776. United Nations. 1960 Public Industrial Management in Asia and the Far East. (A Selection from the Material Prepared for a United Nations Seminar held in New Delhi in December 1959). ST/TAO/M/15. New York. /Asia

4777. United Nations. 1960 Public Industrial Management in Asia and the Far East. New York. /Asia /Public administration /Management /Industrial sector

4778. United Nations. 1962 "As empresas estatais e a opinião pública." Paper presented at the Seminário sobre organização e administração de serviços industriais do estado. Rio de Janeiro: FGV. pp. 45-60. /Public relations

4779. United Nations. 1962 Estudios sobre la electricidad en América Latina. Mexico. V. 1. /Latin America /Electrical utility industry

4780. United Nations. 1964 Estudios sobre la electricidad en America Latina. New York. V. 2. /Latin America /Electrical utility industry

4781. United Nations. 1966 Seminar on Organization and Administration of Public Enterprises, Geneva, 26 September-4 October 1966. Geneva: United Nations. /Management /Public administration / 351.82 Un3r

4782. United Nations. 1967 Report of the United Nations Seminar on Organization and Administration of Public Enterprises. New York. /Public administration /Management /Control process

4783. United Nations. 1969 Financial Aspects of Manufacturing Enterprises in the Public Sector: Report and Proceedings of Interregional Seminar Held in Rome. New York. /Public financing / qHD 3850 F55

4784. United Nations. 1969 Financial Performance of Public Enterprises in India. New York. /India /Public financing /Evaluation / Profits

4785. United Nations. 1969 Final Report of U.N. Expert Working Group on Measures for Improving Performance of Public Enterprises for Developing Countries. Herceg Novi, Yugoslavia: United Nations. /Economic efficiency /Developing nations /Organization change

4786. United Nations. 1972 Proyecto de capacitación de la administración pública uruguaya. New York. /Uruguay /Civil service /Public administration / Training /Administrative reform /OPSS

4787. United Nations. 1974 Comment améliorer les performances des entreprises publiques dans le pays en voie de développement. ST/TAO/M/58. New York. /Developing nations /Management /Economic efficiency

4788. United Nations. Bureau of Flood Control. 1960 A Case Study of the Damodar Valley Corporation and Its Projects. New York. /India /River valley development projects /Case studies

4789. United Nations. Center for Industrial Development. 1965 Organization and Administration of Industrial Services in Ethiopia. Addis Ababa, Ethiopia. /Ethiopia /Industrial sector /Management

4790. United Nations. Commodities Division. 1962 The Role of Marketing Boards for Export Crops in the Developing Countries. New York. /Developing nations /State trading organizations /Export policy

4791. United Nations. DESA. 1958 Integrated River Basin Development. New York. /River valley development projects /Regional development

4792. United Nations. DESA. 1958 Direccín y administración de empresas industriales en los países insuficientemente desarrollados. E/3143; ST/ECA/58. New York. /Developing nations /Industrial sector /Management

4793. United Nations. DESA. 1959 Development of Public Industrial Enterprises in Burma. New York. /Burma /Industrial sector

4794. United Nations. DESA. 1960 Management of Public Enterprises. New York. /Industrial sector /Management

4795. United Nations. DESA. 1960 Management of Public Industrial Enterprises in Japan. New York. /Japan /Industrial sector /Management

4796. United Nations. DESA. 1960 Structure and Operation of Public Enterprises in Indonesia. New York. /Indonesia /Evaluation /Structural characteristics

4797. United Nations. DESA. 1967 The Role of Public Enterprises in the Formulation of Development Plans in Centrally Planned Economy. ST/TAO/M/37. New York. /Economic development

4798. United Nations. DESA. 1967 Informe del seminario de las Naciones Unidas sobre organización y administración de empresas públicas celebrado en Ginebra, Suiza, 26 de Sep. 4 de Oct. 1966. ST/TAO/M/35. New York. /Management

4799. United Nations. DESA. 1968 Organization and Administration of Public Enterprises. New York. /Public administration /Administrative management /Organization formation / Control process /Management

4800. United Nations. DESA. 1973 Legal and Administrative Frameworks for Electricity Enterprises. New York. /Law /Public administration /Electrical utility industry

4801. United Nations. DESA. 1973 Measures for Improving Performance of Public Enterprise in Developing Countries. ST/TAO/M/58. New York. /Evaluation /Developing nations /Productivity

4802. United Nations. DESA. 1974 Organization, Management and Supervision of Public Enterprises in Developing Countries. New York. /Developing nations /Management /Control process /Financing /Evaluation /OPSS

4803. United Nations. DESA. 1976 Financing of Public Enterprises in Developing Countries: Co-Ordination, Forms and Sources. New York. /Public financing /Developing nations / /OPSS

4804. United Nations. DESA. 1977 A Practical Guide to Performance Improvement Programming in Public Organizations. New York. /Evaluation / Productivity

4805. United Nations. DESA. 1977 Handbook on Government Auditing in Developing Countries. New York. /Budget auditing /Accounting

4806. United Nations. Division of Public Administration. 1969 Mejoramiento de la rentabilidad de las empresas públicas en los países en desarrollo. ST/ECLA/Conf.35/L.8. Santiago, Chile. /Developing nations /Evaluation / Profits /

4807. United Nations. Division of Public Administration. 1970 Measures for Improving the Performance of Public Enterprise in Developingg Countries. (Meeting held at Herceg-Novi, Yugoslavia, Oct. 13-24, 1969). ST/TAO/M/49. New York. /Developing nations /Public administration / Productivity /Profits

4808. United Nations. ECA. 1968 Report of the Seminar on the Management of Public Enterprises. (The French-Speaking Group.) Bizerte, Tunisia. /Africa /Management

4809. United Nations. ECA. 1969 Growth of State Enterprise in Zambia. Mauritius. /Zambia /Evaluation / Africa

4810. United Nations. ECA. 1969 Le rôle des entreprises publiques dans la planification et l'exécution des plans: Haute-Volta. Mauritius. /Upper Volta /Evaluation /Planning process / Africa

4811. United Nations. ECA. 1969 The Role of Public Enterprises in Planning and Plan Implementation in Nigeria. Mauritius. /Nigeria /Evaluation /Planning process / Africa

4812. United Nations. ECA. 1969 Report of the Seminar on the Role of Public Enterprises in Planning and Implementation. Mauritius. /Planning process /Goal setting / Africa

4813. United Nations. ECA. 1970 Administration for Development: A Working Paper. Addis Ababa. /Public administration /Economic development /Social development

4814. United Nations. ECA. 1975 "The Role of the Public Enterprise in the Development of African States." In Improving Performance in Public Enterprise, Report of an International Conference, Arusha, Tanzania, 2-5 December. Arusha, Tanzania: East African Community Management Institute, pp. 7-24. /Law /Africa /Nigeria /Cameroon /Case studies

4815. United Nations. ECA. 1978 Regional Seminar on Technical and Managerial Problems of African Public Enterprises, Yaounde, 7-14 August. Yaounde, Cameroon: Economic Commission for Africa; Government of Cameroon. V. 9. /Management /Togo /Algeria /Africa

4816. United Nations. ECA. 1980 "Management Development and Training in African Public Enterprises." Paper presented at the Expert Group Meeting on the Research Project on Education and Training in Public Enterprises in Developing Countries, Ljubljana, Yugoslavia, 17-1122 March. Ljubljana: ICPE. /Africa /Training /Management

4817. United Nations. ECA. 1981 "The Public Sector and the Implementation of the Lagos Plan of Action." Paper presented at the International Workshop on Financial Profitability and Losses in Public Enterprises, Ljubljana, Yugoslavia, 1-5 June. Ljubljana: ICPE. /Public financing / Profits / /Also published in Public Enterprise, Vol. 2, No. 1(1981), pp. 22-29. /OPSS

4818. United Nations. ECA. 1982 "Constraints to the Effective Development of the Entrepreneurial Capabilities and Performance of African Public Enterprises." Paper presented at the ECA/OAU Conference on the Role of the Public Sector in National and Regional Development in the context of the Implementation of the Lagos Plan of Action - Addis Ababa, Ethiopia, 22-27 Nov. /E/ECA/PAMM/PS/82/5. New York. /Financial performance /Management /Africa /OPSS

4819. United Nations. ECA. 1982 "Measures for Enhancing the Effective Performance and Profitability of African Public Enterprises." Paper presented at the ECA/OAU Regional Conference of the Role of the Public Sector in National and Regional Development in the Context of the Implementation of the Lagos Plan of Action, Addis Ababa, Ethiopia, 22-27 Nov. E/ECA/PAMM/PS/82/7 Addis, Ababa: UNECA. /Africa /Profits /Management /OPSS

4820. United Nations. ECAFE. 1953 *Mobilization of Domestic Capital: Report and Documents of the Second Working Party of Experts.* Bangkok, Thailand. /Asia / Investment

4821. United Nations. ECAFE. 1960 *Report of the Seminar on Management of Public Industrial Enterprises in the ECAFE Region.* Bangkok: Thailand. /Asia /Industrial sector

4822. United Nations. ECAFE. 1961 *The Increasing Role of the Public Sector.* Bangkok, Thailand. /Asia /

4823. United Nations. ECAFE. 1964 *State Trading in Countries of Asia and the Far East.* E/CN. 11/665. New York. /Asia /State trading organizations / 382.095 Un3s

4824. United Nations. ECAFE. 1967 *Public Electricity Supply. A Manual on Uniform System of Accounting.* E/CN. 11/759. New York. /Electrical utility industry /Public services /Accounting

4825. United Nations. ECE. 1963 *Economic Methods and Criteria in the Relation of Investment in Electric Power Industry.* Geneva. /Europe /Electrical utility industry /Investment

4826. United Nations. ECLA. 1961 *Movilización de recursos: Las empresas públicas, su significación actual y potencial en el proceso de su desarrollo; la intermediación financiera en América Latina.* Santiago, Chile. /Latin America /Economic development /Investment /Financing

4827. United Nations. ECLA. 1966 *The Process of Industrial Development in Latin America.* E/CN. 12/716/Rev.1. New York. /Latin America /Industrial sector

4828. United Nations. ECLA. 1969 *Inter-Relationships between Public Enterprises and the Central Government: their Implications for Performance. (Summary)* Santiago, Chile. /Latin America /Caribbean Region /Public administration /Control process

4829. United Nations. ECLA. 1969 *Improving Profit Performance of Public Enterprises in Developing Countries.* Santiago, Chile. /Developing nations /Evaluation /Profits / Latin America

4830. United Nations. ECLA. 1969 *Report on the Meeting of Experts on Administration of Public Enterprises in Latin America and the Caribbean.* Santiago, Chile. /Latin America /Caribbean Region /Public administration /Control process /Management

4831. United Nations. ECLA. 1969 *La recepción y transmisión de información en las empresas.* Santiago, Chile. /Latin America /Public administration /Information management

4832. United Nations. ECLA. 1969 "Análisis de la eficiencia de las empresas públicas: Comparación de algunos casos." Paper presented at the meeting of experts on administration of public enterprises in Latin America and the Caribbean, Santiago, Chile, 17-22 Nov. ST/ECLA/Conf. 35/L.7. Santiago, Chile. /Economic efficiency /Comparative analysis

Evaluation /Case studies

4833. United Nations. ECLA. 1969 "Medidas de rentabilidad y eficiencia de las empresas públicas: Breve resumen de la experiencia de los países." Paper presented at the meeting of experts on administration of public enterprises in Latin America and the Caribbean, Santiago, Chile, 17-22 Nov. ST/ECLA/Conf. 35/L. 3. Santiago, Chile. /Latin America /Profits /Economic efficiency

4834. United Nations. ECLA. 1969 "Some Administrative Problems of Public Enterprises." Paper presented at the meeting of experts on administration of public enterpises in Latin America and the Caribbean, Santiago, Chile, 17-22 Nov. ST/ECLA/Conf.35/L1. Santiago, Chile. /Administrative management /Latin America /Caribbean Region /Management /Public administration /OPSS

4835. United Nations. ECLA. 1970 _Informe de la reunión de expertos en administración de empresas públicas en América Latina y el Caribe._ Santiago, Chile. /Latin America /Caribbean Region /Public administration / Control process /Management

4836. United Nations. ECLA. 1971 "Las empresas públicas: Su significación actual y potencial en el proceso de desarrollo." _Boletín Económico de America Latina_ (Santiago, Chile), V. 16, No. 1, pp. 1-62. /Latin America /Economic development /Economic history /G330.9806 Un3 ebs LAC

4837. United Nations. ECLA. 1971 "Public Enterprises: Their Present Significance and Their Potential in Development." _Economic Bulletin for Latin America_ (Santiago, Chile), V. 16, pp. 1-70. /Latin America /Economic development / Economic history / G330.9806 Un 3 eb LAC

4838. United Nations. ECLA. 1971 _Las empresas públicas: Su significación actual y potencial en el proceso de desarrollo._ E/CN. 12/872. Santiago, Chile. /Evaluation /Development process / Economic history / Latin America

4839. United Nations. ECLA. 1972 _Informe de la reunión de consultores sobre administración de empresas públicas._ Santiago, Chile. /Public administration /Management

4840. United Nations. ECLA. 1972 _Bibliografía sobre empresas públicas: Colección bibliográfica._ Santiago, Chile: CLADES - Centro Latinoamericano de Documentación Económica y Social. /Latin America /Bibliography

4841. United Nations. ECLA. 1972 _Meeting of Consultants on Administration of Public Enterprises._ ST/ECLA/Conf. 45/L2. Santiago, Chile. /Latin America /Management /Control process

4842. United Nations. ECOSOC. 1964 "Las relaciones entre las empresas públicas y el gobierno central y su aspecto sobre la eficiencia." ST/ECLA/Conf. 35/L.2. Santiago, Chile. /Control process /Public administration /Economic efficiency

4843. United Nations. ECOSOC. 1969 Usiminas: Un proyecto en desarrollo. SR/ECLA/Conf.35/L.6 Santiago, Chile. /Brazil /Steel industry

4844. United Nations. ECOSOC. 1969 "Precios, rentabilidad y eficiencia de las empresas públicas." Paper presented at the Reunión de expertos en administración de empresas públicas en América Latina y el Caribe, Santiago, Chile, 17 a 22 de nov. ST/ECLA/Conf. 35/L.63. Santiago, Chile. /Latin America /Caribbean Region /Profits /Economic efficiency /Price policy

4845. United Nations. ECOSOC. 1969 The Public Enterprise: Prices, Profitability and Efficiency. Santiago, Chile. /Profits /Price policy / Latin America /Caribbean Region /Economic efficiency

4846. United Nations. ECOSOC. 1973 La interconexión internacional de sistemas de electrificación en América Latina. New York. /Latin America /Regional development /Electrical utility industry

4847. United Nations. ECOSOC. 1974 América Latina y los problemas actuales de la energía. Simposio técnico sobre América Latina y los problemas actuales de la energía. ST/ECLA/Conf.50/L.2. Santiago, Chile. /Latin America /Energy use policy / Electrical utility industry

4848. United Nations. ECOSOC. n.d. La administración de las empresas públicas. Santiago, Chile. /Management

4849. United Nations. EFPE. 1970 Aspectos financieros de las empresas manufactureras del sector público; informe del seminario interregional celebrado en Roma, de 1 a 12 de dez. 1969. New York. V. 1. /Manufacturing industry /Financing

4850. United Nations. FAO. 1968 Agricultural Credit through Co-Ops and Other Institutions. Rome. /Agricultural services /Credit policy

4851. United Nations. ILPES. 1981 "Notas sobre los estilos de planificación y el sector de empresas públicas." Paper presented at the Seminar on Public Enterprises and Planning in Central American and the Caribbean, San José, Costa Rica, 1-3 July. Santiago, Chile. /Planning process /OPSS

4852. United Nations. Resources and Transport Division. 1966 Tariffs as a Tool for the Development of Public Utility Enterprises. Geneva. /Public utility industry /Price policy

4853. United Nations. UNCTAD. 1972 Multinational Shipping Enterprises. New York. /Shipping industry /Multinational corporations

4854. United Nations. UNCTAD. 1973 Current Problems of Economic Integration: State Trading and Regional. New York. /Economic integration / Regional development /Developing nations /State trading organizations

4855. United Nations. UNCTAD. 1978 "Co-operation among State Trading organizations of sub-Saharan African developing countries." (Geneva: UNCTAD). TD/B/C.7/18 /State trading organizations /Africa /OPSS

4856. United Nations. UNDP. 1972 _Las empresas públicas industriales y comerciales en el Uruguay._ DP/SF/UN/75. New York. /Uruguay /Industrial sector /Commercial sector

4857. United Nations. UNIDO. 1969 "Profitability and Efficiency Measures of Public Enterprises." Paper presented at the Meeting of Experts in Administration of Public Enterprises in Latin America and the Caribbean, Santiago, Chile, 17-22 Nov. ST/ECLA/CONF.35/L9 Santiago, Chile. /Profits /Economic efficiency /OPSS

4858. United Nations. TAA. 1956 _International Bibliography of Public Administration._ New York. /Bibliography /Public administration

4859. United Nations. TAA. 1958 _Problemas relativos a la organización y administración de empresas públicas en el sector industrial._ ST/TAA/M/7. New York. /Industrial sector /Management /Public administration

4860. United Nations. TAA. n.d. _Public utilities in Colombia._ ST/TAA/J/Colombia/R.1. New York. /Colombia /Public utility industry

4861. Upadhyay, D. P. 1980 "Morale Building in Public Sector Enterprises." _Lok Udyog_ (New Delhi), V. 13, No. 12, pp. 47-54. /India /Organization behavior /Motivation /354.54 L836 PCL

4862. Upadhyay, K. M. 1977 "Functions of Finance Executives in Selected Public Sector Enterprises." _Lok Udyog_ (New Delhi), V. 11, No. 9, pp. 15-24. /India /Financial management /354.54 L836 PCL

4863. Upadhyaya, K. K. 1978 "Price Formation in Indian Public Sector." In K. R. Gupta, ed(s). _Pricing in Public Enterprises._ New Delhi, India: Atlantic Publishers and Distributors. pp. 127-132. /India /Price policy /HB 236 I4 P75

4864. Upadhyaya, K. K. 1978 "Design, Development & Research Activity in India." _Lok Udyog_ (New Delhi), V. 11, No. 12, pp. 37-44. /India /Research and development /354.54 L836 PCL

4865. Uppal, J. S. 1958 "Accountability of the Nationalized Industries to the Indian Parliament." _Indian Journal of Economics_ V. 39, pp. 77-82. /India /Accountability /Parliament / 330.5 In2

4866. Urciuoli, C. 1962 "A Note on the Nationalization of the Electric Power Industry." _Stato Sociale_ (Rome), V. 6, No. 3, pp. 173-199. /Italy /Nationalization /Electrical utility industry

4867. Uriarte Guerra, H. E. 1980 "L'Etat et le capital international; Un essai sur le rôle de l'Etat dans la transformation de la structure industrielle péruvienne." Paris: Université de Paris. /Peru /Industrialization /Multinational corporations /Nationalism /Foreign investment policy

4868. Uriostegui Miranda, P. 1978 "La administración de recursos humanos y el sistema de capacitación en una empresa pública." Paper presented at the Round Table on Public Enterprise of the Tenth General Assembly of the Latin American Association of Pub. Adm. /Mexico /Electrical utility industry /Training /OPSS.

4869. Urvoy, J. 1969 "The Organization of Public Enterprise." Annals of Public and Cooperative Economy V. 40, No. 1-2, pp. 159-199. /Evaluation /Organization formation / Management /Control process / 330.5 An73

4870. Usher, A. P. 1934 "Colbert and Governmental Control of Industry in 17th Century France." Review of Economic Studies pp. 237-240. /France /Public administration /Industrial sector /Economic history / 330.5 R326

4871. Usher, Dan. 1961 "Government Ownership of Industry in Asia." Malayan Economic Review (Singapore), V. 6, No. 2, pp. 61-67. /Asia /Industrial sector

4872. Uvalic, R. 1954 "La gerencia obrera de las empresas en Yugoslovia." Ekonomika Preduzeca (Belgrade), V. 49, No. 3, pp. 255-275. /Yugoslavia /Worker self management

4873. Uvalic, R. 1954 "The Management of Economic Undertaking by the Workers in Yugoslavia." International Labour Review (Geneva), V. 69, No. 3, pp. 255-275. /Yugoslavia /Worker self management / 331.05 In81 PCL

4874. Uzair, Mohammed. 1955 "Industrial Finance and Initiative in Pakistan." Indian Journal of Economics V. 36. /Pakistan /Industrialization /Public financing / 330.5 In2

4875. Uzair, Mohammed. 1959 "Government Sponsored Finance Corporations in Pakistan." Karachi: Institute of Public and Business Administration. /Pakistan /Financial institutions /332.742 Uzlq

4876. Vacca, S. 1963 "Dimensione ottima dell'impresa pubblica e programazione economica." Risparmio (Rome), pp. 398-420. /Planning process

4877. Vahcic, Ales. 1981 "Management Perspectives and Problem Areas in Jowhar Sugar Factory." Paper presented at the National Workshop of Public Enterprises, Mogadishu, Somalia, 9-13 Aug. Ljubljana: ICPE. /Somalia /Sugar industry /Evaluation /Management /System performance /Productivity /Profits /Case studies /Also published in Public Enterprise, Vol. 2, No. 2(1981), pp. 24-35. /OPSS

4878. Vaid, K. N. 1965 Industrial Production in India. Industrial Relations Statistical Series. No. 3. New Delhi: Shri Ram Centre for Industrial Relations. /India /Case studies

4879. Vaish, M. C. 1954 The Concept of Mixed Economy and India. Agra, India: Nath Publishing House. /India /Mixed enterprises

4880. Vaish, V. R. 1975 "Project Management." Lok Udyog (New Delhi), V. 9, No. 4, pp. 9-18. /India /Project management /354.54 L836 PCL

4881. Vaitsos, Constantino V. 1978 "Las relaciones entre empresas estatales y empresas transnacionales en los países en desarrollo: Proyecto de Investigación." Mexico City: ILET. /Multinational corporations /OPSS

4882. Valcev, T. 1961 "Tendencies in the Development of State Industry in Western Germany and Austria Since the 2nd World War." Ezvestija na Ikonomiceskija Institut (Sofia, Bulgaria), V. 20, No. 3-4, pp. 167-220. /Germany, Federal Rep. of /Austria /Industrial sector / Development process

4883. Valenciar, L. R. 1968 La participación del trabajador en la administración de la empresa; el caso chileno. Santiago, Chile. /Chile /Worker management participation

4884. Valerías, Juan A. 1981 "The Negotiation and Enforcement of Guarantee Clauses: A Case Study on the Construction of the First Argentine Atomic Plant." Ljubljana: ICPE. /Argentina /Technology transfer /Nuclear power / Case studies

4885. Valero Agundez, Urbano. 1970 "La fundación como forma jurídica para empresas del sector público." La empresa pública. Zaragoza, Spain: Publicaciones del Real Colegio de España en Bolonia. /Law

4886. Valle, Faustino 1978 "La comercialización en el sector eléctrico." Paper presented at the fourth general assembly of the Latin American Association of Public Administration, Mexico City, 6-11 Nov. /Mexico /Electrical utility industry /OPSS

4887. Vallina Velarde, Juan Luis. 1971 Régimen jurídico-administrativo del servicio público telefónico. Madrid: Instituto de Estudios Administrativos. /Spain /Law /Telephone industry

4888. Valsan, E. H. 1983 "Public Enterprise in Egypt: Policies, Problems, and Prospects." Paper presented at the 19th International Congress of Administrative Sciences, West Berlin, 19-23 Sept. /Egypt /Control process /OPSS

4889. Van Bol, Jean-Marie R. 1983 "L'entreprise publique comme instrument des politiques de l'Etat: Le cas de la politique industrielle." Administration Publique (Brussels), No. T2, pp. 116-122. /Belgium /Control process /Industrial sector

4890. Van Der Bellen, Alexander. 1972 "A Note on Coordination Between Central Planning Authorities and Public Enterprise. The Case of Zero Prices." Revue de la Société Belge d'Etudes et d'Expansion (Liège), No. 250. /Control process /Price policy

4891. Van Der Bellen, Alexander. 1981 "The Control of Public Enterprises. The Case of Austria." Annals of Public and Cooperative Economy V. 52, No. 1-2, pp. 73-100. /Control process /Austria /330.5 An73

4892. Van Dorn, Harold A. 1926 Government Owned Corporations. New York: Knopf. /United States of America / 338.8 V287g

4893. Van Loo, Maurice. 1958 "The Ghent Town Electricity Service." Annals of Collective Economy V. 29, pp. 641-645. /Belgium /Electrical utility industry / 330.5 An73

4894. Van Reyn, P., and P. Rongy. 1951 "Essai Juridique sur la vie d'un établissement public belge-L'Office de Récuperation Economique." Revue Internationale des Sciences Administratives pp. 687-715. /Belgium /Law

4895. Van der Marel, J. H. 1968 "Some Considerations on Costs, Tariffs and Finance in the Netherlands State Operated PTT Undertaking." Annals of Public and Cooperative Economy V. 39, No. 2. /Netherlands /Costs /Financing /Price policy /Telephone industry / 330.5 An73

4896. Vande-Bosch, Jacques. 1981 "The Public Enterprise and its Personnel." Annals of Public and Cooperative Economy V. 52, No. 1-2, pp. 127-144. /Personnel management /330.5 An73

4897. Vandebosch, Jacques. 1981 "La empresa pública y su personal." Cuadernos de Economía Social V. 3, No. 8, pp. 51-78. /Personnel management / HC 171 C822 LAC

4898. Vandeputte, R. 1967 "The Difficulties of the Public Credit Sector in Belgium." Annals of Public and Cooperative Economy V. 38, pp. 13-16. /Belgium /Financial institutions /330.5 An73

4899. Vanek, Jaroslav. 1963 "Finances of Government Companies, 1961-1962." Reserve Bank of India Bulletin (Bombay), V. 17, No. 10, pp. 1267-1276. /India /Public financing

4900. Vanek, Jaroslav. 1970 The General Theory of Labor-Managed Market Economies. Ithaca: Cornell University Press. /Market economy /Economic theory /Worker self management /658.315 V288g

4901. Vanek, Jaroslav. 1977 "El financiamiento y el derecho de propiedad en un sistema de autogestión." Política y Espíritu (Santiago, Chile), V. 2, No. 332. /Mixed enterprises /Worker self management

4902. Vanrell, R. 1969 "Apuntes sobre la introducción de la administración racional en las empresas estatales." Paper presented at the meeting of experts on administration of public enterprises in Latin America and the Caribbean, Santiago, Chile, 17-22 Nov. ST/ECLA/Conf.35/L.11. /Management

4903. Varadachary, T. R. 1969 "Bank Nationalization - Tasks Ahead." State Bank of India Monthly Review (New Delhi), /India /Financial institutions /Nationalization

4904. Varadan, M. S. S. 1975 "Organisation Development - The HMT Way." Lok Udyog (New Delhi), V. 9, No. 5, pp. 19-30. /India /Organization development /Metal manufacturing industry /Case studies /354.54 L836 PCL

4905. Varangot, Carlos Jorge. 1970 "La empresa pública en la República Argentina." La Empresa Pública. Zaragoza, Spain: Publicaciones del Real Colegio de España en Bolonia. /Argentina / Law

4906. Varela, Julio Alberto. 1978 ´Sistemas de control en las empresas públicas en la Argentina." Paper presented at the fourth general assembly of the Latin American Association of Public Administration, Mexico City, 6-11 Nov. /Argentina /Control process /OPSS

4907. Varga, J. 1966 "La nouvelle réglementation de l´expropriation dans la legislation hongroise." Revue de Droit Hongrois (Budapest), V. 1, pp. 5-17. /Hungary /Law /Nationalization

4908. Vargas, N. 1971 La coparticipación en la toma de decisiones en la empresa chilena: Teoría, práctica y probabilidades. Santiago, Chile. /Chile /Worker management participation

4909. Varma, Satyendra. 1976 "Research in a Fertilizer Industry - An Experience." Lok Udyog (New Delhi), V. 10, No. 8, pp. 43-48. /India /Research and development /Fertilizer industry /354.54 L836 PCL

4910. Varshney, B. G., and B. R. Singh. 1977 "Organizational Development and Training - A Conceptual Framework in Context of Public Sector Companies in India." Lok Udyog (New Delhi), V. 11, No. 7, pp. 5-12. /India /Organization development /Training /354.54 L836 PCL

4911. Varshney, R. L. 1958 "Pricing Policy Under Public Enterprises." Indian Journal of Commerce (Allahabad, India), V. 11, No. 1. /India /Price policy /

4912. Vasquez, S. 1978 "La necesidad de crear un sistema nacional de capacitación y actualización en administracion de empresas públicas." Paper presented at the Round Table on Public Enterprise of the Tenth General Assembly of the Latin American Association of Public Administration, Mexico City. /Mexico /Training /OPSS.

4913. Vaswani, M. H. 1949 "Mixed Economy in Theory and Practice." Indian Journal of Economics V. 30, pp. 161-166. /India /Mixed enterprises / 330.5 In2

4914. Vathsala, S., and Krishna Kumar. 1979 "Top Executive Pay Parity." Lok Udyog (New Delhi), V. 13, No. 3, pp. 41-46. /India /Wages /Management /354.54 L836 PCL

4915. Vautier, M. 1945 "La organización de las personas paraestatales." Revista de la Administración (Madrid), /Spain /Organization formation / Management

4916. Vavpetic, L. 1957 "Algunos problemas planteados por esas relaciones entre órganos de la administración estatal y órganos de autogestión de los trabajores." Le Noveau Droit Yugoslave (Belgrade, Yugoslavia), V. 7, No. 2-4. /Yugoslavia /Public administration /Worker self management

4917. Vazquez, Salvador. 1978 "La necesidad de crear un sistema nacional de capacitación y actualización en administración de empresas públicas." Prepared for the Round Table on Public Enterprise of the 10th General Assembly of the Latin American Association of Public Administration, Mexico City. /Public administration /Training /OPSS

4918. Vedel, Georges. 1946 "La technique des nationalisations." Droit Social (Paris), No. 23. /Nationalization

4919. Vedel, Georges. 1949 "La responsabilité des administrateurs devant la cour de discipline budgétaire." Revue de Science et Legislation Financière (Paris), /Administrative management /Budgetary process / Management

4920. Vedel, Georges. 1955 "Le contrôle par les commissions parlamentaries de la gestion des entreprises nationalisées et des sociétés d'économie." Droit Social (Paris). /France /Mixed enterprises /Parliament /Management /Control process

4921. Vedel, Georges. 1956 Le régime des biens des entreprises nationalisées. CJEG. /Nationalization /Public administration /Law

4922. Vedel, Georges. 1964 "Las empresas públicas en Francia." Revista de Administración Pública (Buenos Aires), V. 3, No. 12, pp. 11-23. /France / JA 5 R483 LAC

4923. Vejvoda, J. 1960 Goods Production in the State Socialist Sector. Prague: Ceskoslovenske Akademie Ved. /Czechoslovakia /Socialist economy

4924. Vela, Eugenio. 1979 "Public Enterprises in Spain." Paper presented at the Regional Meeting of Arab and Mediterraneam Countries on the Role of the Public Sector in Developing Countries, Ljubljana, Yugoslavia, 19-24 Nov. Ljubljana: ICPE. /Spain

4925. Velaerts, A. 1968 Public and Co-operative Economy in Belgium. Liège, Belgium: International Center of Research and Information on Public and Co-operative Economy. /Belgium /Cooperatives /Economic analysis

4926. Velaerts, A. 1968 "L'Etat et les entreprises publiques dans la C.E.E." Annales de l'Economie Collective V. 55, No. 4, pp. 479-518. /European Economic Community /Evaluation

4927. Velaerts, A. 1968 "L'Etat et les entreprises publiques dans la C.E.E." (Second part). *Annales de l'Economie Collective* No. 1-2, pp. 37-54. /European Economic Community /Control process

4928. Velaerts, A. 1969 "El Estado y las empresas públicas en la C.E.E." *Economía Financiera Española* (Madrid), No. 31-3, pp. 4-16. /European Economic Community /Control process

4929. Velarde Fuertes, J. 1964 "Aspectos de la evolución de las empresas públicas en España." *Información Comercial Española* (Madrid), /Spain

4930. Velarde Fuertes, J. 1972 "La empresa pública en una encrucijada." *La Empresa Pública en España* Madrid: Instituto de Estudios Fiscales, Ministerio de Hacienda, /Spain

4931. Velez de Sierra, Cecília, et al. 1980 *Cuánto vale el carbón de el Cerrojón?* Bogotá: Ediciones Tercer Mundo. /Colombia /Coal mining industry /HD 9554 C6 S53 LAC

4932. Velimirovic, J. S. 1969 *The Enterprise and Planning in the System of Selfmanagement.* Herceg Novi: U. N. Public Administration Division. /Planning process /Management

4933. Ven Katesan, S. 1949 "Nationalization of Industries: The Role of Local Bodies (with Special Reference to Hyderabad State)." *Indian Journal of Economics* V. 29, pp. 301-306. /India /Hyderabad, India (State) /Nationalization /Local government / 330.5 In2

4934. Venacio Filho, Alberto. 1968 "Por um teoria da empresas públicas." "Organização e funcionamento das empresas públicas." *A intervenção do Estado no domínio economico: O direito público economico no Brasil.* Rio de Janeiro: FGV. pp. 385-406;415. /Brazil /Law /Economic theory

4935. Venancio Filho, Alberto. 1966 "Bibliografía sobre empresas públicas." *Boletin da Camara dos Deputados* (Brasília), V. 14, No. 3, pp. 609-633. /Bibliography

4936. Venezia, J. C. 1970 "Las empresas públicas en Francia." *La Empresa Pública.* Zaragoza, Spain: Publicaciones del Real Colegio de España en Bolonia. /France

4937. Venezuela. Caracas Public Administration Commission. 1971 *Alternatives Given by the Commissions for the Working of the Council of Autonomous Institutions.* Caracas: Central Office of Coordination and Planning. /Venezuela /Management /Policy analysis

4938. Venezuela. Caracas Public Administration Commission. 1971 *Views Regarding the Integration and Control of Public Enterprise.* Caracas: Central Office of Coordination and Planning. /Venezuela /Control process

4939. Venezuela. Comisión de Administración Pública. 1971 Vistas de una reforma de entidades públicas venezolanas de administración económica. Caracas: Oficina Central de Coordinación y Planeamiento. /Venezuela /Administrative reform

4940. Venezuela. Comisión de Administración Pública. 1971 II Conferencia Venezolana de Empresas Estatales de Servicio Público. Caracas: Comisión de Administración Pública. /Venezuela

4941. Venezuela. Dirección de Estadística Laboral. 1970 Empleo en el sector público (Institutos autónomos, empresas del Estado y gobernaciones de entidades federales). Caracas. /Venezuela /Employment / qHD 5763 A1 V464 LAC

4942. Venkataraman, R. 1969 "Investment and Pricing in Public Enterprises." Lok Udyog (New Delhi), V. 3, No. 7, pp. 823-829. /India /Investment /Price policy /354.54 L836

4943. Venkataraman, Shri R. 1980 "Role of Public Enterprises." Lok Udyog (New Delhi), V. 13, No. 10-1, pp. 3-6. /India /354.54 L836 PCL

4944. Venkataramana, P. 1980 "Some Aspects of Public Enterprises in India, Britain, France and Japan." Institute of Public Enterprises Journal V. 3, No. 1-2, pp. 48-59. /India /United Kingdom /France /Japan

4945. Venkatesan, L. 1961 Bibliography on Public Enterprises in India. New Delhi: Indraprastha Estate. /India /Bibliography

4946. Ventenat, M. 1948 L'expérience des nationalisations. Paris: Librairie de Medicis. /France /Nationalization /HD 4165 V4 HRC

4947. Venu, S. 1972 "Holding Companies and Joint Sector: A Profile." Lok Udyog (New Delhi), V. 6, No. 7, pp. 25-30. /India /Subsidiaries /Holding company /354.54 L836 PCL

4948. Vera Vassallo, Alejandro C. 1974 "La planificación peruana: Conferencia nacional de Perú." Paper presented at the International Seminar '74: Planning in Public Enterprises in Developing Countries, Ljubljana, Yugoslavia, Sept.23-Oct.9. Ljubljana: ICPE. /Peru /Planning process

4949. Vera, J. Bernejo. 1973 "La nacionalización ferroviaria de 1941." Revista de Administración Pública (Madrid), No. 72, pp. 73-125. /Spain /Nationalization /Railway industry

4950. Verdera y Tuells, Evélio. 1970 "La Sociedad de Inversiones Mobiliarias en el Exterior, S. A. - SIMEX." La Empresa Pública. Zaragoza, Spain: Publicaciones del Real Colegio de España en Bolonia. /Spain /Investment /Case studies

4951. Verdier, Jean-Maurice. 1974 "Labor Relations in the Public Sector in France." International Labour Review (Geneva), No. 139, pp. 105-118. /France /Labor relations /331.05 In81 PCL /HD 4811 I65 Pub Aff

4952. Verhulst, H. 1952 Les industries d'utilité publique. Paris: Presses Universitaires de France. /France /Public utility industry

4953. Verma, J. C. 1978 "Role of Public Enterprises in Rural Development." Lok Udyog (New Delhi), V. 12, No. 5, pp. 35-40. /Rural development /354.54 L836 PCL

4954. Verma, Yoginder Singh, and Rajiv Mallik. 1980 "Promotion Policy of Hardwar Unit of Bharat Heavy Electricals Ltd. - An Evaluation." Lok Udyog (New Delhi), V. 13, No. 10-1, pp. 31-40. /India /Personnel management /Case studies /354.54 L836 PCL

4955. Vermeulen, Bruce, and Ravi Sethi. 1982 "Lábor-management conflict resolution in state-owned enterprises: A comparison of public- and private-sector practices in India." In Leroy P. Jones et al., ed(s). Public enterprise in less-developed countries. New York: Cambridge University Press. pp 141-165. /Labor relations /Comparative analysis /Private enterprises /India /HD 3850 P83 PCL

4956. Vernes, J. 1965 "Vers un nouveau système de direction de l'économie en U.R.S.S." Economie et Politique (Paris), No. 131, pp. 61-76. /Union of Soviet Socialist Reps.

4957. Verney, Douglas V. 1959 Public Enterprise in Sweden. Liverpool, England: Liverpool University Press. /Sweden 338.9485 V596p

4958. Verney, Douglas V. 1964 "Public Enterprise." In Julius Gould and William L. Kolb, ed(s). A Dictionary of the Social Sciences. Glencoe, Ill.: Free Press. pp. 260-261. /Bibliography / H 41 G6 REF

4959. Vernon, R. 1963 The Dilemma of Mexico's Development: The Roles of the Private and Public Sectors. Cambridge, Mass: Harvard University Press. /Mexico /Economic development /Private sector / 338.972 V598d

4960. Vernon, R. 1964 Public Policy and Private Enterprise in Mexico. Cambridge, Mass.: Harvard University Press. /Mexico /Planning process /Private enterprises / G330.972 V598p

4961. Vernon, R. 1976 Economic Environment of International Business. Englewood Cliffs, N. J.: Prentice-Hall. /Multinational corporations / HD 2755.5 V47 Pub Aff

4962. Vernon, R. 1981 "State-Owned Enterprises in Latin American Exports." In Werner Baer and Malcolm Gillis, ed(s). Export Diversification and the New Protectionism: The Experiences of Latin America. Champaign, Il.: Bureau of Economic and Business Research, College of Commerce and Business Administration, University of Illinois at Urbana-Champaign. pp. 98-114. /State trading organizations /Latin America /Exports

4963. Vernon, R., and Brian Levy. 1982 "State-owned enterprises in the world economy: the case of iron ore." In Leroy P. Jones et al., ed(s). Public enterprise in less-developed countries. New York: Cambridge University Press. pp. 169-188. /State trading organizations /HD 3850 P83 PCL /Also presented at the Second BAPEG Conference, Boston, April, 1980. /OPSS

4964. Vernon, R., and Yair Aharoni, eds. 1981 State-Owned Enterprise in the Western Economies. New York: St. Martin's Press. /Europe /France /United Kingdom /Italy /Management /Control process /Decision making process /Accountability /HD 3850 S79 PCL

4965. Verre, E. 1965 L'Entreprise industrielle en Union Soviétique. Nouvelles méthodes de gestion. Paris: Sirey. /Union of Soviet Socialist Reps. /Industrial sector /Management / 338.947 V611e

4966. Verruccoli, P. 1950 "Consideraciones jurídico-mercantiles sobre las empresas en mano pública." Revista de Administración Pública (Madrid), No. 3, pp. 155-172. /Law

4967. Viale, Claudio Martín. 1976 "Servicios de aguas corrientes y alcantarillado en la Argentina: Un análisis jurídico." Rio de Janeiro: FGV-EIAP. /Argentina /Sanitation industry /Water supply industry /OPSS

4968. Vickers, Sir G. 1952 "The Accountability of a Nationalized Industry." Public Administration (London), V. 30, pp. 71-80. /Australia /Industrial sector /Accountability /JA 8 P8 Pub Aff

4969. Vickrey, William S. 1980 "Actual and Potential Pricing Practices under Public and Private Operation." In William J. Baumol, ed(s). Public and Private Enterprise in a Mixed Economy. New York: St. Martin's Press. pp. 286-296. /Price policy /Private enterprises /Comparative analysis /HD 3842 P87 PCL

4970. Victor, Mario. 1970 A batalha do petróleo brasileiro. Rio de Janeiro: Civilizacao Brasileira. /Brazil /Oil industry

4971. Vidal Perdomo, J., H. Penaloza, and C. Arana de Ramírez. 1979 "Las empresas públicas en América Latina." Revista Latinoamericana de Administración Pública No. 8-9, pp. 299-309. /Latin America

4972. Vidmar, Milan. 1980 "Macro-Project `Study of Complex Energetics in the Socialist Republic of Slovenia': Approach and Experiences." Paper presented at the Expert Group Meeting on Strategies for Energy Development in Developing Countries--Role for Public Enterprises, Ljubljana, Yugoslavia, 19-22 Feb. Ljubljana: ICPE. /Czechoslovakia /Energy utility industry / Case studies

4973. Vieira, José Paulo Carneiro. 1980 "Padrões de atuação, controle organizacional e controle político das empresas públicas no Brasil." A empresa pública no Brasil: Uma abrodagem multidisciplinar. Brasília: IPEA. pp. 261-321. /Control process /Brazil

4974. Vignier, P. 1951 "La mise en valeur du Delta Central du Niger: L'Office du Niger." Societé Belge d'Etudes et d'Expansion (Liège), No. 148. /Niger /Economic analysis /Case studies / Africa /River valley development projects

4975. Vignocchi, G. I. 1965 "Controli sulle imprese pubbliche." Il Diritto dell'Economia /Italy /Control process

4976. Vignocchi, G. I. 1970 "Los controles sobre las haciendas autónomas y sobre las empresas con participacioness estatales." La Empresa Pública. Zaragoza, Spain: Publicaciones del Real Colegio de España en Bolonia. /Spain /Mixed enterprises /Public administration /Control process

4977. Vijay, K. C. 1980 "Management Training System and Impetus on Organization Development in Public Enterprises: India, Model Reference Instrumentation Ltd., Kota." Paper presented at the Interregional Seminar on Training Management in Public Enterprises in Developing Countries, Ljubljana, Yugoslavia, Sept.29-Oct.10. Ljubljana: ICPE. /India /Training /Management / Case studies

4978. Vijayasaradhi, S. P. 1981 "Problems of Working Capital Management in Public Enterprises." Lok Udyog (New Delhi), V. 14, No. 10, pp. 27-34. /India /Working capital /354.54 L836

4979. Vila, Antun. 1979 "Production Management." paper presented at the Seminar on Production Planning, Mogadishu, Somalia, Feb.26-Mar.3. Ljubljana: ICPE. /Productivity / Also presented at the Seminar on Production Planning, Mogadishu, Somalia, Nov. 24-Dec.3, 1980.

4980. Vila, Antun. 1979 "Preventive Maintenance." Paper presented at the Seminar on Production Planning, Mogadishu, Somalia, Feb.26-Mar.3. Ljubljana: ICPE. /Productivity / Also presented at the Seminar on Production Planning in Mogadishu, Nov. 24 - Dec. 3, 1980.

4981. Vila, Antun. 1979 "General Problems of Organizational Improvement in Industry: Electronics Industry, Yugoslav Case Study." Paper presented at the Interregional Workshop "Developing Problem Solving Skills in Public Enterprises," Ljubljana, Yugoslavia, 2-17 April. Ljubljana: ICPE. /Yugoslavia /Electronics industry /Case studies /Economic efficiency

4982. Vilaghy, M. 1968 "Der staat und sein unternehmen." Acta Juridica (Budapest), V. 10, No. 3-4, pp. 257-274. /Law /Control process

4983. Vilkov, G. 1963 "La nationalisation, droit souverain des Etats indépendants." Vie Internationale (Moscow), V. 3, No. 8, pp. 87-90. /Nationalization /Law

4984. Villa M., Rosa Olivia. 1976 Nacional Financiera: Banco de fomento del desarrollo económico de México. Mexico City: Nacional Financiera. /Mexico /Industrialization /Development banks /Investment /Credit policy / HG 272 M44 N395 LAC

4985. Villani, F. Del. 1959 "Controllo sugli enti sovvenzionati dallo stato." Rivista di Política Economica (Rome), pp. 1392-1410. /Italy /Control process

4986. Villanueva Tavares, Federico José. 1975 "Minas de sal y yeso-CORDE, R.D.: Como aumentar el nivel de producción del yeso triturado a granel, de un promedio de 54,000 toneladas durante los años 1964 a 1968, a un promedio de 186,000 toneledas, durante . . ." Rio de Janeiro: FGV-EIAP. /Dominican Republic /Salt extraction industry /Gypsum mining industry / Holding company /OPSS

4987. Villar Palasi, J. L. 1950 "La actividad industrial del Estado en el derecho administrativo." Revista de Administración Pública (Madrid), No. 3, pp. 53-129. /Spain /Law

4988. Villar Palasi, J. L. 1963 "Aperçc du secteur publique, semi-public et mixte en France." Annales de l'Economie Collective V. 51, No. 4, pp. 625-642. /France /Mixed enterprises

4989. Villar Palasi, J. L. 1964 "La flexibilidad en la administración pública y en la conducción de las empresas públicas." Ciencias Administrativas (Buenos Aires), No. 17, pp. 625-642. /Control process

4990. Villar Palasi, J. L. 1964 La intervención administrativa en la industria. Madrid: I.E.P. /Spain /Industrial sector

4991. Villar Palasi, J. L. 1975 "O setor público brasileiro: Conta corrente e formacão bruta de capital fixo." Conjunture Econômica (Rio de Janeiro), V. 29, No. 6, pp. 82-90. /Brazil /Investment

4992. Villar Palasi, J. L. n.d. "El problema de la tasa de mercado." Revista de Administración Publica /Price policy

4993. Villarreal, Norma Rocío R. de, and René Villarreal. 1980 "Public Enterprises in Mexican Development Under the Oil Perspective in the 1980s." Paper presented at the BAPEG Conference on Public Enterprise in Mixed Economy LDCs, Boston, April. /Mexico /Oil industry /OPSS

4994. Villarreal, René, and Norma Rocío R. de Villarreal. 1977 "La empresa pública." In Gerardo M. Bueno, ed(s). Opciones de política económica en México después de la devaluación. Mexico City: Editorial Tecnos. pp. 81-112. /Mexico /Currency devaluation policy /Planning process / HC 135 0615 LAC

4995. Villarreal, René, and Norma Rocío R. de Villarreal. 1978 "Las empresas públicas como instrumento de política económica en México." Trimestre Económico (Mexico City), V. 45, No. 2, pp. 213-245. /Mexico /Economic policy making /Planning process / G330.972 T735 LAC

4996. Villela, Annibal. 1962 "As empresas do Governo Federal e sua importancia na economia nacional 56/60." Revista Brasileira de Economia (Rio de Janeiro), No. 1, pp. 97-113. /Brazil

/Economic history / G330.5 R326 LAC

4997. Villemor, Claudio Salgado de. 1979 "Contabilidad gerencial en las empresas públicas." In EIAP-FGV, ed(s). Administración de empresas públicas. Mexico City: Editorial Limusa. pp. 385-399. /Accounting HD 3850 A333 LAC

4998. Viloria Vera, Enrique. 1974 "Estado, desarrollo y empresa pública: Conferencia nacional de Venezuela." Paper presented at the International Seminar ´74: Planning in Public Enterprises in Developing Countries, Ljubljana, Yugoslavia, Sept.23-Oct.9. Ljubljana: ICPE. /Venezuela /Planning process /Economic development

4999. Viloria Vera, Enrique. 1974 "Las funciones de la empresa pública en América Latina." Revista Latinaomericana de Administración Pública (Bogotá), No. 2, pp. 20-28. /Latin America /Evaluation

5000. Viloria Vera, Enrique. 1978 "Empresas públicas multinacionales latinoamericanas." Gobierno y empresas públicas en América Latina. Buenos Aires: SIAP. pp. 205-234. /Multinational corporations /OPSS

5001. Viloria Vera, Enrique. 1979 "La Corporación Venezolana de Guyana: Un particular enfoque del desarrollo regional." Ljubljana: ICPE. /Venezuela /Regional development /Development corporation / Case studies

5002. Vinck, François and Jacques Boursin. 1962 "The Development of the Public and Private Sectors of the Coal Mining Industry in Europe: A Comparative Study." Annals of Collective Economy V. 33, pp. 385-490. /Europe /Coal mining industry /Comparative analysis /330.5 An73

5003. Vineza, Emma B., and Mohtadullah Khalid. 1981 "Report of the Regional Workshop on Management Training and Development in Public Enterprises of Developing Countries, 5-15 January 1981, Karachi, Pakistan." Ljubljana: ICPE. /Training /Management /Developing nations

5004. Virally, M. 1950 "Remarques sur le projet de loi portant statut general des entreprises publiques." Revue Administrative (Paris), V. 3, No. 16, pp. 355-364. /France /Law /Administrative law

5005. Virmani, Bal Raj. 1979 Workers´ Participation in Management: A Select Annotated Bibliography. London: Commonwealth Secretariat. /Worker management participation / Bibliography

5006. Virmani, Bal. 1978 Worker´s Participation in Management: Some Experiences and Lessons. New Delhi: MacMillan. /Worker management participation /Case studies /HD 5650 V57 PCL

5007. Virmani, Bharat Bhushan. 1979 "Management and Training in Public Enterprises: Country Report of India." Paper presented at the International Seminar on Management and Training in Public Enterprises in Developing Countries, Ljubljana, Yugoslavia, 1-13 October. Ljubljana: ICPE. /India

/Training /Management

5008. Virmani, Bharat Bhushan. 1980 Man-Power Planning in Public Enterprises in India. Ljubljana: ICPE. /India /Personnel management /Training

5009. Virmani, M. R. 1980 "Autonomy and Accountability of Public Sector Enterprises in India." Lok Udyog (New Delhi), V. 14, No. 4, pp. 17-22. /India /Accountability /Control process /Autonomy /354.54 L836

5010. Virole, J. 1965 "Questions posées par l´interpretation du traité du 21 mars 1957 instituant la Communauté Economique Européenne, à propos de la nationalisation de l´électricité en Italie." Cahiers Juridiques de l´Electricité et du Gaz (Brussels), V. 17, No. 178, pp. 31-51. /Italy /Electrical utility industry /Nationalization / Law

5011. Vitak, R. 1971 "Workers´ Control, the Czechoslovak Experience." Socialist Register (London), pp. 145-264. /Czechoslovakia /Worker self management / 335.058 So12 PCL

5012. Vitello, V. 1959 "Impresa pubblica redditivita aziendale e sviluppo economico." Polit. Ed Econ pp. 20-23. /Italy

5013. Vito, Francesco. 1953 "La pubblica administrazione e l´ativittá economica dello stato moderno." Revista Internazionale de Science Sociali (Milan), No. 4, pp. 311-324. /Public administration

5014. Vito, Francesco. 1958 "The Control of Public Enterprise." Paper presented at the Congress of the International Political Science Association, Rome, Italy, September. /Control process

5015. Vito, Francesco. 1960 "L´Impresa pubblica: Esperienza nazionale e internazionale." Bancaira (Rome), pp. 971-978. /Italy

5016. Vito, Francisco. 1964 "Nota sul concetto e sui limiti dell´impresa pubblica." Revue Internationale des Sciences Administratives pp. 538-548. /Economic theory

5017. Vlasak, Mirko. 1979 "Production Intensification: Metalna TGO-Senovo, Yugoslav Case Study." Paper presented at the Interregional Workshop "Developing Problem Solving Skills in Public Enterprises," Ljubljana, Yugoslavia, 2-17 April. Ljubljana: ICPE. /Yugoslavia /Productivity /Case studies

5018. Vlaskalin, Aleksandar. 1978 "Problèmes des cadres dans les transports maritimes wt portuaires des pays en voie de développement." Paper presented at the Séminaire international sur la gestion et la formation dans les entreprises publiques dans les pays en voie de développement, Ljubljana, Yugoslavia, 3-15 March. Ljubljana: ICPE. /Developing nations /Marine transportation industry /Port authority

5019. Vodusek, Ziga. 1981 "Perspectives and Pathways--ICPE Looks at Public Enterprise." Public Enterprise V. 1, pp. 6-17. /Control process /Financing /Evaluation /Management /OPSS

5020. Vodusek, Ziga. 1981 "Public Enterprise: A Key to National Development, and Instrument of National Policy, a Channel of International Cooperation, a Contribution to Human Resources Development." Paper presented at the Regional Workshop on Research and Teaching of Public Administration in Developing Countries--Problems of State. Owned Enterprises and of Training Programmes, Mexico City. Ljubljana: ICPE. /Economic development /Planning process /Employment policy /Abridged version presented at regional workshop on the evaluation of training packages for public enterprise managers, Bangkok, Thailand, 10-14 Aug. 1981.

5021. Vogel, Klaus. 1970 "Las empresas públicas en la República Federal Alemana." La Empresa Pública. Zaragoza, Spain: Publicaciones del Real Colegio de España en Bolonia. pp. 751-768. /Germany, Federal Rep. of

5022. Voisset, Michele. 1972 "Des nationalisations aux contrats de Progrès le Contrôle gouvernemental la determination des salaires et des conditions de travail dans les entreprises publiques à statut." Bulletin de l´Institut International d´Administration Publique (Paris), No. 21, pp. 17-54. /France /Nationalization /Wages /Working conditions

5023. Vojnovic, Josip. 1974 "Construction de la ville par la réalisation du projet." Paper presented at International Seminar ´74: Planning in Public Enterprises in Developing Countries, Ljubljana, Yugoslavia, Sept. 23 -Oct.9. Ljubljana: ICPE. /Yugoslavia /Planning process /Case studies

5024. Votaw, D. 1964 The Sixlegged Dog: Mattei and E.N.I. A Study in Power. Berkeley and Los Angeles: University of California Press. /Italy /Oil industry / 338.826655 En82Yv

5025. Voubou, Bernard Henri. 1980 "Quelques aspects concernant la formation des cadres au Gabon." Paper presented at the Séminaire international sur la gestion et la formation dans les entreprises publiques dans les pays en voie de développement, Ljubljana, Yugoslavia, 3-15 March. Ljubljana: ICPE. /Gabon /Training

5026. Vranckx, J. 1958 "The National Water Supply Company." Annals of Collective Economy V. 29, pp. 546-549. /Belgium /Water supply industry /Sanitation industry /330.5 An73

5027. Vratusa, Anton. 1974 "Current matters on Planning in Public Enterprise." Paralele Export (Ljubljana), /Planning process

5028. Vratusa, Anton. 1975 "Further Development of Self-Management in Yugoslavia and Its Sociopolitical Aspects." In Ichak Adizes and Elisabeth Mann Borgese, ed(s). Self-Management: New Dimensions to Democracy. Santa Barbara, Cal.; Oxford, England: American Bibliographical Center; Clio Press. pp. 49-56. /Yugoslavia /Worker self management /OPSS

5029. Vratusa, Anton. 1980 "The Role of the Public Enterprise in Efforts to Establish the New International Economic Order." Ljubljana: ICPE. /International economic relations

5030. Vratusa, Anton. 1980 "Socio-Historical Sources of Productivity and Efficiency." Ljubljana: ICPE. /Economic efficiency /Productivity /Cultural system

5031. Vratusa, Anton. 1981 "Labour Participation and Self-Management with Particular Reference to the Experience of Yugoslavia." Paper presented at the International Symposium on Economic Performance of Public Enterprises, Islamabad, Pakistan. Ljubljana: ICPE /Yugoslavia /Worker self management /Worker management participation

5032. Vratusa, Anton. 1981 "Profiles of Workers' Self-Management: The Yugoslav Experience." Paper presented at the Conference on Transition to Workers' Self-Management in Industry as a Strategy for Change in Developing Countries, the Hague, Netherlands. Ljubljana: ICPE /Yugoslavia /Worker self management

5033. Vratusa, Anton. 1981 "Workers' Participation in Public Enterprises." Paper presented at the Semiario INAP/CLAD/CIEP "Análisis de la gestión de las empresas públicas en Nicaragua," Managua, Nicaragua. Ljubljana: ICPE /Nicaragua /Worker management participation

5034. Vrsec, Ernest. 1980 "The Design of Products and Technological Systems." Paper presented at the Seminar on Production Planning, Mogadishu, Somalia, Nov.24-Dec.3. Ljubljana: ICPE. /Productivity /Technology /Also presented at the Seminar on Production Planning, Mogadishu, Somalia, Feb. 26-Mar. 3, 1979.

5035. Vrsec, Ernest. 1980 "How to Determine the Manufacturing Interval by Network Planning Techniques." Paper presented at the Seminar on Production Planning, Mogadishu, Somalia, Nov.24-Dec.3. Ljubljana: ICPE. /Network analysis /Productivity

5036. Vrsec, Ernest. 1980 "Production Planning". Paper presented at the Seminar on Production Planning, Mogadishu, Somalia, Nov.24-Dec.3. Ljubljana: ICPE. /Planning process /Productivity

5037. Vucinich, A. 1952 _Soviet Economic Institutions: The Social Structure of Production Units._ Hoover Institute Studies, Ser. E. Institutions. Stanford, Calif.: Stanford University Press. No. 1. /Union of Soviet Socialist Reps. / Economic organization / 338.947 V972s

5038. Vucinich, W., J. Tomasevich, P. Auty, and M. Zaninovich. 1969 _Contemporary Yugoslavia-Twenty Years of Socialist Experiment._ Berkeley, Calif.: University of California Press. /Yugoslavia /DR 370 U8 Pub Aff /949.7 V9715c PCL

5039. Vukmanovic-Tempo, S. 1964 "Trade Unions and Workers Self Management." _Yugoslav Trade Unions_ (Belgrade), V. 5, No. 14, pp. 3-11. /Yugoslavia /Trade unions /Worker self management

5040. Wade, E. C. S. 1949 "Constitutional Aspects of the Public Corporation." Current Legal Problems (London), V. 2. pp. 172-181. /United Kingdom /Constitutional law

5041. Wadhawan, M. P. 1979 "Public Sector Steel Industry in India - Evaluation of Financial and Physical Performance." Lok Udyog (New Delhi), V. 13, No. 8, pp. 21-30. /India /Economic efficiency /Financial performance /Steel industry /Case studies /354.54 L836 PCL

5042. Wadnva, C. D. 1965 "Concentration of Economic Power in India, 1951-1961." Economic Affairs (Calcutta, India), V. 10, No. 1, pp. 34-50. /India /Economic analysis

5043. Wagner, A. J. 1967 "The Role of Public Enterprise in National Development." Paper presented at the Seminar on Problems of Public Enterprises. Lahore: N.I.P.A. /Economic development

5044. Wahrlich, B. 1979 "Reflexiones de orden administrativo sobre las empresas estatales en el Brasil." Revista Latinoamericana de Administración Pública No. 8-9, pp. 393-410. /Brazil

5045. Wald, Arnoldo. 1953 "As sociedades de economia mista." Revista de Servico Público (Rio de Janeiro), V. 3, No. 2, pp. 46-50. /Brazil /Mixed enterprises

5046. Wald, Arnoldo. 1958 "Controle parlamentar de administração descentralizada no direito norte americano." Revista Direito Público e Ciencia Política (Rio de Janeiro), V. 1, No. 1, pp. 29-40. /United States of America /Parliament /Administrative reform / Decentralization /Control process

5047. Wald, Arnoldo. 1977 "Aplicação da nova lei das sociedades anónimas as sociedades de económia mista." Arquivos do ministério da Justica (Brasília), V. 34, pp. 127-133. /Brazil /Mixed enterprises /Law / G349.81 B7392a LAC

5048. Wald, Arnoldo. 1977 "As sociedades de economia mista e a nova lei das sociedades anónimas." Revista de Informacão Legislativa (Brasília), V. 14, pp. 99-114. /Brazil /Mixed enterprises /Law / G340.05 R3251 LAC

5049. Waline, M. 1952 La distinction du droit privé et du droit public et l´entreprise publique. Paris: Sirey. /France /Law

5050. Waline, M. 1952 De quelques difficultés relatives au champ d´application et a la portée du Statut National du Personnel des Entreprises Electriques et Gazières. C.J.E.G. /France /Electrical utility industry /Gas utility industry / Personnel management /Law

5051. Waline, M. n.d. "Les nationalisations." Droit Social (Paris), No. 3. /France /Nationalization

5052. Waller, Spencer Weber. 1981 "Article 37 of the EEC Treaty: State Trading under Scrutiny." National Journal of International Law and Business V. 3, pp. 662-683. /European Economic Community /Law /State trading organizations

5053. Walrer, K. J. 1970 Workers´ Participation in Management Concepts and Reality. 2C-70/Sect. 11, synthesis report. Geneva: International Industrial Relations Association. 2nd World Congress, 1-4 Sept. 1970. /Worker management participation

5054. Walsh, Annmarie Hauck. 1978 The Public´s Business: The Politics and Practices of Government Corporations. Cambridge, Mass.: MIT Press. /United States of America /Management /Productivity /Public relations /Control process /HD 3887 W34

5055. Walstedt, Bertil. 1980 State Manufacturing Enterprise in a Mixed Economy: The Turkish Case. Baltimore, Md.: The Johns Hopkins University Press. /Turkey /Economic analysis /HD 4276.7 W34 PCL

5056. Walter, Ingo. 1979 State Trading in Iron and Steel by the Developing Countries and Structural Adjustment Problems in the Developed Countries. Les Cahiers du CETAI, No. 79-09. Montreal: Ecole des Hautes Etudes Commerciales. /State trading organizations /Steel industry /OPSS

5057. Wamalwa, W. N. 1980 "The State Training Corporation of Suta." Paper presented at the Regional Workshop on Development of Training Methodologies for Internal Consultants in African Public Enterprises, Addis Ababa, Ethiopia, 1-6 December. Ljubljana: ICPE /Training /Consultant services / Case studies / State trading organizations /Africa

5058. Wanchoo, N. N. 1964 "Advance Planning of Projects." Indian Journal of Public Administration (New Delhi), V. 10, No. 3. /India /Planning process / JA 26 I55 Pub Aff

5059. Wang, Hua. 1954 "The State-Owned Economy of New China." People´s China V. 16, pp. 3-7. /China, People´s Rep. of

5060. Ward, B. 1957 "Worker´s Management in Yugoslavia." Journal of Political Economy V. 65, pp. 373-386. /Yugoslavia /Worker self management / 330.5 J82 PCL

5061. Ward, B. 1965 "The Nationalized Firm in Yugoslavia." American Economic Review V. 55, No. 2, pp. 65-74. /Yugoslavia /Nationalization

5062. Ward, B. 1967 The Socialist Economy, a Study of Organizational Alternatives. New York: Random House. /Socialist economy /Organization theory / HB 97.5 W3 Pub Aff

5063. Warford, J. J. 1966 "Water requirements: The Investment Decision in the Water Supply Industry." Manchester School of Economic and Social Studies V. 34, pp. 87-112. /Water resources development /Economic analysis /Investment

/Reprinted in R. Turvey, Public Enterprise, in an amended version. /338.001 T869e PCL /HD 3850 T89 Pub Aff

5064. Warner, Eldon G. 1969 "Public Enterprises in Trinidad and Tobago." Prepared for the Meeting of Experts on Administration of Public Enterprises in Latin America and the Caribbean, Santiago, Chile: UNECLA. /Trinidad and Tobago /OPSS

5065. Warwick, Donald P. 1980 "A Transactional Approach to the Public Enterprise." Paper presented at the Second BAPEG Conference: Public Enterprise in Mixed Economy LDCs, Boston, Mass., April. /Organization behavior /OPSS

5066. Washington, J. 1960 Las empresas del Estado. Buenos Aires. /Argentina

5067. Wasserstrom, Robert. 1984 "Muebles Nacionales: Oral Histories of a Mexican Worker-Owned Furniture Enterprise." Grassroots Development V. 8, No. 1, pp. 24-29. /Mexico /Worker self management /Furniture manufacturing industry

5068. Waterbury, John. 1976 "Public Versus Private in the Egyptian Economy." Northeast Africa Series. V. 21, No. 5. /Egypt / Comparative analysis

5069. Waterman, Peter. 1976 "The Nigerian State and the Control of Labour: The Case of the Lagos Cargo-Handling Industry." The Hague: Institute of Social Studies. Industrial Relations and Labour Studies Programme. /Nigeria / Marine transportation industry /Labor relations

5070. Watkin, E. E. 1956 "Problems of Nationalized Industries in the United Kingdom." Egypte Contemporaine (Cairo), pp. 5-22. /United Kingdom /Industrial sector / 962.05 Eg98r

5071. Watkin, E. E. 1964 Cost Plus and Full Cost Pricing Techniques in a Public Enterprise. Memo. Cairo: Inst. of National Planning. No. 527. /Price policy /Costs /Accounting

5072. Watkin, E. E. 1964 Some Notes on the Nationalized Industries of U.A.R. and their Pricing Policies. Cairo: Inst. of National Planning. No. 525. /Egypt /Industrial sector /Price policy

5073. Watkins, W. 1967 "Costs, Prices and Efficiency in Nationalized Industries in Great Britain." Annals of Public and Cooperative Economy V. 38, No. 4, pp. 419-420. /United Kingdom /Costs /Price policy /Economic efficiency /330.5 An73

5074. Webb, L. C. 1955 "Statutory Corporations under Review." Public Administration (Sydney, Australia), V. 14, No. 3, pp. 158-165. /Australia

5075. Webb, Michael G. 1971 "Financing Nationalized Industries." Bulletin of the Oxford University Institute of Economics and Statistics V. 33, No. 4, pp. 289-302. /United Kingdom /Financing /310.5 Ox2b

5076. Webb, Michael G. 1973 The Economics of Nationalized Industries: A Theoretical Approach. London: Thomas Nelson and Sons, Ltd. /United Kingdom /Economic efficiency /Economic theory

5077. Webb, Michael G. 1976 Pricing Policies for Public Enterprises. London: MacMillan. /Price policy /Economic theory /Economic policy

5078. Webb, Michael G. 1978 "Policy for Energy Pricing." Energy Policy V. 6, No. 1, pp. 61-63. /Price policy /Electrical utility industry

5079. Webb, Michael G. 1979 "Nationalized Industries." In D. H. Gowland, ed(s). Modern Economic Analysis. Sevenoaks, Eng.: Butterworths. /Economic analysis /United Kingdom /HB 171 M5568

5080. Webb, Michael G. 1980 "A Critical Appraisal of United Kingdom Policy for the Nationalized Industries." In Bridger M. Mitchell and Paul R. Kleindorfer, ed(s). Regulated Industries and Public Enterprise. Lexington, Mass.: D.C. Heath & Company, Lexington Books. pp. 119-138. /United Kingdom /Economic analysis /Investment /Price policy /OPSS

5081. Webber, Y. 1970 "Personnes publiques et fiscalité." Actualité Juridique (Paris), V. 1. /France

5082. Weber, L. 1976 "L´interpretation des comptes des collectivites publiques sous l´angle de leur incidence conjoncturelle." Wirtschaft und Recht V. 28, No. 1, pp. 66-79. /Accounting

5083. Weber, W. 1962 "State-Controlled Enterprise in Austria." International Review of Administrative Sciences No. 2, pp. 192-205. /Austria / JA 1 A1 I6 PCL

5084. Weber, W. 1964 "Données et problèmes des nationalisations industrielles en Autriche." Annales de l´Economie Collective /Austria /Industrial sector /Nationalization

5085. Weber, W. 1967 "Das offentliche unternemen in ost und west." Donauraum (Vienna), pp. 41-52. /Socialist economy /Capitalism /Comparative analysis /943.48 D715 PCL

5086. Weber, W. 1970 "Datos y problemas de las nacionalizaciones industriales en Austria." La Empresa Pública. Zaragoza, Spain: Publicaciones del Real Colegio de España en Bolonia. /Austria /Nationalization /Industrial sector

5087. Weber, W. 1971 "Accroissement rapide de l´activité du secteur nationalisé." Usine Nouvelle (Paris), V. 49, No. 104. /Austria /Nationalization

5088. Weber, W., Stephan Koren, and Karl Socher, eds. 1964 Die verstaatlichung in osterreich. Berlin: Duncker & Humblot. /Austria

5089. Weddigen, W. 1963 "Public Enterprises and Establishments." Finanzarchiv V. 22, No. 2, pp. 204-217. /Evaluation /336.05 F49

5090. Wedin, Constance. 1965 "Development Banks and Corporations." San Juan, P. R.: Government Development Bank for Puerto Rico. /Puerto Rico /Development banks /Economic development

5091. Wegenstein, W. O., and G. W. Kaser. 1954 Management and Organization of the State Monopolies in Turkey. New York: United Nations. /Turkey /Management /Structural characteristics

5092. Wehner, H. J., Jr. 1965 "Marketing Board Performance in Primary Producing Countries." Economia Internazionale (Genoa), V. 18, No. 4, pp. 695-718. /Ghana /Cocoa industry /Marketing boards /State trading organizations /330.5 Ec74i

5093. Weidenbaum, M. L. 1968 "Les entreprises privées a destination publique." Analyse et Prévision (Paris), /Private sector /Nationalization

5094. Weiner, Herbert E. 1960 British Labor and Public Ownership. Washington, D. C.: Public Affairs Press. /United Kingdom /Trade unions 338.942 W431b

5095. Weintraub, Ruth G. 1939 Government Corporations and State Law. New York: Columbia University Press. /United States of America /Law /Local government / HD 3885 W41 Pub Aff

5096. Weintraub, Tina V., and James D. Patterson. 1949 The "Authority" in Pennsylvania, Pro and Con. Philadelphia: Bureau of Municipal Research. /United States of America /Public authority /Pennsylvania (State)

5097. Weisser, G. 1958 "Les entreprises publiques et les entreprises libres d'économie collective ont-elles des tâches et des intérets communs?" Expériences (Paris), No. 1. /Evaluation /Worker management participation /Comparative analysis

5098. Weisser, Gerhard. 1961 "Price Setting in Public Undertakings." Annals of Collective Economy V. 32, pp. 407-416. /Price Policy / 330.5 An73

5099. Weitzell, Everett C. 1960 "Considerations of the Planned Nationalization of Sources of Energy." Rivista di Politica Economica (Rome), V. 50, No. 4, pp. 746-762. /Energy utility industry /Nationalization

5100. Weitzell, Everett C. 1971 "The Rural Telephone Bank--New Financing for Rural Telephone." Public Utility Fortnightly V. 88, No. 9. /United States of America /Telephone industry /Rural development / Banking agency

5101. Weitzell, Everett C. 1971 "Expresas a exámen: Compañía Telefónica Nacional de España." Actualidad Económica (Peru), No. 701. /Spain /Telephone industry

5102. Wells, Donald A. 1971 "ARAMCO: The Evolution of an Oil Concession." In Raymond F. Mikesell, ed(s). Foreign Investment in the Petroleum and Mineral Industries. Baltimore, Md.: Johns Hopkins. /Saudi Arabia /Oil industry /Mixed enterprises /338.23 M589f

5103. Wells, F. A., and W. A. Warmington. 1962 Studies in Industrialization. Nigeria and the Cameroons. London: Oxford University Press. /Nigeria /Cameroon /Industrialization /338.09669 W462s

5104. Wells, Michael, and Walter Hellerstein. 1980 "The Governmental-Proprietary Distinction in Constitutional Law." Virginia Law Review V. 66, pp. 1073-1141. /United States of America /Law

5105. Wenger, K. 1969 The Public Enterprise: A Contribution to the Theory of Economic Management and of Economic Administrative Law. New York: Springer. /Law /Administrative law /Management /Economic analysis / Theoretical framework

5106. Wengert, N. 1952 "Antecedents of TVA: The Legislative History of Muscle Shoals." Agricultural History V. 26, pp. 141-147. /United States of America /River valley development projects / Economic history

5107. Werneck, A. de O. 1969 "As actividades empresariais do Governo Federal no Brasil." Revista Brasileira de Economia (Rio de Janeiro), V. 23, No. 3, pp. 89-110. /Brazil /Government bureaucracy /Entrepreneurial activity / G330.5 R326 LAC

5108. Wesley, E. B. 1932 "The Government Factory System among the Indians, 1795-1822." Journal of Economic Business History V. 4, pp. 487-511. /India /Industrial sector /Economic history

5109. Westrate, C. 1958 "The Effects of Price Control in New Zealand." Economic Review V. 34, pp. 103-108. /New Zealand /Price policy

5110. Wettenhall, R. L. 1965 "Public Ownership in Australia." Political Quarterly (London), V. 36, No. 4, pp. 426-440. /Australia / 320.5 P76p

5111. Wettenhall, R. L. 1966 "The Recoup Concept in Public Enterprise." Public Administration (Sydney, Australia), V. 44, pp. 391-420. /Australia /Control process

5112. Wettenhall, R. L. 1983 "Public Enterprise as an Instruemnt of State Policies: Australian National Report." Paper presented at the 19th International Congress of Administrative Sciences, West Berlin, 19-23 Sept. /Australia /Goal setting /Accountability /Law /OPSS

5113. Whelan, Noel. 1968 "Social Opportunity Cost of Government Investment." Administration (Ibadan, Nigeria), pp. 303-315. /Nigeria /Management /Investment /Cost benefit analysis

5114. Whelan, Noel. 1973 "Organization and Management in the Public Sector." Administration (Dublin), pp. 396-404. /Organization formation /Management

5115. Wheldon, G. F. 1951 "Financing the Nationalized Industries." Law and Contemporary Problems V. 16, No. 4, pp. 620-632. /United Kingdom /Financing

5116. Whenfield, A. A. 1961 "The Public Sector versus Private Sector in Britain." Modern Age V. 6, No. 1, pp. 43-55. /United Kingdom /Private sector / Comparative analysis

5117. White, E. 1973 Empresas multinacionales latinoamericanas. Mexico City: Fondo de Cultura Económica. /Law /Latin America /Multinational corporations /HD 69 I7 W47 LAC

5118. White, E. 1976 La acción internacional de las empresas públicas en América Latina. Rio de Janeiro: FGV-EIAP. /State trading organizations /Multinational corporations /qHD 4010.5 W486 LAC

5119. White, E. 1983 Channels and Modalities for the Transfer of Technology to Public Enterprises in Developing Countries. Ljubljana: ICPE. /Technology transfer /Developing nations

5120. White, E., and J. Campos. n.d. Elementos para el estudio de las empresas conjuntas latinoamericanas. Buenos Aires: BID-INTAL. /Law /Latin America /Multinational corporations /HD 2810.5 W557 LAC

5121. White, E., et al. 1977 Las empresas conjuntas latinoamericanas. Buenos Aires: BID-INTAL. /Latin America /Multinational corporations

5122. White, G. 1961 Nationalization of Foreign Property. London: Stevens. /Nationalization / 341.5 W583n

5123. White, John Alexander. 1972 Regional Development Banks: The Asian, African and Inter-American Development Banks. New York: Praeger; Overseas Development Institute. /Asia /Africa /Latin America /Development banks / HG 4517 W52 LAC

5124. Whiting, Van R., Jr. 1982 "State Intervention in Brazil and Mexico: Theoretical Considerations for a Comparative Study." Paper presented at the 12th World Congress of the International Political Science Association, Rio de Janeiro, 9-14 Aug. /Brazil /Mexico /Political analysis /Comparative analysis

5125. Wijetunge, P. 1981 "Management Training and Development in Public Enterprises in Sri Lanka." Paper presented at the Regional Workshop on Management Training and Development in Public Enterprises of Developing Countries, Karachi, Pakistan, 5-15 January. Ljubljana: ICPE /Sri Lanka /Training /Management

5126. Wilber, C. K. 1969 The Soviet Model and Underdeveloped Countries. London: Oxford University Press. /Union of Soviet Socialist Reps. /Developing nations / 338.947 W641s

5127. Williams, A. 1970 "Cost-Benefit Analysis." In A. Caincross, ed(s). _The Managed Economy._ Oxford: Basil Blackwell. /Cost benefit analysis

5128. Williams, A. T. 1955 "(State Enterprises in) Victoria." In A. H. Hanson, ed(s). _Public Enterprise._ Brussels: IIAS. pp. 482-491. /Australia / HD 3850 H28 Law

5129. Williams, Simon, and James A. Miller. 1973 _Credit Systems for Small-Scale Farmers: Case Histories from Mexico._ Studies in Latin American Business, No. 14. Austin, Tex.: UT Bureau of Business Research. /Mexico /Credit policy /Banking agency /Agricultural sector / HG 2051 M6 W54 LAC

5130. Williamson, Oliver E. 1966 "Peak-load pricing and optimal capacity under indivisibility constraints." _American Economic Review_ V. 56, pp. 810-827. /Price policy / Economic theory / 330.5 Am312 Reprinted in R. Turvey, _Public Enterprise._ /338.001 T869e PCL /HD 3850 T89 Pub Aff

5131. Willis, J. 1928 "Administrative Decision and the Law: The Views of a Lawyer." _Canadian Journal of Economics and Political Science_ (Toronto), V. 24, pp. 502-511. /Public administration /Decision making process /Law / 305 C16

5132. Wilmots, Yves. 1973 "The Public Enterprises in Belgium and the Grand Duchy of Luxemburg." _The Evolution of the Public Enterprises in the Community of the Nine._ Brussels: CEEP Editions. pp. 7-24. /Belgium /Luxemburg /Statistics /OPSS

5133. Wilson, T. 1945 "Price and Outlay Policy of State Enterprise." _Economic Journal_ V. 55, pp. 454-461. /Price policy / 330.5 Ec7

5134. Wiltshire, Kenneth. 1978 "Public Enterprises in Australia." In André Gélinas, ed(s). _Public Enterprise and the Public Interest._ Ontario: The Institute of Public Administration of Canada. pp. 75-103. /Australia /Economic history /Law /Accountability /Control process

5135. Winter, Charles. 1951 "Parliamentary, Ministerial, and Judicial Control of Nationalized Industries in Great Britain." _Law and Contemporary Problems_ V. 16, No. 4, pp. 670-701. /United Kingdom /Control Process /Parliament /340.5 L44

5136. Wiseman, J. 1960 "Nationalization in Britain." _Contemporary Review_ (London), V. 197, pp. 65-77. /United Kingdom /Nationalization / 052 C76

5137. Wiseman, J. 1963 "Guidelines for Public Enterprise: A British Experience." _Southern Economic Journal_ V. 30, No. 1, pp. 39-48. /United Kingdom /Evaluation / HB 1 S6

5138. Witker, Jorge. 1979 "El holding como instrumento de control y coordinación de las empresas públicas, su eventual aplicabilidad a la realidad jurídico-económico de México." Mexico City: Instituto de Investigaciones Jurídicas de la Universidad Nacional Autónoma de México. /Mexico /Control process /Law / Holding company /OPSS

5139. Witte, E., and J. Hauschilot. 1966 *Public Undertakings in Conflicts of Interest. (A Study of Industrial Economics Designed to Give a Definition of the Objectives of Public Undertakings).* Berlin: Gesellschaft fur Offentliche Wirtschaft. /Industrial economy /Economic analysis

5140. Woldayes, Emiru. 1980 "Assessment of Training Needs in Public Enterprises." Paper presented at the Interregional Seminar on Training Management in Public Enterprises in Developing Countries, Ljubljana, Yugoslavia, Sept.29-Oct.10. Ljubljana: ICPE. /Training /Evaluation

5141. Wolf, Robert. 1980 "Regional Development and Public Enterprise: A Monopsonistic Competition Model." Paper presented at the Second BAPEG Conference: Public Enterprise in Mixed Economy LDCs, Boston, Mass., April. /Regional development /Economic theory /OPSS

5142. Wood, D. F. 1958 "The St. Lawrence Seaway: Some Considerations of Its Impact." *Land Economics* V. 34, pp. 61-73. /United States of America /River valley development projects / 305 J824 PCL

5143. Wood, David M. 1952 "Social and Political Problems Presented by Municipal Authorities." Paper presented at the Annual Conference of the Eastern Pennsylvania Group of the Investment Bankers Association of America, Philadelphia, Pennsylvania, April 25. /City government /Local government

5144. World Bank. 1951 *Development Corporations and Related Institutions in Selected Countries.* Washington, D.C. /Developing nations /Economic development

5145. World Bank. 1959 *Data on Development Banks.* Washington, D.C. /Development banks

5146. World Bank. 1978 "The Financing of Public Manufacturing Enterprises." Paper presented at the Interregional Workshop on Financing of Public Enterprises in Developing Countries, Ljubljana, Yugoslavia, 22-26 May. Ljubljana: ICPE. /Public financing /Manufacturing industry

5147. World Bank. 1981 *République Populaire du Congo: Observations de la mission de la Banque Mondiale sur les entreprises publiques, décembre, 1981.* Washington, D.C. /Congo, People's Rep. of /Evaluation /OPSS

5148. World Bank. 1983 "Managing State-Owned Enterprises." In *World Development Report 1983.* New York: Oxford University Press for the World Bank. pp. 74-87. /Management /Economic analysis /Case studies /Comparative analysis /Privatization /Control process /Goal setting /HC 59.7 W659 LAC

5149. Wormald, Avison. 1972 "Growth Promotion: The Creation of a Modern Steel Industry." In Stuart Holland, ed(s). *The State as Entrepreneur.* London: Weidenfeld and Nicolson. pp. 92-105. /Italy /Steel industry /HD 3616 I83 H65 PCL /HD 487

H6 1973 Pub Aff

5150. Wu, Chi-Yuen. 1967 "Public Enterprises as an Instrument of Development." Journal of Local Administration Overseas (London), V. 6, No. 3, pp. 149-158. /Economic development /Management / 352.05 J826

5151. Wyer, R. 1935 "Fact and Fallacy on the St. Lawrence." Harvard Business Review V. 13, pp. 344-352. /United States of America /River valley development projects / HF 5001 H3

5152. Wyrwa, T. 1967 "Notion et problèmes de la propriété socialisée: Modèles soviétiques et polonais." Rivista Internazionale di Scienze Sociali (Milan, Italy), V. 75, No. 4, pp. 349-365. /Union of Soviet Socialist Reps. /Poland /Socialist economy 305 R525 PCL

5153. Wyrwa, T. 1968 "Le rôle des syndicats dans la gestion de l'entreprise socialisée en Pologne." Canadian Slavic Studies V. 11, No. 2, pp. 175-191. /Poland /Trade unions /Worker management participation

5154. Wyrwa, T. 1970 La gestion de l'entreprise socialists: L'expérience polonaise. /Poland /Management

5155. Xavier, Guy Diniz, and José Ruque Rossi. 1969 "Summary: USIMINAS, A Developing Project." Prepared for the Meeting of Experts on Administration of Public Enterprises in Latin America and the Caribbean, Santiago, Chile. /Steel industry /Brazil /OPSS

5156. Yadin, U. 1970 "The Public Corporation in Israel." In W. G. Friedmann and J. F. Garner, ed(s). Government Enterprise, a Comparative Study. New York: Columbia University Press. pp. 248-263. /Israel / 350.0092 G746

5157. Yaffey, M. J. H. 1968 "The Effect of Nationalization on Current External Payments." Economic Papers (Makerere, Uganda), pp. 294-303. /Nationalization /Balance of payments /East Africa

5158. Yaffey, M. J. H., E. R. Rado, and E. J. Wells. 1969 The Effect of Nationalization of Current External Paycosts and Constraints in the Kenya Building Industry. Makerere, Uganda: Institute of Social Research. /Kenya /Construction industry /Nationalization /Economic analysis /East Africa

5159. Yanez, R. Alfonso. 1973 "El control de las empresas públicas en México." Revista de Administración Pública V. 24, pp. 173-174. /Mexico /Control process

5160. Yanowitch, M. 1969 Contemporary Soviet Economics; A Collection of Readings from Soviet Sources. New York: International Arts and Sciences Press. V. 2. /Union of Soviet Socialist Reps. /Economic development

5161. Yao Delon, L. 1969 Le rôle des entreprises publiques ivoiriennes dans la planification et l'exécution des plans en Côte d'Ivoire. Mauritius: UNECA Seminar on Role of Public

Enterprises in Planning and Plan Implementation, September 16-26, 1969. /Ivory Coast /Evaluation /Planning process

5162. Yongkittikul, Twatchai, et al. 1979 "Management and Performance of Public Enterprises in Thailand: Report." Bangkok, Thailand: National Institute of Development Administration. /Thailand /Planning process /Environmental policy /Evaluation /Personnel management /Productivity

5163. Yoshitake, Kiyohiko. 1973 An Introduction to Public Enterprise in Japan. Beverly Hills, Calif.: Sage Publications. /Japan

5164. Young, Edgard B. 1946 "Personnel Administration in the Port of New York." Authority Public Personnel Review pp. 132-140. /New York (State) /Personnel management /Port authority

5165. Young, Rowland L. 1980 "Commerce . . . State-Owned Business." American Bar Association Journal V. 66. /United States of America /Law

5166. Yu, Hoon. 1976 "Coordination of Public Enterprises: Country Study for the Republic of Korea." In A. S. H. K. Sadique, ed(s). Public Enterprise in Asia: Studies on Coordination and Control. Kuala Lumpur, Malaysia: Asian Centre for Development Administration. pp. 337-362. /Korea, Rep. of /Control Process / HD 4276 P8

5167. Yugoslavia. 1958 "El estudio del trabajador en el sistema de gestión obrera; Nueva legislación yugoslava sobre relaciones de trabajo en las empresas." Ekonomska Politika (Belgrade), V. 20, No. 5, pp. 188-197. /Yugoslavia /Worker self management

5168. Yugoslavia. Pharmaceutical Industry "LEK." 1980 "Women as a Factor of Development: Pharmaceutical Industry `LEK.´" Paper presented at the International Expert Group Meeting on Women as a Factor of Development and the Responsibilities of the Public Sector in this Regard, Ljubljana, Yugoslavia, 14-19 April. Ljubljana: ICPE. /Women´s studies /Economic development /Pharmaceutical industry / Case studies

5169. Yuill, Douglas. 1982 Regional Development Agencies in Europe. Brookfield, Vermont: Gower Publishing Co. /Europe /Regional development /Comparative analysis

5170. Yumba, wa Kioni. 1983 "Problème de la rentabilité vis-à-vis de l´intérêt public: Cas des transports en communs à Kinshasa." Paper presented at the 19th International Congress of Administrative Sciences, West Berlin, 19-23 Sept. /Zaire /Kinshasa, Zaire /Mass transportation industry /Public interest /Case studies /OPSS

5171. Yunker, J. 1975 "Economic Performance of Public and Private Enterprise: The Case of U.S. Electric Utilities." Journal of Economics and Business V. 28, No. 1, pp. 60-67. /United States of America /Electrical utility industry / Comparative analysis / HC 101 P452

5172. Yusefu, T. M. 1983 "Labour-management relations in public enterprises in Africa: The Nigerian case." Labour-Management Relations in Public Enterprises in Africa. Geneva: ILO. pp. 33-56. /Labor relations /Personnel relations /Nigeria /Africa /OPSS

5173. Yusof, Misron bin. 1981 "Management Training in L L N: Some Recurring Issues." Paper presented at the Regional Workshop on the Evaluation of Training Packages for Public Enterprise Managers, Bangkok, Thailand, 10-14 August. Ljubljana: ICPE /Training /Management / Case studies

5174. Zakariya, Hasan S. 1978 "State Petroleum Companies." Journal of World Trade Law (Twickenham, England), V. 12, No. 6, pp. 481-500. /Oil industry

5175. Zakariya, Hasan S. 1980 "State Petroleum Enterprises: Some Aspects of their Rationale, Legal Structure, Management, and Jurisdiction." State Petroleum Enterprises in Developing Countries. New York: Pergamon Press. pp. 28-47. /Oil industry /Law /Management

5176. Zaleski, E. 1967 Planning Reforms in the Soviet Union, 1962-1966--An Analysis of Recent Trends in Economic Organization and Management. Chapel Hill: University of North Carolina Press. /Union of Soviet Socialist Reps. /Organization change /Management /Economic analysis /338.947 Z14p

5177. Zambia Government. 1965 The Fourth Inter-African Public Administration Seminar: Planning New Administrative Machinery, Particularly for Public Enterprises. Lusaka, Zambia: Staff Training College, November 7-16, 1965. /Africa /Public administration /Administrative reform

5178. Zammit, Edward L., et al. 1982 Transition to Workers' Self Management. The Hague: Institute of Social Studies; Malta: University of Malta. /Malta /Worker self management /Economic history

5179. Zamora Batiz, J. 1961 "The Development of State Enterprises in Mexico; the Petroleum Industry." Revista de Economía (Mexico City), V. 24, No. 3, pp. 75-107. /Mexico /Oil industry

5180. Zañartu, M. 1969 "Empresas de trabajadores. Elementos de análisis para optar por una estrategia de implantación." Cuadernos de Economía (Santiago, Chile), V. 6, No. 18, pp. 29-37. /Chile /Worker self management / G330.5 C891 LAC

5181. Zañartu, M. 1971 "Análisis de costos sociales en el caso de implantación de la autogestión en algunos sectores de la economía chilena." In A. Foxley et al., ed(s). Chile: Búsqueda de un nuevo socialismo. Santiago, Chile: Ediciones Nueva Universidad. pp. 232-251. /Chile /Worker self management / HX198.5 C5 LAC

5182. Zappa, G. 1968 "Gestione economica e indirizzo politico nelle imprese pubbliche. Il caso dell' IRI." Questitalia

(Venice), V. 2, No. 120-, pp. 62-89. /Italy /Economic policy making / Holding company

5183. Zauberman, A. 1958 Industrial Development in Czechoslovakia, East Germany, and Poland, 1937-1956. Oxford, England: Oxford University Press. /Industrialization /Economic history /Germany, Democratic Rep. of /Poland /Czechoslovakia /338.094 Z19i

5184. Zauschquevich, A. 1964 "ENAMI: Una fábrica de divisas." Revista Chilena de Ingeniería (Santiago, Chile), No. 304, pp. 23-25. /Chile /Mining industry /Case studies

5185. Zelada de Andrés Moreno, Fermín. 1970 "El Banco Exterior de España: Su historia, características y problemática actual." La Empresa Pública. Zaragoza, Spain: Publicaciones del Real Colegio de España en Bolonia. /Spain /Banking agency /Case studies

5186. Zetzchke, A. 1952 "Les participations de l'Etat dans les entreprises en Italie." Problèmes Economiques (Paris), No. 232. /Italy

5187. Zetzchke, A. 1964 "La empresa pública en Alemania." Información Comercial Española (Madrid), /Germany, Federal Rep. of

5188. Zetzchke, A. 1964 "Empresa pública en el Oeste." Información Comercial Española (Madrid), No. 367. /Comparative analysis

5189. Zhivkov, T. 1969 Twenty-Five Years along the Road to Socialism. Sofia, Bulgaria: Sofia Press. /Bulgaria /Socialist economy

5190. Ziegler, J. 1964 "L'autogestion ouvrière en Algérie, problèmes et perspectives." Revue Syndicale Suisse (Berne, Switzerland), V. 56, No. 12, pp. 348-354. /Algeria /Worker self management

5191. Zielinski, J. G. 1967 "Notes on Incentive Systems of Soviet Socialist Enterprises." Economics of Planning (Oslo), V. 7, No. 3, pp. 258-269. /Union of Soviet Socialist Reps. /Incentive systems

5192. Zif, J. 1979 "Decision Analysis with Multiple Objectives: Application to a Product-Mix Problem in a Public Enterprise." Cambridge, Mass.: HIID-BAPEG. /Evaluation /Decision making process

5193. Zif, J. 1980 "Business Versus Politics in State Owned Enterprises." Paper presented at the Second BAPEG Conference: Public Enterprise in Mixed Economy LDCs, Boston, Mass., April. /Management /Israel /OPSS

5194. Zimmermann, F. L., and M. Wendell. 1954 "Representation of the Region in Missouri Basin Organization." American Political Science Review V. 48, No. 1, pp. 152-165. /United States of America /Regional development /Regional planning /320.5 Am31

5195. Zimmermann, Rupert. 1964 Verstastlichung in osterreich: Ihne aufgaben und ziele. Vienna: Verlag der Weiner Volksbuchhandlung. /Austria

5196. Zines, Leslie. 1970 "Federal Public Corporations in Australia." In W.G. Friedmann and J.F. Garner, ed(s). Government Enterprise, A Comparative Study. New York: Columbia University Press. pp. 227-247. /Australia /350.0092 G746

5197. Zinkin, T. 1969 "Financial Performance of Government Corporations in Less Developed Countries." Lok Udyog (New Delhi), pp. 1067-1075. /Developing nations /Financial performance / 354.54 L836

5198. Zuleta Holguin, Hernando. 1971 El Estado empresario. Bogotá: Editorial Revista Colombiana. /Colombia / HD 4104 Z84 LAC

5199. Zupanov, J. 1977 "Participation, Workers' Self-Management and Education." Paper presented at the International Seminar on Management and Training in Public Enterprises in Developing Countries, Ljubljana, Yugoslavia, 10-28 October. Ljubljana: ICPE. /Worker self management /Worker management participation /Also presented at the same seminar in Ljubljana, Sept. 18-Oct. 6, 1978.

5200. Zupanov, J., and A. S. Tannibaum. 1967 "La distribution du contrôle dans quelques organisations industrielles yougoslaves." Sociologie du Travail (Paris), No. 1, pp. 1-23. /Yugoslavia /Industrial sector /Control process /331.05 So14 PCL

5201. Zwass, Adam. 1977 Money, Banking and Credit in the Soviet Union and Eastern Europe. White Plains, N.Y.: M. E. Sharpe. /Eastern Europe /Union of Soviet Socialist Reps. /Banking agency /Credit policy

INDEX